Communion
with
Christ and His People

Communion
with
Christ and His People

The Spirituality of C. H. Spurgeon

Peter J. Morden

With a foreword by
David Bebbington

PICKWICK *Publications* · Eugene, Oregon

COMMUNION WITH CHRIST AND HIS PEOPLE
The Spirituality of C. H. Spurgeon

Copyright © 2013 Peter J. Morden. All rights reserved. Except for brief quotations in critical publications or reviews, no part of this book may be reproduced in any manner without prior written permission from the publisher. Write: Permissions, Wipf and Stock Publishers, 199 W. 8th Ave., Suite 3, Eugene, OR 97401.

First published in Great Britain in 2010 by the Centre for Baptist History and Heritage, Regent's Park College, Pusey Street, Oxford, OX1 2LB.

Pickwick Publications
A Division of Wipf and Stock Publishers
199 W. 8th Ave., Suite 3
Eugene, OR 97401

www.wipfandstock.com

ISBN 13: 978-1-62564-625-5

Cataloging-in-Publication data:

Morden, Peter J.

Communion with Christ and his people : the spirituality of C. H. Spurgeon / Peter J. Morden, with a foreword by David Bebbington.

xii + 163 p. ; 23 cm. Includes bibliographical references.

ISBN 13: 978-1-62564-625-5

1. Spurgeon, C. H. (Charles Haddon), 1834–1892. 2. Evangelicalism—History. 3. Spirituality. I. Bebbington, D. W. (David William), 1949–. II. Title.

BX6495.S7 M59 2013

Manufactured in the U.S.A.
Typeset by Troon & Croft

To Nigel G. Wright and Roger Standing

Contents

Foreword by David W. Bebbington	xi
Preface and Acknowledgements	xiii
Abbreviations	xv
Chapter 1: Introduction	**1**
The Study of Spirituality	2
The Study of Spurgeon	4
Sources Used	8
The Content of this Book	13
Conclusion	15
Chapter 2: Puritan Piety: 'A Calvinistic Creed and a Puritanic Morality'	**16**
Understanding Puritanism	18
Spurgeon's Upbringing: Place, People, and Literature	20
Spurgeon and Bunyan	26
Puritan Commentaries	31
A 'Puritanic Morality'	37
Spurgeon's Theology	39
Conclusion	45
Chapter 3: Evangelical Conversionism: 'Dear spot of ground where Jesus met us! Dear hour which brought us to his feet!'	**47**
Spurgeon's Experience of Conversion	48
Theology of Conversion	55
Early Evangelistic Ministry	62
Later Evangelistic Ministry	66
Spurgeon and Evangelicalism	70
Conclusion	76
Chapter 4: Baptism and the Baptists: 'I firmly believe ... that baptism is the command of Christ'	**77**
Spurgeon's Baptism as a Believer	79
Spurgeon and 'Baptismal Sacramentalism'	84
Reasons for the Rejection of 'Baptismal Sacramentalism'	89
Baptism as an Instructive Symbol	93
Obedience to Christ's Command	94
Baptism as Consecration to Christ	100
Baptism and the Church	101
Conclusion	104

Chapter 5: The Bible: 'O living Christ, make this a living word to me'   **106**
Inspiration and Authority   107
Historical and Cultural Influences   110
Reading the Bible   118
The Bible and Christ   121
The Bible and Preaching   127
The *Treasury of David*   131
Conclusion   135

Chapter 6: Prayer: 'Earnest prayer is the most potent means of winning continued communion'   **137**
Spurgeon's Approach to Prayer   137
Different Dimensions of Prayer   143
Influences   147
Spurgeon's View of Intercession   154
Influences on Intercession   158
Conclusion   163

Illustrations

Chapter 7: The Lord's Supper: 'By faith, I see our Lord standing in our midst'   **165**
The Lord's Supper in Practice   166
Spurgeon's Preaching at the Lord's Supper   173
The Real Presence   178
An 'Accessible ... Method of Fellowship'   184
The Lord's Supper and Active Service   186
Conclusion   188

Chapter 8: Activism: 'A Christian sluggard! Is there such a thing? A *Christian man on half time?*'   **190**
The Course of Spurgeon's Activism   192
Case Study: the Pastors' College   199
Case Study: The Stockwell Orphanage   204
The Orphanage and Communion with Christ's people   212
Activity and Christ   219
Conclusion   221

Chapter 9: Holiness: 'Oh to be Christly! We do desire to live on earth the life of Jesus ...'   **223**
The Central Importance of Holiness   223
Spurgeon's Conception of Holiness   227
Spurgeon and the 'Common Man'   233
Motivation for Holiness   235

Holiness and Eschatology 237
God's Work in Progressive Sanctification 243
The Believer's Struggle for Holiness 246
Spurgeon and Nineteenth-Century teaching on Holiness 248
Spurgeon's Distinctive Approach 253
Conclusion 256

Chapter 10: Suffering: 'Certain of us have had large fellowship with the Lord Jesus in affliction' 258
Spurgeon and Suffering 259
A Theology of Suffering 263
The Benefits of Suffering 268
Influences on Spurgeon's Approach 272
Suffering and Communion with Christ 274
Suffering and Communion with Christ's People 278
The End of Suffering: Perfect Communion 281
Conclusion 284

Chapter 11: Conclusion: 'Love Christ and live Christ; think of Christ and speak of Christ' 286
Diverse Influences 287
A Unifying Theme 290
Integration of Influences 292
Conclusion 294

Bibliography 297

Index 313

Foreword

Charles Haddon Spurgeon, the greatest of Victorian preachers, is rightly remembered as a doughty Calvinist. He firmly believed in the doctrines of the Reformed faith, not following the growing fashion for vagueness of belief in the later nineteenth century. He upheld what he called 'the old theology', the divinity that he read in the authors of the seventeenth century, and wanted the tutors who taught in his college to be 'Puritans themselves'.[1] Yet Spurgeon was no extremist. He rejected 'Hyper-Calvinism' and took comfort from the circumstance that men trained in his college who took the Arminian path away from Calvinism still remained 'earnestly evangelical'.[2] His primary concern was that preachers should proclaim the gospel. 'To waver upon the atonement, or the work of the Holy Spirit, or salvation by grace', he wrote, 'is not merely dangerous but fatal to a preacher's usefulness.'[3] The atoning work of Christ on the cross redeemed sinners, the Holy Spirit applied the benefits of Christ's sacrifice to the lives of individuals and the whole process was the result of divine bounty, not of human merit. These evangelical convictions were the motor of Spurgeon's ministry.

It was not only the Reformed tradition, however, that moulded Spurgeon. It is one of the merits of this book by Peter Morden that it brings out the diversity of the factors that affected the great preacher. Alongside the seventeenth-century Puritan influences were the intellectual currents flowing from the Enlightenment of the eighteenth century. Spurgeon appealed to reason, the most characteristic stance of an Enlightenment thinker. He asserted the strong form of the doctrine of assurance that had come into vogue during the eighteenth century. There was a powerful dose of pragmatism, another prominent symptom of the Enlightenment, about Spurgeon. And he insisted on the importance of common sense, that cardinal virtue of the enlightened age. The opposite, as so often in Spurgeon's compositions, was lampooned. He ridiculed preachers who 'affect obscurity', quoting the latest thinkers, however unorthodox.[4] They were abandoning the solid, practical common sense that Spurgeon so much admired. Altogether, Peter Morden shows, Spurgeon cannot be understood unless he is located as a Victorian figure deeply swayed by the intellectual legacy of the previous century.

Nor did Spurgeon remain immune to the influences of his own day. While resisting the liberal theological tendencies of the times, Spurgeon was swayed by expressions of the Romantic taste that was growingly attractive in the Victorian era.

---

[1] *Annual Paper descriptive of the Lord's Work connected with the Pastors' College during the Year 1870* (London: Passmore & Alabaster, 1871), p. 14.

[2] *Annual Paper descriptive of the Lord's Work connected with the Pastors' College during the Year 1871* (London: Passmore & Alabaster, 1872), p. 5.

[3] *Annual Paper descriptive of the Lord's Work connected with the Pastors' College during the Year 1870* (London: Passmore & Alabaster, 1871), p. 5.

[4] *Annual Paper descriptive of the Lord's Work ... during the Year 1870*, p. 7.

Thus he was friendly with the Romantic art critic John Ruskin, condemned the unpoetic age in which he lived and sometimes gave free rein to his imagination in the interpretation of scripture. Spurgeon esteemed High Church Anglicans who were deeply affected by contemporary cultural trends and, despite his stern anti-Catholicism, even appreciated the writings of the Roman Catholic convert F.W. Faber whose writings were steeped in Romantic sensibility. Spurgeon's theological perspective was tinctured by the same approach. He believed in funding Christian ventures by the faith principle that had emerged in the Romantic milieu earlier in the century. His college, he claimed, had 'nothing to rely on but the hand of the Lord'.[5] Although on occasion he was willing to appeal for funds, Spurgeon normally wished to demonstrate the radical faith that looked to the Almighty to provide. Peter Morden demonstrates that such contemporary attitudes intermingled with the other elements in the formation of Spurgeon's complex understanding.

The result was the rich spirituality that this book expounds with cogency and clarity. Here we find much about prayer and the Bible, about conversion, baptism and the Lord's Supper and about holiness, suffering and Christian service. Spurgeon displayed passionate beliefs about these matters because each was a component of the believer's devotion. Once when listing the qualities of a training college for pastors, he wrote, as his final point, that it should be a place where 'spiritual life is highly esteemed and carefully fostered'.[6] The aim of preparation for ministry should be to produce not just sound preachers but godly people. At his own college Spurgeon added the requirement that trainees should join in the life of his church, the Metropolitan Tabernacle, by attending, for instance, its prayer meetings. Spirituality could best be nurtured in the fellowship of a specific Christian community. That is why Peter Morden can contend that a good summary of Spurgeon's approach to the spiritual life is 'communion with Christ and his people'. The author's case is highly persuasive.

David Bebbington
University of Stirling,
September 2010.

---

[5] *Outline of the Lord's Work by the Pastor's College and its Kindred Organisations at the Metropolitan Tabernacle* (London: Passmore & Alabaster, 1867), p. iii.

[6] *Annual Paper descriptive of the Lord's Work connected with the Pastors' College during the Year 1870* (London: Passmore & Alabaster, 1871), p. 15.

Preface to the Pickwick Edition

This book is a revised version of my PhD thesis. The desire to pursue doctoral research on the spirituality of Charles Haddon Spurgeon was initially stimulated by Ian Randall, who subsequently became my supervisor. His insightful comments on different drafts of my work have been invaluable. Pieter Lalleman read the whole of the original thesis and his detailed notes saved me from a number of errors. Anil Den and Amanda Woolley read and commented on the chapter on suffering and offered valuable insights based on their respective expertise in psychiatry and psychology. I am especially grateful to Amanda, who went into labour whilst reading the chapter! She later told me, 'At the time I was not convinced by Spurgeon's theology of suffering!' Thank you to Amanda, her husband, Euan, and their beautiful daughter, Anya. I am indebted to my PhD examiners, David Bebbington and Crawford Gribben, and to the chair of my *viva voce*, Peter Stevenson, for their encouragement. I am honoured that David Bebbington agreed to write the Foreword to this book. Of course, I alone am responsible for all the opinions expressed in this study and the errors that doubtless remain.

My research took me to a number of different libraries and archives. I acknowledge the assistance I have received from Steve Taylor of the Evangelical Library, London; Susan Mills and Emma Walsh of The Angus Library and Archives, Regent's Park College, Oxford; and Jean Bowerman and Brett Pitchfork of 'Spurgeons' (formerly known as Spurgeon's Childcare), Rushden. The majority of my research took place in the Heritage Room at Spurgeon's College and I am especially grateful to Judy Powles, the indefatigable college librarian, for all the help she gave me.

This book was originally published by the Centre for Baptist History and Heritage, Regent's Park College, Oxford, in 2010. I especially want to acknowledge the generous help of Anthony R. Cross, the original editor, and I am grateful to Rob Ellis, Principal of Regent's Park, for permission for the study to be reprinted in this Pickwick edition. The illustrations that appear in the book are drawn from the Heritage Room at Spurgeon's College, and are used with permission. Thank you to Dave Lock for his help preparing this illustrative material. I am also grateful to Wipf & Stock for bringing out this Pickwick edition, and for doing such a splendid job with it. I particularly want to record my thanks to Robin Parry, an editor of the Pickwick imprint, Christian Amondson, and Laura Poncy.

Some of the material which takes its place in this study had already appeared in various articles and papers prior to the book's publication in 2010. The substance of chapter 3 was published in the *Baptist Quarterly* as 'C. H. Spurgeon and Baptism; Part 1: The Question of Baptismal Sacramentalism', and 'C. H. Spurgeon and Baptism: The Importance of Baptism', respectively. An early version of chapter 6 appeared as 'The Lord's Supper and the Spirituality of C. H. Spurgeon' in *Baptist Sacramentalism 2*, edited by Anthony R. Cross and Philip E. Thompson and published by Paternoster. I read a paper on 'The Spirituality of C. H. Spurgeon' to the Academic and Theological Workgroup of the Baptist World Alliance (BWA) at the annual gathering of the BWA in Mexico City in 2006, and spoke on 'Spurgeon and Prayer' at a meeting of the Scottish Baptist History Project in Glasgow in 2007. I also read drafts of different chapters at various Spurgeon's College research seminars. On all the occasions when I have written or presented material I received stimulating feedback. Writing my 'popular' book, *C. H. Spurgeon: The People's Preacher*, published by Christian World Revival (CWR), also informed this study. I remain very grateful to all at CWR, especially Lynette and Mick Brooks.

Since 2010 I have produced articles on Spurgeon and prayer for the *Evangelical Quarterly* and Spurgeon and suffering for the *Evangelical Review of Theology*. The J. D. Hughey lectures I gave at the International Baptist Theological Seminary in Prague in the Autumn of 2010 on the subject of Spurgeon's spirituality were revised and have been published in a special edition of *Baptistic Theologies*. I also taught an intensive elective at Golden Gate Theological Seminary, San Francisco, California, in the summer of 2013. So I have continued to think, write, and speak on the great preacher. Nevertheless, as I have reviewed the MS of *'Communion with Christ and His People'* it still expresses the heart of what I want to say about his spirituality. Hence this reprint.

In September 2007 I started work as Tutor in Church History and Spirituality at Spurgeon's College, and in September 2013 I became the college's Vice Principal. Consequently, much of my research and writing into Spurgeon has been undertaken whilst working for the institution he founded in 1856, which now bears his name. Spurgeon's is an extremely stimulating place to work and I am grateful to all the staff and students for their warm and ongoing support. Most of all, I have to thank my wonderful wife, Anne, and my two wonderful children, Rachel and Joseph. I am grateful to them for more than I could ever say.

This Pickwick edition is dedicated to the two Principals I have been privileged to serve under since 2007, Nigel G. Wright and, from September 2013, Roger Standing. In different ways they have both given me tremendous help and encouragement, and continue to do so. I give thanks to God for all he has done in and through Spurgeon's College in the past, and look forward to the future with great expectancy.

Peter J. Morden
Spurgeon's College, London
Christmas 2013

Abbreviations

MTP   *Metropolitan Tabernacle Pulpit*
NPSP   *New Park Street Pulpit*
Sword and Trowel   *The Sword and the Trowel*

Charles Haddon Spurgeon in 1868.
The engraving appeared in the *Metropolitan Tabernacle Pulpit* issue 808 (1868).
(Digital image courtesy of the author and used with permission of Spurgeon's College, London.)

CHAPTER 1

Introduction

On 9 October 1880 the *Boy's Own Paper* published silhouettes of those it considered to be the greatest 'celebrities' of late-Victorian England. Unsurprisingly, the collection included the two most notable prime ministers of the age, William Gladstone and Benjamin Disraeli, as well as the poet-laureate, Alfred, Lord Tennyson, and the essayist Thomas Carlyle. Also pictured, in the centre of the nine silhouettes, was the Baptist pastor Charles Haddon Spurgeon (1834–92).[1] The bracketing of Spurgeon and, say, Gladstone can seem strange to modern commentators but, as Patricia Kruppa observes, 'many Victorians would have found it appropriate'.[2] As David Bebbington states, Spurgeon was by far 'the most popular preacher of the day' in an era when religion bulked large in the life of the nation.[3] As such he was a 'personality of national standing' in Victorian Britain.[4]

Principally because of the circulation of his printed sermons, Spurgeon's reputation and influence travelled far beyond his British base. As early as 1858, when Spurgeon was only twenty-four, the *North American Review* was reporting that Americans returning from a trip to England were invariably asked two questions, namely, 'Did you see the Queen?' and 'Did you hear Spurgeon?' The paper went on to declare that there was 'scarcely any name more familiar' than Spurgeon's in America.[5] By 1875 his sermons had been translated into languages as varied as French, Dutch, Telugu and Maori.[6] Soon to follow were some Russian editions of a

---

[1] *Boy's Own Paper*, 9 October 1880, in C.H. Spurgeon, *Autobiography: Compiled from his Diary, Letters, and Records by his Wife and his Private Secretary* (4 Vols; London: Passmore and Alabaster, 1897–99), Vol. 4, p. 185. The other silhouettes were of the Marquis of Hartington, John Ruskin, the Duke of Argyle and John Bright.

[2] P.S. Kruppa, *Charles Haddon Spurgeon: A Preacher's Progress* (New York: Garland Publishing, 1982), p. 1.

[3] D.W. Bebbington, *Evangelicalism in Modern Britain: A History from the 1730s to the 1980s* (London: Unwin Hyman, 1989), p. 145.

[4] D.W. Bebbington, *The Dominance of Evangelicalism: The Age of Spurgeon and Moody* (Leicester: IVP, 2005), p. 57.

[5] *North American Review* (Boston: Crosby and Nicholls, 1858), p. 275.

[6] C.H. Spurgeon, 'Twenty Years of Published Sermons', in C.H. Spurgeon (ed.), *The Sword and The Trowel: A Record of Combat With Sin and Labour For The Lord* (*Sword and Trowel*) (London: Passmore and Alabaster, 1865–92), January 1875, p. 7; C. Ray, *A Marvellous Ministry: The Story of Spurgeon's Sermons* (London: Passmore and Alabaster, 1905), pp. 27-28.

few select messages. These were passed by the Tsarist censor and approved by the Orthodox Church for official distribution.[7] A staggering one million copies were printed.[8] Spurgeon also made a significant impact in Australia where he became, as Australian Baptist historian Ken Manley states, a 'household name'.[9] Many additional examples could be adduced to demonstrate his truly global reach.[10] C.H. Spurgeon was a figure of international importance in the nineteenth century.

This study makes a detailed examination of the spirituality of this remarkable and significant Baptist minister. This brief introductory chapter establishes a working understanding of the term 'spirituality', considers the current state of Spurgeon scholarship and surveys the primary evidence which will constitute the raw material of this study, as well as indicating the direction the argument will take. After some deliberation I have not included a biographical sketch of Spurgeon. Rather, biographical details will be built up step-by-step as the chapters unfold, with the basic timeline of Spurgeon's life established in chapter 2. Each of the nine main chapters (chapters 2 to 10) will examine in detail an aspect of Spurgeon's spirituality and my aim in all of them is to throw fresh light on both the man and his ministry.

The Study of Spirituality

As Philip Sheldrake observes, 'spirituality is one of those subjects whose meaning everyone claims to know until they have to define it'.[11] As I have suggested elsewhere, the problem of definition is greater because the term has a secular and general religious use as well as a Christian one.[12] But there are also many and varied

---

[7] One of these, published in 1880, is held in Spurgeon's College. See 'Spurgeon's Scrapbooks, Numbered Volumes', Spurgeon's College, Heritage Room (2G), Vol. 4, p. 58 b. The extant numbered volumes of Scrapbooks are, Vol 1, 1856–January 1879; Vol. 2, January 1879–December 1879; Vol. 4, August 1880–July 1881; Vol. 5 June 1881–March 1882; Vol. 6 January 1882–October 1882; Vol. 7, October 1882–April 1883; Vol. 9, October 1883–June 1884; Vol. 12, October 1884–May 1885. Vols 3, 8, 10 and 11 appear to have been broken up and the material placed in different 'Loose-Leaf Scrap Folders'. The three loose leaf folders I have cited from in this study are on shelf 2H. There are also two unnumbered volumes of scrapbooks in similar binding to the numbered ones, 'Spurgeon's Scrapbooks, Two Unnumbered Volumes', 1880–1890; 1890 (2G).

[8] I.H. Murray (ed.), *C.H. Spurgeon: The Full Harvest 1860–1892* (London: Banner of Truth, 1973), pp. 353-54; M. Hopkins, *Nonconformity's Romantic Generation: Evangelical and Liberal Theologies in Victorian England* (Carlisle: Paternoster, 2004), p. 155.

[9] K.R. Manley, *From Woolloomooloo to 'Eternity': A History of Australian Baptists: Growing an Australian Church (1831–1914)* (Milton Keynes: Paternoster, 2006), p. 109. For more on Spurgeon's influence in the Antipodes, see Spurgeon, *Autobiography*, Vol. 3, pp. 324-29; P.J. Morden, 'C.H. Spurgeon and Baptism Part 1: The Question of Baptismal Sacramentalism', *Baptist Quarterly* Vol. 43, No. 4 (October 2009), pp. 213-14.

[10] Spurgeon, 'Twenty Years of Published Sermons', p. 7.

[11] P. Sheldrake, *Spirituality and History* (London: SPCK, 1991), p. 32.

[12] P.J. Morden, *Offering Christ to the World: Andrew Fuller (1754–1815) and the Revival of Eighteenth Century Particular Baptist Life* (Carlisle: Paternoster, 2003), p. 157.

ways of understanding specifically Christian spirituality.[13] A few of these are so broad as to encompass almost all of human experience and hardly help to establish conceptual limits for the term. On the other hand, other approaches that focus exclusively on prayer and what are termed the spiritual exercises are too narrow for the purposes of this study. Helpfully, as Linda Wilson notes, there is a growing trend among commentators on Christianity to define spirituality as consisting of more than just the interior life.[14] Wilson herself argues that, used in a Christian context, spirituality should be understood as both 'the way in which a person develops his or her relationship with God', and also 'the outworking of that [relationship] in his or her life, both public and private'.[15] Alister McGrath's understanding exhibits similar concerns. For him, Christian spirituality is to do with 'the quest for a fulfilled and authentic Christian existence'. It involves the 'bringing together of the fundamental ideas of Christianity and the *whole experience of living on the basis of and within the scope of the Christian faith*'.[16] According to these writers, Christian spirituality should be understood as encompassing more than just the interior life of the soul. The concrete ways this interior life is expressed and lived are also important.

The study of C.H. Spurgeon's spirituality undertaken here follows this broader, but still focused, approach. Using a framework proposed by Sheldrake, spirituality is understood as being concerned with the conjunction of theology, prayer and practical Christianity.[17] This model is helpful in that it encompasses both the inner and outer aspects of the Christian life. Sheldrake's framework also gives due weight to theology, although it needs to be stressed that theology is not considered in an abstract fashion apart from relationship with God and practical action. Rather, the emphasis, in Sheldrake's three-dimensional model and in this study, is on how theology and practical action both shape and are shaped by experience.[18] It ought to be noted that the framework for understanding spirituality set out by Sheldrake and adopted here would have been alien to Spurgeon himself who, when he used the term 'spirituality', meant by it something akin to piety or devotion, thus focusing on the

---

[13] For a brief and helpful survey see A.E. McGrath, *Christian Spirituality* (Oxford: Blackwell, 1999), pp. 1-7.

[14] L. Wilson, *Constrained by Zeal: Female Spirituality Among Nonconformists 1825–1875* (Carlisle: Paternoster, 2000), p. 4. Cf. S.M. Schneiders, 'Christian Spirituality: Definition, Methods and Types', in P. Sheldrake (ed.), *The New SCM Dictionary of Christian Spirituality* (London: SCM, 2005), p. 1; J.M. Gordon, *Evangelical Spirituality: From the Wesleys to John Stott* (London: SPCK, 1991), p. vii.

[15] Wilson, *Constrained by Zeal*, p. 4.

[16] McGrath, *Christian Spirituality*, p. 2, italics added.

[17] Sheldrake, *Spirituality and History*, p. 52. Cf. I.M. Randall, *Evangelical Experiences: A Study in the Spirituality of English Evangelicalism 1918–1939* (Carlisle: Paternoster, 1999), p. 2.

[18] Cf. the similar comments of Randall, *Evangelical Experiences*, p. 2.

inner dimension of the spiritual life.[19] But this is not really the problem it might appear to be and the adoption of this different, more recent, model for the study of spirituality is both legitimate and helpful, allowing as it does for an analysis of a wide range of Spurgeon's 'lived experience'.[20] What I am understanding as 'spirituality' was vitally important to Spurgeon and it is my own conviction that he cannot be adequately understood without reference to it. 'Spirituality', as defined by Sheldrake, was of crucial importance to the life and ministry of C.H. Spurgeon.

The Study of Spurgeon

Spurgeon has not received anything like the scholarly coverage he deserves. During his lifetime a number of popular biographies were written[21] and his death in 1892 led to a rush of such books.[22] Few of these works rise above the level of hagiography.[23] The opening words of J.D. Douglas's *The Prince of Preachers* give a flavour of the sort of writing many of these books contain. Douglas introduced his subject by stating that Spurgeon 'was in no respect' ordinary. Rather, 'He was great as a man; great as a theologian; great as a preacher; great in private with God; and great in public with his fellow men.'[24] Some of these 'tombstone' biographies, for example Douglas's own work and a volume by William Williams, are useful because the writers knew their subject personally and insights can be gleaned from them with regards Spurgeon's personality and friendships.[25] The official biography was by G. Holden Pike. Originally published in three volumes, this was a straightforward description of Spurgeon's life and ministry. Described by a contemporary, not unfairly, as 'laborious',[26] Pike's work is almost devoid of analysis.[27] The four

---

[19] See, e.g., Spurgeon, *Autobiography*, Vol. 1, p. 145, 'Oh that my spirituality may be revived! My matchless Immanuel, let me see once more Thy face in the temple of my heart.' This quotation from Spurgeon's diary is n.d., but is probably from late 1850 or early 1851.

[20] Schneiders, 'Christian Spirituality: Definition, Methods and Types', p. 1. Cf. Randall, *Evangelical Experiences*, p. 2.

[21] The first book length treatment seems to be G.J. Stevenson, *A Sketch of the Life and Ministry of the Reverend C.H. Spurgeon* (New York: Sheldon and Blakeman, 1857). Cf. the comments of Kruppa, *Spurgeon*, pp. 2-3.

[22] See, e.g., R. Shindler, *From The Pulpit To The Palm-Branch: A Memorial of C.H. Spurgeon* (London: Passmore and Alabaster, 1892); G.C. Lorimer, *C.H. Spurgeon, The Puritan Preacher In The Nineteenth Century* (Boston: James H. Earle, 1892).

[23] [Anon.], *Charles Haddon Spurgeon: A Biographical Sketch And An Appreciation By One Who Knew Him Well* (London: Andrew Melrose, 1903), was one of the few works which was occasionally critical of Spurgeon. See, e.g., pp. vii-viii.

[24] J.D. Douglas, *The Prince of Preachers: A Sketch; A Portraiture; And A Tribute* (London: Morgan and Scott, n.d. [1893]), p. v.

[25] W. Williams, *Personal Reminiscences of Charles Haddon Spurgeon* (London: Religious Tract Society, 1895).

[26] [Anon.], *Charles Haddon Spurgeon*, p. v.

[27] G.H. Pike, *The Life and Work of Charles Haddon Spurgeon* (3 Vols; London: Cassell, n.d. [1892–93]). Throughout this study I have cited from a later six-volume edition of the

volume *Autobiography* appeared at the end of the nineteenth century, compiled by C.H. Spurgeon's wife, Susannah, and his private secretary, Joseph W. Harrald. This comprises material from Spurgeon (both his preaching and writing) which had been previously published in a number of places, together with material written specially by him with an autobiography in mind.[28] Harrald and, especially, Susannah Spurgeon inserted their own comments at a number of points but, again, there is hardly any analysis. Used with care, the works cited in this paragraph can provide the researcher with much useful source material, but for critical evaluation one must turn elsewhere.[29]

Two biographies of Spurgeon produced in the first half of the twentieth century attempt some critical appraisal. These are the studies by William Y. Fullerton and John C. Carlile, published in 1920 and 1933 respectively.[30] Both men, like William Williams, were former students of the Pastors' College who had known Spurgeon personally and these books certainly contain some useful personal reminiscences of Spurgeon. The evaluative material they do include often tells the reader more about the author than his subject.[31] Other works from this period tend merely to repeat the hagiography of the previous century.[32] The second half of the twentieth century saw the appearance of a number of biographies of Spurgeon. The longest of these is Lewis Drummond's *Spurgeon, Prince of Preachers*[33] which, unfortunately, is seriously flawed, not least by factual inaccuracies. The best book-length scholarly study is Patricia Kruppa's *Charles Haddon Spurgeon: A Preacher's Progress*. Kruppa breaks new ground in seeking to set her subject in the context of his times, but her work is still limited. It is especially weak in its treatment of Spurgeon's theology.[34] One unpublished PhD study worth noting is H.F. Colquitt's study of Spurgeon's soteriology. This is based on a thorough reading of Spurgeon's published

---

same text, *The Life and Work of Charles Haddon Spurgeon* (6 Vols; London: Cassell, 1894). Pike had also written an earlier one-volume work, *Charles Haddon Spurgeon: Preacher, Author, Philanthropist* (London: Hodder and Stoughton, 1886).

[28] See the comments of J.W. Harrald in 'Mr Spurgeon's Autobiography. An Interview with Mr Harrald', *British Weekly* 30 September 1897, in 'Maroon Bound Scrapfolders', Vol. 3, Spurgeon's College, Heritage Room, p. 146. The *Autobiography* was also issued in 'monthly shilling parts', the first of which was available in December 1897.

[29] It is only fair to acknowledge that many of the works cited or alluded to in this paragraph never set out to offer critical analysis of their subject. Therefore, the comment that they contain little such analysis should perhaps be regarded as more of an observation than a criticism.

[30] W.Y. Fullerton, *C.H. Spurgeon: A Biography* (London: Williams and Norgate, 1920); J.C. Carlile, *C.H. Spurgeon: An Interpretative Biography* (London: Kingsgate Press, 1933).

[31] See, e.g., Carlile's comments on Spurgeon's theology. See *Spurgeon*, pp. 132-51.

[32] See, e.g., A. Cunningham Burley, *Spurgeon And His Friendships* (London: Epworth, 1933).

[33] L. Drummond, *Spurgeon, Prince of Preachers* (Grand Rapids: Kregel, 1992).

[34] Cf. the comments of Hopkins, *Nonconformity's Romantic Generation*, p. 11.

sermons, but Colquitt's comments are rarely incisive.[35] I have written a biography of Spurgeon, *C.H. Spurgeon: The People's Preacher*, which is designed to be an accessible introduction to Spurgeon's life for the general reader.[36] Over a hundred years after Spurgeon's death, both a comprehensive study of his theology and a definitive critical biography are badly needed.[37]

There are a number of smaller studies which reflect on a particular dimension of Spurgeon's life and ministry, and with profit. These include Brian Stanley's examination of Spurgeon's relationship with the Baptist Missionary Society,[38] Andrew Bradstock's study of Spurgeon and Victorian 'manliness',[39] Tim Grass and Ian Randall's analysis of Spurgeon's approach to the sacraments,[40] and David Bebbington's work on Spurgeon and the 'common man'.[41] Bebbington has also written, in various places, on the relationship between Spurgeon and the Enlightenment.[42] I have interacted with all these scholars in this study, often seeking to build on the insights they offer. In my view, the best scholarly work on Spurgeon currently available is by Mark Hopkins. His *Nonconformity's Romantic Generation* contains two chapters on Spurgeon, one of which is a fine, suggestive exposition of his theology.[43] At various points in this study I have taken issue with some of Hopkins' judgements, but his work is undoubtedly the place to start for any serious student of Spurgeon. All of the scholars cited in this paragraph have contributed to an understanding of the man and his ministry. Spurgeon was, however, such a complex character that it is not possible to capture the essence of him in a shorter study. Through detailed analysis of the different aspects of his spirituality, this

---

[35] H.F. Colquitt, 'The Soteriology of Charles Haddon Spurgeon Revealed in his Sermons and Controversial Writings' (unpublished PhD dissertation, University of Edinburgh, 1951).

[36] P.J. Morden, *C.H. Spurgeon: The People's Preacher* (Farnham: CWR, 2009).

[37] At the time of writing, Christian George is pursuing PhD research into Spurgeon's theology at St Andrews University, Scotland. As far as Spurgeon's theology is concerned, this thesis is likely to go some way to filling the scholarly lacuna.

[38] B. Stanley, 'C.H. Spurgeon and the Baptist Missionary Society 1863–1866', *Baptist Quarterly* Vol. 20, No. 3 (July 1982), pp. 319-28.

[39] A. Bradstock, '"A Man of God is a Manly Man": Spurgeon, Luther and "Holy Boldness"', in A. Bradstock, S. Gill, A Hogan and S. Morgan (eds), *Masculinity and Spirituality in Victorian Culture* (Basingstoke: Macmillan, 2000), pp. 209-25.

[40] T. Grass and I.M. Randall, 'C.H. Spurgeon on the Sacraments', in A.R. Cross and P.E. Thompson (eds), *Baptist Sacramentalism* (Carlisle: Paternoster, 2003), pp. 55-75.

[41] D.W. Bebbington, 'Spurgeon and the Common Man', *Baptist Review of Theology* Vol. 5, No. 1 (Spring 1995), pp. 63-75. Bebbington has also contributed 'Spurgeon and British Evangelical Theological Education', in D.G. Hart and R.A. Mohler, Jr (eds), *Theological Education in the Evangelical Tradition* (Grand Rapids: Baker, 1996), pp. 217-34.

[42] See, e.g., D.W. Bebbington, *Holiness in Nineteenth-Century England* (Carlisle: Paternoster, 2002), pp. 48-49; 'Gospel and Culture in Victorian Nonconformity', in J. Shaw and A. Kreider (eds), *Culture and the Nonconformist Tradition* (Cardiff: University of Wales Press, 1999), pp. 57-58.

[43] Hopkins, *Nonconformity's Romantic Generation*, pp. 125-66.

present work seeks to paint a more complete picture of this multifaceted man and uncover the forces that shaped and drove him.

A number of more general works give a degree of attention to Spurgeon. Bebbington's *The Dominance of Evangelicalism: The Age of Spurgeon and Moody* is especially important.[44] Another book which includes some helpful analysis is Horton Davies' *Worship and Theology in England*.[45] Usually, however, the coverage given to Spurgeon in both general and religious histories of the nineteenth century is remarkably thin. There are only two references to him in John Wolffe's *God and Greater Britain: Religion and National Life in Britain and Ireland 1843–1945*,[46] and none at all in Boyd Hilton's *The Age of Atonement* (which only covers the period 1785–1865).[47] These are fine works but, given Spurgeon's importance and influence, admittedly as a purveyor of popular religion, the lack of notice accorded to him seems surprising.

Finally, it is important to note the welter of popular and semi-popular books, pamphlets, papers and, more recently, web-based articles, which highlight Spurgeon's Calvinism and speak of him, by turns, as the 'heir of the Puritans' or the 'last of the Puritans'. This tradition was already established by the end of the nineteenth century, in works with subtitles like *The Puritan Preacher*.[48] Ernest Bacon provides an example of this approach from the second half of the twentieth century. In his biography of Spurgeon, subtitled *Heir of the Puritans*, Bacon states that his subject 'was completely moulded and fashioned by those spiritual giants of the sixteenth and seventeenth centuries, the Puritans. He stood in their noble tradition, in the direct line of their theology and outlook.'[49] The writing in this vein is usually polemical and often focuses on the Downgrade Controversy of 1887–88 and Spurgeon's decision to resign from the Baptist Union. This is then used as ammunition to score points in favour of a separatist ecclesiology.[50] Some studies in this genre, for example those by Iain Murray, undoubtedly contribute to an

---

[44] Bebbington, *Dominance of Evangelicalism*.

[45] H. Davies, *Worship and Theology in England: From Watts and Wesley to Martineau, 1690–1900* (Grand Rapids: Eerdmans, 1996 [1961–62]), pp. 333-45.

[46] J. Wolffe, *God and Greater Britain: Religion and National Life in Britain and Ireland 1843–1945* (London: Routledge, 1994), pp. 89, 166.

[47] B. Hilton, *The Age of Atonement: The Influence of Evangelicalism on Social and Economic Thought, 1785–1865* (Oxford: Clarendon Press, 1988).

[48] See, e.g., Lorimer, *Spurgeon*, with his subtitle, *The Puritan Preacher In The Nineteenth Century*.

[49] E.W. Bacon, *Spurgeon: Heir of the Puritans* (London: George Allen and Unwin, 1967), p. 102.

[50] Spurgeon's name was invoked in similar ways by Baptist fundamentalists in inter-war Britain. See D.W. Bebbington, 'Baptists and Fundamentalism in Inter-War Britain', in K. Robbins (ed.), *Protestant Evangelicalism: Britain, Ireland, Germany and America, c.1750–c.1950* (Oxford: Blackwell, 1990), pp. 303-304. Cf. H.H. Harris, *Fundamentalism and Evangelicals* (Oxford: Clarendon, 1998), p. 46.

understanding of Spurgeon.⁵¹ Comments such as those cited from Bacon, however, are simply wrong, as this study will show.

Overall, then, the published literature on Spurgeon is uneven in quality and a major, satisfying scholarly study is lacking.⁵² The best of the secondary literature offers insights into particular aspects of Spurgeon, but the whole picture is not painted. What there is plenty of is hagiography and polemic, a significant amount of which is marked by misinformation and lack of depth. There is a consistent failure to capture a picture of Spurgeon which does justice to the cross-currents which fed his life and ministry and get to the heart of the man. This present book seeks to make a contribution to the study of Spurgeon by considering him both in depth and breadth.

Sources Used

As already indicated, I have worked in the main from primary data. This includes the aforementioned four-volume *Autobiography* and the biographies written by those who knew Spurgeon, mainly men who had studied at the Pastors' College. The sixty-three volumes of the *New Park Street / Metropolitan Tabernacle Pulpit*, which contain the vast majority of Spurgeon's printed sermons, are indispensable.⁵³ From 1855 Spurgeon's preaching was taken down verbatim by stenographers and then edited, until the last years of his life by Spurgeon himself, for publication. After his death a large cache of sermons remained unissued and so publication continued, ending only in 1917, the final message issued being number 3563.⁵⁴ In his preaching

---

⁵¹ See, e.g., I.H. Murray, *The Forgotten Spurgeon* (London: Banner of Truth, 1966), and *Heroes* (Edinburgh: Banner of Truth, 2009), pp. 261-96.

⁵² Hopkins' *Nonconformity's Romantic Generation* is the work that comes closest to this, but his study of Spurgeon covers only two of seven main chapters. See pp. 125-66 and pp. 193-248.

⁵³ C.H. Spurgeon, *New Park Street Pulpit (NPSP) / Metropolitan Tabernacle Pulpit (MTP)* (London: Passmore and Alabaster, 1855–1917). These are now supplemented by T.P. Crosby (ed.), *C.H. Spurgeon's Sermons Beyond Volume 63: An authentic supplement to the Metropolitan Tabernacle Pulpit* (Leominster: Day One, 2009). The majority of the forty-five sermons in this volume appeared in the *Baptist Messenger* between 1877 and 1881.

⁵⁴ C.H. Spurgeon, 'A Cheering Congratulation', *MTP*, Vol. 63, S. No. 3563, Psalm 32.1, n.d., pp. 217-27. There are not quite 3568 sermons. Some of the early sermons were too long for a single issue and were issued in two parts. See, e.g., 'Christ Crucified', *NPSP*, Vol. 1, S. Nos 7-8, 1 Corinthians 1.23,24, delivered 11 February 1855, pp. 49-60. Furthermore, there were a few issues which did not actually contained a sermon. Examples of these include, *NPSP*, Vol. 5, Nos 268-70, pp. 345-68, which are detailed reports of 'The Ceremony Of Laying The First Stone Of The New Tabernacle …', 16 August 1859; and Vol. 6, S. Nos 331-32, pp. 357-72, which contain 'The Proceedings Of The Great Meeting In The Metropolitan Tabernacle, Newington', 2 September 1860. Finally, there are sermons in *NPSP*, Vol. 7 which are not by Spurgeon himself, e.g., the expositions of various Calvinistic doctrines which partly make up Nos 385-88, one of which was delivered by C.H. Spurgeon's brother, J.A. Spurgeon, on 'Particular Redemption', pp. 313-18. The meeting at which these expositions was given was on 11 April 1861. When Spurgeon died many sermons remained

Introduction   9

Spurgeon sought to stick closely to the biblical text but was also often highly autobiographical. The printed sermons are, therefore, very revealing both of Spurgeon's overall conception of the Christian life and of his spirituality. I have sought to read widely in this vitally important body of material. However, some studies of Spurgeon concentrate on these sermons almost to the exclusion of other sources.[55] I have tried not to do this and have used a range of other material as well.

Many sermons, talks and 'meditations' by Spurgeon were published outside of the *New Park Street / Metropolitan Tabernacle Pulpit*. His book of communion meditations, entitled *Till He Come*, is a vital resource.[56] A book of prayer meeting addresses was also published,[57] as were some of the Friday afternoon lectures Spurgeon gave to his Pastors' College students.[58] Like the sermons in the *New Park Street / Metropolitan Tabernacle Pulpit*, these messages were taken down by stenographers and other personal aides and later revised for publication. But Spurgeon also wrote a large number of books. An early work, *The Saint And His Saviour*, is significant in that it sets out his conception of the Christian life.[59] Spurgeon wrote in a popular, accessible style. His two volumes of daily devotional readings, *Morning By Morning* and *Evening By Evening*,[60] and two books written under the *nom de plume* of 'John Ploughman'[61] stand perhaps as the supreme examples of this approach. These small, affordable books enjoyed significant sales. Just three years after its publication *Morning By Morning* had sold more than 20,000 copies.[62] The agricultural John Ploughman's avowed aim was to communicate in both 'plain speech' and 'mirthful vein'.[63] By 1897 more than 500,000 copies of the

---

still to be issued. Publication ceased on 10 May 1917 because of 'difficulties due to war conditions'. See the notices announcing 'Suspension of Publication' in *MTP*, Vol. 63, pp. 216, 228.

[55] See, especially, Colquitt, 'The Soteriology of Charles Haddon Spurgeon', despite his claim that he has made 'extensive use' of 'many other of Spurgeon's publications', p. ii. In Colquitt's chapters 2 and 3, all the references to primary Spurgeon material except one are, directly or indirectly, from *NPSP / MTP*. See pp. 54-112.

[56] C.H. Spurgeon, *Till He Come: Communion Meditations And Addresses* (London: Passmore and Alabaster, 1896).

[57] C.H. Spurgeon, *Only a Prayer Meeting: Forty Addresses at the Metropolitan Tabernacle and Other Prayer Meetings* (London: Passmore and Alabaster, 1901).

[58] C.H. Spurgeon, *Lectures To My Students* (3 Vols; London: Passmore and Alabaster, n.d.).

[59] C.H. Spurgeon, *The Saint And His Saviour: The Progress Of The Soul In The Knowledge Of Jesus* (London: Hodder and Stoughton, 1889 [1857]).

[60] C.H. Spurgeon, *Morning By Morning: Or, Daily Readings for the Family or the Closet* (London: Passmore and Alabaster, 1865); *Evening By Evening: Or, Readings at Eventide for the Family or the Closet* (London: Passmore and Alabaster, 1868).

[61] C.H. Spurgeon, *John Ploughman's Talk; Or, Plain Advice for Plain People* (London: Passmore and Alabaster, n.d.); *John Ploughman's Pictures; Or, More of his Plain Talk for Plain People* (London: Passmore and Alabaster, 1880).

[62] See Spurgeon, *Evening By Evening*, Preface, pp. vii-viii.

[63] Spurgeon, *John Ploughman's Pictures*, Preface, p. 3.

two John Ploughman books had been sold.[64] Spurgeon was shaping the views and devotional habits of countless Victorian Christians not only through his published preaching but also through his writing. There were many other books, including two biblical commentaries, *The Gospel of the Kingdom*,[65] which was on Matthew's Gospel, and the multi-volume *Treasury of David*,[66] which was on the Psalms. The latter work is a particularly important and neglected resource. The production and publication of the seven volumes which made up the *Treasury of David* spanned over sixteen years and in many ways the commentary was Spurgeon's *magnum opus*. These different and varied books yield insights into Spurgeon's spirituality which could not be gleaned elsewhere and I have drawn from all of them, with a special focus on the *Treasury*, which is invaluable because of the way Spurgeon reflected on the nature of spiritual experience as he worked his way through the different Psalms.

Further printed material is available. Spurgeon began his monthly magazine, *The Sword and The Trowel* (referred to as the *Sword and Trowel* in all subsequent references in the main text of this book) in January 1865. He was its editor from its inception to his death, contributing numerous articles and reviews himself.[67] The *Sword and Trowel* is another vital resource for this study. In 1866 Spurgeon edited and published a hymnal for his church, the Metropolitan Tabernacle, which was entitled *Our Own Hymn Book*.[68] The hymns and shorter verses included were selected with great care by the book's editor, who also composed a number of the hymns.[69] *Our Own Hymn Book* is, once again, both a neglected and a revealing resource for the student of Spurgeon. Similarly neglected and even more important are the records of the prayers Spurgeon prayed in the Metropolitan Tabernacle Sunday services. Spurgeon famously rejected any formal liturgy or set prayers and refused to include written prayers in his books of daily readings.[70] But records of his public, extempore prayers survive because it became Spurgeon's practice, from at

---

[64] See *John Ploughman's Almanack* (London: Passmore and Alabaster, 1897). The Almanack was produced on a single sheet.

[65] C.H. Spurgeon, *The Gospel of the Kingdom. A Popular Exposition of the Gospel According to Matthew* (London: Passmore and Alabaster, 1893). Spurgeon completed this commentary in the last few months of his life. See Susannah Spurgeon's 'Introductory Note', pp. iii-iv.

[66] C.H. Spurgeon, *The Treasury Of David: Containing An Original Exposition Of The Book Of Psalms; A Collection Of Illustrative Extracts From The Whole Range Of Literature; A Series Of Homiletical Hints Upon Almost Every Verse; And Lists Of Writers Upon Each Psalm* (7 Vols; London and Edinburgh: Marshall Brothers, n.d. [London: Passmore and Alabaster, 1869–1885]).

[67] Spurgeon (ed.), *Sword and Trowel*.

[68] C.H. Spurgeon (ed.), *Our Own Hymn Book* (London: Passmore and Alabaster, 1866).

[69] Spurgeon (ed.), *Our Own Hymn Book*, Preface, pp. vi-x. A supplement was produced after Spurgeon's death which included some hymns Spurgeon had written after the publication of the original hymnal. See [Anon.] (ed.), *Supplement To Our Own Hymn Book* (London: Passmore and Alabaster, 1898), p. ii.

[70] Spurgeon, *Morning By Morning*, Preface, p. vii.

Introduction 11

least the early 1860s, to have his Tabernacle stenographers take these down verbatim, apparently to enable him to reflect on his own practice of public prayer.[71] He would have strongly resisted any attempts at publication, but after his death two collections of prayers quickly appeared based on these records.[72] The stenographers' transcripts were still extant and in possession of the publishers Marshall, Morgan and Scott when Charles T. Cook prepared his edition of Spurgeon's hymns and prayers in the early 1930s.[73] I have not seen these prayers cited in any scholarly study of Spurgeon. They are essential reading if his spirituality is to be understood.

This study also seeks to utilise a vast corpus of unpublished material. I have drawn from the archives of 'Spurgeons' (formerly known as 'Spurgeon's Childcare') at Rushden and there is also some helpful manuscript material held at the Angus Library and Archives, Regent's Park College, Oxford. In the main, however, I have worked with the unpublished, primary sources which are held in the Heritage Room (also known as the 'Spurgeon Archive') at Spurgeon's College. Important are the bound scrapbooks and loose-leaf scrapfolders which are held in different places in the archive.[74] Most appear to have been originally compiled by Spurgeon family members, for example, his sister, Emily.[75] They contain cuttings from newspapers and magazines and a wealth of other printed material relevant to C.H. Spurgeon, but they also include many letters, both to and from Spurgeon, the majority of which are not catalogued.[76] Also, there are three bound volumes of letters from Spurgeon which together contain over 400 letters and cards.[77] In addition to these, there are

---

[71] C.T. Cook (ed.), *Behold the Throne of Grace: C.H. Spurgeon's Prayers and Hymns* (Marshall, Morgan and Scott: London, n.d. [1934]), pp. 10-11.

[72] [Anon.] (ed.), *The Pastor in Prayer: Being a Selection of C.H. Spurgeon's Sunday Morning Prayers* (London: Elliot Stock, 1893); D.T. Young (ed.), *C.H. Spurgeon's Prayers* (London: Passmore and Alabaster, 1905). Prayers recorded in *The Pastor in Prayer* are particularly valuable for being dated.

[73] Cook (ed.), *Behold the Throne of Grace*, p.11.

[74] In addition to 'Spurgeon's Scrapbooks, Numbered Volumes', 'Spurgeon's Scrapbooks, Two Unnumbered Volumes' and the 'Loose-Leaf Scrap Folders', see the four volumes of 'Maroon Bound Scrapfolders', Spurgeon's College, Heritage Room. In the bibliography of this study I have included all these scrapbooks and scrapfolders under the heading, 'Manuscript Material', as they contain written as well as printed matter. Also, of course, the scrapbooks and scrapfolders themselves are unpublished.

[75] See 'Cuttings on C.H. Spurgeon', Spurgeon's College, Heritage Room (H1.01 and 02). Some were compiled by Susannah Spurgeon, see Spurgeon, *Autobiography*, Vol. 2, p. 33.

[76] The Heritage Room is a difficult archive to work in. Through no fault of the excellent and overworked librarian many items are not properly catalogued. In the 1980s there was an attempt to tidy up the archive. Some of the changes were positive, with much material being properly logged for the first time. Other changes, for example the breaking up of some of the scrapbooks and the placing of material in ring binders, have been less helpful. I have noted where in the archive the material I am citing is currently held, although it is highly possible that a future reorganisation of the archive will render these references obsolete.

[77] 'Original Correspondence of Charles Haddon Spurgeon' 1851–1893 (Vol. 1); 1863–1868 (Vol. 2); 1887–1892 (Vol. 3), Spurgeon's College, Heritage Room (4G). Volume One

many other of Spurgeon's letters which are not in the bound volumes or the scrapbooks or folders, but scattered throughout the archive. In letters to his family and close friends Spurgeon often wrote in an unguarded way about issues relevant to this study. Letters written to Spurgeon, together with handwritten recollections of his personality and ministry, also bring insights.[78]

The manuscript materials I have found most illuminating for the early period of Spurgeon's ministry are the notebooks containing outlines of his unpublished, pre-London, Cambridgeshire sermons. Eight volumes are extant,[79] containing just under 350 'skeletons' from which he preached. Many of these outlines are considerably longer than the ones from which he preached in his London ministry.[80] A few of the 'skeletons' are included in Volume 1 of the *Autobiography*, and these give an impression of the sort of detail he could include.[81] As with the published prayers, I am not aware of any study that has utilised the wealth of information these outlines contain relative to the formative years of Spurgeon's Cambridgeshire ministry.

The Heritage Room archive has been used by researchers before. For example, Mike Nicholls made use of a number of photographs and drawings to illustrate his book on Spurgeon, which also includes some facsimiles of letters and a sermon outline.[82] Ian Randall has drawn from the archive in his history of Spurgeon's College[83] and in a short paper which examines responses to the more restrictive basis of the College Conference introduced in the aftermath of the Downgrade Controversy, where he makes excellent use of a collection of letters written by members of the Conference.[84] Both Kruppa and Hopkins spent some time in the archive and cite some of the published and unpublished material in their respective studies, but they do so only sparingly. I do not think that the unpublished manuscript sources have had any significant, shaping influence on their work, with the sole (but very important) exception of Hopkins' chapter and articles on the Downgrade

---

contains a number of letters not written by C.H. Spurgeon, one from as late as 1909 and one, written by C.H. Spurgeon's father, from 1821. Therefore the description of this volume is not accurate. See, e.g., the letters numbered 161 and 168.

[78] E.g. T. Cox, 'Notes on C.H. Spurgeon', Spurgeon's College, Heritage Room (B1.17).

[79] C.H. Spurgeon, 'Notebook Containing Early Sermon Skeletons, Vol. 1', Spurgeon's College, Heritage Room (K1.5); 'Notebooks With Sermon Outlines, Vols 2, 4-9', Spurgeon's College, Heritage Room (U.1). Volume 3 is missing, which seems to have contained 54 outlines, is missing, and appears not to be extant. Volume 8 closes with outline number 377.

[80] See the comments in Spurgeon, *Autobiography*, Vol. 1, pp. 214, 277.

[81] Spurgeon, *Autobiography*, Vol. 1, pp. 214-26; 277-84.

[82] M.K. Nicholls, *C.H. Spurgeon: The Pastor Evangelist* (Didcot: Baptist Historical Society, 1982), pp. 29-30; 38-39.

[83] I.M. Randall, *A School of the Prophets: 150 Years of Spurgeon's College* (London: Spurgeon's College, 2005).

[84] I.M. Randall, 'Charles Haddon Spurgeon, the Pastors' College and the Downgrade Controversy', in K. Cooper and J. Gregory (eds), *Discipline and Diversity: Papers Read at the 2005 Summer Meeting and the 2006 Winter Meeting of the Ecclesiastical History Society* (Woodbridge, Suffolk: Boydell, 2007), pp. 366-76.

Controversy.[85] I have sought to make good use of the archive in each of the main chapters of this study. Moreover, I have tried to allow the unpublished resources in the Heritage Room to inform and shape the argument rather than merely using them to illustrate conclusions arrived at by another route. This material has been helpful in overturning some of the established opinions about Spurgeon and in bringing new features to light. This study, then, works with a diverse range of primary evidence – from published sermons and books to unpublished letters and notes – in order to build up a picture of Spurgeon's spirituality.

The Content of this Book

Examination of Spurgeon's spirituality is made in nine main chapters. Chapters 2, 3 and 4 focus in the main on issues of spiritual formation. Chapter 2 considers the oft spoken of 'Puritan atmosphere' in which Spurgeon was brought up and the way 'Puritanism' had a continuing influence on him. Chapter 3 analyses his evangelical conversion and the ways that 'conversionism' shaped his subsequent life and ministry. Chapter 4 examines his baptism as a believer and the ways that this and his overall approach to baptism was important for his spirituality. Chapters 5 to 7 focus especially on how spirituality was sustained, with detailed consideration given to the Bible (chapter 5), prayer (chapter 6) and the Lord's Supper (chapter 7), all of which were crucial in nurturing Spurgeon's spirituality. Chapters 8 to 10 consider, broadly speaking, the outworking of his spirituality. His 'activism' is examined and the link between such activism and spirituality is analysed (chapter 8). His approach to personal holiness and his engagement with a range of other approaches to 'sanctification' which were current in the nineteenth century are evaluated (chapter 9). The final main chapter (chapter 10) deals with Spurgeon's experience of suffering and concludes with an examination of his conception of life beyond the grave where, for the Christian, all suffering would be over. It should also be noted that there are big themes which cross the chapters. Examples of these include the atonement and 'spiritual friendship'.

The analysis of Spurgeon's spirituality undertaken in this study reveals him to be a far more complex, multi-faceted figure than is usually supposed. Each main chapter contributes to an understanding of this complexity. Approaches to Spurgeon which portray him as the reincarnation of sixteenth- and seventeenth- century Puritanism, or, conversely, as a typical Victorian fail to grasp either the man or his ministry. Attempts to interpret Spurgeon as an Enlightenment figure standing against Romantic trends in nineteenth-century religious life are, on their own, inadequate, but neither is it right to describe him, without severe qualification, as 'Romantic'.

---

[85] Hopkins, *Nonconformity's Romantic Generation*, pp. 193-248; M.T.E. Hopkins, 'The Downgrade Controversy: New Evidence', *Baptist Quarterly* Vol. 35, No. 6 (April 1994), pp. 262-78; 'Spurgeon's Opponents in the Downgrade Controversy', *Baptist Quarterly* Vol. 32, No. 6 (April 1988), pp. 274-94.

There is important truth in these and other pictures, but, by themselves, they do not capture the angularity, complexity and richness of Spurgeon.

Analysis of Spurgeon's spirituality suggests an alternative theme, one which helps to make sense of the man and his ministry. One of Spurgeon's communion meditations, included in *Till He Come*, was given the suggestive title of 'Communion With Christ And His People'.[86] In this message Spurgeon set out different ways in which communion, or fellowship, firstly with Christ and secondly with Christ's people, was to be attained, sustained and deepened. What I will aim to show in this study is that the phrase 'communion with Christ and his people' actually represents the integrating theme of Spurgeon's spirituality.[87]

I will argue Spurgeon's spirituality was thoroughly christocentric, with an overriding stress on communion with Christ. This was true both of the inner and outer dimensions of his spirituality. At the point of conversion Spurgeon began to experience communion with Christ and his subsequent spiritual journey represented a quest for yet deeper communion. Even Christian activity, for Spurgeon a crucial outworking of his experience of communion or fellowship with Christ was, in and of itself, a way of experiencing closer communion with Jesus. The Christian life was, for Spurgeon, the 'progress of the soul in the knowledge of Jesus'.[88] Spurgeon also pursued fellowship with Christ's people. He was not a 'solitary' but sought to live out his faith in close connection with others. For Spurgeon, communion with Christ was often experienced in the presence of other, like-minded believers and for him Christianity had to be lived out, in the church and the wider world. Spurgeon is certainly a more complex figure than is often supposed. His spirituality was moulded by a range of different influences – religious, cultural and temperamental. Nevertheless, analysis of his spirituality reveals a single, integrating theme, albeit one that was kaleidoscopic rather than monochrome. 'Communion with Christ and his people' is the theme which helps us makes sense of the different dimensions of Spurgeon's life and ministry.

---

[86] C.H. Spurgeon, 'Communion With Christ And His People', 1 Corinthians 10.16,17, in *Till He Come*, pp. 313-27.

[87] In this study, where I am referring to the sermon 'Communion With Christ And His People', I begin each word with an upper case letter, but I do not do this when I am using the phrase in a more general sense. Overall, in all quotations from different sources I follow the capitalisation and grammar of the original. In the quotations which appear at the beginning of each chapter, I do not provide a footnote reference if that quotation appears later in the chapter. On the two occasions when the quotation does not appear again I do provide a reference. One further point about quotations can be made. Spurgeon did not use inclusive language. I have quoted Spurgeon accurately but have sought to use inclusive language myself in my own writing in this study.

[88] The subtitle of Spurgeon's *The Saint And His Saviour*.

Conclusion

This book makes a detailed examination of the spirituality of Charles Haddon Spurgeon. Studies of this significant figure in the religious and cultural life of Victorian Britain have failed to do justice to his complexity. Analysis of his spirituality using a range of primary data illuminates the different dimensions of Spurgeon's life and ministry and shows how they fit into the whole. It will be argued that 'communion with Christ and his people' is the integrating theme which ties together and makes sense of the different, and sometimes seemingly contradictory, aspects of Spurgeon's life and work. In this way, this study aims to make a contribution to Spurgeon studies and, more broadly, to an understanding of religion in nineteenth-century Britain.

CHAPTER 2

Puritan Piety:
'A Calvinistic creed and a Puritanic morality'

Charles Haddon Spurgeon was born on 19 June 1834 in the small village of Kelvedon, Essex, the first child of John and Eliza Spurgeon (née Jarvis).[1] John was pastor of a small Independent congregation in nearby Tollesbury, but had to supplement his income by working as a clerk to a coal merchant in Colchester. Within a year of Charles Spurgeon's birth the family moved to Colchester and, following the arrival of Eliza, who was born in January 1836,[2] Charles was sent to live with his paternal grandparents, James and Sarah, in Stambourne, also in Essex. By the time the infant Charles arrived in rural, isolated Stambourne, grandfather James had been minister of the Independent chapel there for twenty-five years. Charles was to stay in the manse with his grandparents, and their unmarried daughter Ann, until 1841. As an adolescent, he would regularly return to his grandparents' home for long holidays and other visits.[3] As Mark Hopkins states, the influence of James and Sarah on the young C.H. Spurgeon was 'considerable'.[4]

Charles Spurgeon returned to Colchester to live with his parents and their growing family in August 1841.[5] He was taught locally at Stockwell House, but in 1848 he was sent to Maidstone, Kent, to attend an Anglican agricultural school. In 1849 he

---

[1] For biographical details included in this paragraph, unless otherwise stated, see C.H. Spurgeon, *Autobiography: Compiled from his Diary, Letters, and Records by his Wife and his Private Secretary* (4 Vols; London: Passmore and Alabaster, 1897–99), Vol. 1, pp. 10-31, 43, 47-55, 96-115; G.H. Pike, *The Life and Work of Charles Haddon Spurgeon* (6 Vols; London: Cassell, 1894, [1892–93]), Vol. 1, pp. 6-31.

[2] 'Family Register' in 'Spurgeon Family Bible' (*The Holy Bible with the Commentaries of [Thomas] Scott and [Matthew] Henry* ... (Glasgow: W.R. M'Phun, 1852), Spurgeon's College, Heritage Room (Display Case 2).

[3] Spurgeon, *Autobiography*, Vol. 1, p. 43.

[4] M. Hopkins, *Nonconformity's Romantic Generation: Evangelical and Liberal Theologies in Victorian England* (Carlisle: Paternoster, 2004), p. 125.

[5] By 1841 James Archer Spurgeon (June 1837) and Emily J. Spurgeon (April 1839) had been born. See C.H. Spurgeon's handwritten notes reproduced in facsimile, in W.M. Higgs, *The Spurgeon Family: Being An Account Of The Descent And Family Of Charles Haddon Spurgeon* (London: Elliot Stock, 1906), p. viii. There were seventeen children in all, although nine died in infancy. See Higgs' chart, 'Pedigree of the Spurgeon ... Family', attached between pp. 32-33 in his *The Spurgeon Family*, and C.H. Spurgeon's handwritten note in the 'Family Register', in 'Spurgeon Family Bible'.

became an usher, or 'junior instructor', at a school in Newmarket, Suffolk. In January 1850 Charles had an evangelical conversion experience, while he was back in Colchester for his holidays. This will be analysed in detail in chapter 3. In the September of 1850 he moved again, to Cambridge, where he taught in another school. Both in Newmarket and Cambridge C.H. Spurgeon stayed with committed, Nonconformist Christians.

As should already be clear, C.H. Spurgeon had a staunchly religious upbringing which predated his conversion. The first half of this chapter examines the influence aspects of that upbringing had on his later spirituality. The focus is on how 'Puritanism' moulded him. After a discussion on the nature of Puritanism, the so-called 'Puritan atmosphere' in which Spurgeon was brought up is considered. It is true that his family were also evangelical, and this evangelicalism and its impact on him will be examined in chapter 3.[6] Nevertheless, the family were evangelicals of a particular stripe, seeking to stand within what they understood to be the Puritan tradition. The mature Spurgeon identified himself strongly with this tradition. Puritanism is, therefore, a good place to start in any consideration of his spirituality.

The second half of the chapter considers some of the particular ways Puritanism helped to mould Spurgeon. As noted in chapter 1, too much has been claimed in respect of the connection between Spurgeon and the Puritans. Nevertheless, Puritanism was still very significant for his spirituality. It helped shape his approach to the Christian life in both its inner and outer dimensions. This will be shown in detail as the chapter unfolds but some quotations from Spurgeon are helpful in establishing the basic point. In a sermon entitled 'All Of Grace', based on Ephesians 2.8 and originally included in the *Sword and Trowel* for January 1887, Spurgeon stated that the doctrines he preached were those of the Puritans. Furthermore, he stated that his 'experience' endeared these doctrines to him.[7] On another occasion he wrote of the 'vigorous personal piety of the Puritanic period'.[8] This was something he admired and sought to emulate. Puritanism was foundational to Spurgeon's spirituality.

---

[6] In which a discussion and definition of the nature of evangelicalism will also be offered.

[7] C.H. Spurgeon, 'All Of Grace', in C.H. Spurgeon (ed.), *The Sword and The Trowel: A Record of Combat With Sin and Labour For The Lord* (London: Passmore and Alabaster, 1865–92) (*Sword and The Trowel*), January 1887, p. 4. The paragraph in which these comments occur was omitted from the version of this message that was eventually published in the *Metropolitan Tabernacle Pulpit*. See 'All Of Grace', *New Park Street Pulpit (NPSP) / Metropolitan Tabernacle Pulpit (MTP)* (London: Passmore and Alabaster, 1855–1917), *MTP*, Vol. 61, S. No. 3479, Eph. 2.8, p. 470. All subsequent references to 'All Of Grace' are from the version published in the *Sword and Trowel*.

[8] Spurgeon (ed.), *Sword and Trowel*, August 1871, p. 368.

Understanding Puritanism

As John Coffey and Paul Lim state, 'Defining Puritanism has become a favourite parlour game for early modern historians.'[9] Lawrence Sasek writes that the terms 'Puritan' and 'Puritanism' pose 'great and possibly unique difficulties for modern scholarship'.[10] Having noted the difficulties, however, it is necessary to arrive at a working understanding of Puritanism for the purposes of this chapter and, indeed, for the study as a whole. Coffey and Lim suggest the following,

> Puritanism is the name we give to a distinctive and particularly intense variety of early modern Reformed Protestantism which originated within the unique context of the Church of England but spilled out beyond it, branching off into divergent dissenting streams, and overflowing into other lands and foreign churches.

Coffey and Lim then proceed to comment on this statement. Firstly, Puritanism was *Protestant*. Puritans affirmed the sixteenth-century Reformation 'slogans' – *sola fide, sola gratia, sola scriptura* (although there was disagreement as to exactly what these entailed in practice) and rejected Roman Catholicism. Indeed, Puritan 'anti-Popery' was especially 'intense'. Secondly, Puritanism was *Reformed*. That is, Puritans aligned themselves with the continental Calvinists rather than the Lutherans.[11] Puritans tended to have a Calvinistic theology (although there were exceptions).[12] Usually doctrines such as predestination, election and final perseverance were important, as was the idea of God entering into 'covenant' with his people.[13] The overarching stress was on God's sovereignty in salvation. Simplicity in worship was also a feature, with Puritans recoiling with 'iconophobic horror from images and elaborate rituals'.[14] All this was recognisably Reformed. Thirdly, *Puritanism originated within the Church of England*, that is, it was formed in the tensions of that particular environment, being, as Patrick Collinson has written, 'one half of a stressful equation'.[15] The Puritans regarded the Reformation in

---

[9] J. Coffey and P.C.H. Lim, 'Introduction', in J. Coffey and P.C.H. Lim (eds), *The Cambridge Companion to Puritanism* (Cambridge: Cambridge University Press, 2008), p. 1.

[10] L.A. Sasek (ed.), *Images of English Puritanism: A Collection of Contemporary Sources 1589–1646* (Louisiana: Louisiana State University Press, 1989), p. 1.

[11] Coffey and Lim, 'Introduction', pp. 2-3.

[12] J. Coffey, *John Goodwin and the Puritan Revolution: Religion and Intellectual Change in Seventeenth-Century England* (Woodbridge, Suffolk: Boydell, 2008 [2006]). Goodwin was, unusually, a 'pugnacious proponent of Arminian theology', p. 199.

[13] The importance of covenant theology for the Puritans, and the nuances of some of the different Puritan approaches to the covenant, with special reference to the situation in Ireland, is highlighted by C. Gribben, 'Defining the Puritans? The Baptism Debate in Cromwellian Ireland, 1654-56', *Church History* Vol. 73, No. 1 (2004), pp. 81-85.

[14] Coffey and Lim, 'Introduction', p. 2.

[15] As cited by Coffey and Lim, 'Introduction', p. 4. Cf. P. Collinson, *The Birthpangs of Protestant England* (Basingstoke: Macmillan, 1988), p. 143, and *The Puritan Character: Polemics and Polarities in Early Seventeenth-Century English Culture* (Los Angeles: University of California, 1989).

the Church of England as half finished and, as Mark Noll has stated, they wanted 'to finish the Reformation and finish it now'.[16] In this they were unsuccessful, but in the heat of battle the language of Puritanism was forged and the identity of those who described themselves as the 'godly' ('Puritan' was, originally, a term of abuse used by opponents) was consolidated.[17] Fourthly, Puritanism came to *spill out beyond the Church of England*; indeed, Coffey and Lim describe Puritanism as a 'uniquely fissiparous' and 'remarkably fluid' variety of the Reformed faith. Independents and Baptists who separated from the Church of England and Presbyterians who were excluded from it retained their Puritan identity. The godly 'spilled out' not only beyond the boundaries of the established church in England but beyond the boundaries of England itself, most notably as different groups of pilgrims sailed for the New World. Finally, Coffey and Lim note that Puritanism has 'had an enduring legacy, one that fed into Protestant Dissent and Evangelicalism'.[18] Puritanism, then, was complex and multi-faceted. Nevertheless, although it is extremely difficult to define there are identifiable, distinguishing features. The basic understanding stated and expounded by Coffey and Lim is the one that is worked with in this study.

Coffey and Lim give some attention to Puritanism as a movement of spirituality,[19] and K.M. Kapic and R.C. Gleason argue that Puritans were, to a significant degree, concerned with spirituality.[20] Certainly, the godly practised a particular form of practical, personal piety, one that was especially intense, with a stress on 'experimental religion'. Personal and family devotions were emphasised, spiritual diaries were kept and an 'experimental predestinarianism' was fostered as encouragement was given to the believer to seek evidence that they were truly one of the elect.[21] There was also a strong emphasis on communion with God. Geoffrey Nuttall has spoken of Puritanism as a 'movement towards immediacy in relation to God'.[22] This core concern of Puritanism – experimental, Godward-facing piety – was very important for Spurgeon, as will be shown.

It is also important to consider Spurgeon's own understanding of Puritanism. As Patricia Kruppa observes, Spurgeon himself used the words 'Puritan' and 'Puritanism' loosely, a point illustrated by the fact that he could describe George

---

[16] M.A. Noll, *A History of Christianity in the United States and Canada* (London: SPCK, 1992), p. 32. Noll's focus is on Puritanism in North America, but in this statement he is speaking specifically of English Puritanism.

[17] Coffey and Lim, 'Introduction', p. 3.

[18] Coffey and Lim, 'Introduction', pp. 5-7.

[19] Coffey and Lim, 'Introduction', p. 4.

[20] K.M. Kapic and R.C. Gleason, 'Who Were the Puritans?', in K.M. Kapic and R.C. Gleason (eds), *The Devoted Life: An Invitation to the Puritan Classics* (Leicester: IVP, 2004), pp. 23-32. Cf., T. Schwanda, 'Soul Recreation: Spiritual Marriage And Ravishment In The Contemplative-Mystical Piety of Isaac Ambrose' (unpublished PhD dissertation, University of Durham, 2009), p. 12.

[21] Coffey and Lim, 'Introduction', p. 4.

[22] G. Nuttall, *The Holy Spirit in Puritan Faith and Experience* (Oxford: Basil Blackwell, 1947), p. 134. Cf. Kapic and Gleason, 'Who Were the Puritans?', p. 25.

Whitefield (1714–70) and even John Wesley (1703–91) as being 'part of a great chain of Puritan divines'.[23] In the aforementioned sermon, 'All Of Grace', Spurgeon declared that the doctrines of grace he associated with the Puritans were also the doctrines of Calvin, Augustine, the apostle Paul, the 'Holy Ghost' and Jesus.[24] Spurgeon's understanding of Puritan theology could, at times, be breathtakingly broad. His approach was also selective. He had little interest in the political concerns of sixteenth- and seventeenth- century English Puritanism, for example. In a review of a biographical study of Oliver Cromwell for the *Sword and Trowel*, Spurgeon chose to comment for the most part on Cromwell's 'Calvinistic faith'. 'It is time', Spurgeon stated, 'that Cromwell's religion were (sic) in vogue again, that we might see its power under more genial circumstances than those of civil war.' Aspects of Cromwell's Calvinism that Spurgeon highlighted included God's sovereignty, predestination, the covenant and its 'certainty', 'grace' and 'glory', and the Bible, which was the authoritative word of God.[25] This understanding of Puritanism, which was by turns both broadly conceived and highly selective, is, of course, part of the problem of identifying Spurgeon uniquely with Puritanism. Nevertheless, when Spurgeon spoke of the Puritans he usually did mean the English men and women of the sixteenth and seventeenth century who fit within the parameters of Puritanism proposed by Coffey and Lim. Moreover, when Spurgeon spoke of Puritanism he tended to have in mind a theology that was both Calvinistic and 'experimental', one which emphasised communion with God and the practical outworking of that communion. When Spurgeon used the term Puritan, then, he had a particular vision of doctrinal, experiential, practical piety in mind. It was this vision that, for him, was the crucial aspect of the Puritan legacy.

Spurgeon's Upbringing: Place, People and Literature

Various aspects of Spurgeon's upbringing helped mould his later, Puritan-influenced, spirituality. Firstly, the shaping influence of *place* can be considered. The history of Essex from the Reformation to the mid-nineteenth century was steeped in 'determined and earnest Protestant Nonconformity'.[26] Essex was a main centre of Protestant resistance during the Marian persecutions and during the reign of Elizabeth I the county's Protestantism was further bolstered when large numbers of Dutch and Flemish *émigrés* settled there having fled Roman Catholic persecution in continental Europe. Essex later welcomed Puritan rule. The Independent

---

[23] P.S. Kruppa, *Charles Haddon Spurgeon: A Preacher's Progress* (New York and London: Garland Publishing, 1982), p. 380.

[24] Spurgeon, 'All Of Grace', p. 4. Cf. C.H. Spurgeon to J.A. Spurgeon, 13 February 1855, 'C.H. Spurgeon Letter to J.A. Spurgeon, 13 February 1855', Angus Library, Regent's Park College, Oxford (D/SPU 5), 'My daily labour is to revive the old doctrines of Gill, Owen, Calvin, Augustine and Christ.'

[25] Spurgeon, *Sword and Trowel*, January 1883, p. 37.

[26] J.C. Cox and H. Round, *Victoria County History of Essex* (London: n.p., 1907), Vol. 2, p. 34, as cited by Kruppa, *Spurgeon*, p. 9.

congregation at Stambourne had been founded following the Act of Uniformity and the 'great ejection' of 1662. Henry Havers, the Rector of Stambourne, was one of the clergymen forced to leave the Church of England.[27] Taking most of his congregation with him, he supervised the building of the manse and large meeting house, described by Charles as 'the old Puritanic chapel'.[28] This history was celebrated by the Spurgeon family who also held (seemingly without hard evidence) that at least some of their ancestors were among the Flemish and Dutch settlers, who often worked in the manufacture of different kinds of cloth. 'I daresay our fathers were poor weavers', C.H. Spurgeon surmised in the *Autobiography*, 'but I would far rather be descended from one who suffered for the faith than to bear the blood of all the emperors in my veins.'[29] Kruppa both exaggerates and simplifies when she says that the young Spurgeon was 'enveloped by the shadows of a staunchly Puritan past'.[30] Nevertheless, a sense of place contributed to Spurgeon's self-understanding and helped mould his later spirituality.

Secondly, and more importantly, there was the influence of *people*. Even in rural Stambourne, James Spurgeon cut an eccentric, 'old fashioned figure in black silk stockings, knee breaches and buckled shoes'.[31] He was proud to stand in Havers' tradition and preached a Calvinistic gospel,[32] one that was shaped by the Puritan commentaries and works of theology that were the staple of his library.[33] This library had been bequeathed to his successors in the Stambourne pastorate by the Cambridge-educated Havers.[34] At James's funeral in 1864, C.H. Spurgeon averred

---

[27] B. Beddow, 'Memories of Stambourne. Stencillings by Benjamin Beddow', in B. Beddow and C.H. Spurgeon, *Memories of Stambourne* (London: Paternoster and Alabaster, 1891), p. 33. This book consists of a number of different pieces from Spurgeon and Beddow, who was the grandson of another Benjamin Beddow who had been minister of the Stambourne chapel from 1776 to 1810. For another reference to Havers, see P. Adam, 'A Church "Halfly Reformed" – The Puritan Dilemma', The 1998 St Antholin Lecture, p. 2. www.masg.net.au/Documents/08_Adam_ChurchHalflyReformed.pdf, accessed 9 August 2009.

[28] Spurgeon, *Autobiography*, Vol. 1, p. 18.

[29] Spurgeon, *Autobiography*, Vol. 1, p. 8; cf. C.H. Spurgeon, *A Good Start: A Book for Young Men and Women* (London: Passmore and Alabaster, 1898), p. 318. Higgs, *The Spurgeon Family*, pp. 3, 32-34; and 'Pedigree of the Spurgeon … Family', was unable to find any evidence for such a link, despite tracing family records back to the fifteenth century.

[30] Kruppa, *Spurgeon*, p. 10.

[31] Kruppa, *Spurgeon*, p. 18. Cf. Pike, *C.H. Spurgeon*, Vol. 1, p. 15.

[32] Beddow, 'Memories of Stambourne. Stencillings …', p. 63. In describing James Spurgeon's Calvinism, Beddow draws on the recollections of J.C. Houchin, who succeeded James Spurgeon as pastor at Stambourne.

[33] R. Shindler, *From the Usher's Desk to the Tabernacle Pulpit: The Life and Labours of Pastor C.H. Spurgeon* (London: Passmore and Alabaster, 1892), p. 16, speaks of James Spurgeon 'holding firmly to a Puritan theology'. The proofs of Shindler's work were revised under Spurgeon's own supervision at Mentone in 1891 and this suggests Shindler's views reflected C.H. Spurgeon's own. See title page.

[34] Spurgeon, *Sword and Trowel*, December 1873, p. 534.

that every line of some hymns his grandfather had written could have been quoted without embarrassment in front of the Westminster Assembly, at least as far as the theology was concerned.[35]

Spurgeon's comments about his grandfather's hymns hint that some may have been published, but I have been unable to locate a copy, or any manuscript material, so it has not been possible to check C.H. Spurgeon's claim about their theology. It is worth asking the question, how much of the writing and speaking about C.H. Spurgeon's 'Puritan past' was actually a later gloss, an idealised picture painted by Spurgeon and his associates which made up part of the 'Spurgeon myth'? G.H. Pike's comments are particularly suspect. Pike enthusiastically compared James Spurgeon to a 'Puritan Greatheart of the Commonwealth era' and recorded, almost inevitably, that some at Stambourne regarded James as 'the last of the Puritans'.[36] A certain amount of 'overpainting' needs to be allowed for when reading such descriptions. It fitted the image the mature Spurgeon wanted to project if his Puritan roots were 'talked up'. Nevertheless, there is still a large body of evidence to support the contention that James Spurgeon had a theology and a spirituality which was redolent of the Puritan volumes which had been passed down to him by his ministerial predecessors. Regarding James' spiritual experience, in 1842 he wrote a 'memorandum' to himself which took the form of an extended reflection on Philippians 4.19 and the phrase, 'My God shall supply all your needs', encouraging himself to greater trust as he 'meditated upon this precious promise of [his] covenant God'. The memorandum was later included by C.H. Spurgeon in the *Sword and Trowel*. James clearly struggled with periodic doubts and in his meditation he declared,

> I cannot say how soon I will be shut up in Doubting Castle again; but I most sincerely pray God that I may never, if it be his will, dishonour him again by unbelief as I have done: for even when I am low in spirits, he will supply all my need ... Oh, the sweetness I felt when I was thus musing! I cannot convey to others the joy which filled my soul![37]

A number of features of Puritan piety are evident: the confessional style of writing, the reference to *Pilgrim's Progress* ('Doubting Castle'), the struggle for assurance, the focus on the sovereignty of God and the experimental piety.[38] Moreover, C.H. Spurgeon, writing in the last month of his life, regarded the

---

[35] C.H. Spurgeon, 'Funeral Sermon for a Grand Old Man', in Beddow and Spurgeon, *Memories of Stambourne*, pp. 81-82. C.H. Spurgeon was less convinced by the poetry of his grandfather's compositions.

[36] Pike, *C.H. Spurgeon*, Vol. 1, pp. 9-10.

[37] The 'memorandum' is quoted at length in C.H. Spurgeon, 'Sweet Experiences in 1842 and 1892', in *Sword and Trowel*, January 1892, pp. 3-5.

[38] Cf. a comment cited by Pike, *C.H. Spurgeon*, Vol. 1, p. 16, from a 'devout working man' who was a member of James Spurgeon's congregation: 'He was always so experimental. You felt as if you had been inside of a man.'

manuscript 'as a precious fragment of experience, full of grace and truth'. Unable because of his illness to articulate what he really felt at that time, Spurgeon found that the 'memorandum' spoke for him. The feelings James Spurgeon had had in 1842 effectively formed a liturgy which helped his grandson express his own feelings in 1892. The legacy of a spirituality shaped, in a number of important ways, by the Puritans, had been passed down from grandfather to grandson.

C.H. Spurgeon was also influenced by his parents. His father, John, emphasised Puritan themes in his preaching, such as the covenant of grace, and consistently displayed, according to his eldest son, a 'fidelity to the old gospel'.[39] But it was C.H. Spurgeon's mother, Eliza, who is especially significant here.[40] As has already been noted, in 1841 C.H. Spurgeon returned home to live with his parents, where his mother took the lead in bringing up him and his siblings, his father often being absent due to work or church duties. Eliza Spurgeon regularly led family prayers. A fragment of her spiritual journal survives in some short extracts copied out by her eldest son. The original entry was dated 2 June 1843.

> [W]hile reading the 55 chap of Isa. And speaking a few words upon it Charles was much affected. Dear Jesus hear and answer prayer for him and teach him to pray for himself. Oh! let not these impressions die away. Thank thee <u>dear Saviour</u> that this day has been a blessed day of good things, and if it is thy will to spare me on earth, grant me many more happy [...] of thy presence. Lord I do desire to love thee more.[41]

Once again, the influence of the Puritans can be seen in the pattern of family prayer in the home and the keeping of a spiritual journal. Also relevant are the stress on God's sovereignty ('if it is thy will ...') and the focus on experience ('Lord, I ... desire to love thee more'). In a message preached in 1864, Spurgeon noted that at these times of family prayer his mother often included readings from Joseph Alleine's *Alarm To The Unconverted* and Richard Baxter's *Call To The Unconverted*.[42] The lineaments of a Puritan-influenced piety can clearly be seen.

The extracts from Eliza Spurgeon's diary cited in the previous paragraph were possibly transcribed by her eldest son in 1857.[43] The reasons why C.H. Spurgeon chose to copy these particular extracts is clear enough – they relate to his mother's prayers for his conversion and his own religious 'impressions' which came as a result of her reading. The son, once he was converted, was sure he owed his mother a significant debt. He wrote to her on 1 May 1850, just a few months after his

---

[39] C.H. Spurgeon, 'Rev. John Spurgeon', in Spurgeon (ed.), *Sword and Trowel*, September 1884, p. 471.

[40] C.H. Spurgeon said as much himself. See *Autobiography*, Vol. 1, p. 69.

[41] C.H. Spurgeon, 'Extracts made ... from his mother's diary', Spurgeon's College, Heritage Room (Display Case 2).

[42] C.H. Spurgeon, 'Children Brought To Christ, Not To the Font', *MTP*, Vol. 10, S. No. 581, Mark 10.13-16, delivered 24 July 1864, p. 418.

[43] The notepaper C.H. Spurgeon used was pasted onto a picture of him which bears that date.

conversion experience, declaring, 'Your kind, warning Sabbath-evening addresses were too deeply settled on my heart to be forgotten. You, by God's blessing, prepared the way for the preached Word ...'.[44] Spurgeon believed that his mother had been instrumental in his eventual conversion.

The 'Puritan' influence on C.H. Spurgeon was thus wider than that which he experienced in the Stambourne manse of his grandparents. In Colchester, he 'played' at preaching to his brother and sisters, standing on top of a hay rack in a barn to address them. When C.H. Spurgeon was eleven he produced a handwritten 'magazine' for the 'Home Juvenile Society' he had formed. As well as organising a tea party and holding 'business meetings' the 'society' also organised prayer meetings in the home which were additional to the times led by his mother. 'Blessings come through prayer', the eleven-year-old boy wrote.[45] This was the atmosphere in which C.H. Spurgeon was brought up.

As already indicated, Henry Havers' Puritan library was at Stambourne, and C.H. Spurgeon's encounter with this needs to be noted. Spurgeon used to go into the room in which this library was kept and first look at, then later read, the books. He said it was here that he first engaged with John Foxe's stories of the 'martyrs, and specially with "Old Bonner" who burned them' and John Bunyan's (1628–88) *Pilgrim's Progress*.[46] The influence of Bunyan on Spurgeon will be given an extended treatment later in this chapter. Foxe, a moderate Puritan, was also important. His *Actes and Monuments* (i.e., Foxe's *Book of Martyrs*) was originally published in 1563. In the Victorian era the book, simplified and abridged, was a popular one and the majority of the population would have been at least familiar with it,[47] but its effect on Spurgeon personally was significant. Foxe's work was an illustrated 'catalogue' of Christian martyrs, with a particular focus on the Marian persecutions of 1553–58.[48] It provided Spurgeon with models of Christians who were 'heroically' committed to Christ. As Spurgeon suffered what he regarded as persecution – vitriolic press comment, for example – he identified with those such as the Marian martyrs who had suffered for Christ in the past.[49] Foxe's *Book of Martyrs* also contributed to Spurgeon's anti-Catholicism, helping shape the opinions which found expression in a prize-winning essay, 'Antichrist And Her Brood; Or, Popery

---

[44] C.H. Spurgeon to E. Spurgeon (mother), 1 May 1850, in 'Original Correspondence of Charles Haddon Spurgeon' 1851–1893 (Vol. 1), Spurgeon's College, Heritage Room, (4G), No. 171. Cf. Spurgeon, 'Children Brought To Christ, Not To The Font', p. 418.

[45] *C.H. Spurgeon's M.S. Magazine, Written by Himself, When a Boy, Under 12 Years of Age. Facsimile Reproduction* (London: J. Barton, n.d.). The original magazine was written in April 1846.

[46] Spurgeon, *Autobiography*, Vol. 1, pp. 22-23. 'Old Bonner' was Edmund Bonner, the sixteenth-century Bishop of London.

[47] J. Wolffe, *The Protestant Crusade in Great Britain, 1829–1860* (Oxford: Clarendon Press, 1991), p. 112.

[48] M. Pearse, 'John Foxe', in T. Larson (ed.), *Biographical Dictionary of Evangelicals* (Leicester: IVP, 2003), p. 237.

[49] For samples of this press comment, see Spurgeon, *Autobiography*, Vol. 2, pp. 43-60.

Puritan Piety 25

Unmasked', which Spurgeon wrote a few months before his conversion.[50] The titles of some of the seventeen chapters of 'Antichrist And Her Brood ...', for example, 'Popery, a Ravenous Wolf' and 'Popery, a Gigantic Horseleach', give a flavour of the visceral anti-Catholicism the young Spurgeon had imbibed.[51]

Spurgeon believed the anti-Catholicism of Foxe's *Actes and Monuments* was timeless. Indeed, he believed it was especially relevant for Victorian Britain. He reviewed some of the many editions which appeared after 1865 for the *Sword and Trowel*, warmly commending them to his readers. One such review, in December 1866, urged his constituency to aid distribution of the 'precious volume', suggesting it would be a wonderful Christmas present for children. Given what Spurgeon described as the 'threatened revival of Popery' and the 'pernicious nonsense of Ritualism' (i.e., the Oxford Movement in the Church of England),[52] the dissemination of Foxe's book was vital work.[53] Although, as we shall see, there were many other factors which fed Spurgeon's anti-Catholicism, nevertheless Foxe and other Puritan writers were important in shaping and sustaining this. Spurgeon always viewed Roman Catholic ecclesiology, theology and ritual as being inimical to true spirituality, militating against real communion with Christ and his people. Such anti-Catholicism was fashioned in part by Foxe's *Book of Martyrs* and also by other Puritan works.[54]

The remainder of this chapter makes more detailed examination of some of the specific ways Puritanism was significant for Spurgeon's spirituality. This will be done in four separate sections. Firstly, the influence of John Bunyan and especially *Pilgrim's Progress* will be examined. Secondly, the attraction that Puritan commentaries had for Spurgeon will be analysed. Thirdly, the influence 'Puritanism' had on Spurgeon's conception of holiness will be examined. Finally, recognisably

---

[50] C.H. Spurgeon, 'Antichrist And Her Brood; Or, Popery Unmasked', Spurgeon's College, Heritage Room (A2.06). Material from at least two earlier drafts appears to survive. There are 295 handwritten pages in the final version. Cf. *Autobiography*, Vol. 1, pp. 57-66. Pike, *C.H. Spurgeon*, Vol. 1, pp. 18-19, directly links 'Antichrist and her Brood' with Spurgeon's reading of Foxe.

[51] Spurgeon, 'Antichrist And Her Brood; Or, Popery Unmasked', chapters 5 and 15. The letter informing Spurgeon he had won a prize (although not first prize) in the competition he had entered was copied out by Spurgeon and fixed inside the cover of the bound copy of the essay. G. Smith to C.H. Spurgeon, 23 December 1851 (Spurgeon's copy). Cf. Spurgeon, *Autobiography*, Vol. 1, p. 58.

[52] For which see, especially, chapters 4 and 6 of this study.

[53] Spurgeon (ed.), *Sword and Trowel*, December 1866, p. 564. For another, positive review, see *Sword and Trowel*, August 1872, p. 384. G.H. Pike contributed an article entitled 'John Foxe the Martyrologist' to *Sword and Trowel*, March 1878, pp. 122-30.

[54] With regard to the influence of other Puritan works on Spurgeon's anti-Catholicism, see, e.g., C.H. Spurgeon, *Morning By Morning: Or, Daily Readings for the Family or the Closet* (London: Passmore and Alabaster, 1865), 5 November, and the comments on Matthew Henry's annual sermons preached on this day, the anniversary of the failure of the Gunpowder Plot in 1605 and the landing of William of Orange at Torbay in 1688.

'Puritan' elements of Spurgeon's theology will be considered, especially as revealed in his preaching.

Spurgeon and Bunyan

Important as Foxe's *Book of Martyrs* was to Spurgeon, John Bunyan's works were of greater significance.[55] *Pilgrim's Progress* was the Bunyan book which had the greatest impact, but others, such as the spiritual autobiography *Grace Abounding to the Chief of Sinners* and the allegorical *Holy War*, were also of consequence.[56] By the time Spurgeon lived at Newmarket in 1849–50 he could recite long passages from *Grace Abounding* from memory.[57] *Pilgrim's Progress* left its imprint on 'Antichrist And Her Brood'. At the end of the first chapter, which was entitled 'Popery, the Apostate Spirit', Spurgeon declared,

> What a monument to the frailty of earthly greatness is the Papacy! Compare Pope Alexander in the act of putting his foot on an emperor's neck, with a Pope imprisoned by Napoleon ... How vapid a descent hath this monster made from the pinnacle of glory ... to the condition of Bunyan's giant who sat biting his nails, and grinning at the pilgrims who passed by without having the power to hunt them however much they spoke against him.[58]

Pilgrim's Progress thus provided some of the words and characters which helped Spurgeon give vent to his anti-Catholicism.

More importantly, Bunyan's language, metaphors and imagery became crucial to the way Spurgeon described his spiritual experience, crucial, indeed, to his conception of the Christian life. This can be seen from Spurgeon's writing in the months immediately following his conversion. Spurgeon kept a spiritual diary between April and June 1850, at which point it appears he discontinued this practice. The entries he did make are valuable for the way they reveal his spirituality at that time. On 26 April he wrote, 'I have had a pretty good day. Fear, Mistrust and Timorous are yet at sword's length. May I be Valiant-for-Truth, and live and die in my Master's glorious war!' On 30 April, referring to Newmarket, he wrote, 'How

---

[55] On *Pilgrim's Progress* as a Puritan work, see N.H. Keeble, 'The Pilgrim's Progress: A Puritan Fiction', *Baptist Quarterly* Vol. 28, No. 7 (July 1980), pp. 321-336, especially p. 322. Cf. R. Pooley, 'The Wilderness of the World – Bunyan's Pilgrim's Progress', *Baptist Quarterly* Vol. 27, No. 7 (July 1978), p. 290. Pooley describes *Pilgrim's Progress* as 'Puritan art'.

[56] J. Bunyan's *Grace Abounding* was originally published in 1666. *Holy War* was originally published in 1682.

[57] Pike, *C.H. Spurgeon*, Vol. 1, p. 43. Pike is drawing from the written recollections of J.D. Everett, who was also an usher or 'articled pupil' at Newmarket and shared a room with Spurgeon.

[58] Spurgeon, 'Antichrist And Her Brood', pp. 21-22.

much like Vanity Fair is this place!'[59] Such language was not confined to Spurgeon's diary. In a letter to his mother, written on 19 February 1850, he wrote that he had been in 'the miry slough of despond'.[60] As Spurgeon wrote of his spiritual experience he was heavily indebted to Bunyan.

This indebtedness continued to be felt in the period of Spurgeon's pre-London ministry. This period of ministry can be briefly described. Following his baptism as a believer, which was on 3 May 1850 (see chapter 4), Spurgeon moved to Cambridge, as already noted, where he joined St Andrew's Street Baptist Church in the city.[61] From here Spurgeon had his first experiences of preaching, going out to different village congregations under the auspices of the local lay-preachers' association. Soon he became known as the 'Boy preacher of the Fens' and was called by the Baptist church at Waterbeach, which was six miles from Cambridge, to be their pastor. Spurgeon, despite having no formal theological training, accepted the call. He first started to preach there in October 1851 and enjoyed conspicuous success, with the small chapel soon packed to overflowing Sunday-by-Sunday. The boy preacher had become the boy minister.

Spurgeon's early sermons provide clear evidence of the continuing influence of Bunyan. Spurgeon preached a message entitled 'The Fight And The Weapons', taking as his text 2 Corinthians 10.4, in the second half of 1851.[62] As he spoke of the Christian life in terms of a 'fight', he made notes to himself to illustrate his points with 'Instances in Pilgrim's Progress'. Topics which could be thus illuminated included 'pride', 'sloth', 'drowsiness', 'forgetfulness' and 'carnality'. *Pilgrim's Progress* provided the imagery by which the teenage pastor could speak to others about the Christian life.

In January 1854 Spurgeon received a call to the historic New Park Street Chapel, Southwark, London.[63] It was at this point that Spurgeon's career began to veer, as

---

[59] C.H. Spurgeon, 'Diary, April to June, 1850', in *Autobiography*, Vol. 1, pp. 133-34. The town Spurgeon was referring to was Newmarket. Susannah Spurgeon had been handed the diary by her husband with the comment, '[T]hat book contains a record of some of my past spiritual experiences', *Autobiography*, Vol. 1, p. 127. Susannah transcribed a number of the entries. The original is not extant.

[60] C.H. Spurgeon to Eliza Spurgeon, 19 February 1850, in *Autobiography*, Vol. 1, p. 118.

[61] For biographical details included in this paragraph, see Spurgeon, *Autobiography*, Vol. 1, pp. 185, 199-206, 227-40.

[62] C.H. Spurgeon, 'The Fight And The Weapons', in 'Notebook Containing Early Sermon Skeletons, Vol. 1', Spurgeon's College, Heritage Room (K1.5), S. No. 37. Few messages in pre-London sermon notebooks are dated and so it is not possible to know when Spurgeon first preached them with any precision. The earliest date in Vol. 1 is 9 February 1851, which was when Spurgeon preached the second message in the notebook, 'Necessity Of Purity For An Entrance To Heaven', S. No. 2, Revelation 21.27, at Barton. Nos 28 and 29, 'Heaven's Preparations', John 14.2 and 'Beginning At Jerusalem', Luke 24.47, were preached on 31 August at Dunmow and 6 September and Balsham respectively, although these may not have been the first occasions Spurgeon delivered these messages.

[63] For C.H. Spurgeon's own appreciation of this history, see *The Metropolitan Tabernacle: Its History And Work* (London: Passmore and Alabaster, 1876), pp. 9-64.

Hopkins puts it, from the 'unusual to the exceptional'.[64] Within a year the large New Park Street building was so full on a Sunday that people were being turned away. Other buildings were rented for services, first the Exeter Hall in the Strand and then the Surrey Gardens Music Hall. In 1861 the purpose-built Metropolitan Tabernacle was opened in Newington Butts. The 'Tab' could comfortably seat 4600 people, but it was not uncommon for considerably more to be present so that there was standing room only.[65] The scene was set for the sort of national and global fame spoken of in the opening paragraphs of the introductory chapter of this study.

Spurgeon the London pastor continued to be indebted to the man he described as his 'old friend John Bunyan'.[66] When Spurgeon wanted to give a gift to the woman who would later become his wife (the as yet unconverted Susannah Thompson), the pastor of New Park Street Chapel chose an illustrated copy of *Pilgrim's Progress*, writing in the front, 'Miss Thompson, with desires for her progress in the blessed pilgrimage ... Ap[ril] 20, 1854.'[67] The couple were married on 8 January 1856. As editor of the *Sword and Trowel*, Spurgeon wrote numerous, enthusiastic reviews of different publications of *Pilgrim's Progress* stating, on one occasion, that 'there cannot be too many editions of Bunyan's Pilgrim'[68] and, on another, that 'next to the Bible comes Bunyan's Allegory'.[69] Other Bunyan works were also repeatedly commended,[70] and Spurgeon himself reprinted Bunyan's *Water Of Life*, describing it as a 'homely' and 'precious' treatise which pointed readers to Christ and his cross.[71] Spurgeon made regular reference to Bunyan in his London preaching.[72] We might add that Bunyan also influenced Spurgeon's plain prose style. The Bedford tinker's language, said Spurgeon, was 'the best of earth' for it was 'Saxon'.[73] Bunyan's works remained extremely important for Spurgeon throughout his ministerial career.

Bunyan gave Spurgeon the language which enabled the latter to describe his spirituality *in extremis*. On 19 October 1856 Spurgeon led his first service at the

---

[64] Hopkins, *Nonconformity's Romantic Generation*, p. 128.

[65] I.H. Murray (ed.), *C.H. Spurgeon: The Full Harvest 1860–1892* (London: Banner of Truth, 1973), p. 48; W.H.C. James, *A Souvenir of Spurgeon's Tabernacle* (London: Hart and Straker, n.d., [1898]), p. 9.

[66] C.H. Spurgeon, 'Christ Crucified', *NPSP*, Vol. 1, S. Nos 7-8, 1 Corinthians 1.23,24, delivered 11 February 1855, p. 56.

[67] Spurgeon, *Autobiography*, Vol. 2, p. 7.

[68] Spurgeon (ed.), *Sword and Trowel*, April 1887, p. 194.

[69] Spurgeon (ed.), *Sword and Trowel*, April 1874, p. 186.

[70] For a review of an edition of Bunyan's complete works see *Sword and Trowel*, October 1882, p. 542. 'All Bunyan's books are precious', said Spurgeon.

[71] J. Bunyan, *The Water Of Life; Or, A Discourse Showing The Richness And Glory Of The Grace And Spirit Of The Gospel ... With Preface By C.H. Spurgeon* (London: Passmore and Alabaster, 1868), p. vi. The *Water of Life* was originally published in 1688, the last year of Bunyan's life.

[72] In addition to the sermons cited elsewhere in this section, see, e.g., C.H. Spurgeon, 'Baptismal Regeneration', *MTP*, Vol. 10, S. No. 573, Mark 16.15,16, delivered 5 June 1864, p. 314. The apostles' commission was to a 'Holy War'.

[73] Spurgeon (ed.), *Sword and Trowel*, December 1866, p. 566.

Surrey Gardens Music Hall. The building was packed with a large crowd outside unable to gain access. After the service started there was a panic (possibly caused by cries of 'Fire!' and / or that the galleries were collapsing). As many people rushed to exit the building a stairway collapsed. Seven people were killed and many others injured.[74] Spurgeon was initially unaware that there had been any fatalities and for a short while tried to continue with the service. This was in response to encouraging shouts from some at the front of the crowd who had not moved from their seats, but it was a move widely condemned in the press.[75] This incident and the recollection of it would profoundly affect Spurgeon for the rest of his life. Speaking about the tragedy years after the event, he confided to his friend, William Williams, 'There are dungeons beneath the Castle of Despair as dreary as the abodes of the lost, and some of us have been in them.'[76] Bunyan's vivid imagery was deployed to describe one of the lowest points of Spurgeon's Christian 'pilgrimage'.

The material surveyed in this section suggests two important ways in which Bunyan influenced Spurgeon's spirituality. Firstly, Bunyan's writing (and especially his *Pilgrim's Progress*) gave Spurgeon a framework for understanding the Christian life, which was viewed as a pilgrimage towards the heavenly reward, a journey along the 'divine track' to a 'better country'.[77] 'Pilgrimage', said Spurgeon, was 'one of the leading ideas of Christianity'.[78] Spurgeon saw himself as Bunyan's Christian, passing through the 'Valley of the Shadow of Death',[79] seeking to be Valiant-for-Truth, heading towards the 'gates of the celestial city'.[80] Thus Bunyan provided Spurgeon with a map of Christian experience so that, at whatever point he was at in his 'earthly pilgrimage', he could locate himself on the journey. Crucially, the journey was conceived as one that was with Christ and to Christ. The weary pilgrim would one day cross the 'stream of death' and behold Christ's 'glory'.[81] And Bunyan not only provided the framework for Spurgeon's own spiritual journey or the pilgrimage of a

---

[74] C.H. Spurgeon, 'Our First Seven Years', in Spurgeon (ed.), *Sword and Trowel*, April 1876, pp. 162-63.

[75] Spurgeon, 'Our First Seven Years', p. 163; *Autobiography*, Vol. 2, p. 204. A supporter wrote of the 'virulent mendacity of the London Press'. See J. Campbell, *Mr Spurgeon Defended: Being a Series of Articles from the British Banner* ... (London: Passmore and Alabaster, n.d. [1856]), pp. 6-10.

[76] W. Williams, *Personal Reminiscences of Charles Haddon Spurgeon* (London: The Religious Tract Society, 1895), p. 166.

[77] C.H. Spurgeon, 'The First Setting Up Of The Brazen Serpent', *MTP*, Vol. 29, S. No. 1722, Numbers 21.4-9, delivered 10 May 1883, pp. 289-90.

[78] C.H. Spurgeon, *The Saint And His Saviour: The Progress Of The Soul In The Knowledge Of Jesus* (London: Hodder and Stoughton, 1889 [1857]), p. 244.

[79] C.H. Spurgeon, 'Breaking The Long Silence, Two Brief Addresses ... on the last evening of 1891, and the first morning of 1892', in Spurgeon (ed.), *Sword and Trowel*, February 1892, p. 49, cf. p. 55.

[80] C.H. Spurgeon, 'Good News', *MTP*, Vol. 50, S. No. 2866, Prov. 25.25, delivered 6 January 1876, p. 36.

[81] Spurgeon, 'Good News', p. 36.

few select saints; Bunyan's vision of the Christian life was relevant to all. In a sermon in which Spurgeon described the book of Numbers as 'Moses's Pilgrim's Progress', he averred that Numbers and *Pilgrim's Progress* were alike in that they both mapped out the spiritual journey, not only of one person or of one nation, but of 'all God's people'.[82] All faithful believers were on a journey through various trials to the promised land and the celestial city. Bunyan's plain, accessible prose helped emphasise that the Christian life was open to all. *Pilgrim's Progress*, then, gave all Christians a basic orientation for their life of discipleship. This was conceived of as a journey, with Christ and towards Christ. Moreover, it was one that was undertaken by all of Christ's true people.

Secondly, Bunyan helped Spurgeon make sense of particular experiences that occurred along a Christian's journey. For example, Bunyan helped shape Spurgeon's understanding of the ideal conversion which marked the beginning of real communion with Christ and his people. 'Any true conversion is good', Spurgeon stated, 'but we confess our liking to the old-fashioned Bunyan-like experience.'[83] As has already been shown, Bunyan helped Spurgeon understand his own times of struggle and depression, which he came to view as part of normal Christian experience. The Christian life was not a serene progress to journey's end; it was characterised by great joy, it was true, but it was also a life in which struggle and battle were important motifs. This was particularly relevant with regard to Spurgeon's approach to questions of holiness (see chapter 8) and suffering (see chapter 10). Bunyan, then, provided a route map for the Christian pilgrimage, providing basic orientation but also filling out the contours and giving shape to the landmarks along the way, warning against wrong turnings and alerting the believer to other potential dangers. Bunyan provided an invaluable guide to Christian spirituality. Of course, Bunyan, as well as Foxe, was widely read in nineteenth-century England.[84] Spurgeon was just one of many whose piety was moulded by Bunyan's works. But the point still needs to be made that Bunyan had an important, shaping effect on Spurgeon's spirituality. It can be added that, even in the context of the nineteenth century, Spurgeon believed Bunyan's works needed to be more deeply imbibed by his contemporaries. Writing in 1877, he stated that both *Pilgrim's Progress* and the *Holy War* were 'allegories … powerfully descriptive of a type of true godliness from which, it is feared, the church is fast receding'.[85] Bunyan's Puritan vision of true, rugged godliness was one Spurgeon was determined to keep alive in respect of his own spirituality, and he was also determined to commend this vision to others.

---

[82] Spurgeon, 'The First Setting Up Of The Brazen Serpent', p. 289.

[83] Spurgeon (ed.), *Sword and Trowel*, February 1883, p. 60. Spurgeon would have been thinking of Bunyan's spiritual autobiography, *Grace Abounding to the Chief of Sinners* and Bunyan's struggle with sin and doubt pre-conversion. In certain respects this mirrored Spurgeon's experience, as will be seen in chapter 3.

[84] J. Coffey, 'Puritan Legacies', in Coffey and Lim (eds), *Cambridge Companion to Puritanism*, p. 336.

[85] Spurgeon (ed.), *Sword and Trowel*, May 1877, p. 234.

Puritan Commentaries

When Spurgeon moved to London to take up the pastorate of New Park Street Chapel in 1854 he set about acquiring a collection of Puritan writings which would surpass even his grandfather's at Stambourne. J.C. Carlile surmised that Spurgeon's collection of Puritan literature had become, by the time of his subject's death, probably 'the most extensive possessed by any private individual' of the Victorian period.[86] Spurgeon became well known amongst the capital's booksellers as someone who, either in person or through his associates, would regularly scour their shops for original editions of Puritan works. He was not above appealing in print for help in tracking down a particularly rare volume.[87] Spurgeon's collection included works of theology. In 1867 he himself reissued Elisha Coles' seventeenth-century work, *A Practical Discourse of God's Sovereignty*. Coles' treatise dealt with Calvinistic themes such as election, redemption, effectual calling and perseverance. The book was a core text at the Pastors' College Spurgeon established in 1856.[88] Spurgeon, the President of the College, wrote a preface for his new edition, stating that the book had been of 'great assistance' to him personally 'in the earliest days of [his] religious thought'.[89] Spurgeon's specific debt to Coles was recognised by others.[90] The doctrines Coles expounded were ones by which Spurgeon said his soul continued to live 'happily', indeed he believed they formed a crucial part of the 'truth as it is in Jesus'.[91] But Spurgeon was a preacher, not a systematic theologian, and it was Puritan biblical commentaries which were especially important to him. This can be seen by an analysis of *Commenting and Commentaries*, Spurgeon's 'catalogue' of biblical commentaries and expositions.

Commenting and Commentaries was published in 1876. It was designed 'for the use of ministers of average attainments', that is, it was to be of practical help to

---

[86] J.C. Carlile, *C.H. Spurgeon: An Interpretive Biography* (London: The Religious Tract Society and The Kingsgate Press, 1933), p. 132; cf. Spurgeon, *Autobiography*, Vol. 4, p. 280.

[87] C.H. Spurgeon, *Commenting and Commentaries* (London: Banner of Truth, 1969 [London: Passmore and Alabaster, 1876]), p. 184. Regarding W. Bradshaw, *A Plaine and Pithy Exposition of 2 Thessalonians* (1620), Spurgeon wrote, 'As we cannot get a sight of this, perhaps some reader will present us with a copy'.

[88] E. Coles, *A Practical Discourse on God's Sovereignty, with Other Material Points Derived Thence: Viz:- of the Righteousness of God, of Election, of Redemption, of Effectual Calling, of Perseverance, with Brief Preface by C.H. Spurgeon* (London: Passmore & Alabaster, 1885 [1867]), Preface, p. vi. For the date of Spurgeon's edition, see the Preface to *MTP*, Vol. 13, p. vii. Coles' original work was first published in 1678.

[89] Coles, *A Practical Discourse ... with Brief Preface by C.H. Spurgeon*, Preface, pp. v-vi. Spurgeon also reprinted Thomas Watson's *A Body of Divinity, Contained in Sermons Upon the [Westminster] Assembly's Catechism ... With a Preface and an Appendix by Pastor C.H. Spurgeon* (London: Passmore and Alabaster, 1898 [1890?]). Watson's original work was first published in 1692.

[90] Spurgeon, *Autobiography*, Vol. 2, p. 38.

[91] Coles, *A Practical Discourse ... with Brief Preface by C.H. Spurgeon*, Preface, p. vi.

ministers in their preaching, rather than an academic survey.[92] Spurgeon ranked the commentaries into three categories: 'heartily recommended', 'good, but more ordinary' and 'the least desirable'. A different size typeface was assigned to each category. Spurgeon also offered 'brief reviews' of the different commentaries listed.[93] Unsurprisingly, Puritan works featured strongly in the catalogue, and were almost always warmly commended. In the section on Hosea, for example, all of the five works placed in the 'heartily recommended' category were written in the seventeenth century, with Spurgeon singling out the Puritan expositions of Richard Sibbes and Jeremiah Burroughes for special praise. Spurgeon described the latter work as 'masterly'.[94] Occasionally Spurgeon would include some historical details of the writer whose work was being considered, for example informing his readers that Thomas Taylor 'was a preacher at Paul's Cross during the reigns of Elizabeth and James I, and a voluminous writer'. Taylor's commentary on Titus would 'well repay the reader'.[95]

Rarely do Puritan works fail to win Spurgeon's unqualified approval in *Commenting and Commentaries*. An exposition of Hebrews 11 by William Perkins was too prolix even for Spurgeon, who was wearied by the long digressions into past controversies.[96] Even so, he still placed this work in the 'good, but more ordinary' section. This was the same rating given to an exposition of Malachi 3 by Thomas Watson, even though at the time of writing Spurgeon had not actually seen a copy. 'This would be a great find', he lamented, 'if only we could come at it.'[97] *Commenting and Commentaries* also gave a strong place to other Reformed literature. Of the various commentaries and expositions of John Calvin, whose image Spurgeon had kissed when in Geneva in the summer of 1860,[98] he stated, 'You will find forty-two or more goodly volumes worth their weight in gold.'[99] But it was Puritan works that were most consistently commended. Even the notes in the margins

---

[92] Cf. Spurgeon's comments in his own review of *Commenting and Commentaries* in Spurgeon (ed.), *Sword and Trowel*, March 1876, p. 137.

[93] Spurgeon, *Commenting and Commentaries*, pp. 33.

[94] Spurgeon, *Commenting and Commentaries*, pp. 132-33. J. Burroughes, *Exposition of the Prophecie of Hosea* (4 Vols; London, 1643–1651); R. Sibbes, *The Returning Backslider, or a Commentary upon Hosea XIV* (London, 1639).

[95] Spurgeon, *Commenting and Commentaries*, p. 185. T. Taylor, *Commentarie upon Titus* (Cambridge, 1619).

[96] Spurgeon, *Commenting and Commentaries*, p. 190. W. Perkins, *A Cloud of Faithful Witnesses: Commentary on Hebrewes XI* (n.pl. or provenance, 1622).

[97] Spurgeon, *Commenting and Commentaries*, p. 140.

[98] W.Y. Fullerton, *C.H. Spurgeon: A Biography* (London: Williams and Norgate, 1920), p. 117; T. George, 'Controversy and Communion: The Limits of Baptist Fellowship from Bunyan to Spurgeon', in D.W. Bebbington (ed.), *The Gospel in the World: International Baptist Studies* (Carlisle: Paternoster, 2002), p. 57.

[99] C.H. Spurgeon, 'A Chat About Commentaries', Lecture 1 prefixed to *Commenting and Commentaries*, p. 4. Two lectures preceded the catalogue, the second entitled 'On Commentating', see pp. 1-32.

Puritan Piety 33

were 'as rich as the books themselves'. They were 'the dust of gold', Spurgeon declared, 'of the same metal as the ingots in the centre of the page'.[100]

What was it about the Puritan commentators which caused Spurgeon to view them so positively? Spurgeon's brief 'reviews' of their works cast considerable light on this. First of all, the Puritan works he commended were thoroughgoing in their commitment to Calvinistic orthodoxy. For example, John Barlow's *Exposition of 2 Timothy I and II* was commended as 'soundly doctrinal',[101] a phrase Spurgeon used as shorthand for the leading Calvinistic doctrines and for a substitutionary view of the atonement.[102] He also quoted with approval Thomas Chalmers' appreciation of John Owen's multi-volume *Exposition of Hebrews*. Chalmers had written of Owen's work that, 'He who hath mastered it is very little short … of being an erudite and accomplished theologian.'[103] The Puritan authors also focused on the text of scripture, working hard on exegesis. So George Hutcheson's *Exposition upon Job* was commended because Hutcheson 'distils the text'.[104] These Puritan commentaries paid close, detailed attention to scripture, which was interpreted within a Calvinistic framework.

What Spurgeon particularly appreciated about the Puritan commentaries he was reviewing, however, was the way they married theology and experience. Barlow's *Exposition of 2 Timothy I and II*, already referred to, was not only soundly doctrinal, it was also 'deeply experimental'.[105] Similarly, Burroughes' four-volume commentary on Hosea was a 'vast treasure house of experimental exposition'.[106] David Dickson's *Brief Explanation of the Psalms*, published in three volumes, was a 'rich volume, dropping fatness'. Concerning this last work, Spurgeon wrote, 'Having read it and re-read it, we can speak of its holy savour and suggestiveness. We commend it with much fervour.'[107] All these expositions were Calvinistic in doctrine, but Spurgeon did not find these works dry. Rather the theology was heart-warming

---

[100] Spurgeon, 'A Chat About Commentaries', in *Commenting and Commentaries*, p. 5.

[101] Spurgeon, *Commenting and Commentaries*, p. 184. J. Barlow, *Exposition of 2 Timothy, I and II* (London, 1632).

[102] See, e.g., C.H. Spurgeon, 'The Effects Of Sound Doctrine', *NPSP*, Vol. 6, S. No. 324, Matthew 24.24, delivered 22 April 1860, pp. 301-308. The 'sound doctrine' in view on this occasion was election. At the beginning of the chapter, 'A Defence of Calvinism', in *Autobiography*, Vol. 1, p. 167, Spurgeon speaks of 'good solid doctrine'.

[103] Spurgeon, *Commenting and Commentaries*, p. 188. J. Owen, *Exposition of Hebrews* (4 Vols; London, 1668–74). Cf. Spurgeon's own comments on Owen's *A Practical Exposition on the One Hundred and Thirtieth Psalm* (2 Vols; London, 1669 and 1680), in *Commenting and Commentaries*, p. 103.

[104] Spurgeon, *Commenting and Commentaries*, p. 78. G. Hutcheson, *An Exposition upon Job, being the sum of 316 Lectures* (London, 1699).

[105] Spurgeon, *Commenting and Commentaries*, p. 184.

[106] C.H. Spurgeon, *Commenting and Commentaries*, p. 132. Burroughes, *Exposition of the Prophesie of Hosea*.

[107] Spurgeon, *Commenting and Commentaries*, p. 84. D. Dickson, *A Brief Explanation of the Psalms* (3 Vols; London, 1655).

and consistently related to human experience. Commentaries which could be described as combining both 'marrowy doctrine' and 'holy thought' were deemed 'excellent, beyond all praise'.[108] The marrying together of these qualities Spurgeon found supremely in Puritan works.

Spurgeon prized Puritan commentaries for the way they sought to foster communion with Christ as the central element of Christian experience. As far as this was concerned, Spurgeon particularly appreciated Puritan expositions of the Song of Songs. It was the Puritan James Durham's *Clavis Cantici; or, an Exposition of the Song of Solomon* which Spurgeon believed provided the 'key' which unlocked the Song.[109] Spurgeon was here referring to an essay entitled 'A Key, Useful For Opening Up The Song' with which *Clavis Cantici* began. In the essay, Durham advocated an allegorical approach, insisting that the Song spoke of the 'mutual love and spiritual union, and communion that is betwixt Christ and his church'.[110] That Spurgeon followed this approach himself can be seen from his preaching, for example that contained in a volume of sermons on the Song, entitled *The Most Holy Place*.[111] For Spurgeon, this was an 'allegorical song' describing the communion which could be enjoyed between Christ and his people.[112] Interpreted in the typological, christological way advocated and modelled by Durham, the Song was an extremely important book for Spurgeon.[113]

Richard Sibbes' commentary on chapters 4 to 6 of the Song of Songs, which was subtitled *A Discovery of Neere and Deere Love, Union and Communion betwixt Christ and the Church*, was one of the Puritan commentaries enthusiastically commended by Spurgeon. 'Sibbes never writes ill', Spurgeon enthused in his remarks on Sibbes' commentary.[114] Works such as Sibbes' informed Spurgeon's approach to the Song.

Analysis of Sibbes' exposition (the commentary is based upon a series of twenty sermons) reveals the following emphases. Sibbes insisted that persons must first be

---

[108] Spurgeon, *Commenting and Commentaries*, p. 161. G. Hutcheson, *Exposition of John* (London, 1657).

[109] Spurgeon, *Commenting and Commentaries*, pp. 112-13. J. Durham, *Clavis Cantici; or, an Exposition of the Song of Solomon ... With a Preface by the Rev Gavin Parker* (Aberdeen: George and Robert King, 1840 [original work, London, 1668 and 1723]).

[110] Durham, *Clavis Cantici*, pp. 32-33.

[111] C.H. Spurgeon, *The Most Holy Place: Sermons on the Song of Solomon* (London: Passmore and Alabaster, 1896)

[112] C.H. Spurgeon, 'Altogether Lovely', in *Most Holy Place*, S. No. 1001, Song of Songs 5.16, delivered 23 July 1871, p. 409; 'Come My Beloved', in *Most Holy Place*, S. No. 2360, Song of Songs 8.14, delivered 4 March 1888, p. 559.

[113] C.H. Spurgeon, 'The Church's Love To Her Loving Lord', *MTP*, Vol. 11, S. No. 636, p. 349, 'We see our Saviour's face in almost every page of the Bible, but here [the Song of Songs] we see his heart and feel his love for us.'

[114] Spurgeon, *Commenting and Commentaries*, p. 116.

united to Christ before they could know communion.[115] He exhorted his hearers and readers to pursue communion with Christ,[116] and reminded them that Christ desired 'a further and further communion' with them, his church.[117] Sibbes also dealt with various hindrances to communion,[118] and assured people that the 'sweetest' communion with Christ was sometimes experienced 'under the greatest crosses'.[119] Finally, Sibbes looked forward to the time Christians would enjoy a 'glorious communion' in heaven with Christ.[120] Moreover, according to Sibbes' exposition, Christians experienced communion with one another as well as with Christ. '[T]he children of God love the communion and fellowship one of another', he declared.[121] It was not only communion with Christ but also 'communion of saints' that was sweet.[122] As will become clear as this study unfolds, these were all points that Spurgeon emphasised in his own preaching and that were crucial to his own spiritual experience. It was entirely natural that Spurgeon should warmly commend Sibbes 'discovery' – that the Song of Songs spoke of the love and communion which existed between Christ and his church – to the readers of *Commenting and Commentaries*.[123] Spurgeon's own use of the Song, one of his favourite books of the Bible, will be referred to again in chapter 6 and analysed in more detail in chapter 7. Suffice to say here that Spurgeon's approach to this book was one which emphasised communion with Christ and which was guided by the Puritan works he so warmly commended.

Finally, the Puritan commentaries Spurgeon commended were, he insisted, thoroughly practical and helpful. This was true with regard to sermon preparation, which was what Spurgeon had particularly in view in *Commenting and Commentaries*, and also for daily living. Dickson's aforementioned commentary on the Psalms was 'invaluable to the preacher', and John Rogers in his *Fruitful Exposition upon all the First Epistle of Peter* was both 'wisely experimental' and 'earnestly practical'.[124] By contrast with these practical, applied works, many commentaries published in Spurgeon's lifetime were tersely dismissed, with remarks such as 'of no consequence' and 'utter rubbish'. Such dismissals were not just because these works were judged 'anti-Calvinistic in doctrine', indulging in what

---

[115] R. Sibbes, *Bowels Opened; Or: A Discovery of Neere and Deere Love, Union and Communion betwixt Christ and the Church*, in A.B. Grosart (ed.), *Complete Works of Richard Sibbes* (7 Vols; Edinburgh: James Nichol, 1862-64), Vol. 2, p. x. *Bowels Opened* was originally published in 1639.

[116] Sibbes, *Bowels Opened*, p. vi; S. No. 14, p.135.

[117] Sibbes, *Bowels Opened*, S. No. 5, p. 58; cf. S. No. 6, p. 70.

[118] Sibbes, *Bowels Opened*, S. No. 5, p. 59; S. No. 7, p. 87.

[119] Sibbes, *Bowels Opened*, S. No. 19, p. 180.

[120] Sibbes, *Bowels Opened*, S. No. 5, p. 58.

[121] Sibbes, *Bowels Opened*, S. No. 7, p. 80.

[122] Sibbes, *Bowels Opened*, S. No. 16, p. 152.

[123] Spurgeon, *Commenting and Commentaries*, p. 116.

[124] Spurgeon, *Commenting and Commentaries*, pp. 84, 193. Rogers' commentary was published in 1650.

Spurgeon viewed as speculative theology (although such tendencies would certainly earn his condemnation), but also because they were 'dry and sapless', with little about them that was 'experimental', and because they were of little practical use, either for pulpit preparation or for living the Christian life.[125] Speaking positively, Matthew Henry's *An Exposition of all the Books of the Old and New Testament* was perhaps the most warmly commended of all the commentaries Spurgeon reviewed. It was, he declared, 'first among the mighty for general usefulness'. For Spurgeon this multi-volume work exhibited all the qualities he prized so highly in Puritan commentaries, being 'most pious and pithy, sound and sensible, suggestive and sober, terse and trustworthy', as well as 'profitable' and 'practical'. Such a commentary was, according to Spurgeon, 'deeply spiritual'.[126]

To sum up, the three overlapping qualities Spurgeon saw in these Puritan commentaries were sound biblical doctrine, experimental piety, and plain, practical application. All three of these qualities were essential to Spurgeon's spirituality. Biblical theology was crucial because, as he famously put it, 'the coals of orthodoxy' were 'necessary to the fires of piety'.[127] Theology and experience were closely linked. 'Experimental' religion was vital for Spurgeon. Doctrine had to be experienced, and it had to draw the believer closer to Christ. The communion with Christ which Spurgeon sought was a felt communion which could be enjoyed.[128] And, if this relationship with Christ was real, then it would be worked out in practical action. The Puritans provided a framework for spiritual experience which was biblically and theologically grounded, deeply experiential and practically applied.

Moreover, Spurgeon appreciated the Puritans for the way they sought to magnify Christ. In Spurgeon's book, *The Saint And His Saviour*, he cited Richard Sibbes,

> The special work of our ministry is to lay open Christ, to hold up the tapestry and unfold the mysteries of Christ. Let us labour therefore to be always speaking somewhat about Christ, or tending that way. When we speak of the law, let it drive us to Christ; when of moral duties, let them teach us to walk worthy of Christ. Christ, or something tending to Christ, should be our theme, and mark to aim at.[129]

---

[125] Spurgeon, *Commenting and Commentaries*, pp. 184-85, 169-70.

[126] Spurgeon, *Commenting and Commentaries*, p. 2; Spurgeon's Preface to the reprint, *Matthew Henry's Commentary on the New Testament* (10 Vols; London: William MacKenzie, n.d.), Vol. 1, pp. iii-iv. Cf. Spurgeon's comments in his Preface to his reprint of Thomas Watson's *A Body of Divinity*, p. iii, 'There is a happy union of sound doctrine, heart searching experience and sound wisdom throughout all his works'.

[127] As cited by J.M. Gordon, *Evangelical Spirituality: From the Wesleys to John Stott* (London: SPCK, 1991), p. 169. Cf. Spurgeon, *Autobiography*, Vol. 1, p. 178, 'A man cannot have an erroneous belief without by-and-by having an erroneous life. I believe the one thing naturally begets the other.'

[128] C.H. Spurgeon, 'The Bridegroom's Parting Word', *MTP*, Vol. 29, S. No. 1716, Song of Songs 8.13, delivered 15 April 1883, pp. 218-19.

[129] Spurgeon, *The Saint And His Saviour*, n.p.

Sibbes' avowed desire to approach scripture and to engage in ministry in a way which kept the focus firmly on Christ. This quotation was one of two Spurgeon included as standalone quotations, placed before the title page of *The Saint And His Saviour*, evidence that he identified closely with the words. Spurgeon appreciated the christocentric spirituality of a man like Sibbes. Overall, through their books, the Puritans had a shaping effect on Spurgeon's spirituality.

A 'Puritanic Morality'

Speaking in 1888, Spurgeon said that, alongside his 'Calvinistic creed', he preached to his people what he termed a 'Puritanic morality'. 'That is what they want', he insisted, 'and that is what they get.'[130] One of Spurgeon's daily reflections in *Evening By Evening* helps fill out what Spurgeon understood by a 'Puritanic morality'. He stated, 'Professors are no longer strict and Puritanical, questionable literature is read on all hands, frivolous pastimes are currently indulged, and a general laxity threatens to deprive the Lord's peculiar people of those sacred singularities which separate them from sinners.'[131] One of the 'frivolous pastimes' which Spurgeon believed incompatible with 'Puritanic morality' was theatregoing. His attitude to this particular practice can be considered in more detail.

Visiting the 'play-house' was, to Spurgeon, anathema. In a sermon entitled 'The Holy Road', preached in August 1886, he noted, in language that echoed that used earlier in *Evening By Evening*, that

> Professing Christians are becoming less and less strict as to their amusements. We hear of Christian ministers doing that which those who formerly occupied their pulpits never dreamed of doing themselves, nor countenancing in others. Is there to be an open door from the pulpit to the theatre? Are men to go from exercising the sacred ministry to the playhouse? Time was when this would have seemed utterly incredible. God help his church when the leaders of religion come to this![132]

One of Spurgeon's targets in this attack was Joseph Parker, the minister of the City Temple in London, who had 'sanctioned' Nonconformist ministers' theatregoing and attended a performance himself.[133] In a letter dated 2 March 1887, Spurgeon, in explaining his refusal to cooperate with Parker in a putative conference the pastor of the City Temple wanted to organise, declared that the 'view of religion which takes you to theatre is so far off mine that I cannot commune with you therein' (i.e., join in

---

[130] *The Pall Mall Gazette*, Vol. 39 (19 July 1884), p. 12, cited by Kruppa, *Spurgeon*, p. 159.

[131] C.H. Spurgeon, *Evening By Evening: Or, Readings at Eventide for the Family or the Closet* (London: Passmore and Alabaster, 1868), 20 August, p. 235.

[132] 'The Holy Road', *MTP*, Vol. 32, S. No. 1912, Isaiah 35.8, delivered 1 August 1886, p. 413.

[133] Kruppa, *Spurgeon*, p. 449.

the proposed conference).[134] It was reported in September 1886 that Spurgeon had told students at the Pastors' College that if any were found attending the theatre it would be their 'first and last time'.[135] Spurgeon's stance in relation to theatregoing was uncompromising.

It is important to note that Spurgeon's attitudes were shaped by a number of factors, not just Puritanism. Eighteenth-century evangelicals – both Calvinistic and Arminian – were opposed to the theatre and this opposition, as Doreen Rosman shows, continued well into the nineteenth century.[136] Moreover, there were many in Victorian Britain, not just evangelicals, who were negative about the theatre. Speaking of Regency London, Rosman comments that evangelicals' attitudes to the theatre 'mirrored that of their contemporaries' to a significant degree.[137] The same was true of the years following the Regency period. Nevertheless, ways of thinking with regard to the theatre, even amongst those who could be considered broadly evangelical and 'respectable', were changing as the nineteenth century wore on, as Parker's actions illustrate. In contrast to this new mood, Spurgeon remained implacably opposed to the theatre. His outlook continued to be shaped by the norms of an earlier generation of Christians, namely the Puritans and the older evangelicals (who were, of course, themselves significantly shaped by the Puritan heritage). With them, Spurgeon believed that theatregoing and lax morality went hand-in-hand.[138] Crucially, he held that communion with God and 'likeness to Christ' could not be promoted by 'tragedies or comedies'.[139] For Spurgeon, rejecting the theatre was a matter of spirituality. He could not conceive of communing with God in a playhouse and he did not want to commune with those Christians who thought theatregoing was an acceptable practice.

This commitment to a 'Puritanic morality' helps explain other attitudes Spurgeon held which can seem puzzling. As Patricia Kruppa notes, by contrast with many other evangelicals, Spurgeon was late in embracing the temperance cause, resisting it for much of his ministry. In a review of *The Temperance Alphabet for Bands of Hope* in 1871 he had some fun at the publication's expense, describing it as 'ghastly' and commenting on the illustrations, '*The snakes* are on every page, and seem to be fond of coiling round bottles with the corks in; we think they are more likely to be there when the corks are out.'[140] To the annoyance of teetotallers he resisted attempts

---

[134] Spurgeon to J. Parker, 2 March 1887, in Fullerton, *C.H. Spurgeon*, p. 299.

[135] *Kentish Mercury*, 24 September 1886, in 'Loose-Leaf Scrap Folder, March – October 1886', p. 65, Spurgeon's College, Heritage Room (2G).

[136] D.M. Rosman, *Evangelicals and Culture* (London: Croom Helm, 1984), pp. 76-77. For the rejection of theatre-going, novel-reading and social dancing among the majority of Nonconformists up to 1859, see M.R. Watts, *The Dissenters: Volume II, The Expansion of Nonconformity* (Oxford: Clarenden Press, 1995), p. 209.

[137] Rosman, *Evangelicals and Culture*, p. 76.

[138] See, e.g., Spurgeon, 'The Holy Road', p. 413

[139] Spurgeon (ed.), *Sword and Trowel*, April 1877, p. 162.

[140] Spurgeon (ed.), *Sword and Trowel*, October 1871, p. 476.

to persuade him to take the pledge for many years.[141] By 1882 he had accepted the temperance cause and a Tabernacle 'Total Abstinence Society' was promptly formed.[142] Kruppa suggests that Spurgeon became a total abstainer for health reasons, although I have found no evidence for this.[143] More likely, Spurgeon took the pledge because he recognised the havoc male drunkenness wreaked on many poorer families.[144] But his support for the temperance cause was still lukewarm, as shown by his comments to the Tabernacle's Total Abstinence Society, that they should not 'wear a lot of ... putty medals', or be 'always trying to convert the moderate drinkers'.[145] Such late and equivocal support for a cause which was becoming closely identified with Nonconformist life can be explained, in part, by the fact that beer was the 'Puritan drink'.[146] Other attitudes held by Spurgeon were also redolent of the Puritans, for example his partiality to the 'Puritan game of bowls', the only exercise, apart from walking, that he took.[147] Spurgeon's attitudes to the different 'amusements' noted in this section were shaped by a range of factors, but he believed that in upholding them he was remaining true to a 'Puritanic morality'. He was self-consciously 'Puritan' and 'Puritanism' helped determine the way he conceptualised and practised the Christian life.

Spurgeon's Theology

Spurgeon's theology can now be considered. The essentially Calvinistic, Puritan shape to Spurgeon's theology is shown most clearly by an analysis of his preaching. Early sermons are full of expositions of what Spurgeon, standing in the English Calvinistic tradition, repeatedly termed the 'doctrines of grace'. Examples from Volume 1 of the sermon notebooks include: No. 8, 'Final Perseverance'; No. 10, 'Election'; No. 13, 'Free Grace'; and No. 18, 'God's Sovereignty'.[148] Such expositions continued in subsequent volumes of the notebooks, for example, Volume 2, No. 82, 'Final Perseverance Certain'.[149] In a message in Volume 5 of the notebooks, Spurgeon ranged over a number of different Calvinistic doctrines and

---

[141] Kruppa, *Spurgeon*, pp. 222-24.

[142] Kruppa, *Spurgeon*, p. 223.

[143] Kruppa, *Spurgeon*, p. 222.

[144] A point made repeatedly by 'John Ploughman'. See, e.g., *John Ploughman's Pictures; Or, More of his Plain Talk for Plain People* (London: Passmore and Alabaster, 1880), chapter 39, 'He has a hole under his nose and his money runs into it', pp. 39-45. See also the positive reviews of temperance literature in Spurgeon (ed.) *Sword and Trowel*, July 1880, p. 355; February 1885, p. 90.

[145] Kruppa, *Spurgeon*, p. 223.

[146] Kruppa, *Spurgeon*, p. 220. For the growth of the temperance movement among Nonconformists from the 1820s, see Watts, *The Dissenters*, Vol. 2, pp. 211-22.

[147] Spurgeon, *Autobiography*, Vol. 4, p. 54; Fullerton, *C.H. Spurgeon*, pp. 169, 201.

[148] Spurgeon, 'Notebook Containing Early Sermon Skeletons, Vol. 1'. Spurgeon's texts for these messages were Psalm 94.14, Ephesians 1.4, Revelation 21.6 and Psalm 10.16.

[149] Spurgeon, 'Notebooks With Sermon Outlines, Vols 2, 4-9', Vol. 2, Philippians 1.6.

related them explicitly to Christ. The message was entitled 'The Nail In A Sure Place' and was probably preached in 1853.[150] Spurgeon's text was Isaiah 22.23-24. His notes record that he stated, 'Every doctrine derives glory from him [i.e., Christ].' The young preacher then proceeded to list a number of these doctrines, relating them explicitly to Christ,

> Election – we are elect in him as our head.
> Redemption – we are purchased in his blood.
> Justification – a righteousness we find in him.
> Perseverance – is mainly through his intercession.
> Resurrection – is after the model of his resurrection.
> Judgment – He will judge both quick and dead.
> Glory – would be no glory without him.
> All in all he is – Alpha & Omega.[151]

As Spurgeon expounded the Calvinistic themes of election and perseverance, he had a strong christological focus.

Messages that were very similar in overall theme and content to the pre-London sermons appear in the early volumes of the *New Park Street Pulpit*. Examples from Volume 1 of the series include Nos 41-42, 'Election' and No. 52, 'Free-Will – A Slave'.[152] This last named message contained a particularly fierce anti-Arminian polemic. As well as these extended expositions of Calvinistic doctrines, Calvinistic emphases pervaded Spurgeon's preaching on a range of different themes.[153] Spurgeon was proud to be known as a preacher who had strong views on the 'divine sovereignty of God and his divine electings (sic.) and special love towards his own people'.[154] Spurgeon was self-consciously standing in the Puritan tradition he believed was his birthright, as exhibited, especially, in the example of his grandfather. Indeed, in Spurgeon's sermon, 'All Of Grace', he related that he had once preached a joint sermon with his grandfather on Ephesians 2.8 and the

---

[150] Spurgeon, 'Notebooks With Sermon Outlines, Vols 2, 4-9', Vol. 5, begins with a note dated 26 February 1853, '"J____h. Jireh." _ _ "I am ever with you".'

[151] C.H. Spurgeon, 'The Nail In A Sure Place', 'Notebooks With Sermon Outlines, Vols 2, 4-9', Vol. 5, S. No. 236, Isaiah 22.23,24.

[152] C.H. Spurgeon, 'Election', *NPSP*, Vol. 1, S. Nos 42-43, 2 Thessalonians 2.13-14, delivered 2 September 1855, pp. 311-22; 'Free-Will – A Slave', S. No. 52, John 5.40, delivered 2 December 1855, pp. 395-402. Cf. from other *NPSP* volumes, 'Effectual Calling', Vol. 2, S. No. 73, Luke 19.5, delivered 30 March 1856, pp. 153-60; 'Divine Sovereignty', Vol. 2, S. No. 77, Matthew 20.15, delivered 4 May 1856, pp. 185-92; 'Particular Election', Vol. 3, S. No. 123, 2 Peter 1.10,11, delivered 22 March 1857, pp. 129-36.

[153] See, e.g., C.H. Spurgeon, 'A Wise Desire', *NPSP*, Vol. 1, S. No. 33, Psalm 47.4, delivered 8 July 1855, pp. 253-60; 'The Power Of The Holy Ghost', S. No. 30, Romans 15.13, delivered 17 June 1855, pp. 229-36; 'The Comer's Conflict With Satan', Vol. 2, S. No. 100, Luke 9.42, delivered 24 August 1856, pp. 370-76.

[154] C.H. Spurgeon, 'False Professors Solemnly Warned', *NPSP*, Vol. 2, S. No. 102, Philippians 3.18,19, delivered 24 August 1856, p. 391.

'doctrines of grace'. The two men took turns at preaching on themes such as the 'weakness and inability of human nature' and the 'certainty that salvation could not be of ourselves' each giving way to the other. Speaking in 1887, Spurgeon declared that if his grandfather could return to earth and hear his grandson preaching, he would find him 'where he left me' – true to the 'same form of doctrine' and preaching the same gospel.[155]

It is important to note that there was some development in Spurgeon's theology, despite his comments in 'All Of Grace'. Mark Hopkins has shown that although Spurgeon's theology remained 'fundamentally Calvinistic, by the end of the 1850s it was of a lower variety than in his earlier preaching'.[156] Use of terms such as 'lower' and 'higher' is fraught with difficulty in a debate concerning Calvinism, but Hopkins is surely correct in asserting that there were some changes in Spurgeon's approach which can be dated to the beginning of the 1860s.[157] By the 1870s the shifts of emphasis had become even more pronounced. In the *Sword and Trowel* in 1874, Spurgeon stated that 'the truth of God is wider than either of the two great systems [i.e., Calvinism and Arminianism]).' He went on to observe that 'Calvinism, pure and simple ... is not perfect, for it lacks some of the balancing truths of a system which arose as a remonstrance against its mistakes.' It was not, Spurgeon assured his readers, that he had thrown away the five points. These continued to be vitally important for him, anchoring his spiritual life. But, he stated, he 'may have gained [an]other five'. If the truth lay 'in the valley between two camps', or if the truth had 'both sides' of the valley in view, then the truth should be followed – wherever it might lead.[158] The attacks on Arminians were toned down and full-scale expositions of Calvinistic tenets were largely absent from Spurgeon's preaching in the Metropolitan Tabernacle.[159] There were, then, some important adjustments made to Spurgeon's Calvinism in the course of his ministry.

---

[155] Spurgeon, 'All Of Grace', pp. 3-4. C.H. Spurgeon's joint sermon with his grandfather is n.d. and the place where it was preached is not recorded (C.H. Spurgeon merely said it was in a 'certain town in the Eastern Counties'). Almost certainly the event described in 'All Of Grace' took place in the 1850s as James Spurgeon rarely preached in the last few years of his life.

[156] Hopkins, *Nonconformity's Romantic Generation*, p. 140.

[157] See, e.g., C.H. Spurgeon, 'Election and Holiness', *NPSP*, Vol. 6, S. No. 302, Deuteronomy 10.14,15,16, delivered 11 March 1860, p. 133, 'It is time that the systems were broken up ... We know no difference between high doctrine and low doctrine.' As the title of this sermon indicates, however, Spurgeon was still working within a basically Calvinistic framework.

[158] C.H. Spurgeon, 'The Present Position Of Calvinism In England', in Spurgeon (ed.), *Sword and Trowel*, February 1874, pp. 49-53; cf. 'High Doctrine And Broad Doctrine', *MTP*, Vol. 30, S. No. 1762, John 6.37, n.d., pp. 49-50.

[159] Although see *NPSP*, Vol. 7, and the expositions of various Calvinistic doctrines which partly make up Nos 385-88, pp. 304-28. These were not by Spurgeon, although he was certainly in fundamental agreement with the material his invited speakers delivered.

Nevertheless, Hopkins' comment that Spurgeon's theological framework remained 'fundamentally Calvinistic' is an important one. Election, final perseverance and the covenant of grace were all tenets of Calvinistic theology which remained highly significant to Spurgeon. The chapter in the *Autobiography* entitled 'A Defence of Calvinism' represents his mature view.[160] Although Spurgeon softened his approach on Arminianism, the contours of his theological topography remained recognisably Calvinistic and these in turn continued to shape the contours of his spirituality.

Perhaps the most important and enduring way this Calvinistic framework moulded Spurgeon's spirituality was in providing security for the Christian journey. In a communion meditation entitled 'The Spiced Wine Of My Pomegranate: Or, The Communion Of Communication', which was preached on Song of Songs 8.2, Spurgeon stated that the 'immovable basis' of communion with Christ was 'laid of old in the eternal union which subsisted between Christ and His elect'.[161] Spurgeon's emphasis was redolent of that contained in the a Puritan commentaries on the Song by Sibbes and Durham,[162] which have already been analysed in this chapter. In another message, entitled 'Bands Of Love; Or, Union To Christ', Spurgeon declared, 'The believer was in the loins of Jesus Christ the mediator when in old eternity the covenant settlements of grace were decreed, ratified and made sure forever.'[163] James Gordon is right to speak of the 'Calvinistic tenor of Spurgeon's spiritual experience' in relation to these extracts.[164] A Christian believer's relationship with Christ was firmly grounded in the election which had taken place in 'old eternity'. Consequently, the basis of the relationship was 'immovable'.

Spurgeon's insistence on final perseverance flowed out from this fundamental conviction concerning the indissoluble union between Christ and the believer. This union, sealed as it was by the blood of Christ shed on the cross, simply had to be eternal. 'I will be an infidel at once when I can believe that a saint of God can ever fall finally', he insisted.[165] In a sermon, 'The Rocky Fortress And Its Inhabitant', preached in 1884, in the last decade of Spurgeon's ministry, he insisted that such a

---

[160] Spurgeon, *Autobiography*, Vol. 1, pp. 167-78.

[161] C.H. Spurgeon, 'The Spiced Wine Of My Pomegranate: Or, The Communion Of Communication', Song of Songs 8.2, John 1.16, n.d., in *Till He Come: Communion Meditations* (London: Passmore and Alabaster, 1896), p. 183.

[162] As evidenced by, e.g., the subtitle of Sibbes' work, ... *Neere and Deere Love, Union and Communion betwixt Christ and the Church* and Sibbes' insistence that true communion with Christ had to based on prior union. See *Bowels Opened*, p. x.

[163] C.H. Spurgeon, 'Bands Of Love; Or, Union To Christ', Hosea 11.4, n.d., in *Till He Come*, p. 183. Cf. *Autobiography*, Vol. 1, pp. 170-71; 'No condemnation', in T.P. Crosby (ed.), *C.H. Spurgeon's Sermons Beyond Volume 63: An authentic supplement to the Metropolitan Tabernacle Pulpit* (Leominster: Day One, 2009), Romans 1.8, n.d., p. 335. Those who took hold of God's covenant 'by simple faith in his unswerving fidelity' could know they were eternally free from condemnation.

[164] Gordon, *Evangelical Spirituality*, p. 163.

[165] Spurgeon, *Autobiography*, Vol. 1, p. 172.

view was based on the 'guarantees of everlasting faithfulness' God had given in his word. Indeed, God's 'covenant, made up of promises ... and ratified by blood' was like a 'bulwark' behind which believers sheltered, a 'line of defence' which could not be breached. A believer was eternally secure and they could know that security now. Spurgeon wanted to emphasise that this security could be known by his hearers even as they heard and responded in their hearts to his words. The preacher quoted John 10.28 and Romans 8.35 before declaring, dramatically, 'We challenge earth and hell, time and eternity, to dissolve the blessed union between Christ and his people ... If your confidence be in the living God, who shall put you to shame?' The passage in 'The Rocky Fortress ...' which deals with final perseverance can be summed up in Spurgeon's exclamation, 'Oh, the blessed security of a child of God!'[166]

This was a security that Spurgeon depended on himself. Indeed, he stated, 'If I did not believe the doctrine of the final perseverance of the saints, I think I should be of all men most miserable, because I should lack any ground of comfort.'[167] But Spurgeon did believe the doctrine and so, however difficult the road became for him in his 'earthly pilgrimage', he believed he would endure to the end. Communion would not ultimately be broken, for that communion was based on the 'immutable' decree of God.

It ought to be stressed that this Calvinistic theology was not just influenced by sixteenth- and seventeenth-century Puritans or even, more broadly, the 'Puritanism' of his family. As already noted, C.H. Spurgeon's family were evangelical Calvinists and their evangelicalism, and the evangelicalism Spurgeon imbibed from other influences, shaped him too. In particular it needs to be emphasised that the assurance he derived from the Calvinistic decrees would not necessarily have been shared by many of the seventeenth-century godly who, as David Gillett notes, often went through a long 'struggle' for assurance. Gillett cites Thomas Brooks. For Brooks, the Christian who wanted to attain assurance 'must work, and sweat and weep ... He must not only dig, but he must dig deep before he can come to the golden mine. Assurance is such precious gold, that a man must win it before he can wear it.'[168] Assurance and the joy which follows was seen, as Gillett notes, as 'an exceptional possession rather than a normal experience'.[169] The quotation from Brooks carries evidence of the 'experimental predestinarianism' highlighted by Coffey and Lim – a

---

[166] C.H. Spurgeon, 'The Rocky Fortress And Its Inhabitant', *MTP*, Vol. 30, S. No. 1764, Isaiah 33.15,16, delivered 3 February 1884, pp. 79-81.

[167] Spurgeon, *Autobiography*, Vol. 1, p. 173.

[168] D.K. Gillett, *Trust and Obey: Explorations in Evangelical Spirituality* (London: Darton, Longman and Todd, 1993), p. 43; T. Brooks, *Heaven on Earth* (London: Banner of Truth, 1961 [1654]), p. 139. Cf. the discussion in D.W. Bebbington, *Evangelicalism in Modern Britain: A history from the 1730s to the 1980s* (London: Unwin Hyman, 1989), pp. 42-47, and the supporting cluster of Puritan works cited on p. 44.

[169] Gillett, *Trust and Obey*, p. 43. For an extended discussion of Puritan approaches to assurance, see J. Von Ruhr, *The Covenant of Grace in Puritan Thought* (Atlanta: Scholars, 1986), pp. 155-91.

tendency to regular, detailed self-examination in order to find assurance that one was truly part of the elect.[170] This was a tendency to which Spurgeon's grandfather appears to have been prone.[171] In 1864 Spurgeon reprinted some selections from Thomas Brooks,[172] entitled *Smooth Stones Taken from Ancient Brooks*, but he did not follow Brooks in his approach to assurance. Spurgeon's was a more confident view shaped by an evangelical reading of the Puritan legacy. The importance to Spurgeon of evangelical approaches to assurance will be considered in more detail in chapter 3.

Nevertheless, despite Spurgeon's debt to eighteenth-century evangelicalism in respect of his understanding of assurance, his approach to the question was still shaped in significant degree from Puritan works that provided (once viewed through the lens of a more confident evangelicalism) the basis for his assurance. Overall, I am convinced the evidence shows that Spurgeon's theology owed the Puritans a substantial debt. That his Calvinism, consciously adopted as it was,[173] was shaped to a real degree by the Puritanism which he encountered through his grandfather at Stambourne and through his wider family is shown by the evidence assembled in this chapter. His Calvinism was not derived directly from John Calvin (in fact I can find no evidence of Spurgeon engaging directly with Calvin in his pre-London period).[174] John Gill, the Baptist High Calvinist, is another possible source for Spurgeon's Calvinism. As a young Cambridgeshire pastor, Spurgeon purchased a set of Gill's works and when he moved to London he was conscious that Gill was one of the previous pastors of the church that was now meeting at New Park Street.[175] Yet Spurgeon did not follow Gill into High Calvinism. This subject will be dealt with in more detail in chapter 3. Suffice to say here that, in the very first sermon in Volume

---

[170] Coffey and Lim, 'Introduction', p. 4. Elsewhere, Coffey shows that the Puritan approach to assurance was more diverse than has often been supposed whilst admitting that the view I have described as typically Puritan was still the mainstream one. See J. Coffey, 'Puritanism, Evangelicalism and the Evangelical Protestant Tradition', in M.A.G. Haykin and K.J. Stewart (eds), *The Emergence Of Evangelicalism: Exploring Historical Continuities* (Leicester: IVP, 2008), pp. 265-66. Cf. the comments of D.W. Bebbington, 'Response', in the same volume, p. 421.

[171] See Spurgeon, 'Sweet Experiences in 1842 and 1892', pp. 3-5. James Spurgeon, according to his grandson, was 'liable to many a doubt as to his own spiritual condition'.

[172] C.H. Spurgeon (ed.), *Smooth Stones Taken from Ancient Brooks ... Being a Collection of Sentences, Illustrations, and Quaint Sayings, from the Works of that Renowned Puritan, Thomas Brooks* (London: Dean and Son, 1864).

[173] This is Hopkins' point in *Nonconformity's Romantic Generation*, pp. 132-33. I agree that Spurgeon's Calvinism was consciously adopted, but think Hopkins underplays the influence of his family background in the adoption of this Calvinism.

[174] This does not mean he did not engage directly with Calvin, of course, but I have been unable to track down evidence of this in his early preaching notes and letters. Certainly, a reading of Calvin does not seem to have been at all significant in the development of Spurgeon's thought.

[175] Spurgeon, *Autobiography*, Vol. 1, pp. 254-53.

1 of the notebooks Spurgeon makes an appeal 'to saints and sinners'.[176] By the time he was pastor at Waterbeach he was actively and explicitly opposing the High Calvinism which denied the propriety of offering such appeals, and which was strongly associated with Gill. In another early sermon, in Volume 4 of the notebooks, Spurgeon declared, 'It is to be feared that old Gill-ism is not so productive of heat and life as ... the religion which has a spice of Wesley in it.'[177] The evidence suggests that Gill was not an important shaping factor for Spurgeon's Calvinism. Those that Spurgeon met in Newmarket and Cambridge would have helped him. These included Mary King, a Strict Baptist cook at the house in which Spurgeon stayed. Mary King was, said Spurgeon, an avid reader of the *Gospel Standard* who liked 'good, strong Calvinistic doctrine'. Spurgeon certainly said he owed her a debt although her influence is hard to quantify.[178]

Certainly, forces that were not strictly Puritan helped shape Spurgeon's Calvinism. Nevertheless, the mature Spurgeon delved ever more deeply into the Puritans and, in his private study at 'Westwood', his final home in South Norwood, he surrounded himself with his Puritan books.[179] Spurgeon encouraged his own congregation to read the Puritans for themselves,[180] and it was Puritan works of theology that were reprinted and taught at the Pastors' College,[181] with an avowed desire to train a new generation of ministers who 'would continue the Puritanical succession'.[182] Spurgeon believed he was bound by no system, but his theology was still substantially marked by a particular form of Calvinism, one which was linked, both indirectly and directly, to the Puritans. Because this theology was deeply a part of him, it was also part of his spirituality.

Conclusion

Spurgeon's upbringing had elements to it that were recognisably Puritan. This upbringing had an important, shaping effect on his later spirituality. There is substantial evidence, both from Spurgeon's Cambridgeshire ministry and also from his London ministry, of Puritan influence on his spiritual life. John Bunyan's *Pilgrim's Progress* provided both an overarching vision of the Christian life as a pilgrimage and also the metaphors and imagery which helped Spurgeon make sense

---

[176] C.H. Spurgeon, 'Adoption', 'Notebook Containing Early Sermon Skeletons, Vol.1', S. No. 1, Ephesians 1.5.

[177] C.H. Spurgeon, 'Nonconformity', 'Notebooks With Sermon Outlines, Vols 2, 4-9', Vol. 4, S. No. 223, Romans 12.2.

[178] Spurgeon, *Autobiography*, Vol. 1, p. 53.

[179] Spurgeon, *Autobiography*, Vol. 4, p. 295-96.

[180] C.H. Spurgeon, 'Paul – His Cloak And His Books', *MTP*, Vol. 9, S. No. 542, 2 Timothy 4.13, delivered 29 November 1863, p. 668.

[181] Fullerton, *C.H. Spurgeon*, p. 235.

[182] Spurgeon, *Autobiography*, Vol. 4, p. 296. Cf. Spurgeon's comments about John Owen, made at the annual Pastors' College conference in 1884, as reported by the *Christian World*, 24 April 1884. See 'Loose-Leaf Scrap Folders', April–June 1884, p. 3.

of particular experiences along the journey. Puritan commentaries provided a framework for the Christian life that was complementary to Bunyan's. Sound, Calvinistic doctrine was wedded to an experimental piety which flowed out in a host of practical applications. Also, the Calvinistic theology which, the evidence assembled in this chapter shows, owed a substantial debt to the Puritans and their legacy, provided (once it had been considered from an evangelical perspective) a secure basis from which to grow into communion with Christ. Communion was based on the eternal union with Christ which was guaranteed by God's decree and by the atonement. Spurgeon believed he was eternally secure, a belief which affected the whole tenor of his spiritual experience.

The Puritans also provided Spurgeon with an example of those who had actively sought the communion with Christ that union with him made possible. Indeed, the Puritans delighted in their experiences of 'sweet' communion with Christ. In *Smooth Stones from Ancient Brooks* Spurgeon included the flowing extract,

> Christ is a most precious commodity, he is better than rubies or the most costly pearls ... Christ is to be sought and bought with any pains, at any price; we cannot buy this gold too dear. He is a jewel more worth than a thousand worlds, as all know who love him. Get him, and get all; miss him, and miss all.

The emphases on Christ ('a jewel more worth than a thousand worlds') and on experience ('as all know who love him') surface in other extracts from Brooks selected by Spurgeon, for example, 'Souls that know by experience what the bosom of Christ is, what spiritual communion is, and what the glory of heaven is, will not be put off by things that are mixed, mutable, and momentary.'[183] Spurgeon himself was to make the single-minded pursuit of 'spiritual communion' his life's goal. The dimensions of Puritan piety outlined in these quotations from Brooks and present in other Puritan works that Spurgeon imbibed were vitally important to his spirituality.

---

[183] Spurgeon (ed.), *Smooth Stones*, pp. 30, 10. Cf., e.g., p. 55.

CHAPTER 3

Evangelical Conversionism:
'Dear spot of ground where Jesus met us! Dear hour which brought us to his feet!'

Communion with Christ was based on the eternal union with Christ wrought by God's decree and Christ's work on the cross. But for communion with Christ to be experienced by a person, conversion to Christ had to take place. Conversion is here being understood as a 'turning to Christ and finding a relationship with him'.[1] For Spurgeon, sinners were not 'friends' with Jesus until their hearts were changed by regeneration and they came to him in repentance and faith.[2] This was a view that was shaped by his own experience. Spurgeon was, as we have seen, extremely grateful for his Christian upbringing and recognised that this was significant in moulding him.[3] Nevertheless, he believed that as a child he had not known Christ in his 'innermost soul'.[4] It was when he was converted, he believed, that his experience of communion with Christ truly began. Furthermore, conversion was also the moment that marked the beginning of true communion with Christ's people. In coming to Christ and entering into fellowship with him, Spurgeon entered into fellowship with others who had similarly come to Christ. Conversion, then, was the essential gateway to an experience of 'communion with Christ and his people'.

This chapter analyses Spurgeon's conversion experience and also the way he later retold it. I will seek to establish that the mature version of his conversion narrative was a carefully crafted account in which he, consciously or unconsciously, highlighted a number of theological and practical motifs which were important to him. His theology of conversion, which was intimately bound up with his own experience and how he later understood it, is then examined. In the second half of

---

[1] I.M. Randall, *What a Friend We Have in Jesus: The Evangelical Tradition* (London: Darton, Longman and Todd, 2005), p. 26. This is the classic evangelical understanding, which Spurgeon shared.

[2] C.H. Spurgeon, 'The Friends Of Jesus', *New Park Street Pulpit (NPSP) / Metropolitan Tabernacle Pulpit (MTP)* (London: Passmore and Alabaster, 1856–1917), *MTP*, Vol. 26, S. No. 1552, John 15.14, delivered 8 August 1880, p. 445. Sinners were not 'friends' of Jesus until their hearts were changed.

[3] C.H. Spurgeon, *Autobiography: Compiled from his Diary, Letters, and Records by his Wife and his Private Secretary* (4 Vols; London: Passmore and Alabaster, 1897–99), Vol. 1, p. 102, 129.

[4] Spurgeon, *Autobiography*, Vol. 1, p. 98.

the chapter Spurgeon's evangelistic preaching ministry is accorded special consideration, with coverage given to his pre-London preaching as well as to his later ministry. As was argued in chapter 2, 'Puritanism' was an important element in his spiritual formation, and aspects of this can be also be discerned in the material handled in this chapter. But what I especially aim to show here is that Spurgeon was influenced by forces associated with the eighteenth-century Evangelical Revival and the broader evangelical movement which flowed out of the Revival. Evangelicalism both shaped the way that communion with Christ was conceived and moulded the way Christ was shared with others.

Spurgeon's Experience of Conversion

Spurgeon held that his conversion took place on 6 January 1850 at a Primitive Methodist chapel in Artillery Street, Colchester.[5] The fullest description he gave of his conversion and the events leading up to it was that contained in the *Autobiography*. This in turn was largely based on a small eight-page booklet, entitled *How Spurgeon Found Christ*, published in 1879 as part of the celebrations to mark Spurgeon's twenty-five years of ministry in London.[6] In the account in Volume 1 of the *Autobiography*, Spurgeon related how he had experienced deep conviction of sin with accompanying 'darkness and despair' for a number of years.[7] In the *Autobiography* he did not specify the length of time, although elsewhere he spoke of 'five years of conviction'.[8] This contention receives some support from the extract from Eliza Spurgeon's diary which was noted in chapter 2 which, as we saw, spoke of C.H. Spurgeon being spiritually 'affected' as early as 1843.[9] Spurgeon clearly engaged with a number of books which related to conversion during this period. These included the two Puritan works that his mother had read to him – Baxter's *Call to the Unconverted* and Alleine's *Alarm to Sinners* – but Spurgeon also read Philip Doddridge's *Rise and Progress of Religion in the Soul*[10] and John Angell James' *Anxious Enquirer*.[11] Despite engaging with this literature Spurgeon

---

[5] Spurgeon, *Autobiography*, Vol. 1, pp. 107-108.

[6] C.H. Spurgeon, *How Spurgeon Found Christ* (London: James E. Hawkins, n.d. [1879]).

[7] Spurgeon, *Autobiography*, Vol. 1, pp. 98, 105.

[8] C.H. Spurgeon, 'Fellowship With God', *MTP*, Vol. 7, S. No. 407, 1 John 1.3, delivered 15 September 1861, p. 495. The extract from Eliza Spurgeon's diary entry from 1843, which her son later copied, speaks of C.H. Spurgeon being spiritually 'affected' as early as 1843. C.H. Spurgeon, 'Extracts made ... from his mother's diary', Spurgeon's College, Heritage Room (Display Case 2).

[9] C.H. Spurgeon, 'Extracts made ... from his mother's diary'.

[10] See Spurgeon, *Autobiography*, Vol. 1, pp. 80, 104. Doddridge's *Rise and Progress* was originally published in 1745.

[11] Spurgeon, *Autobiography*, Vol. 1, p. 104. Angell James' *The Anxious Enquirer after Salvation Directed and Encouraged* was originally published in 1834.

was unable to find relief. 'I panted and longed to understand how I might be saved', he said.[12] The evidence indicates that his period of conviction was long and deep.

The leading features of Spurgeon's lengthy conversion narrative, as it appeared in the *Autobiography*, are as follows.[13] Spurgeon was heading to an unspecified place of worship in Colchester but was unable to reach his intended destination because of what he described as 'the goodness of God in sending a snowstorm'. He turned down Artillery Street and came to a small Primitive Methodist chapel which was attended, on that Sunday, by 'a dozen or fifteen people'. Spurgeon said he had 'heard of the Primitive Methodists, how they sang so loudly they made people's heads ache'. This did not matter, however. What was important was that they might be able to tell him how he could be 'saved'. If they were able to do this, then the style of worship would be of little consequence. Spurgeon stated that the minister 'did not come that morning', surmising that he must have been snowed in. 'At last', Spurgeon said, 'a very thin looking man, a shoemaker, or tailor, or something of that sort, went up into the pulpit to preach.'

Spurgeon described the preacher in unflattering terms. The man was 'really stupid', obliged to keep closely to his text 'for the simple reason he had little else to say'. The unlearned preacher did not even pronounce the words of Isaiah 45.22 properly when he read them. Nevertheless, there was, said Spurgeon, 'a glimpse of hope' for him in the text. Spurgeon averred that the preacher began his message thus,

> 'My dear friends, this is a very simple text indeed. It says, "Look." Now lookin' don't take a great deal of pains. It ain't liftin' your foot or your finger; it is just, "Look." Well, a man needn't go to College to learn to look. You may be the biggest fool, and yet you can look. A man needn't be worth a thousand a year to be able to look. Anyone can look; even a child can look. But then the text says, "Look unto *Me*" Ay!' said he, in broad Essex, 'many on ye are lookin' to yourselves. Some look to God the Father. No, look to him by-and-by. Jesus Christ says, "Look unto *Me*." Some on ye say, "We must wait for the Spirit's workin'". You have no business with that just now. Look to *Christ*. The text says, "Look unto *Me*".'

The preacher continued in this vein for about ten minutes repeatedly urging his hearers to look to Christ. Then events took a dramatic turn. The preacher stared at Spurgeon and addressed the young man directly, saying that he looked very 'miserable'. Then, the preacher lifted up his hands and shouted, '"Young man, look to Jesus Christ. Look! Look! Look! You have nothin' to do but to look and live!"' Spurgeon described his own response thus, 'I saw at once the way of salvation'. He 'looked' to Christ, he declared, 'until [he] could almost have looked [his] eyes away'. The 'darkness' had gone and Spurgeon said that he could have stood at 'that instant' and sung of the 'precious blood' of Jesus and of the 'simple faith' which looked 'only to him'.

---

[12] Spurgeon, *Autobiography*, Vol. 1, pp. 104-105.

[13] The information and quotations in this and the following two paragraphs are taken from Spurgeon, *Autobiography*, Vol. 1, pp. 105-108.

Spurgeon's description of his conversion can now be analysed. His account was presented in the *Autobiography* as a factual record of what had actually happened.[14] Nevertheless, there are solid reasons for doubting that certain features of this later retelling of events are accurate. Firstly, there is evidence to suggest that the preacher of the 'Look' sermon was not actually a layman but an experienced Primitive Methodist circuit minister. As Spurgeon's fame grew following his move to London, and as the basic outline of his conversion narrative became known, at least three men claimed to be the preacher of the sermon in question.[15] Spurgeon said he did not recognise any of those who were presented to him, but almost certainly one of these claimants, the Rev. Robert Eaglen, was the man in question. The evidence in favour of Eaglen was assembled by Danzy Sheen, a Primitive Methodist who trained at the Pastors' College. Sheen used his contacts in Primitive Methodism to glean much information about Spurgeon's conversion.[16] That Eaglen was the preacher was the testimony of at least three members of Artillery Street Chapel, including the most important church officer, and their testimony was supported by other Primitive Methodist ministers in the area. Eaglen had been suffering from 'pulmonary consumption' in January 1850, but had regained his health and put on weight by the time he was presented to Spurgeon as the preacher who was instrumental in his conversion. This meeting was probably in 1854.[17] Eaglen's improvement in health, Sheen surmised, may have been the reason Spurgeon failed to identify him, insisting that Eaglen was not the man. The suspicion must be, however, that it was convenient for Spurgeon for the preacher to remain anonymous.[18] Indeed, speaking to an audience of Primitive Methodists meeting at the Metropolitan Tabernacle in 1861 Spurgeon stated, 'I was converted in one of your chapels, not under one of your regular ministers, but under a local preacher whose features I shall never look upon again until the morning of the resurrection.'[19] Just eleven years after the event, Spurgeon appeared surprisingly sure that he would never, in this life, meet the preacher who had given the 'Look' sermon. Nevertheless, the evidence assembled by Sheen strongly suggests that Eaglen – a minister not a layman – was the preacher.

Secondly, Spurgeon was probably mistaken concerning the date of his conversion, despite his confident avowals to the contrary.[20] 13 January 1850 rather than 6 January 1850 was the most likely date. This was the Sunday the circuit plan indicated Eaglen was preaching in Colchester and meteorological evidence cited by

---

[14] See, e.g., the comment by the compilers of the *Autobiography* concerning the date of Spurgeon's conversion, Vol. 1, p. 108.

[15] Spurgeon, *Autobiography*, Vol. 1, p. 105.

[16] D. Sheen, *Pastor C.H. Spurgeon: His Conversion, Career, And Coronation* (London: J.B. Knapp, 1892), pp. 14-51; and cf. T. McCoy, 'The evangelistic ministry of C.H. Spurgeon: Implications for a contemporary model of pastoral evangelism' (unpublished PhD dissertation, Southern Baptist Theological Seminary, 1989), Appendix D, pp. 323-50.

[17] Sheen, *Pastor C.H. Spurgeon*, pp. 39-40.

[18] So McCoy, 'The evangelistic ministry of C.H. Spurgeon', Appendix D, pp. 348-49.

[19] Sheen, *Pastor C.H. Spurgeon*, p. 20.

[20] Spurgeon, *Autobiography*, Vol. 1, p. 108.

Timothy McCoy, although not absolutely conclusive, indicates there was snow over the weekend of 12–13 January but not over the previous weekend.[21] Spurgeon appears mistaken with regard to an important detail of his conversion, one which appeared in his later, developed accounts of the event.[22]

Thirdly, and most importantly, there has to be serious doubt as to the accuracy of Spurgeon's *reportage* of the sermon itself. That Spurgeon was almost certainly mistaken about the identity of the preacher and the date of his conversion are facts which in themselves suggest he did not recall the event as clearly as he later claimed. Moreover, I have not been able to find any evidence that he wrote or preached about the details of his conversion until 1855, that is, five years after it actually happened. There are no sermons on Isaiah 45.22 in Spurgeon's extant Cambridgeshire outlines. Moreover, I have found no evidence, despite a close reading of all the relevant extant notebooks, that Spurgeon spoke about the details of his conversion in any of these pre-London sermons.[23] The earliest instance I have discovered of Spurgeon referring to the details of his own conversion is in a message preached to an estimated crowd of 12,000 people in a field in Hackney, north London, in September 1855.[24] This message was included in Volume 1 of the *New Park Street Pulpit*, where it is entitled 'Heaven And Hell'.[25] There is a further reference in this first volume of Spurgeon's published preaching, in a sermon entitled 'Healing For The Wounded' which was preached on 11 November 1855.[26] These early accounts were much briefer than the ones in the *Autobiography* and in *How Spurgeon Found Christ*. In 'Heaven And Hell' the only words spoken by the Primitive Methodist preacher were those of his text and the direct appeal 'Look, look, look',[27] and in 'Healing For The Wounded' Spurgeon tellingly said that he did not 'recollect what [the preacher] said in the sermon'.[28] Yet from 1856 onwards Spurgeon began to speak about his conversion publicly on a regular basis, and at length. Extended references to his conversion in the *New Park Street / Metropolitan Tabernacle*

---

[21] McCoy, 'The evangelistic ministry of C.H. Spurgeon', Appendix D, pp. 343, 350. The evidence provided was for London, not Colchester, hence its inconclusive nature. As to the date of Spurgeon's conversion, see also the evidence assembled by Sheen, *Pastor C.H. Spurgeon*, pp. 28-29.

[22] And in the majority of biographies of Spurgeon. See, e.g., C. Ray, *A Marvellous Ministry: The Story of Spurgeon's Sermons* (London: Passmore and Alabaster, 1905 [1903]), pp. 64-65.

[23] C.H. Spurgeon, 'Notebook Containing Early Sermon Skeletons, Vol. I', Spurgeon's College, Heritage Room (K1.5); 'Notebooks With Sermon Outlines, Vols 2, 4-9', Spurgeon's College, Heritage Room (U.1). Of course, Volume 3 is missing.

[24] Sheen, *Pastor C.H. Spurgeon*, pp. 16-17.

[25] C.H. Spurgeon, 'Heaven And Hell', *NPSP*, Vol. 1, S. Nos 39-40, Matthew 8.11,12, delivered 4 September 1855, pp. 301-10.

[26] C.H. Spurgeon, 'Healing For The Wounded', *NPSP*, Vol. 1, S. No. 53, Psalm 147.3, delivered 11 November 1855, pp. 403-10.

[27] Spurgeon, 'Heaven And Hell', p. 310.

[28] Spurgeon, 'Healing For The Wounded', p. 407.

Pulpit occur in, for example, 'Sovereignty And Salvation' (delivered 6 January 1856),[29] 'Turn Or Burn' (delivered 7 December 1856)[30] and 'The Life-Look' (delivered 9 January 1876).[31] An account of Spurgeon's conversion also appeared in the *Christian World* in 1857 and this was reproduced by Sheen in his biography.[32]

Of course, the fact that there appears to be no reference to the events surrounding Spurgeon's conversion in the pre-London notebooks does not conclusively show that Spurgeon did not speak about it when preaching. The Cambridgeshire 'skeletons' are an incomplete record of what Spurgeon preached in this period. Nevertheless, the lack of a clear reference is surprising, as is the fact that Spurgeon does not appear to have preached at all on Isaiah 45.22 in his pre-London ministry. Moreover, his comment, made in November 1855, that he did not 'recollect' the words of the preacher further suggests that later detailed 'recollections' of the event may have owed a significant amount to imaginative reconstruction.

Furthermore, and as already indicated, the earlier accounts lack the detail and colour of the later ones. Regarding the basic facts, the different accounts are broadly congruent (although in both 'Sovereignty And Salvation' and 'Turn Or Burn' the Primitive Methodist preacher is described as a 'minister').[33] There was clearly some fine-tuning to suit the needs of a particular audience. For example, in 'Turn Or Burn', which was preached to his New Park Street congregation, the Primitive Methodists were a 'peculiar sect'; in *How Spurgeon Found Christ*, which was for wider consumption and also a later and more considered account, they were a 'very useful body'.[34] The addition of much detail strongly suggests that the account printed in the *Autobiography* does not contain the *ipsissima verba* of the Primitive Methodist preacher and, in a number of respects, probably not the *ipsissima vox* either. Overall, by the time Spurgeon did begin to speak about his conversion regularly it was his more mature reflections on his experience which were given voice, with certain theological notes sounded with particular clarity. The story was subsequently both expanded and honed until the carefully fashioned, dramatised account of the event in *How Spurgeon Found Christ* was published, designed to instruct, inspire, score theological points and, perhaps most importantly, be instrumental in the conversion of others. Large quantities could be obtained for evangelistic distribution from depots in London, Glasgow and Dublin at a generous

---

[29] C.H. Spurgeon, 'Sovereignty And Salvation', *NPSP*, Vol. 2, S. No. 60, Isaiah 45.22, pp. 49, 56.

[30] C.H. Spurgeon, 'Turn Or Burn', *NPSP*, Vol. 2, S. No. 106, Psalm 7.12, p. 423.

[31] C.H. Spurgeon, 'The Life-Look', *MTP*, Vol. 50, S. No. 2867, Isaiah 45.22, pp. 37-38. Spurgeon declared in this sermon that he had preached 'a good many times' from Isaiah 45.22 (see p. 37). For another example, in which Spurgeon refers to his own conversion only briefly, see 'Life For A Look', *MTP*, Vol. 50, S. No. 2805, delivered 22 March 1877, pp. 541-52.

[32] See Sheen, *Pastor C.H. Spurgeon*, pp. 18-20.

[33] Spurgeon, 'Sovereignty And Salvation', p. 49; 'Turn Or Burn', p. 424.

[34] Spurgeon, 'Turn Or Burn', p. 424; *How I Found Christ*, p. 4.

reduction.[35] Thus Spurgeon's testimony was not only celebrated, it was also packaged and marketed as an aid to evangelism. Spurgeon's mature conversion account was one which had been moulded and re-moulded by a range of theological and practical concerns.

Spurgeon's later account of his conversion is in the classic evangelical pattern and before exploring this in a more detailed fashion, some consideration of what is meant by the term 'evangelical' is necessary. David Bebbington, in his landmark study of 1989 entitled *Evangelicalism in Modern Britain*, defines the distinctive hallmarks of the movement as being 'biblicism', 'crucicentrism', 'conversionism' and 'activism'.[36] In an essay entitled 'Towards an Evangelical Identity', he speaks more simply of a 'zeal for conversion', 'proclamation of the cross', 'devotion to the Bible' and 'unbounded activism'.[37] These four 'special marks' form a 'quadrilateral of priorities which together make up the basis of Evangelicalism'.[38] Bebbington's approach has gained much scholarly support. To cite just one example, G.M. Ditchfield describes Bebbington's analysis as 'the most convincing summary of evangelical characteristics by a modern historian'.[39] Indeed, Bebbington's understanding of evangelicalism has become widely accepted. In 2008 a collection of essays appeared under the title *The Emergence of Evangelicalism*. The essays in this volume all engage with aspects of Bebbington's work. The first main chapter is by Timothy Larsen, who offers a wide-ranging review of the various responses to *Evangelicalism in Modern Britain*. As Larsen notes, the definition of evangelicalism Bebbington offers has become the 'standard one'.[40] In this study I am following the understanding of evangelicalism proposed by Bebbington.

In *Evangelicalism in Modern Britain* David Bebbington further argues that evangelicalism is 'a popular Protestant movement which has existed in Britain since the 1730s'.[41] In other words, it was the eighteenth-century Evangelical Revival which signalled the emergence of evangelicalism. This contention has attracted significant criticism from those who want to date the beginnings of evangelicalism

---

[35] Spurgeon, *How Spurgeon Found Christ*, p. 8 (Publisher's note).

[36] D.W. Bebbington, *Evangelicalism in Modern Britain: A history from the 1730s to the 1980s* (London: Unwin Hyman, 1989), pp. 5-17.

[37] D.W. Bebbington, 'Towards an Evangelical Identity', in S. Brady and H.H. Rowden (eds), *For Such A Time As This* (London: Scripture Union, 1996), p. 44.

[38] Bebbington, *Evangelicalism in Modern Britain*, pp. 2-3.

[39] G.M. Ditchfield, *The Evangelical Revival* (London: UCL Press, 1998), p. 26. Cf. J. Wolffe, *The Expansion of Evangelicalism, The Age of Wilberforce, More, Chalmers and Finney* (Leicester: IVP, 2006), p. 19.

[40] T. Larsen, 'The Reception given to *Evangelicalism in Modern Britain*', in M.A.G. Haykin and K.J. Stewart (eds), *The Emergence of Evangelicalism: Exploring Historical Continuities* (Leicester: IVP, 2008), pp. 24-29. Cf. D.J. Tidball, *Who Are The Evangelicals?* (London: Marshall Pickering, 1994), p. 14; and David Bebbington's own comments in his 'Response' to various essays engaging with his work in Haykin and Stewart (eds), *The Emergence of Evangelicalism*, pp. 425-26.

[41] Bebbington, *Evangelicalism in Modern Britain*, p. 1. Cf. p. 21.

earlier. In the aforementioned *The Emergence of Evangelicalism*, a number of contributors attempt to challenge Bebbington's work on this point.[42] In response to their arguments, Bebbington admits, firstly, that there was a little more continuity between evangelicalism and earlier religious movements, such as Puritanism, than he previously allowed and, secondly, that 'the changes wrought by the Evangelical Revival were in some quarters more delayed' than he originally proposed.[43] Nevertheless, in his 'Response' he restates his essential case, that the eighteenth-century transatlantic Evangelical Revival still broadly demarcates the beginning of a new movement, 'modern evangelicalism'. He shows that, although there was significant continuity with the past (something Bebbington always allowed),[44] there was real discontinuity as well.[45] I find the evidence in favour of this approach overwhelming. At least some of the essays in *The Emergence of Evangelicalism* are shaped by a rather obvious polemical intent, and a focus on Calvinistic evangelicals as opposed to Wesleyan Methodists, despite the fact that the latter were more numerous in Britain, further skews the volume.[46] This study understands evangelicalism as a movement which, for all the important connections which have quite rightly been drawn with its Protestant past, was also recognisably different from that past, constituting what can properly be described as something new.

As far as the evangelical conversion narrative is concerned, Bebbington distinguishes some of the strands that generally made up the fabric of such narratives. The basic pattern was one of 'agony, guilt and immense relief'. Conversions were often 'ardently sought' and they could stir up 'intense emotion'.[47] Bruce Hindmarsh, in his study of evangelical conversion narratives, has demonstrated important continuities between the eighteenth-century accounts and those produced by seventeenth-century Puritan Dissenters. Indeed, this is one of the areas in which there was greater continuity between seventeenth-century Protestantism and eighteenth-century evangelicalism than *Evangelicalism in Modern*

---

[42] See, e.g., A.T.B. McGowan, 'Evangelicalism in Scotland From Knox to Cunningham', pp. 73-83; and G.J. Williams, 'Enlightenment Epistemology and Eighteenth-Century Evangelical Doctrines of Assurance', pp. 345-74, in Haykin and Stewart (eds), *The Emergence of Evangelicalism*. Cf. K.J. Stewart, 'Did Evangelicalism Predate the Eighteenth Century? An Examination of David Bebbington's Study', *Evangelical Quarterly* Vol. 77, No. 2 (April 2005), pp. 135-53.

[43] Bebbington, 'Response', p. 427-28.

[44] See Bebbington, *Evangelicalism in Modern Britain*, pp. 34-35.

[45] See Bebbington, 'Response', pp. 428-32.

[46] See Bebbington's 'Response', pp. 424-25. An extended discussion of these issues is beyond the scope of this study. Williams' essay, 'Enlightenment Epistemology and Eighteenth-Century Evangelical Doctrines of Assurance', pp. 345-74, provides the best example of what I am concerned about. Williams' desire to sideline Arminian evangelicals skews his handling of the evidence.

[47] Bebbington, *Evangelicalism in Modern Britain*, p. 5.

Britain intimated.[48] Spurgeon was influenced by accounts of conversion which arose out of Puritan Dissent (for example, and as already noted, Bunyan's spiritual autobiography *Grace Abounding*)[49] and also by later, more recognisably evangelical works on conversion. Despite Spurgeon's avowed resistance to Doddridge's *Rise and Progress* he still described it, in a letter to his mother, as that 'Holy Book'.[50] Doddridge was an important figure bridging 'Old Dissent' and eighteenth-century evangelicalism.[51] John Angell James' *Anxious Enquirer* was a nineteenth-century work that was an evangelical standard on conversion.[52] C.H. Spurgeon was strongly influenced by what he witnessed of his mother's prayers for his conversion and her exhortations as to the vital importance of this step of faith, as indicated in chapter 2,[53] and in Eliza Spurgeon the Puritan and evangelical strands of thinking were closely woven together.[54] Spurgeon's conversion narrative fits Bebbington's pattern perfectly, a pattern that began in the seventeenth century and developed in the eighteenth.

Theology of Conversion

Spurgeon's conversion narrative exhibits a number of dominant theological motifs which are suggestive of the main features of his mature theology of conversion. First of all, the stress on the sovereignty of God in conversion can be noted. That this was the point Spurgeon wanted to emphasise by allowing the preacher of the 'Look'

---

[48] D.B. Hindmarsh, *The Evangelical Conversion Narrative: Spiritual Autobiography in Early Modern England* (Oxford: Oxford University Press, 2005), pp. 16-60, and his 'The antecedents of evangelical conversion narrative: spiritual autobiography and the Christian tradition', in Haykin and Stewart (eds), *The Emergence of Evangelicalism*, pp. 327-44. Cf. Bebbington's comments in 'Response', p. 427. Hindmarsh, 'The antecedents of evangelical conversion narrative', p. 344, states, 'The conversion narrative 'emerged especially during the [Puritan] Commonwealth and among the gathered churches in the context of testimonies required for admission to membership.'

[49] Cf. Spurgeon, *Autobiography*, Vol. 1, p. 108.

[50] C.H. Spurgeon to Eliza Spurgeon, 1 May 1850, in 'Original Correspondence of Charles Haddon Spurgeon 1851-1893', Spurgeon's College, Heritage Room, (4G), No. 171. This comment may indicate that *Rise and Progress* was originally read to Spurgeon by his mother, as was the case with the works by Baxter and Alleine.

[51] See Bebbington, *Evangelicalism in Modern Britain*, p. 34.

[52] Angell James was a Congregational minister at Carr's Lane, Birmingham.

[53] C.H. Spurgeon to Eliza Spurgeon, 1 May 1850; 'Extracts made ... from his mother's diary', Spurgeon's College, Heritage Room (Display Case 2).

[54] Indeed, in another extract from the diary, Eliza Spurgeon's diary wrote, 'Oh! for a light to shine upon the road that leads to God.' See Spurgeon, 'Extracts made ... from his mother's diary'. This is a clear reference to William Cowper's eighteenth-century hymn, 'Oh! for a closer walk with God' with its lines, 'A light to shine upon the road / that leads me to the Lamb.' This was an evangelical standard. See W. Cowper, *Olney Hymns: In Three Parts* (London: Thomas Nelson, 1856 [1779]), in which 'Oh! for a closer walk with God' is hymn no. 3 in Book 1. I am grateful to David Bebbington for pointing out this reference to me.

sermon to remain anonymous is suggested by a number of writers, for example Patricia Kruppa.[55] This suspicion is borne out by Spurgeon's November 1855 sermon, 'Healing For The Wounded'. It was God and 'only God', Spurgeon declared, who had 'healed' his heart through conversion. Although elsewhere Spurgeon stressed that preaching was an instrumental means of people's conversion,[56] the only means he seemed prepared to allow in 'Healing For The Wounded' were the bare words of Isaiah 45.22 which were, for him, the very words of God.[57] Spurgeon emphasised that he did not know the man who had repeated this text and clearly it suited his purposes not to know. The same concern – Spurgeon's desire to underline that his conversion was a supernatural act of a sovereign God – shaped the later, more developed accounts. The heavy emphasis on the 'really stupid' nature of the preacher, the contention that he was 'unlettered',[58] and the playing up of the countrified accent (one can imagine Spurgeon employing his considerable powers of mimicry to good effect as he imitated the preacher), all serve to magnify God's sovereign action and minimise the part played by the human agent.[59] This emphasis on God's sovereignty was present in Spurgeon's preaching on conversion more generally. As noted in chapter 2, Spurgeon held that sinners only came to Christ if they were predestined to do so by God.[60] Spurgeon, in his conversion narrative, came to Christ because the 'eternal purpose of Jehovah had decreed it'.[61]

The second aspect of Spurgeon's theology of conversion which can be noted was his stress on the atonement. In his conversion narrative the cross of Christ featured strongly, even though the Old Testament text he was preaching from did not, of course, mention Christ, the atonement or indeed any of the sacrifices which might be said to prefigure the cross. At one point the Primitive Methodist preacher urged his hearers to look to Christ who was 'sweatin' great drops of blood' and was 'hangin' on the cross'. The moment after Spurgeon 'looked' to Jesus he said he had wanted to stand and sing 'with the most enthusiastic [of the Primitive Methodists] of the precious blood of Christ'.[62] In Spurgeon's overall theology of conversion the

---

[55] P.S. Kruppa, *Charles Haddon Spurgeon: A Preacher's Progress* (New York: Garland Publishing, 1982), pp. 41-42. Cf. Drummond, *Spurgeon, Prince of Preachers*, p. 119; McCoy, 'The evangelistic ministry of C.H. Spurgeon', Appendix D, p. 349.

[56] See, e.g., C.H. Spurgeon, 'The Minister's Commission', 'Notebook Containing Early Sermon Skeletons', Vol. 2, S. No. 110, Matthew 28.19,20. Cf. *NPSP*, Vol. 1, Preface, n.p. [first page].

[57] Spurgeon, 'Healing For The Wounded', p. 407.

[58] Spurgeon, 'The Life-Look', p. 37.

[59] See, especially, Spurgeon, *Autobiography*, Vol. 1, pp. 105-108; *How Spurgeon Found Christ*.

[60] For another message which emphasised this, see C.H. Spurgeon, 'A Testimony To Free And Sovereign Grace', *MTP*, Vol. 33, S. No. 1953, Psalm 37.39, n.d. [in or after 1861, as preached at the Metropolitan Tabernacle], pp. 159-160.

[61] Spurgeon, *Autobiography*, Vol. 1, p. 109.

[62] Spurgeon, *Autobiography*, Vol. 1, p. 106.

atonement was central and at the heart of his view of the atonement was the doctrine of penal substitution.[63] Christ died in the place of sinners, enduring the righteous wrath of God against sin on their behalf. Any attempt to water down penal substitution elicited Spurgeon's strongest condemnation.[64] As Michael Walker states, Spurgeon believed that 'the vicarious, substitutionary and atoning death of Christ' was 'the central truth of the Christian faith'.[65]

Spurgeon's deep commitment to a substitutionary view of the atonement was closely linked to his own conversion and his later reflections on what had happened. He held that nothing but the sacrifice of Christ could have bridged the gap between a holy God and a sinful human being such as him.[66] If it were not for the cross, understood in terms of penal substitution, then Spurgeon believed he could not have been 'saved'. Salvation had many dimensions: a sinner was justified,[67] redeemed,[68] reconciled to God[69] and forgiven.[70] But in Spurgeon's thought all of these different aspects of salvation were inextricably bound up with the atonement. The cross of Christ was the fulcrum around which a right understanding of salvation must revolve. Spurgeon believed this not on the basis of the scriptures alone but also because of his own experience.

Consequently, when Spurgeon spoke of his commitment to penal substitutionary atonement he did so as if his very life depended on it, as indeed he thought it did.[71] In a sermon entitled 'The Sacred Love Token', based on the phrase in Exodus 12.13,

---

[63] C.H. Spurgeon, 'Letter From Mr Spurgeon [to his congregation from Mentone]', *MTP*, Vol. 35, 11 February 1889, p. 96. Cf. *Autobiography*, Vol. 1, p. 113; 'Redemption Through Blood, The Gracious Forgiveness Of Sins', *MTP*, Vol. 37, S. No. 2207, Ephesians 1.7, n.d., pp. 305-306. Although Spurgeon strongly emphasised substitution, on at least one occasion he stated, 'I feel ... substitution does not cover the whole of the matter ... no human conception can completely grasp the whole of the dread mystery.' See W.Y. Fullerton, *C.H. Spurgeon: A Biography* (London: Williams and Norgate, 1920), pp. 181-82.

[64] See C.H. Spurgeon, 'The Word Of The Cross', *MTP* Vol. 27, S. No. 1611, 1 Corinthians 1.18, delivered 31 July 1881, pp. 425-36, for a particularly stinging rebuke.

[65] M.J. Walker, *Baptists at the Table: The Theology of the Lord's Supper amongst English Baptists in the Nineteenth Century* (Didcot: Baptist Historical Society, 1992), p. 170.

[66] Cf. the comments of Mark Hopkins, *Nonconformity's Romantic Generation: Evangelical and Liberal Theologies in Victorian England* (Carlisle: Paternoster, 2004), p. 146.

[67] C.H. Spurgeon, 'Messrs. Moody And Sankey Defended; Or, A Vindication Of The Doctrine Of Justification By Faith', *MTP*, Vol. 21, S. No. 1239, Galatians 5.24, n.d., p. 327; 'None But Jesus', *NPSP*, Vol. 7, S. No. 361, John 3.18, delivered 17 February 1861, pp. 111-112.

[68] C.H. Spurgeon, 'The Common Salvation', *MTP*, Vol. 27, S. No. 1592, Jude 3, delivered 10 April 1881, p. 200.

[69] C.H. Spurgeon, 'Plain Directions To Those Who Would Be Saved From Sin', *MTP*, Vol. 34, S. No. 2033, Psalm 4.4,5, delivered 15 July 1888, p. 391.

[70] C.H. Spurgeon, 'Bankrupt Debtors Discharged', *MTP*, Vol. 29, S. No. 1739-40, Luke 7.42, delivered 16 September 1883, pp. 493; 499-502; *Autobiography*, Vol. 1, pp. 108, 110.

[71] See Spurgeon, *Autobiography*, Vol. 1, pp. 99; 113.

'When I see the blood, I will pass over', Spurgeon defended penal substitution with all his might. 'The blood upon the lintel said, "someone has died here instead of us"', he declared. This truth had saved Spurgeon and he did not just 'hold' to it, he 'rested' in it. The preacher continued, 'We dwell beneath the blood mark, and rejoice that Jesus for us poured out his soul unto death when he bare the sins of many.'[72] Similar emphases were present in a message, 'Redemption By Price', based on 1 Corinthians 6.19-20. Over and against those who objected to the 'idea of substitution and vicarious sacrifice', Spurgeon insisted that on the cross Christ bore 'divine wrath in our stead'. He continued, 'No truth within the circle of theology is so eminently consolatory to souls burdened with sin', adding dramatically, 'I nail my colours to the cross.'[73] Spurgeon spoke of the 'atoning sacrifice of Christ' as being nothing less that the 'marvellous mystery of the gospel' and 'the greatest of all revealed truths'.[74] Put another way, it was only because of the cross that a relationship with Christ could be established and enjoyed. Spurgeon believed this had been his own experience and this was what he preached.

The third aspect of Spurgeon's theology of conversion which can be highlighted is his focus on regeneration, or the 'new birth'. A sinner's salvation was grounded in God's electing grace and purchased by the atonement, but regeneration was necessary to awaken the conscience of an individual thus enabling them to exercise saving faith. Men and women were spiritually 'dead' and incapable of 'vital godliness'.[75] It was the Holy Spirit who convinced them of sin and 'awakened the conscience',[76] renewing the 'heart' by an 'act of divine grace' at the time of God's choosing.[77] Although the 'processes' which led up to the point of regeneration could be long and drawn out, the actual 'spiritual quickening', when it came, was 'instantaneous'.[78] Spurgeon's view of the fundamental importance of regeneration is driven home by a quotation from a sermon, revealingly entitled 'Jesus Known By Personal Revelation'. It was entirely possible, Spurgeon declared, for someone to go on 'hearing, reading, and thinking' about religion but still fail to 'discern the Lord's Christ'. This was because a saving knowledge of Christ came only 'by revelation of the Spirit'. Spurgeon pressed home his point,

---

[72] C.H. Spurgeon, 'The Sacred Love Token', *MTP*, Vol. 21, S. No. 1251, Exodus 12.13, delivered 22 August 1875, pp. 483-84.

[73] C.H. Spurgeon, 'Redemption By Price', *MTP*, Vol. 26, S. No. 1554, 1 Corinthians 6.19-20, delivered 22 August 1880, pp. 469-70.

[74] Spurgeon, 'The Life-Look', p. 45.

[75] C.H. Spurgeon, 'Man Humbled, God Exalted', *MTP*, Vol. 59, S. No. 3369, Isaiah 2.17, delivered 4 October 1886, p. 411.

[76] C.H. Spurgeon, 'Conversion And Character', *MTP*, Vol. 59, S. No. 3372, Acts 16.24-34, n.d., p. 452

[77] C.H. Spurgeon, 'Faith And Life', *MTP*, Vol. 10, S. No. 551, 2 Peter 1.1-4, delivered 24 January 1864, pp. 50-51.

[78] C.H. Spurgeon, 'A Sermon For The Worst Man On Earth', *MTP*, Vol. 33, S. No. 1949, Luke 18.13, delivered 20 February 1887, p. 119.

> Can you follow me experimentally in this? Has the Father revealed Christ to you *by a birth in you?* ... A spiritual faculty must be created in us, by which we are enabled to perceive the Son of God ... You must be begotten again of the Father; otherwise Jesus Christ will be as little known to you as the light of the sun is known to dead men.[79]

Without regeneration someone might know about Jesus, but it was impossible they could know him personally. It was this personal knowledge that was at the heart of Spurgeon's understanding of conversion and at the heart of his spirituality.

As we have seen, this emphasis on the necessity of regeneration was woven into the fabric of Spurgeon's own conversion narrative where it was closely allied with the first point about God's sovereignty in conversion. A snow storm had driven Spurgeon to the Artillery Street chapel where a lay preacher took the place of the minister who had 'probably' been snowed in. These were not random, coincidental happenings but events providentially arranged by God; Spurgeon was sure that all had been 'wisely ordered'.[80] During the service the Holy Spirit had 'enabled' Spurgeon to believe and, consequently, in a 'moment' he had looked to Christ and been saved.[81] Spurgeon had heard the gospel many times before, but, because the Spirit had not taken the message into his heart on these previous occasions, he had not believed.[82] The difference this time was that this was the moment God had ordained for his conversion. Spurgeon held that there were true Christians who were unable to remember the exact time of they were converted,[83] but as far as he was concerned he believed he knew the day and indeed the hour he became regenerate[84] (although, as it happens, he was almost certainly a week out). At Artillery Street Spurgeon had experienced the new birth.[85]

The fourth aspect of Spurgeon's theology of conversion that can be examined is his view of the nature of saving faith. Given Spurgeon's repeated stress on God's action in salvation, it is unsurprising that he regarded both repentance and faith as given by God. Where true repentance and faith were present in a person, that proved that the person concerned was a 'regenerate character',[86] for not one 'grain' of

---

[79] C.H. Spurgeon, 'Jesus Known By Personal Revelation', *MTP*, Vol. 34, S. No. 2041, Matthew 16.13-17, delivered 26 August 1888, p. 487.

[80] Spurgeon, *Autobiography*, Vol. 1, p. 108.

[81] Spurgeon, *Autobiography*, Vol. 1, pp. 109, 111.

[82] Spurgeon, *Autobiography*, Vol. 1, p. 102.

[83] Spurgeon, *Autobiography*, Vol. 1, p. 108.

[84] C.H. Spurgeon, 'The Marvellous Magnet', *MTP*, Vol. 29, S. No. 1717, John 12.32,33, n.d., p. 237; 'Sovereignty And Salvation', p. 49; *Autobiography*, Vol. 1, p. 108.

[85] This point is particularly suggestive of evangelical influences. See, e.g., J. Wesley, *Sermons*, Vol. 1, Sermon 15, 'The Great Privilege of those that are Born of God', p. 300, as cited by A. Skevington Wood, *The Burning Heart, John Wesley: Evangelist* (Calver: Cliff College Publishing, 1993 [1967]), pp. 243-44. On the new birth, see, also, H.S. Stout, *The Divine Dramatist: George Whitefield and the Rise of Modern Evangelicalism* (Grand Rapids: Eerdmans, 1991), e.g. p. xx.

[86] C.H. Spurgeon, 'Pleading And Encouragement', *MTP*, Vol. 30, S. No. 1795, Ezekiel 18.32; 33.11, delivered 17 August 1884, p. 455.

saving faith existed 'in all the world' which had not been created by Christ.[87] But Spurgeon also reflected on what happened in conversion as experienced by the person who was coming to Christ. Such a person needed to exercise faith. Spurgeon's definition of faith was a christocentric one. Faith was to be understood as 'believing the testimony of God concerning his Son, and trusting in the Lord Jesus as he is set forth in the Scriptures'.[88] In a sermon preached in 1881, entitled 'Faith: What Is It? How Can It Be Obtained?', Spurgeon spoke of saving faith as being made up of three elements, 'knowledge, belief and trust'. Knowledge was defined as having some awareness of what the Scriptures teach about Christ, especially regarding the atonement, whilst 'belief' was here understood as accepting 'that these things are true'. Trust was the third crucial ingredient needed to 'complete faith'. As far as this final dimension of faith was concerned, Spurgeon said,

> Commit yourself to the merciful God; rest your hope on the gracious gospel; trust your soul to the dying and living Saviour; wash away your sins in the atoning blood; accept his perfect righteousness, and all is well. Trust is the life-blood of faith; there is no saving faith without it.

In making this point he sought to illustrate it to the Tabernacle congregation by leaning his weight on the pulpit rail, saying 'even thus lean upon Christ'. But the illustration would have been more accurate, Spurgeon declared, if he had instead stretched himself out 'full length'.[89] This, he said, was what the Puritans described as 'recumbency'.[90] 'Fall flat upon Christ', he urged his hearers, 'Cast yourself upon him, rest in him, commit yourself to him. That done, you have exercised saving faith.'[91] Elsewhere Spurgeon spoke of faith in terms of 'falling into Christ's arms',[92] and of 'resting'[93] and 'rolling upon' Christ.[94] The images were slightly different, but

---

[87] C.H. Spurgeon, 'The Search For Faith', *MTP*, Vol. 33, S. No. 1963, Luke 18.8, delivered 15 May 1887, p. 279.

[88] C.H. Spurgeon, Preface to J. Norcott, *Baptism Discovered Plainly and Faithfully According to the Word of God: A New Edition, Corrected and Somewhat Altered* (London: Passmore and Alabaster, 1878), p. iii. Norcott's original work was first published in 1672.

[89] C.H. Spurgeon, 'Faith: What Is It? How Can It Be Obtained?', *MTP*, Vol. 27, S. No. 1609, Ephesians 2.8, delivered 17 July 1881, pp. 402-403.

[90] For the use of this word by Puritans, see J. Spurr, *English Puritanism, 1603–1689* (Basingstoke: Macmillan, 1998), p. 164.

[91] Spurgeon, 'Faith: What Is It? How Can It Be Obtained?', pp. 402-403.

[92] C.H. Spurgeon, 'The Ploughman', *MTP*, Vol. 59, S. No. 3383, Isaiah 28.24, n.d., p. 586.

[93] C.H. Spurgeon, 'Baptismal Regeneration', *MTP*, Vol. 10, S. No. 573, Mark 16.15,16, delivered 5 June 1864, p. 324.

[94] C.H. Spurgeon, 'Witnessing At The Cross', *MTP*, Vol. 59, S. No. 3363, Luke 23.39-43, n.d., p. 341.

the essential meaning was the same. The object or focus of faith was Christ, and true believers were those who trusted in him completely.[95]

This was the wholehearted faith Spurgeon exercised in his own conversion, as related in his conversion narrative. True, it was a simple 'look' to Christ, but he also described his act of faith in terms of trusting Christ and also of clinging and clasping to Christ.[96] Indeed, the look itself was not a passing glance for, as already noted, Spurgeon said he looked until he 'almost could have looked [his] eyes away'.[97] Faith, then, was not mental assent to a set of truths; it was complete trust in Christ for salvation. Those who exercised it were regenerate, because only those who were regenerate could possibly have such faith. Being regenerate and having received a new nature, they would certainly go on to live in a way that was in harmony with their Christian profession. Spurgeon himself spoke of a new hatred of sin that accompanied his conversion,[98] and in his thinking true conversion was always accompanied by a desire to live a holy life.[99] Indeed, in 'Life For A Look', also preached on Isaiah 45.22, Spurgeon maintained that the 'free grace of God' and the 'necessity of change in heart and life' were two doctrines that were entirely congruent with one another. The vital importance of holiness for Spurgeon, and its relationship to communion with Christ and Christ's people, will be followed up in detail in chapter 9. Suffice to say here that, for Spurgeon, the pursuit of holiness always followed true conversion.

Spurgeon's spirituality was thus 'conversionist', but it should be emphasised that Spurgeon's conversion related to the other three points of the quadrilateral identified by Bebbington as well. Firstly, the scriptures – in Spurgeon's case Isaiah 45.22 – were important in leading him to conversion. Secondly, conversion was made possible by the work of Christ on the cross. Thirdly, at the point of conversion Spurgeon was active, exercising saving faith. Such faith prepared the way for a life of Christian activism.

It should further be noted that in the different dimensions of Spurgeon's theology of conversion examined in this section – God's sovereignty in conversion, the atonement, the necessity of regeneration, the exercise of saving faith – the focus on Christ was resolutely maintained. God's sovereign will was that the elect sinner came to Christ; salvation was purchased by the blood of Christ shed on the cross; regeneration was the revelation of Christ, by the Spirit, to the sinner; and, finally, saving faith was faith in Christ. What is striking about the chapter in the *Autobiography*, entitled 'The Great Change.—Conversion', which contains Spurgeon's conversion narrative and some further reflections on it, is how strong the concentration on Christ is. In conversion Christ had become Spurgeon's 'Saviour'

---

[95] Cf. C.H. Spurgeon, 'Salvation By Knowing The Truth', *MTP*, Vol. 26, S. No. 1516, 1 Timothy 2.3,4, n.d., p. 55.
[96] Spurgeon, *Autobiography*, Vol. 1, pp. 108, 110, 112.
[97] Spurgeon, *Autobiography*, Vol. 1, p. 106.
[98] Spurgeon, 'Messrs. Moody And Sankey Defended', pp. 337, 339, 341.
[99] Spurgeon, *Autobiography*, Vol. 1, p. 99.

and 'Master'; there was now nothing so true to him as 'those bleeding hands' and 'thorn-crowned head'.[100] The chapter contains a wealth of material in this vein.[101] Conversion was the establishment of a personal, 'experimental' relationship with Christ. The moment faith was exercised communion with Christ was inaugurated and there was the promise of more and deeper communion to come.

Early Evangelistic Ministry

Spurgeon closes the chapter, 'The Great Change. – Conversion', with the sentence, 'Would that I knew more of [Christ], and that I could tell it out better!'[102] Spurgeon had trusted and experienced Christ but he had an accompanying desire: to share Christ with others that they too might know him. Spurgeon believed that all Christians should be engaged in evangelism.[103] As far as ministers were concerned, 'soul winning' was to be their 'chief business'.[104] Spurgeon the pastor threw himself into a ministry of calling others to look to Christ as he had done. I aim now to show that sharing Christ with other people was a vital dimension of Spurgeon's spirituality from the beginning of his ministry.

In Spurgeon's conversion narrative he cites Bunyan wanting 'to tell the crows on the ploughed land all about his conversion', saying that he understood what Bunyan meant.[105] Nevertheless, Mark Hopkins argues that in Spurgeon's preaching he was for a while 'fettered' in his inclination to give a 'free invitation' to respond to the gospel. Hopkins attributes this to an idea that he says was 'then common among Calvinistic Baptists following Richard Baxter and other Puritans, that only sinners who displayed some evidence that the Holy Spirit was convicting them should be invited to believe'.[106] It would have been more accurate if Hopkins had traced the line of descent of this theology as coming, not from Baxter but from Tobias Crisp through Joseph Hussey and then on to the Baptists John Skepp and John Gill.[107] This was the 'High Calvinism' (or, more pejoratively, 'hyper-Calvinism'), which was prevalent in many Particular Baptist churches, especially in the eighteenth century

---

[100] Spurgeon, *Autobiography*, Vol. 1, p. 109.

[101] Cf., e.g., Spurgeon, *Autobiography*, Vol. 1, pp. 114-15.

[102] Spurgeon, *Autobiography*, Vol. 1, p. 115.

[103] C.H. Spurgeon, *Speeches at Home and Abroad* (London: Passmore and Alabaster, 1878), p. 120.

[104] C.H. Spurgeon, *The Soul-Winner; Or, How To Lead Sinners To The Saviour* (London: Passmore and Alabaster, 1895), p. 11; cf. p. 43.

[105] Spurgeon, *Autobiography*, Vol. 1, p. 108.

[106] Hopkins, *Nonconformity's Romantic Generation*, p. 140.

[107] Cf. J.H.Y. Briggs, 'Baptists in the Eighteenth Century', in J.H.Y. Briggs (ed.), *Pulpit and People: Studies in Eighteenth-Century Baptist Life and Thought* (Milton Keynes: Paternoster, 2009), pp. 3-4. Hussey provided a systematic exposition of High Calvinism, entitled *God's Operations of Grace, But no Offers of Grace* (1707). For Hussey, see A.P.F. Sell, *The Great Debate: Calvinism, Arminianism and Salvation* (Worthing: H.E. Walter, 1982), pp. 52-54.

(although the teaching continued into the nineteenth century, and indeed beyond). Unconverted sinners were not morally obliged to believe the gospel because total depravity had rendered them incapable of doing so. The logical corollary of this view was that ministers should not openly 'offer' the gospel to the unconverted. To exhort the unconverted to believe would be a nonsense and such appeals carried with them the danger that those who were not elect might make false professions which could sully the purity of the church.[108] It might be legitimate for a minister to encourage an individual to believe if there was evidence that God was truly convicting this person and leading them towards faith. But so-called 'indiscriminate' appeals, whereby the gospel was offered to a whole congregation, were unacceptable.

There is in fact little evidence for the contention that Spurgeon was ever 'fettered' by this High Calvinistic teaching. The only sermon Hopkins cites, 'The Power Of The Holy Ghost', which was preached at New Park Street on 17 June 1855, certainly contains the attack on freewill that Hopkins speaks of, together with a strong denial of the power of a minister to save (which is of a piece with Spurgeon's mature conversion narrative, as has been shown).[109] More importantly for the purposes of this discussion, the message closes with an appeal which is addressed to sinners who show some evidence of the Holy Spirit's work in their lives. Spurgeon asks, 'Has [the Holy Spirit] gone so far as to make you desire his name, to make you wish for Jesus?' Expecting an answer in the affirmative, he continues, 'Then, O sinner! Whilst he draws you, say, "Draw me, I am wretched without thee".'[110] This seems to fit Hopkins' contention. His case falls, however, as there are far more direct appeals in sermons which Spurgeon gave earlier than June 1855.

One of these appeals occurs at the close of a message preached on 21 January 1855. The sermon was entitled 'The Comforter'. Spurgeon declared,

> 'He that believeth and is baptized shall be saved, and he that believeth not shall be damned.' Weary sinner, hellish sinner, thou who art the devil's castaway, reprobate, profligate, harlot, robber, thief, adulterer, swearer, Sabbath-breaker—list! I speak to thee as well as the rest. I exempt no man. God has said there is no exemption here. '*Whosoever* believeth in the name of Jesus Christ shall be saved.' Sin is no barrier; thy guilt is no obstacle. Whoever ... this night believes, shall have every sin forgiven ...

---

[108] See P.J. Morden, *Offering Christ to the World: Andrew Fuller (1754–1815) and the Revival of Eighteenth Century Particular Baptist Life* (Carlisle: Paternoster, 2003), pp. 12-13. The best full-scale exposition of High or 'hyper' Calvinism is probably still P. Toon, *The Emergence of Hyper Calvinism in English Nonconformity, 1689–1765* (London: Olive Tree, 1967).

[109] C.H. Spurgeon, 'The Power Of The Holy Ghost', *NPSP*, Vol. 1, S. No. 30, Romans 15.13, pp. 233-34.

[110] Spurgeon, 'The Power Of The Holy Ghost', p. 236.

shall be saved in the Lord Jesus Christ, and shall stand in heaven safe and secure. That is the glorious gospel.[111]

It is true that Spurgeon concluded this appeal with the sentence, 'God apply it home to your hearts, and give you faith in Jesus!' It is also true that New Park Street Chapel, which was full to bursting point, was the scene of much emotion that Sunday, with people in the congregation weeping and crying out to God phrases such as 'have mercy upon me a sinner'. 'A great work is going on in this chapel', the preacher commented,[112] and this could be interpreted as evidence that the Holy Spirit was clearly at work, thus perhaps legitimising some sort of appeal in the eyes of a High Calvinist. But Spurgeon's words in 'The Comforter' constitute a direct and powerful evangelistic challenge to all who were present in the crowded auditorium. The appeal was explicitly indiscriminate: no one was exempted, not even the 'devil's castaway' or, astonishingly, the 'reprobate'. Earlier in the message Spurgeon had quoted George Whitefield, saying, 'Well might Whitfield [sic] call out, "O earth, earth, earth, hear the Word of the Lord!"'[113] Spurgeon certainly believed that the Holy Spirit needed to be at work for people to respond truly to the gospel, and his words in both 'The Power Of The Holy Ghost' and 'The Comforter' are reminders of this. Nevertheless, Spurgeon wanted to follow the eighteenth-century Methodist Whitefield's example and call all people to trust in Christ.

In fact, evangelistic appeals in Spurgeon's preaching ministry can be traced even further back than his time at New Park Street. There are clear indications in the pre-London sermon outlines that Spurgeon engaged in direct, invitational evangelism in his early preaching. This fact was noted in chapter 2, but more space can be given to establishing the evidence for it here. Spurgeon's notes for a sermon entitled 'Despisers Warned', which is in Volume 1 of the notebooks, close with the startlingly direct words, 'Jesus is the only Saviour – Turn or die – Repent or Perish.'[114] Another message in the same volume indicates that Spurgeon gave an 'exhortation' both to the 'vilest' and also to 'little sinners' to 'come' to Christ.[115] An appeal in Volume 4 of these notebooks echoes that given in 'Despisers Warned': 'Turn or die. Repent or perish. Believe or be damned.'[116] In 'No Wise Cast Out', a further sermon in this fourth volume, Spurgeon recorded his desire to 'Read, write, print [and] shout' the message that God would not 'cast out' any who came to him.

---

[111] C.H. Spurgeon, 'The Comforter', *NPSP*, Vol. 1, S. No. 5, John 14.26, delivered 21 January 1855, p. 40.

[112] C.H. Spurgeon, 'The Sin Of Unbelief', *NPSP*, Vol. 1, S. No. 3, 2 Kings 7.19, delivered 14 January 1855, p. 23.

[113] Spurgeon, 'The Comforter', p. 40.

[114] C.H. Spurgeon, 'Despisers Warned', 'Notebook Containing Early Sermon Skeletons, Vol. 1', S. No. 26, Proverbs 29.1.

[115] C.H. Spurgeon, 'Beginning At Jerusalem', 'Notebook Containing Early Sermon Skeletons, Vol. 1', S. No. 29, Luke 24.47.

[116] C.H. Spurgeon, 'Zephaniah's Warning', 'Notebook Containing Early Sermon Skeletons, Vol. 4', S. No. 222, Zephaniah 4.5,6.

Evangelical Conversionism

Spurgeon wrote at the end of the sermon what may have been his closing exhortation, 'Believe & thou shalt be saved.'[117] Similar outlines, apparently forming the basis of strong evangelistic appeals, pepper the different Cambridgeshire volumes.[118] One further message can be cited here. In Volume 4 of the notebooks there is a three-page, closely written outline for a sermon on Isaiah 1.18. In his notes Spurgeon insisted that 'none' were 'excluded' from the gospel invitation to come to Christ and trust in him except those who excluded themselves. The invitation was to 'all sinners'. 'Come. now,' Spurgeon urged.[119] There were High Calvinists at Waterbeach who thought Spurgeon's preaching far too 'invitational', describing Spurgeon as a 'Fullerite' after the eighteenth-century evangelical Calvinist Andrew Fuller whose theology did much to wean many Particular Baptists away from the High Calvinism that was associated with Gill.[120] It is easy to see why this 'charge' was made. There is also evidence that such invitations were successful; for example, the crowded services at Waterbeach and the records of specific conversions which had taken place.[121]

The overarching point is that Spurgeon was engaged in invitational, evangelistic preaching from the beginning of his ministry.[122] For Spurgeon there was an imperative to share Christ that served to override any temptation he might have had to bend to the High Calvinistic thinking he encountered at Waterbeach and, later, in London, where his invitational preaching drew the ire of James Wells, the Strict Baptist and High Calvinist who was pastor of the Surrey Tabernacle. Wells accused Spurgeon, in January 1855 (i.e., months before Spurgeon preached the sermon cited by Hopkins), of passing by the 'essentials of the work of the Holy Ghost' in his

---

[117] C.H. Spurgeon, 'No Wise Cast Out', 'Notebook Containing Early Sermon Skeletons, Vol. 4', S. No. 212, John 6.37. Cf. *Autobiography*, Vol. 1, p. 225.

[118] For further examples see, for instance, C.H. Spurgeon, 'The Rending Of The Veil' 'Notebook Containing Early Sermon Skeletons, Vol. 2', S. No. 96, Mark 15.38; 'The Stronghold of Refuge'; 'Vol. 5', S. No. 246, Zechariah 9.12. In 'Keeping The Ordinances', Vol. 7, S. No. 333, 1 Corinthians 11.2, Spurgeon noted, approvingly, 'The Wesleyan loves to invite sinners to Jesus'.

[119] C.H. Spurgeon, 'Come & Let Us Reason Together', 'Notebook Containing Early Sermon Skeletons, Vol. 4', S. No. 193, Isaiah 1.18. Underlining original.

[120] Spurgeon, *Autobiography*, Vol. 1, p. 256. For Fuller, see P.J. Morden, 'Andrew Fuller and the *Gospel Worthy of All Acceptation*', in Briggs (ed.), *Pulpit and People*, pp. 128-51; *Offering Christ to the World, passim*.

[121] Spurgeon, *Autobiography*, Vol. 1, pp. 232-32, 256.

[122] For one further piece of evidence, see C.H. Spurgeon to John Spurgeon, n.d. [December 1853?], 'C.H. Spurgeon. Letters to his Father and Mother, 1850-84', No. 15, 'The London people [i.e., New Park Street] are rather higher in Calvinism than myself, but I have succeeded in bringing one church to my own views and will trust with divine assistance to do the same with another.' By early 1854 Spurgeon had changed his view of New Park Street. See C.H. Spurgeon to John Spurgeon, 25 January 1854, 'C.H. Spurgeon. Letters to his Father and Mother, 1850-84', No. 16, 'The church in London exactly agrees with my sentiments. They are Calvinists, not hyper cold and dry.'

ministry at New Park Street.[123] Spurgeon remained unrepentant with regard to his invitational preaching.[124] The comment the Primitive Methodist preacher makes in Spurgeon's mature conversion narrative, that his hearers had no business saying, 'We must wait for the Spirit's workin'', may well have been a blow aimed by Spurgeon in the direction of High Calvinists. What is certain is that the personal relationship with Christ that Spurgeon had experienced was something he was determined to offer to all; indeed, it was an integral part of Spurgeon's spirituality for him to disseminate the gospel message as widely as possible, especially in preaching. From the beginning of Spurgeon's public ministry, he wanted to share his own experience of communion with Christ with other people.

Later Evangelistic Ministry

Spurgeon continued to give himself to evangelism throughout his London ministry. He engaged in a range of evangelistic activity. One example of this is the work of his Colportage Society, founded in 1866 for the sale of Christian literature.[125] Spurgeon regarded such literature as important,[126] nevertheless, as Hopkins rightly states, 'Preaching never strayed from its central place in Spurgeon's life and work.'[127] Consequently, this brief consideration of Spurgeon's later evangelistic ministry, which concentrates on the period after the opening of the Metropolitan Tabernacle in 1861, concentrates on his preaching.

Spurgeon's preaching post-1861 is consistently revealing of an evangelistic concern. Even in messages which were aimed mainly at instructing or encouraging Christians, the preacher would often still close with an evangelistic appeal. Spurgeon

---

[123] Spurgeon, *Autobiography*, Vol. 2, pp. 37-40. Wells wrote a long letter about Spurgeon and his ministry which was published in the *Earthen Vessel* in January 1855 under the pseudonym 'Job'. On this dispute, see K. Dix, *Strict and Particular: English Strict and Particular Baptists in the Nineteenth Century* (Didcot: Baptist Historical Society, 2001), pp. 208-17. Cf. I.H. Murray, *Spurgeon Versus Hyper Calvinism: The Battle for Gospel Preaching* (Edinburgh: Banner of Truth, 1995).

[124] See C.H. Spurgeon, 'The Echo', *MTP*, Vol. 13, S. No. 767, Psalm 27.8, n.d., pp. 469-70, for a clear repudiation of High Calvinistic teaching. Saving faith was only present in the regenerate, but it was still the 'duty of man' to respond to the gospel. For this argument in the context of the eighteenth-century debates on High Calvinism, see Morden, *Offering Christ*, pp. 12-13; 23-27.

[125] Spurgeon, *Autobiography*, Vol. 3, pp. 161-66. It should be noted that one of the aims of this society was to distribute works which opposed what Spurgeon described as the 'disguised Romanism' of the Oxford Movement. Nevertheless, the society sold and gave out a wide range of evangelistic literature and many conversions resulted. See Spurgeon, *Autobiography*, Vol. 3, pp. 161, 164-65.

[126] See [Anon.], Preface, in C.H. Spurgeon (ed.), *The Sword and The Trowel: A Record of Combat With Sin and Labour For The Lord* (*Sword and Trowel*) (London: Passmore and Alabaster, 1865–92), 1892, p. iv. Following Spurgeon's death, the editorial work for the *Sword and Trowel* was carried on by an editorial team.

[127] Hopkins, *Nonconformity's Romantic Generation*, p. 152.

was so concerned that people turned to Christ he poured himself into such appeals, which could be costly for him on an emotional level.[128] This is illustrated by a message Spurgeon delivered in 1867 to a vast crowd at the Agricultural Hall, Islington. In the course of this Spurgeon declared,

> Have pity on thyself, my hearer. I have pity on thee. Oh if my hand could pluck thee from that flame, how cheerfully would I do it! ... Oh if my pleadings should by God's grace persuade you to trust in Christ this morning, I would plead with you while voice, and lungs, and heart, and life held out![129]

The appeal, as with so many of Spurgeon's evangelistic appeals, was emotionally charged. For him, nothing was more important than that men and women responded to the gospel message. The preacher's love for Christ and compassion for people fused together as he implored his hearers to trust in Christ. The flame to which he referred in this message was the flame of judgment that would be experienced by sinners in hell. Spurgeon moved away from the lengthy, lurid descriptions of hell which he had indulged in during his pre-London ministry and in his earlier years at New Park Street.[130] Nevertheless, his essential beliefs about the reality of hell and the eternal punishment of the impenitent did not change.[131] He still wept over those who did not know Christ and who would, consequently, be eternally separated from him, and he could not see why all Christians did not do the same.[132] The fate of the 'lost' was a great spur to Spurgeon's evangelistic appeals,[133] but, for such a sensitive man, giving these passionate invitations could be extremely draining.

There was, however, a further motivation for Spurgeon's evangelistic preaching, one that was far more positive for him. People could experience happiness 'here and hereafter' if they came to Christ. Spurgeon believed such happiness was 'beyond description', although this did not stop him trying to expound it.[134] Communion with Christ in the present and a 'resting' in the promises of God for eternal life were his

---

[128] Cf. Spurgeon, *Soul-Winner*, pp. 101, and the comments of Hopkins, *Nonconformity's Romantic Generation*, p. 129, which relate to Spurgeon's preaching more generally, not just to his evangelistic preaching.

[129] C.H. Spurgeon, 'A Sermon To Open Neglecters And Nominal Followers Of Religion', *MTP*, Vol. 13, S. No. 742, Matthew 21.28-32, delivered 24 March 1867, p. 176.

[130] For an example of one of these descriptions, see C.H. Spurgeon, 'Harvest Time', *MTP*, Vol. 50, S. No. 2896, 1 Samuel 12.17, delivered (at New Park Street Chapel) August 1854, pp. 393-94.

[131] See, e.g., the passage headed 'The Appropriate Punishment' in C.H. Spurgeon, 'The Pleading Of The Last Messenger', *MTP*, Vol. 33, S. No. 1951, Mark 12.6-9, delivered 6 March 1887, pp. 142-44.

[132] Spurgeon, *Soul-Winner*, p. 110.

[133] C.H. Spurgeon, 'One Lost Sheep', *MTP*, Vol. 35, S. No. 2083, Matthew 18.12,13, delivered 28 April 1889, p. 246. For a comment on this from a prayer meeting address, see *Soul Winner*, p. 210.

[134] C.H. Spurgeon, 'The Parable Of The Wedding Feast', *MTP*, Vol. 17, S. No. 975, Matthew 22. 2,3,4, delivered 12 February 1871, p. 95.

own deepest joys. So his appeals to his hearers to trust in Christ proceeded out of his own, intensely felt experience of communion and his personal hope for deeper, unbroken communion to come beyond the grave. 'The Statute Of David For The Sharing Of The Spoil' was a message which was shot-through with Spurgeon's own experience.[135] It was actually the last sermon he ever preached at the Tabernacle, on 7 June 1891.[136] He assured his hearers that it was 'heaven to serve Jesus' who was 'superabundant in love'. How did Spurgeon know this? 'These forty years and more have I served him, blessed be his name! and I have had nothing but love from him.'[137] His joyful experience of what a relationship with Christ meant in practice was thus to the fore at the close of his London ministry, as he exhorted others to trust in Christ. The joy he experienced in knowing Christ was deepened when it was shared by others.

It is worth emphasising again that Spurgeon's repeated stress on conversion as a 'coming to Christ', a stress which bound his theology of conversion together and which was the hallmark of his early ministry,[138] was an emphasis which was sustained throughout his later ministry too. Although he did speak of coming to God the Father through Christ,[139] his usual habit was to talk in terms of simply 'believing', 'trusting' and 'resting' on Jesus.[140] This was in line with the preacher in his conversion narrative, who urged his congregation not to look to the Father, but to Christ.[141] It was sermons which were 'full of Christ', Spurgeon believed, that were most likely to lead to conversions.[142] The aforementioned 'The Statute Of David ...' serves as an example of the Christ-centred evangelistic preaching in which he delighted. It included a reference to his conversion[143] and closed with an evangelistic appeal. In the appeal Spurgeon depicted himself as the 'recruiting sergeant' looking for new soldiers for Christ. He insisted that Christ was 'the most magnanimous of

---

[135] See, C.H. Spurgeon, 'The Statute Of David For The Sharing Of The Spoil', *MTP*, Vol. 37, S. No. 2208, 1 Samuel 30.21-25, delivered 7 June 1891, e.g., pp. 315-16, 321.

[136] See, Spurgeon, *Autobiography*, Vol. 4, p. 356. At the time, of course, Spurgeon did not know this was the last occasion he would preach at his church.

[137] Spurgeon, 'The Statute Of David For The Sharing Of The Spoil', pp. 323-24.

[138] A good example is C.H. Spurgeon, 'Come Let & Us Reason Together', 'Notebooks Containing Sermon Outlines, Vols 2, 4-9', Vol. 4. Whatever the question an enquirer might have about salvation, the answer would be found by going 'to Jesus'.

[139] In C.H. Spurgeon to T.W. Medhurst, 14 July 1854, *Autobiography*, Vol. 2, p. 144, Spurgeon urged the as yet unconverted Medhurst (the man who would become the first student at the Pastors' College), to 'look, in prayer, to the sacred three-in-one God, and then you will be delivered', although he had previously urged him, typically, to look to the 'cross, and the bleeding God-man upon it'.

[140] C.H. Spurgeon, 'Conversions Encouraged', *MTP*, Vol. 22, S. No. 1283, Deuteronomy 4.29-31, delivered 12 March 1876, p. 151. For a further example of an evangelistic appeal which was focused on Christ and his work, see 'Pleading And Encouragement', *MTP*, Vol. 30, S. No. 1795, Ezekiel 18.32; 33.11, delivered 17 August 1884, p. 456.

[141] Spurgeon, *Autobiography*, Vol. 1, p. 106.

[142] Spurgeon, *Soul-Winner*, p. 108.

[143] Spurgeon, 'The Statute Of David For The Sharing Of The Spoil', p. 321.

captains', before adding, 'His service is life, peace, joy. Oh, that you would enter into it at once! God help you to enlist under the banner of Jesus even this day!'[144] The final words of his appeal were later printed on a card which could be given to unbelievers.[145] His final preached words at the Tabernacle were a fitting close to a ministry which was consistently evangelistic and focused on Christ.

This later evangelistic preaching also shows how the mature Spurgeon continued to come to Christ as a 'sinner'. In 'The Whole Gospel In A Single Verse', preached in 1889, he spoke in the following way: 'My dear friend, I am a poor sinner still; and I have to look to Christ every day as I did at the very first. Come along with me ... I wish that ... some soul would look to him and live.'[146] The message contains yet another reference to Spurgeon's own conversion (possibly brought on by the fact that it was a snowy day).[147] It is cited here, however, because of the way, in the extract just quoted, Spurgeon held up the pattern of his conversion as his pattern of daily living. Every day, he said, he came to Christ as a sinner. This was in order for confession of sin to take place and so he could admit complete dependence on Christ, effectively looking to him once again.[148] As he declared elsewhere, in a sermon entitled 'Redemption Through Blood, The Gracious Forgiveness Of Sins', the one 'that has the mind of Christ within him must still come to his Lord, just as he came at first'. Spurgeon quoted lines from Augustus Toplady's hymn, 'Rock of Ages',

> Nothing in my hand I bring,
> Simply to thy cross I cling.

Spurgeon then insisted that, as a mature Christian, he was not an 'inch forwarder' as to the ground of his trust than at the time of his conversion. Toplady's couplet expressed Spurgeon's own, continuing Christian experience.[149] His daily pattern of relating to Christ was a pattern which was shaped by his conversion.

Overall, it should be clear that Spurgeon's later ministry was both thoroughly evangelistic and resolutely focused on Christ. Part of his *raison d'être* was to call others to come to Christ and experience conversion as he had done. This was essential if a sinner was to escape eternal separation from Christ and enter into an experience of communion with him. Moreover, his evangelistic preaching reveals that he believed that the pattern of coming to Christ as a dependent sinner, established at conversion, was the only valid way forward for faithful Christian living. Spurgeon's 'conversionism' shaped a pattern of piety in which looking to Christ and sharing Christ were central motifs.

---

[144] Spurgeon, 'The Statute Of David For The Sharing Of The Spoil', pp. 323-24.

[145] 'C.H. Spurgeon's Last Words at the Tabernacle', in *Autobiography*, Vol. 4, p. 356.

[146] C.H. Spurgeon, 'The Whole Gospel In A Single Verse', *MTP*, Vol. 39, S. No. 2300, 1 Timothy. 1.15, delivered 28 February 1889, p. 142.

[147] Spurgeon, 'The Whole Gospel In A Single Verse', p. 142.

[148] Cf. Spurgeon *Autobiography*, Vol. 1, p. 113.

[149] Spurgeon, 'Redemption Through Blood, The Gracious Forgiveness Of Sins', p. 311.

Spurgeon and Evangelicalism

The material covered in this chapter is suggestive of some of the ways evangelicalism shaped Spurgeon. A number of important points have already been noted. The way his conversion narrative fits the established, evangelical framework for such narratives and connects with each point of Bebbington's quadrilateral has been highlighted. Spurgeon's pre-conversion reading of Doddridge's *Rise and Progress* and Angell James' *Anxious Enquirer* are, as already stated, suggestive of evangelical influences, as was the influence of his mother. Much more can be said, however. The fact that he was converted among the Primitive Methodists, an Arminian grouping with its roots firmly in the Wesleyan Evangelical Revival, is certainly relevant. Spurgeon had an extremely high regard for Wesley himself,[150] the Methodist leader's Arminianism notwithstanding.[151] His engagement with Wesley will be further considered in chapter 9, in which questions of holiness are examined. Suffice to say at this point that his appreciation of eighteenth-century Methodism certainly extended to the Arminian Wesley.

Thinking more broadly about Spurgeon's evangelistic ministry, evangelical influences abound. Although he had a warm estimate of Wesley, of the eighteenth-century revivalists it was the Calvinistic George Whitefield whom Spurgeon most admired. One suggestive reference to Whitefield in a Spurgeon sermon has already been cited in this chapter.[152] In fact, he made many more admiring comments, not only in Sunday sermons but also in midweek preaching[153] and in books.[154] In a revealing comment, he said to his students at the Pastors' College, 'Study the most successful models ... I made Whitefield my model years ago. Buy his sermons.'[155] Similarities between Whitefield and Spurgeon were pointed out early in Spurgeon's London ministry by observers on both sides of the Atlantic, in books[156] and in newspapers.[157] Some of the similarities between the two men (in addition to the extraordinary popularity they both enjoyed) include a clear, powerful voice, the

---

[150] Spurgeon (ed.), *Sword and Trowel*, August 1871, p. 380.

[151] Spurgeon, *Autobiography*, Vol. 1, p. 176.

[152] Spurgeon, 'The Comforter', p. 40.

[153] C.H. Spurgeon, *Only A Prayer Meeting: Forty Addresses at the Metropolitan Tabernacle and Other Prayer-Meetings* (London: Passmore and Alabaster, 1901), p. 14.

[154] Spurgeon, *Soul-Winner*, p. 96.

[155] W. Williams, *Personal Reminiscences of Charles Haddon Spurgeon* (rev. and ed. M. Williams; London: Religious Tract Society, n.d. [1933]), p. 57. Cf. Spurgeon, *Autobiography*, Vol. 2, p. 66.

[156] E.L. Magoon, *'The Modern Whitefield': Sermons of the Rev. C.H. Spurgeon, of London; With an Introduction and Sketch of his Life* (New York: Sheldon, Blakeman and Co., 1857). See also 'Spurgeon's Scrapbooks, Numbered Volumes', Spurgeon's College, Heritage Room (2G), Vol. 1, p.'a', and the extract from an unnamed 'American Paper (about 1856)'.

[157] *Glasgow Examiner*, 21 July 1855, as cited in Spurgeon, *Autobiography*, Vol. 2, p. 105; *Morning Advertiser*, 19 February 1855; and *Daily Bulletin*, 16 July 1855, as cited in *Autobiography*, Vol. 2, pp. 66 and 104 respectively.

ability to speak in the language of the people[158] and a certain theatrical, melodramatic style.[159] The way Spurgeon's conversion narrative became part of the Spurgeon myth and was marketed to a wide and growing constituency was also redolent of Whitefield, memorably described by Frank Lambert as a 'pedlar in divinity'.[160] Whitefield's entrepreneurial style found many other echoes in Spurgeon's ministry, as will be seen in other chapters of this study. We might also note Harry Stout's comment on Whitefield, that his piety was moulded 'by a conversion experience that, he passionately believed, was unmerited and of divine initiative'.[161] Spurgeon's view of his own conversion mirrored this exactly and, as we have seen, it had a similar shaping effect on his piety. The way that Spurgeon's conversion decisively moulded his subsequent life and ministry is a revealing indicator of his evangelicalism.

Spurgeon's approach to the question of assurance further illuminates his evangelicalism. In Spurgeon's mature conversion narrative the young convert received assurance of salvation immediately. 'I felt as sure that I was forgiven as before I felt sure of condemnation', he said.[162] There is evidence to suggest the reality may not have been quite as straightforward. Letters C.H. Spurgeon wrote to his father on 30 January, 12 March and 6 April 1850 contain references to 'doubts', 'fears' and 'darkness'.[163] Nevertheless, Spurgeon certainly came to a more confident view of assurance and his diary entries for May and June 1850 suggest this happened reasonably quickly, with his baptism on 3 May being perhaps the crucial turning point.[164]

Spurgeon's mature approach to assurance was that it was the birthright of every believer. In a sermon preached in 1888, entitled 'The Blessing Of Full Assurance', he set out his views. He was careful to say that possession of assurance was not 'essential to salvation'.[165] He did, however, insist that assurance was vital for a believer's peace, patience in suffering, desire for holiness and zeal. These were all qualities that Spurgeon believed were essential elements of true godliness. He declared,

---

[158] Spurgeon held Whitefield up as an example of this. See *Soul-Winner*, p. 96.

[159] Spurgeon, *Autobiography*, Vol. 2, pp. 51, 65-66, 77, 104-105, 116, 243-44.

[160] F. Lambert, *Pedlar in Divinity* (Princeton: Princeton University Press, 1994).

[161] Stout, *The Divine Dramatist*, p. xxiii.

[162] Spurgeon, *Autobiography*, Vol. 1, p. 111. Cf. p. 112.

[163] C.H. Spurgeon to J. Spurgeon, 30 January 1850, 'C.H. Spurgeon. Letters to his Father and Mother, 1850–84', Angus Library, Regent's Park College, Oxford (D/SPU), No. 3; C.H. Spurgeon to J. Spurgeon, 12 March and 6 April 1850, in *Autobiography*, Vol. 1, pp. 120-22.

[164] See, e.g., entries for 3, 21, 22, 31 May 1850, in Spurgeon, *Autobiography*, Vol. 1, pp. 135-41. Spurgeon was moving towards a more confident view of assurance before his baptism. See, e.g., C.H. Spurgeon to E. Spurgeon, 12 March 1850, 'C.H. Spurgeon. Letters to his Father and Mother, 1850–84', No. 4.

[165] C.H. Spurgeon, 'The Blessings Of Full Assurance', *MTP*, Vol. 34, S. No. 2023, 1 John 5.13, delivered 13 May 1888, p. 266.

Brethren, full assurance will give us the full result of the gospel ... Do not paddle about the margin of the water of life, but first wade in up to your knees, and then plunge into the waters to swim in. Beware of contentment with shallow grace. Prove what the power of God can do for you by giving yourself up to its power.[166]

The spiritual life which was not fed by a confident assurance would become malnourished. Assurance might not be essential for salvation, but it was essential if the Christian were to make solid progress in the spiritual life.

How was this assurance to be achieved and sustained? Spurgeon's early answer to this question involved self-examination. As noted in chapter 2, Puritan preachers tended to encourage ongoing, rigorous self-examination as the way to gain assurance, with one of their favourite texts being 1 Peter 1.10, with its the injunction to 'make your calling and election sure'.[167] Thomas Brooks, in his *Precious Remedies Against Satan's Devices*, offered a checklist of ten signs of grace to look for, and other preachers supplied similar lists, often with strong emphasis on 'works'.[168] Spurgeon, too, practised self-examination and recommended it for a time, as some of his early sermon outlines, with titles such as 'Self Examination' and 'Examine Yourselves', indicate.[169] In this last named message Spurgeon encouraged his hearers to look for a range of 'experimental' and 'practical' evidences which might give indication that they were truly saved. Examples of 'experimental' questions a believer could ask themselves included, 'Dost thou ever enjoy his divine presence and smile?' and 'Hast thou been upheld & comforted in trouble?' Examples of questions which might uncover 'practical' evidences included, 'Dost thou frequent the house of prayer and love to do so?', and 'Dost thou live honestly, soberly, & righteously?'[170] Spurgeon also preached under the title 'Self-Examination' at the Surrey Garden Music Hall in 1858, stating 'if you are in doubt now, the spediest [sic] way to get rid of your doubts and fears is by self-examination'.[171]

---

[166] Spurgeon, 'The Blessings Of Full Assurance', pp. 273-276. Cf. *Autobiography*, Vol. 1, p. 164.

[167] As noted in chapter 2, J. Coffey, 'Puritanism, Evangelicalism and the Evangelical Protestant Tradition', in Haykin and Stewart (eds), *The Emergence of Evangelicalism*, pp. 265-66, highlights some different Puritan views of assurance which contrast with the mainstream one.

[168] D.K. Gillett, *Trust and Obey: Explorations in Evangelical Spirituality* (London: Darton, Longman and Todd, 1993), p. 43; Bebbington, *Evangelicalism in Modern Britain*, p. 44.

[169] C.H. Spurgeon, 'Examine Yourselves', in 'Notebooks With Sermon Outlines, Vols 2, 4-9', Vol. 4, S. No. 214, 2 Corinthians 13.5; 'Self Examination', Vol. 9. S. No. 380, 2 Corinthians 13.5; Cf. 'Calling Of Election Sure', Vol. 3, S. No. 135, 1 Peter 1.10,11.

[170] Spurgeon, 'Examine Yourselves'.

[171] C.H. Spurgeon, 'Self-Examination', *NPSP*, Vol. 4, S. No. 218, 2 Corinthians 13.5, delivered 10 October 1858, p. 431. Spurgeon did close this message with a more confident affirmation, however, 'If Jesus be in thy heart, though thy heart sometimes be so dark that thou canst scarcely tell he is there, yet thou art accepted in the beloved, and thou mayest "rejoice with joy unspeakable and full of glory".' See p. 432.

This commitment to self-examination does not seem to have affected Spurgeon's confident view of his own assurance. He may well have persisted with sermons such as those cited in the previous paragraph because he was concerned, with the rush of new converts both at Waterbeach and New Park Street, that some of his hearers would be emotionally swept along with the tide, making professions of faith without having truly exercised saving faith.[172] Thus he emphasised the importance of changed lives. Nevertheless, by at least 1858, the self-examination advocated by Spurgeon was not to be as protracted as many Puritans suggested. As the quotation from the Surrey Gardens sermon cited in the previous paragraph indicates, if certain evidences *were* present, doubts might be quickly dispelled.

As Spurgeon's ministry progressed he grew increasingly cautious about self-examination, without repudiating it entirely. In the *Autobiography* he stated,

> Self-examination is a very great blessing, but I have known self-examination carried on in a most unbelieving, legal, and self-righteous manner; *in fact I have so carried it on myself*. Time was when I used to think a vast deal more of marks, and signs, and evidences, for my own comfort, than I do now, for I find that I cannot be a match for the devil when I begin dealing in these things.

In making these comments, Spurgeon explicitly distanced himself from his earlier approach. Spurgeon's mature view was that his early attempts to 'try' himself only succeeded in putting unnecessary 'stumbling-blocks' in his path. Any kind of self-examination which would take a believer away 'from the cross-foot' was to be eschewed, for it proceeded in entirely the 'wrong direction'.[173]

In 'Redemption Through Blood, The Gracious Forgiveness Of Sins', Spurgeon was if anything even more negative about self-examination. In this sermon (which although not dated, must have been preached in or after 1861)[174] he said that he did not believe those who felt themselves very poor would get rich by looking through all their 'empty cupboards'. 'No, no; if our graces are to be revived, we must begin with a renewed consciousness of pardon through the precious blood.' The only way to get this, said Spurgeon, was for the believer to go to the cross again, as they had

---

[172] See, e.g., the comment in C.H. Spurgeon, 'The Faith Of Simon Magus', 'Notebooks With Sermon Outlines, Vols 2, 4-9', Vol. 5, S. No. 237, Acts 8.13 and 21, 'In the Wesleyan & Primitive Methodist bodies are men professing to be converted worked upon by excitement, noise & earnestness – but they soon turn again.' Spurgeon describes some of the characters who were attracted to his ministry but not, in the preacher's estimate, truly converted, in *Soul Winner*, pp. 35-39.

[173] Spurgeon, *Autobiography*, Vol. 1, pp. 161-62. In the long quotation the italics are added. Spurgeon also stated, 'While I can believe the promise of God, and while I can trust my Saviour because He is God, and therefore mighty to save, all goes well with me; but I do find, when I begin questioning myself about this and that perplexity, thus taking my eye off Christ, that all the virtue of my life seems oozing out at every pore.'

[174] Because it was preached 'at the Metropolitan Tabernacle'. The message was published in 1891.

done 'at first'.[175] In both 'Redemption Through Blood ...' and the *Autobiography* the approach to assurance was essentially the same. Believers were not to look inside themselves for internal evidences of their salvation; rather they were to look away from 'self' towards Christ and his cross.[176] The look which led to conversion was paralleled by the look which led to continued assurance. Good works were still important in the Christian life, but looking to them was not the way assurance was gained. Rather, a believer was simply to trust Christ and his saving work and believe the accompanying promises of salvation for all who did so. If they did this, there was nothing to stop them knowing an assurance that was immediately given and which was also 'abiding' and 'eternal', assuming the focus on Christ was maintained.[177]

Spurgeon's mature, confident approach to assurance was one of the characteristic features of evangelicalism.[178] One of the sources shaping this evangelical doctrine of assurance was certainly the eighteenth-century Enlightenment.[179] It is increasingly recognised that the Enlightenment was a complex and diverse phenomenon.[180] Consequently, it is difficult to nail down a precise definition of what it meant to be 'enlightened'. Nevertheless, it certainly involved, as Bebbington's states, an assertion of 'the ability of human reason to discover truth'. Enlightenment empiricism encouraged free enquiry in an effort to ascertain the facts of whatever the matter under examination might be. That which had been 'found by investigation' could then 'be known with confidence'.[181] It is not difficult to see connections

---

[175] Spurgeon, 'Redemption Through Blood, The Gracious Forgiveness Of Sins', p. 311.

[176] Cf. Spurgeon, *Autobiography*, Vol. 1, p. 173: 'I believe that the happiest of Christians and the truest of Christians are those who never dare to doubt God, but take his Word simply as it stands, and believe it, and ask no questions, just feeling assured that if God has said it, it will be so.'

[177] Spurgeon, 'The Blessings Of Full Assurance', pp. 270-73.

[178] Even if examples of a confident approach to assurance can be found in the seventeenth century and even if some eighteenth-century evangelicals, such as John Newton, had a more 'Puritan' approach to assurance. On Newton and assurance, see D.B. Hindmarsh, *John Newton and the English Evangelical Tradition* (Oxford: Clarendon Press, 1996), chapter 6. Nevertheless, as Bebbington states, it is surely true that, 'on the evidence so far available it seems likely that the predominant view on the subject in the seventeenth century was less confident than what was normally professed in the eighteenth'. See 'Response', p. 422.

[179] This association has been challenged. See, e.g., Williams, 'Enlightenment Epistemology and Eighteenth-Century Evangelical Doctrines of Assurance', pp. 344-74. Nevertheless, although the Enlightenment was perhaps 'less the inspiration' for the typical evangelical view of assurance than was previously thought, it was still important. See Bebbington, 'Response', p. 422. Mark Noll has written that 'evangelicalism revealed its closest affinities to the Enlightenment ... in a dramatically heightened concern for the assurance of salvation.' See M.A. Noll, *The Rise of Evangelicalism: The Age of Edwards, Whitefield and the Wesleys* (Leicester: IVP, 2004), p. 141.

[180] See, e.g., B.K. Ward, *Redeeming the Enlightenment: Christianity and the Liberal Virtues* (Grand Rapids: Eerdmans, 2010), pp. 2-3.

[181] D.W. Bebbington, *Holiness in Nineteenth-Century England* (Carlisle: Paternoster, 2000), pp. 33, 35. Cf. Bebbington, *Evangelicalism in Modern Britain*, p. 48. In addition to

between Spurgeon's approach to assurance and such 'enlightened' patterns of thinking. Take the following from the *Autobiography* as an example.

> Has Jesus saved me? I dare not speak with any hesitation here; I know He has. His word is true, therefore I am saved. My evidence that I am saved does not lie in the fact that I preach, or that I do this or that. All my hope lies in this, that Jesus Christ came to save sinners. I am a sinner, I trust Him, then He came to save me, and I am saved; I live habitually in the enjoyment of this blessed fact, and it is long since I have doubted the truth of it, for I have His own word to sustain my faith.[182]

Spurgeon's argument reveals an 'enlightened' confidence that truth could be known. The particular truth in question, assurance of salvation, was based on Christ and his word and verified in Spurgeon's own experience. Elsewhere he could state, 'True Christian assurance is not a matter of guesswork, but of mathematical precision. It is capable of logical proof, and is no rhapsody or poetical fiction.'[183] In speaking in this way Spurgeon showed himself to be influenced to a significant degree by enlightened ways of thinking.

This confident, evangelical, Enlightenment-influenced approach to assurance was vitally important for Spurgeon's spirituality. One can imagine the debilitating effect ongoing self-examination in the mainstream Puritan mould might have had on Spurgeon who had a sensitive disposition with, as will be shown, a tendency to depression. Similarly, the Wesleyan teaching that it was possible to fall from grace, if Spurgeon had believed it, would have shaped his spirituality in a very different way. Spurgeon once stated, 'I do not believe how some people, who believe a Christian can fall from grace, manage to be happy.'[184] Spurgeon was instead moulded by an enlightened evangelical Calvinism which drew from Puritanism, but was marked by a more confident epistemology than that which typically characterised Puritan thinking. Spurgeon was *sure* that he knew Christ and was eternally saved.[185] Doubt was inappropriate, for God had promised in his word to give salvation and security to all who trusted in his Son. Protracted self-examination was unnecessary; indeed, it was unhelpful since it took the focus away from Christ and his cross. Spurgeon's sense of assurance was strong enough to remain, even through times of prolonged physical illness and bouts of depression (the one exception I could find is noted in chapter 10 in the discussion of Spurgeon and

---

empiricism and rationalism, Enlightenment characteristics include: the importance of free public discussion, the refusal to take on trust inherited opinions, tolerance, and progress. Alexander Brodie writes of the 'concept of Enlightenment' as 'a process in which reason is exercised in free public debate'. He further states that 'if reason leads one might expect real progress'. See his 'Introduction – What was the Scottish Enlightenment?' in A. Brodie (ed.), *The Scottish Enlightenment: An Anthology* (Edinburgh: Canongate, 1997), p. 17.

[182] Spurgeon, *Autobiography*, Vol. 1, p. 112.
[183] Spurgeon, 'The Blessings Of Full Assurance', p. 268.
[184] Cf. Spurgeon's comments in *Autobiography*, Vol. 1, p. 173.
[185] C.H. Spurgeon, 'The Security of Believers; Or, Sheep who Shall Never Perish', *MTP*, Vol. 35, S. No. 2120, John 10.27-30, delivered 5 September 1889, pp. 689-96.

suffering).[186] Given the firm base this assurance gave him, communion with a trustworthy Christ who kept his promises to save could be enjoyed and the energy which might have been expended in introspective soul-searching could be directed instead towards unstinting activity in the cause of Christ. Assurance of salvation was an important, even central feature of Spurgeon's spirituality, one which had great implications for both the inner and outer dimensions of his Christian life.

Conclusion

On 11 February 1892 Spurgeon's funeral service took place, following which his coffin was conveyed to Norwood cemetery for the committal. Throughout the five-mile journey from Newington Butts to Norwood, his pulpit Bible lay open on the top of the casket, with a marker pointing to the text of Isaiah 45.22.[187] The act was suggestive of the crucial importance of his conversion to his life and ministry. Spurgeon's conversion signalled the beginning of his experience of communion with Christ. It was, moreover, foundational to all subsequent 'felt' communion. Consequently, his theology of conversion was crucial to him. This theology was rooted in his own experience. His conversion, and how he had come to understand it, shaped his theology and the mature retellings of the events of January 1850. And, just as Spurgeon's theology was shaped by his conversion, so his evangelistic preaching was moulded by it. Spurgeon's 'experimental' knowledge of communion with Christ impelled him to offer the gospel to others from the beginning of his public ministry to the end. In this ministry, Spurgeon was effectively sharing, in sermon after sermon, both the gospel message and his own, personal encounter with it.[188] For him, the possibility of rich communion with Christ simply had to be shared with other people.

Spurgeon's conversionist, 'twice-born' spirituality was shaped by an evangelicalism which, although it had clear affinities with Puritanism, was not synonymous with it. Just one of the ways evangelicalism showed itself in Spurgeon was in his confident view of assurance. In tracing how Spurgeon's spirituality was impacted by evangelicalism and the Enlightenment, it can be seen that he was influenced by more than 'Puritanism', however important this was and however broadly the phenomenon of Puritanism might be conceived. His approach to assurance, affected by enlightened patterns of thinking, was a vital dimension of his spirituality which provided the motor which drove much of his Christian activity. Spurgeon's spirituality was thoroughly conversionist and thoroughly evangelical.

---

[186] Williams, *Personal Reminiscences* (rev. edn.), p. 32. Williams' recollection of Spurgeon's struggle is n.d.. Even here, Spurgeon soon rallied.

[187] R. Shindler, *From The Pulpit To The Palm-Branch. A Memorial of C.H. Spurgeon ... Including The Official Report Of The Services in Connection With His Funeral* (London: Passmore and Alabaster, 1892), p. 205.

[188] Spurgeon himself was clear that this was what he often did. See, *Soul-Winner*, p. 103.

CHAPTER 4

Baptism and the Baptists:
'I firmly believe ... that baptism is the command of Christ'

Spurgeon the new convert wanted to waste no time in being baptized as a believer. On 30 January 1850, just weeks after his conversion, he wrote a letter to his father which contained the following lines,

> From the Scriptures, is it not apparent that, immediately upon receiving the Lord Jesus, it is a part of duty openly to profess him? I firmly believe and consider that baptism is the command of Christ, and shall not feel quite comfortable if I do not receive it. I am unworthy of such things, but so am I unworthy of Jesu's love.[1]

Spurgeon believed that baptism was associated with the beginnings of the Christian life and that it should follow as soon as possible after conversion. Any account of Spurgeon's Christian initiation, therefore, needs to give due weight to his baptism.

Spurgeon was baptized as a believer by immersion on 3 May 1850. This took place at Isleham Ferry, north of Newmarket, the service being conducted by William Cantlow, a Baptist minister.[2] This was a significant, shaping event for the young Spurgeon, and the continuing importance of baptism to him can be seen from the emphasis he put on the rite throughout his subsequent ministry. It is true that, in 1859, Spurgeon stated that he 'seldom' mentioned the subject of baptism in his preaching, believing that the Holy Spirit applied the truth about the ordinance to people's hearts without his help,[3] but the reality was somewhat different. Indeed, there are numerous references to baptism in Spurgeon's published preaching. In only

---

[1] C.H. Spurgeon to J. Spurgeon, 30 January 1850, 'C.H. Spurgeon. Letters to his Father and Mother, 1850–84', Angus Library, Regent's Park College, Oxford (D/SPU), No. 3. Cf. C.H. Spurgeon, *Autobiography: Compiled from his Diary, Letters, and Records by his Wife and his Private Secretary* (4 Vols; London: Passmore and Alabaster, 1897–99), Vol. 1, p. 118.

[2] Spurgeon, *Autobiography*, Vol. 1, pp. 151-53.

[3] C.H. Spurgeon, 'Who Should Be Baptized?', *New Park Street Pulpit (NPSP) / Metropolitan Tabernacle Pulpit (MTP)* (London: Passmore and Alabaster, 1856–1917), *MTP*, Vol. 13, S. No. 2737, Acts 8.37, delivered (at New Park Street) in the 'summer of 1859', p. 349. Cf. T. Grass and I.M. Randall, 'C.H. Spurgeon on the Sacraments', in A.R. Cross and P.E. Thompson (eds), *Baptist Sacramentalism* (Carlisle: Paternoster, 2003), p. 58.

the fourth sermon published in the *New Park Street Pulpit*, Spurgeon lamented the fact that the New Park Street baptismal pool was covered.[4] When the Metropolitan Tabernacle was built he made it clear that the new baptistery would normally be left open as a sign that he and his church were 'not ashamed' to declare their commitment to believers' baptism.[5] On another occasion Spurgeon said, 'We Baptists are generally thought to lay great stress on Baptism ... I sometimes think we do not value it enough!'[6] In addition to his preaching on the ordinance, he also edited and republished two older works on baptism by Baptists. These were John Norcott's *Baptism Discovered*[7] and William Shirreff's *Lectures on Baptism*[8] respectively, Spurgeon adding his own Preface in each case. Also, Spurgeon's edition of Thomas Watson's *Body of Divinity* included an appendix in which he dissociated himself from the seventeenth-century Puritan's views on baptism and set out his own approach.[9] Baptism was vitally important to Spurgeon and he made no secret of this, or of his particular views on the rite.[10]

This chapter considers the role baptism played in Spurgeon's spirituality. His baptism as a believer took place at a crucial, formative time in his Christian journey, and this is analysed. This baptism was vital in setting the trajectory of his subsequent Christian life. Spurgeon's mature understanding of baptism which, like his theology of conversion, was closely bound up with his own experience, is also examined. His theology of baptism is especially revealing of the store he set on committed Christian discipleship. As with his approach to conversion, a strong stress on communion with Christ will be seen to pervade his approach to baptism. Consideration is also given to what baptism reveals about Spurgeon's ecclesiology. For him, commitment to the

---

[4] C.H. Spurgeon, 'The Personality Of The Holy Spirit', *NPSP*, Vol. 1, S. No. 4, John 14.16,17, delivered 21 January 1855, p. 26.

[5] I.H. Murray (ed.), *C.H. Spurgeon: The Full Harvest 1860–1892* (London: Banner of Truth, 1973), p. 37.

[6] C.H. Spurgeon, 'A Glorious Church', *MTP*, Vol. 11, S. No. 628, Ephesians 5.25-27, delivered 7 May 1865, p. 260.

[7] J. Norcott, *Baptism Discovered Plainly and Faithfully According to the Word of God: A New Edition. Corrected and Somewhat Altered by Charles Haddon Spurgeon* (London: Passmore and Alabaster, 1878). Norcott's *Baptism Discovered* was originally published in 1672. Norcott served as pastor of the Baptist church at Wapping from 1670 to 1678.

[8] W. Shirreff, *Lectures on Baptism ... with a Preface by C.H. Spurgeon* (London: Passmore and Alabaster, 1884 [1878]). Shirreff had been a Church of Scotland minister before becoming convinced of the need for believers' baptism. He gave his lectures soon after his own baptism as a believer, which took place in 1823.

[9] T. Watson, *A Body of Divinity, Contained in Sermons Upon the [Westminster] Assembly's Catechism ...* (London: Passmore and Alabaster, 1898 [1890?]). Watson's work was originally published in 1692.

[10] I have written further on Spurgeon and baptism in P.J. Morden, 'C.H. Spurgeon and Baptism Part 1: The Question of Baptismal Sacramentalism', *Baptist Quarterly* Vol. 43, No. 4 (October 2009), pp. 196-220, and 'C.H. Spurgeon and Baptism: The Importance of Baptism', *Baptist Quarterly* Vol. 43, No. 7 (July 2010), pp. 388-409.

church, the body of Christ, was essential. The Christian life, rightly conceived, was not a solitary affair. Rather, it had to be lived out in the midst of Christ's people.

Spurgeon's Baptism as a Believer

As will already be clear, C.H. Spurgeon was not 'brought up' a Baptist. He was baptized as an infant by his grandfather in the back parlour of his parents' home[11] and his conversion took place among the paedobaptist Primitive Methodists. Some account of his adoption of 'Baptist' views of baptism is therefore necessary. According to Spurgeon himself, the turning point was an encounter with an Anglican clergyman who, as Tim Grass and Ian Randall put it, 'inadvertently' challenged Spurgeon's inherited views of baptism.[12] The encounter, which was not precisely dated in the *Autobiography*, took place sometime in the academic year 1848–49, when Spurgeon was attending the Anglican school in Maidstone, Kent.[13] The point to emphasise is that this encounter was *before* Spurgeon's evangelical conversion experience just analysed in chapter 3. During a lesson on the Prayer Book Catechism, the Catechism's assertion that 'faith and repentance' were necessary for baptism was discussed. The young Spurgeon found himself directly challenged, the clergyman taking the lesson declaring, 'Spurgeon, you were never properly baptized.' In the *Autobiography* Spurgeon's recollection of the ensuing exchange between teacher and student is recorded thus,

> S[purgeon].—Oh, yes sir, I was [baptized]; my grandfather baptized me in the little parlour, and he is a minister, so I know he did it right!
> C[lergyman].—Ah, but you had neither faith nor repentance, and therefore ought not to have received baptism!
> S.—Why, sir, that has nothing to do with it! All infants ought to be baptized.
> C.—How do you know that? Does not the Prayer Book say that faith and repentance are necessary before baptism? ... Now, Charles, I shall give you till next week to find out whether the Bible does not declare faith and repentance to be necessary qualifications before baptism.[14]

The clergyman's aim had been to lead Spurgeon to see the necessity of godparents who would make promises on behalf of the infant, in the process scoring a point against the Independents, who did not require the involvement of godparents as sponsors. As the clergyman said in the following week's lesson, '[Your grandfather] baptizes in the very teeth of Scripture; and I do not ... for I require a

---

[11] For the reference to Spurgeon's infant baptism, see *Autobiography*, Vol. 1, p. 48.

[12] Grass and Randall, 'C.H. Spurgeon on the Sacraments', p. 56.

[13] See C.H. Spurgeon, 'God's Pupil, God's Preacher – An Autobiography', *MTP*, Vol. 39, S. No. 2318, delivered 28 July 1889, p. 354. This message contains a briefer retelling of the incident at Maidstone, see pp. 354-55.

[14] Spurgeon, *Autobiography*, Vol. 1, p. 48. Cf. Grass and Randall, 'C.H. Spurgeon on the Sacraments', p. 56.

promise, which I look upon as an equivalent of repentance and faith, to be rendered in future years.'[15] Spurgeon was not convinced by this argument, but he had been convinced, through the study of the scriptures which he had undertaken in the intervening week, that 'faith and repentance' were indeed 'necessary qualifications' for baptism in the New Testament. Spurgeon and the clergyman differed in that, as far as the young Spurgeon could see, what was required was the personal faith of the one being baptized.

Consequently, Spurgeon came to the view that his own 'baptism' as an infant was invalid. If ever he was to 'have repentance and faith', he resolved, he would be 'properly baptized' (i.e., baptized as a believer) himself.[16] His desire was simply to be obedient to the biblical teaching and he was explicit in saying that there was no 'Baptist' influence on his new commitment. He stated that when he had first come to believe that personal repentance and faith were necessary for baptism he had not known any Baptists.[17] As to the mode of baptism, Spurgeon said that further biblical study, which included learning 'a little Greek', convinced him that the word βαπτίζω meant to immerse rather than to sprinkle.[18] It was this, he concluded, that was the appropriate mode of baptism. Spurgeon was not so clear as to when this Greek study took place, although it is at least implied that it was very soon after his encounter with the clergyman.[19] According to the explanation of Spurgeon's conversion to baptistic views given in the *Autobiography*, the influence of Baptist Christians was non-existent. The first service of believers' baptism Spurgeon ever saw, he insisted, was his own.[20]

The account Spurgeon gave of his actual baptism as a believer which is included in the *Autobiography* first appeared in the *Sword and Trowel* in April 1890.[21] Spurgeon wrote that the minister, Cantlow, was Baptist pastor at Isleham, which was about eight miles from Newmarket where Spurgeon was then living. He had agreed to baptize Spurgeon, who had been unable to discover a Baptist church any nearer to

---

[15] Spurgeon, *Autobiography*, Vol. 1, p. 49.

[16] Spurgeon, *Autobiography*, Vol. 1, p. 50; Spurgeon, 'God's Pupil, God's Preacher – An Autobiography', pp. 354-55.

[17] Spurgeon, 'God's Pupil, God's Preacher – An Autobiography', pp. 354-55.

[18] Spurgeon, *Autobiography*, Vol. 1, p. 148.

[19] See, especially, Spurgeon, *Autobiography*, Vol. 1, pp. 148, 150.

[20] Spurgeon, *Autobiography*, Vol. 1, p. 152; Grass and Randall, 'C.H. Spurgeon on the Sacraments', p. 57.

[21] Cf. C.H. Spurgeon, 'Baptizing at Isleham Ferry', in C.H. Spurgeon (ed.), *The Sword and The Trowel: A Record of Combat With Sin and Labour For The Lord* (*Sword and Trowel*) (London: Passmore and Alabaster, 1865–92), April 1890, pp. 157-61, and *Autobiography*, Vol. 1, pp. 151-54. All details and quotations which appear in this and the following paragraph are taken from this account, unless otherwise stated. Spurgeon had earlier written to his father asking for any notes he had made about the baptism at the time, or any letters the son had written about it that were in the father's possession. See C.H. Spurgeon to John Spurgeon, 14 November 1889, in 'Original Correspondence of Charles Haddon Spurgeon, 1851–1893', Spurgeon's College, Heritage Room (4G), No. 100.

his home base. Isleham Ferry was on the banks of the River Lark and it was in the river that Spurgeon's baptism took place. Many people had gathered to watch the baptisms and Spurgeon initially felt timid and anxious. He was asked to help two women who were being baptized with him into the water, but he declined, being afraid, he said, of 'making some mistake'. His own vivid description of what happened when it was his turn to be baptized is as follows:

> The wind blew down the river with a cutting blast, as my turn came to wade into the flood; but after I had walked a few steps, and noted the people on the ferry-boat, and in boats, and on either shore, I felt as if heaven and earth and hell might all gaze upon me, for I was not ashamed, then and there, to own myself a follower of the Lamb. My timidity was washed away; it floated down the river into the sea, and must have been devoured by the fishes, for I have never felt anything of the kind since. Baptism also loosed my tongue, and from that day it has never been quiet. I lost a thousand fears in that River Lark, and found that in 'keeping His commandments there is great reward.'
> ... God be praised for his deserving goodness which allows me to write of it with delight so long afterwards.

The last sentence of this extract makes it absolutely clear that this represents Spurgeon's mature reflections on his earlier experience, as does his account of his pre-conversion adoption of Baptist views. Consequently, and as was the case with Spurgeon's conversion narrative, what appears in the *Autobiography* needs to be examined very carefully before being accepted as an accurate record of what actually happened. Spurgeon's description of how he came to adopt baptistic views of baptism can be considered first. Certainly, we should not suppose that his dramatic reconstruction of his conversations with the clergyman gives us the actual words which were spoken at the time. Here there is a clear parallel with Spurgeon's later, detailed 'recollections' of the words spoken by the Primitive Methodist preacher, which were offered in his mature conversion narrative.

What about Spurgeon's basic contention, that it was his encounter with the clergyman and the study of the scriptures this provoked which were the sole reasons for his change of views on baptism? His insistence that there was no 'Baptist' influence on his journey is certainly open to question. John Swindell, with whom Spurgeon lived in Newmarket on moving there in the summer of 1849, was a Baptist with whom Spurgeon could have, by his own admission, 'good religious conversations'.[22] Also, as already noted in chapter 2, the cook in Swindell's home, Mary King, was a Strict Baptist whom Spurgeon knew well.[23] Post-January 1850 Spurgeon also knew Robert Langford, the pastor of Eld Lane Baptist Church in Colchester. Spurgeon described Langford, in a letter to his mother, dated 20 April

---

[22] C.H. Spurgeon to J. Spurgeon, 30 January 1850, in C. Spurgeon (ed.), *The Letters of Charles Haddon Spurgeon* (London: Marshall Brothers, n.d. [1923?]), p. 13.

[23] Spurgeon, *Autobiography*, Vol. 1, p. 53. There appears to have been no Strict Baptist chapel in Newmarket, so Mary King attended the same Congregational church as Spurgeon. It is not clear where Swindell attended.

1850, as his 'friend' and advised her to attend his church.[24] Could these Baptists have influenced Spurgeon as to the need for believers' baptism?

The data available is too incomplete and fragmentary for a confident answer to be offered to this question. But there is evidence from the early 1850s which gives some support for Spurgeon's later account. A careful reading of the letters C.H. Spurgeon wrote to his parents between January and May 1850 does not reveal any statement from him which suggests the influence of Baptists on his desire to undergo believers' baptism.[25] Perhaps more importantly, there is nothing to indicate that Spurgeon's parents suspected any such influence on their son's decision to be, as they saw it, rebaptized.[26] The reasons C.H. Spurgeon did give for his decision were set out in the letter to his father which was written on 30 January 1850 and cited in the opening paragraph of this chapter.[27] Just a few weeks after his conversion, Spurgeon's mind was made up as far as being baptized as a believer was concerned and the reason offered for this decision was the teaching of scripture, with a special focus on the need for obedience to Christ's command. Furthermore, there is a reference to the Prayer Book Catechism in relation to baptism in a sermon in the pre-London notebooks. This occurs in the outline for a message, entitled simply 'Baptism', which was preached at a baptismal service at Waterbeach, probably in the first half of 1853.[28] Spurgeon wrote, 'The Prayer-book declares faith & repentance to be necessary before Baptism. & certainly there is no instance [in the New Testament] of any being baptized who did not profess to have each of these things.'[29] In Spurgeon's sermon, his argument that baptism was only for believers is predicated on the Prayer Book and on the New Testament.

---

[24] C.H. Spurgeon to Eliza Spurgeon, 20 April 1850, in Spurgeon, *Autobiography*, Vol. 1, p. 122. Langford was pastor of Eld Lane between 1842 and 1872. See H. Spyvee, *Colchester Baptist Church – The First 300 years, 1689–1989* (Colchester: Colchester Baptist Church, 1989), p. 53. Spyvee pays some attention to the connection with Spurgeon, pp. 59-61. Spurgeon preached for Langford in Colchester on 13 April 1859. See the advertisement in 'Maroon Bound Scrapfolders', Vol. 1, Spurgeon's College, Heritage Room, p. 40.

[25] The closest is Spurgeon's comment, already cited, that he could get 'good religious conversations' with Swindell.

[26] They clearly did express a concern that their son might be 'trusting' in baptism. The idea was anathema to C.H. Spurgeon. He wrote in his diary, on 26 April 1850, 'How my father's fears lest I should trust to baptism stir up my soul! My God, Thou knowest that I hate such a thought!' See *Autobiography*, Vol. 1, p, 133. Cf. C.H. Spurgeon to J. Spurgeon, 6 April 1850, 'C.H. Spurgeon. Letters to his Father and Mother, 1850–84', No. 5.

[27] C.H Spurgeon to John Spurgeon, 30 January 1850, 'C.H. Spurgeon. Letters to his Father and Mother, 1850–84', No. 3.

[28] C.H. Spurgeon, 'Baptism' in 'Notebooks With Sermon Outlines, Vols 2, 4-9', Spurgeon's College, Heritage Room (U1), Vol. 5, S. No. 276. Spurgeon commenced Volume 5 of his 'Notebooks' on 26 February 1853.

[29] Spurgeon, 'Baptism'. As noted in chapter 3, I did not find any evidence from the notebooks in support of Spurgeon's mature conversion narrative. There is another reference to the Prayer Book Catechism's teaching on baptism in Spurgeon, 'Who Should Be Baptized?', p. 351. This was, as already noted, was preached in the summer of 1859.

Spurgeon's claim to have discovered that baptism meant 'immersion' through a close study of the New Testament in Greek, and no other means, receives some background support from a letter to his mother, written on 19 February 1850, which indicates that Spurgeon had commenced learning Greek sometime before this date.[30] Of course, this in itself does not corroborate Spurgeon's later claim. Nevertheless, when all the available evidence is considered, there seems no compelling reason to reject the essential veracity of Spurgeon's account of his 'conversion' to baptistic views. This is true with regard to both the mode of baptism and also (and this is the more important point), the proper subjects of the rite. It is hard to believe, at least for this writer, that the Baptists Spurgeon knew in 1849–50 did not have a role in confirming and strengthening his views, but I have found no evidence to say for certain that this happened. Certainly, there is good evidence to say that a study of the scriptures really was formative for Spurgeon's change of mind on baptism. Unsurprisingly, for Spurgeon personally, commitment to the Bible became what he thought should be a fundamental Baptist distinctive.[31] He was keen not to be seen as a 'sectarian' Baptist;[32] indeed, following his baptism at Isleham he became for a time increasingly involved in his Congregational church in Newmarket.[33] Spurgeon's baptism in the River Lark was not primarily to do with a shift of allegiance from the Independents to the Baptists. True, this shift did take place soon after, when Spurgeon joined St Andrew's Street Baptist Church in Cambridge in September 1850,[34] and Spurgeon's baptism as a believer would have important implications for his ecclesiology, as we shall see. But his baptism in the River Lark was more to do with a desire to be faithful to what Spurgeon believed the Bible taught and especially to what Christ commanded concerning baptism.

As far as Spurgeon's later description of his actual baptism is concerned, the issue of reliability is more straightforward. By contrast with his conversion narrative the basic facts – the date, the identity of the minister, the outline of what happened at the service – are easily established, verified as they are not only by Spurgeon's contemporaneous letters and diary entries but also by the testimonies of others who were present at the service.[35] Even the names of those who were baptized with him are known.[36] It is harder to judge whether his baptism meant to him at the time

---

[30] C.H. Spurgeon to Eliza Spurgeon, 19 February 1850, in C. Spurgeon (ed.), *The Letters of C.H. Spurgeon*, p. 16.

[31] Spurgeon, *Autobiography*, Vol. 1, p. 155.

[32] See, e.g., Spurgeon, *Autobiography*, Vol. 1, p. 154.

[33] See the evidence of Spurgeon's diary, April to June 1850, in, *Autobiography*, Vol. 1, pp. 129-45. Of course, this was probably partly due to the fact that Spurgeon could find no Baptist church close enough for him to attend easily.

[34] C.H. Spurgeon to John Spurgeon, 19 September 1850, 'C.H. Spurgeon. Letters to his Father and Mother, 1850–84', No. 7; Spurgeon, *Autobiography*, Vol. 1, p. 185, and as already noted.

[35] See, e.g., C.H. Spurgeon to Eliza Spurgeon, 1 May 1850, in 'Original Correspondence of Charles Haddon Spurgeon, 1851–1893', No. 171; *Autobiography*, Vol. 1, pp. 135, 153-54.

[36] Diana Wilkinson and Eunice Fuller. See Spurgeon, *Autobiography*, Vol. 1, p. 152.

exactly what he later said it did – a public confession of Christ which had nothing to do with salvation but much to do with discipleship, and which was necessary before he could, in good conscience, take part in the Lord's Supper. But, once again, there is evidence which can be cited in support of Spurgeon. In 1850 he was sure that baptism played 'no part' in salvation, although it was vitally important to be baptized because this was Christ's command to all who had believed in him.[37] The fact that baptism was a public declaration of commitment to Christ which might provoke ridicule was also vital to him at the time of his baptism: his avowal of Christ in an 'open river' would be, he wrote to his mother, 'a good confession before many witnesses'.[38] As such it would require 'courage'[39] and constitute a very public 'bond' between him and his 'Master', 'Saviour' and 'King'.[40] His desire to do something for Christ was all-consuming in the months immediately following his conversion.[41] Baptism conceived of as public confession clearly gave concrete expression to that desire: here was something difficult he could 'do' for his Lord. Finally, Spurgeon refused to join in the Lord's Supper until after his baptism at Isleham (although he had, interestingly, already joined the Congregational church as a member), believing that baptism was necessary before he could unite with the Lord's people in Communion.[42] As the young convert stepped nervously into the River Lark baptism was for him fundamentally a matter of obedient discipleship by which he identified himself publicly as a follower of Christ and united himself with Christ's people.

Spurgeon and 'Baptismal Sacramentalism'

The beliefs Spurgeon held about baptism in 1850 were those he would carry with him for the rest of his life. Spurgeon the London pastor continued to emphasise the need for baptism as a crucial early step for all believers who wanted to live as true disciples of Christ. His conviction that there was nothing saving about baptism also continued to find expression. For example, in 1885 he preached a sermon, 'The Good Ananias, A Lesson For Believers', taking as his text Acts 9.10. In the course of this message he declared,

> Do not make any mistake, and imagine that immersion in water can wash away sin; but do remember that if the Lord puts outward profession side by side with the washing

---

[37] C.H. Spurgeon to Eliza Spurgeon, 19 February 1850, in C. Spurgeon (ed.), *Letters of C.H. Spurgeon*, p. 16.

[38] C.H. Spurgeon to Eliza Spurgeon, 20 April 1850, in C. Spurgeon (ed.), *Letters of C.H. Spurgeon*, pp. 21-22.

[39] C.H. Spurgeon to Eliza Spurgeon, 1 May 1850.

[40] C.H. Spurgeon to Eliza Spurgeon, 20 April 1850.

[41] C.H. Spurgeon to John Spurgeon, 12 March 1850, in C. Spurgeon (ed.), *Letters of C.H. Spurgeon*, pp. 17-18.

[42] Spurgeon, *Autobiography*, Vol. 1, p. 129.

away of sins it is not a trifling matter ... Faith must be followed by obedience, or it cannot be sincere: do, then, what Jesus bids you.[43]

The emphases, in a sermon from the last decade of Spurgeon's ministry, were remarkably similar to those of his earliest reflections on baptism. The focus was resolutely on the believer's faith. Baptism was an act of obedience to Christ, an 'outward profession' which was evidence of the 'sincerity' of inward faith. Crucially, baptism was sharply distinguished from the actual 'washing away' of sin. In another message, entitled 'Fencing The Table', Spurgeon went further. The 'plunge into the water' did not confer 'any grace' on the person baptized.[44] Spurgeon insisted that baptism played 'no part' in salvation, but he also wanted to contend for a much broader notion, that it did not mediate any grace. If we understand sacraments as 'means of grace' or 'media that transmit the grace of God to bodily creatures'[45] (and this is what I have in mind when I use the terms 'sacrament' and 'sacramental' in this study), then it should be clear that, in 'The Good Ananias ...' and 'Fencing The Table' at least, Spurgeon was not advocating a 'sacramental' view of baptism.

In fact, Spurgeon's preaching contains numerous statements similar to those just cited.[46] A survey of his published sermons reveals that he was remarkably clear and consistent in avoiding any statement that could be interpreted as suggesting that baptism conveyed grace. Sermons with initially promising titles such as 'Baptism, Belief, Blessing' will be searched in vain by anyone seeking to discover a strand of sacramentalism in Spurgeon's baptismal theology. The preacher's text on this particular occasion was Acts 16.33,34. As Spurgeon expounded the story of the Philippian jailor's conversion and baptism, he observed that God was at work in a number of ways in the story. God was active in the miracle of Paul and Silas' release, through their preaching and, of course, in the jailor's conversion. As he closed his message, Spurgeon emphasised that salvation was 'by the working of sovereign grace'. The one point in the story where it appears Spurgeon did not believe God was at work was in the jailor's baptism. This was described entirely in terms of human response to grace previously received.[47]

This rejection of baptismal sacramentalism can further be shown by a consideration of Spurgeon's attitude to baptismal hymns. The hymnbook which Spurgeon had used at Waterbeach, and which was also in use at New Park Street / Metropolitan Tabernacle prior to the introduction of *Our Own Hymn Book* in 1866,

---

[43] C.H. Spurgeon, 'The Good Ananias, A Lesson For Believers', *MTP*, Vol. 31, S. No. 1838, Acts 9.10, delivered 26 April 1885, p. 251.

[44] C.H. Spurgeon, 'Fencing The Table', *MTP*, Vol. 50, S. No. 2865, 1 Corinthians 11.28, delivered 2 January 1876, p. 13.

[45] C.H. Pinnock, *Flame of Love: A Theology of the Holy Spirit* (Downers Grove: IVP, 1996), p. 122.

[46] See, e.g., Spurgeon, 'Who Should Be Baptized?', p. 355-56.

[47] C.H. Spurgeon, 'Belief, Baptism, Blessing', *MTP*, Vol. 38, S. No. 2275, Acts 16.33,34, delivered 9 February 1890, pp. 457-65.

was John Rippon's famous *Selection*.[48] Rippon, who, like John Gill, was a previous pastor of Spurgeon's London congregation,[49] had included a number of hymns invoking the descent of the Holy Spirit at baptism in his *Selection*.[50] These included 'Descend, celestial dove' by John Fellows (No. 468), as well as the following from Benjamin Beddome (No. 460),

> Eternal Spirit! heavenly dove!
>   On these baptismal waters move!
> That we through energy divine
>   May have the substance with the sign.[51]

In *Our Own Hymn Book*, Spurgeon omitted all such hymns. This was despite his taking over a range of other material from Rippon.[52] Undoubtedly, for Spurgeon, it would have been a conscious choice to exclude such verses.

Another book from which Spurgeon drew selectively in compiling *Our Own Hymn Book* was one edited by James Upton.[53] This book, which first appeared at the

---

[48] J. Rippon (ed.), *Selection of Hymns, from the best authors, Intended to be an Appendix to Dr Watts's Psalms and Hymns* (London, 1787). As indicated in the title, Rippon's *Selection* was intended to be used in conjunction with Isaac Watts' *Psalms and Hymns*. See C.H. Spurgeon (ed.), *Our Own Hymn Book* (London: Passmore and Alabaster, 1866), Preface, p. v. Rippon edited a copy of *Psalms and Hymns* himself. See J. Rippon (ed.), *An Arrangement of the Psalms, Hymns, and Spiritual Songs of Rev. Isaac Watts D.D....* (London, 1801). An edition of Watts' *Hymns* was first published in 1707; an edition of his *Psalms* first appeared in 1719.

[49] Rippon was an evangelical Calvinist Baptist pastor who had trained at the Bristol Academy and who had been pastor of the congregation between 1773 to 1836. For more on Rippon, see K.R. Manley, *Redeeming Love Proclaim: John Rippon and the Baptists* (Carlisle: Paternoster, 2004), *passim*.

[50] Although these sat alongside others which spoke of baptism as an act of obedience. See the analysis in Manley, *Redeeming Love Proclaim*, pp. 109-10.

[51] Rippon (ed.), *Selection*. These two songs (Beddome's is just a verse, to be sung either immediately before or after the act of baptism) are in the first edition and also later (e.g., 1874) editions. Beddome was pastor of the Baptist church at Bourton-on-the-Water from 1743 until his death in 1795. A collection of 822 hymns and eight doxologies were published by Robert Hall, Jr, as B Beddome, *Hymns adapted to Public Worship, or Family Devotion* (London: Button, 1818). See M.A.G. Haykin, 'Benjamin Beddome (1717–1795): His Life and His Hymns', in J.H.Y. Briggs (ed.), *Pulpit and People: Studies in Eighteenth-Century Baptist Life and Thought* (Milton Keynes: Paternoster, 2009), pp. 93-111, who also gives further detail on Beddome's life and hymnody. Haykin does not refer to Beddome's baptismal sacramentalism.

[52] The fact that Spurgeon excluded the sacramental hymns of Rippon's *Selection* when editing *Our Own Hymn Book* is noted by Grass and Randall, though no specific examples are given. See 'C.H. Spurgeon on the Sacraments', pp. 57-58.

[53] Upton was pastor, from 1785 to 1834, of the Baptist church which met in Green Walk (later renamed Church Street) in Southwark. See S.J. Price, *Upton: The Story of One Hundred and Fifty Years, 1785–1935* (London: Carey Press, 1935), pp. 50, 113, 123.

beginning of the nineteenth century, contained a particularly large number of hymns relating to baptism, with various compositions containing material which ranged right across the 'sacramental' / 'non-sacramental' spectrum. The theology in some of these hymns flatly contradicts that contained in others and one struggles to see what criteria, if any, Upton applied as he chose which baptismal verses to include in his *Collection*.[54] Faced with Upton's eclectic selection, Spurgeon studiously avoided any hymn which suggested that grace was imparted, or that God was active in any way in baptism (like Rippon, Upton had included 'Descend, celestial dove'). But Spurgeon did select Upton's No. 277, 'Come, ye who bow to sovereign grace', for *Our Own Hymn Book*. This included the verse,

> No trust in water do we place,
> 'Tis but an outward sign;
> The great reality is grace,
> The fountain, blood divine.

Spurgeon added an additional verse to this polemic (beginning with the words, 'Here we declare in emblem plain ...') crediting the authorship of the hymn jointly to Upton and himself, proof enough (if any were needed) that it represented his own theology.[55] For Spurgeon, although baptism symbolised much, it mediated nothing.

Although, as Anthony R. Cross states, the 'memorialist' position had become the 'denominational norm' for nineteenth-century Baptists, there were still a minority who espoused some form of baptismal sacramentalism.[56] Indeed, the presence of verses such as Beddome's in popular hymnals was indication that there were at least some who believed that baptism was more than just a believer's subjective response to grace received on some previous occasion.[57] One such, Baptist Wriothesley Noel, was a former Anglican who seceded from the Church of England in 1848, submitting to believers' baptism in 1849.[58] Noel, commenting on Acts 2.38, stated that baptism was 'closely connected' with the remission of sins, indeed it was 'necessary' to this.

Spurgeon had a high estimate of Upton, believing that he had 'presided' over the church 'right worthily'. See C.H. Spurgeon's Preface to W. Williams, *Upton Chapel Sermons: A Centenary Memorial* (London: Passmore and Alabaster, 1885), p. xi.

[54] J. Upton (ed.), *A Collection of Hymns Designed As A Supplement To Dr Watts' Psalms And Hymns* (London: Button and Gale, 1814).

[55] Upton (ed.), *Collection*, No. 277; Spurgeon (ed.), *Our Own Hymn Book*, No. 923. This hymn suggests that Upton himself did not have a sacramental theology of baptism, despite his willingness to include more sacramental verses in his *Collection*.

[56] See A.R. Cross, *Baptism and the Baptists: Theology and Practice in Twentieth-Century Britain* (Carlisle: Paternoster, 2000), pp. 10-11, 16-17.

[57] A third edition of Upton's *Collection* appeared in 1818; Rippon's *Selection* went through numerous editions, both before and after the compiler's death. On Rippon's *Selection*, see Manley, *Redeeming Love Proclaim*, pp. 82-138.

[58] For Noel, see D.W. Bebbington, 'The Life of Baptist Noel: Its Setting and Significance', *Baptist Quarterly* Vol. 24, No. 8 (October 1972), pp. 389-411.

Repentance and baptism were 'declared in the text to secure the gift of the Holy Ghost'.[59] Noel emphasised baptism as a 'seal of regeneration', language which, as Stanley Fowler notes, locates Noel in the tradition of 'Calvinistic sacramentalism'.[60] Fowler suggests, in his treatment of Spurgeon on baptism, that Spurgeon might not have been averse to this concept of baptism as a seal of regeneration.[61] But Spurgeon's sermons and other writings on baptism show conclusively that he did not support such a view. Not that Spurgeon was against using the language of sealing in relation to baptism. In 'Baptism – A Burial', a message preached in 1881, he declared, 'Now, by being buried with Christ in baptism, *we set our seal* to the fact that the death of Christ was on our behalf, and that we were in him, and, in token of our belief, we consent to the watery grave, and yield ourselves to be buried according to his command.'[62] Thus, the concept of a seal was used but, yet again, it was the believer's action, rather than God's, which was in view.

The only possible exceptions which might be cited to counter this seemingly all-pervasive focus on baptism as human response were the occasions when Spurgeon reflected on his own experience at Isleham Ferry, which, as Spurgeon's recollections of this event show, had been deeply meaningful for him. His diary entry for 3 May 1850, completed after he had returned to his lodgings at Newmarket following his baptism, spoke of the 'Blest pool' which was the 'sweet emblem' of his death to the world.[63] Over seventeen years later his language was hardly less joyful: the recollection of that 'happy' day was still 'fragrant'.[64] In the account in the *Autobiography* which has already been cited, Spurgeon spoke of his fears being washed away and his tongue being 'loosed'.[65] In his own experience, then, baptism and God's blessing do appear to be tied together. But closer examination of the way Spurgeon wrote about his baptism shows that he believed it was *his own obedience* that God was blessing. It was still, fundamentally, the human action that was in view. God's 'reward' had certainly come, but it had come because he had faithfully kept Christ's command to be baptized.[66] Spurgeon frequently averred that God generally

---

[59] B.W. Noel, *Essay on Christian Baptism* (London: James Nisbet, 1849), p. 99, as cited by Cross, *Baptism and the Baptists*, pp. 11-12.

[60] S.K. Fowler, *More Than a Symbol: The British Baptist Recovery of Baptismal Sacramentalism* (Carlisle: Paternoster, 2002), pp. 72-75. Cf. A.R. Cross, 'Baptismal Regeneration', in A.R. Cross and P.E. Thompson (eds), *Baptist Sacramentalism 2* (Milton Keynes: Paternoster, 2008), p. 157. In Fowler's discussion of Noel's theology he is drawing from B.W. Noel, *Sermons on Regeneration, with Especial Reference to the Doctrine of Baptismal Regeneration* (London: 'The Pulpit' Office, 2nd edn., n.d.).

[61] Fowler, *More Than a Symbol*, p. 82.

[62] C.H. Spurgeon, 'Baptism – A Burial', *MTP*, Vol. 27, S. No. 1627, Romans 6.3,4, delivered 30 October 1881, p. 619, italics added.

[63] Spurgeon, *Autobiography*, Vol. 1, p. 135.

[64] C.H. Spurgeon, 'Songs Of Deliverance', *MTP*, Vol. 13, S. No. 763, Judges 5.11, delivered 28 July 1867, p. 423.

[65] Spurgeon, *Autobiography*, Vol. 1, pp. 151-54.

[66] Spurgeon, *Autobiography*, Vol. 1, p. 152.

rewarded Christian obedience. The one who obeyed would know 'joy', 'freedom', 'comfort' and 'grace'. Obedience to Christ's command to be baptized would lead to such blessing, but so would responding positively to a host of other 'orders' which Christ had given.[67] In short, there was no objective sacramental significance to baptism. The blessing which might be experienced by a believer through baptism was not different in essence to the blessing believers might receive on obeying any command of Christ. I have taken some time to establish the extent and depth of Spurgeon's rejection of baptismal sacramentalism. I have done so partly because there are hints in the secondary literature that this rejection might not have been as thoroughgoing as it actually was,[68] but also, and more importantly, because this rejection was fundamental to Spurgeon's approach to baptism. The question, 'Did Spurgeon have a sacramental view of baptism?' should be answered firmly in the negative.

Reasons for the Rejection of 'Baptismal Sacramentalism'

How can Spurgeon's vehement rejection of baptismal sacramentalism be explained? A crucial reason for Spurgeon's dismissal of baptismal sacramentalism was his anti-Catholicism, a strand in his thinking which has already been commented on in this study, in chapter 2. Such anti-Catholicism was a feature of evangelical, Nonconformist life in the nineteenth century, one which was heightened by the progress of the Oxford Movement in the Church of England from the beginning of the 1830s. The Oxford Movement was often known as 'Tractarianism' after the *Tracts for the Times* its leaders published between 1833 and 1841, or, more pejoratively, as 'Puseyism' after Edward Bouverie Pusey, one of the Movement's most important leaders. As Peter Nockles has stated, the Tractarians sought to defend the Church of England as a 'divine institution', as a branch of the 'church Catholic', and as a 'repository of apostolical succession and sacramental grace'.[69] Ritual was not initially important to the Oxford Movement, but became more so later, particularly from the 1860s.[70] As Michael Walker states, this High Church,

---

[67] C.H. Spurgeon, 'Obeying Christ's Orders', *MTP*, Vol. 39, S. No. 2317, John 2.5, delivered 13 June 1889, pp. 342-45.

[68] In addition to Fowler, *More Than a Symbol*, pp. 82-83, a few of the statements of Grass and Randall, 'C.H. Spurgeon on the Sacraments' are open to question. See, especially, p. 55: 'For Spurgeon the ordinances [i.e., both the Lord's Supper *and* baptism] were associated with God's gracious activity.'

[69] P.B. Nockles, 'The Oxford Movement', in J. Hill (ed.), *The History of Christianity* (Oxford: Lion, 2007), p. 366. For more on the Oxford Movement and the wider tradition of Anglican High Churchmanship, see P.B. Nockles, *The Oxford Movement in Context: Anglican High Churchmanship 1760–1857* (Cambridge: Cambridge University Press, 1994). For High Church spirituality, see D.W. Bebbington, *Holiness in Nineteenth-Century England* (Carlisle: Paternoster, 2002), pp. 7-28.

[70] M. Chandler, *An Introduction to the Oxford Movement* (London: SPCK, 2003), pp. 107-21.

'Anglo-Catholic', movement tended to confirm for Baptists that Anglicanism was 'incurably biased towards Rome'.[71] As has already been noted, Spurgeon's own antipathy to Roman Catholicism and the Oxford Movement was firmly established long before his conversion.[72] The sacerdotalism which Spurgeon saw in the baptismal theology of both Roman Catholicism and the Oxford Movement (which he referred to as 'Anglicised Popery')[73] undoubtedly served to inure him against sacramental views of baptism.[74] In a sermon outline for a Waterbeach message entitled 'Keeping The Ordinances', which was preached at a baptismal service, Spurgeon wrote that 'Baptismal Regeneration & all its accompanying Puseyism' was, rather than a 'keeping' of the ordinances, a 'prostitution' of them.[75] In Spurgeon's ministry, his opposition to 'Romanising influences' was linked in his preaching with antipathy to the idea that any spiritual power was conveyed in baptism.

The so-called baptismal regeneration dispute of 1864 is particularly important here. This controversy was sparked off by a sermon Spurgeon preached on 5 June 1864 in which he declared that 'baptismal regeneration' (which was the title of his message) was 'the great error which we have to contend with throughout England'. This doctrine was a nonsense, Spurgeon insisted, for 'Baptism without faith saves no one'.[76] On 24 July Spurgeon fanned the flames of what by this point had already become an acrimonious controversy by preaching a message, 'Children Brought To Christ, Not To the Font', which was, if anything, even more provocative than 'Baptismal Regeneration'.[77] Spurgeon's attack (and this is not too strong a term) was more focused on the evangelical party in the Church of England than it was on the Tractarians or Roman Catholics. He believed that the baptismal service in the Church of England Prayer Book taught baptismal regeneration; evangelical clergy who did not believe in baptismal regeneration were, therefore, being hypocritical by remaining within a Church which plainly subscribed to such an erroneous doctrine.[78]

---

[71] M.J. Walker, *Baptists at the Table: The Theology of the Lord's Supper amongst English Baptists in the Nineteenth Century* (Didcot: Baptist Historical Society, 1992), p. 85.

[72] As illustrated by, for example, C.H. Spurgeon, 'Antichrist and her Brood; or, Popery Unmasked', Spurgeon's College, Heritage Room (A2.06).

[73] C.H. Spurgeon, 'The Priest Dispensed With', *MTP*, Vol. 21, S. No. 1250, 1 John 5.10, delivered 15 August 1875, p. 469.

[74] That this was the case with many Baptists has been widely recognized. See, e.g., J.H.Y. Briggs, *The English Baptists of the Nineteenth Century* (Didcot: Baptist Historical Society, 1994), p. 46; Cross, *Baptism and the Baptists*, pp. 10, 15-16; Fowler, *More Than a Symbol*, p. 58.

[75] C.H. Spurgeon, 'Keeping The Ordinances', 'Notebooks With Sermon Outlines, Vols 2, 4-9', Vol. 7, S. No. 333, 1 Corinthians 11.2.

[76] C.H. Spurgeon, 'Baptismal Regeneration', *MTP*, Vol. 10, S. No. 573, Mark 16.15,16, delivered 5 June 1864, p. 315.

[77] C.H. Spurgeon, 'Children Brought To Christ, Not To the Font', *MTP*, Vol. 10, S. No. 581, Mark 10.13-16, delivered 24 July 1864, pp. 413-24.

[78] Spurgeon, 'Baptismal Regeneration', pp. 316-17.

Spurgeon was touching on an issue that was extremely sensitive for evangelical Anglicans.[79] The precise details of the controversy and the intense pamphlet war that it generated will not be rehearsed here.[80] What must be noted in respect of the dispute is Spurgeon's belief that any form of infant baptism and / or baptismal sacramentalism left the door open to baptismal regeneration, a step on the slippery slope towards 'Popery' and, crucially, an undermining of the necessity of personal conversion. These concerns were a feature of Spurgeon's preaching long after the baptismal regeneration dispute had run its course. So, in 1873 he declared, in a message entitled 'Signs Of The Times',

> As long as you give baptism to an unregenerate child, people will imagine that it must do the child good; for they will ask, If it does not do it any good, why is it baptized? The statement that it puts children into the covenant, or renders them members of the visible church, is only a veiled form of the fundamental error of Baptismal Regeneration. If ye keep up the ordinance, you will always have men superstitiously believing that some good cometh to the babe thereby, and what is this but sheer Popery?[81]

This is a statement which is worthy of extended comment. All paedobaptism, whatever the theology accompanying it, undermined what for Spurgeon was the vital point, that regeneration and the exercise of personal saving faith needed to precede any valid baptism. Even an approach to infant baptism which set it within the framework of Puritan covenant theology, with baptism regarded as the new covenant 'antitype' of circumcision in the Old Testament, failed to safeguard the essential link between regeneration and personal faith. For Spurgeon, it was *faith* that was the New Testament antitype of circumcision, not baptism.[82] Arguing that baptism did the infant some 'good' in a sense that stopped short of actual regeneration (the covenantal view of his parents and the majority of the Puritans[83]) was still unacceptable, for it left the door open, in Spurgeon's mind, to baptismal regeneration and 'Popery'.

---

[79] D.W. Bebbington, *Evangelicalism in Modern Britain: A history from the 1730s to the 1980s* (London: Unwin Hyman, 1989), pp. 9-10.

[80] There is a significant amount of secondary literature available. The best treatments are Grass and Randall, 'C.H. Spurgeon on the Sacraments', pp. 63-67; and Fowler, *More Than a Symbol*, pp. 79-83. 200,000 copies of Spurgeon's 'Baptismal Regeneration' sermon had been sold by 1876. See C.H. Spurgeon, *The Metropolitan Tabernacle: Its History And Work* (London: Passmore and Alabaster, 1876), p. 80.

[81] C.H. Spurgeon, 'Signs Of The Times', *MTP*, Vol. 19, S. No. 1135, Luke 12.54-57, delivered 5 October 1873, p. 556.

[82] Grass and Randall, 'C.H. Spurgeon on the Sacraments', p. 60.

[83] There were some in the seventeenth century who would have been regarded as 'Puritan' but would not have held to the covenantal approach that Spurgeon was rejecting. See, e.g., C. Gribben, 'Defining the Puritans? The Baptism Debate in Cromwellian Ireland, 1654–56', *Church History*, Vol. 73, No. 1 (2004), pp. 63-89.

Given this line of reasoning, Spurgeon was not about to suggest that any form of baptism, including believers' baptism, did any 'good' in an objective, sacramental sense. In 'Children Brought To Christ, Not To The Font', Spurgeon declared, 'If you have baptism after you have come to Christ, well and good.' But, he warned, to think of such baptism as 'being inevitably connected with Christ, or as being the place to find Christ' was to go back 'to the beggarly elements of the old Romish harlot'.[84] Only when baptism was understood as the confessing believer's response to grace received earlier at conversion could both church and nation be proofed against the encroachment of Popery, and only then could the truth Spurgeon regarded as fundamental be safeguarded: regeneration took place immediately before conversion.

Spurgeon's antagonism to baptismal sacramentalism, then, was not just because of a culturally conditioned antipathy to Roman Catholicism and the Oxford Movement. Of course, and as I have argued, Spurgeon's opposition was certainly related to his antagonism both to 'Popery' and what he regarded as its Anglicised form, but it was more sharply focused, homing in on a particular aspect of High Church teaching. In speaking of baptism as the moment of regeneration, Roman Catholics and Anglican High Churchman alike were, in his opinion, guilty of minimizing the importance of conversion. It was *evangelical conversion* which was the essential beginning of communion with Christ and the only basis of future communion. The Roman Catholic and Tractarian approaches to baptism (and, in Spurgeon's view, any practice of infant baptism) blurred this fundamental truth, replacing it with 'ceremony' and 'superstition'.[85] The issue was non-negotiable for Spurgeon. For him, anything which obscured the centrality of conversion obscured Christ.

The title of Spurgeon's aforementioned sermon, 'Children Brought To Christ, Not To The Font', is, therefore, deeply revealing of his overriding concern. In this message, coming to Christ and infant baptism were set in direct opposition. It was crucial that children were brought to Christ as they grew up. By this Spurgeon meant that they should be prayed for, taught about Christ and shown that personal faith in Christ was the only way to a living relationship with him. Spurgeon's exposition was replete with praise for his mother and with exhortations to Christian parents.[86] By contrast, infant baptism, rather than making it more likely that the infant would exercise personal saving faith later in life, took the focus away from the need for such faith. In a telling comment Spurgeon declared, 'There is a mighty distinction ever to be held between the font and Christ, between the sprinkling of the priest and living faith in the Lord Jesus Christ.'[87] Conversion was the route to a living relationship with Jesus; infant baptism was a superstitious nonsense which kept people from exercising personal faith in Christ, encouraging them instead to trust in

---

[84] Spurgeon, 'Children Brought To Christ Not To The Font', p. 421.

[85] Spurgeon's emphasis on the 'superstition' he believed attached to infant baptism betrays an Enlightenment influence. In 'Who Should Be Baptized?' he tellingly said that he did not see how any 'rational creature' could endorse infant baptism. See pp. 351-52.

[86] Spurgeon, 'Children Brought To Christ, Not To The Font', pp. 417-18.

[87] Spurgeon, 'Children Brought To Christ, Not To The Font', p. 416.

'magic' and ceremony. Spurgeon expressed this with startling bluntness: 'Faith is the way to Jesus, baptism is not.'[88]

All this means that Spurgeon did not believe that baptism was a communion with Christ in a sacramental sense – it was not 'the place to find Christ'. But it also shows that Spurgeon was not prepared for anything which appeared to obscure the route to true communion to go unchallenged. If baptism was not the place to find Christ then anything that hinted that it might be (baptismal sacramentalism or any form of infant baptism) was to be resolutely resisted, since finding and knowing Christ through the true route of conversion was of the essence of Christianity. And, more positively, baptism did connect with Spurgeon's stress on communion with Christ in a number of different, and very significant ways, as an exposition of what Spurgeon did believe about baptism will show.

Baptism as an Instructive Symbol

In Spurgeon's thinking baptism was, first of all, an instructive symbol which 'set forth' the central saving events of the gospel, namely the death and resurrection of Christ. The centrality of the cross for Spurgeon has already been made clear in this study. But the resurrection was also vital, not least because it was the 'confirmation' that the cross was accepted by God the Father 'for full atonement'.[89] Indeed, it was the 'seal to all [Christ's] claims'.[90] To question the historicity of the resurrection was, Spurgeon warned, to question 'the whole of our faith'.[91] He was adamant that it was only through trust in Christ and these great saving events that salvation could be found.[92] The cross and the resurrection were the two closely related, indispensable truths which were at the heart of the Christian gospel.

Spurgeon believed that in baptism these fundamental gospel truths were set forth with particular clarity. Believers' baptism, with its dying and rising imagery, portrayed to Christians their own 'death, burial, and resurrection with Jesus'.[93] In his sermon, 'Baptism – A Burial', Spurgeon spoke at some length of how baptism pictured the Christian's 'representative union' with Christ. A believer was not baptized into Christ's life or example, but into his death. Full immersion showed

---

[88] Spurgeon, 'Children Brought To Christ, Not To The Font', p. 419; cf. p. 421.

[89] C.H. Spurgeon, 'Mouth And Heart', *MTP*, Vol. 32, S. No. 1898, delivered 25 April 1886, p. 249. Cf. C.H. Spurgeon, 'The First Appearance Of The Risen Lord To The Eleven', *MTP*, Vol. 33, S. No. 1958, Luke 24.36-44, delivered 10 April 1887, p. 223.

[90] C.H. Spurgeon, 'The Resurrection Of Our Lord Jesus', *MTP*, Vol. 28, S. No. 1653, 2 Timothy 2.8, delivered 9 April 1882, p. 197.

[91] Spurgeon, 'The First Appearance Of The Risen Lord To The Eleven', p. 223.

[92] Spurgeon, 'Mouth And Heart', pp. 250-52.

[93] Spurgeon, *Evening By Evening*, p. 281. This was emphasised in letters given to those baptized at the Tabernacle. See 'Printed Letter from Susannah Spurgeon Addressed to Women Candidates for Baptism at the Tabernacle', Spurgeon's College, Heritage Room (Display Case 7).

dramatically that a confessing believer shared in the benefits of the atonement.[94] But Christ had not only died and been buried on behalf of believers, he had also been raised on their behalf. A believer's rising up out of the water symbolised that he or she was now spiritually alive: they had received 'resurrection-life in Christ Jesus'.[95] Such baptism also spoke of how salvation was a work of grace. In an evangelistic message, preached in 1873 and entitled 'Good News For The Lost', Spurgeon stated that it was impossible for people to save themselves, for it was *dead* people who were buried with Christ in baptism. There was 'no improving the old nature', he insisted. Rather, it had to die and be buried. The scriptural command was not, 'Ye must be improved', but, 'Ye must be born again.'[96]

Of course, for Spurgeon baptism did not effect what it symbolised; it was merely an illustration of what it set forth. Baptism spoke of the need for regeneration but it did not convey the benefits of regeneration, just as it proclaimed a believer's union with Christ but played no part in effecting such a union. For baptism to be an instructive symbol it had to point away from itself and point to Christ. And, crucially, the one being baptized had to be a committed believer who had already received all the benefits of which baptism spoke. Any other approach to baptism would, for Spurgeon, blur the focus on the gospel, rather than clarifying it. Nevertheless, Spurgeon believed that if the rite was (to his mind) properly understood and practised, then it was an invaluable aid in helping to illustrate, explain and apply fundamental gospel truths. Baptism was an 'embodied creed' which showed the way to communion with Christ. As such it spoke powerfully to believers and unbelievers alike.[97]

Obedience to Christ's Command

When someone responded to the gospel which believers' baptism so vividly illustrated, it was vital that they went on to submit to baptism themselves. Spurgeon argued this with reference to the preaching of the apostles and the examples of conversions and baptisms recorded in Acts.[98] There was also the baptism of Christ to consider. Believers were bound to imitate the example of their Lord who, in submitting to John's baptism, had himself shown obedience to his Father.[99] Finally,

---

[94] C.H. Spurgeon, 'Baptism – A Burial', p. 619.

[95] Spurgeon, 'Baptism – A Burial', p. 620. Cf. C.H. Spurgeon, 'What Doth Hinder Me To Be Baptized?', in 'Notebooks With Sermon Outlines, Vols 2, 4-9', Vol. 5, S. No. 241, Acts 8.36.

[96] C.H. Spurgeon, 'Good News For The Lost', *MTP*, Vol. 19, S. No. 1100, Luke 19.10, delivered 9 March 1873, pp. 141-42.

[97] Spurgeon, 'Baptism – A Burial', p. 621.

[98] See, e.g., Spurgeon, 'Belief, Baptism, Blessing', pp. 457-65.

[99] C.H. Spurgeon, 'Voices From The Excellent Glory', *MTP*, Vol. 16, S. Nos 909-10, Matt 3.16,17; Matt 17.5; John 12.28, delivered 9 January 1870, p. 23; *Autobiography*, Vol. 1, p. 154; *The Gospel of the Kingdom. A Popular Exposition Of The Gospel According to Matthew* (London: Passmore and Alabaster, 1893), pp. 12-13. Many of the baptismal hymns in

and most importantly, on the basis of texts such as Matthew 28.19-20 and especially Mark 16.16 from the long ending of Mark's Gospel Spurgeon insisted that to be baptized was a clear command of Christ himself to the new believer.[100] For Spurgeon, it was axiomatic that all such commands had to be obeyed promptly.

It was rare for Spurgeon to make any extended comment about baptism without emphasising the close connection he believed there to be between submitting to the rite and obedience to Christ. As already noted, this was Spurgeon's stress in 'The Good Ananias, A Lesson For Believers', despite his text being from Acts 9. In another message, 'Elijah's Plea', preached in 1884 from 1 Kings 18.36 and the words 'Let it be known that I have done all these things at thy word', Spurgeon issued the following challenge,

> [W]ill you be obedient to Jesus in everything? If you would have Christ as Saviour, you must also take him for a King. Therefore it is that he puts it to you: 'He that believeth and is baptized shall be saved.' Will baptism save me? Assuredly not, for you have no right to be baptized until you are saved by faith in Jesus Christ; but remember, if Christ gives you the command – if you accept him as King – you are bound to obey him.[101]

This was typical of Spurgeon's thinking. There was no connection between baptism and salvation but there was a very important connection between baptism and faithful discipleship. Any Christian who resisted the clear command of Christ to be baptized was being disobedient to their King. If Christians were not willing to obey Christ in 'everything' they were not, by definition, living as faithful disciples. Because baptism was, as the title to a message preached in 1889 declared, 'Essential To Obedience', it was essential to faithful Christian living as well.[102]

For Spurgeon the issue was, of course, *believers'* baptism. It was not enough for a Christian to point to their baptism as an infant and claim that the command of Christ had been fulfilled in their life, for a Christian was bound to do as Christ commanded in the order he commanded it.[103] Consequently, it can seem surprising that Spurgeon had a high regard for the piety of many paedobaptists. These included, of course, seventeenth-century Puritans, such as Thomas Brooks and Richard Sibbes, as well as eighteenth-century evangelicals, such as George Whitefield and John Wesley, but his admiration for evangelical paedobaptists was not confined to the church triumphant.

Spurgeon (ed.), *Our Own Hymn Book* spoke of Christ's example and the need for Christians to follow. See, e.g., Nos 925 and 927.

[100] See, e.g., C.H. Spurgeon, 'The Power Of The Risen Saviour', *MTP*, Vol. 20, S. No. 1200, Matthew 28.18-20, delivered 25 October 1874, p. 611; and 'Preach, Preach, Preach Everywhere', *MTP*, Vol. 15, S. No. 900, Mark 16.15,16, n.d., pp. 628-29.

[101] C.H. Spurgeon, 'Elijah's Plea', *MTP*, Vol. 31, S. No. 1832, 1 Kings 18.36, delivered 9 November 1884, p. 179. Cf. 'To You', *MTP*, Vol. 50, S. No. 2899, Acts 13.26, delivered 9 July 1876, p. 429.

[102] C.H. Spurgeon, 'Baptism Essential To Obedience', *MTP*, Vol. 39, S. No. 2339, Mark 16.16, delivered 13 October 1889, pp. 601-12.

[103] C.H. Spurgeon, 'Waiting Only Upon God', *NPSP*, Vol. 3, S. No. 144, Psalm 62.5, delivered 2 August 1857, p. 300; 'Baptism Essential To Obedience', p. 605.

His relationships with his own parents and grandparents remained very strong and Spurgeon appointed two Independents, George Rogers and Vernon Charlesworth, to be, respectively, principal of his Pastors' College and headmaster of his Stockwell Orphanage.[104] Although Charlesworth was later baptized as a believer at the Tabernacle, Rogers remained a lifelong paedobaptist. Spurgeon had an extremely close working relationship with Rogers and described his principal as not only 'orthodox in doctrine', but also 'earnest', 'devout' and 'liberal of spirit'.[105] How did Spurgeon reconcile his view – that believers' baptism was essential to obedience and thus to faithful discipleship – with his warm estimate of someone like Rogers?

Spurgeon squared the circle by allowing that everyone needed to be convinced of the necessity of believers' baptism in their own 'consciences'.[106] This Enlightenment stress on the individual conscience had been present in his letters to his family written around the time of his own baptism as a believer. For example, on 11 June 1850 Spurgeon had written to his mother stating that, in the matter of baptism, they 'ought both to follow our own consciences'.[107] This approach gave him some latitude and made it possible for him to maintain close working friendships with evangelical paedobaptists who were at one with him in other ways. But Spurgeon still insisted on calling all paedobaptists 'unbaptized'[108] and, as we have seen, he could speak vehemently against infant baptism. What is clear is that, as to his *own* conscience Spurgeon was fully persuaded that to be baptized as a believer was Christ's command. People who worked closely with him had to accept that he would not soften his line on this and that they might face some uncomfortable moments as a result. The compilers of the *Autobiography* regarded the appointments of Rogers and Charlesworth as evidence of Spurgeon's 'catholicity of spirit'.[109] One is tempted to suggest that it actually said more for the 'liberal spirit' of a man like Rogers, who was willing to accept that Spurgeon's distaste for infant baptism would not remain hidden.

If Spurgeon could make allowances for paedobaptists whose consciences had led them to conclude in favour of infant baptism, he had no patience with those who regarded believers' baptism as simply unimportant and who could not see the need for it. In the course of 'Elijah's Plea' he declared,

> If instead of saying 'Be baptized' [Christ] had simply said, 'Put a feather in your cap', you might have asked, 'Will putting a feather in my cap save me?' No, but you are

---

[104] See Spurgeon, *Autobiography*, Vol. 2, pp. 147-48; Vol. 3, p. 177. Rogers first became actively involved in helping Spurgeon in 1857; Charlesworth was appointed to his role at the Orphanage in 1869.

[105] Spurgeon (ed.), *Sword and Trowel*, April 1870, p. 146.

[106] Cf. Grass and Randall, 'C.H. Spurgeon on the Sacraments', p. 58.

[107] C.H. Spurgeon to Eliza Spurgeon, 11 June 1850, in Spurgeon, *Autobiography*, Vol. 1, p. 125.

[108] See, e.g., Spurgeon's remarks in 'Meeting Of Our Own Church', *MTP*, Vol. 7, 8 April 1861, p. 260.

[109] Spurgeon, *Autobiography*, Vol. 3, p. 177.

bound to do it because he bids you. If he had said, 'Put a stone in your pocket, and carry it with you'; if that were Christ's command, it would be needful that you take the stone, and carry it with you. The less there seems to be of importance about a command, often the more hinges on it ... I want you, if you would be Christ's, to be just like the brave men that rode at Balaclava.[110]

In the final sentence of this extract Spurgeon was referring to the incident when, at the 1854 battle of Balaclava in the Crimean War, Lord Cardigan had led the British light cavalry in a suicidal charge against Russian artillery positions. Cardigan had misunderstood an order from his superior, Lord Lucan, and the ensuing charge was pointless, resulting only in great loss of life. Yet this tragic instance of British military bungling had become immortalised as an example of bravery and heroism partly thanks to Tennyson's famous poem, 'The Charge of the Light Brigade'. This Spurgeon proceeded to invoke,

> Yours not to reason why;
> Yours but to do and die.[111]

Spurgeon's point was this: where a clear command of Christ was concerned unconditional, even unquestioning, obedience was required, however unimportant the command appeared to be.

Spurgeon's language, particularly his comparisons with picking up stones and putting feathers in caps, might seem to suggest that baptism was of little importance to him. His comparison with the Light Brigade could even be read as implying that baptism itself was, somehow, pointless. But such a reading would be mistaken. Careful consideration of the context indicates that Spurgeon's comments were aimed particularly at those who were saying that, if baptism was not essential to salvation, then, consequently, there was no need for it at all. Spurgeon believed wholeheartedly in the first part of this proposition, baptism was not essential for salvation. But the second part of the proposition, the idea that baptism was, therefore, optional, most certainly did not follow in his thinking. Indeed, it was anathema to Spurgeon, giving rise to his rather scornful argument *ad hominem* even the seemingly trivial commands of Christ ought to be obeyed. Saying this did not mean that he himself regarded baptism as trivial, or that the command to be baptized was a trivial one, merely that, if any Christian did (wrongly) think in these ways, that was still no reason to play fast and loose with Christ's 'orders'. The quotation from 'Elijah's Plea' is evidence not of a low view of the importance of baptism (although it is certainly yet further confirmation that his view was not sacramental) but of an

---

[110] Spurgeon, 'Elijah's Plea', p. 179.

[111] Spurgeon, 'Elijah's Plea', p. 179. Tennyson's actual lines were: 'Theirs not to reason why / Theirs but to do and die.' The poem was written in 1854, the same year as the battle of Balaclava itself.

extremely high view of the importance of obedience to Christ.[112] It was not the grim reality of the events at Balaclava that Spurgeon had in mind when he declared, 'Yours not to reason why ...' Rather it was the heroic bravery of Tennyson's Light Brigade, who obeyed their leader wholeheartedly and unquestioningly, that Spurgeon was invoking. Baptism was effectively the 'badge' of such obedient, faithful, full-blooded discipleship.[113]

Obedience to Christ was extremely important to Spurgeon's understanding of communion with Christ. In a message on John 15.14, 'Ye are my friends, if ye do whatsoever I command you', Spurgeon, declared, firstly, that to be called the friend of Christ was 'the highest honour in the world' and, secondly, that active obedience to Christ 'set the seal' on the friendship begun at conversion and was the means of access to the 'circle of [Christ's] personal friendship'. An appreciation of these truths should 'transfigure' a believer's attitude to obedience. The obverse, of course, was also true. Those who did not obey Christ were not his friends. Overall, the message was clear: those who wanted to get into and maintain 'full fellowship' with Christ had to be obedient to him.[114]

Spurgeon's message on John 15.14, which was entitled 'The Friends Of Jesus', did not mention baptism explicitly, although there was perhaps an echo of Spurgeon's own experience of baptism in his comment that obedience to Christ could be difficult when it clashed with the wishes of loved parents.[115] By contrast, in the sermon 'Baptism Essential To Obedience' the focus on baptism was, obviously, overt. In this message Spurgeon used an illustration which would have resonated with many of the solid middle-class families who formed a significant portion of those who filled the pews of the Tabernacle. If someone asked a servant to do something for them and the servant refused, then what would be the result? The servant would be asked to leave the family's employment and consequently the family home.[116] Servants of Jesus needed to take note, for the implication was clear. Those who wanted to remain under Christ's roof, in close contact with him, needed to obey him, not least in baptism.

---

[112] This is also true of other instances where Spurgeon deployed similar arguments. See, e.g., C.H. Spurgeon, 'Open Profession Required', 'Notebooks With Sermon Outlines, Vols 2, 4-9', Vol. 3, S. No. 158, Matthew 10. 32,33: 'Men should not get into a habit of enquiring the "why" and "wherefore" of a plain and positive command – let them rather obey.' An earlier comment made it clear that one area which Spurgeon had in view was 'submission to the ordinances'. Cf. Spurgeon, 'Baptism Essential To Obedience', p. 608: '(I)f the Lord Jesus Christ had said, "Pick up six stones off the ground ..." Somebody would have said, "That stone picking is non-essential." It becomes essential as soon as Christ commands it.' But in neither message did Spurgeon want to minimize baptism. In 'Open Profession Required', a list of additional reasons why submission to the ordinances was important was provided.

[113] Cf. Spurgeon, 'Preach, Preach, Preach Everywhere', p. 628.

[114] C.H. Spurgeon, 'The Friends Of Jesus', *MTP*, Vol. 26, S. No. 1552, John 15.14, delivered 8 August 1880, pp. 445-49.

[115] Spurgeon, 'The Friends Of Jesus', p. 451.

[116] Spurgeon, 'Baptism Essential To Obedience', p. 607.

Baptism loomed large in Spurgeon's thinking as a test of obedience for a number of reasons. Firstly, Spurgeon did believe that the rite should ordinarily follow soon after someone's conversion experience.[117] Baptism, then, was an early and vital test of a believer's commitment. If Christians were not willing to be obedient to this command then their lives as disciples would be starting off on the wrong trajectory. Secondly, believers' baptism was a very public act. When Spurgeon commented, on one of the anniversaries of his own baptism, that it was 'exactly twenty-four years this night that I put on the Lord Jesus Christ publicly in baptism, avowing myself to be his servant', the word 'publicly' was a crucial one.[118] His had been an open avowal in an open river. Thirdly, such a public commitment was costly. 'It seemed like coming away from all the Christian people I knew',[119] Spurgeon said of his own baptism, which had been difficult for him in other ways as his accounts of his 'timidity' as he approached his baptism bear out.[120] But, he declared in 1889, although his baptism had been a 'trial' at the time it had taken place, it had proved hugely beneficial to his character.[121] He suspected that because baptism could be difficult and demand sacrifices some Christians drew back from it, preferring 'cowardly quietness' to outward profession.[122] Although he was prepared to allow that some of these secret believers were truly regenerate, he insisted that saving faith, as portrayed in the scriptures, was 'confessing', 'open' and 'working'.[123] In 'Baptism Essential To Obedience', Spurgeon quoted two texts which he repeatedly cited when speaking of baptism: Matthew 10.32-33 and Romans 10.9, with their emphases on public 'acknowledgement' and confession of Christ coupled with faith in him.[124] He was sure that baptism was 'God's way of openly confessing our faith', going so far as to say that God 'required it to be added' to faith.[125] In short, although any command of Christ had to be obeyed, there were particular reasons why Spurgeon gave special attention to the command to be baptized. Failure to obey in this would most likely lead to loss of communion with Christ and feeble, half-hearted Christian living. Conversely, obedience at this point would be character-building and would

---

[117] C.H. Spurgeon, 'He That Believeth Shall Not Make Haste', 'Notebooks With Sermon Outlines, Vols 2, 4-9', Vol. 5, S. No. 255, Isaiah 28.16; 'Belief, Baptism, Blessing', p. 461.

[118] C.H. Spurgeon, 'The Ear Bored With An Aul', *MTP*, Vol. 20, S. No. 1174, Exodus 21.5,6, p. 293. The sermon is n.d., assuming Spurgeon's recollection was correct, it was delivered on 3 May 1878.

[119] C.H. Spurgeon, 'Pressing Questions Of An Awakened Mind', *MTP*, Vol. 26, S. No. 1520, Acts 9.5,6, n.d., p. 91.

[120] Spurgeon, *Autobiography*, Vol. 1, p. 152.

[121] C.H. Spurgeon, 'Filling With The Spirit, And Drunkenness With Wine', *MTP*, Vol. 35, S. No. 2111, Ephesians 5.18, delivered 26 May 1889, pp. 587-88.

[122] C.H. Spurgeon, 'Loyal To The Core', *MTP*, Vol. 26, S. No. 1512, 2 Samuel 15.21, n.d., pp. 8-9.

[123] Spurgeon, 'Baptism Essential To Obedience', pp. 601-607.

[124] For another example, see C.H. Spurgeon, 'The Dying Thief In A New Light', *MTP*, Vol. 32, S. No. 1881, Luke 23.40-42, delivered 23 August 1885, pp. 606-607.

[125] Spurgeon, 'Baptism Essential To Obedience', pp. 605-607.

likely lead on to a life of active, faithful discipleship springing from deep communion.

Baptism as Consecration to Christ

Closely related to Spurgeon's belief in the importance of baptism as obedient public profession was his conviction that it was a solemn pledge of absolute commitment to Christ as Lord. In a sermon entitled 'Loyal To The Core' he declared,

> It is best to begin the Christian life with thorough consecration ... This should be one of the earliest forms of our worship of our Master – this total resignation of ourselves to him. According to his word, the first announcement of our faith should be by baptism, and the meaning of baptism, or immersion in water, is death, burial and resurrection. As far as this point is concerned, the avowal is just this: 'I am henceforth dead to all but Christ, whose servant I now am. Henceforth let no man trouble me, for I bear in my body the marks of the Lord Jesus. The watermark is on me from head to foot. I have been buried with him in baptism unto death to show that henceforth I belong to him.'[126]

A number of Spurgeon's emphases here have been encountered already, for example, baptism understood as an open 'avowal' of Christ. But there was also a new note, at least one which had not been sounded as clearly in previously cited extracts, that of complete consecration to Christ. Believers were to consecrate themselves thoroughly to Christ as his servants and the way to do this was through baptism. The 'watermark' was a sign that Christians had pledged all to their saviour. Spurgeon applied the image of the 'watermark' explicitly to himself and his own baptism. In an autobiographical fragment contained in an undated message entitled 'Holding Fast Our Profession', he declared, 'I bear in my body that watermark'. He had, he said, risen from the 'liquid grave' and from that point onwards his life was 'consecrated' to God. Consequently, he was now bound to 'bear a life-long testimony'.[127] The baptized believer was fully consecrated to their Saviour. They had crossed the Rubicon and there was now no turning back.[128]

Consecration was extremely important to Spurgeon in his overall conception of the Christian life. He wrote and preached about it on numerous occasions[129] and, in Puritan fashion, he had written a prayer of consecration soon after his conversion. This was dated 1 February 1850 (i.e., before his baptism) and placed at the head of his diary. But Spurgeon came to regard his baptism – the 'watermark' that was on

---

[126] Spurgeon, 'Loyal To The Core', p. 7.

[127] C.H. Spurgeon, 'Holding Fast Our Profession', *MTP*, Vol. 32, S. No. 1897, Hebrews 10.23, n.d., p. 234.

[128] C.H. Spurgeon, 'The Way To Honour', *MTP*, Vol. 19, S. No. 1118, Proverbs 27.18, n.d., p. 353; cf. Spurgeon, *Autobiography* 1, p. 149.

[129] E.g. C.H. Spurgeon, 'Consecration Of Our Substance', in Spurgeon (ed.), *Sword and Trowel*, September 1876, p. 426; 'Consecration To God – Illustrated By Abraham's Circumcision', *MTP*, Vol. 14, S. No. 845, Genesis 17.1,2, delivered 13 December 1868, pp. 685-96.

him 'from head to foot' – as his true moment of consecration. Spurgeon's consecration prayer contained themes and language ('I yield myself up to Thee ... I would be for ever, unreservedly, perpetually, Thine')[130] which were later taken up into his thinking about baptism, and when he spoke of his own consecration it was his baptism, not his earlier prayer, to which he invariably referred.[131] Indeed, in 'Loyal To The Core', he went so far as to say,

> In Dr Doddridge's 'Rise and Progress of Religion in the Soul' there is a very solemn form of consecration, which he recommends young men to sign when they give themselves to Christ. I cannot say that I can commend it, though I practised it, for I fear there is something of legality about it, and that it may bring the soul into bondage.[132]

Spurgeon believed in the importance of consecration but he had come to disagree with the eighteenth-century Independent Doddridge, and the Puritans upon whom Doddridge was at this point leaning, as to the way consecration should be made. In the *Autobiography* Spurgeon stated, 'Mr Doddridge has recommended a solemn covenant between the soul and God, to be signed and sealed with due deliberation and most fervent prayer ... I conceive that burial with Christ in baptism is a far more Scriptural and expressive sign of dedication.'[133] Here Spurgeon turns his back on an aspect of Puritan spirituality, as mediated through Doddridge, replacing it with something more 'Baptist'. Referring again to his own baptism, Spurgeon declared the memory of it had 'often operated' as both a 'spur to duty' and a 'seal of consecration'.[134] His baptism at Isleham Ferry had been the scene of his entire consecration and 'surrender' to Christ. It set the tone for the way he wanted to live his life: complete surrender to Christ his Lord.[135]

Baptism and the Church

The material covered so far in this chapter focuses on the relationship between baptism and the individual. But Spurgeon believed that an important relationship also existed between baptism and the church. In 'Baptism Essential To Obedience', Spurgeon declared that the open confession that baptism represented was vital because it was 'necessary to the very existence of the church of God'. Spurgeon sought to draw out what he believed were the logical consequences of a faith that was not openly confessed:

---

[130] Spurgeon, *Autobiography*, Vol. 1, p. 129.
[131] See, e.g., Spurgeon, 'The Way To Honour', p. 353.
[132] Spurgeon, 'Loyal To The Core', p. 8.
[133] Spurgeon, *Autobiography*, Vol. 1, pp. 150-51. Cf. *The Saint And His Saviour*, p. 262.
[134] Spurgeon, *Autobiography*, Vol. 1, p. 153.
[135] The importance of baptism as a time of complete surrender and consecration to Christ was also part of Spurgeon's preaching to others. See, Spurgeon, 'Who Should Be Baptized?', pp. 357-58.

[I]f I may be a believer, and never confess my faith, you may be a believer, and never confess your faith, and all round we should have a company of men believing, and none of them confessing; and where would be the outward ordinances of the Church of Christ at all? Where would be any minister? Where would be the setting up and growing of the kingdom of Christ? [136]

By the phrase 'the outward ordinances of the Church of Christ' Spurgeon was not referring to baptism or the Lord's Supper, which he normally described as 'ordinances of Christ', but to a broader range of churchly activities (for example, preaching and prayer) and offices (for example, that of deacon).[137] Baptism was the open confession of faith which was necessary for the existence of the church and its different 'ordinances'. This was vital because it was the church, here conceived of as gathered congregations of freely confessing baptized believers,[138] that was the instrument of the 'setting up' and 'growing' of Christ's kingdom.

Spurgeon was also clear that commitment to a church was absolutely necessary for believers themselves. True, for Spurgeon, faith and discipleship were deeply personal. There was a strong 'enlightened' emphasis in Spurgeon's thinking on the individual and this could be seen in his approach to baptism – personal repentance and faith must precede personal baptism.[139] This stress on the individual could lead to comments which, taken in isolation, appear to minimize the importance of the church. Mark Hopkins cites one such statement from a Spurgeon sermon entitled 'The Man Of Sorrows' which was preached in 1873. In this message Spurgeon declared, 'The church is only the aggregation of individuals, and if any good is to be done it must be performed by individuals.' Spurgeon even went on to refer to the church as an 'abstraction'.[140] On the basis of this comment, Hopkins suggests

---

[136] Spurgeon, 'Baptism Essential To Obedience', p. 607.

[137] In a message in Volume 7 of the early sermon notebooks, Spurgeon distinguished between ordinances of 'God's House' (e.g., public worship, the ministry), ordinances of the church (e.g., excommunication, deacons), and 'ordinances of Christ' (of which there were only two, baptism and the Lord's Supper). See C.H. Spurgeon, 'Keeping The Ordinances', 'Notebooks With Sermon Outlines, Vols 2, 4-9', Vol. 7, S. No. 333, 1 Corinthians 11.2. For a similar, inclusive use of the word 'ordinance', see *The Baptist Catechism: Commonly Called Keach's Catechism* (Philadelphia: American Baptist Publication Society, 1851 [1677]), as cited by Fowler, *More Than a Symbol*, p. 18. For a further instance of Spurgeon referring to baptism as an 'ordinance of Christ', see *Autobiography*, Vol. 1, p. 154.

[138] For more insight into Spurgeon's ecclesiology, see C.H. Spurgeon, 'Abram's Call; Or, Half-Way And All The Way', *MTP*, Vol. 34, S. No. 2011, Genesis 11.31; 12.5, delivered 26 February 1888, pp. 122-23.

[139] For an especially strong and sustained stress on this point, see Spurgeon, 'Who Should Be Baptized?', pp. 351-55.

[140] C.H. Spurgeon, 'The Man Of Sorrows', *MTP*, Vol. 19, S. No. 1099, Isaiah 53.3, delivered 2 March 1873, p. 131. Cf. M. Hopkins, *Nonconformity's Romantic Generation: Evangelical and Liberal Theologies in Victorian England* (Carlisle: Paternoster, 2004), p. 149. In making this statement, Spurgeon may have wanted to emphasise a gathered church ecclesiology over against a parish system. The previous week a lecture by Spurgeon had been

Spurgeon had a weak ecclesiology, although he is careful to note that Spurgeon still attached 'a high practical importance' to the 'Church's fellowship and work'.[141] But even with this important qualification, the contention that Spurgeon's ecclesiology was 'weak' ought to be challenged.

The fundamental point to make is that the quotation from 'The Man Of Sorrows' was not Spurgeon's usual way of describing the church, which he often spoke of as a glorious institution.[142] Although Spurgeon did stress the importance of the individual he was also aware that such an emphasis could tend to 'isolation' and to a believer forgetting they had 'any connection with other people'.[143] To counter this danger Spurgeon regularly underlined the importance of commitment to a local church. Faith was personal but it was not private; it had to be expressed through active involvement in a local body of believers. And baptism was not just individual and personal; it was also 'Christ's own way' of entering the visible church and was the 'mark of distinction between the Church and the world'.[144] Although New Park Street / Metropolitan Tabernacle had an open communion policy, with all Christians able to join in the celebration of the Lord's Supper, it also operated a 'closed membership', with only those baptized as believers able to join. Spurgeon had inherited this dual policy when he became pastor, but he thoroughly approved of it. Indeed, he said he would 'rather give up his pastorate' than admit anyone into church membership who had 'not been obedient to [their] Lord's command' to be baptized.[145] The church, conceived of as a gathered church of baptized believers, was vitally important for Spurgeon, whose ecclesiology was stronger than Hopkins allows.

A significant number of nineteenth-century Baptists, as Cross states, had an 'unecclesial view' of baptism.[146] In 1833, Isaiah Birt stated that he viewed baptism as a personal contract, 'an affair wholly between God and the individual'[147] and, in

---

published which attacked the link between church and state. See the notice in *MTP*, Vol. 19, p. 120. The lecture was originally delivered at the Metropolitan Tabernacle on 28 January 1873.

[141] Hopkins, *Nonconformity's Romantic Generation*, p. 149.

[142] In addition to the other messages cited in this paragraph, see, e.g., C.H. Spurgeon, 'The Glory, Unity, And Triumph Of The Church', *MTP*, Vol. 25. S. No. 1472, John 22.22-23, delivered 4 May 1879, pp.253-64. For Spurgeon's love for his own church, the Metropolitan Tabernacle, see 'Crowning Blessings Ascribed To God, *MTP*, Vol. 25. S. No. 1475, Psalm 65.11, delivered 18 May 1879, pp. 289-300. This last named message was the second sermon Spurgeon preached to celebrate his twenty-five years of ministry in London.

[143] C.H. Spurgeon, 'The Light Of The World', *MTP*, Vol. 19, S. No. 1109, Matthew 5.14, delivered 27 April 1873, p. 244.

[144] Spurgeon, *Autobiography*, Vol. 1, pp. 149, 152. Cf. Grass and Randall, 'C.H. Spurgeon on the Sacraments', p. 61.

[145] Spurgeon, 'Meeting Of Our Own Church', p. 260.

[146] Cross, *Baptism and the Baptists*, p. 13.

[147] I. Birt, *Personal Religion Vindicated in Relation to Christian Baptism* (London: G. Wightman, 1836 [1833?]), pp. 13-14, as cited by Briggs, *English Baptists of the Nineteenth Century*, p. 53.

1877, John Clifford declared that baptism in the scriptures was 'uniformly and exclusively ... prescribed as a solemn transaction between the soul and the Saviour'. Therefore, baptism was not necessary 'in order to entrance [sic] upon a church state'.[148] It has already been shown that Spurgeon's emphasis on the corporate dimension of discipleship led him to reject this unecclesial approach. To sum up, Spurgeon argued that baptism was needed, firstly, because for the church to exist faith obviously had to be publicly professed and, secondly, because individuals must take their places within a local church if they were to live as faithful disciples of Christ. These two arguments were different sides of the same coin and both highlight the centrality of the church in God's purposes. Once again, the importance of baptism to Spurgeon is underlined, and this time the rite was significant because of the connection it made between the believer and Christ's people.

Conclusion

Spurgeon's own baptism had been the moment when he had confessed his new-found faith in Christ in obedience to Christ's command. Furthermore, baptism was the point at which he had consecrated himself wholly and publicly to Christ, declaring that he would serve him in the church and in the world. These emphases were at the heart of his mature theology of baptism. He was adamant that baptism was not the place to find Christ although, paradoxically, this insistence is actually revealing of the overriding importance of communion with Christ to him. Spurgeon was convinced that communion with Christ began at conversion, and he was further convinced that both infant baptism and any form of sacramentalism in respect of baptism took the focus away from conversion, thus obscuring the only route to true communion. As a consequence, he was determined that both infant baptism and baptismal sacramentalism should be rigorously opposed. But if baptism was not the way to find Christ, it was still vital to be baptized as a believer in order for the Christian to enjoy continuing communion with Christ. Even the trivial commands of Christ had to be obeyed in order for communion to be maintained and deepened, and baptism which, in reality, was far from a trivial matter in Spurgeon's thinking, was most definitely commanded by Christ. How could believers hope to experience fellowship with Christ if they were disobedient to him? Certainly, Spurgeon regarded his own baptism as a believer as being essential to ongoing communion with his Lord.

Spurgeon's approach to baptism was, in one sense, deeply personal. But his stress on the individual did not mean he neglected the church. He held to a gathered-church ecclesiology in which baptism played a central part. Uniting visibly with the church of Christ, something which took place in the act of believers' baptism, was not an optional extra, rather it was vital. Following his conversion, Spurgeon had held that

---

[148] J. Clifford in the *General Baptist Magazine*, December 1877, pp. 448-49, as cited by Briggs, *English Baptists of the Nineteenth Century*, p. 135. Cf. Cross, *Baptism and the Baptists*, p. 14.

he could not in conscience enjoy fellowship with Christ's people at the Lord's Supper until he had been baptized as a believer. Once he had been baptized he could begin to enjoy communion with Christ's people in a richer way.

As we prepare to switch focus – from considering issues of spiritual formation to analysing how spirituality was sustained – a brief summary statement is in order. Spurgeon's upbringing had prepared him for his conversion. Although he believed that his union with Christ, and its security, had been established by God's eternal decree, he also believed that it was at the time of his conversion that his personal relationship with Christ began. Being baptized as a believer was a crucial next step following conversion, establishing him on the path of discipleship, a 'pilgrimage' that was both with Christ and to Christ. Baptism also led to a visible uniting with the people of Christ and to vigorous involvement in the life of the church and the world. As Spurgeon came up out of the River Lark on 3 May 1850, the trajectory of his life from that point onward had been set.

CHAPTER 5

The Bible:
'O living Christ, make this a living word to me'

It has been shown that Spurgeon's upbringing, conversion and baptism were fundamental to his early spiritual formation, and it has also been shown that they remained important to him throughout his life. The Puritan-influenced piety of his family continued to shape Spurgeon, with the books he had first discovered in his grandfather's house becoming the staple of his own library in London. Spurgeon's conversion experience, in which he came to Christ as a sinner, formed the pattern by which he would continue to approach Christ and enjoy communion with him. Spurgeon's baptism, which he experienced as public consecration to Jesus, was something he sought to live in the light of as he served Christ both in the church and in the wider world. Thus his upbringing, conversion and baptism all had ongoing significance in sustaining his spirituality.

Nevertheless, as Spurgeon's Christian life and ministry unfolded, a number of spiritual disciplines were also vital in sustaining his spiritual life. Prayer and frequent observance of the Lord's supper were extremely important in this regard, and these will be dealt with in chapters 6 and 7 respectively. But it was the Bible that was foundational to the nurturing of Spurgeon's spirituality and so this will be considered first. Indeed, the Bible was crucial for the whole of his Christian life and ministry. As far as spiritual formation was concerned, we have already seen that the Bible was central in Spurgeon's upbringing and that it was through the Bible being preached that he experienced conversion. Also, Spurgeon's desire to be baptized as a believer was decisively shaped by his consideration of various biblical passages. Later, in chapters 8 to 10 it will be shown that the Bible shaped the ways his spirituality was worked out in the church and the world. The scriptures were crucial to the spirituality of C.H. Spurgeon. This present chapter examines in detail the role the Bible played in sustaining his spiritual life.

To begin with, Spurgeon's approach to questions of biblical inspiration and authority will be analysed, together with the various factors – historical and cultural – which shaped this. The way Spurgeon read the scriptures will also be examined. The fact that the Bible was so crucial to Spurgeon could be regarded as undercutting the argument which is at the centre of this study, namely that 'communion with Christ and his people' is the integrating theme which helps us makes sense of Spurgeon's spirituality. How can the essence of Spurgeon's spiritual life be captured in a phrase which does not make explicit reference to the Bible? The second half of this chapter addresses this question, doing so through consideration of Spurgeon's

The Bible

method of biblical interpretation and by analysis of his ministry as a preacher and Bible commentator. Illumination of the ways he interpreted and used the Bible strengthens rather than weakens the argument of this study.

Inspiration and Authority

On one level, Spurgeon's views of biblical inspiration and authority are not difficult to state. With regard to inspiration, the approach he took at the beginning of his ministry can be seen from a sermon outline from Volume 2 of the pre-London notebooks. Spurgeon's text was Ephesians 6.17 and the message was entitled 'The Sword Of The Spirit'. It is possible this was from as early as 1851 and it is certainly no later than the first half of 1852.[1] The Holy Spirit, said Spurgeon, 'dictated' the words of scripture, acting as the 'great executive' for the 'glorious Trinity'. Spurgeon warned his agricultural, village hearers that, just as 'edged tools' were not to be played with, so they were to be careful with the sword of the word. Certainly, the 'measure of the blade' was not to be altered.[2] In another early sermon, contained in Volume 1 of the *New Park Street Pulpit*, Spurgeon repeated his conviction that the Bible was 'dictated by the Holy Spirit', indeed, 'each letter was penned with an Almighty finger'. In this sermon, preached on 15 March 1855 and entitled, simply, 'The Bible', Spurgeon went on to declare that the whole of scripture was 'untainted by any error'.[3] Spurgeon maintained this commitment to verbal inspiration throughout his ministry. For example, in a message preached in or after 1861 he affirmed his belief that the 'Spirit of God...dictated' the scriptures,[4] and in August 1888 he spoke of the 'infallible wisdom [of God]' dictating 'every syllable'.[5] In this last message Spurgeon was speaking specifically of the promises of Christ as revealed in the Bible, but his words were clearly reflective of an underlying attitude

---

[1] C.H. Spurgeon, 'The Sword Of The Spirit', 'Notebooks With Sermon Outlines, Vols 2, 4-9', Spurgeon's College, Heritage Room' (U.1), Vol. 2, S. No. 79, Ephesians 6.17. With regard to dating, this outline is the second in the notebook, although, as with all the outlines in this volume, it is n.d. There is a note at the back of the book which is dated 19 June 1852. Spurgeon recorded that he preached S. No. 128 in this book, 'The Corner Stone', Psalm 118.22, at various places in the summer of 1852, but it might possibly have been composed and originally given before this time.

[2] Spurgeon, 'The Sword Of The Spirit'.

[3] C.H. Spurgeon, 'The Bible', *New Park Street Pulpit (NPSP) / Metropolitan Tabernacle Pulpit (MTP)* (London: Passmore and Alabaster, 1856–1917), *NPSP*, Vol. 1, S. No. 15, Hosea 8.12, delivered 18 March 1855, pp. 110-12.

[4] C.H. Spurgeon, 'Renewing Strength', *MTP*, Vol. 29, S. No. 1756, Isaiah 40.31, n.d., p. 700. The earliest this could have been preached was 1861 as it was given in the Metropolitan Tabernacle. Cf. 'The Secret Food And The Public Name', *MTP*, Vol. 18, S. No. 1079, Jeremiah 15.16, n.d., p. 616.

[5] C.H. Spurgeon, 'The Message Of Our Lord's Love', *MTP*, Vol. 34, S. No. 2060, Mark 16.7, delivered 5 August 1888, p. 711. Cf. 'Search The Scriptures', *NPSP*, Vol. 4, S. No. 172, Isaiah 8.20, delivered 17 January 1858, p. 63.

that encompassed the whole of scripture and he was sure that both the Old and the New Testaments were in and of themselves the 'infallible' word of God.[6]

Spurgeon's estimate of the authority of scripture was couched in similar terms; indeed, he was certain the infallible word gave correspondingly 'infallible' direction for believers.[7] Tradition was not authoritative, neither was human reason. It was the Bible, and the Bible alone, which was the authority for the church and for individual Christians in all matters of doctrine and practice. As will be shown, all scripture had to be interpreted christologically and this governed the way the Bible functioned as an authority for Spurgeon. Nevertheless, his basic convictions are clear enough: firstly, God, through the agency of the Holy Spirit, had dictated every word of scripture from Genesis to Revelation and, secondly, scripture was authoritative for Christians.

Spurgeon's comments concerning the infallibility of the Bible should be taken as applying to scripture as originally given,[8] and he was clear that the Authorized Version (AV) contained errors of translation.[9] Nevertheless, Patricia Kruppa is right to note Spurgeon's strong commitment to the AV,[10] and he was usually content to accept its wording when preaching.[11] This was so even with regard to a verse like Job 19.25, rendered in the AV, 'I know that my Redeemer liveth, and that he shall stand at the latter day upon the earth.' Spurgeon was aware of some of the difficulties posed by the Hebrew text of this verse and yet, at the beginning of a sermon preached in 1876, he declared himself 'quite satisfied' with the AV translation.[12] The ensuing sermon was entitled 'Job's Sure Knowledge'.[13] Spurgeon's approach to biblical inspiration was not subtle and he always preferred to deal in certainties.

What role did Spurgeon ascribe to the human authors of scripture? Perhaps surprisingly, given his espousal of a dictation theory of biblical inspiration, the 'humanity' of the scriptures was very important to Spurgeon. This emphasis was

---

[6] C.H. Spurgeon, 'Paul – His Cloak And His Books', *MTP*, Vol. 9, S. No. 542, 2 Timothy 4.13, delivered 29 November 1863, p. 669.

[7] C.H. Spurgeon, 'The Talking Book', *MTP*, Vol. 17, S. No. 1017, Proverbs 6.22, delivered 22 October 1871, p. 590. Cf. 'Eyes Right', *MTP*, Vol. 34, S. No. 2058, Proverbs 4.25, delivered 14 July 1887, p. 694.

[8] C.H. Spurgeon, 'The Bible Tried And Proved', *MTP*, Vol. 35, S. No. 2084, Psalm 12.6, delivered 5 May 1889, p. 257.

[9] Spurgeon, 'Search The Scriptures', p. 59; 'The Bible Tried And Proved', p. 257.

[10] P.S. Kruppa, *Charles Haddon Spurgeon: A Preacher's Progress* (New York: Garland, 1982), pp. 190-91.

[11] For C.H. Spurgeon's positive estimate of the AV see, e.g., 'The Secret Food And The Public Name', p. 616.

[12] C.H. Spurgeon, 'Job's Sure Knowledge', *MTP*, Vol. 50, S. No. 2909, Job 19.25, delivered 10 September 1876, p. 541. Cf. *My Sermon Notes: A Selection From Outlines Of Discourses Delivered At The Metropolitan Tabernacle... From Genesis To Proverbs I to LXIV* (New York: Fleming H. Revell, n.d. [1884]), No. 40, Job 19.25, p. 243.

[13] Spurgeon, 'Job's Sure Knowledge', pp. 541, 549-50.

especially to the fore in his teaching on the Psalms. Writing in his Preface to Volume 6 of the *Treasury of David*, he described the book of Psalms, taken as a whole, as the 'tongue of saints'. By this Spurgeon meant that the book helped the Christian give voice to feelings which otherwise would have 'found no utterance'. The Psalms said what Christians themselves 'wished to say', Spurgeon declared.[14] The Psalter helped Christians vocalize their feelings of praise, thankfulness and petition.[15] It also helped believers express their penitence for sin. In his Preface to Volume 2 of the *Treasury*, Spurgeon wrote of his experience of commenting on Psalm 51. 'The Psalm is very human', he declared, 'its cries and sobs are of one born of a woman.'[16] For Spurgeon, the human author of this Psalm was unquestionably David and the occasion which had led to its composition was the exposure, by the prophet Nathan, of the act of adultery committed by the King with Uriah's wife, Bathsheba.[17] In Spurgeon's exposition of Psalm 51 he identified strongly with the penitent King both in his sense of sinfulness and in his trust in God for forgiveness.[18] Taken as a whole the Psalms provided a 'map' of spiritual experience, one that was complementary to *Pilgrim's Progress* and which, like Bunyan's allegory, traversed the valleys as well as the high points of the Christian life.[19] The experience of frail, indeed fallible human authors who gave voice not only to their triumphs but also to their failures provided a pattern for Christian believers whose own pilgrimage would also run the whole gamut of spiritual experience.

Nevertheless, in expounding the Psalms in a way that emphasised their humanity Spurgeon was careful to affirm that they were the word of God. Psalm 51, whilst being authentically 'human' was also 'freighted with an inspiration all divine'. Indeed, it was 'as if the Great Father were putting words into his child's mouth'.[20] A dictation theory of biblical inspiration thus coexisted with an exposition which stressed the humanity of the Psalm. Hopkins has noted Spurgeon's tendency to set different lines of thought alongside one another 'with little of the synthesis which might reduce their tension'. This was the case with regard to Spurgeon's Christology, as Hopkins shows. The deity and humanity of Christ are both stressed by Spurgeon with little thought as to how these might hold together at the centre.[21]

---

[14] C.H. Spurgeon, *The Treasury Of David: Containing An Original Exposition Of The Book Of Psalms; A Collection Of Illustrative Extracts From The Whole Range Of Literature; A Series Of Homiletical Hints Upon Almost Every Verse; And Lists Of Writers Upon Each Psalm* (7 Vols; London and Edinburgh: Marshall Brothers, n.d. [London: Passmore and Alabaster, 1869-1885]), Vol. 6, p. vii.

[15] See, e.g., C.H. Spurgeon, 'The Singing Pilgrim', *MTP*, Vol. 28, S. No. 1652, Psalm 119.54, n.d., pp. 181-92.

[16] Spurgeon, *Treasury of David*, Vol. 2, Preface, p. v.

[17] 2 Samuel 11.1 – 12.14; Spurgeon, *Treasury of David*, Vol. 2, p. 449.

[18] Spurgeon, *Treasury of David*, Vol. 2, pp. 449-56.

[19] Spurgeon, *Treasury of David*, p. vii.

[20] Spurgeon, *Treasury of David*, Vol. 2, Preface, p. v.

[21] M. Hopkins, *Nonconformity's Romantic Generation: Evangelical and Liberal Theologies in Victorian England* (Carlisle: Paternoster, 2004), p. 144.

Spurgeon's approach to the question of the authorship of scripture is another prime example of this tendency. The divine and human authorship of the Bible were both strongly affirmed and these two emphases were developed independently of one another with little thought given as to how they might cohere.

Where the two emphases – the divine and human aspects of scripture – do unite is in Spurgeon's understanding of the Bible as the Christian's fundamental authority. What was contained in the scriptures, whether it was a verse which began, 'Thus saith the Lord...', or whether it was a text which contained the words of a repentant sinner addressed directly to God, was fully *authoritative* for Christians. If a passage revealed truths about God, then those truths needed to be fully embraced; if it contained commands, then they needed to be obeyed (once they had been interpreted christologically); if it described the experience of a sinner returning to God, then this would provide a pattern for believers in a similar situation. The experiences and words of obviously ungodly characters were warnings to believers, revealing truths about the human condition and God and his dealings with the world. Whatever tensions there might be in Spurgeon's approach to the scriptures, this much was entirely consistent: he believed the Bible was authoritative. This commitment puts the Bible at the heart of his spirituality.

Historical and Cultural Influences

Spurgeon's views on the Bible were influenced by a range of historical and cultural factors. First of all, it should be noted that he appealed to a diverse array of historical figures as he defended his adherence to scripture as his infallible authority. In a message, 'The Word A Sword', preached in May 1887, Spurgeon made reference to a pantheon of Protestant and evangelical 'heroes' as he set out his commitment to the Bible and this sermon can be given an extended treatment.

'The Word A Sword' spanned just eleven pages in its printed form, making it slightly shorter than the average length for a published Spurgeon sermon. Yet within the space of these eleven pages there were references to John Owen, John Calvin, Martin Luther, George Whitefield, Isaac Watts and Augustine. Spurgeon also made a general reference to 'the Reformers' and evoked John Bunyan without actually naming him.[22] It was rare for Spurgeon to make this number of references to different historical figures in a sermon and his doing so on this occasion was significant. It is true that he did not mention all these men for precisely the same reasons. For example, Owen and Calvin were cited because of their careful exegesis of Spurgeon's text, Hebrews 4.12; Luther because of the theological 'conversion' he underwent through his engagement with the scriptures; and Whitefield because Spurgeon used an illustration of a man who had been converted when he had tried to imitate Whitefield's preaching. Some of the other references add to this diversity and

---

[22] C.H. Spurgeon, 'The Word A Sword', *MTP*, Vol. 34, S. No. 2010, Hebrews 4.12, delivered 17 May 1887, pp. 109 (Calvin and Owen), 113 (Luther), 115 (Whitefield), 117 (Watts), 118 (Augustine), 114 (Bunyan), and 120 (the 'Reformers').

certainly the different men are invoked in different ways within the sermon. Nevertheless, the preacher believed there was a common thread which linked all those cited together and made their collective use in this sermon especially appropriate. He was sure they all supported his basic commitment to the Bible as the authoritative, powerful word of God. The cumulative effect of the illustrations and references was to build a picture of a particular heritage, one in which the Protestant, Reformed, Puritan and evangelical were linked together. Spurgeon's suggestion was that throughout the ages this had been the tradition within which faithful, fruitful Christians had stood and, of course, it was with this tradition that he himself identified profoundly.[23]

Spurgeon showed no obvious awareness in 'The Word A Sword' of any of the nuances which distinguished the views of the scriptures held by the diverse array of figures he was citing. In spite of the differences between these men, all were co-opted to serve a common cause: Spurgeon's fight against the nineteenth-century figures he believed were betraying the scriptures. When the pastor of the Metropolitan Tabernacle appealed at the end of his message for his hearers to let the 'gospel of the Reformers' be their own gospel (with the word 'Reformers' used, it seems clear, without any real precision), it was an appeal to identify with a tradition the essence of which Spurgeon believed he could trace from Augustine through the different expressions of Reformed Protestantism and evangelicalism he had referred to.[24] This heritage was important to Spurgeon as he articulated his views on the Bible and it certainly helped shape his fundamental commitment to the scriptures.

Secondly, Spurgeon's views on the scriptures were influenced by Enlightenment thought. Enlightened patterns of thinking were to the fore in some of Spurgeon's arguments for his views of biblical inspiration and authority. Commenting on Psalm 119.129 in the *Treasury of David*, Spurgeon wrote that God's 'testimonies' are 'free from all error' and bear 'within themselves overwhelming self-evidence of their truth' being always 'clear', 'full', 'gracious' and 'mighty'. Immediately they enter the 'soul', Spurgeon added, 'they enlighten it'. In other words, the inherent qualities of the scriptures witnessed to their own truthfulness. Spurgeon's prayer was that the words of scripture might enter through the 'window' of his own understanding 'like the beams of the sun', thus illuminating the darkness of his mind.[25] Hopkins states that Spurgeon came to believe in the 'bankruptcy of reason and conscience' with 'rational philosophical arguments' virtually abandoned by 1860.[26] It is certainly true

---

[23] Cf. C.H. Spurgeon's comments in his 'Address to students of the Pastors' College, 1885' as cited in *Autobiography: Compiled from his Diary, Letters, and Records by his Wife and his Private Secretary* (4 Vols; London: Passmore and Alabaster, 1897-99), Vol. 4, p. 254.

[24] Spurgeon, 'The Word A Sword', p. 120.

[25] Spurgeon, *Treasury of David*, Vol. 6, p. 283. This volume was first published in 1882, see Preface, p. ix.

[26] Hopkins, *Nonconformity's Romantic Generation*, pp. 134-35. For reason as an important 'enlightened' characteristic, see H. Rosenblatt, 'The Christian Enlightenment' in S.J. Brown and T. Tackett (eds), *The Cambridge History of Christianity: Enlightenment,*

that Spurgeon could be negative about the power of human reason,[27] but, in the light of this material from the *Treasury of David*, Hopkins' view needs to be qualified.

The impress of enlightened thinking can also be discerned in the following quotation from a sermon on Jeremiah 15.15, 'Thy words were found, and I did eat them....' In this message, entitled 'The Secret Food And The Public Name', Spurgeon declared that the Bible was 'God's inspired teaching, infallible, and infinitely pure'. But how did he know this? Spurgeon continued,

> We accept it as the very word of the living God ... because we discern an inward evidence in the words themselves. They have come to us with a power that no other words had in them and we cannot be argued out of our conviction of their superlative excellence and divine authority ... When we speak God's truth, we speak what we do know, what we have tasted, and handled, and tested, and proved.[28]

The first sentence of this quotation links with the material from the *Treasury of David* cited in the previous paragraph: the scriptures carry within themselves evidence of their truthfulness. The final sentence is also shot through with 'enlightened' thinking, but here the scriptures have not only illuminated the 'darkness' of the 'mind' (Spurgeon's words from the *Treasury*) they have been tried and proved in his lived experience. Spurgeon's dominant argument for the truth and power of the scriptures was this experiential one.[29] Spurgeon spoke elsewhere of how the 'instructed believer' had 'imbibed' and 'assimilated' scripture to such an extent that its teaching flowed though his or her soul as blood flowed through the body.[30] Spurgeon urged all his hearers to take the Bible into their hearts and live it out.[31] When this happened all the truths of scripture would be 'verified' in their own lives.[32] Speaking personally, Spurgeon insisted that the Bible had 'proved' its own inspiration by inspiring him 'with its spirit', adding, 'We now live in the Word as fish in the stream; it is the element of our spiritual life.'[33] He held to the authority of the scriptures as tenaciously as he did primarily because the Bible was so deeply imbedded in his own experience. This is further evidence for locating the scriptures at the heart of Spurgeon's spirituality. It is also further evidence of Enlightenment thinking.

Reawakening and Revolution 1660-1815 (Cambridge: Cambridge University Press, 2006), pp. 284-88.

[27] For an example, see C.H. Spurgeon, 'Great Spoil', *MTP*, Vol. 28, S. No. 1641, Psalm 119.162, delivered 22 January 1882, p. 58.

[28] Spurgeon, 'The Secret Food And The Public Name', p. 619.

[29] As Hopkins notes, *Nonconformity's Romantic Generation*, pp. 135-36.

[30] Spurgeon, 'The Lover Of God's Law Filled With Peace', p. 39.

[31] Spurgeon, 'The Lover Of God's Law Filled With Peace', p. 38.

[32] C.H. Spurgeon, 'The Infallibility Of Scripture', *MTP*, Vol. 34, S. No. 2013, Isaiah 1.20, delivered 11 March 1888, p. 158.

[33] Spurgeon, 'The Lover Of God's Law Filled With Peace', p. 39.

The Bible

Thirdly, another cultural influence, namely Romanticism, was at work shaping Spurgeon's views. The Romantic movement was far more important to Spurgeon than has often been recognised, and delineating some its leading features is important for this study. Romanticism, like the Enlightenment, is not easy to define.[34] It arose in part as a reaction against enlightened thinking, certainly against rationalism.[35] Whereas the Enlightenment emphasised reason, Romanticism exalted the will and emotion, and tended to dwell on concepts such as 'awe', 'wonder' and 'mystery'.[36] Nature was important (indeed for some Romantics this could tip over into pantheism),[37] and the 'ancient' was usually preferred to the 'modern',[38] with a particular penchant for 'medievalism'.[39] In the British Isles, such a mood was represented in art by the critic, John Ruskin, in prose by the novelist, Sir Walter Scott, and in poetry by the lake poets, Samuel Taylor Coleridge and William Wordsworth.[40] What Douglas Hedley describes as the 'noumenal seas, mountains and lakes' of Coleridge's the *Ancient Mariner* are deeply revealing of the Romantic stress on nature, for example.[41] Thus, for all its diversity, those who were imbued with the Romantic temper tended to exhibit certain distinguishing features.

How did Romanticism shape Spurgeon's approach to the scriptures? David Bebbington has shown that eighteenth- and early nineteenth- century evangelicals who were not influenced by Romanticism, such as Philip Doddridge and Henry Martyn, did not believe in verbal inspiration.[42] Doddridge had written of different 'modes' of inspiration, only one of which, according to Doreen Rosman, was 'divine dictation'.[43] Indeed, Charles Simeon, a man with impeccable evangelical credentials,

---

[34] B.M.G. Reardon, *Religion in the Age of Romanticism: Studies in Early Nineteenth Century Thought* (Cambridge: Cambridge University Press, 1985), p. 1.

[35] S. Gilley, 'Introduction', in S. Gilley and B. Stanley (eds), *World Christianities, c.1815–c. 1914* (Cambridge: Cambridge University Press, 2006), p. 3.

[36] Gilley, 'Introduction', p. 3; D.W. Bebbington, *Holiness in Nineteenth-Century England* (Carlisle: Paternoster, 2000), p. 13.

[37] Reardon, *Religion in the Age of Romanticism*, p. 5.

[38] Bebbington, *Holiness in Nineteenth-Century England*, p. 13.

[39] Reardon, *Religion in the Age of Romanticism*, pp. 11-12.

[40] For examples of Wordsworth's poetry which exemplify Romantic sensibilities, see the extracts from *Tintern Abbey*, *The Excursion* and *The Prelude* which are cited by Reardon, *Religion in the Age of Romanticism*, pp. 4-5.

[41] D. Hedley, 'Theology and the revolt against the Enlightenment', in Gilley and Stanley (eds), *World Christianities, c.1815–c.1914*, p. 30.

[42] D.W. Bebbington, *Evangelicalism in Modern Britain: A history from the 1730s to the 1980s* (London: Unwin Hyman, 1989), pp. 86-87. This argument has not been overturned by K.J. Stewart, 'The evangelical doctrine of Scripture, 1650–1850: a re-examination of David Bebbington's theory', in M.A.G. Haykin and K.J. Stewart (eds), *The Emergence of Evangelicalism: Exploring Historical Continuities* (London: IVP, 2008), pp. 394-413. See Bebbington's 'Response' in the same volume, pp. 423-44.

[43] D. Rosman, *Evangelicals and Culture* (London: Croom Helm, 1984), p. 40. Rosman is citing from P. Doddridge, *Works* (1803 edn.), Vol. 4, pp. 168-98; Vol. 5, pp. 93-106. Cf. Bebbington, *Evangelicalism in Modern Britain*, p. 87.

could declare that the Bible contains 'inexactnesses in reference to philosophic and scientific matters'.[44] However, as the nineteenth century wore on a different approach to inspiration became popular among evangelicals. Partly in response to what Bebbington calls 'misty Romantic notions' that scripture is inspired in the same way as poetry, evangelicals such as Robert Haldane contended for the 'infallibility' and 'perfection' of the scriptures which should be received as something 'mysterious'.[45] This might be regarded purely as a reaction against Romanticism. But, as Bebbington shows, to insist on biblical infallibility 'was to counter one Romantic attitude with another – the assertion that men should "receive with adoring faith and love what they could not comprehend"'.[46] Thus, Spurgeon's insistence on the plenary inspiration and infallibility of the scriptures was fashioned, to an important degree, by Romanticism. He not only used the language of infallibility and maintained that the Bible was 'perfect', but he also said this was a mystery that should be believed, not argued over.[47] Certainly the appropriate attitude towards the scriptures was 'adoring faith and love'. Spurgeon's commitment to the verbal inspiration of the scriptures needs to be set firmly in the context of the Romanticism which was permeating through nineteenth-century Britain.

Fourthly, we need to take notice of some nineteenth-century developments in biblical studies and theology. These developments further shaped the context within which Spurgeon articulated his views of the Bible and played a significant role in moulding the way these views were expressed. John Rogerson writes, 'It is no exaggeration to say that in the period 1815 to 1914 the study of the Bible experienced the biggest changes that had ever occurred in its history.' Rogerson further notes that these changes were 'particularly marked in Britain'.[48] The second half of the nineteenth century saw the inflow of liberal biblical criticism from Germany into British religious life, as represented by the publication of *Essays and Reviews* in 1860.[49] Associated with these new approaches to the Bible were changing

---

[44] A.W. Brown, *Recollections of the Conversation Parties of the Rev. Charles Simeon* (London: Hamilton, Adams, 1863), p. 100, as cited by Bebbington, 'Response', pp. 423-24.

[45] Bebbington, *Evangelicalism in Modern Britain*, p. 87. Bebbington is citing from R. Haldane, *The Evidence and Authority of Divine Revelation* (Edinburgh, 1816), pp. 134 ff, and A. Haldane, *The Lives of Robert Haldane of Airthrey, and his Brother, James Alexander Haldane*, 5th edn. (Edinburgh, 1855), chapter 18, especially p. 412.

[46] Bebbington, *Evangelicalism in Modern Britain*, p. 87; Haldane, *The Lives of Robert Haldane of Airthrey ...*, chapter 18, especially p. 412.

[47] See, e.g., Spurgeon's statements in 'The Infallibility Of Scripture', pp. 145-46.

[48] J. Rogerson, 'History and the Bible', in Gilley and Stanley (eds), *World Christianities, c.1815–c.1914*, p. 195.

[49] See, e.g., S. Neill and N.T. Wright, *The Interpretation of the New Testament, 1861-1986*, rev. edn. (Oxford; Oxford University Press, 1989 [1964]), pp. 20-34. For further background, see D.W. Bebbington, *The Dominance of Evangelicalism: The Age of Spurgeon and Moody* (Leicester: IVP, 2005), pp. 162-72. See, also, M.A. Noll, *Between Faith and Criticism: Evangelicals, Scholarship and the Bible* (Leicester: IVP, 1991), pp. 62-68, who gives some attention to Spurgeon's response.

approaches to theology. Within Nonconformity the mood was represented by men such as the Congregational leader, J. Baldwin Brown.[50] Spurgeon expressed his unhappiness with Baldwin Brown's theology in 1860, following the publication of Congregationalist's *The Divine Life of Man*.[51] Liberal biblical criticism, with its denial of biblical infallibility, gained ground in Nonconformist life in the period from 1860 to 1886 and Spurgeon's concern deepened.[52] The very title of the *Treasury of David* is indicative of Spurgeon's anti-critical stance. Spurgeon derided the tendency of modern, critical writers 'to take every Psalm away from David'. Because such critics were invariably 'unsound' and 'unspiritual', Spurgeon's own instinct, he wrote, was to 'gravitate in the opposite direction'. Even Psalms which did not have titles attributing them to David, for example Psalm 119, were ascribed to Israel's King in the *Treasury*.[53] Spurgeon's opposition to prevailing trends in biblical studies and theology came to a head in 1887-88. These were the years of the so-called Downgrade Controversy which saw him resign from the Baptist Union. This was in protest at what he believed was the adoption of the new views by many younger ministers within the denomination.[54]

It is important to recognise that in the Downgrade Controversy Spurgeon was not just contending against new, critical attitudes towards the Bible. Crucial to his concern was his belief that the atonement was being 'downgraded', with penal substitution being displaced by other understandings of the cross. But the fact that, as he saw it, the 'inspiration of scripture was [being] derided' was still one of the great issues for him in the dispute.[55] In the course of the Downgrade Controversy

---

[50] See D.A. Johnson, *The Changing Shape of English Nonconformity 1825–1925* (Oxford: Oxford University Press, 1999), pp. 125-62, for some of the views Spurgeon stood against, including those of Baldwin Brown. Cf. Hopkins, *Nonconformity's Romantic Generation*, pp. 17-45.

[51] See Spurgeon, *Autobiography*, Vol. 2, pp. 269-81. *The Divine Life of Man* was originally published in 1859 with a second edition in 1860. See Hopkins, *Nonconformity's Romantic Generation*, p. 22.

[52] See, e.g., C.H. Spurgeon, 'Eternal Faithfulness Unaffected By Human Unbelief', *MTP*, Vol. 25, S. No. 1453, 2 Timothy 2.13, n.d., pp. 25-36; C.H. Spurgeon, 'Commendation For The Steadfast', *MTP*, Vol. 30, S. No. 1814, Revelation 3.8,10, n.d., pp. 676-77. Although neither of these messages is dated, they were clearly given in or after 1861, as they were delivered at the Metropolitan Tabernacle. The first was published in 1879, the second in 1884.

[53] See Spurgeon, *Treasury of David*, Vol. 6 (Psalm 119), pp. 2-3.

[54] For a reliable account of the Downgrade Controversy, see Hopkins, *Nonconformity's Romantic Generation*, pp. 193-248, and 'The Down Grade Controversy: New Evidence', *Baptist Quarterly* Vol. 35, No. 6 (April 1994), pp. 262-78. Cf. 'The Downgrade Controversy: reflections on a Baptist earthquake' (G.R. Beasley-Murray Memorial Lecture presented at the Baptist Union Assembly, Brighton, 6 May 2007, unpublished photocopy), Spurgeon's College, Heritage Room (J2.28).

[55] C.H. Spurgeon (ed.), *The Sword and The Trowel: A Record of Combat With Sin and Labour For The Lord* (London: Passmore and Alabaster, 1865–92) (*Sword and Trowel*), July 1887, p. 363; August 1887, p. 397. In a letter written on 7 November 1883 to W. Blockridge,

Spurgeon repeatedly affirmed his unshakable commitment to all the 'infallible book' revealed; indeed, he wanted to affirm his commitment to the infallible book itself.[56] This was in direct contrast to the purveyors of 'modern thought', who dared to question and doubt passages from 'Holy Writ'.[57] Spurgeon regularly asserted his belief in the Bible's infallibility in the course of the Downgrade. Eight sermons in the 1887 volume of the *Metropolitan Tabernacle Pulpit* contain clear declarations of biblical infallibility, and the corresponding volume for 1888 has eleven sermons which include such statements.[58] Many of these statements are lengthy, and the 1888 volume includes one sermon, the aforementioned 'The Infallibility Of Scripture', which was devoted to this theme.[59] By contrast there is just one brief reference to biblical infallibility in Volume 3 of the *New Park Street Pulpit*, which was published in 1857.[60]

As we have seen, Spurgeon's commitment to a 'dictation theory' of biblical inspiration was in place long before the 1880s or even the 1860s. Moreover, the Bible was his foundational authority from the beginning of his ministry. These fundamental convictions about the scriptures undergirded all his early preaching, even if those convictions were not often stated explicitly. It was because he sensed

---

a Baptist pastor in Gillingham, Spurgeon spoke of a 'great fight...coming on for the cross & the word'. See 'Various Spurgeon Letters', Spurgeon's College, Heritage Room (K1.9).

[56] C.H. Spurgeon, 'The Lover Of God's Law Filled With Peace', *MTP*, Vol. 34, S. No. 2004, Psalm 119.165, delivered 22 January 1888, p. 44. Cf. Spurgeon, 'The Infallibility Of Scripture', *passim*.

[57] Spurgeon, 'The Infallibility Of Scripture', p. 145.

[58] C.H. Spurgeon, *MTP*, Vol. 33, S. Nos 1955, 1956, 1963, 1970, 1979, 1980, 1986, 1991; Vol. 34, S. Nos 2004, 2009, 2010, 2013, 2017, 2019, 2023, 2032, 2047, 2058, 2060.

[59] Spurgeon also gave more attention to articulating his basic commitment to the Bible towards the end of his ministry than he did at the beginning. Appended to a 1904 edition of his posthumously published *The Gospel of the Kingdom. A Popular Exposition Of The Gospel According to Matthew* (London: Passmore and Alabaster, 1905 [1893]), is an 'index of subjects' for the first fifty-one volumes of the *New Park Street / Metropolitan Tabernacle Pulpit* (i.e. those published between 1855 and 1904). There are thirty-nine separate sermons listed under the subject heading 'The Word Of God' (There are forty-one separate entries on the list, but two messages are included twice). These thirty-nine messages were all sermons in which Spurgeon gave considerable attention to the nature or function of the scriptures. Of these thirty-nine, only four sermons are from the first twenty volumes in the series (published between 1855-1865). By contrast, thirty-two of the sermons appear in volumes twenty-seven to fifty-one (published between 1881-1904). Of this last group, four messages are not dated, but all the other sermons from this later set of volumes were definitely given in the final ten years of Spurgeon's ministry. In short, twenty-eight of the thirty-nine sermons listed as dealing with 'The Word Of God' are certainly from the last decade of Spurgeon's ministry. Tellingly, nine of them were preached in 1887-88.

[60] C.H. Spurgeon, 'Particular Election', *NPSP*, Vol. 3, S. No. 123, 2 Peter 1.10,11, delivered 22 March 1857, p. 133: 'Get, if you can, a system of divinity out of God's Bible. Put the doctrines together. Get real, theological knowledge, founded upon the infallible word.'

that scripture was under attack that he stated his position increasingly and at more length. Sermons like the 'Great Spoil' and 'The Infallibility Of Scripture' were preached explicitly against what Spurgeon regarded as the sacrilegious blasphemies of 'modern thought'. Such messages are very revealing of the importance of the Bible to Spurgeon. In 'The Infallibility Of Scripture' he pleaded with his hearers,

> Where are we if our Bibles are gone? Where are we if we are taught to distrust them? If we are left in doubt as to which part is inspired and which is not, we are as badly off as if we had no Bible at all. I hold no theory of inspiration; I accept the inspiration of the Scriptures as a fact.[61]

Earlier in the same message he had declared, 'I cannot speak out my whole heart on this theme which is so dear to me ...'.[62] Spurgeon struggled to express himself coherently when issues which he believed were foundational to his whole way of relating to God were at stake. He did not have the patience or the emotional capacity for careful, detailed argument. He regarded the battle lines as sharply drawn and lumped all biblical critics together, demonising his opponents with slogans, fighting with a bludgeon rather than a rapier. As has often been noted, Spurgeon was not at his best in a controversy.[63] William Young Fullerton perceptively stated that, 'Mr Spurgeon was too earnest, too intent on the eternal meaning of things, too sure of his own standing, to be a good controversialist.'[64] The side of Spurgeon highlighted by Fullerton was clearly in evidence as he sought to defend his approach to the Bible in the heat of the Downgrade Controversy. The dispute provides yet further evidence that the inspiration and authority of the Bible were crucial to him, so crucial that he became emotional and angry when he saw the Bible treated, as he saw it, with irreverence. This emotion was a factor in his struggles to express himself coherently on the subject.

To summarise, I have sought to show that Spurgeon's approach to the inspiration and authority of the scriptures was shaped by a matrix of interconnected factors, religious, historical, cultural and temperamental. Spurgeon was sure he was standing in a long line of 'Reformed' thinkers on scripture, a line which included the Puritans. But his precise views were also moulded both by Enlightenment patterns of thinking and by Romanticism, two different and in many ways contrasting cultural movements. New developments in biblical studies and theology, developments which were unwelcome to Spurgeon, provided the context in which he expressed his views, often speaking with intense emotion. Thus, the influences on his approach to the scriptures were various: it is true that Puritan thinking was significant but much

---

[61] Spurgeon, 'The Infallibility Of Scripture', p. 152.
[62] Spurgeon, 'The Infallibility Of Scripture', p. 149.
[63] See, e.g., J.C. Carlile, *C.H. Spurgeon: An Interpretive Biography* (London: Religious Tract Society and Kingsgate Press, 1933), pp. 243-44; M.K. Nicholls, *C.H. Spurgeon: The Pastor Evangelist* (Didcot: Baptist Historical Society, 1992), p. 143.
[64] W.Y. Fullerton, *C.H. Spurgeon: A Biography* (London: Williams and Norgate, 1920), p. 303.

more needs to be taken into account; the Enlightenment was important, but this was not the only cultural movement at work. It needs to be recognised that different factors came together to shape Spurgeon's approach. As the Bible was clearly crucial to Spurgeon's spirituality, this is further evidence that 'Puritanism' alone cannot be the integrating theme of this spirituality, although it was undoubtedly significant for him. A view of Spurgeon which sees him as an enlightened figure resisting the encroachment of Romanticism into evangelical life, whilst insightful in many respects, also needs to be qualified. Certainly his spirituality, taken as a whole, cannot be described simply as enlightened.

Reading the Bible

What approach did Spurgeon adopt and advocate as far as reading the Bible was concerned? A number of sermons deal with this question directly. One of these was entitled 'How To Read The Bible' and was based on Matthew 12.3-7.[65] In this message, which was published in 1879, Spurgeon outlined a step-by-step process by which his hearers could engage with the scriptures. 'How To Read The Bible' merits a detailed treatment. To begin with, he wanted to stress the importance of actually reading the scriptures. He believed it was necessary to underline this obvious point as, in 'contrast to the old Puritanic times', his was 'not so much a Bible reading age as it ought to be'.[66] But what Spurgeon really wanted to emphasise at the beginning of his message was the danger of people reading without 'understanding'. If someone thought they had benefited from reading a Bible passage they had not understood it then they were merely being superstitious. The 'benefit' of reading had to come to the 'soul' by way of the mind. It was vital, of course, that the Holy Spirit illuminated the meaning of the scriptures to a reader, and so prayer was crucial.[67] But Spurgeon also wanted to assert the need to give time to scripture reading.[68] He declared,

> Do not many of you read your Bible in a hurried way—just a little bit, and off you go? Do you not soon forget what you have read, and lose what effect it seemed to have? How few of you are resolved to get at its soul, its juice, its life, its essence, and to drink in its meaning.[69]

Thus the encouragement was to diligent, focused, slow reading of the Bible with the mind fully engaged in the activity. This might mean in-depth study of a passage and

---

[65] C.H. Spurgeon, 'How To Read The Bible', *MTP*, Vol. 25, S. No. 1503, Matthew 12.3-7, n.d., pp. 625-36. For another sermon on this theme, see 'Understandest Thou What Thou Readest?', *MTP*, Vol. 30, S. No. 1792, Acts 8.30-33, delivered 11 May 1884, pp. 409-20.

[66] Spurgeon, 'How To Read The Bible', p. 626.

[67] Spurgeon, 'How To Read The Bible', pp. 627-29.

[68] Cf. C.H. Spurgeon, 'Samuel And The Young Man Saul', *MTP*, Vol. 26, S. No. 1547, 1 Samuel 9.27, n.d., pp. 393-96.

[69] Spurgeon, 'How To Read The Bible', p. 631.

The Bible 119

for this all 'means and helps' should be used to aid understanding. Spurgeon appeared to have in mind both biblical commentaries and the words of faithful preachers.[70] But his fundamental aim was to encourage meditation on the text of scripture itself.[71] Through such careful, prayerful wrestling with the scriptures their essential meaning could be grasped.[72]

This was a vital first step to engaging with the scriptures but, as Spurgeon warmed to his theme in 'How To Read The Bible', there was much more he wanted to say. Having reached a measure of understanding with regard to a particular text or passage, he insisted that its message must be appropriated yet more deeply. Understanding was good, but it was possible to have this and for the Bible to remain a 'dead book' and the reader a 'dead soul'. Consequently, and characteristically, Spurgeon emphasised the importance of knowing the Bible 'experimentally'. A sound creed was all very well, but that creed needed to be written on the 'tablets of [the] heart'; the 'doctrines of grace' were good, but the 'grace of the doctrines' was better.[73] It was vital that meditation did not stop once a good level of understanding had been reached. In the *Gospel of the Kingdom*, Spurgeon echoed an Anglican collect when he encouraged his readers not only to 'read', 'mark' and 'learn' the scriptures but also to 'inwardly digest' them, turning them over repeatedly in the mind so that the 'soul' grew strong.[74] Elsewhere in the same commentary he made a similar point with the help of language derived from Bunyan's *Holy War*, 'Do not be content merely to open ear-Gate; but rest not satisfied until the King himself comes riding through that gate right up to the very citadel of the town of Mansoul, and takes possession of the castle of your heart.'[75]

In 'How To Read The Bible' Spurgeon gave an example to illustrate his general point. 'The doctrine of election is one thing', he said, 'but to know that God has predestined you, and to have the fruit of it in the good works to which you are ordained, is quite another thing.'[76] An understanding of the doctrine needed to be followed by the personal knowledge that one was the recipient of God's electing grace (and all who believed the gospel and trusted Christ could have this knowledge), followed in turn by fruitful Christian living.[77] The power of the doctrine needed to be felt and a changed life needed to result. If these experiential steps were missed then the doctrine of election had not properly been appropriated by the Bible reader. Spurgeon's approach, in tune with enlightened thinking, was both 'experimental' and practical.

---

[70] Spurgeon, 'How To Read The Bible', p. 630, cf. p. 626.

[71] Cf. C.H. Spurgeon, *Evening by Evening: Or, Readings At Eventide For The Family or the Closet* (London: Passmore and Alabaster, n.d. [1868]), 10 June, John 5.39, p. 161.

[72] Cf. Spurgeon, 'Understandest Thou What Thou Readest?', pp. 411-12.

[73] Spurgeon, 'How To Read The Bible', p. 633-34.

[74] Spurgeon, *Gospel of the Kingdom*, p. 497.

[75] Spurgeon, *Gospel of the Kingdom*, p. 493.

[76] Spurgeon, 'How To Read The Bible', pp. 631-33.

[77] C.H. Spurgeon in the *Church Union*, 12 May 1881, 'Spurgeon's Scrapbooks, Numbered Volumes', Spurgeon's College, Heritage Room, Vol. 4 (2G), p. 4.

What was essential in order for a reader to imbibe the Bible spiritually was for Jesus to be present and working by the Holy Spirit.[78] As Spurgeon proceeded with his exposition in 'How To Read The Bible' he cried out, 'O living Christ, make this a living word to me. Thy word is life, but not without the Holy Spirit.'[79] The presence of Christ mediated by the Spirit would enable the believer to read and respond appropriately to the word. Thus a commitment to biblical infallibility was held side-by-side with a view which insisted on the need for Christ, by his Spirit, to make the word come alive. If the scriptures were encountered in this way, the believer would find they received a 'thousand helps out of that wondrous book'.[80] Spurgeon was clear that this was his own experience. In a remarkable passage in 'The Word A Sword' he made this absolutely explicit, as he spoke of the Bible in the following terms,

> It moves, it stirs itself, it lives, it communes with living men as a living Word. Solomon saith concerning it, 'When thou goest, it shall lead thee; when thou sleepest, it shall keep thee; and when thou awakest, it shall talk with thee.' Have you never known what that means? Why the Book has wrestled with me; the Book has smitten me; the Book has comforted me; the Book has smiled on me; the Book has frowned on me; the Book has clasped my hand; the Book has warmed my heart. The Book weeps with me, and sings with me, it whispers to me; and it preaches to me; it maps my way, and holds up my goings; it was to me the Young Man's Companion, and it is still my Morning and Evening Chaplain. It is a live Book: all over alive; from its first chapter to its last word it is full of a strange mystic vitality, which makes it have pre-eminence over every other writing for every living child of God.[81]

The passage gets close, I consider, to expressing the essence of what Spurgeon thought and felt regarding the Bible. The emotional language ('weeps', 'sings', 'whispers') allied with the practical thrust ('it maps my way, and holds up my goings') captures well his experimental, applied approach. The comment that the Bible was full of a 'strange mystic vitality' gives evidence of the Romantic dimension of Spurgeon's approach. Also worth noting here is Spurgeon's stress that the whole of the Bible was vital for the whole of life. The sorts of expressions contained in this extract, especially the repeated personification of the scriptures, laid Spurgeon open to the accusation of bibliolatry. He was well aware of the charge but was dismissive of it. Bibliolatry, he said, was a crime of his critics 'own inventing'. In his view, few who had been accused of this had ever been guilty of it and, in any case, if 'there be such things as venial sins, surely an undue reverence of Holy Scripture is one of them'. He continued, 'To me the Bible is not God, but it is God's voice, and I do not hear it without awe.'[82]

---

[78] Cf. Spurgeon, 'Understandest Thou What Thou Readest?', p. 418.
[79] Spurgeon, 'How To Read The Bible', pp. 633-34.
[80] Spurgeon, 'How To Read The Bible', p. 636.
[81] Spurgeon, 'The Word A Sword', p. 109.
[82] Spurgeon, 'The Word A Sword', p. 114.

As noted in the introduction to this chapter, the fact that the Bible was so crucial to Spurgeon's spirituality seems to undercut the argument that 'communion with Christ and his people' is the integrating theme of his spirituality. This, however, is to underestimate both the extent to which he knew communion with Christ through the scriptures and also the extent to which other people loomed large in his overall approach to the Bible. These issues will be addressed in the rest of this chapter, with the relationship between the Bible and Christ in Spurgeon's thinking examined first.

The Bible and Christ

In showing how the concept of communion with Christ related to Spurgeon's approach to the scriptures we need to note, first of all, that Spurgeon believed that the whole Bible pointed to Christ. Speaking on John 20.30,31, Spurgeon declared that the apostle John had produced his own 'life of Christ' which was designed to lead people to faith in Jesus. Indeed, what was stated in John 20.31 could actually be applied to the whole of scripture. Spurgeon declared, 'We may begin at Genesis and go on to the Book of Revelation, and say of all the holy histories, "These are written that ye might believe that Jesus is the Christ, the Son of God."' Bible readers who had never trusted Christ had read 'in vain'. What was crucial was not faith in a creed but faith in the 'person, offices, nature, and work of Jesus'.[83] It was to him that all of scripture pointed. In the earlier discussion of Spurgeon's sermon, 'How To Read The Bible', his strong emphasis on discerning the 'spiritual meaning' of scripture was highlighted. As Spurgeon drew his message on John 20.30,31 to a close, he wanted to make the point that this spiritual meaning was found in Christ. He used the following analogy. Leading out of every village in England there was always a road a traveller could take which would eventually, through a series of different interconnected roads, lead them to London. In the same way, from every text of the Bible there was a 'road' which led, directly or indirectly, to Christ.[84] Whether it was the Old Testament or the New, Spurgeon's approach to the Bible had a strong christological focus.[85] He advised his students that Christ should be the 'diamond setting' of every sermon.[86] This was advice that Spurgeon himself followed. As

---

[83] C.H. Spurgeon, 'The Main Matter', *MTP*, Vol. 27, S. No. 1631, John 20.30,31, delivered 6 November 1881, pp. 654-60. The comment about the 'life of Christ' related to the many such lives that were produced during the Victorian era.

[84] Spurgeon, 'How To Read The Bible', p. 634.

[85] For a specific example of C.H. Spurgeon moving from an Old Testament passage to Christ in a commentary, see *Treasury of David*, Vol. 6 (Psalm 119.41), p. 113; for a corresponding instance of him making this journey in a sermon, see 'Job's Sure Knowledge', pp. 541-50. Of course, such examples are legion and occur from the very beginning of his ministry. See, e.g., 'The Second Psalm', 'Notebooks With Sermon Outlines, Vols 2, 4-9', Vol. 2. S. No. 101, Psalm 2, 'This Psalm was written by David and doubtless with an eye to Christ in every word of it.' See also 'Jacob's dreams', 'Notebooks With Sermon Outlines, Vols 2, 4-9', Vol. 4, S. No. 194, where Jacob is 'a type of Jesus'.

[86] Williams, *Personal Reminiscences* (rev edn.), p. 65.

Tabernacle elder Thomas Cox remembered, in his pastor's preaching, 'No matter what the text ... it became a pedestal for Christ.'[87]

One outworking of this christological focus was Spurgeon's typological approach to the Old Testament. In a sermon entitled 'David's First Victory', ostensibly preached on 1 Samuel 17.50 but in reality ranging over the whole David and Goliath narrative as recorded in 1 Samuel 17, Spurgeon not only stated his belief that David was an 'eminent type' of Christ but also spoke more generally about his attitude to typologising.[88]

With regard to the specific example of David, Spurgeon was sure that David prefigured Christ and that he did so in a number of different ways. For example, Goliath's conqueror had been anointed by oil several times (some specific references from the books of Samuel were noted: 1 Samuel 16.13; 2 Samuel 2.4; 5.3). David's anointing pointed to Christ who himself 'was anointed of God, is anointed of his saints, and shall be anointed of the whole church'.[89] Also, as David had been sent to comfort his brothers only to be mistreated by them, so Christ had been sent to his 'brethren' and been rejected by them, a rejection which culminated in the cross. This last point provided Spurgeon with a platform from which he launched into some reflections on the passion of Christ, with Luke 23.34, Hebrews 12.3 and Isaiah 53.3 all cited. Spurgeon then proceeded to draw out yet further 'correspondences' between David's experiences and the cross of Christ. David's intense love for God and his people 'plainly foreshadowed' the love of Christ shown supremely on the cross. David represented his people as he went into battle with Goliath; Christ represented his people as he went to the cross on their behalf. David had rejected the offer of Saul's armour and won a great victory; Christ's greater victory had been won in weakness and without the weapons of human wisdom. Still the parallels were not exhausted. The fact that Goliath was struck 'effectually' on the 'forehead of his pride', was suggestive of how Christ had 'projected his atoning sacrifice as a stone that has smitten sin and all its powers upon the forehead'.[90] The whole narrative needed to be interpreted spiritually. Truly, for Spurgeon the 'road' from this passage led to Christ and, especially, his atoning work.

With regard to Spurgeon's overall approach to what he called 'typical analogies', he was ready to sound some notes of caution. He was clear that a number of the early

---

[87] T. Cox, 'Notes on C.H. Spurgeon', Spurgeon's College, Heritage Room (B1.17), p. 3. These handwritten notes are not bound but the pages are numbered. Cox joined the Tabernacle in 1870 and became an elder in 1882. See T. Spurgeon, 'A Loving Tribute To The Memory of Mr. Thomas Cox...', Spurgeon's College, Heritage Room (B1.17), which was delivered at Chatsworth Baptist Church on 19 March 1914 following Cox's death.

[88] C.H. Spurgeon, 'David's First Victory', *MTP*, Vol. 50, S. No. 2913, 1 Samuel 17.50, n.d., p. 589.

[89] Spurgeon, 'David's First Victory', pp. 589-90. Spurgeon gave no references for these different 'anointings'. Probably he had in mind texts such as Matthew 3.13-17, Luke 7.38,46, Mark 16.1 and, perhaps, with regard to a future 'anointing' by the whole church, a passage like Revelation 5.8-14.

[90] Spurgeon, 'David's First Victory', pp. 590-94.

church Fathers had overreached themselves with some rather fanciful typologising. By seeking to draw spiritual truths out of every tiny detail of a story they had brought typologising and 'spiritualising' into disrepute. Origen was noted as an example of this tendency in 'David's First Victory'.[91] Elsewhere, in one of Spurgeon's *Lectures* to his students, Spurgeon also dissociated himself from some of the spiritualising of John Gill, citing, amongst other examples, Gill's exposition of the parable of the Good Samaritan in which the two coins given to the innkeeper were the Old and New Testaments.[92] Spurgeon believed, then, that typologising should only take place within certain limits.

Having said this, Spurgeon was not especially clear as to what the limits to such typologising were. In his Pastors' College lecture on this theme, entitled 'On Spiritualizing', Spurgeon spoke merely of the need to use 'discretion and judgement' without elaborating further.[93] In practice, Spurgeon's doctrinal commitments (especially with regard to the person and work of Christ) combined with common sense (Gill's approach was described, at one point, as 'absurd')[94] and a desire to avoid speculation for the sake of it to provided a framework within which he made connections between the Old Testament narratives and Christ. The 'common consent' of evangelical Christians was also a factor in determining what was and what was not an acceptable piece of typologising – the fact that David was viewed as a type of Christ by a range of Puritan and evangelical commentators gave Spurgeon confidence to pursue this line himself; where there was a less of a consensus, he was more cautious.[95] Certainly he was clear that care needed to be taken when developing 'typical analogies'.

Nevertheless, Spurgeon was sure that the search for types and 'allegories' in scripture was important. Indeed, in what he described, in Romantic vein, as the 'mechanical and unpoetic times' in which he and his hearers lived, Spurgeon wanted to reassert the validity of this approach.[96] In his own preaching, the sort of detailed allegorising found in 'David's First Victory' was not uncommon. One is tempted to conclude that he overstepped the bounds he set for his own students on a number of occasions. Even in 'On Spiritualizing' Spurgeon spoke of his appreciation of John Bunyan's allegory of Solomon's Temple, despite the fact that this was, the lecturer had to admit, a 'little strained' and 'far-fetched' in places. What saved Bunyan's implausible allegory for Spurgeon was the fact that it focused on the heart of the

---

[91] Spurgeon, 'David's First Victory', pp. 589-90. For Origen's approach to the scriptures, see J.B. Rogers and D.K. McKim, *The Authority and Interpretation of the Bible: An Historical Approach* (San Francisco: Harper and Row, 1979), pp. 11-16.

[92] C.H. Spurgeon, *Lectures To My Students* (3 Vols; London: Passmore and Alabaster, n.d.), Vol. 1, Lecture 7, 'On Spiritualizing', p. 112.

[93] Spurgeon, 'On Spiritualizing', p. 116. In this lecture Spurgeon covered typologising but also ranged more widely.

[94] Spurgeon, 'On Spiritualizing', p. 112.

[95] Spurgeon, 'David's First Victory', p. 590.

[96] Spurgeon, 'David's First Victory', pp. 589-90.

gospel – Christ and his work.[97] Also significant was the fact that Bunyan was regarded by Spurgeon as being deeply spiritual. Enlightened and Romantic influences can be seen as being in tension here. Common sense and practical application were important and fanciful speculation was to be avoided, but, in what Thomas Carlyle had referred to as the 'mechanical age',[98] poetry and the imagination were also vital.[99] It is surely significant that Spurgeon enjoyed a friendship with John Ruskin, the Romantic art critic already mentioned in this chapter. Ruskin appreciated Spurgeon's preaching, and the two men met on a number of occasions.[100] Spurgeon was imbued with a good measure of the spirit of Romanticism and his own imagination was vivid and creative.[101] This, together with his commitment to seeing Christ in all the scriptures, often led him to reading a considerable amount of colourful christological detail into some rather unlikely passages.

Spurgeon's christological focus is further shown by the fact that, for him, the scriptures not only pointed to Christ, they were closely identified with Christ. 'The Word A Sword' was, as already noted, preached on Hebrews 4.12, 'For the word of God is quick …'. But to what or to whom does the phrase 'the word of God' refer as it is used in this text? Does it refer to the incarnate Word, Christ, or the written word of the scriptures? Spurgeon posed this question in the introduction to his sermon and noted that different biblical commentators came down on either side of the debate. This was the specific issue upon which Spurgeon had consulted Owen and Calvin. Owen believed the reference was to the incarnate Son, whereas Calvin thought that what the writer meant was the 'revelation of God in the book'.[102] Spurgeon's own solution was as follows,

> I have been greatly instructed by the mere fact that it should be difficult to know whether in this passage the Holy Ghost is speaking of the Christ of God, or the Book of God. This shows us a great truth, which we might not otherwise have so clearly noted. How much can be said of the Lord Jesus may also be said of the inspired volume! How closely are these two allied! How certainly do those who despise the one reject the

---

[97] Spurgeon, 'On Spiritualizing', pp. 112-13.

[98] T. Carlyle, 'The Mechanical Age', was first published in the *Edinburgh Review* in 1829: 'Were we required to characterise this age of ours by any single epithet, we should be tempted to call it, not an Heroical, Devotional, Philosophical, or Moral Age, but, above all others, the Mechanical Age.'

[99] Spurgeon, 'On Spiritualizing', p. 112. With regard to Bunyan, Spurgeon tellingly said that 'men of rare poetical temperament' ought to be given some latitude in spiritualizing.

[100] See Spurgeon, *Autobiography*, Vol. 2, pp. 288-90; Vol. 3, pp. 194-196; Vol. 4, pp. 94-95; J. Ruskin to C.H. Spurgeon, 25 November 1862, Spurgeon's College Heritage Room (D.1.8). In the late 1850s Ruskin frequently attended Spurgeon's services at the Surrey Gardens Music Hall. Ruskin once embraced the pastor with 'tender affection and tears' on a visit to the Spurgeons' home.

[101] As noted by Hopkins, *Nonconformity's Romantic Generation*, pp. 130-31.

[102] Spurgeon, 'The Word A Sword', p. 109. The summary of Calvin's comment was Spurgeon's own.

other! How intimately are the Word made flesh, and the Word uttered by inspired men, joined together! It may be most accurate to interpret this passage as relating both to the Word of God incarnate, and the Word of God inspired.[103]

This was far more than a preacher failing to do exegesis properly or being determined to find good in two different, seemingly competing, interpretations. The extended quotation from 'The Word A Sword' reflected what for Spurgeon was a deeply held belief: Christ and the scriptures were, as he put it, closely 'allied'. As Spurgeon went on he insisted that 'Christ and his Word must go together'. So, 'it is only because Jesus is not dead that the Word becomes living and effectual ... If you leave Christ out of the Scripture, you have left out the essential truth which it is written to declare.' But the reverse was also true: it was not possible to have Christ without the word. Spurgeon castigated biblical critics who began their works with great professions of loyalty to Christ and then proceeded to cast doubt on the substitutionary nature of the atonement, which he believed was central to Christ's saving work as defined by the scriptures.[104] For Spurgeon, the biblical critics were talking about 'Jesus' whilst in reality casting away the 'real Jesus, namely his gospel, and his inspired Word'. In strong language he declared that such behaviour was analogous to Judas betraying Christ with a kiss.[105] The Christ with whom Spurgeon had communion was the Christ whom the scriptures revealed. Any other 'Christ' was merely a product of people's imaginings. The 'Revealer' could not be separated from 'his own revelation'.[106]

For Spurgeon, then, there was an extremely close association between Christ and the Bible. This close connection regularly surfaced in his writing and preaching. Commenting in the *Treasury of David* on Psalm 33.4, 'For the word of the Lord is right', Spurgeon moved seamlessly between the written word and the incarnate Word.[107] In a sermon entitled 'Feeding On The Word', Spurgeon declared, 'Oh, what a blessed thing it is when a soul is enabled to feed upon the Word of God, to feed upon the Christ of God, to feed upon the grace of God!' The context makes it clear that the preacher's reference to the 'Word of God' was a reference to the

---

[103] Spurgeon, 'The Word A Sword', pp. 109-10.

[104] Spurgeon, 'The Word A Sword', pp. 109-10. I am not unaware that the biblical basis for penal substitutionary atonement has been strongly challenged. For the recent debate among evangelicals in Britain, see D. Hilborn, J. Thacker and D. Tidball (eds), *The Atonement Debate: Papers from the London Symposium on the Theology of Atonement* (Grand Rapids: Zondervan, 2008). The papers from the symposium, which was held in July 2005, are on the Evangelical Alliance website: http://www.eauk.org/theology/key_papers/Atonement accessed 03 / 07 / 09.

[105] Spurgeon, 'The Word A Sword', p. 110. Cf. Spurgeon's comments on Matthew 22.18 in *Gospel of the Kingdom*, pp. 196-7.

[106] Spurgeon, 'The Word A Sword', p. 110.

[107] Spurgeon, *Treasury of David*, Vol. 2 (Psalm 33.4), p. 116; cf. the comments on 33.6, p. 117.

Bible.[108] Consequently, feeding on the scriptures, on Christ and on grace were all of a piece. In some places it was less than clear how Spurgeon was using the phrase the 'Word of God'. Commenting in the *Treasury* on Psalm 107.20, 'He sent his word and healed them', Spurgeon stated that, 'Sin-sick souls should remember the power of *the Word*, and be much in hearing and meditating upon it.'[109] The description of 'the Word' as 'it' seems to point, fairly conclusively, to this being a reference to the written word. However, the use of the upper-case 'W' and the way the phrase was printed in italics cast doubt.[110] So does the fact that in the very next paragraph Spurgeon wrote of 'Christ, the eternal Word', the one who would come with healing and saving power to all who cried out to him.[111] Spurgeon himself may have deliberately intended to give *the Word* a double meaning as he believed was warranted in Hebrews 4.12. Even if this was not Spurgeon's intention, it is my contention that he would not have been concerned about the ambiguity. In practice, much that was said about Christ could also be said about the Bible.

Spurgeon's understanding of communion with Christ was, then, indissolubly bound up with the scriptures. It was through the scriptures that Christ could truly be known and fellowship with him truly experienced. It would not be true to say that such communion could only be known through the scriptures for, and as will be shown, communion could be experienced through prayer (chapter 6) and the Lord's supper (chapter 7), as well as through Christian service (chapter 8), by holy living (chapter 9) and in suffering (chapter 10). Spurgeon's approach to communion with Christ, as noted in the introduction to this study, was not monochrome, but kaleidoscopic. Nevertheless, there was something foundational about the scriptures as far as his understanding and experience of fellowship with Christ was concerned. Spurgeon's understanding of Christ was defined by what he believed the scriptures said about his person and work. It was the Christ the scriptures revealed with whom communion was experienced. Also, the way Spurgeon approached other means of communion was moulded in significant measure by what he believed the scriptures said about these various routes to closer fellowship.

This is not to suggest that Spurgeon somehow achieved a reading of the scriptures which was free from presuppositions. As I have argued, Spurgeon's interpretation of scripture betrays the clear impress of his heritage (Protestant, Calvinistic, Puritan and evangelical), culture (both 'enlightened' and Romantic) and specific context (for example, reaction against the prevailing liberal biblical criticism). But he was

---

[108] C.H. Spurgeon, 'Feeding On The Word', *MTP*, Vol. 38, S. No. 2278, Isaiah 40.2, delivered 8 May 1890, p. 497. For the context, see also p. 495.

[109] Spurgeon, *Treasury of David*, Vol. 5 (Psalm 107.20), p. 120.

[110] Although, both in Spurgeon's published preaching and in his writing, an upper-case 'W' was often used even when it seems obvious that a reference to the Bible rather than Christ was intended. Two examples from Spurgeon's published sermons, both of which have already been cited in this chapter, are 'Search The Scriptures', p. 63, and 'The Word A Sword', pp. 109-10. For an example from the *Treasury of David*, see Vol. 1 (Psalm 1.2), p. 2.

[111] Spurgeon, *Treasury of David*, Vol. 5 (Psalm 107.20), p. 120. Cf. some of the comments on v20 that were reproduced in the 'Explanatory Notes' section, p. 135.

consciously seeking to be faithful to the scriptures, pursuing communion with the Christ he believed the scriptures revealed in the ways he believed the scriptures encouraged. The Bible was fundamental to Spurgeon's experience of communion with Christ.

The Bible and Preaching

Spurgeon's engagement with the scriptures not only linked strongly with his stress on communion with Christ, but also with his focus on Christ's people. This can be seen in his approach to preaching. First of all, his method of sermon preparation, which was recognised by contemporaries as being unusual, even idiosyncratic,[112] deserves some comment. Spurgeon used to spend only a few hours on a Saturday evening (for the Sunday morning service) and a Sunday afternoon (for the Sunday evening service) in composing the brief outlines from which he preached at the Tabernacle.[113] Thousands of these brief outlines are held in Spurgeon's College Heritage Room. In contrast to the written notes from which he gave his pre-London messages, the majority of these later outlines contain little more than bare headings and sub-headings, with some of them written on the front of envelopes.[114] Such an approach to sermon preparation surprised many, but it was only possible because Spurgeon had spent many other hours reading and reflecting.[115] This reading included commentaries and works of theology but was primarily in the scriptures themselves. The Bible that Spurgeon habitually used in his study from 1856 onwards was worn to pieces by 1870 when it was sent for rebinding.[116] Although he could find his mode of preparation challenging – particularly when it was late on a Saturday evening and he had still not settled on a text from which to preach the next morning – he clearly derived much joy from this work as well.[117] The point to note is

---

[112] See, e.g., Fullerton, *C.H. Spurgeon*, p. 217; [Anon.], *Charles Haddon Spurgeon: A Biographical Sketch And An Appreciation, By 'One Who Knew Him Well'* (London: Melrose, 1903), pp. 106-107.

[113] Spurgeon, *Autobiography*, Vol. 4, pp. 65, 73; Fullerton, *Spurgeon*, pp. 217-18; C.H. Spurgeon, *My Sermon Notes: A Selection From Outlines Of Discourses Delivered At The Metropolitan Tabernacle ... From Genesis To Proverbs I to LXIV* (New York: Fleming H. Revell, n.d. [1884]), Preface, p. 6.

[114] 'Miniature Cabinet with many of C.H. Spurgeon's pulpit notes', Spurgeon's College, Heritage Room (L2.1); Williams, *Personal Reminiscences* (rev. edn.), p. 100. When Spurgeon wrote for publication, the evidence suggests he wrote the text out himself in long hand. See, e.g., his manuscript for *The Cheque Book Of The Bank Of Faith: Being Promises Arranged for Daily Use With Brief Experimental Comments* (London: Passmore and Alabaster, 1895). 'Original manuscript of "The cheque book of the bank of faith",' Spurgeon's College, Heritage Room (Display Case 8).

[115] Cf., Nicholls, *C.H. Spurgeon*, p. 36.

[116] Spurgeon, *Autobiography*, Vol. 4, p. 66.

[117] Spurgeon, *Autobiography*, Vol. 4, p. 68. Texts to preach from were sometimes suggested by friends. See Williams, *Personal Reminiscences* (rev. edn.), pp. 97-98.

that Spurgeon did not spend many hours on his own in sermon preparation. During the week he habitually worked with different secretaries, for example with Joseph W. Harrald, his private secretary, and John L. Keys, his literary secretary, at his side.[118] Spurgeon's method allowed him to keep the time he spent alone composing the actual outline to a minimum.

Comments that callers were not allowed to see Spurgeon on a Saturday can create the impression that the preacher spent most of this day in solitude,[119] but such was not the case. Students from the Pastors' College would come and see him on Saturday mornings for 'an hour or two' (at least in the 'early days' of the College),[120] but it was in the afternoon when there were most visitors. G. Holden Pike first met Spurgeon in 1869 and in 1872 became part of the 'inner circle' when he was appointed a sub-editor of the *Sword and Trowel*.[121] Pike described a typical Saturday afternoon for the pastor of the Metropolitan Tabernacle, speaking of the time the Spurgeons lived in Nightingale Lane, Clapham Common.[122] Saturday afternoon was a time when C.H. Spurgeon met with a host of 'intimate' friends. These often included, according to Pike, his publishers, Joseph Passmore and James Alabaster, heads of the various Tabernacle 'departments', including George Rogers, Pastors' College principal, and Spurgeon's deacons. The group could be swelled by other preachers known to Spurgeon, as well as other guests, for example visitors from America. Pike's description makes it clear that C.H. Spurgeon revelled in these occasions[123] which continued after the Spurgeons had moved to 'Westwood', Upper Norwood, in 1880.[124] Both in Nightingale Lane and at Westwood those who had remained late into the afternoon would be invited to stay for tea and join family prayers.[125]

At six o'clock all callers would leave and Spurgeon would work on his sermon.[126] But even after he had retreated to his study, he would re-emerge to speak with

---

[118] Fullerton, *C.H. Spurgeon*, p. 172; cf. the illustration reproduced in R. Shindler, *From The Usher's Desk To the Tabernacle Pulpit: Pastor C.H. Spurgeon, His Life And Work* (London: Passmore and Alabaster, 1892), p. 282, which shows Spurgeon in his study at Westwood with Harrald. John Lewis Keys worked with Spurgeon on all his publications from 1867 to 1891, including the printed sermons and the *Sword and Trowel*. The compilers of the *Autobiography* stated that when Spurgeon died, Keys 'lost his best earthly friend'. See Spurgeon, *Autobiography*, Vol. 3, pp. 200-201.

[119] G.H. Pike, *The Life And Work Of Charles Haddon Spurgeon* (6 Vols; London: Cassell, 1894 [1892-93]), Vol. 4, p. 376.

[120] Fullerton, *C.H. Spurgeon*, p. 169. Fullerton does not say when this practice stopped.

[121] Pike, *C.H. Spurgeon*, Vol. 4, pp. 309-10; Vol. 5, p. 37.

[122] This was from 1857 to 1880 and so Pike would have been talking about the period 1869-80. Spurgeon, *Autobiography*, Vol. 2, p. 284; Vol. 4, p. 49.

[123] Pike, *C.H. Spurgeon*, Vol. 4, p. 377.

[124] Spurgeon, *Autobiography*, Vol. 4, p. 64.

[125] Pike, *C.H. Spurgeon*, Vol 4, p. 384; Spurgeon, *Autobiography*, Vol. 4, p. 64.

[126] Spurgeon, *Autobiography*, Vol. 4, p. 64. Fullerton, *Spurgeon*, p. 217, suggests callers did not have to leave until seven o'clock.

Susannah if he was struggling to find a text ('Wifey, what shall I do?') or just to talk with her more generally. He would also call on her to read to him from commentaries after his text had been chosen and this appears to have been his regular practice.[127] Thus, even in these hours of preparation, Spurgeon was not really alone. Biographers tend to put Spurgeon's particular method of preparing sermons down to his brilliant mind and to the fact that he had been, in effect, getting ready to preach throughout the week by reflecting on possible texts and other material as he went about his ministry.[128] But it is not fanciful to suggest another reason behind Spurgeon's unusual approach to sermon preparation: he drew strength from being with people, especially people who he sensed loved Christ and who saw the Christian life in similar ways to himself. Spending, say, eight hours in seclusion as he worked on sermon material would not have suited him temperamentally. The importance of other people to Spurgeon is underlined. Overall, Spurgeon's engagement with the biblical text involved also engaging with many different people. As he understood it, these included both the church triumphant (he sensed a bond with biblical commentators and even the biblical authors themselves) and the church militant (his faithful band of helpers and those for whom he wrote and preached). Through his engagement with the Bible in preaching preparation, he experienced communion with Christ *and* his people.

The importance of other people to Spurgeon is further shown by a consideration of the act of preaching itself. For him, it was essential for all Christians that they were actively engaged in the service of Christ and of others. The nature and extent of an individual Christian's service was determined by the particular gifts God had given them and the opportunities for activity he had provided. Spurgeon believed that he had been gifted and called to preach and that this was fundamental to the way God wanted him to serve. Consequently, the fact he was a preacher was central to his self-understanding and central to his spirituality. He found preaching to others both a necessity and a joy. Sermon delivery was a time when a deep connection with his hearers was forged, as together they 'commune[d]' around the text of scripture.[129]

It is true that, for Spurgeon, sermon delivery was often emotionally draining. Hopkins notes this fact: the experience of preaching could be 'costly' and 'wearing' for him. But Hopkins is careful to balance this judgement by stating that Spurgeon also found preaching thrilling.[130] Spurgeon's own comments show that he was often exhilarated by preaching. For example, as he reflected on his early years in London he said,

---

[127] Spurgeon, *Autobiography*, Vol. 4, pp. 65, 68; J.J. Ellis, *Charles Haddon Spurgeon* (London: James Nisbet, n.d. [although internal evidence shows this was published after 1888 and before 1892, see pp. v-vii]), p. 178.

[128] So Fullerton, *C.H. Spurgeon*, pp. 217-18.

[129] C.H. Spurgeon, 'For The Sick And Afflicted', *MTP*, Vol. 22, S. No. 1274, Job 34.31,32, n.d., p. 38: '[D]ear friends, let us commune together upon the text.'

[130] Hopkins, *Nonconformity's Romantic Generation*, p. 129. Hopkins comments on Spurgeon's struggles in both preparation and delivery.

> Some of my ministerial brethren used to mourn over the heavy burden that rested upon them because they had to deliver their Master's message twice on the Sabbath, and once on a week-night; but I could not sympathize with them in their complaints, for the more often I preached, the more often I found joy in the happy service.[131]

In the 1850s (and this comment would also have held true for most of the 1860s) the more Spurgeon preached the more fulfilled and joyful he felt. Consequently, in the first phase of his ministry in London Spurgeon gave himself to midweek services in the capital and beyond in addition to his ministry to his own congregation.

From 1867 onwards, as will be established in chapter 8, ill-health curtailed the number of midweek engagements he could fulfil and also led to him being absent from the Tabernacle pulpit for months at a time.[132] Preaching when unwell, which he often did, caused him great strain. But being unable to preach caused great strain and unhappiness too.[133] Although preaching could make Spurgeon 'weary', not preaching made him wearier still. In the last decade of his life sermon delivery became perhaps less of a joy because of his health problems, but it was no less important to him than it had been at the beginning of his ministry. Preaching was both a solemn honour and a 'great responsibility', an activity into which Spurgeon put all of his effort. 'Woe unto us if we dare to speak the Word of the Lord with less than our whole heart, and soul, and strength!' he declared in the 'Infallibility Of Scripture'.[134] His understanding of preaching as a proclamation, not of human reason but of the word of Christ which gives life to men and women, was at the heart of this attitude. He insisted that,

> If we had common themes to speak about, we might leave the pulpit as a weary pleader quits the forum; but as, 'The mouth of the Lord hath spoken it,' we feel his Word to be as fire in our bones, and we grow more weary with refraining than with testifying. O my brethren, the Word of the Lord is so precious that we must in the morning sow this blessed seed, and in the evening we must not withhold our hands. It is a living seed and the seed of life, and therefore we must diligently scatter it.[135]

Spurgeon could be, as Thomas Cox remembered, 'intensely earnest / at times terribly so'.[136] This long quotation from 'The Infallibility Of Scripture' is an

---

[131] Spurgeon, *Autobiography*, Vol. 2, p. 82.

[132] For an account of Spurgeon's illness of 1867 that underlines the seriousness of the situation, see Pike, *C.H. Spurgeon*, Vol. 4, pp. 222-24. For more detail on Spurgeon's health see chapters seven and nine of this study.

[133] See C.H. Spurgeon, 'A Short Sermon For The New Year. From The Sick Chamber Of C.H. Spurgeon', n.d., pp. 1-4; 'The Sick Man Left Behind', *MTP*, Vol. 25, S. No. 1452, 2 Timothy 4.20, 'A Short Sermon From The Sick Room Of C.H. Spurgeon', 12 January 1879, pp. 13-16; 'To My Beloved Church and Congregation', *MTP*, Vol. 25, p. 36. This last reference was a letter from Spurgeon to the Tabernacle congregation, reprinted in the *MTP*.

[134] Spurgeon, 'The Infallibility Of Scripture', p. 146.

[135] Spurgeon, 'The Infallibility Of Scripture', p. 149.

[136] Cox, 'Notes on C.H. Spurgeon', p. 2.

example of this earnestness. The word burned deep within Spurgeon and he felt compelled to share it however weary he felt. As long as he was able to, he had to preach. The word had given him life by pointing him to Jesus. He now had the high calling of 'scattering' the 'seed' of word in preaching that others might also look to Christ. The true message of Christ that was at the heart of the scriptures had to be shared with Christ's people.

The *Treasury of David*

Spurgeon's approach to writing the *Treasury of David* further shows the extent to which other people were important to him. Firstly, to a degree, Spurgeon considered the Psalms themselves to be 'friends' with whom he could 'commune'. In the Preface to Volume 6 of the *Treasury* he wrote,

> No man needs better company than the Psalms; therein he may read and commune with friends human and divine; friends who know the heart of man towards God, and the heart of God towards man; friends who perfectly sympathise with us and our sorrows, friends who never betray or forsake.[137]

The Psalms were reliable friends who understood, supported and strengthened him. Spurgeon had a deep need for companionship and suffered an acute sense of loss when he felt let down by those he had trusted. The Downgrade Controversy provides useful material to illustrate the general point. In 1888 Spurgeon effectively disbanded the Pastors' College conference – the fellowship of former students – reconstituting it as a new grouping with a tightened the basis of faith, one which explicitly excluded anyone who espoused universalism or the possibility of 'probation after death' (repentance and salvation in the after-life).[138] The refusal of some former students of the Pastors' College to sign the revised basis, thus splitting the old College Conference, was described by the Conference president as 'the sorest wound' he experienced in the whole dispute.[139] For Spurgeon, by contrast with this sort of disloyalty, the Psalms were life-long friends who would never 'betray' or

---

[137] Spurgeon, *Treasury of David*, Vol. 6, Preface, p. vii.

[138] *Freeman*, 10 February 1888, p. 81, as cited by I.M. Randall, 'Charles Haddon Spurgeon, the Pastors' College and the Downgrade Controversy', in K. Cooper and J. Gregory (eds), *Discipline and Diversity: Papers Read at the 2005 Summer Meeting and the 2006 Winter Meeting of the Ecclesiastical History Society* (Woodbridge, Suffolk: Boydell, 2007), p. 368.

[139] Spurgeon (ed.), *Sword and Trowel*, March 1888, p. 148. Cf. C.H. Spurgeon to an unnamed 'friend', 21 February 1888, in 'Original Correspondence of Charles Haddon Spurgeon, 1887-1892, Spurgeon's College, Heritage Room (4G), No. 93, in which Spurgeon speaks of the 'desertion of his own men'. Randall, 'Spurgeon, the Pastors' College and the Downgrade Controversy', shows that many of the College alumni who felt they could not sign the new basis of faith were also deeply hurt by the split. Randall is drawing on 'Downgrade Controversy: Various letters in answer to questionnaire of 1888', Spurgeon's College, Heritage Room (B1.16).

'forsake'. As has already been noted in this chapter, he felt a kinship with the human authors of scripture, such as David,[140] and with the passages of scripture themselves. The Psalter, indeed the whole Bible, was not only an infallible guide but an infallible friend.

Spurgeon also felt a sense of communion with the various biblical commentators he consulted as he worked on the *Treasury*. In his Preface to Volume 1 he claimed 'originality' for his comments insisting that he had consulted only a 'few authors' before penning his own exposition.[141] But the reality was different. In this first volume of the *Treasury*, the 'Index Of Authors Quoted Or Referred To', printed immediately after the Preface, covers six pages of the Marshall's edition.[142] Corresponding indices in subsequent volumes are of similar length.[143] The majority of the references are to pages in the sections entitled 'Explanatory Notes And Quaint Sayings'. These are appended to the main exposition of each Psalm and consist of edited quotations and occasional summaries of the work of others.[144] The material in these 'Explanatory Notes …' sections in Volume 1 was largely culled from Spurgeon's own reading. Given the 'bulk' of his accumulated notes, only 'specimens' of the whole could be given. Spurgeon made it clear that he was far from endorsing all that was said in his sources. Nevertheless, he believed that nothing 'evil' had been included and his hope was that the extracts might prove 'serviceable' to others.[145]

Many different authors were cited. In Volume 1 Spurgeon drew liberally from Augustine (twenty-nine references), Martin Luther (thirty-one references) and John Calvin (seventeen references). Puritan commentators featured prominently. These included Stephen Charnock (seventeen references), William Gurnall (twenty-eight references), Matthew Henry (sixteen references) and John Trapp, whom Spurgeon would later eulogise in *Commenting and Commentaries* and who, with fifty-eight separate recorded references, was the most quoted authority in this volume of the *Treasury*.[146] Eighteenth-century evangelicals were also represented, for example George Whitefield (two references) and Andrew Fuller (seven references). But Spurgeon had engaged with a broader range of authors than those just cited. These

---

[140] Spurgeon, *Treasury of David*, Vol. 6, Preface, p. vii: 'Oh, to be shut up in a cave with David, with no other occupation but to hear him sing, and to sing with him.'

[141] Spurgeon, *Treasury of David*, Vol. 1, Preface, p. v.

[142] Spurgeon, *Treasury of David*, Vol. 1, 'Index Of Authors Quoted Or Referred To', pp. vii-xii.

[143] Cf. Spurgeon, *Treasury of David*, Vol. 2, pp. vii-xii (six pages); Vol. 6, pp. xi-xvi (just over five pages).

[144] From Spurgeon, *Treasury of David*, Vol. 5, onwards, this section was re-titled, 'Explanatory Notes'. See, e.g., Vol. 5, p. 13. For instances where extracts have been 'condensed', see Vol. 5, pp. 193, 199.

[145] Spurgeon, *Treasury of David*, Vol. 1, Preface, p. v.

[146] Spurgeon, *Treasury of David*, Vol. 1, 'Index Of Authors Quoted Or Referred To', pp. vii-xii. Cf. C.H. Spurgeon, *Commenting and Commentaries* (London: Banner of Truth, 1969 [London: Passmore and Alabaster, 1876]), pp. 7-8; 43.

included the Caroline divine Lancelot Andrewes (six references), and leading Oxford Movement figures John Keble (two references), and John Mason Neale (eighteen references).[147] Although the 'Explanatory Notes And Quaint Sayings' sections can seem somewhat removed from the main exposition, Spurgeon clearly drew on a great range of commentators, both dead and living, as he wrote on the various Psalms. With reference to Psalm 119 he stated, 'Several great authors have traversed this region and left their tracks behind them, and so far the journey has been all the easier for me; but yet to me and my helpers it has been no mean feat of patient authorship and research.'[148] Spurgeon leant on a range of commentators as he worked his way through the Psalter.

Spurgeon's reference to 'my helpers' in the previous paragraph alerts us to the fact that he did not pursue the task of exposition alone. He was happy to state this explicitly in the Preface to Volume 1 of the *Treasury*. Spurgeon was assisted by his 'friend and amanuensis' J.L. Keys who had helped the author track down various books and references. '[W]ith his help I have ransacked books by the hundred', Spurgeon wrote.[149] By the time Spurgeon had finished Volume 3 (completed in March 1872) he was also drawing on the services of David Gracey, the classics tutor at the Pastors' College,[150] who helped translate Latin commentators and the principal, George Rogers, who provided much material for another section which appeared for each of the Psalms, 'Hints To The Village Preacher'.[151] Volume by volume the number of helpers increased. By Volume 5 they included E.T. Gibson of Crayford, who helped translate both Latin and German authors and, by Volume 6, various ministers who had trained at the Pastors' College, who had provided a number of the sermon outlines in the 'Hints ...' sections.[152] Those College trained ministers who supplied outlines included, for Volume 6, F.G. Marchant, W.H.J. Page, C.A. Davis and William Williams,[153] and for Volume Seven, C.A. Davis

---

[147] Spurgeon, *Treasury of David*, Vol. 1, 'Index Of Authors Quoted Or Referred To', pp. vii-xii.

[148] Spurgeon, *Treasury of David*, Vol. 6, Preface, p. vi; cf. C.H. Spurgeon, *The Golden Alphabet Of The Praises Of Holy Scripture...Being A Devotional Commentary Upon The One Hundred And Nineteenth Psalm* (London: Passmore and Alabaster, 1898 [1887]), p. 8. The *Golden Alphabet* was mainly composed of material extracted from Vol. 6 of the *Treasury of David*. A list of ten works specifically on Psalm 119 is given immediately following the 'Notes On Separate Verses' section in the *Treasury of David*, Vol. 6, pp. 397-98. These include J. Calvin, *Two and Twentie Sermons of Maister John Calvin* (trans. T[homas] S[tocker]; London: John Harrison and Thomas Man, 1580), and T. Manton, *One Hundred and Ninety Sermons on the Hundred and Nineteenth Psalm* (London, 1725).

[149] Spurgeon, *Treasury of David*, Vol. 1, Preface, pp. v-vi; cf. Vol. 3, Preface, p. vi.

[150] Gracey became principal of the College in 1881. I.M. Randall, *A School of the Prophets: 150 Years of Spurgeon's College* (London: Spurgeon's College, 2005), p. 4.

[151] Spurgeon, *Treasury of David*, Vol. 3, Preface, pp. v-vi.

[152] Spurgeon, *Treasury of David*, Vol. 5, 'Preface', pp. vii-viii; Vol. 6, Preface, pp. vi-vii.

[153] Spurgeon, *Treasury of David*, Vol. 6, pp. 360-61, 389. These outlines on verses from Psalm 119 were subsumed in a section headed 'Notes on Separate Verses' which covered pp. 359-97. C.A. Davis of Reading was one of the ministers who protested in 1888 about the

(again), W.B. Haynes and John Field.[154] There is evidence that Spurgeon was very close to a number of these men, for example Williams and Page. In 1884 Spurgeon brought Page 'a complete set of Calvin' as a token of his esteem.[155] Williams had 'many memories' of times spent at Westwood and elsewhere. He also went on holiday with Spurgeon to Scotland.[156] Spurgeon enjoyed friendships with these men which were fostered by their shared work on the *Treasury*.

The writing of the *Treasury of David* was, therefore, a team effort. This was so from the beginning of the enterprise, but it was especially the case for later volumes. In his Preface to Volume 7 Spurgeon acknowledged that he was now 'editor in chief, and not much more' for the sections containing extracts from other works. These were now collected by others.[157] The hints to village preachers were also largely written by others, as Spurgeon once again acknowledged.[158] He wrote the expositions for this volume and corrected the proofs, as his original handwritten expositions and the heavily annotated proofs, which are both extant, show.[159] This material shows that Spurgeon was fully engaged in writing the *Treasury*, but it also offers further evidence that the finished product was very much a joint effort. Spurgeon relied heavily on the relationship that he had with his publishers, Passmore and Alabaster. The existence of the carefully prepared proofs and the fact that Spurgeon's (sometimes barely legible) comments on these were carefully incorporated into the final version bears testimony to this fact. Comparison of the corrected proofs of Spurgeon's exposition of Psalm 150 with the published version shows that all Spurgeon's detailed corrections and additions were carefully incorporated into the final text.[160] Spurgeon's relationship with his publishers was one of deep mutual regard and, indeed, complete trust. Joseph Passmore was a

---

new, restricted basis of membership of the College Conference. See C.H. Spurgeon to C.A. Davis, 18 February 1888, in Pike, *C.H. Spurgeon*, Vol. 6, pp. 297-98. Cf. in 'Downgrade Controversy, Various Letters ...', G. Smith to Profs Gracey and Ferguson, 21 February 1888; E. Compton to Profs Gracey and Ferguson, 14 February 1888, 'I have no sympathy with...Davis and Co.'.

[154] Spurgeon, *Treasury of David*, Vol. 7, pp. 11, 27, 43, 99. George Rogers remained a regular contributor to the 'Hints ...' section. See, e.g., p. 68 where Rogers contributed three of the nine outlines on Psalm 129, and cf. Spurgeon's own comments in the Preface, pp. vi-vii. For more of Davis's contributions, see, e.g., Vol. 6, pp. 356-57. For John Field's positive estimate of his 'beloved President', see J. Field to Profs Gracey and Ferguson, 10 February 1888, in 'Downgrade Controversy, Various letters ...'.

[155] C.H. Spurgeon to W.H.J. Page, 17 June 1884, in 'Original Correspondence of Charles Haddon Spurgeon, 1863-1886', Spurgeon's College, Heritage Room (4G), No. 50.

[156] See Williams, *Personal Reminiscences* (rev edn.), p. 37. The book as a whole offers much evidence of Williams' closeness to Spurgeon, which will be highlighted again in chapter nine of this study.

[157] Spurgeon, *Treasury of David*, Vol. 7, Preface, p. vi.

[158] Spurgeon, *Treasury of David*, Vol. 7, Preface, pp. vi-vii.

[159] C.H. Spurgeon, 'Manuscripts. Treasury of David. Vol. VII', Spurgeon's College, Heritage Room (Display Case 8)

[160] Spurgeon, 'Manuscripts. Treasury of David. Vol. VII'.

Tabernacle deacon (from 1862) and especially close friend.[161] Overall, although Spurgeon was obviously central to the *Treasury*, he relied on a host of others. This was Spurgeon's own judgement. In writing the different volumes he said he owed, in the first place, 'all to God' and, in the second place, 'very, very much to those generous friends who find a delight in making my efforts successful'.[162]

To sum up, Spurgeon leaned on the commentators he consulted and relied on his close band of living helpers as he worked on the *Treasury of David*. Moreover he felt a sense of spiritual kinship, not only with the living helpers and the best of the commentators, but also with David himself. Undoubtedly, Spurgeon's reliance on men like Keys, Rogers and Passmore was necessitated, to a degree, by his health problems which, as will be shown, affected his ministry especially from 1867. But his preference for working with others ran much deeper than this. It was linked to issues of character and temperament. Spurgeon was not attracted to a solitary life or to thought of working in isolation. He wanted to have other people close by and to work with others. As far as the *Treasury of David* was concerned, the message of Christ the Psalter contained was only shared with the help of significant and varied input from Christ's people.

Conclusion

In 'The Talking Book', Spurgeon made the following comment about 'the law of God', a phrase which he understood in terms of 'the whole run of scripture, and, especially the gospel of Jesus Christ'.

> The law of God should be so dear to us, that it should be bound about the most vital organ of our being, braided about our heart ... We are to love the word of God with all our heart, and mind, and soul, and strength; with the full force of our nature we are to embrace it; all our warmest affections are to be bound up with it.[163]

Thus, Spurgeon declared his love for the scriptures, even daring to rework Mark 13.30 and parallels so that they spoke of love for God's word rather than God himself. What we have seen in this chapter, and what this quotation reinforces once again, is that the Bible was central to the sustaining of Spurgeon's spirituality. The Bible was for Spurgeon an infallible 'guide' to the Christian life and a trustworthy 'friend' along the way.

---

[161] In speaking of Passmore, Spurgeon moved seamlessly between words and phrases such as 'faithful (member) of the church' and 'friendship...of the most intimate character'. Work and friendship were all of a piece, something that was perhaps summed up by Spurgeon's comment that he and Passmore enjoyed 'fellowship through the printing press'. *Christian Herald*, 22 August 1895, in 'Maroon Bound Scrapfolders', Vol. 2, Spurgeon's College, Heritage Room, p. 69.

[162] Spurgeon, *Treasury of David*, Vol. 6, Preface, pp. vi-vii. Spurgeon's comment related first to the writing of the *Treasury* but also, he said, held good for all his other 'labours'.

[163] Spurgeon, 'The Talking Book', p. 589.

Further analysis of Spurgeon's approach to the Bible shows that this was influenced by a complex matrix of factors – to do with religion, culture and temperament. But, despite this complexity, our analysis of Spurgeon's use of the Bible shows that the theme 'communion with Christ and his people' binds together Spurgeon's thinking and practice. With regard to communion with Christ, there was an extremely close correlation in Spurgeon's thinking between Christ and the Bible. The Bible led Spurgeon to Christ, revealed Christ and was closely identified with Christ. With regard to communion with Christ's people, the church (both militant and triumphant) was crucial to the task of biblical interpretation. Moreover, it was a vital part of Spurgeon's spirituality that he disseminate the message of the Bible (which for him was the message of Christ) far and wide, through preaching and writing. The gospel of Christ was to be shared with Christ's people, and those who did not yet know Christ were encouraged to look to him. In summary, for Spurgeon, the 'quintessence of the word of God [the Bible] is Christ',[164] and his own calling was to appropriate that word ever more deeply and then 'go forth and prove its power in the hearts' of others.[165]

---

[164] C.H. Spurgeon, *Evening By Evening*, 10 June, John 5.39, p. 162.
[165] Spurgeon, *Gospel of the Kingdom*, Matthew 8.8-9, p. 48.

CHAPTER 6

Prayer:
'Earnest prayer is the most potent means of winning continued communion'

The Bible was foundational for the sustaining of Spurgeon's spiritual life, but prayer was vitally important as well. Prayer is an aspect of Spurgeon's life and ministry that has rarely been examined or given its due weight. For example, Patricia Kruppa, in her biography of Spurgeon, hardly ever mentions prayer, despite the importance her subject attached to it.[1] For Spurgeon, prayer was 'as much a necessity' for his own spiritual life as breath was for his natural life. 'We cannot live', he insisted, 'without asking favours of the Lord.'[2] Spurgeon was referring here especially to intercession and this vital dimension of his prayer life is considered at length in this chapter. But other aspects of prayer – praise and thanksgiving, confession and quiet contemplation – were also important to him and these are analysed too. This chapter builds on previous ones by further illuminating the diverse and complex set of influences which came together to shape Spurgeon's spirituality, and it sheds additional light on the integrating theme of his spiritual life, 'communion with Christ and his people'.

Spurgeon's approach to Prayer

Spurgeon defined prayer as nothing less than the approach of the human soul 'by the Spirit of God to the throne of God'. Prayer was not merely the 'utterance of words', neither was it 'alone the feeling of desires'. Rather it was 'the advance of [those] desires to God, the spiritual approach of our nature towards the Lord our God'.[3] He believed that many people thought they were praying when they were, in point of fact, just repeating 'pious language' which was merely a caricature of true prayer. This was a central reason why he rejected all liturgy and set prayers. He held that the practice of reading prayers, whether in private or family worship, encouraged empty,

---

[1] P.S. Kruppa, *Charles Haddon Spurgeon: A Preacher's Progress* (New York: Garland, 1982).

[2] C.H. Spurgeon, 'The Secret Of Power In Prayer', *New Park Street Pulpit (NPSP)/Metropolitan Tabernacle Pulpit (MTP)* (London: Passmore and Alabaster, 1856–1917), *MTP*, S. No. 2002, Vol. 34, John 15.7, delivered 8 January 1888, p. 15.

[3] C.H. Spurgeon, 'The Throne Of Grace', *MTP*, S. No. 1024, Vol. 17, Hebrews 4.16, delivered 19 November 1871, p. 673.

'formal' devotions, so militating against prayer from the 'heart'.[4] The stress on true prayer as coming from the heart was a repeated one.[5] In speaking about prayer from the heart, Spurgeon wanted to insist that it was vital for the mind and the emotions to be fully engaged. Any words used had to be the believer's own and they had to spring from deep within.[6] In one sermon he stressed what was one of his major emphases by way of an epigram, 'Prayer with the heart is the heart of prayer.'[7]

Spurgeon was also clear that approaching God in prayer was only possible because of the sacrifice of Christ, who was the Christian's great high priest. Because of Christ's 'once for all time' sacrifice, continued access to the Father in prayer was now possible for someone who had been brought into a saving relationship with God. The presence and work of the Holy Spirit was also crucial if true 'heart' prayer was to take place, for only the Spirit could give proper life and shape to a Christian's desires and enable real 'spiritual fellowship'.[8] Thus Spurgeon had a theology which set prayer within a trinitarian framework and, unsurprisingly, many of his recorded prayers are explicitly addressed to the Father, through the Son, by the Spirit.[9]

Nevertheless, Spurgeon tended to focus on Christ in prayer – at least this is what the evidence of his published prayers shows. Much space is given in these prayers to extended reflections on Christ's person and especially his work. The following passage, from a prayer later entitled 'The Wonders of Calvary', is typical,

> We ... bless Thee, O God, as the God of our redemption, for Thou hast so loved us as to give even Thy dear Son for us. He gave Himself, His very life for us that He might redeem us from all iniquity and separate us unto Himself ... The wonders of Calvary

---

[4] C.H. Spurgeon, *Morning By Morning: Or, Daily Readings for the Family or the Closet* (London: Passmore and Alabaster, 1865), p. vii; 'A Loving Entreaty', *MTP*, S. No. 1743, Vol. 29, Isaiah 43.26, delivered 7 October 1883, p. 551.

[5] See, e.g., C.H. Spurgeon (ed.), *The Sword and The Trowel: A Record of Combat With Sin and Labour For The Lord* (*Sword and Trowel*) (London: Passmore and Alabaster, 1865–92), October 1871, p. 453; 'Unanswered Prayer', *MTP*, Vol. 59, S. No. 3344, Psalm 22.2, delivered 20 September 1866, p. 115; *Lectures To My Students* (3 Vols; London: Passmore and Alabaster, n.d.), Vol. 1, Lecture 4, 'Our Public Prayer', p. 61.

[6] C.H. Spurgeon, 'Prayer To God In Trouble An Acceptable Sacrifice', *MTP*, S. No. 1505, Vol. 19, Psalm 50.15, delivered 9 November 1879, p. 653.

[7] C.H. Spurgeon, 'Thought-Reading Extraordinary', *MTP*, Vol. 30, S. No. 1802, Psalm 10.17, delivered 5 October 1884, p. 536.

[8] Spurgeon, 'The Throne Of Grace', pp. 673-74.

[9] See, e.g., C.H. Spurgeon, 'Boldness at the Throne of Grace', in D.T. Young (ed.), *C.H. Spurgeon's Prayers* (London: Passmore and Alabaster, 1905), Prayer 21, p. 117; 'A Word To The Heart', in C.T. Cook (ed.), *Behold the Throne of Grace: C.H. Spurgeon's Prayers and Hymns* (London: Marshall, Morgan and Scott, n.d. [1934]), 19 April 1863, p. 16. The titles given to these prayers and excerpts from prayers were not original to Spurgeon.

never cease to be wonders, they are growingly [sic] marvellous in our esteem as we think of Him who washed us from our sins in His own blood.[10]

The atoning sacrifice of Christ made true prayer possible. It also provided the content of much of Spurgeon's public praise.[11]

Spurgeon's focus on Jesus is also shown by the frequency with which he prayed directly to Christ. Despite his trinitarian framework for prayer and the fact that he habitually began his prayers by addressing the Father, it is striking how many recorded prayers also contain sections in which Christ is addressed. Sometimes the Holy Spirit is also addressed in prayer,[12] but it was much more usual for Spurgeon to speak to Christ. So, in the course of a prayer prayed at the Tabernacle on 9 September 1887, Spurgeon exclaimed, 'Above all, blessed Jesus, our redeemer, let Thy love to us fire us with love to Thee. Stamp Thy dear image on our hearts, and let us never wander from the path of complete obedience to Thy will.'[13] The themes are similar to those Spurgeon dealt with in the extract from 'The Wonders of Calvary' – redemption through the cross and separation to Christ for a life of holiness – but whereas before God the Father was worshipped for the work of his Son, here it was Jesus himself who was addressed and praised.

Spurgeon's prayers at the Tabernacle provide many such examples of him speaking to Christ, rather than to the Father through Christ. The first twelve prayers included in the compilation entitled *The Pastor in Prayer* provide a sample of how he prayed in Sunday morning services. The prayers are from twelve separate services, all of which took place in the period 1877–78. On each occasion he began by addressing God as 'Father' or 'Lord', but in ten of the twelve prayers there are unambiguous examples of particular petitions or outbursts of praise being offered to Christ directly.[14] His love for Christ effectively led him to step outside his own theological framework for prayer. Indeed, the constant pull to focus on Christ could

---

[10] See, e.g., C.H. Spurgeon, 'The Wonders of Calvary', in Young (ed.), *C.H. Spurgeon's Prayers*, Prayer 6, p. 34. For another example of the focus on Christ, see 'The Blood-Besprinkled Mercy Seat', in Cook (ed.), *Behold the Throne of Grace*, pp. 119-20.

[11] Cf. Young (ed.), *C.H. Spurgeon's Prayers*, Introduction, p. viii. Reflecting on Spurgeon's public prayers, Young states, 'Precious to him beyond compare was the Divine Redeemer. The blood of our redemption was his glory.' See also Cook (ed.), *Behold the Throne of Grace*, Foreword, p. 12.

[12] Spurgeon, 'The Wonders of Calvary', in Young (ed.), *C.H. Spurgeon's Prayers*, Prayer 6, p. 35.

[13] C.H. Spurgeon, 'Ejaculatory Prayer', in [Anon.] (ed.), *The Pastor in Prayer: Being a Selection of C.H. Spurgeon's Sunday Morning Prayers* (London: Elliot Stock, 1893), Prayer 4, 9 September 1887, p. 27.

[14] See [Anon.] (ed.), *The Pastor in Prayer*, Prayer 1, p. 8; Prayer 2, pp. 14-17; Prayer 3, p. 22; Prayer 4, p. 27; Prayer 5, p. 34; Prayer 6, p. 39; Prayer 7, p. 41; Prayer 8, p. 50; Prayer 11, pp. 67, 69; Prayer 12, p. 76. In Prayer 9 Christ is not directly addressed on his own, although there is prayer to 'the Triune God of Israel', p. 54. In Prayer 10 there is no clear instance of prayer offered to Christ.

lead to some awkward grammar, as was the case in Prayer 15 in this volume, 'The Foot-Washing'. In this Spurgeon prayed,

> Oh Lord and Master, thou who didst wash Thy disciples' feet of old, still be very patient toward us, very condescending towards our provoking faults, and go on with us, we pray Thee, till Thy great work shall be completed, and we shall be brethren of the First-born, like unto Him.[15]

The reference to the washing of the disciples' feet (John 13.1-17) makes it clear that, at the beginning of this sentence, it is Christ who was being addressed. But by the end of the prayer Spurgeon had reverted to speaking of Christ in the second person, as he expressed his desire to be 'like unto Him [i.e., Jesus]', the 'First-born' (cf. Colossians 1.15-20). Both theology and grammar were strained by his ubiquitous desire to concentrate on Christ as the one with whom communion was to be enjoyed.

As to the daily rhythm of Spurgeon's prayer life, a set time of prayer early in the morning and another in the evening constituted his pattern. He sought to observe this discipline for himself and stated his belief, near the beginning of his public ministry, that 'Secret prayer is the test of a Christian.'[16] But his daily habit of prayer also included, from at least the time of his marriage onwards, leading morning and evening prayers for his own household. In these times hymn singing was included alongside scripture reading and prayer.[17] Spurgeon saw no contradiction between the blanket rejection of liturgy and the enthusiastic espousal of hymn singing. He had a strong commitment to 'family prayers' and this pattern of piety was frequently endorsed in sermons and shorter addresses.[18] For example, he told the students at the Pastors' College that it was essential that 'morning and evening sacrifice' should 'sanctify' their homes.[19] Although he believed it was unwise to 'make family exercises long',[20] to neglect them was 'Eli's sin', and such an attitude would be likely to bring with it the judgment of God.[21]

It is also important to recognise that, alongside this daily rhythm, Spurgeon also had a weekly rhythm of prayer. Crucial to this were the corporate prayer meetings

---

[15] Spurgeon, 'The Foot-Washing', in [Anon.] (ed.), *The Pastor in Prayer*, Prayer 15, p. 93.

[16] C.H. Spurgeon, 'The Pure Language', in 'Notebooks With Sermon Outlines, Vols 2, 4-9', Spurgeon's College, Heritage Room (U1), Vol. 4, S. No. 221, Zephaniah 3.9.

[17] C.H. Spurgeon, *Autobiography: Compiled from his Diary, Letters, and Records by his Wife and his Private Secretary* (4 Vols; London: Passmore and Alabaster, 1897–99), Vol. 1, p. 286.

[18] See, e.g., C.H. Spurgeon, 'Intercessory Prayer', *MTP*, S. No. 1049, Vol. 18, Psalm 141.5, delivered 5 May 1872, p. 260; Preface, *MTP*, Vol. 11, 1865, p. vii.

[19] Spurgeon, *Lectures To My Students*, Vol. 1, Lecture 3, 'The Preacher's Private Prayer', p. 40, cf. p. 41.

[20] Spurgeon, *Morning By Morning*, Preface to the section, 'Hymns for Morning Worship in the Family', n.p.. In my edition of *Morning By Morning* this section is an appendix to the main book.

[21] C.H. Spurgeon, 'Hindrances To Prayer', *MTP*, S. No. 1192-3, Vol. 20, 1 Peter 3.7, delivered 13 September 1874, p. 506.

which were part of the life of his church. Focusing on the life of the Tabernacle post-1861, it can be noted that, firstly, Spurgeon led prayers in the different Tabernacle worship services. There were two services which took place morning and evening on a Sunday, and a further service every Thursday evening. Spurgeon was famously reluctant to delegate the 'long prayer' which was offered on these occasions to another person, saying, 'I would sooner yield up the sermon than the prayer'.[22] Consequently, when he was present at a Tabernacle service, he invariably led in prayer. Secondly, Spurgeon was closely involved with the prayer meetings which preceded these different services.[23] Thirdly, he put special emphasis on the church's main prayer meeting which took place on a Monday night. There were usually over a thousand people present at this meeting, a level of attendance which he regarded as a sure sign of the health of the church.[24] Thomas Cox recorded what typically happened at the Monday night prayer meeting. There was usually at least one hymn and what Cox described as an 'impromptu' message from Spurgeon, who would then ask different men to pray. Much of the praying was done from the platform, although sometimes Spurgeon would invite someone to pray while they were still in the main body of the meeting. According to Cox, Spurgeon was careful to keep out 'cranks' and only 'call on those who could be heard'.[25] Clearly, he maintained a high level of involvement in these Monday night meetings and at the same time exercised a considerable amount of control over them.

Spurgeon was deeply committed to all of the different Tabernacle prayer meetings and he found the times when he had to miss them extremely difficult. With regard to the Monday night meetings he once said,

> I think that many of these ... meetings for prayer will never be forgotten by us who have been privileged to be present at them ... I know that, very often, as I have gone home, I have felt that the spirit of prayer has been so manifestly poured out in our midst that we have been carried right up to the gates of Heaven.[26]

The Monday evening meeting for corporate, extempore prayer was for Spurgeon a 'means of grace' and, specifically, a means of communion with God.[27] In the meetings before the various services, too, the 'mount of communion [with God]'

---

[22] Cook (ed.), *Behold the Throne of Grace*, Foreword, p. 10.

[23] C.H. Spurgeon, 'The Pastor's Need Of The People's Prayers', 2 Corinthians 1.11, in *Only a Prayer Meeting: Forty Addresses at the Metropolitan Tabernacle and Other Prayer Meetings* (London, Passmore and Alabaster, 1901), pp. 207-208; Spurgeon (ed.), *Sword and Trowel*, November 1883, p. 609.

[24] Spurgeon, 'Prayer Meetings; – As They Were, And As They Should Be', in *Only a Prayer Meeting*, p. 27; Spurgeon (ed.), *Sword and Trowel*, November 1883, p. 609.

[25] T. Cox, 'Notes on C.H. Spurgeon', Spurgeon's College, Heritage Room (B1.17), pp. 4-5.

[26] Spurgeon, 'Prayer Meetings; – As They Were, and as They Should Be', pp. 31; 27. For similar comments, see Spurgeon (ed.), *Sword and Trowel*, November 1883, p. 609.

[27] Spurgeon, 'Prayer Meetings; – As They Were, and as They Should Be', pp. 31; 27.

could be 'exceedingly glorious'.[28] He enjoyed rich communion with God in Tabernacle prayer meetings. The importance of corporate prayer to Spurgeon can further be seen from his belief that intercession offered by the church together was 'more effectual' than that offered by believers praying on their own.[29] As far as his own ministry was concerned, he was convinced that this was dependent on the prayers of others, saying at one Monday night meeting that he craved 'beyond all things' the 'constant prayers' of God's people.[30] Finally it can be added that he found participation in these different meetings for prayer personally invigorating. Such meetings were vital to his spirituality.

In addition to these daily and weekly rhythms Spurgeon sought to integrate prayer as fully as possible into the fabric of his daily life and work.[31] He told his students,

> We cannot always be on the knees of the body, but the soul should never leave the posture of devotion. The habit of prayer is good, but the spirit of prayer is better. Regular retirement is to be maintained, but continued communion with God is to be our aim. As a rule, we ministers ought never to be many minutes without actually lifting up our hearts in prayer.[32]

The comment 'the habit of prayer is good' is important. Spurgeon wanted to assert the importance of the sort of disciplines he himself observed and could be scathing about Christians who had 'no appointed time' in the day set aside for prayer.[33] But he also wanted to insist on the importance of maintaining continued communion with God through prayer throughout the day.[34] This involved quiet contemplation and wordless prayer, as will be shown, but it was verbal prayer – with words spoken either in the mind or out loud – which Spurgeon especially had in mind as he addressed his students. Regarding his own practice he said, 'Some of us could

---

[28] [Anon.] (ed.), *The Contemporary Pulpit Library: Sermons by the Rev. C.H. Spurgeon* (London: Swan, Sonnenschein & Co., 1892), Prayer 1, p. 115. This volume contains a number of Spurgeon's prayers, none of which is dated. The only detail is 'At the Metropolitan Tabernacle. Specially Reported.' In the prayer I have cited Spurgeon was explicitly referring to the pre-service prayer meeting.

[29] C.H. Spurgeon, 'Spiritual Knowledge and its Practical Results', *MTP*, S. No. 1742, Vol. 29, Colossians 1.9-10, delivered 30 September 1883, p. 532; 'The Importunate Widow', in *Sermons on our Lord's Parables* (London: Passmore and Alabaster, 1908), S. No. 856, Luke 18.1-8, delivered 21 February 1869, p. 105.

[30] Spurgeon, 'The Pastor's Need of the People's Prayers', pp. 201-202.

[31] C.H. Spurgeon, 'Prayer Without Ceasing', *MTP*, Vol. 18, S. No. 1039, 1 Thessalonians 5.17, delivered 10 March 1872, pp. 134-35, 142; 'The Importunate Widow', p. 98.

[32] Spurgeon, *Lectures To My Students*, Vol. 2, Lecture 1, 'The Holy Spirit in Connection with our Ministry', p. 13. Cf. 'John's First Doxology', *MTP*, Vol. No. 29, S. No. 1737, Revelation 1.5,6, delivered 2 September 1883, p. 470, where Spurgeon encouraged Christians to be always ready for prayer and to seek actively opportunities for this.

[33] Spurgeon, 'Hindrances To Prayer', p. 509.

[34] Cf. C.H. Spurgeon, 'Good News', *MTP*, Vol. No. 50, S. No. 2866, Proverbs 25.25, delivered 6 January 1876, p. 32.

honestly say that we are seldom a quarter of an hour without speaking to God.'[35] William Young Fullerton recorded examples of his subject praying with friends on walks and at railway stations and before and after reading books. He reckoned that 'Spurgeon seldom wrote a letter without raising his heart to God for guidance.'[36] Once again, it can be noted that communion with God in prayer was something Spurgeon often experienced together with others. This was so whether the context was a Monday night prayer meeting with a thousand present, working with one of his secretaries, or a walk with a friend.

In summary, examination of Spurgeon's approach to prayer is deeply revealing of the vital place of prayer in his life. Analysis of his practice of prayer reveals a stress on experimental 'heart' religion and a particular focus on the cross of Christ. Prayer was an essential means to communion with God. This was sometimes conceived of as communion with the Father through the Son,[37] but often as direct communion with Christ.[38] Spurgeon's desire for communion with Christ was repeatedly given voice in his published prayers.[39] Also, although he believed wholeheartedly in praying on his own, he accorded an important place to the corporate. Prayer – both solitary and corporate – was a means by which intense communion with Christ was regularly experienced.

Different Dimensions of Prayer

Spurgeon's practice of particular aspects of prayer – namely praise, thanksgiving and confession – can now be analysed in more detail. Because a significant number of Spurgeon's prayers at the Tabernacle are extant, this can be done with reference to his actual prayer life (at least his public prayer life), not just in relation to his preaching and writing about the subject. The importance of quiet contemplation to his spirituality is also considered in this section.

With regard to praise, the three main volumes of Spurgeon's prayers all contain a vast amount of material, as some of the titles given to various prayers by the different editors – 'To The King Eternal', 'The Music Of Praise', 'Bless the Lord, O My Soul!'[40] and 'Let All The People Praise Thee'[41] – indicate. Often, as already noted, this praise was centred on Christ, as in 'The Love of the Firstborn',[42] with a

---

[35] Spurgeon, 'The Holy Spirit in Connection with our Ministry', p. 13.

[36] W.Y. Fullerton, *C.H. Spurgeon: A Biography* (London: Williams and Norgate, 1920), pp. 178-79.

[37] See, e.g., Young (ed.), *C.H. Spurgeon's Prayers*, 'God's Unspeakable Gift!', Prayer 19, pp. 105-06.

[38] See, e.g. [Anon.] (ed.), *The Pastor in Prayer*, 'Take Fast Hold', 9 June 1878, p. 67.

[39] See, e.g., Young (ed.), *C.H. Spurgeon's Prayers*, 'O, for more Grace!', Prayer 18, p. 101.

[40] Young (ed.), *C.H. Spurgeon's Prayers*, Prayer 5, pp. 25-31; Prayer 10, pp. 55-59; Prayer 14, pp. 79-83.

[41] Cook (ed.), *Behold the Throne of Grace*, p. 101.

[42] Cook (ed.), *Behold the Throne of Grace*, p. 105.

special focus on the atonement, as in 'The Great Sacrifice' and the aforementioned 'The Wonders of Calvary'.[43] Nevertheless a vast array of themes was covered, from creation[44] to the future new heavens and new earth.[45] One prayer of praise which ranges widely, given the title 'The Adorable Trinity' by Charles Cook, can be considered in more detail.

The prayer begins with Spurgeon exclaiming, 'O Lord, we feel as if we must just stand before you in adoration.'[46] Spurgeon's strong desire to praise God in prayer, a desire which he often expressed,[47] and which others noted,[48] was here to the fore. Spurgeon's language throughout the ensuing prayer was emotional and earnest, an indication of the extent to which the praise he expressed proceeded from his own felt experience. Adoration was offered to the God who had revealed himself in 'trinity as well as in unity'. Father, Son and Holy Spirit were directly addressed and praised in turn. The Spirit was praised for 'condescending' to 'dwell in such poor tenements as our nature'[49] and, unsurprisingly, Christ was praised as the 'Lamb' with the focus once again on his saving work. Language which would have been recognised by Christians down the ages (Christ identified as the 'Lamb' of God) mixed with other language ('tenements') which was drawn from the immediate context of the London he and his hearers inhabited. What is especially noteworthy is the fact that when the Father was praised the focus was largely on Christ. Spurgeon led his congregation in adoration of God the Father who was the 'Father of Jesus' and 'of all that we are in Jesus'. Because Christ had been sent into the world, those who had embraced the gospel had a new relationship with God and could use the word 'Father' when addressing him. This was a mode of address that even Abraham had not been able to use. That Christians could use it was all thanks to the coming of the 'Lamb'. The relationship to God was different under the new covenant which Jesus had inaugurated. Thus, although Spurgeon was praising the Father, the focal point of this section of his prayer was still Christ.[50]

When Spurgeon engaged in thanksgiving, this was similarly concentrated on Christ. Cook includes a short section entitled 'Thanksgiving' in *Behold the Throne of Grace* which includes excerpts from eight prayers.[51] The first of these which was entitled 'Father, Son and Holy Spirit' contains a section very similar to the one from 'The Adorable Trinity'. Spurgeon spoke to God as 'Father', thankful that this was not an 'empty title'. Rather, this mode of address was deeply meaningful for, through

---

[43] Young (ed.), *C.H. Spurgeon's Prayers*, Prayer 20, pp. 111-16; Prayer 6, pp. 33-37.

[44] Cook (ed.), *Behold the Throne of Grace*, 'The Cross and the Throne', p. 103.

[45] Young (ed.), *C.H. Spurgeon's Prayers*, 'He Ever Liveth', Prayer 16, p. 93.

[46] Cook (ed.), *Behold the Throne of Grace*, 'The Adorable Trinity', p. 99.

[47] Cf. Cook (ed.), *Behold the Throne of Grace*, 'Let All the People Praise Thee!', p. 101; 'The Blood-Besprinkled Mercy Seat', p. 119.

[48] E.g., A.T. Pierson, as cited by Cook (ed.), *Behold the Throne of Grace*, Foreword, p. 10.

[49] Cook (ed.), *Behold the Throne of Grace*, 'The Adorable Trinity', p. 100.

[50] Cook (ed.), *Behold the Throne of Grace*, 'The Adorable Trinity', p. 99.

[51] Cook (ed.), *Behold the Throne of Grace*, pp. 111-12. The book also includes a section entitled 'Adoration' (pp. 99-108) from which 'the Adorable Trinity' was taken.

belief in Jesus, Christians had been adopted into God's family. Those present who were believers could 'feel' the spirit of adoption in them, enabling them to cry, 'Abba, Father'. God the Father was approached and thanked but again the fulcrum of the prayer was Christ and his work.[52]

In another prayer in this section, 'The Blood-Besprinkled Mercy Seat', there was thanksgiving offered for the atonement, described as 'the great expiatory Sacrifice'. Standing before his vast Tabernacle congregation, Spurgeon declared,

> [W]e [would] compass Thine altar, O God. We come sprinkled with the blood to a blood-sprinkled Mercy seat, and are not afraid to come when we can make mention of the righteousness of Christ and His Atonement. We feel that we are reconciled unto God by the death of His Son.[53]

Once more, the familiar themes are present in this prayer, which was in reality more a prayer of approach than one of thanksgiving. The themes were Christ, the cross, and a 'felt' sense that the benefits of the atonement were truly enjoyed. This was experimental religion which was focused on the person and work of Christ.

As far as prayers of confession were concerned, I have been unable to find one which does not make reference to the sacrifice of Christ.[54] It was only through the atonement that confession and cleansing were possible. One example of a prayer of confession can be adduced:

> [H]elp everyone here to make an acceptable confession of sin ... here we stand, Lord, a company of publicans and sinners, with whom Jesus deigns to sit down. Heal us, Emanuel! [sic] Here we are needing that healing. Good physician, here is scope for Thee; come and manifest Thy healing power! There are many of us who have looked unto Jesus and are lightened, but we do confess that our faith was the gift of God. We had never looked with these blear eyes of ours to that dear cross, unless first the heavenly light had shone, and the heavenly finger had taken the thick scales away ... Lord, maintain the faith Thou hast created, strengthen it, let it be more and more simple.[55]

Once more, Spurgeon switches between addressing the Father in the first sentence and prayer to Jesus in the second and third sentences with prayer offered to 'Emanuel' and the 'Good physician'. He then returns to addressing the Father again. Yet again, the focus is on Christ and the cross. The references to regeneration and 'looking' to the cross carry with them echoes of his own conversion. The way that forgiveness was received at the time of initial conversion was also the way daily

---

[52] Cook (ed.), *Behold the Throne of Grace*, 'Father, Son And Holy Spirit', pp. 111.

[53] Cook (ed.), *Behold the Throne of Grace*, p. 119.

[54] Passages of confession include, Young (ed.), *C.H. Spurgeon's Prayers*, 'Boldness at the Throne of Grace', Prayer 21, p. 118; 'The Look of Faith', Prayer 23, pp. 132-33; [Anon.] (ed.), *The Pastor in Prayer*, 'Your Adversary', Prayer 18, pp. 110-11.

[55] [Anon.] (ed.), *The Pastor in Prayer*, Prayer 1, pp. 8-9.

forgiveness was to be received. Spurgeon's practice of public praise, thanksgiving and confession were not only christocentric but also crucicentric.

As far as quiet contemplation was concerned, Spurgeon put a high priority on this and James Gordon is mistaken when he says that 'Spurgeon had no patience with the more passive forms of devotion.'[56] In the sermon, 'Communion With Christ And His People', Spurgeon spoke at length of his own experience of silent prayer:

> I like sometimes in prayer, when I do not feel I can say anything, just to sit still, and look up; then faith spiritually descries the Well-beloved, and hears His voice in the solemn silence of the mind. Thus we have intercourse with Jesus of a closer sort than words could possibly express. Our soul melts beneath the warmth of Jesus' love, and darts upward her own love in return. Think not that I am dreaming, or am carried off by the memory of some unusual rhapsody: no, I assert that the devout soul can converse with the Lord Jesus all the day, and can have as true fellowship with Him as if He still dwelt bodily among men. This thing comes to me not by the hearing of the ear but by personal experience: I know of a surety that Jesus manifests Himself unto His people as He doth not unto the world.[57]

The quotation is revealing of the important place contemplation held in Spurgeon's practice of prayer, something that is supported by statements he made on other occasions.[58] Spurgeon felt unable to express in words the close communion he felt he experienced with Christ on these occasions. Christ was present to him to such an extent that he believed it bore comparison with Christ's bodily presence. This was a mystical experience of Christ but, crucially, it was available to all. This was not some 'unusual rhapsody'. Rather close communion with Christ could be experienced by any 'devout soul'. Christ manifested himself not just to Spurgeon or indeed to a few select saints. Communion with Christ could be known by 'his people'.

Overall, Spurgeon's prayer life was made up of a number of different dimensions. Adoration, thanksgiving, confession and contemplation have been considered in this section; intercession will be treated in more detail later in the chapter. Spurgeon's practice of prayer was, in some ways, diverse: it could be corporate or solitary, verbal or non-verbal. But the different dimensions of prayer and the different ways they were practised were united by the stress on experience and, especially, the emphasis on Christ. He was the focus of Spurgeon's adoration, the means of confession and forgiveness, the object of contemplation and the one with whom 'true fellowship' could be known.

---

[56] J.M. Gordon, *Evangelical Spirituality: From the Wesleys to John Stott* (London: SPCK, 1991), p. 168.

[57] C.H. Spurgeon, 'Communion With Christ And His People', 'An Address at a Communion Service at Mentone', 1 Corinthians 10.16-17, in *Till He Come: Communion Addresses and Meditations* (London: Passmore and Alabaster, 1896) p. 315.

[58] See, e.g., Spurgeon, 'Pray Without Ceasing', p. 134; cf. p. 141.

Influences

If Spurgeon's prayer life is held together by some unifying themes, it nevertheless shows evidence of a range of different influences. The impact of Puritanism can certainly be discerned, for example, in the commitment to family prayers. As was shown in chapter 2 of this study, family prayers in the Puritan pattern were practised by Spurgeon's mother and paternal grandfather. Spurgeon was shaped by these occasions, as evidenced by the handwritten 'Juvenile Magazine', which was cited in chapter 2, and the culture of family prayer in the Puritan mould became deeply ingrained in him.[59] In 1874 he made explicit reference to the Puritans as he sought to encourage commitment to regular family worship, declaring that

> In the good old Puritan times, it was said, that if you had walked down Cheapside you would have heard in every house the voice of a Psalm at a certain hour of the morning and evening, for there was no house then of professed Christians without family prayer.[60]

Spurgeon's picture of Puritan London was certainly idealised, but it was undoubtedly true that Puritan preachers were committed to morning and evening family prayers as an important expression of piety.[61] Spurgeon also drew on the example of the Puritans more generally, believing them to have been 'abundant in meditation and prayer', giving a priority to prayer that was rarely seen in his own day.[62] Again, it was an idealised version of Puritanism which was being invoked, but undoubtedly Puritan spirituality helped shape Spurgeon's prayer life.

If the influence of Puritanism was important then that of evangelicalism was crucial, indeed, the stress on family devotions (as well as being a Puritan emphasis) was, as David Bebbington states, 'a bastion of Evangelical spirituality'.[63] Daily family prayers were an example of the 'disciplined spirituality' which Cheryl Sanders notes has always been a 'characteristic feature' of evangelicalism.[64] The place of family prayer also helped to define nineteenth-century evangelical spirituality over and against High Church spirituality which, whilst being

---

[59] *C.H. Spurgeon's M.S. Magazine, Written by himself, when a boy, under 12 years of age. Facsimile Reproduction* (London: J. Barton, n.d. [original 1846]).

[60] Spurgeon, 'Hindrances To Prayer', p. 506.

[61] See, e.g., P. Benedict, *Christ's Churches Purely Reformed: A Social History of Calvinism* (New Haven/London: Yale University Press, 2002), p. 326; H. Davies, *The Worship of the English Puritans* (London: Dacre Press, 1946), pp. 278-85.

[62] Spurgeon, 'Only a Prayer Meeting', in *Only a Prayer Meeting*, p. 19.

[63] D.W. Bebbington, *Holiness in Nineteenth-Century England* (Carlisle: Paternoster, 2002), p. 44.

[64] C. Sanders, 'Disciplined Spirituality', in M.A. Noll and R.F. Thiemann (eds), *Where Shall My Wond'ring Soul Begin: The Landscape of Evangelical Piety and Thought* (Grand Rapids: Eerdmans, 2000), p. 61.

correspondingly 'disciplined', tended to stress a daily service in a church building.[65] Tellingly, Spurgeon contrasted his own advocacy of daily family prayers with what he called the 'theory' that prayer was 'most acceptable in the parish church'. The latter approach to daily prayer took away 'the priesthood from the father of the family' and made a 'vacancy for a superstitious priesthood'. Spurgeon drove home what was another attack on the Tractarians by calling family prayers a 'bulwark of Protestantism'.[66] Spurgeon's relationship with High Church spirituality was more subtle and complex than has often been supposed, as will be shown. But here Spurgeon's prayer life can be seen to be distinctively evangelical as opposed to High Church.

Spurgeon's emphasis on extempore prayer, in public and private, was also typically evangelical (whilst not being so typically Puritan).[67] Caution regarding the use of set prayers regularly surfaced within evangelicalism. Whitefield, for example, lamented that when 'the spirit of prayer began to be lost, then forms of prayer were invented'.[68] John Wesley, too, was decidedly cool regarding the use of written prayers.[69] The rejection of set prayers was certainly not uniform amongst evangelicals, as John Wolffe notes, and some evangelicals took a different approach from Spurgeon, producing books of prayers for use in family worship.[70] But even J.C. Ryle, the evangelical Bishop of Liverpool, cautioned against an over-reliance on written prayers in his widely read *Practical Religion*, published in 1878, two years before he became a bishop. The reasons given, namely that it was too easy to pray such prayers 'by rote' with little thought as to their meaning, were remarkably similar to those put forward by Spurgeon.[71] This is not to suggest any direct dependence, merely that Ryle and Spurgeon were part of the same evangelical milieu. Eighteenth-century evangelicals could also prize contemplation. Whitefield thought of meditation as 'a kind of silent prayer, whereby the soul is frequently as it

---

[65] For the emphasis in the Oxford Movement on the need for 'daily opportunities for common prayer in church', see G. Mursell, *English Spirituality: From 1700 to the Present Day* (London: SPCK, 2001), pp. 199-200.

[66] C.H. Spurgeon, 'Hindrances To Prayer', pp. 506-507. Cf. 'Family Reformation', *MTP*, Vol. 24, S. No. 1395, Genesis 35.1, n.d., p. 55.

[67] Davies, *Worship of the English Puritans*, pp. 115-61, although Puritans certainly shared an antipathy to 'merely formal' religion. So M.A. Noll, *The Rise of Evangelicalism: The Age of Edwards, Whitefield and the Wesleys* (Leicester: IVP, 2004), p. 48.

[68] G. Whitefield, *George Whitefield's Journals* [Seventh Journal: 25 June 1740–11 March 1741] (London: Banner of Truth, 1959 [1741]), p. 483.

[69] A. Skevington Wood, *Burning Heart: John Wesley, Evangelist* (Calver: Cliff College, 2001 [1967]), pp. 63, 102; I.M. Randall, *What a Friend We Have in Jesus: The Evangelical Tradition* (London: Darton, Longman and Todd, 2005), pp. 77, 79-80.

[70] J. Wolffe, *The Expansion of Evangelicalism: The Age of Wilberforce, More, Chalmers and Finney* (Leicester: IVP, 2006), pp. 148-49.

[71] J.C. Ryle, *Practical Religion* (Cambridge: James Clark, 1959 [1878]), p. 64. Ryle wrote, 'I believe that there are tens of thousands whose prayers are nothing but a mere form – a set of words repeated by rote, with no thought to their meaning.'

were carried out of itself to God',[72] and John Wesley said that although a faithful believer would not always be 'on his knees', yet he or she would be 'praying without ceasing'. Crucially, this was not always with words, but, as Ian Randall states, through 'silence, groans, adoration and a constant sense of God's presence'.[73] Thus, many aspects of Spurgeon's approach to prayer were representative of the evangelical tradition.

More needs to be said, however, for when Spurgeon spoke of silence and contemplation he often referred to other influences. To the students at the Pastors' College, he spoke of the importance of 'time spent in quiet prostration of the soul before the Lord'. Such practice was a reliable means to communion with God. This was because the King 'in his beauty' deigned to walk in the 'hallowed courts' of 'quietude'. This was of a piece with Spurgeon's thinking in 'Communion With Christ And His People': the importance of quiet contemplation was highlighted as a vital means to communion. But in speaking to his students Spurgeon linked this practice explicitly with the Quakers. 'Do you think me a Quaker?', he asked. 'Well, be it so. Herein I follow George Fox most lovingly.'[74] Fox, the most influential of the early Quaker leaders, had at one point sought spiritual guidance from a number of seventeenth-century Puritan separatist leaders, but had been disappointed by the counsel he received.[75] Although Quakers were linked with the Puritans, and some broad definitions of the movement include them within it,[76] it seems right to distinguish them from Puritanism. Silence is described by Michael Birkel as a 'pillar' of Quaker spirituality. According to Birkel, worship in this tradition has always been 'fundamentally receptive and contemplative', as well as being 'mystical in orientation'.[77] Spurgeon was willing to affirm this central aspect of Quaker spirituality, and his appreciation of Fox and the Quakers ran surprisingly deep.[78] A further influence on Spurgeon's practice of prayer can therefore be discerned.

---

[72] G. Whitefield, *Sermons on Important Subjects* (London: H. Fisher and Son, and P. Jackson, 1835), p. 52, as cited by Randall, *What a Friend*, p. 81.

[73] J. Wesley, 'The Character of a Methodist', in T. Jackson (ed.), *The Works of John Wesle* (Kansas: Beacon Hill Press, 3rd edn, 1978), Vol. 8, p. 404, as cited by Randall, *What a Friend*, p. 77.

[74] Spurgeon, 'The Preacher's Private Prayer', p. 50.

[75] M.L. Birkel, *Silence and Witness: The Quaker Tradition* (London: Darton, Longman and Todd, 2004), p. 18. For a short, alternative summary of the central tenets of Quaker spirituality, see L. Bouyer, *A History of Christian Spirituality, Vol. 3, Orthodox Spirituality and Protestant and Anglican Spirituality* (Tunbridge Wells: Burns and Oates, 1968 [French edn. 1965]), pp. 160-64.

[76] Quakers are sometimes viewed as being on the radical wing of Puritanism. See B.C. Lane, 'Puritan Spirituality', in P. Sheldrake (ed.), *The New SCM Dictionary of Christian Spirituality* (London: SCM, 2005), p. 519.

[77] Birkel, *Silence and Witness*, pp. 38, 15.

[78] See, especially, Spurgeon's lengthy and appreciative review of F.E. Budge, *Annals of the Early Friends: A Series of Biographical Sketches* (London: Samuel Harris, 1877), in Spurgeon (ed.), *Sword and Trowel*, October 1877, pp. 484-85. The review indicates that Spurgeon preferred the spiritual experience of early 'Friends' to that of nineteenth-century

Also, and surprisingly given Spurgeon's general attitude to Roman Catholicism and the Oxford Movement, the influence of High Church spirituality can be traced. As the College President continued speaking of silence and contemplation in 'The Preacher's Private Prayer', he observed,

> [T]he Romanists are accustomed to secure what they call 'Retreats', where a number of priests will retire for a time into perfect quietude, to spend the whole of the time in fasting and prayer, so as to inflame their souls with ardour. We may learn from our adversaries.[79]

Spurgeon's basic anti-Catholicism is indicated by his description of Roman Catholics as 'our adversaries'. But his willingness to recognise the note of authentic Christian experience, even in Roman Catholics, is in evidence as well. Spurgeon also spoke warmly of the work of Madame (Jeanne) Guyon, the seventeenth-century Roman Catholic mystic, and included four of her hymns in *Our Own Hymn Book* (see Nos 777–779 and 781).[80] These hymns are all in the crucial section, 'The Golden Book Of Communion With Jesus' (Nos 764–820) and they all express desires for continued and deeper communion with Christ in mystical terms. One hymn (No. 781) includes the lines,

> All hearts are cold, in every place,
>   Yet earthly good with warmth pursue;
>
> Dissolve them with a flash of grace,
>   Thaw these of ice, and give us new!

Spurgeon, as already shown, used remarkably similar language to this himself. It is true that all of Guyon's hymns included in *Our Own Hymn Book* are in translations by William Cowper, and so it could be argued that they were part of the common coinage of evangelical worship.[81] Nevertheless, Spurgeon's appreciation of Madame Guyon has rarely been recognised.[82] Moreover, this appreciation went beyond his appropriation of her hymnody and surfaces regularly in his works.[83] It

---

Quakers. The title page of Budge's work included a quotation from George Fox, 'We are nothing, Christ is all.' For another appreciative reference to Fox, see C.H. Spurgeon, 'The Personality Of The Holy Ghost', *NPSP*, Vol. 1, S. No. 4, John 14.16,17, delivered 21 January 1855, p. 30.

[79] Spurgeon, 'The Preacher's Private Prayer', p. 51.

[80] C.H. Spurgeon (ed.), *Our Own Hymn Book* (London: Passmore and Alabaster, 1866).

[81] Cf. Mursell, *English Spirituality*, p. 22. Guyon was also read by John Newton.

[82] Indeed, I am not aware of any study which has recognised it.

[83] In addition to the other references in this chapter, see, e.g., C.H. Spurgeon, 'The Church's Love To Her Loving Lord', in *The Most Holy Place: Sermons on the Song of Solomon* (London: Passmore and Alabaster, 1896), S. No. 636, Song of Songs 1.7, n.d., p. 72; 'Better than Wine', in *Most Holy Place*, S. No. 2459, Song of Songs 1.2, delivered 2 June 1872, p. 3.

was Guyon's approach to contemplation – her spending 'many a day and ... month in the sweet enjoyment of the love of Jesus' – together with her mysticism which particularly attracted Spurgeon.[84] She was, he said, a 'very mother of the mystics'.[85]

High Church works could be commended if they encouraged contemplation and communion with Christ. In *Commenting and Commentaries*, Spurgeon recommended a volume on the Song of Songs by John Baptist Elias Avrillon which, he informed his readers, was one of a series of reissues of 'Romish authors' by. Pusey. It was, Spurgeon stated, 'a deeply spiritual work', after the manner of the mystics. Indeed, 'it might have been written by Madame Guyon'. He admired the book because, despite its 'occasional Popery and sacramentarianism', it contained 'much choice devotional matter'.[86] Another work on the Song he commended was by John Mason Neale, the nineteenth-century Anglican High Churchman. Neale's printed sermons on the Song, said Spurgeon, smelt of 'Popery'. Nevertheless, 'the savour of our Lord's good ointment [could not] be hid'. Many a 'devout thought' had come to him whilst reading these sermons which, as the title of Neale's work announced, had been 'preached in a religious house'.[87] Again, a distinction was being made between ecclesiology and 'sacramentarianism' on the one hand and devotional writing which emphasised contemplation of Christ on the other. The former was rejected as superstitious nonsense; the latter was embraced as an aid to communion.

Mark Hopkins states that Spurgeon 'had long recognized spirituality in the High Church when he had come into contact with it', but argues that Spurgeon's 'last years' of illness and 'controversy' (Hopkins is thinking particularly of the Downgrade Controversy) 'brought something more'. The suggestion is that, as Spurgeon turned his sights on theological liberalism, he became more eirenic towards High Churchmen, and generally more 'catholic' in tone.[88] Hopkins, as usual, is perceptive, and undoubtedly there was a development in Spurgeon's views along the lines suggested. Speaking at the close of 1891, Spurgeon declared,

---

[84] Spurgeon, 'Better than Wine', p. 3.

[85] Spurgeon (ed.), *Sword and Trowel*, p. 38.

[86] C.H. Spurgeon, *Commenting and Commentaries* (London: Banner of Truth, 1969 [London: Passmore and Alabaster, 1876]), p. 111. Spurgeon was commending Avrillon's *The Year of Affections; or, Sentiments on the love of God, drawn from the Canticles, for every day of the year* (London and Oxford: Parker, 1847).

[87] Spurgeon, *Commenting and Commentaries*, p. 115. J.M. Neale's work was *Sermons on the Canticles, preached in a Religious House. By a Priest of the Church of England* (London: J. Masters, 1857). Cf. the comments Spurgeon made on another work, R.F. Littledale's *A Commentary. From Ancient and Mediaeval Sources* (London: J. Masters, 1869), also on p. 115 of *Commenting and Commentaries*. Littledale, said Spurgeon, was a close follower of Neale and had to be read with caution. Nevertheless, if 'discretion' was used, 'jewels' of 'silver' and 'gold' could be extracted from this book.

[88] M. Hopkins, *Nonconformity's Romantic Generation: Evangelical and Liberal Theologies in Victorian England* (Carlisle: Paternoster, 2004), p. 160.

> During the past year I have been made to see that there is more love and unity among God's people than is generally believed ... We mistake our divergences of judgment for differences of heart; but they are far from being the same thing ... For my part I believe that all spiritual persons are already one.[89]

Thus Spurgeon speaks of a shift in his own thinking. This is a crucial quotation, one which indicates some movement in his thought at the end of his life, and which suggests that some of the views he expressed in the heat of the Downgrade Controversy might not have been the ones he took to his grave. But while this quotation is certainly evidence of Spurgeon developing a more catholic tone in the final year of his life, my contention is that Spurgeon did more than just 'recognize' spirituality in the High Church in his earlier years of ministry. Rather, from at least the mid-1860s he could be warmly appreciative of such spirituality, and, crucially, influenced by it. Certainly the nature and extent of that influence was limited; indeed, it can be defined with a good degree of precision. He was influenced by some High Church practices and, especially, some mystical, High Church figures who through their writing and example helped him practice and experience communion with Christ. He was *not* influenced – at least in any positive sense – by Anglo-Catholic and Roman Catholic ecclesiology, sacerdotalism and ritual, because these all obscured Christ. They did this by trapping people in superstition and by interposing something or someone else, whether inappropriate symbolism or a priest acting as a mediator, between a person and Christ. The issue was simple: did the practice or attitude in question foster communion with Christ or did it militate against it? Moreover, in applying this test, Spurgeon was not just thinking of himself. The issue was also whether these practices and attitudes helped or hindered other people in their communion with Christ. The phrase 'communion with Christ and his people' thus helps us make sense of Spurgeon's seemingly contradictory attitudes to High Church spirituality. Spurgeon's appreciation of some High Church devotional literature is important, and this theme will be returned to in chapter 7. Here it can be noted that he was not afraid to embrace such literature when it connected positively with the integrating theme of his spirituality.

As already noted, Guyon used mystical language as she expressed her devotion to Christ. Given Spurgeon's comments in respect of her and other 'mystical' writers, it comes as little surprise to see this mystical strain evident in his prayers.[90] Indeed, the

---

[89] C.H. Spurgeon, 'Breaking the Long Silence', *Sword and Trowel*, February 1892, p. 52. This address, from 31 December 1891, is also in R. Shindler, *From The Pulpit To The Palm-Branch: A Memorial of C.H. Spurgeon* (London: Passmore and Alabaster, 1892), pp. 25-26.

[90] I am understanding mysticism here with Geoffrey Nuttall as 'a sense of being carried out beyond the things of time and space into unity with the infinite and eternal, in which the soul is filled with a deep consciousness of love and peace.' Nuttall further speaks of the passionate love language (he actually uses the term 'erotic') as the language which is often drawn on to express intimate unity with the divine. See 'Puritan and Quaker Mysticism' in G.F. Nuttall, *Studies in English Dissent* (Weston Rhyn: Quinta, 2002), pp. 83-84.

passionate 'love language' he used when speaking of Christ was, at times, startling. In 1878 he prayed,

> Oh to love the Saviour with a passion that can never cool ... Oh to delight in God with a holy overflowing rejoicing that can never be stopped, so that we might live to glorify God at the highest bent of our powers, living with enthusiasm, burning, blazing, being consumed with the indwelling God who worketh all things in us according to his will.[91]

Numerous other prayers in this vein could be cited (together with similar passages from his preaching).[92] In another prayer, also from 1878, Spurgeon expressed his longing for an increased devotion to Christ and focuses on the cross as the place where Christ's love for people is supremely shown.

> Oh, were there not a stone in our hearts we should melt in love to thee ... Give us more tenderness of heart, give us to feel the wounds of Jesus till they wound our sins to death. Give us to have a heart pierced even as his was, with deep sympathy for his griefs, and an all consuming love for his blessèd person.[93]

Gordon, in his treatment of Spurgeon in *Evangelical Spirituality*, points out that this sort of language and imagery – 'burning', 'blazing', 'being consumed with the indwelling God', and melting – was 'the standard vocabulary of the mystic'.[94] As already shown, similar language can be identified in Guyon's hymns. It was passages like those just quoted which led J.C. Carlile to devote a whole chapter of his biography of Spurgeon to his subject's 'mysticism',[95] and William Robertson Nicoll, the editor of the *British Weekly* from 1886, to bracket Spurgeon with Bunyan as one of the two greatest 'Evangelical mystics'.[96] This facet of Spurgeon simply has to be recognised if a true estimate of his prayer life is to be held. Devotion to Christ was expressed in distinctly mystical vein.

Robertson Nicoll's comparison of Spurgeon and Bunyan is helpful in that it reminds us that there is a mystical strand running through Puritanism.[97] Along with

---

[91] [Anon.] (ed.), *The Pastor in Prayer*, Prayer 1, 4 November 1878, p. 10.

[92] See, e.g., C.H. Spurgeon, 'The Well Beloved', in *Till He Come*, Song of Songs 5.16, 'A Communion Address at Mentone', pp. 101-102.

[93] [Anon.] (ed.), *The Pastor in Prayer*, Prayer 2, 18 November 1878, p. 14.

[94] Gordon, *Evangelical Spirituality*, p. 162. Gordon was commenting specifically on Spurgeon, 'The Well Beloved', pp. 101-102.

[95] J.C. Carlile, *C.H. Spurgeon: An Interpretative Biography* (London: Kingsgate Press, 1933), pp. 268-86. Cf. the comments of Fullerton, *C.H. Spurgeon*, pp. 181-82.

[96] T.H. Darlow, *W. Robertson Nicoll: Life and Letters* (London: Hodder and Stoughton, 1925), p. 402. This quotation has been used before in the secondary literature on Spurgeon. See, e.g., Hopkins, *Nonconformity's Romantic Generation*, p. 129; Gordon, *Evangelical Spirituality*, p. 161.

[97] On this, see the excellent discussion in T. Schwanda, 'Soul Recreation: Spiritual Marriage And Ravishment In The Contemplative-Mystical Piety of Isaac Ambrose'

Bunyan, Samuel Rutherford could be regarded as an exemplar of this tradition. Spurgeon's regard for Rutherford, especially his *Letters*, was great.[98] Indeed, in the same sermon on the Song of Songs in which Spurgeon commended Guyon's experience of communion with Christ through contemplation, he also enthused about Rutherford and for the same reason.[99] It is important to emphasise that I am not suggesting that Spurgeon's mysticism was influenced by High Church spirituality alone, or even that it was primarily influenced from this direction. The Puritan mysticism represented by Bunyan and Rutherford was a much more likely primary link, one that can be demonstrated from Spurgeon's own writings. But the connection between Spurgeon and High Church mysticism, although secondary, can also be demonstrated. Spurgeon's own brand of mysticism locates him within a broader stream of spirituality than Puritanism alone.

Examination of Spurgeon's prayer life thus strengthens the argument that his spirituality was moulded by a range of factors. Puritanism was certainly one of these, but evangelicalism was also important and, crucially, other influences, namely the Quakers and Roman Catholic and High Church writings, can also be identified, thus adding to the picture of a complex and diverse set of shaping factors which helped fashion Spurgeon's spiritual life. In fact, detailed analysis of Spurgeon's approach to intercession adds further to this complex web of influences, whilst further illuminating the central theme of this study.

Spurgeon's View of Intercession

In line with the mystical strain in Spurgeon, and his stress on the importance of contemplation, it should be emphasised that not all of Spurgeon's intercession was verbal. He believed that, 'We may cry into God's ear most effectually, and yet never say a word.'[100] Indeed, *in extremis*, prayer might be incoherent, consisting of, for example, groans and broken cries. In a message, entitled 'Concerning Prayer', preached on a Thursday evening at the Tabernacle, he declared,

> Prayers that are indistinct, inharmonious, broken, made up of sighs and cries, and damped with tears – these are the prayers which win heaven. Prayers that you cannot pray, pleadings too big for utterance, prayers that stagger the words, and break their backs, and crush them down – these are the very best prayers our God ever hears.[101]

(unpublished PhD dissertation, University of Durham, 2009), pp. 14-25. Cf., Nuttall, 'Puritan and Quaker Mysticism', pp. 81-108.

[98] See Spurgeon's review of Andrew Bonar's *Letters of Samuel Rutherford, With a Sketch of his Life, and Biographical Notices of his Correspondents* (Edinburgh and London: Oliphant, Anderson and Ferrier, 1891), in *Sword and Trowel*, June 1891, p. 342.

[99] Spurgeon, 'Better Than Wine', p. 3.

[100] Spurgeon, 'Pray Without Ceasing', p. 134.

[101] C.H. Spurgeon, 'Concerning Prayer', *MTP*, S. Nos. 2053-54, Vol. 34, Psalm 86.6-7, delivered Thursday evening 23 August 1888, p. 626. Cf. 'The Secret of Power in Prayer',

Praying such as this was most likely difficult, flowing as it probably did from a painful experience or situation. As such it would be deeply felt and, in Spurgeon's thinking, for this reason it was likely to be deeply efficacious – it was from the 'heart'. He spoke even more strongly of the value of this sort of praying in the *Treasury of David*. He wrote that there was an experience in prayer which was an 'intense longing', a time of 'waiting and fainting'. This sort of prayer was well known by 'full grown saints' and it was an experience that was not satisfied 'to express itself by the lips'. Rather, said Spurgeon, it 'speaks with the eyes'. He continued, once again using mystical language,

> Eyes can speak right eloquently; they use both mutes and liquids, and can sometimes say more than tongues ... A humble eye lifted to heaven in silent prayer may flash such a flame as shall melt the bolts which bar the entrance of vocal prayer, and so heaven shall be taken by storm with the artillery of tears.[102]

Undoubtedly Spurgeon's struggles with physical pain (see chapters 8 and 10) and with depression (see chapter 10) shaped his prayers; indeed all his comments concerning 'cries', 'sighs' and 'wordless prayers' were shot through with autobiography. Spurgeon's personal intercession encompassed non-verbal prayer and was certainly moulded by his suffering.

Having made this point, it is important to emphasise that Spurgeon's normal method of interceding for various concerns was to vocalize his prayers. Yet, despite the use of words, these requests were still brief and to the point and one gains the impression that the fewer words spoken the better. In a prayer meeting address Spurgeon declared his belief in what he termed 'business prayers'. These he described with the use of the following illustration.

> We should not think of going to the bank, and then coming away without the coin we needed; but we should lay before the clerk the promise to pay the bearer a certain sum, tell him in what form we wished to take the amount, count the cash after him, and then go our way to attend to other business. That is just an illustration of the method in which we should draw supplies for the Bank of Heaven. We should seek out the promise which applies to that particular case, plead it before the Lord in faith, expect to

---

MTP, S. No. 2002, Vol. 34, John 15.7, delivered 8 January 1888, p. 16, 'A single groan before God may have more fullness of prayer in it than a fine oration of great length.'

[102] C.H. Spurgeon, *The Treasury of David: Containing An Original Exposition Of The Book Of Psalms; A Collection Of Illustrative Extracts From The Whole Range Of Literature; A Series Of Homiletical Hints Upon Almost Every Verse; And Lists Of Writers Upon Each Psalm* (7 Vols; London and Edinburgh: Marshall Brothers, n.d. [London: Passmore and Alabaster, 1869–1885]), Vol. 6, p. 202.

have the blessing to which it relates; and then having received it, let us proceed to the next duty devolving upon us.[103]

Fullerton noted that Spurgeon often used this image, that of cashing a cheque at a bank, to describe his approach to intercessory prayer.[104] In the analogy the cheque was the prayer offered in faith to God who presided over the 'bank of heaven'. Because the guarantee that the 'cheque' would be accepted was the 'honoured name' of Christ and the relevant biblical promise, believers could be confident as they presented their requests. The point Spurgeon made about pleading biblical promises in prayer is important.[105] He was not advocating a form of intercession which consisted of bringing peremptory demands to God on an arbitrary range of subjects. In another prayer meeting address entitled 'Why We Have Not', Spurgeon affirmed that the scriptures encouraged the supplicant to use Christ's name and hence his authority in prayer and went on to say that this meant that believers 'ought not to pray anything' they could not imagine Jesus praying.[106] Intercessory prayer was to be tied to the character and will of God, as well as to the specific promises in the Bible (which Spurgeon believed were all fulfilled in Christ).[107] Believers were to seek out these promises in the scriptures and present their requests accordingly. As he told a Baptist Missionary Society (BMS) prayer meeting in 1885, although personal, temporal concerns were a proper subject for intercession, a Christian's prayer life, viewed in the round, should be 'proportionate'. For Spurgeon, this meant that the primary focus of a Christian's intercessory prayers was to be the concerns of Christ and his kingdom,[108] and, in practice, he especially emphasised prayers for the conversion of others.[109]

Spurgeon, then, believed a Christian should pray short, bold, faith-filled prayers that were focused on Christ's kingdom and then wait for the answer. He expressly wanted to avoid 'beating about the bush' in intercessory prayer.[110] There was no need for excessive and lengthy 'pleading' in prayer, for 'the name (of Christ) itself'

---

[103] C.H. Spurgeon, 'Business Prayers', in *Only a Prayer Meeting*, p. 32. Cf. *The Cheque Book of the Bank of Faith: Being Promises Arranged for Daily Use With Brief Experimental Comments* (London: Passmore and Alabaster, 1895), Preface, p. v.

[104] Fullerton, *C.H. Spurgeon*, p. 179.

[105] Cf. C.H. Spurgeon, 'Growth In Faith', *MTP*, Vol. 59, S. No. 3384, Luke 17.5, delivered 12 December 1867, p. 597; J.D. Douglas, *The Prince of Preachers: A Sketch; A Portraiture; And A Tribute* (London: Morgan and Scott, n.d. [1893]), p. 98.

[106] C.H. Spurgeon, 'Why We Have Not', James 4.2, in *Only a Prayer Meeting*, p. 218.

[107] C.H. Spurgeon, 'Keep In Mercy's Way', in [Anon.] (ed.), *The Pastor in Prayer*, pp. 161-63.

[108] C.H. Spurgeon, 'The World For Christ', address delivered 'at the Baptist Missionary Society Prayer Meeting at Bloomsbury Chapel', as reported in *The Christian World*, 28 April 1885, 'Spurgeon's Scrapbooks, Numbered Volumes', Spurgeon's College, Heritage Room (2G), Vol. 12, pp. 108-109.

[109] Spurgeon, 'Intercessory Prayer', p. 264.

[110] Spurgeon, 'Business Prayers', in *Only a Prayer Meeting*, p. 31.

Prayer 157

pleaded.[111] This approach to intercession is illustrated by his own prayers in the Tabernacle services.

Intercession for unbelievers was a regular feature of these recorded prayers.[112] Many of these petitions are good examples of Spurgeon 'pleading the promises' and the character of God in prayer. In the morning service on 5 July 1863 he expressed an emotional plea to see sinners converted. 'We thirst and pant for more numerous conversions', he declared. What was the basis of this request? Spurgeon continued,

> We have one argument that Thou wilt hear. It is that Jesus died ... Remember Jesus, O Thou mighty Father ... Canst Thou deny us? Wilt Thou not hear us when we have such a plea as this? If the preacher urged aught that he has said, or aught that his hearers have done, well mightest Thou turn Thy back upon us.[113]

Spurgeon had cried out to God in prayer with great boldness. But his confidence was based on the truth of the atonement as revealed in the scriptures. As he put it in prayer in the evening service later on that day, 'Our soul pleadeth with Thee for the dying sons of men. Jesus, is not Thy blood able to cleanse?'[114] Thus, if God had revealed something about himself through his word, either a promise or an aspect of his character, then he was emboldened to ask God to act in accordance with the scriptures.

As befitted Spurgeon's 'business' approach to intercession, many of his prayers appear brief to the point of terseness.[115] On occasion he simply listed a whole range of different concerns in quick succession, particularly when focusing on the multi-faceted work of the Tabernacle. Prayers such as, 'Bless all the agencies – the Sabbath School, the City Mission, the Bible women, street preachers and tract distributors ...' were not uncommon.[116] Sometimes he could deal in generalities, as in a prayer for God to bless 'all the thousand and one things which constitute the activities of the churches at large'.[117] This was in spite of advice he gave elsewhere about avoiding 'hackneyed prayers for everything in general and nothing in

---

[111] Fullerton, *C.H. Spurgeon*, p. 179.

[112] See, e.g. [Anon.] (ed.), *The Pastor in Prayer*, 'Intercession For One Another', Prayer 22, p. 137; 'An Evening Prayer', Prayer 25, p. 155; 'An Evening Prayer', Prayer 26, p. 159.

[113] Cook (ed.), *Behold the Throne of Grace*, 5 July (morning) 1863, pp. 32-33. For further examples of prayers for unbelievers from this volume, see, e.g., 28 September 1884, pp. 66-67; 13 October 1889, pp. 79-80.

[114] Cook (ed.), *Behold the Throne of Grace*, 5 July (evening), 1863, p. 38.

[115] There is nothing to suggest that these particular sections have been edited to make them shorter. Generally, the presence in the different volumes of Spurgeon's prayers of 'Spurgeonisms', for example, 'Oh to be Christly [sic]!' and awkward sentences, 'O Lord, we feel as if we must just stand before you in adoration', suggests that major editing of Spurgeon's words did not take place. Some of the prayers included in Cook's volume were excerpts from longer prayers.

[116] [Anon.] (ed.), *Sermons by the Rev. C.H. Spurgeon*, Prayer 6, n.d., p. 130.

[117] [Anon.] (ed.), *The Pastor in Prayer*, Prayer 9, 5 May 1878, p. 57.

particular'.[118] But more often he was specific. On 4 November 1877, within the space of what must have been a few minutes, he prayed for the Pastors' College, that 'every brother sent out be clothed with power', for the boys at the Orphanage, that all might be converted to Christ, and for the colporteurs, that they might be 'graciously guided to speak a word for Jesus'.[119] Spurgeon's normal practice of intercessory prayer was congruent with the teaching he gave to others. Intercession was to be thoroughly 'businesslike'.

Influences on Intercession

What were the factors which helped shape Spurgeon's 'business' approach to intercession? Certainly relevant was his astonishing speed of thought. He once confided to Fullerton that he could think of 'twenty things in five minutes'.[120] Spurgeon's quick mind and fertile imagination were important factors as he developed this model of intercession. An Enlightenment-influenced, evangelical pragmatism can also be discerned, as can an evangelical activism. Time was at a premium. It suited Spurgeon to pray briefly and then move on to his next 'duty'. In addition, particularly in relation to the stress on 'pleading the promises of God', the Puritan strand can once again be seen as important. In a sermon entitled 'The Covenant Pleaded', Spurgeon spoke of the 'covenant of grace' that God had made with 'the second Adam, our federal head, Jesus Christ' and through him with his people. This covenant of grace emphasised the commitment of God to his people and the certainty of his promises to them. A particular stress Spurgeon wanted to make in this message was on the confidence Christians could have in prayer as they pleaded the covenant promises and truly prayed in the name of Christ.[121] Enlightenment epistemology and Puritan covenant theology fused together to help shape Spurgeon's approach to intercession.

But the influence of what became known as the 'faith principle' on Spurgeon's approach to intercession also needs to be considered. The faith principle was being advocated by a number of influential evangelicals, particularly those who had links with the Brethren, as Spurgeon began his ministry in London. The proponents of this principle held that funds for Christian work should be sought, as Brian Stanley notes, 'primarily through the instruments of faith and prayer'.[122] When applied to overseas mission, as it often was, the faith principle involved a rejection of the pragmatism and 'prudence' which characterised the evangelical missionary societies which had

---

[118] Spurgeon, 'Incense and Light', p. 152.

[119] [Anon.] (ed.), *The Pastor in Prayer*, Prayer 1, 4 November 1877, p. 11.

[120] Fullerton, *C.H. Spurgeon*, p. 218.

[121] C.H. Spurgeon, 'The Covenant Pleaded', *MTP*, Vol. 25, S. No. 1451, Psalm 74.20, n.d., pp. 5-6.

[122] B. Stanley, 'C.H. Spurgeon and the Baptist Missionary Society 1863–1866', *Baptist Quarterly* Vol. 20, No. 7 (July, 1982), p. 320; cf. Bebbington, *Dominance of Evangelicalism*, pp. 174-79.

been established at the end of the eighteenth century.[123] As Stanley shows, Edward Irving was significant in advocating this approach through a sermon given to the London Missionary Society (LMS) in 1824.[124] The two best known exponents of 'living by faith' in the second half of the nineteenth century were probably George Müller (1805–98) and J. Hudson Taylor (1832–1905), both of whom put their principles into practice – Müller through his orphanage work in Bristol and Taylor, the so-called 'father' of faith missions, through his pioneering China Inland Mission (CIM).[125] Müller's stated approach was to pray for funds without directly appealing for them, trusting that God would provide what he needed at just the right time.

Spurgeon enjoyed friendships with both Müller and Taylor. Spurgeon first met Müller in 1855, when he visited Bristol to see the orphanages,[126] and he met Taylor in May 1864, when Taylor came to the Metropolitan Tabernacle to hear Spurgeon preach and the two spoke together after the service.[127] Spurgeon's friendship with Taylor was important and the 'principles of faith in God' upon which the CIM was conducted commended themselves to Spurgeon's 'innermost soul'.[128] Taylor attended and spoke at prayer meetings at the Tabernacle, for example in April and October 1883,[129] and his publications were reviewed enthusiastically in the *Sword and Trowel*.[130] Taylor's commitment to the faith principle clearly impressed Spurgeon, but Müller, whom Spurgeon had first met when he was only twenty-two, was the greater influence. The impact of Müller's orphanage work on Spurgeon's own Stockwell Orphanage is especially significant and will be discussed in chapter 7. But what is important to recognise at this point is the way Müller shaped

---

[123] Bebbington, *Dominance of Evangelicalism*, p. 174.

[124] Stanley, 'C.H. Spurgeon and the BMS', p. 319.

[125] See K. Fiedler, *The Story of Faith Missions* (Oxford: Regnum Books, 1994), p. 32. For more on the 'faith principle', see H.H. Rowdon, 'The Concept of "Living by Faith"', in A. Billington, A.N.S. Lane and M. Turner (eds), *Mission and Meaning: Essays presented to Peter Cotterell* (Carlisle: Paternoster, 1995), pp. 339-56; T. Larsen, '"Living by Faith": A short history of Brethren practice', *Brethren Archivists and Historians Network Review* Vol. 1, No. 2 (Winter 1998), pp. 67-102. Taylor had a passage from Irving's 1824 LMS sermon reprinted in his own magazine, *China's Millions*. See C.E.M. Wigram, *The Bible and Mission in Faith Perspective: J. Hudson Taylor and the Early China Inland Mission* (Zoetermeer: Boekencentrum, 2007), p. 66.

[126] A. Cunningham Burley, *Spurgeon and his Friendships* (London: Epworth, 1934), pp. 103-104; I.M. Randall, '"Ye men of Plymouth ...": C.H. Spurgeon and the Brethren', unpublished paper, November 2006.

[127] A.J. Broomhall, *Hudson Taylor and China's Open Century* (4 Vols; London: Hodder & Stoughton, 1982), Vol. 3, p. 390; I.M. Randall, '"The World is our Parish": Spurgeon's College and World Mission, 1856–1892', in A.R. Cross and I.M. Randall (eds), *Baptists and Mission: Papers from the Fourth International Conference on Baptist Studies* (Milton Keynes: Paternoster, 2007), p. 70.

[128] C.H. Spurgeon, 'The Apostolic Work in China', in Spurgeon (ed.), *Sword and Trowel*, January 1869, p. 32.

[129] Spurgeon (ed.), *Sword and Trowel*, May 1883, p. 247; November 1883, p. 609.

[130] See, e.g., Spurgeon (ed.), *Sword and Trowel*, June 1869, p. 283; July 1875, p. 342.

Spurgeon's approach to intercession. Spurgeon described Müller as 'mighty in prayer' and believed that in this regard 'none of us are worthy to be placed beside him'.[131] The principle of praying in 'faith' and then waiting for the answer to come, which Spurgeon believed he saw exemplified in Müller, helped mould his own practice. A comment from Spurgeon, that Müller had 'tried and proved the promises of God', is especially suggestive when put alongside Spurgeon's own approach.[132] Spurgeon believed that he too had 'tried and proved' the promises of God as he prayed with faith. The faith principle, proved in his own experience of prayer, helped shape his theology and practice of intercession.

Spurgeon's espousal of the faith principle is another instance of a connection between Spurgeon and Romanticism. Irving, who was crucial to the development of this approach, was clearly shaped by the Romantic temper, as has been widely recognised.[133] Relying on prayer and faith was idealistic and heroic when contrasted with the more prosaic and practical approach characteristic of the Enlightenment, and which marked the BMS and the LMS, voluntary societies established at the end of the eighteenth century. A comment from Spurgeon, that Müller's work was 'a romance of Christian confidence in God in this prosaic, unbelieving, nineteenth century', is revealing in this regard.[134] The faith principle, and Spurgeon's attraction to it, were linked with the prevailing Romantic mood.

Reflecting back on material covered earlier in this chapter, we can see that other aspects of Spurgeon's prayer life also reveal affinities with Romanticism. His sympathy with some aspects of High Church spirituality is relevant, with the influence of Romanticism on the Oxford Movement generally accepted.[135] Spurgeon's approach to contemplation and mystical communion with Christ was also tinged with Romanticism. A quotation from one of Spurgeon's Friday lectures to his students helps emphasise this. Spurgeon stated,

---

[131] Spurgeon, 'The Pastor's Need of the People's Prayers', p. 209.

[132] Spurgeon (ed.), *Sword and Trowel*, October 1889, p. 576. For detail on Müller, see F.R. Coad, *A History of the Brethren Movement* (Exeter: Paternoster, 1976 [1968]), pp. 36-58.

[133] Stanley, 'Spurgeon and the BMS', p. 320, speaks of Irving's 'romantic idealism', a description that is also applied to Taylor. On Irving and Romanticism, see also D.W. Bebbington, *Evangelicalism in Modern Britain: A History from the 1730s to the 1980s* (London: Unwin Hyman, 1989), pp. 78-80; T.F.C. Stunt, *From Awakening to Secession: Radical Evangelicals in Switzerland and Britain 1815–1835* (Edinburgh: T.&T. Clark, 2000), p. 34.

[134] Spurgeon (ed.), *Sword and Trowel*, March 1884, p. 141. Cf. Randall, '"Ye men of Plymouth ..."'. For links between Taylor and Romanticism, see Wigram, *Bible and Mission in Faith Perspective*, pp. 53-57.

[135] For links between the Oxford Movement and Romanticism, see G. Rowell, *The Vision Glorious: Themes and Personalities of the Catholic Revival in Anglicanism* (Oxford: Oxford University Press, 2001 [1983]), pp. 10; 26-27; D. Hedley, 'Theology and the revolt against the Enlightenment', in S. Gilley and B. Stanley (eds), *World Christianities, c.1815–c.1914* (Cambridge: Cambridge University Press, 2006), pp. 37-38.

> I saw the other day in an Italian grotto a little fern, which grew where its leaves continually glistened and danced in the spray of a fountain. It was always green, and neither summer's drought nor winter's cold affected it. So let us for ever abide under the sweet influence of Jesus' love. Dwell in God, brethren; do not occasionally visit him, but abide in him.[136]

The nature imagery Spurgeon employs here is suggestive of Romanticism. The invitation to abide in Christ was expressed in Romantic idiom.

A further quotation, similarly autobiographical, helps to define and limit the particular way the Romantic cultural mood impinged on Spurgeon. This is from a sermon entitled 'My Lord And My God', based on the words of the disciple Thomas in John 20.28. In the course of this message Spurgeon stated,

> When we have been musing, the fire has burned ... Though not after the flesh, yet in very deed and truth we have seen the Lord. On a day which I had given up to prayer, I sat before the Lord in holy peacefulness, wrapped in solemn contemplation, and though I did not see a vision, nor wish to see one, yet I so realised my Master's presence that I was borne away from all earthly things, and knew of no man save Jesus only. Then a sense of his Godhead filled me till I would fain have stood up where I was and have proclaimed aloud, as with the voice of a trumpet, that he was my Lord and my God. Such times you also have known.[137]

The quotation relates what can only be described as a mystical experience born out of quiet contemplation, but ends with a significant twist, the comment, 'Such times you also have known.' Spoken to the vast congregation at the Tabernacle, these words can seem surprising, indeed incongruous, particularly as earlier in this message Spurgeon had stated that many true Christians were also 'weak in faith'.[138] But, crucially, it illustrates Spurgeon's view noted earlier in this chapter, that such intense experiences of God's 'presence' were not the preserve of the few, but were in fact open to all believers. The remark, 'I did not see a vision, or wish to see one' is also significant. Spurgeon was careful to describe his experience in such a way that it did not seem out of reach of ordinary people. This approach was of a piece with his championing of the 'common man' which will be dealt with in more detail in chapter 9.[139] The experience of close communion with God, described in mystical terms and with a distinctly Romantic tincture, was a possibility for all. This was not the Romanticism of high culture, or the mysticism of a few, experienced saints. Spurgeon's was a mysticism of the common people.

---

[136] Spurgeon, *Lectures To My Students*, Vol. 2, Lecture 2, 'The Necessity of Ministerial Progress', p. 35.

[137] C.H. Spurgeon, 'My Lord And My God', *MTP*, Vol. No. 30, S. No. 1775, John 20.28, delivered 13 April 1884, p. 214.

[138] Spurgeon, 'My Lord And My God', p. 207.

[139] So D.W. Bebbington, 'Spurgeon and the Common Man', *Baptist Review of Theology*, Vol. 5 No. 1 (Spring 1995), pp. 63-75. Cf. Bebbington, *Dominance of Evangelicalism*, p. 40.

Returning to Spurgeon's approach to intercession, yet further influences can be discerned. Kruppa states that Spurgeon was, in many ways, an archetypal Victorian 'self-made man' who embodied the typical values of the dominant middle class.[140] Kruppa overstates her case, in particular presenting too simplistic an analysis of the multi-faceted Spurgeon. But undoubtedly Spurgeon did reflect some of the entrepreneurial values which were highly influential in Victorian Britain. This was something Spurgeon shared with Hudson Taylor, who, according to Randall, exhibited 'a faith-filled entrepreneurial energy that mirrored [Spurgeon's] own'.[141] As Kruppa notes, Spurgeon was an admirer of Samuel Smiles, whose hugely popular work *Self Help* had sold over 250,000 copies by 1904. Smiles preached a gospel of thrift, hard work and perseverance in the face of adversity.[142] Spurgeon described Smiles as 'one of the ablest authors of our time',[143] and it was quite natural that he should commend him. Virtues which *Self Help* exalted included 'promptitude in action' and 'economical use of time'.[144] These are principles which clearly fit Spurgeon's 'businesslike' approach to the practice of intercession.

In fact, the language of Victorian business and industry regularly surfaced when Spurgeon was talking about prayer. In a message entitled 'The Golden Key Of Prayer', praying Christians were compared to 'spiritual merchantmen', and encouraged to pray in the following terms, 'The market is high, trade much; thy profit shall be large.'[145] Elsewhere, Spurgeon compared the Tabernacle alternately to a large factory or a great ocean steamer. In both these analogies the prayer meeting was the engine, upon which the whole enterprise depended. Developing the factory image with the help of his considerable imaginative powers he declared,

> If you visit a factory, you may see thousands of wheels revolving, and a host of hands employed. It is a wonderful sight. Where is the power which keeps all this running? Look at that slated shed! Come into this grimy place smelling with oil. What is it? It is the engine house. You do not think much of it. This is the centre of power. If you stop that engine every wheel will stand still.[146]

My contention is that Spurgeon's 'business' approach to intercessory prayer was effectively a fusion of a number of quite complex and, at first sight, not especially

---

[140] Kruppa, *Spurgeon*, pp. 146-47.

[141] Randall, 'Ye men of Plymouth ...'

[142] S. Smiles, *Self Help: With Illustrations of Character, Conduct, and Perseverance* (Oxford: Oxford University Press, 2002 [1859]), p. vii.

[143] Spurgeon, *Autobiography*, Vol. 1, p. 7. This comment is also noted by Kruppa, *Spurgeon*, p. 167.

[144] Smiles, *Self Help*, p. 229.

[145] Spurgeon, 'The Golden Key Of Prayer', Jeremiah 33.3, in *The Pastor in Prayer*, p. 160. Spurgeon was encouraging praying Christians that, if they sensed a special desire to pray, they should take that as a sign that God was about to answer, and therefore redouble their efforts in prayer.

[146] C.H. Spurgeon, 'Fighting and Praying: A Bugle Blast', in Spurgeon (ed.), *Sword and Trowel*, November 1889, p. 590.

compatible factors. These included Spurgeon's temperament and certain Puritan and 'enlightened' evangelical emphases, and they also included the Romantic faith principle, as exemplified by George Müller. In addition, some of the language and values of the Victorian business world were important. Puritan covenant theology and evangelical activism were being reinterpreted and recast in ways which reflected the prevailing culture and the world of the Victorian entrepreneur. And yet, despite this complex matrix of influences, Spurgeon's focus in intercession remained clear. Prayers that communion with Christ might be more deeply known, that Christians might be conformed to the will of Christ and that more might know conversion to Christ predominate. Spurgeon wanted to know communion with Christ in prayer, believing that prayers were 'roads wherein the Saviour walketh'. Moreover, a burden of his intercession was that others would turn to Christ and thus experience such ongoing communion for themselves.[147]

Conclusion

Analysis of Spurgeon's prayer life has revealed much diversity. The different influences which shaped his prayer life can be thought of as various strands – Puritan and evangelical, High Church, different aspects of nineteenth-century culture – which come together to form a complex, interconnected web. But examination of Spurgeon's prayer life also reveals much unity. That unity is based around the focus on Christ, which is present in all of the dimensions of Spurgeon's prayer life, and the focus on others. With regard to the focus on Christ, some extracts from a prayer which was entitled 'O, for more Grace!' form a fitting conclusion. In the course of the prayer Spurgeon declared,

> [M]ay we know the Christ and have Him to be our all in all ... He is everything to us; more than all in Him we find. We do accept Thee, Lord Jesus, to be made unto us wisdom, righteousness, sanctification, and redemption. We will not look out of Thee for anything, for everything is in Thee.[148]

Spurgeon mixed both petition and praise, two of the dimensions of prayer we have seen were important to him, yet the focus of the whole was Christ and Christ alone. Soon in 'O, for more Grace!', Christ was being addressed directly.

> O Saviour, reveal Thyself anew, teach us a little more, help us to go a little deeper into the divine mystery. May we grip Thee and grasp Thee; may we suck out of Thee the

---

[147] C.H. Spurgeon, 'Keep In Mercy's Way', in [Anon.] (ed.), *The Pastor in Prayer*, pp. 161-63. These are written thoughts from Spurgeon on prayer rather than an example of an actual prayer.

[148] C.H. Spurgeon, 'O, for more Grace!', in Young (ed.), *C.H. Spurgeon's Prayers*, Prayer 18, p. 101.

nutriment of our spirit; may we be in Thee as a branch is in the stem, and may we bear fruit from Thee. Without Thee we can do nothing.[149]

Communion with Christ was the content of Spurgeon's prayer. Moreover, it was petitions such as this which led observers to insist that Spurgeon actually experienced such communion as he led in prayer.

With regard to the focus on others, the prayer was, of course, offered in a corporate setting. Spurgeon enjoyed communion with Christ in the midst of the congregation of which he was pastor. The prayer also moved towards urgent petition for those who did not know Christ. '[L]ook in great mercy upon those who are unconverted; Lord save them … May they cease their seeking by finding everything in Christ'.[150] Once again Spurgeon expressed his desire for others to know Christ as he did, and once again the central theme of this study is reinforced.

---

[149] Spurgeon, 'O, for more Grace!', in Young (ed.), *C.H. Spurgeon's Prayers*, Prayer 18, pp. 101-102.

[150] Spurgeon, 'O, for more Grace!', in Young (ed.), *C.H. Spurgeon's Prayers*, Prayer 18, pp. 103-104.

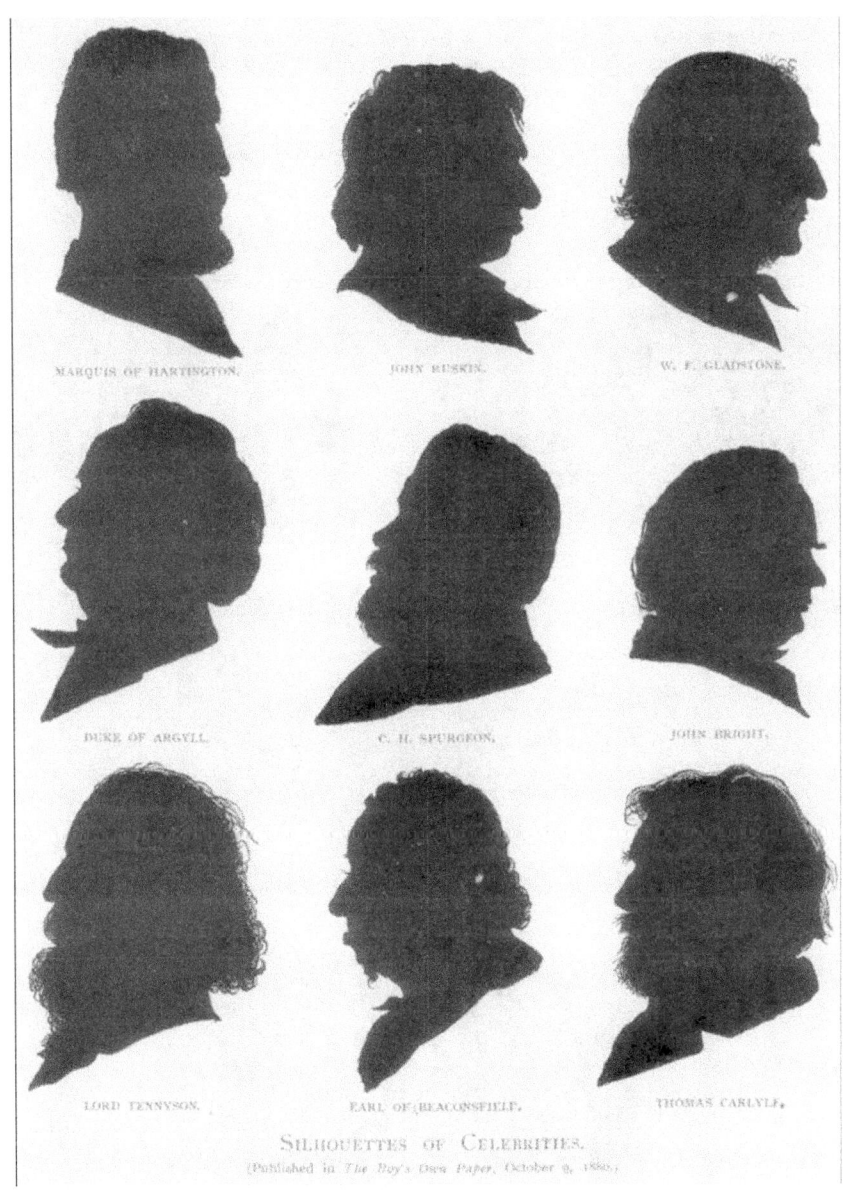

'Silhouettes of Celebrities', published by the *Boy's Own Paper*, 9 October 1880. Spurgeon is surrounded by other nineteenth-century luminaries such as W.E. Gladstone, the Earl of Beaconsfield (Benjamin Disraeli), John Ruskin, John Bright, and Thomas Carlyle. (Digital image courtesy of Spurgeon's College, London, and used with permission.)

C.H. Spurgeon's paternal grandfather, James.   Spurgeon's mother, Eliza.

Spurgeon's father, John.
(Photographs by the author and used with permission of Spurgeon's College, London.)

Robert Eaglen, the Primitive Methodist Minister who was almost certainly the preacher at Spurgeon's conversion.
A handwritten note on the back of the original photo says it was taken in 1853.
(Digital image courtesy of Dave Lock and used with permission of Spurgeon's College, London.)

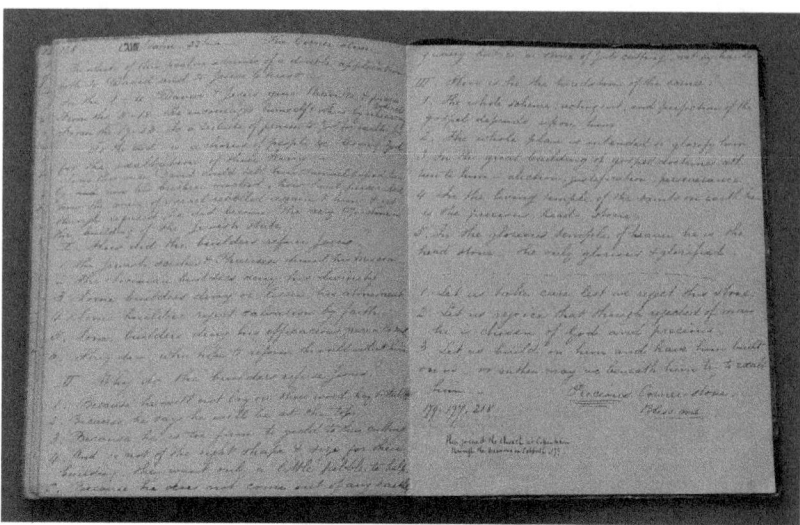

Spurgeon's sermon number 128, entitled 'The Cornerstone', from the second of the pre-London notebooks. Spurgeon's notes show that the message was first preached at Cottenham in June 1852. Spurgeon also records that 'three joined the church at Cottenham' as a result of hearing this message.

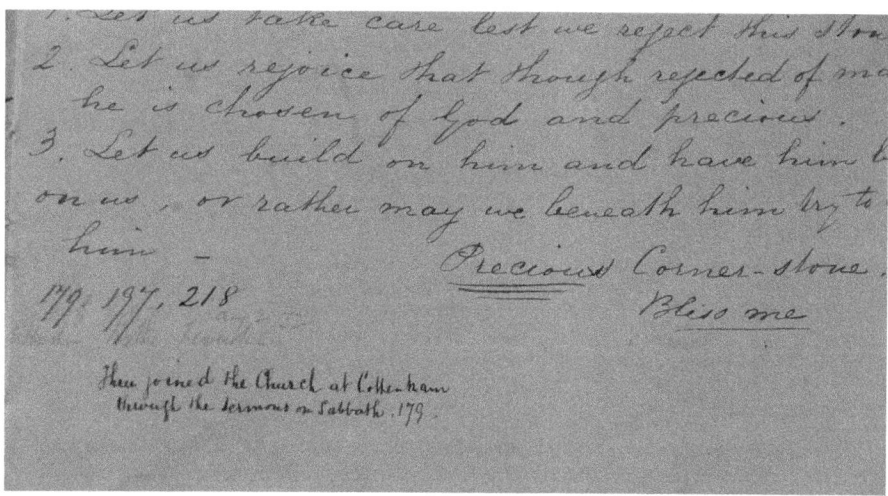

Note also the prayer appended to the sermon notes, 'Precious Corner-stone, Bless me'.
(Digital images courtesy of Dave Lock and used with permission of Spurgeon's College, London.)

New Park Street Chapel, Southwark.
(Digital image courtesy of Spurgeon's College, London, and used with permission.)

An engraving of C.H. Spurgeon, c.1855.
(Digital image courtesy of Dave Lock and used with permission of Spurgeon's College, London.)

The Slow Coach.

The Fast Train.
In 'The Slow Coach and The Fast Train' the Churchman drives a coach pulled by the two horses of 'Church' and 'State'. The pastor of New Park Street Chapel rides the speedy locomotive, 'The Spurgeon'. The caricatures date from the mid-1850s and were included in Spurgeon's *Autobiography*, Vol. 2, pp. 48 and 49.
(Digital images courtesy of the author and used with permission of Spurgeon's College, London.)

The exterior of the Surrey Gardens Music Hall, scene of some of Spurgeon's greatest preaching triumphs, and his greatest tragedy.

Spurgeon preaching at the Surrey Gardens Music Hall.
(Digital images courtesy of Spurgeon's College, London, and used with permission.)

Susannah Spurgeon (née Thompson).
(Digital image courtesy of Dave Lock and used with permission of Spurgeon's College, London.)

Thomas W. Medhurst, who, in 1855, was Spurgeon's first student, photographed later in life with a bust of his mentor.
(Digital image courtesy of Dave Lock and used with permission of Spurgeon's College, London.)

The original interior of the Metropolitan Tabernacle. The building was opened in 1861.

The exterior of the Metropolitan Tabernacle.
(Digital images courtesy of Dave Lock and used with permission of Spurgeon's College, London.)

Spurgeon in 1868. The engraving was intended for the title page of *Metropolitan Tabernacle Pulpit* issue 808 (1868), but the publishers decided to use the image reproduced on p. xvi.
(Digital image courtesy of the author and used with permission of Spurgeon's College, London.)

A caricature of Spurgeon from 1870, printed in the old British publication, *Vanity Fair*. The accompanying comment reads, 'No one has succeeded like him in sketching the comic side of repentance and regeneration.'
(Digital image courtesy of the author and used with permission of Spurgeon's College, London.)

The Temple Street building which was home to the Pastors' College from 1874.

Spurgeon said, 'This is my life's work, to which I believe God has called me.'
(Digital images courtesy of Dave Lock and used with permission of Spurgeon's College, London.)

Spurgeon and his deacons in 1878.
(Digital image courtesy of Spurgeon's College, London, and used with permission.)

George Rogers, Principal of the Pastors' College until 1881.
(Digital image courtesy of Spurgeon's College, London, and used with permission.)

James Archer Spurgeon, 'co-pastor' of the Metropolitan Tabernacle from 1868.
(Digital image courtesy of Dave Lock and used with permission of Spurgeon's College, London.)

The Orphanage at Stockwell.
(Digital image courtesy of Dave Lock and used with permission of Spurgeon's College, London.)

The Spurgeon Memorial, originally sited at the Stockwell Orphanage, but later broken up and dispersed. (Photograph held by Spurgeon's College, photographer unknown.)

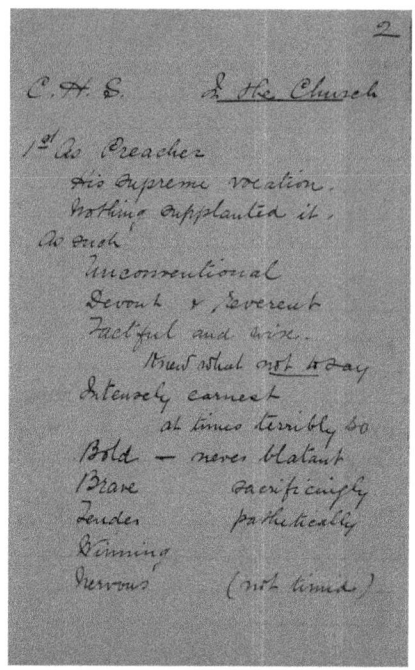

A page from Tabernacle elder Thomas Cox's comments on Spurgeon. Note the remark that Spurgeon could be 'Intensely earnest / at times terribly so.'

Cover of Spurgeon's book, *The Way of Salvation*.
(Digital images courtesy of Dave Lock and used with permission of Spurgeon's College, London.)

Caricature of Spurgeon preaching from 9 August 1890. Note the comment of the chair, 'Sunday is not much of a day of rest for me!' It originally appeared in *Moonshine* 9 August 1890, p. 61.
(Digital image courtesy of the author and used with permission of Spurgeon's College, London.)

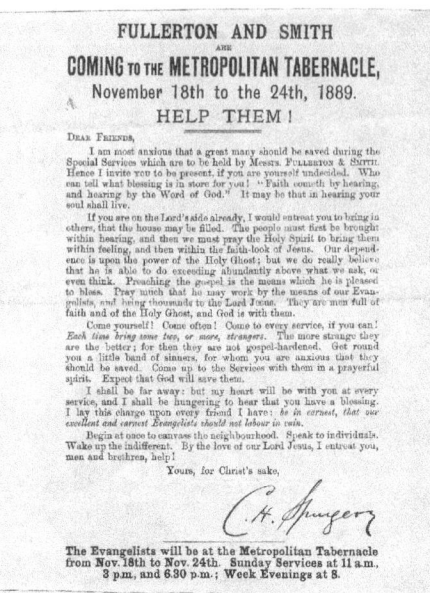

Spurgeon enthusiastically supported evangelistic mission, here W.Y. Fullerton and J. Manton Smith's visit to the Metropolitan Tabernacle, 18-24 November 1889.
(Digital image courtesy of and used with permission of Spurgeon's College, London.)

The Colportage Room in the Temple Street building.
(Digital image courtesy of Dave Lock and used with permission of Spurgeon's College, London.)

Charles Haddon Spurgeon (1834–92)
(Digital image courtesy of Dave Lock and used with permission of Spurgeon's College, London.)

The last photo of C.H. Spurgeon, taken during his final trip to Mentone.
(Digital image courtesy of Dave Lock and used with permission of Spurgeon's College, London.)

CHAPTER 7

The Lord's Supper:
'By faith, I see our Lord standing in our midst'

Spurgeon's spirituality was sustained through his engagement with the Bible and through his practice of prayer. It was also nurtured through regular celebration of the Lord's Supper. The importance of the Supper to Spurgeon is indicated by some comments he made as president of the Lambeth Auxiliary of the London Sunday School Union for 1882.[1] This inter-denominational Union (as well as Baptists it included Anglicans, Wesleyan Methodists and Independents)[2] was part of the movement founded by Robert Raikes which existed to promote Sunday school work – a cause close to Spurgeon's heart.[3] In his capacity as president of the Union, Spurgeon led a Communion service at the Metropolitan Tabernacle for over a thousand teachers.[4] He told the meeting of his 'intense joy' that those assembled had come 'not only to hear a little address from me but to see a sermon, for there is no sermon like the Lord's Supper'.[5] From one who consistently sought to emphasise the importance of preaching, and who has been so frequently styled the 'prince of

---

[1] The London Sunday School Union was founded in 1803 at a meeting held in the schoolrooms of the Congregational Surrey Chapel. The Lambeth Auxiliary, which included the districts of Newington and Camberwell, was formed in 1818. See W.H. Watson, *The Sunday School Union, Its History And Work* (London: Sunday School Union, 1869), pp. 6-7, 18. The 'Lord's Supper' was the usual way that Spurgeon described Holy Communion and I have tended to refer to the rite in this way as well in this chapter, also using the word 'Supper' as a shorthand. Occasionally I have used the words 'Communion' and 'Eucharist' for stylistic reasons.

[2] For the interdenominational (yet thoroughly Protestant) character of the London Union, see Watson, *Sunday School Union*, p. 8. See *South London Press*, 8 April 1882, 'Spurgeon's Scrapbooks, Numbered Volumes', Vol. 6, Spurgeon's College, Heritage Room (2G), p. 25, for Wesleyan involvement in the Lambeth Auxiliary.

[3] For Raikes, see J.C. Power, *The Rise and Progress of Sunday Schools, A Biography of Robert Raikes and William Fox* (New York: Sheldon, 1863), *passim*.

[4] *Lambeth Auxiliary of the London Sunday School Union: Annual Prayer And Communion Service ... Monday, February 13th, 1882* (Printed Hymn Sheet), 'Spurgeon's Scrapbooks, Numbered Volumes', Vol. 6, p. 8b; *Sunday School Chronicle*, 17 February 1882, 'Spurgeon's Scrapbooks, Numbered Volumes', Vol. 6, p. 8. Another 700 to 800 attended the service but did not take Communion.

[5] *Sunday School Chronicle*, 17 February 1882, 'Spurgeon's Scrapbooks, Numbered Volumes', Vol. 6, p. 8.

preachers' by others,[6] this might seem a surprising statement. Nevertheless, it was entirely consistent with what Spurgeon said about Communion elsewhere, as will be shown in this chapter. Spurgeon had an extremely high view of the Lord's Supper and he believed it played a vital role in nurturing his spiritual life. Accordingly, this chapter makes a detailed examination of Spurgeon's approach to the Supper. Once again, the theme of 'communion with Christ and his people' emerges as central.

The Lord's Supper in Practice

Spurgeon's basic practice of celebrating the Lord's Supper needs to be established. A number of points can be made. To begin with, it should be noted that Spurgeon believed the Supper should be celebrated frequently. At the Metropolitan Tabernacle it was Spurgeon's practice to hold a Communion service every Sunday evening. On the first Sunday of the month this was a full service – the so-called 'Great Communion' – and on other Sundays a shorter, half-hour celebration followed the main evening service.[7] Spurgeon's own commitment to a weekly celebration was such that when he was away from London he habitually sought to share in a Communion service with other Christians every Sunday.[8] Often he would arrange and lead such a service himself. He told the Sunday school teachers who had gathered for the Lambeth Union meeting, 'It has been my joy wherever I may have been on the first day of the week – at Mentone, at Rome, at Naples, at Venice, – to get together as many as I could of the Lord's servants, and to join with them in the breaking of bread ...'[9] When Spurgeon was at Mentone he would hold regular Sunday afternoon Communion services in his sitting room at the Hôtel Beau Rivage. These informal meetings were in addition to the Communion services at the Presbyterian church in Mentone which Spurgeon would, when well enough, also attend, occasionally preaching or even taking the whole service.[10] Thus, on at least some occasions, he would take Communion twice on a Sunday. Spurgeon believed in meeting with other Christians around the Communion table at other times too. For

---

[6] Timothy Larsen notes that at least nine different books about Spurgeon have been published with 'prince of preachers' in their titles or sub-titles. See T. Larsen, 'Charles Haddon Spurgeon's Reading of the Sermon on the Mount', in T. Larsen, J.P. Greenman and S.R. Spencer (eds), *Reading the Sermon on the Mount through the Centuries* (Grand Rapids: Brazos, forthcoming).

[7] C.H. Spurgeon, *Autobiography: Compiled from his Diary, Letters, and Records by his Wife and his Private Secretary* (4 Vols; London: Passmore and Alabaster, 1897–99), Vol. 4, p. 72; T. Grass and I.M. Randall, 'C.H. Spurgeon on the Sacraments', in A.R. Cross and P.E. Thompson (eds), *Baptist Sacramentalism* (Carlisle: Paternoster, 2003), p. 72.

[8] Spurgeon, *Autobiography*, Vol. 4, p. 72.

[9] *Sunday School Chronicle*, 17 February 1882, 'Spurgeon's Scrapbooks, Numbered Volumes', Vol. 6, p. 8.

[10] Spurgeon, *Autobiography*, Vol. 4, p. 216.

example, he sometimes did so on a Friday afternoon with his students at the Pastors' College.[11] Spurgeon believed in frequently celebrating the Lord's Supper.

This commitment to frequent Communion was not the norm amongst Baptists in the second half of the nineteenth century.[12] In a sermon entitled 'The Greatest Exhibition Of The Age', which was preached towards the end of his ministry in 1889, Spurgeon referred to other Christians (Baptists and those of other denominations) who celebrated the Supper far less often than was his own custom:

> I love to come every Lord's-day to the communion table; I should be very sorry to come only once a month, or, as some do, only once a year. I could not afford to come as often as that. I need to be reminded, forcibly reminded, of my dear Lord and Master very often ... How is it with you, my brethren? I know that it is thus with me.[13]

This statement which, as Grass and Randall who also cite this passage note, was 'deeply personal',[14] is yet further evidence that Spurgeon's basic practice was regular, weekly celebration of the Lord's Supper. It also gives an insight as to the reasons behind his repeated observance of the Supper. He needed to 'remember' or, as he put it here, be 'forcibly reminded' of his Lord. Spurgeon's regular celebration of the Supper was bound up with his desire to focus on Christ and to do so together with other Christians.

Spurgeon also believed that observance of the Lord's Supper should be simple. Indeed, in a message entitled 'Christ And His Table Companions', which is included in *Till He Come*, he insisted that the Lord's Supper, rightly understood and celebrated, was 'simplicity itself'.[15] He held that simplicity was what Christ himself had ordained, for there was nothing of 'elaborate ceremonial' in the 'regulations' that he had laid down for the observance of the Supper, as recorded, for example, in Matthew 26.26-28.[16] Christian believers were to meet together round a table, break bread and drink wine (the 'wine' served in the Tabernacle was non-alcoholic, despite rumours to the contrary[17]) in remembrance of their Lord.[18] Nothing else was needed.

---

[11] Spurgeon, *Autobiography*, Vol. 4, p. 89.

[12] J.H.Y. Briggs, *The English Baptists of the Nineteenth Century* (Didcot: Baptist Historical Society, 1994), p. 67.

[13] C.H. Spurgeon, 'The Greatest Exhibition Of The Age', *New Park Street Pulpit (NPSP) / Metropolitan Tabernacle Pulpit (MTP)* (London: Passmore and Alabaster, 1855–1917), *MTP*, Vol. 39, S. No. 2307, 1 Corinthians 11.26, delivered 5 May 1889, p. 220.

[14] Grass and Randall, 'C.H. Spurgeon on the Sacraments', p. 72.

[15] C.H. Spurgeon, 'Christ And His Table Companions', Luke 22.14, in *Till He Come: Communion Meditations And Addresses* (London: Passmore and Alabaster, 1896), p. 266. Spurgeon was also referring to baptism at this point. Cf. Grass and Randall, 'C.H. Spurgeon on the Sacraments', p. 71. 'Christ And His Table Companions' was also printed in *MTP*, Vol. 54, where it is S. No. 3107, pp. 409-18.

[16] C.H. Spurgeon, *The Gospel of the Kingdom. A Popular Exposition of the Gospel According to Matthew* (London: Passmore and Alabaster, 1893), Matthew 26.26-28, p. 235.

[17] Spurgeon, *Autobiography*, Vol. 4, p. 135.

Spurgeon made this point about simplicity on a regular basis in his Communion sermons and meditations.[19] As he did so, he habitually contrasted the simple and plain approach he was advocating with the elaborate practices of both Roman Catholics and Tractarians, often making these observations as he began his address. So, in the opening words of 'Communion With Christ And His People', Spurgeon lamented the fact that the 'simple ordinance' of the Lord's Supper had been 'complicated' by the addition of 'genuflexions, adornments, and technical phrases'. He asked those who had gathered with him in Mentone, 'Can anyone see the slightest resemblance between the Master's sitting down with the twelve, and the mass of the Roman community?'[20] To Spurgeon the answer to this question was self-evidently 'no'. Here the contrast was between ritual and Christ's example as well as his instructions. Christ's celebration of the Supper was simple; Christians' celebration of the Supper must be simple too. Spurgeon was certain that both Roman Catholics and Tractarians were perverting Christ's ordinance as it was both instituted and practised in the scriptures.[21] To call the plate a 'paten', the cup a 'chalice' and the table an 'altar' was to 'super-impose ritual' over the plain, straightforward rite that Christ had intended.[22] When Spurgeon spoke in this way about Roman Catholic and High Church Anglican practices he usually levelled the charge of 'superstition' against his opponents and he was not slow to do so on in 'Communion With Christ And His People'. The practices he had described were, he declared, the 'incrustations of superstition'.[23] They had nothing to do with the rite of the Supper and nothing to do with the gospel.

Spurgeon would have much to say against the eucharistic theology of both Roman Catholics and Tractarians, but it should be noted that he was also implacably opposed to their eucharistic practice (which, of course, flowed from their theology). He could, however, and as we have seen, be sympathetic to certain aspects of Roman Catholic and Tractarian spirituality. Michael Walker states that Spurgeon held 'an attitude of uncompromising antipathy' towards the Roman Catholic Church, an antipathy which he is fully aware extended to the Tractarians. Whilst saying this,

---

[18] C.H. Spurgeon, 'In Remembrance', *MTP*, Vol. 55, S. No. 3130, 1 Corinthians 11.24,25, delivered 5 January 1873, p. 61.

[19] See, e.g., C.H. Spurgeon, 'The Lord's Supper', *MTP*, Vol. 50, S. No. 2872, delivered 1861, p. 102; 'The Lord's Supper, Simple But Sublime!', *MTP*, Vol. 55, S. No. 3151, 1 Corinthians 11.25-26, delivered 1866, p. 314.

[20] C.H. Spurgeon, 'Communion With Christ And His People', 1 Corinthians 10.16,17, in *Till He Come*, p. 313. Cf. 'The Lord's Supper', p. 102.

[21] Cf. C.H. Spurgeon's exposition of Matthew 26.17-30 and 1 Corinthians 11.18-34 in *MTP*, Vol. 50, pp. 22-24, in which he repeatedly contrasted the witness of scripture with the practices of the 'Romanists'. The exposition itself is undated, but is attached to 'Fencing the Table', *MTP*, Vol. 50, S. No. 2865, 1 Corinthians 11.28, delivered 2 January 1876, pp. 13-22.

[22] Spurgeon, 'Communion With Christ And His People'. Cf. C.H. Spurgeon, 'The Double Forget Me Not', *MTP*, Vol. 54, S. No. 3099, 1 Corinthians 11.24, delivered 5 July 1874, p. 318.

[23] Spurgeon, 'Communion With Christ And His People', pp. 313-14.

The Lord's Supper 169

Walker takes care to note that Spurgeon was nevertheless indebted to certain Roman Catholic devotional writers. He cites what he describes as a 'rare reference' in which Spurgeon himself acknowledged this indebtedness, a reference which actually occurs in 'Communion With Christ And His People'.[24] Walker is perceptive and almost exactly right – Spurgeon was implacably opposed to the Roman Catholic Church as an institution, whilst at the same time drawing significantly from a number of Roman Catholic devotional writers. Walker is only mistaken in his contention that positive references to Roman Catholic devotional literature from Spurgeon are 'rare'. As has already been shown in our examination of Spurgeon's prayer life, Spurgeon freely acknowledged his debt to Madame Guyon and to certain High Church Anglican writers. In addition to the references cited in chapter 6, Spurgeon's appreciation of the medieval Catholic Bernard of Clairvaux can be highlighted. In a Communion meditation, Spurgeon declared that Bernard's canticles 'flamed with devotion',[25] whilst in another Communion address he quoted the hymn, 'O Sacred Head Once Wounded'.[26] Described by Spurgeon as 'Holy Bernard', the twelfth-century Catholic was a writer the pastor of the Metropolitan Tabernacle deeply prized.[27]

Walker does not discuss how Spurgeon held together this obvious tension in his thinking – acknowledging his affection for selected Roman Catholic devotional writers on the one hand whilst describing their eucharistic practice in such insulting terms on the other. As argued in chapter 6, Spurgeon's ubiquitous desire for 'communion with Christ and his people' is the interpretative key that allows us to make sense of this seemingly irreconcilable contradiction. In the message which was entitled 'Communion With Christ And His People', Spurgeon declared,

> In perusing a deeply spiritual book of devotion, you have been charmed and benefited, and yet upon looking at the title-page it may be you have found that the author

---

[24] M.J. Walker, *Baptists at the Table: The Theology of the Lord's Supper amongst English Baptists in the Nineteenth Century* (Didcot: Baptist Historical Society, 1992), p. 165; Spurgeon, 'Communion With Christ And His People', p. 324.

[25] C.H. Spurgeon, 'The Well-beloved's Vineyard', Isaiah 5.1, 'An Address To A Little Company Of Believers, In Mr Spurgeon's Own Room At Mentone', in *Till He Come*, p. 149.

[26] C.H. Spurgeon, 'Jesus, The Object Of Great Astonishment', in *Till He Come*, p. 167.

[27] Spurgeon, 'The Well-beloved's Vineyard', p. 149. For another reference, see C.H. Spurgeon, *Lectures To My Students* (3 Vols; London: Passmore and Alabaster, n.d.), Vol. 1, Lecture 3, p. 340. For a further appreciative reference to High Church spirituality, see the reviews in C.H. Spurgeon (ed.), *The Sword and The Trowel: A Record of Combat With Sin and Labour For The Lord* (London: Passmore and Alabaster, 1865–92) (*Sword and Trowel*), January 1888, p. 38; October 1880, p. 532. This last mentioned review of *Practical Reflections on every verse of the Holy Gospels* (London: Rivingtons, [1880?]), a book by an anonymous High Churchman, included the words, 'It does us good to read genuinely godly works by men of schools of thought from which we differ; it sets in motion a new set of ideas, and brightens up our old ones.' I have been unable to locate a copy of this book but [Anon.], *Practical Reflections on every verse of the New Testament* (2 Vols; London: Rivingtons, 1882) appears to be an expanded version of this earlier work. The 1882 book includes a preface by the High Churchman H.P. Liddon.

belonged to the Church of Rome. What then? Why, then it has happened that the inner life has broken all barriers, and your spirits have communed. For my own part, in reading certain precious works, I have loathed their Romanism, and yet I have had close fellowship with their writers in weeping over sin, in adoring at the foot of the cross, and in rejoicing in the glorious enthronement of our Lord. Blood is thicker than water, and no fellowship is more inevitable and sincere than fellowship in the precious blood, and in the risen life of our Lord Jesus Christ. Here, in the common reception of the one loaf, we bear witness that we are one; and in the actual participation of all the chosen in the one redemption, that unity is in very deed displayed and matured in the most substantial manner. Washed in the one blood, fed on the same loaf, cheered by the same cup, all differences pass away, and 'we, being many, are one body in Christ, and every one members one of another.'[28]

This suggestive quotation is illustrative of a side to Spurgeon that is rarely commented upon. Certain works by Roman Catholic authors were 'precious' to him. He certainly regarded those authors as real Christians, 'chosen' members with him of the people of God. Indeed they were Christians of a high calibre. Spurgeon appreciated these authors' focus on Christ and his cross, but it was the way they focused on these themes that was all important. In these books Spurgeon discovered an approach that was worshipful, spiritual and engaged as opposed to dry and detached. Here was 'weeping', 'adoring' and 'rejoicing' over Christ and his work. Felt communion with Christ was enjoyed by these writers and they enabled Spurgeon to experience such communion too. Moreover, as the writers led Spurgeon to the 'foot of the cross' he enjoyed what he was unashamed to call 'fellowship' with them. The 'inner life' which had its focal point in fellowship with Christ broke down the barriers between Christians, even evangelical Nonconformist and Roman Catholic ones. True fellowship was enjoyed across the confessional divide. The tangible expression of that unity and fellowship was the Lord's Supper. I am not aware of any occasion when Spurgeon shared the Supper with a Roman Catholic and suspect, given his hatred of 'Romanism' and the ecclesial climate of his day, that he would not have done so (even in the highly unlikely event of a Roman Catholic being willing). Nevertheless, Spurgeon explicitly stated that he regarded himself as being in 'close fellowship' with authors who belonged to the 'Church of Rome'. The 'blood' of true spiritual union and felt communion was thicker than confessional 'water'.

The interpretative key that is 'communion with Christ and his people' thus helps us understand his love for certain Roman Catholic devotional writers, but it also sheds light on why he 'loathed' Roman Catholic and High Church Anglican eucharistic practice. As far as Spurgeon was concerned, Roman Catholicism's approach to the Eucharist obscured both Christ (by, for example, interposing layers of ritual between Christ and the communicants) and also fellowship with other Christians (by, for example, replacing a 'table' with an 'altar' and withholding the

---

[28] Spurgeon, 'Communion With Christ And His People', p. 324.

cup from the 'laity').[29] Such practices did not, as Roman Catholics believed, act as aids to devotion; rather they were accretions which had collected around the pure and simple rite which Christ had instituted. Consequently they needed to be scrubbed off so that the Supper and its spiritual meaning could be seen and experienced.[30] It is instructive that, even as Spurgeon spoke of enjoying spiritual fellowship with all God's people at the Lord's Supper in the long extract just cited, he described the Supper in Protestant terms. It was one 'loaf', not a number of individual wafers, which 'displayed and matured' the unity of all God's true people.

Analysis of Spurgeon's approach to Roman Catholic devotional writing and eucharistic practice highlights the importance of the integrating theme of this study to him. His shrill denunciations of Roman Catholic eucharistic practice and his embracing of certain Roman Catholic devotional literature were, in his mind, entirely consistent. Fellowship with Christ and his people was enabled by some 'precious' Roman Catholic devotional writings, but was obscured by Roman Catholic and Tractarian eucharistic practice. The former were to be embraced just as the latter were to be rejected.

As should already be clear, Spurgeon's approach to the Supper was not only to celebrate it frequently and with simplicity, he also wanted to celebrate it with Christ's people. This aspect of his practice can now be considered further. I have not been able to find one example of Spurgeon ever taking Communion on his own, even when he was seriously ill. The Supper was always to be celebrated with others. 'I must have you with me', he once said to his congregation at the Tabernacle in the course of a Communion service, 'I cannot do without you.'[31] He felt a great affinity with his church and spoke of communing with them around the Lord's Table, comparing the experience to a family gathering. Once again, he contrasted this approach with Roman Catholic practice. '[T]he most spiritually minded of you, if you shut yourselves up in a cell, and try to play the monk ... cannot keep this ordinance.' In a suggestive phrase Spurgeon declared that if someone wanted to be truly spiritual he or she 'must come down among the saints'. The monk isolated in his cell was not the exemplar of biblical spirituality, but quite the reverse. Those who were faithful to the command of Christ would desire to experience fellowship with one another at the Supper.[32] Spurgeon's vision and practice of the Supper was thoroughly communitarian.

Spurgeon's fellowship with other Christians around the Communion table extended beyond his own church members. As already noted in chapter 4, New Park Street / Metropolitan Tabernacle had a policy of closed membership but of open

---

[29] For Spurgeon's comments on the practice of withholding the cup from the laity, see C.H. Spurgeon, 'The Object Of The Lord's Supper', *MTP*, Vol. 51, S. No. 2942, 1 Corinthians 11.26, delivered 2 September 1877, p. 314.

[30] Spurgeon, 'Communion With Christ And His People', p. 324.

[31] Spurgeon, 'The Lord's Supper, Simple But Sublime!', pp. 315-16. Cf. Grass and Randall, 'C.H. Spurgeon on the Sacraments', p. 71.

[32] Spurgeon, 'The Lord's Supper, Simple But Sublime!', pp. 315-16.

Communion.³³ Consequently, those whom Spurgeon regarded as unbaptized were able to join in the Sunday night celebrations of the Lord's Supper which Spurgeon led at the Tabernacle.³⁴ As already shown in this chapter, he was ready to share the Supper with those gathered for the interdenominational Lambeth Union meeting, and he celebrated Communion in the Presbyterian church at Mentone. This ecumenical approach found yet broader expression in the Communion services he led in his hotel room at the French resort, where persons from a range of different denominations (as well as different nationalities) would be present.³⁵ Spurgeon spoke about these occasions, and other informal services he had held at different places on his travels, to the teachers who made up the Lambeth Union. 'I have had my Master's presence there', Spurgeon said, 'though, perhaps, scarcely two of us belonged to any one church or denomination.' He continued,

> I have not found the Lord absent because I have had two or three Clergymen of the Church of England. I have not found him stop away because some of the brethren were not baptised. I have not found He has been absent because of any fault in them so long as they have loved him, served him, and desired communion with him.³⁶

Spurgeon's repeated stress on the presence of Christ at the Lord's Supper is one that will be followed up later in this chapter. What can be noted here is his truly expansive, pan-denominational vision of the Supper. Whilst he might not have celebrated the Supper with a Roman Catholic, he certainly did celebrate it with Anglicans. He was fully aware that there were some who objected to his inter-denominational approach but he told the Lambeth Union bluntly that he did not understand those objections.³⁷ Only Christians could come to the Table, of course,³⁸ but all true believers who desired communion with Christ were welcome to come and share the bread and wine. Significant differences in ecclesiology were no barrier

---

³³ See C.H. Spurgeon's remarks in 'Meeting Of Our Own Church', *MTP*, Vol. 7, 8 April 1861, p. 260. For Spurgeon's general belief in this approach, see C.H. Spurgeon to unnamed friend, 22 July 1880, 'Original Correspondence of Charles Haddon Spurgeon, 1863–1886', Spurgeon's College, Heritage Room (4G), No. 31.

³⁴ It should be noted that by the mid-nineteenth century this approach had become the norm amongst Baptists. See A.R. Cross, *Baptism and the Baptists: Theology and Practice in Twentieth-Century Britain* (Carlisle: Paternoster, 2000), p. 9.

³⁵ [Anon.], 'Prefatory Note', to Spurgeon, *Till He Come*, n.p.. Probably this was written by J.W. Harrald who, together with Susannah Spurgeon, was C.H. Spurgeon's literary executor.

³⁶ *Sunday School Chronicle*, 17 February 1882, 'Spurgeon's Scrapbooks, Numbered Volumes', Vol. 6, p. 8.

³⁷ *Sunday School Chronicle*, 17 February 1882, 'Spurgeon's Scrapbooks, Numbered Volumes', Vol. 6, p. 8. An earlier piece in the *Sunday School Chronicle*, 10 February 1882, 'Spurgeon's Scrapbooks, Numbered Volumes', Vol. 6, pp. 7-8, further indicates that the service was controversial for some.

³⁸ Spurgeon, 'The Lord's Supper', p. 104.

to shared experience.[39] Spurgeon's approach to the Supper can rightly be called 'catholic' with a lower case 'c'. In summary, Spurgeon believed in a celebration of the Supper that was frequent, simple and 'open', emphasising the importance of fellowship with other believers.

Spurgeon's Preaching at the Lord's Supper

Spurgeon's preaching at the Lord's Supper can now be analysed. The central theme of Spurgeon's Communion addresses and meditations was, unsurprisingly, the cross.[40] Preaching at the Supper afforded Spurgeon ideal opportunity to assert his belief in the centrality of the atonement for soteriology. In a message entitled simply, 'The Lord's Supper', Spurgeon observed that the cross was the focal point of the Supper and declared that this showed that it was the 'most important part of all that [Christ] did or suffered'.[41] In another message entitled 'The Object Of The Lord's Supper', preached in 1877 at one of the 'Great Communion' services at the Tabernacle, Spurgeon stated, 'It is the death of Christ which is set forth by this memorial supper. Why was that chosen? *I answer, because it is the most vital of all truths* ... The atoning death of Christ once put away, you have taken the sun out of the Church's heavens.'[42] Spurgeon did not want to 'depreciate' Christ's incarnation, life or resurrection, but it was the cross that was central. Had not Christ said as much by instituting a memorial to his death but not to other aspects of his ministry?[43] The Lord's Supper was proof to Spurgeon that the atonement was at the heart of the Christian gospel.

The Supper was a setting in which Spurgeon regularly proclaimed his particular theology of the cross, that of penal substitution. For example, in 'The Sin Bearer', which was published in *Till He Come*, Spurgeon defended his views on the atonement in some detail. The preacher's text was 1 Peter 1.24-25, and he was quite certain that the statement that Christ 'bare our sins in his own body on the tree' was a plain declaration of penal substitutionary atonement. Spurgeon set out a whole series of other scriptures which all pointed in the same direction, including Hebrews 9.28, 'Christ was once offered to bear the sins of many', and 2 Corinthians 5.21, 'Christ hath redeemed us from the curse of the law, being made a curse for us...' In a comment which reflected his belief in the verbal inspiration of scripture he stated, 'I cannot imagine that the Holy Spirit would have used language so expressive if He had not intended to teach us that our Saviour really did bear our sins, and suffer in our stead.' Those advocates of 'modern thought' who rejected penal substitution were, for Spurgeon, 'modern haters of the cross', so clearly were they denying what

---

[39] Cf. C.H. Spurgeon, 'Mysterious Visits', Psalm 17.3, 'An Address To A Little Company At The Communion Table At Mentone', in *Till He Come*, p. 12.

[40] See the comment in [Anon.], 'Prefatory Note', to Spurgeon, *Till He Come*, n.p..

[41] Spurgeon, 'The Lord's Supper', p. 100.

[42] Spurgeon, 'The Object Of The Lord's Supper', p. 317.

[43] Cf. Spurgeon, 'The Lord's Supper', pp. 99-100.

the 'word of God' taught about the death of Christ.[44] Other addresses in *Till He Come* contain much material in a similar vein. In 'The Memorable Hymn', Spurgeon concluded his message with an unambiguous declaration of penal substitution, repeatedly using the word 'punish' for rhetorical effect. 'Christ was punished in the room, place, and stead of every man and woman who will believe on Him. If you believe on Him ... God cannot punish you, for he has punished Christ ahead of you, and He will never punish twice for the same offence.'[45] Preaching at the Lord's Supper was a context in which Spurgeon affirmed his commitment to the centrality of the atonement and defended and expounded his theology of the cross.

Furthermore, it is striking how often Spurgeon's preaching on the importance and nature of the atonement at the Lord's Supper was closely tied to his own experience. Undoubtedly his theology was, in Eugene Peterson's terms, a spiritual theology, that is one that was 'lived', the antithesis of a theology 'depersonalised into information about God'.[46] This can be seen with particular clarity in 'The Sin Bearer'. In the introduction to this message Spurgeon stated that, 'We ourselves now know *by experience* that there is no place for comfort like the cross.'[47] Later on in the sermon he declared,

> Beloved friends, we very calmly and coolly talk about this thing [the atonement], but it is the greatest marvel in the universe; it is the miracle of earth, the mystery of heaven, the terror of hell. Could we fully realise the guilt of sin, the punishment due to it, and the literal substitution of Christ, it would work in us an intense enthusiasm of gratitude, love, and praise. I do not wonder our Methodist friends shout, "Hallelujah!" This is enough to make us all shout and sing, as long as we live, "Glory, glory to the Son of God!"[48]

Once again, the theology was penal substitution, but here it is especially clear that the 'punishment' due to sin and the 'literal substitution of Christ' were not abstract concepts to be debated but truths that were living and vital, to be believed in ever more deeply. If the atonement were truly appreciated it would 'work in' the believer intense feelings of 'gratitude' and 'love' to God, feelings which could not help being expressed in praise. To Spurgeon's mind, for someone to discuss the atonement in a detached way was a sure sign that they had not understood it, and for a person to reject penal substitution was proof that they had not only an inadequate knowledge of their own sinfulness but also a shallow appreciation of God's holiness. For

---

[44] C.H. Spurgeon, 'The Sin Bearer', 1 Peter 2.24-25, 'A Communion Meditation At Mentone', in *Till He Come*, pp. 333-34.

[45] C.H. Spurgeon, 'The Memorable Hymn', Matthew 26.30, in *Till He Come*, p. 229.

[46] E.H. Peterson, *Christ Plays in Ten Thousand Places: A Conversation in Spiritual Theology* (London: Hodder and Stoughton, 2005), p. 1. Elsewhere Peterson speaks of 'Spiritual Theology' as to do with 'prayer' and 'spiritual formation', linked with reading the Bible 'formationally, not just intellectually'. See E.H. Peterson, *Subversive Spirituality* (Vancouver: Regent College, 1997), p. 259.

[47] Spurgeon, 'The Sin Bearer', p. 334. Italics added.

[48] Spurgeon, 'The Sin Bearer', p. 338.

The Lord's Supper

Spurgeon, who had a profound and deep sense of both, the work of Christ on the cross by which the guilty sinner and a holy God were reconciled was indeed a source of 'great comfort', as well as being a spur to heartfelt, evangelical worship – singing and shouting praises to God. In point of fact, to speak 'coolly and calmly' about the cross was quite beyond Spurgeon, and statements about its 'preciousness' for the believer were never far away from any of his expositions of the atonement.[49] The Lord's Supper provided a vital context for these passionate, 'intense' reflections, turning as it did the thoughts of both preacher and congregation to Christ's cross and its meaning.[50]

When preaching at the Lord's Supper, Spurgeon would often take a text from the Song of Songs. *Till He Come* contains twenty-one separate addresses and meditations, six of which are based, in whole or in part, on verses from the Song.[51] As shown in chapter 2, Spurgeon followed Puritans such as Richard Sibbes and James Durham in understanding the Song as an allegory which depicted the relationship between Christ and his Church.[52] For Spurgeon, the Song was one of the 'high places of Scripture' because he believed it spoke with particular richness and suggestiveness of the communion Christians could enjoy with Christ. For those not taught in this 'school of communion' the book was 'sealed', but for 'full grown Christians', who knew what it was to experience closeness to Christ, the spiritual meaning of the Song would be clear 'from the first verse to the last'.[53] Spurgeon's preaching on the Song at the Lord's Supper further illuminates the intense communion he believed could exist between Christ and his church. In the following analysis, the focus will be on messages on the Song of Songs printed in *Till He Come*.

Spurgeon's preaching on the Song at the Supper was, first of all, an opportunity for him to speak about Christ's love for the church. In 'Fragrant Spices From The

---

[49] Cf. C.H. Spurgeon, 'The Well Beloved', Song of Songs 5.16, in *Till He Come*, pp. 104-105; 'The Object Of The Lord's Supper', p. 316.

[50] Cf. C.H. Spurgeon, 'A Holy Celebration', *MTP*, Vol. 19, S. No. 1092, n.d., Exodus 12.42, pp. 1-2.

[51] See C.H. Spurgeon, 'Under His Shadow', Psalm 91.1, Isaiah 31.2, Song of Songs 2.3, Psalm 63.7, Isaiah 49.2, pp. 11-20; 'Under The Apple Tree', Song of Songs 2.3, pp. 37-53; 'Over The Mountains', Song of Songs 2.16,17, pp. 57-70; 'The Well-Beloved', Song of Songs 5.16, pp. 95-113; 'Fragrant Spices From The Mountains Of Myrrh', Song of Songs 4.7, pp. 73-93. These are in addition to 'The Spiced Wine Of My Pomegranate' which has already been cited in this chapter. In *Till He Come*, p. 22, the text for 'Under His Shadow' is given as Psalm 91.1 only, but the four additional texts are listed on the contents page of the book.

[52] See, e.g., C.H. Spurgeon, 'The Lily Among The Thorns', in C.H. Spurgeon, *The Most Holy Place: Sermons on the Song of Solomon* (London: Passmore and Alabaster, 1896), S. No. 1525, delivered 29 February 1880, Song of Songs 2.2, p. 125.

[53] C.H. Spurgeon, 'A Bundle Of Myrrh', in Spurgeon, *Most Holy Place*, S. No. 558, delivered 6 March 1864, Song of Songs 1.13, pp. 89-90.

Mountains Of Myrrh', which was based on Song of Songs 4.7,[54] he spoke of this theme in some detail. The words of the text, 'Thou art all fair, My love; there is no spot in thee', spoken by the lover to his beloved were interpreted as words spoken by Christ to his Church. Spurgeon proceeded to expound the verse on this basis, speaking of Christ's 'high esteem' for his Church. Christ regarded the Church with 'rapturous delight' as 'superlatively' lovely and his love for her was like that of a 'fond mother' for her child.[55] In further daring language Spurgeon declared,

> The beauty which He admires is *universal*, He is as much enchanted with her temples as with her breasts. All her offices, all her pure devotions, all her earnest labours, all her constant sufferings, are precious to His heart. She is 'all fair'. Her ministry, her psalmody, her intercessions, her alms, her watching, all are admirable to Him, when performed in the Spirit ... He loves and admires her everywhere.[56]

The references to 'temples' and 'breasts' hark back to Song of Songs 4.3, 'Thy temples are like a piece of a pomegranate within thy locks' and 4.5, 'Thy two breasts are like two young roes that are twins'. Spurgeon believed the woman in the Song was the Church personified and his overarching point in this extract was that Christ loves his Church in every aspect of her 'person' and life. The language and imagery Spurgeon employed speaks of the intensity of that love.

Of course, Spurgeon was fully aware that the Church did not always act 'in the Spirit', indeed, she was deeply sinful and this Christ 'abhorred'.[57] Christ's love for the Church and his estimate of it as 'all fair' were consistent with his people's sinfulness, however, in the light of the cross. The doctrine of imputed righteousness was crucial here. In 'Fragrant Spices From The Mountains Of Myrrh' Spurgeon quoted James Durham's comments on Song of Songs 1.6, stating,

> As Durham says, these words are spoken 'in respect of the imputation of Christ's righteousness wherewith they are adorned, and which they have put on, which makes them very glorious and lovely, so that they are beautiful beyond all others, through His comeliness put upon them.'

The Church, imperfect and sinful, was viewed as spotless by Christ because, when he looked on his Church he saw his own imputed righteousness, not the sin of unfaithful believers. The beauty, or 'comeliness' of the Church to Christ was effectively his own beauty, conferred on believers as they put their trust in Christ and in his cross. Through faith in the 'blood of Jesus' every 'stain' had been 'removed'.[58] Consequently, Christians could be sure that they were loved by Christ.

---

[54] In reality C.H. Spurgeon did not confine himself to this text, but ranged much more widely through the Song. See, e.g., 'Fragrant Spices From The Mountains Of Myrrh', pp. 74-75.

[55] Spurgeon, 'Fragrant Spices From The Mountains Of Myrrh', pp. 76-77, 87.

[56] Spurgeon, 'Fragrant Spices From The Mountains Of Myrrh', p. 77.

[57] Spurgeon, 'Fragrant Spices From The Mountains Of Myrrh', p. 74.

[58] Spurgeon, 'Fragrant Spices From The Mountains Of Myrrh', pp. 80-81.

Furthermore, Christ's love was communicated to the Church in ways that led to times of deep, felt communion. In 'Fragrant Spices From The Mountains Of Myrrh' Spurgeon spoke of such times from personal experience,

> I have sometimes, when the Lord has assured me of His love, felt as if I could not contain more joy and delight. My eyes ran down with tears of gratitude. I fell upon my knees to bless Him, but rose again in haste, feeling as if I had nothing more to ask for, but must stand up and praise Him; then have I lifted my hands to heaven, longing to fill my arms with Him; panting to talk with Him, as a man talketh with his friend, and to see Him in His own person, that I might tell Him how happy He had made His unworthy servant, and might fall on my face, and kiss His feet in unutterable thankfulness and love.[59]

The intensity of Spurgeon's experience is illustrated by his tears as well as by words and phrases such as 'longing', 'panting', 'kiss His feet' and 'unutterable thankfulness and love'. Christ's love for Spurgeon opened the door to passionate, felt communion. Moreover, Spurgeon was sure these experiences were open to all true believers, even 'dwarfish Littlefaiths'. Christ loved the imperfect, sinful Church and so all Christians could seek him and find him. 'The importunate pleader shall not lack his reward', Spurgeon assured his congregation. 'Haste thee to Him, O timid one, and tell Him that nothing will content thee but a smile from His own face, and a word from His own lips!' Spurgeon was sure that such requests would be answered.[60] He himself came to Christ at the Supper as a repentant sinner, and he experienced communion with Christ. Other sinners could come in the same way and, together with Spurgeon, they could experience communion too.

This corporate dimension of the Lord's Supper, which we saw was crucial to Spurgeon's practice of the Supper, is also highlighted by the extracts just cited from 'Fragrant Spices From The Mountains Of Myrrh'. It was Christ's people, gathered round the Table, who together experienced communion with their Lord. Spurgeon was explicit that as Christ's people came together in this way they would experience communion not only with Christ but also with one another. In another sermon on the Song, 'The Spiced Wine Of My Pomegranate', which was subtitled, 'The Communion Of Communication', Spurgeon gave an extended reflection on the fellowship or κοινωνία (the word was written in Greek in the printed text of Spurgeon's sermon) which Christians could enjoy. This included κοινωνία with Christ himself, of course; indeed this was the burden of Spurgeon's message. But κοινωνία could also be enjoyed between Christians on the basis of their shared union with Christ as they came together around the table. Spurgeon spoke of how it was his practice to have a collection for the poor when he led a Communion service, as a tangible expression of this κοινωνία. In the act of giving and receiving, real communion was known and this reflected the fellowship that was shared between Christ and his people at the Supper which was also based on giving and receiving –

---

[59] Spurgeon, 'Fragrant Spices From The Mountains Of Myrrh', pp. 89-90.
[60] Spurgeon, 'Fragrant Spices From The Mountains Of Myrrh', p. 91.

Christ had given his body and blood which was received into the lives of the gathered believers who ate and drank in faith.[61] The vertical and the horizontal dimensions of fellowship were thus held together.

In 'Christ And His Table Companions' (which was not preached on the Song of Songs), Spurgeon spoke further of the corporate dimension of the Supper. The act of believers eating and drinking together was a 'pledge' of faithfulness, not only to Christ, but also to 'one another'. Moreover, the Supper was a place where 'hearty brotherhood' was set forth and could be enjoyed, where all came as equals. Spurgeon picked up on the phrase, 'Liberty, Equality, Fraternity', the motto of the French Revolution. The reality of which this phrase spoke could not be realised in a political republic, but it could be known at the Supper, for in the family of Christ all were equals and all were free. A Christian should not speak of the first apostles as 'saints' unless they were also prepared to speak of '*Saint* William and *Saint* Jane sitting over yonder'.[62] Christians were bound together with each other and enjoyed real and rich communion with one another as they met as 'brothers', and hence as equals, around the Lord's Table. Thus Spurgeon's preaching at the Supper spoke of both the communion which could be enjoyed with Christ and also of the communion all those who were 'in Christ' could know around the Table. Both dimensions of this κοινωνία were described with an intensity and passion which sprang directly from Spurgeon's own experience at the Supper.

The Real Presence

It will already be clear that Spurgeon believed Christ was powerfully present at what was his table. He believed in the 'real presence' of Christ at the Table: Jesus met with his people in bread and wine as they ate and drank in faith. Of course, as has already been shown in a number of places in this book, he rejected the sacerdotalism of Roman Catholicism and of the Oxford Movement. He regarded the doctrine of transubstantiation with particular 'horror' and 'contempt'. He attacked it, in a sermon preached at the Metropolitan Tabernacle entitled 'The Witness Of The Lord's Supper', in terms that were redolent of his critique of Roman Catholic baptismal theology (see chapter 4). Spurgeon declared that transubstantiation was a 'foolish superstition' and an affront to both 'reason' and the 'spiritual nature'.[63] In 'Mysterious Visits', which was given at Mentone, he asserted that although 'the Romish church' said much about the 'real presence' of Christ at the Mass, what they actually believed in was Christ's 'corporeal presence'.[64] This teaching was abhorrent to Spurgeon and he never ceased to take opportunities to denounce it, doing so throughout his ministry.

---

[61] See Spurgeon, 'The Spiced Wine Of My Pomegranate', pp. 118-19.

[62] Spurgeon, 'Christ And His Table Companions', pp. 279. Italics original.

[63] C.H. Spurgeon, 'The Witness Of The Lord's Supper', *MTP*, Vol. 59, S. No. 3338, 1 Corinthians 11.26, n.d., pp. 37-38.

[64] Spurgeon, 'Mysterious Visits', p. 17.

Nevertheless, despite this vehement rejection of sacerdotalism, Spurgeon strongly resisted the prevailing drift among nineteenth-century Protestants towards what Timothy George describes as 'eucharistic minimalism'.[65] This trend towards viewing the Supper as primarily a 'memorial to an absent saviour' had actually begun in the last quarter of the eighteenth century, even amongst Calvinistic Baptists.[66] By the mid-nineteenth century many evangelicals were reacting against Roman Catholic and Tractarian views by capitulating to an eviscerated memorialism as far as their approach to the Supper was concerned.[67] A Baptist such as John Clifford responded to sacerdotalism in a way that left him, as Walker states, 'hardly within reach of a viable eucharistic theology'.[68] By contrast, Spurgeon repeatedly affirmed his belief in the 'real presence' of Christ at the Supper. Certainly, Spurgeon did speak of the Lord's Supper as a 'memorial' of Christ's death,[69] but he was also clear that it was much more than this. He referred to the 'real presence' in both the messages cited in the previous paragraph. In 'The Witness Of The Lord's Supper' he stated, 'We believe in the real presence ... We believe that Jesus Christ spiritually comes to us and refreshes us.'[70] In 'Mysterious Visits' Spurgeon expounded in some detail what he meant by the 'real presence',

> By spiritual we do not mean unreal ... I believe in the true and real presence of Jesus with His people: such presence has been real to my spirit. Lord Jesus, thou Thyself hast visited me. As surely as the Lord Jesus came really as to His flesh to Bethlehem and Calvary, so surely does He come really by His Spirit to His people in the hours of their communion with Him. We are as conscious of that presence as of our own existence.[71]

Although Christ's presence was not 'corporeal', it was nonetheless 'true' and 'real'. It was not that he took a mediating position between the Roman Catholic and the merely memorialist views, a sort of middle way between two extremes. Spurgeon was working within a different paradigm. Christ's body was in heaven, but Christ was present by the Holy Spirit (described by Spurgeon as 'His [i.e., Christ's] Spirit') as the bread was broken and the wine poured out. Christ's presence was thus spiritual and yet it was made tangible by the material signs of bread and wine which

---

[65] T. George, 'Controversy and Communion: The Limits of Baptist Fellowship from Bunyan to Spurgeon', in D.W. Bebbington (ed.), *The Gospel in the World: International Baptist Studies* (Carlisle: Paternoster, 2002), p. 56.

[66] See M.A.G. Haykin, '"His Soul Refreshing Presence": The Lord's Supper in Calvinistic Baptist Thought and Experience in the "Long" Eighteenth Century', in Cross and Thompson (eds), *Baptist Sacramentalism*, pp. 177-93.

[67] See D.W. Bebbington, *The Dominance of Evangelicalism: The Age of Spurgeon and Moody* (Leicester: IVP, 2005), pp. 146-49, for the 'diminution' of the significance of the sacraments (i.e., Communion and baptism) amongst evangelicals as a reaction against the rise of High Churchmanship. Pp. 147-49 deal with Communion specifically.

[68] Walker, *Baptists at the Table*, pp. 193-94.

[69] See, e.g., Spurgeon, 'The Lord's Supper', p. 98.

[70] Spurgeon, 'The Witness Of The Lord's Supper', p. 38.

[71] Spurgeon, 'Mysterious Visits', p. 17.

the believer ate and drank in faith. The materiality of the signs was important to Spurgeon for, as he said in a sermon entitled 'The Double Forget-Me-Not', Christians were still linked with what he called 'materialism'; they were not yet 'purely spiritual'. Thus the linking of the 'spiritual' and 'material' in the Supper was important, both as an aid to faith for embodied creatures and also as an affirmation of the physical, which would one day, at the return of Christ, be itself 'lifted up' and 'reunited with the spiritual' as Christians received their new resurrection bodies and took their place in the new heavens and the new earth.[72] Christ's presence at the Supper was thus spiritual, but nonetheless real, made tangible by the materiality of the signs. This was how Spurgeon experienced Christ's presence around the Table. The spiritual, real presence of Christ at the Supper led to correspondingly spiritual and real communion with him.

Walker, who also cites this passage from 'Mysterious Visits', argues for the influence of John Calvin on Spurgeon's theology of the Supper.[73] Although it would be more strictly correct to say that Spurgeon was influenced by Calvin as mediated through the English Calvinistic and Puritan heritage, undoubtedly there was a link between Calvin, Calvinism and Spurgeon's views, and Walker's study was groundbreaking in pointing this out. But Randall and Grass are surely right to highlight the roles also played by reason (transubstantiation, said Spurgeon, made no sense to someone who was 'rational' and 'enlightened')[74] and, especially, experience in shaping and sustaining Spurgeon's approach.[75] It was Spurgeon's clear testimony that 'the more frequently he obeyed his Lord's command, "This do in remembrance of me," the more precious did his Saviour become to him.'[76] So, although Spurgeon was preaching that communion was a 'means of grace' very early in his public ministry, his approach undoubtedly grew more 'sacramental' as that ministry progressed. This can be seen by comparing his preaching on the Lord's Supper in the 1850s with his preaching on the same subject in the 1870s and 1880s.[77] Spurgeon's

---

[72] Spurgeon, 'The Double Forget-Me-Not', p. 315. On the linking of the 'spiritual' and 'material' in the Supper, see also C.H. Spurgeon, 'Mealtime In The Cornfields', in *Farm Sermons* (London: Passmore and Alabaster, 1900), pp. 266-67. The Supper was 'literally' as well as 'spiritually' a meal.

[73] Walker, *Baptists at the Table*, pp. 174-75.

[74] Spurgeon, 'The Witness Of The Lord's Supper', p. 38.

[75] Randall and Grass, 'C.H. Spurgeon on the Sacraments', p. 69.

[76] This is from the unsigned 'Prefatory Note' in Spurgeon, *Till He Come*. For this stress on experience as shaping and sustaining Spurgeon's sacramental view of the Supper, see also C.H. Spurgeon, 'Baptism – A Burial', *MTP*, Vol. 27, S. No. 1627, Romans 6.3-4, delivered 30 October 1881, p. 618, 'In heavenly things we see as much as we have within ourselves. He who has eaten Christ's flesh and blood spiritually is the man who can see this (truth) in the sacred Supper'; *Autobiography*, Vol. 4, p. 72; 'Mealtime in the Cornfields', p. 267.

[77] Cf. C.H. Spurgeon, 'Preparation Necessary For Communion', *MTP*, Vol. 45, S. No. 2647, 1 Corinthians 11.28, delivered Autumn 1857, pp. 530-36 with 'Communion With Christ And His People', pp. 313-27.

regular experience of celebrating Communion led him to assert ever more strongly that he believed in the real but spiritual presence of Christ at the Table.

This realisation of the importance of experience in shaping and sustaining Spurgeon's belief in the real presence of Christ at the Lord's Supper helps explain the bifurcation between his approach to baptism (Christ is not present in any objective sense) and the Supper (Christ is spiritually and really present). Believers' baptism, as a once for all time never-to-be-repeated rite, was by definition not experienced by Spurgeon in the same, continuing way as the Lord's Supper was. Of course, he did conduct numerous baptismal services – at least at Waterbeach and in the first phase of his London ministry. But from 1868 onwards he effectively stopped baptizing. On 1 January of that year, Spurgeon's brother, James Archer Spurgeon, was appointed 'co-pastor' of the Metropolitan Tabernacle.[78] James' duties included baptizing candidates at the regular weeknight baptismal services at the Tabernacle. As the figures which appeared each month in the *Sword and Trowel* show, Charles hardly ever baptized following his brother's appointment. Figures for two different six-month periods prove the point. In the first six months of 1868 there were nineteen baptismal services at the Metropolitan Tabernacle, with two hundred and seventy-seven people baptized, according to the statistics printed in the *Sword and Trowel*.[79] All the candidates at these services were baptized by J.A. Spurgeon. In a later six-month period, the second half of 1874, there were twelve baptismal services with a total of one hundred and ninety-four baptisms. J.A. Spurgeon was responsible for eleven of these services and one hundred and ninety-two of the baptisms.[80] C.H.

---

[78] In reality J.A. Spurgeon was his brother's assistant, as the carefully worded terms of appointment made abundantly clear. See G.H. Pike, *James Archer Spurgeon D.D. LL.D. Preacher, Philanthropist, and Co-Pastor With C.H. Spurgeon at the Metropolitan Tabernacle* (London: Alexander and Shepheard, 1894), pp. 85-89.

[79] See Spurgeon (ed.), *Sword and Trowel*, February 1868, p. 94: two services, nineteen baptized; March 1868, p. 142: one service, eighteen baptized; April 1868, p. 191: four services, fifty-one baptized; June 1868, p. 286: six services, 102 baptized; July 1868, p. 333: two services, thirty-one baptized; August 1868, p. 383: two services, twenty-three baptized; September 1868, p. 431: two services, thirty-three baptized. The May issue did not carry any information about baptismal services. J.A. Spurgeon was already baptizing at the Tabernacle before he officially took up his appointment. For example, he officiated at six different services in November and December 1867, baptizing a total of eighty-three people. See *Sword and Trowel*, January 1868, p. 47; February 1868, p. 94; March 1868, p. 142. It could take time for a service to be recorded in the magazine; hence figures for the end of 1867 were logged in the first three months of 1868. There also seems to have been some 'double counting' as the *Sword and Trowel* struggled to record accurately what was an unusually large number of baptisms. It appears that a backlog had built up before J.A. Spurgeon's involvement. Services on 2 January and 20 January, when there were fifteen and four baptisms respectively, appear to have been recorded in both the February and March issues of the magazine. I have counted these figures only when they first appear in the February issue.

[80] Spurgeon (ed.), *Sword and Trowel*, October 1874, p. 491: three services, forty-six baptized; November 1874, p. 543: two services, thirty-three baptized; December 1874, p.

Spurgeon baptized only two candidates, both of them on 21 September 1874.[81] These were his twin sons, Thomas and Charles.[82] I have not been able to find any other instances of C.H. Spurgeon baptizing at the Tabernacle in the 1870s or, indeed, beyond.[83] If J.A. Spurgeon did not conduct the baptisms, then someone else would be called in to do so.[84] Doubtless, C.H Spurgeon's stepping back from baptizing was related to his deteriorating physical health, although, clearly, he could still make the effort for the occasion of his sons' baptism. But, whatever the reasons, the effect was to distance himself from the act, and the experience, of baptism.

C.H. Spurgeon would still preach at baptismal services when he was present: the account of his preaching at his sons' baptism in the *South London Press* suggests the burden of his message on that occasion was a particularly strident attack on infant baptism and baptismal regeneration.[85] But his usual practice was to preach, lead in prayer and then 'step from the rostrum', at which point James would take over.[86] As the 1870s wore on, Charles was increasingly absent from these services.[87] The disparity between C.H. Spurgeon's regular experience of the Lord's Supper and his corresponding lack of experience of baptisms thus became even starker. Certainly there were additional reasons for the bifurcation between Spurgeon's views of baptism and the Lord's Supper. In my analysis of Spurgeon's approach to baptism in chapter 4 I argued that Spurgeon's evangelical stress on the supreme importance of personal conversion militated against a theology of baptism as a means of grace. Because the Lord's Supper was not linked with conversion in the same way that baptism was, it was easier for Spurgeon to maintain that God was present and active through the Supper. Nevertheless, his theology of the 'real presence' was undoubtedly grounded in significant degree in his own repeated experience of communion with Christ at the Supper, just as his approach to baptism was confirmed by his lack of continuing experience of that particular ordinance.

582: three services, forty-three baptized; January 1875, p. 44: three services, forty-nine baptized; February 1875, p. 92: one service, twenty-three baptized.

[81] Spurgeon (ed.), *Sword and Trowel*, October 1874, p. 491.

[82] 'Baptism of Mr. Spurgeon's Sons', *South London Press*, 26 September 1874, in 'Spurgeon's Scrapbooks, Numbered Volumes', Vol. 1, p. 6.

[83] From the beginning of 1879 the *Sword and Trowel* stopped including the name of the person who conducted the Tabernacle baptisms. But I have found no evidence, in newspapers or elsewhere, that C.H. Spurgeon baptized in the period from 1879 to his death. If he did so at all, it was certainly a rare occurrence.

[84] E.g., Vernon Charlesworth, the headmaster of Spurgeon's Stockwell Orphanage. See Spurgeon (ed.), *Sword and Trowel*, September 1874, p. 439.

[85] 'Baptism of Mr. Spurgeon's Sons', *South London Press*, 26 September 1874, in 'Spurgeon's Scrapbooks, Numbered Volumes', Vol. 1, p. 6.

[86] 'My Visit to Spurgeon's Tabernacle, Thursday 25 February 1886', by 'Saladin' (Angus Library, Regent's Park College, D/SPU 9). This is a very negative handwritten description of 'One of Pastor [C.H.] Spurgeon's dipping nights'. The author might well be William Stewart Ross, a Scottish educationalist and secularist, who frequently used the pseudonym 'Saladin', but I have been unable to verify this.

[87] Something clearly implied by Pike, *J.A. Spurgeon*, p. 125.

The Lord's Supper

Spurgeon's experimental knowledge of the presence of Christ at the Lord's Supper is in many ways summed up in the words of his hymn, 'Amidst us Our Belovèd Stands'. This was written specifically for use in Communion services and included in *Our Own Hymn Book*. The first three verses are cited here,

> AMIDST us our Belovèd stands,
>   And bids us view His piercèd hands;
> Points to His wounded feet and side,
>   Blest emblems of the Crucified.
>
> What food luxurious loads the board,
>   When at His table sits the Lord!
> The wine how rich, the bread how sweet,
>   When Jesus deigns the guests to meet!
>
> If now with eyes defiled and dim,
>   We see the signs but see not Him,
> Oh, may His love the scales displace,
>   And bid us see Him face to face![88]

The focus on the atonement, the description of Christ as the 'Belovèd' echoing the language of the Songs of Songs and, supremely, the presence of the risen Christ, spiritual but nonetheless real and substantial, are all apparent in this, the most enduring of Spurgeon's hymns. It should be emphasised that Spurgeon did not have an *ex opere operato* understanding of the Supper. Christ had to 'deign' to meet with his people and the food was only 'luxurious' when Christ sat at the table. His presence could not be presumed upon and God could not be manipulated. Moreover, it was possible for the communicant to see only the 'signs' and miss the reality to which they pointed. But when the 'eye' of faith was able to look through the symbols of bread and wine, then Christ, who had promised to be present by his grace, could be perceived and experienced as he met with his humble, trusting, expectant people. This, for Spurgeon, was the heart of the Lord's Supper. Christ was present with his people and invited them to participate in fellowship that was so deep and rich that it could even be described as 'face-to-face' communion with him.

In fact, so rich was Spurgeon's experience of Christ's presence at the Supper that it enjoyed a special place in his thinking about communion with Christ. There were, of course, many routes to such communion and Spurgeon dealt with some of these in 'Communion With Christ And His People'. Different avenues to fellowship with Christ mentioned include those already covered in the study: meditation on the scriptures, intercessory prayer and contemplation of Christ. He also considered two

---

[88] C.H. Spurgeon (ed.), *Our Own Hymn Book* (London: Passmore and Alabaster, 1866), No. 939. Cf. *Till He Come*, p. 359. In *Our Own Hymn Book* the hymn was headed 'Jesu's Presence Delightful'.

routes to communion which will be examined in chapters 8 and 10 of this study (namely, activity and suffering). He believed these different means of communion all represented 'windows of agate and gates of carbuncle' through which the earnest believer 'might come to the Lord',[89] and he certainly did not believe that Christ's presence was tied to the sacramental table. Nevertheless, in 'Communion With Christ And His People' at least, Spurgeon insisted that 'the ordinance of the Lord's Supper sets forth a way which surpasses' all other means to communion. This was because it was a 'receiving of Christ into our souls'.[90] So, although the Bible was foundational to his thinking about communion with Christ, the Supper enjoyed a special place in his experience of such communion. In respect of the Lord's Supper if not of baptism, it is right to speak of Spurgeon as having a sacramental spirituality.

An 'Accessible ... Method of Fellowship'

There are two other areas that need to be considered, both of which highlight how the Lord's Supper helped believers who were struggling in their Christian lives. These two areas will be examined in two shorter sections. Spurgeon himself experienced struggles in his Christian life, and so these two sections show ways in which the Supper connected with his own spirituality. Spurgeon was acutely aware of other believers who might also be experiencing difficulties. He was keen to assert that the Supper was a place where all could come and be sustained in their spiritual lives.

First of all, Spurgeon insisted that the Lord's Supper was a place where those who were conscious of their own sin and weakness could come and receive assurance of salvation and, furthermore, know that communion with Christ really was for them. This was of a piece with his view, as expressed in 'Fragrant Spices From The Mountains Of Myrrh', that the Table was somewhere where 'dwarfish Littlefaiths' could come. As far as Spurgeon himself was concerned, he was acutely aware of his own sin and yet he had frequently known felt communion with Christ at the Supper. In 'Communion With Christ And His People', Spurgeon stated that the Lord's Supper was 'the most accessible and the most effectual method of fellowship [with Christ]'. It is the word 'accessible' which is especially important to the argument here. Spurgeon pictured a believer saying, 'I do not feel that I can get near to Christ. He is so high and holy, and I am a poor sinner.' Spurgeon could do nothing but approve of such an attitude for he felt it himself. But this was precisely why the Lord's Supper was so helpful and so vital. Here Christ was presented as the saviour of *sinners*. The gulf separating the holiness of God and the sinfulness of men and women seemed impossibly wide, but in the atonement this gulf had been bridged: God and the sinner were now reconciled. In the Supper this truth was set forth in a solid, objective way. Spurgeon declared, 'This table sets before you His great sacrifice. Jesus has offered it; will you accept it? He does not ask you to bring

---

[89] Spurgeon, 'Communion With Christ And His People', pp. 318; 314.
[90] Spurgeon, 'Communion With Christ And His People', pp. 318; 314.

anything, – no drop of blood, no pang of flesh; all is here, and your part is to come and partake of it.'[91] Here every repentant sinner, however wretched they might feel, could come to Christ with nothing but their faith and receive from Christ, thus being assured of his love.[92]

The Lord's Supper spoke of how the sinful believer could know that communion with Christ was, for them, 'eternal'. Spurgeon stated,

> No power upon earth can henceforth take from me the piece of bread which I have just now eaten, it has gone where it will be made up into blood, and nerve, and muscle, and bone. It is within me, and of me. That drop of wine has coursed through my veins, and is part and parcel of my being. So he that takes Jesus by faith to be his Saviour has chosen the good part which shall not be taken away from him. He has received the Christ into his inward parts, and all the men on earth, and all the devils in hell, cannot extract Christ from him ... By our sincere reception of Jesus into our hearts, an indissoluble union is established between us and the Lord, and this manifests itself in mutual communion.[93]

This is an astonishing passage, one which, yet again, shows Spurgeon's powerful imagination at work. The Lord's Supper set forth with particular clarity the permanent nature of the believer's union with Christ which, as Spurgeon said elsewhere in *Till He Come*, was the 'immovable basis' of communion.[94] The elements, once ingested, could not be separated from the believer's body. The eating of the bread and drinking of the wine in faith signified the reception of Christ into the 'inmost soul' of the believer, and the way the elements became an integral part of him or her set forth the 'indissoluble' bond between the communicant and Christ. Spurgeon saw the closest possible correlation between the signs (the bread and the wine) and the one signified (Christ himself), so that he could speak without qualification of receiving *Christ* into 'the inward parts'. Here, then, was an objective and effectual sign for the timid believer: Christ really was in them and they in Christ. The assurance that we saw Spurgeon believed was the birthright of every convert to Christ was nurtured by participation in the Supper.

This assurance of the reality and permanence of a believer's union with Christ could then act as a springboard to felt communion. The believer who was acutely conscious of his or her sin and weakness could still know that they were united with Christ. Because the 'indissoluble union' was established, 'mutual communion' could follow. Once again, it should be evident that Spurgeon's spirituality was not an elitist

---

[91] Spurgeon, 'Communion with Christ and His People', pp. 318-19.

[92] For another passage on this theme, see Spurgeon, 'The Lord's Supper', pp. 105-106. It was entirely appropriate that this sermon was placed alongside an exposition of Romans 8.18-39, with its stress on assurance of salvation, in the *Metropolitan Tabernacle Pulpit*. See Vol. 50, pp. 106-108. It is not clear, from the *MTP*, that Spurgeon gave this exposition in the same service as the one in which he preached 'The Lord's Supper'.

[93] Spurgeon, 'Communion With Christ And His People', pp. 319-20.

[94] Spurgeon, 'The Spiced Wine Of My Pomegranate', p. 117. Cf. C.H. Spurgeon, 'Bands Of Love; Or, Union To Christ', in *Till He Come*, Hosea 11.4, pp. 181-83.

spirituality. The assurance of salvation and communion with Christ set forth and experienced at the Supper were not the preserve of the few but were accessible to the many. Spurgeon's vision of the Supper was an egalitarian one.

The Lord's Supper and Active Service

A second way the Lord's Supper could help struggling believers was by reviving them for active service. *Till He Come* closes with a sermon entitled 'Swooning And Reviving At Christ's Feet'. This message was unique in the collection in that it was delivered at the close of one of the Pastors' College conferences, with many of the ministers present at the service about to return to demanding, difficult pastorates. Although not dated in *Till He Come*, this message first appeared in the *Sword and the Trowel* in October 1882 and was in fact delivered at the close of the conference of that year, on the evening of Friday 21 April.[95]

Spurgeon took as his text Revelation 1.17-18, and focused in particular on the picture of the apostle John first falling and then 'reviving' at the feet of the glorified Christ. Spurgeon sought to apply this image to those present in a number of ways which related to pastoral ministry. With the Communion table set, Spurgeon believed that Christ was with them, and so the falling and reviving before Christ of which the text spoke could be the experience of all those who were present. As Spurgeon began his address he spoke first of all of the importance of 'swooning' at the feet of Christ. Those who were making progress in the life of holiness or experiencing success in ministry needed to be brought back to the necessity of 'daily cleansing'. A right appreciation of the Lord's Supper would do this, as well as engendering the humility Spurgeon believed simply had to be present if they rightly thought of 'Gethsemane and Calvary'. An experience of Christ granted at the Supper would also show that a believer, let alone a pastor, 'could not live an hour spiritually without Him who is not only bread, but life'. Just as 'natural bread' was essential for daily living so, spiritually, none of them could ever grow out of their need of feeding on a 'present Christ'. Thus the Supper spoke of the need for complete dependence on Christ, in ministry and life in general.[96] The Lord's Supper might be an accessible means of communion for those who were conscious of their failings; it was also an essential means of communion for those who felt strong, bringing them back to the heart of the gospel. The Supper 'forcibly reminded' (to pick up Spurgeon's phrase in 'The Greatest Exhibition Of The Age' cited earlier)[97] both the weak and the strong that all, without exception, needed to fall at the feet of Christ.

---

[95] Spurgeon (ed.), *Sword and Trowel*, October 1882, pp. 505-10; *Christian World*, 27 April 1882, 'Spurgeon's Scrapbooks, Numbered Volumes', Vol. 6, p. 47.

[96] C.H. Spurgeon, 'Swooning And Reviving At Christ's Feet', Revelation 1.17-18, 'An Address Delivered at the Close of One of the Pastors' College Conferences', in *Till He Come*, pp. 349-52.

[97] Spurgeon, 'The Greatest Exhibition Of The Age', p. 220.

Spurgeon then proceeded to speak of the ways Christ revived his people. The first and primary way by which it was possible to 'get alive again' spiritually was through being 'brought into contact' with Jesus. Spurgeon noted that in Revelation 1.17 Christ 'laid his right hand upon' the apostle. Thinking of this action in relation to himself and his hearers, he asked why Christ did not 'lay his foot upon' them, treading them down 'as the mire of the streets'. As the image of the text combined with Spurgeon's fertile imaginative powers he had an answer, which was that the foot in question had been 'pierced for [them]'. Therefore it was inconceivable that it should 'trample them in His wrath'. Rather than trampling them down, Christ showed his love to his people by laying his 'right hand' upon them, and so his love could be felt, restoring and 'reviving' the 'fainting disciple'. This renewing power could be experienced at the Lord's Supper because there the gracious self-giving of Christ in the atonement was set forth so clearly and effectually. Those present who entered into the 'true meaning' of what they were about to celebrate could expect to be 'revived and vitalized'. Indeed, there was the promise, in word and sacrament (although Spurgeon did not use this latter term), that Christ would be with the believer through every future 'dark hour'. Even the prospect of death should hold no fears for them because, as both text and Supper proclaimed, Christ himself had died and risen again. 'Onward, soldiers of the cross', Spurgeon encouraged the conference members, 'for our immortal Captain leads the way'.[98]

Another address printed in *Till He Come*, entitled 'The Well Beloved's Vineyard', was given in a quite different setting, his 'own room' at Mentone. To the small group who had come together to celebrate Communion Spurgeon spoke, in optimistic mood, of the many opportunities he saw all around them for fruitful Christian service,

> Each one of us may find work for the Master; there are capital opportunities around us. There never was an age in which a man, consecrated to God, might do so much as he can at this time. There is nothing to restrain the most ardent zeal. We live in such happy times that, if we plunge into a sea of work, we may swim, and none can hinder us. Then, too, our labour is made, by God's grace, to be so pleasant to us. No true servant of Christ is weary of the work, though he may be weary in the work: it is not the work that he ever wearies of, for he wishes that he could do ten times more.[99]

How was this desire, and the activity itself, to be sustained? Yet again, an important part of the answer was the Lord's Supper. Later on in his message, referring to the 'table of blessing', Spurgeon stated, 'This hallowed ordinance, I am sure, is a spot where hopes grow bright, and hearts grow warm, resolves become firm, and lives become fruitful, and all the clusters of our soul's fruit ripen for the Lord.'[100] A faithful believer was sustained for the work he or she had been called to do, in part, through participating in the Lord's Supper which would grant them fresh strength

---

[98] Spurgeon, 'Swooning And Reviving At Christ's Feet', pp. 353-56.
[99] Spurgeon, 'The Well-beloved's Vineyard', p. 147.
[100] Spurgeon, 'The Well-beloved's Vineyard', p. 149.

from Christ. As Spurgeon put it elsewhere, just as people were renewed as to their 'bodily strength' by eating good food, so those who came to 'wait upon the Lord...by feeding upon the body and blood of Christ' would be renewed spiritually for active service.[101] Again, those who ate the bread and the wine in faith would, as they depended on Christ, find him to be 'nutriment' to their souls, sustaining their ongoing spiritual life.[102] In summary, flowing out of Spurgeon's theology of the 'real presence' was an emphasis that a direct encounter with Christ at the Supper revitalised believers for practical activity in his cause, as well as strengthening them to face whatever might befall them along the way. Thus the Lord's Supper links once again with a crucial aspect of Spurgeon's spirituality. Spurgeon believed this was not only the case for him personally, but for every 'servant' of Christ.

Conclusion

Spurgeon believed that the Lord's Supper should be celebrated often. He stressed the importance of frequent celebration because he believed it was central to the Christian life, a belief which was based, in significant degree, on his experience at the Table. He also held that the Supper should be celebrated simply and with other Christians. Approaches which detracted from this simplicity or the corporate nature of the Lord's Supper, such as those associated with Roman Catholicism or High Church Anglicanism, marred the Supper. Indeed, they obscured the very purposes for which Christ instituted it. What Spurgeon believed these purposes were is illustrated by some further remarks he made about the Lord's Supper to the Lambeth Union in 1882. He declared,

> I find [Christ] will have communion with His erring children or else, full sure, He would never have communion with me. I think it is a blessed thing to break through all the little walls that separate us and come together and see if there is a place where we are one. If there be such a place it is in Christ and in showing forth his death till he come.[103]

Several of Spurgeon's central emphases concerning the Lord's Supper are present in this extract. The Supper as an accessible, effectual means of communion with Christ is one such emphasis; the Supper as a place where Christians know fellowship with each other is a further one. At the table Spurgeon believed that the walls that separated believers from each other could be broken through and (although he did

---

[101] C.H. Spurgeon, 'Renewing Strength', *MTP*, Vol. 29, S. No. 1756, Isaiah 40.31, n.d., 'Suitable for the close of the year', p. 706. Cf. 'The Blessing Of Full Assurance', *MTP*, Vol. 34, S. No. 2023, 1 John 5.13, delivered 13 May 1888, p. 269, 'Do you know the quickening, restoring, cheering, power of the precious blood of Christ which is set forth in the Lord's Supper by the fruit of the vine?'

[102] Spurgeon, 'The Double Forget-Me-Not', p. 317.

[103] *Sunday School Chronicle*, 17 February 1882, 'Spurgeon's Scrapbooks, Numbered Volumes', Vol. 6, p. 8.

not say so explicitly in this extract) the walls that separated believers from Christ too. The Lord's Supper thus takes us to the heart of Spurgeon's spirituality. As the bread was broken and the wine poured out Spurgeon knew 'communion with Christ and his people'.

CHAPTER 8

Activism:
'A Christian sluggard! Is there such a thing? A *Christian* man on half time?'[1]

The previous three chapters of this study have focused on how Spurgeon's spirituality was sustained through the Bible, through prayer and through the Lord's Supper. The final three main chapters examine how this spirituality was to be lived out in Christian activity, in personal holiness and as he faced suffering. This chapter considers Spurgeon's activism.

Numerous events from Spurgeon's life could be cited to show the central importance of Christian service to him. One such event was the annual fête of his Stockwell Orphanage for 1879, which was held on 19 June. Speakers at the evening meetings included Thomas Barnardo, whose Stepney Orphanage band had provided some of the entertainment earlier in the day, and also Burman Cassin, Rector of 'Old St. George's', Southwark.[2] Spurgeon enjoyed a good personal relationship with Cassin, who was a strong supporter of the Stockwell Orphanage.[3] For the occasion, and in honour of Spurgeon, the Rector had composed an acrostic poem which he proceeded to recite,

> **S**ervant of God, whose hand
> **P**rovides thy every need,
> **U**ndaunted thou shalt stand,
> **R**enowned for word and deed.
> **G**lory shall crown above
> **E**ach act of faith below.

---

[1] C.H. Spurgeon, 'The Sluggard's Farm', Proverbs 24.30-32, in *Farm Sermons* (London: Passmore and Alabaster, 1882), p. 18.

[2] *Christian World*, 27 June 1879; *Baptist*, 27 June 1879, in 'Spurgeon's Scrapbooks', Vol. 2, Spurgeon's College, Heritage Room (2F), pp. 77-78.

[3] W.Y. Fullerton, *C.H. Spurgeon: A Biography* (London: Williams and Norgate, 1920), p. 237; *Christian World*, 27 June 1879, in 'Spurgeon's Scrapbooks', Vol. 2, p. 77. Cassin would later lead in prayer at the graveside of William Olney when the Metropolitan Tabernacle's senior deacon was buried in Norwood cemetery. See C.H. Spurgeon, 'Living, Loving, Lasting Union', *New Park Street Pulpit (NPSP) / Metropolitan Tabernacle Pulpit (MTP)* (London: Passmore and Alabaster, 1856–1917), *MTP*, Vol. 38, S. No. 2245, Ephesians 5.30, delivered 22 October 1890, p. 98.

> Orphans who share thy love
> Nor want nor care shall know.[4]

The poem was appropriate for a number of reasons and it is no surprise that the handwritten original was carefully kept and inserted in the 'Scrapbooks', where it appears next to a photograph of the author.[5] Cassin, in a popular 'homely' style that was entirely fitting, had captured something that was at the heart of Spurgeon's spirituality, portraying his subject as actively living out his Christian faith not in 'word' only but also in 'deed'. Spurgeon would have heartily agreed with Cassin: deeds or 'acts of faith' springing from a deep dependence on God were what the Lord required of his 'servants'. The fact that Spurgeon himself was regarded as exemplifying such vigorous practical piety would have been much appreciated by the president of the Orphanage. Newspaper accounts indicate that the whole day brought Spurgeon much joy. The *Christian World* reported that Spurgeon 'looked well and happy' and the *Essex Telegraph* described him greeting people in the Orphanage grounds with a 'beaming smile of delight on his face'.[6] As Spurgeon surveyed the fruit of much activity and contemplated the possibility of further work (the day's events were punctuated by frequent appeals for funding for the newly proposed girls' wing for the Orphanage),[7] he was in his element.

In considering this crucial dimension to Spurgeon's spirituality, his activism, I have not attempted a detailed survey of every area of Christian work he was involved in. An overview of how his activism was expressed in different periods of his ministry is given, but the focus of this chapter is on an examination of how Spurgeon's activism related to his spirituality. Two 'case studies' of his activity are offered, with the Pastors' College and the Stockwell Orphanage both subjected to scrutiny. Because the life and work of the College has been analysed in some detail before,[8] more space is given here to the Orphanage, which will be dealt with in two

---

[4] 'An acrostic addressed to Rev C.H. Spurgeon', 19 June 1879, in 'Spurgeon's Scrapbooks', Vol. 2, p. 74a. The punctuation is Cassin's own. It appears the reporter from the *Christian World* misheard Cassin, as he quoted the Southwark Rector as saying 'unwearied' rather than 'undaunted'. See *Christian World*, 27 June 1879, in 'Spurgeon's Scrapbooks', Vol. 2, p. 77.

[5] 'Spurgeon's Scrapbooks', Vol. 2, p. 74b. Both the handwritten acrostic and Cassin's photograph are clipped, rather than pasted, into the Scrapbook. They are numbered 74a and 74b respectively by the compiler(s) as a result.

[6] *Christian World*, 27 June 1879; *Essex Telegraph*, 24 June 1879, in 'Spurgeon's Scrapbooks', Vol. 2, pp. 76-77.

[7] *South London Press*, 21 June 1879, in 'Spurgeon's Scrapbooks', Vol. 2, p. 75.

[8] See, especially, I.M. Randall, *A School of the Prophets: 150 Years of Spurgeon's College* (London: Spurgeon's College, 2005). Cf. M.K. Nicholls, *Lights to the World: A History of Spurgeon's College, 1856–1992* (Harpenden: Nuprint, 1994), and *C.H. Spurgeon: The Pastor Evangelist* (Didcot: Baptist Historical Society, 1992), pp. 69-114.

sections.⁹ The chapter closes with a section analysing Spurgeon's Christ-centred theology of activism as revealed in his preaching.

The Course of Spurgeon's Activism

Spurgeon did not work at the same pace and in the same way in every period of his ministry. Broadly speaking, four periods of activity can be traced. These are 1850–53, 1854–66, 1867–79 and 1879–92. The first period covers the years of Spurgeon's pre-London ministry. Between 1850 and 1853 activism was established as a crucial dimension of his spirituality. Spurgeon the young convert gave himself to Christian service. According to his diary, in the week which followed his baptism on 3 May 1850, he taught in his Newmarket church's afternoon Sunday school, went visiting with another church member, attended a teachers' prayer meeting, a teachers' business meeting and a missionary prayer meeting.¹⁰ Part of the diary entry he made at the beginning of the following week, on Sunday 12 May, reads, 'Went to Sunday-school at 9, stayed till service at 10.30, out at 12.15; Sunday-school at 1.45, service 3 till 4, visiting till 5.' Spurgeon was not exaggerating when he remarked that the day had been 'closely occupied'.¹¹ He found such activism exhilarating. Following some time spent distributing tracts on 18 May, Spurgeon was ecstatic. At the beginning of this activity he had, he wrote, been 'all but dumb concerning spiritual things'. However, as he gave out his booklets, seeking to commend Christ through personal conversation as well as by handing out the literature, he quickly felt 'the working of the Lord'. The relevant diary entry contains the following burst of praise which was also a prayer for other similar experiences, 'Blessed be His holy name for ever and ever ... Give me more of the entrancing visions of Thy face, the looks of Thy love, and more constant communion with Thee!'¹² Activity was a route to great joy, a joy that was bound up, in Spurgeon's early experience, with increased communion with God.

Soon after Spurgeon's move to Cambridge he began preaching in the villages around the city, as noted in chapter 2, walking for miles across fields in all weathers in order to conduct midweek as well as Sunday services.¹³ In Spurgeon's preaching, both as an itinerant and as pastor at Waterbeach, he urged others to engage wholeheartedly in Christian work themselves. One early sermon, based on 2 Corinthians 10.4 and entitled 'The Fight' in Spurgeon's notebook, was originally preached in the summer of 1851. Here Spurgeon urged on his hearers 'habits of devotion' and 'meditation' which would flow out in 'energy' and 'activity for God'.

---

⁹ Although some good work has been done by P. Shepherd, 'Spurgeon's Children', *Baptist Quarterly* Vol. 42, No. 2: Part 1 (April 2007), pp. 89-102.

¹⁰ Diary entries for 4 May, 5 May, 6 May and 8 May 1850, in C.H. Spurgeon, *Autobiography: Compiled from his Diary, Letters, and Records by his Wife and his Private Secretary* (4 Vols; London: Passmore and Alabaster, 1897–99), Vol. 1, pp. 135-36.

¹¹ Diary entry for 12 May 1850, in Spurgeon, *Autobiography*, Vol. 1, p. 137.

¹² Diary entry for 18 May, in Spurgeon, *Autobiography*, Vol. 1, p. 138.

¹³ Spurgeon, *Autobiography*, Vol. 1, p. 204.

The Holy Spirit was a Christian's 'strength' and Jesus Christ a Christian's 'captain' for the fight.[14] Unsurprisingly, other early sermon outlines contain similar material.[15] Often the focus was on evangelistic activity – 'holy labour for souls' – but all acts of Christian 'charity' and 'liberality' were commended.[16] According to Spurgeon, the most important thing was that, in 'some way or other ... all who believe in Jesus serve our God right heartily'.[17] Such service was just as important as singing hymns to God. Indeed, Christian work which flowed from deep devotion to Christ should be understood as an act of worship. Thus, when Spurgeon exhorted his hearers to be like the woman who anointed Christ, 'loving much, since we have had much forgiven', it was Christian service – he specifically mentioned tract distribution and Sunday school teaching – that he had in view as an appropriate expression of love and devotion.[18]

The close relationship between the inner and outer dimensions of the Christian life – between 'habits of devotion' and 'activity for God' – can be seen in these quotations from Spurgeon's early sermon outlines. On the one hand, activity for Christ could not be engaged in apart from daily dependence on him. On the other hand, if devotion to Christ was real, that devotion would certainly work itself out in practical service.

Spurgeon's call to London ushered in the second period of his activity, which ran from 1854 to 1866. During this period he gave himself even more fully to the work of preaching. The late 1850s were the most hectic years of all in this regard, as Spurgeon preached around the country with a view to raising funds for the new Metropolitan Tabernacle. During a three year period (1858–60) he conducted thousands of midweek services, all in addition to his regular Sunday ministry, an effort which was remarkable even by his standards.[19] Spurgeon was also closely involved, from 1855, in preparing his sermons for publication every week. In addition to preaching and publishing, Spurgeon met with thousands of individuals in the course of his ministry. The sort of visitation which Spurgeon engaged in when he

---

[14] C.H. Spurgeon, 'The Fight', S. No. 37, 2 Corinthians 10.4, 'Notebook Containing Early Sermon Skeletons, Vol. 1', Spurgeon's College, Heritage Room (K1.5). This particular sermon is n.d., but dates elsewhere in the notebook suggest 'The Fight' was originally preached in August or early September 1851.

[15] C.H. Spurgeon, 'God Glorified In The Saved', S. No. 56, Galatians 1.24, 'Notebook Containing Early Sermon Skeletons, Vol. 1'. Here Spurgeon spoke of the need for 'activity in God's service'.

[16] C.H. Spurgeon, 'Praise Ye The Lord', S. No. 327, Psalm 148.1, 'Notebooks With Sermon Outlines, Vols 2, 4-9', Vol. 7, Spurgeon's College, Heritage Room (U1). For this outline, see also *Autobiography*, Vol. 1, pp. 281-84.

[17] Spurgeon, 'Praise Ye The Lord'; *Autobiography*, Vol. 1, p. 283.

[18] Cf. Luke 7.36-50. Spurgeon, 'Praise Ye The Lord'; *Autobiography*, Vol. 1, p. 283.

[19] Spurgeon, *Autobiography*, Vol. 2, pp. 336-52.

first came to London[20] soon became an impossibility given the numerical growth his church experienced.[21] Nevertheless, he continued to have numerous meetings with individuals one-to-one throughout this second period of activism. As late as January 1865 he was still seeing every applicant for membership at the Tabernacle personally, with the number of 'admissions' during Spurgeon's pastorate up to and including that point standing at 3569.[22] Taken as a whole, his activity still brought great delight[23] although sometimes the dynamic – activism leads to joy – could be stretched almost to breaking point by the sheer busyness and accompanying tiredness.[24] The compilers of the *Autobiography* probably captured something of Spurgeon's mood when they described a particular duty (seeing enquirers and candidates for baptism) as being, at one and the same time, both 'congenial' and 'exhausting' for the busy pastor.[25]

The period 1854–66 also saw Spurgeon establish and develop a number of organisations and institutions which greatly broadened the scope of his activity. The Pastors' College was founded in 1856 for the training of evangelistically minded ministers who would be equipped both to serve existing churches and engage in pioneering ministry in places where no Baptist or evangelical work existed.[26] Spurgeon's Colportage Society, which, as already noted in chapter 3, was founded in 1866, also had a focus on evangelism.[27] In addition, Spurgeon involved himself in social projects. One example of his social action was the Tabernacle's collection of 'almshouses'. These had actually been established in 1803 by John Rippon, but when Spurgeon became pastor of New Park Street he readily embraced this aspect of the church's work.[28] The almshouses provided accommodation for the 'aged poor' (in reality those helped were all women). When the Tabernacle was built and the original homes were deemed too far from the new site, Spurgeon had new houses erected near the Elephant and Castle, with seventeen built to replace Rippon's six.[29] These different projects were all important expressions of Spurgeon's activism. In

---

[20] See, e.g., Spurgeon, *Autobiography*, Vol. 1, pp. 371-73, and Spurgeon's response to a cholera outbreak in London towards the end of 1854. He visited numerous families who had been affected by the outbreak.

[21] Randall, *School of the Prophets*, p. 19.

[22] G. Rogers, 'Metropolitan Tabernacle Statistics', in C.H. Spurgeon (ed.), *The Sword and The Trowel: A Record of Combat With Sin and Labour For The Lord* (London: Passmore and Alabaster, 1865–92) (*Sword and Trowel*), January 1865, p. 31. The figure of 3,569 includes those admitted into membership when the church was still based at New Park Street.

[23] See, e.g., Spurgeon, *Autobiography*, Vol. 3, p. 164.

[24] See, e.g., Spurgeon, *Autobiography*, Vol. 4, p. 74.

[25] Spurgeon, *Autobiography*, Vol. 4, p. 79. The compilers were, of course, Susannah Spurgeon and J.W. Harrald.

[26] Randall, *School of the Prophets, passim*.

[27] Spurgeon, *Autobiography*, Vol. 3, pp. 161-66.

[28] C.H. Spurgeon, *The Metropolitan Tabernacle: Its History And Work* (London: Passmore and Alabaster, 1876), pp. 52-53, 93-95.

[29] Spurgeon, *Autobiography*, Vol. 1, pp. 313-314; Nicholls, *Spurgeon*, pp. 56-57.

1865 Spurgeon began his magazine, the *Sword and Trowel*, one of the central purposes of which was to encourage financial and prayer support for the different works he and his church were engaged in. As Spurgeon stated in the first number of the magazine, he was committed to doing 'practical service' himself and to exciting others to similar 'active exertion'.[30] During this second period of activism, then, Spurgeon engaged in an increasing range of Christian activity and encouraged others to join with him.

Spurgeon's third period of activity ran from the end of 1867 to 1879. In the autumn of 1867 he had been taken seriously ill and found, to his consternation, that he was unable to preach for a number of successive Sundays.[31] He was told he had rheumatic gout although, in fact, he was also suffering from the onset of kidney disease. This was diagnosed, in the last years of Spurgeon's life, as 'Bright's disease', that is, chronic nephritis.[32] In the closing months of 1867 Spurgeon was in agony. He visited Mentone in the south of France for the first time in the winter of 1867–68 in order to recuperate.[33] The visit was a success and he would return to the French Riviera most winters from this point on to his death, usually spending between one and three months in Mentone.[34] Nevertheless, there would, from 1868 onwards, be few times in his life when he was entirely pain-free. The beginning of 1868 saw, as already noted, the appointment of James Archer Spurgeon as 'co-pastor' of the Tabernacle, to help ease the pressure on his brother. C.H. Spurgeon's suffering, which was not just physical, and the way this related to his spirituality will be dealt with at length in chapter 10. What is important to note here is that his physical condition forced Spurgeon to slacken seriously the pace at which he worked.[35] He had to cut back on his outside engagements and, as will be shown, he became increasingly dependent on other people.

Nevertheless, Spurgeon continued to engage in much Christian activity. A further institution was established in the shape of the Stockwell Orphanage, with the main

---

[30] C.H. Spurgeon, 'Our Aims And Intentions', in Spurgeon (ed.), *Sword and Trowel*, January 1865, p. 2.

[31] C.H. Spurgeon, 'The Editor's Illness', in Spurgeon (ed.), *Sword and Trowel*, November 1867, pp. 526-27. Cf. 'On My Back', in *Sword and Trowel*, December 1867, p. 539.

[32] The *Times* gave the cause of Spurgeon's death as 'congestion of the kidneys complicated by gout'. The *Times*, 1 February 1892, 'Charles Haddon Spurgeon: Obituaries – Newspaper Cuttings' (held at Spurgeons [Spurgeon's Childcare], Rushden), p. 1.

[33] Spurgeon, *Autobiography*, Vol. 3, pp. 237-39. This 1867–68 visit was part of a longer European tour which also took in, amongst other places, Venice and Rome. In subsequent winters Spurgeon would head straight for the south of France.

[34] According to the *Autobiography*, Vol. 4, p. 198, Spurgeon made 'about twenty' separate visits to the Riviera between 1868 and 1892.

[35] See, e.g., C.H. Spurgeon to an unnamed friend, September 1873, in 'Original Correspondence of Charles Haddon Spurgeon, 1863–1886, Spurgeon's College, Heritage Room (4G), No. 10. Turning down a request to preach, Spurgeon said, 'I am only staggering along under my load and more I cannot attempt without being a suicide.'

buildings for boys and staff completed by 1870.[36] Spurgeon was particularly active in church planting during this third period of activity, usually working through students and former students of his College. Thus the social and evangelistic dimensions of his activism continued to find expression.

Did Spurgeon's activity also have a prominent political dimension? This has been argued by Patricia Kruppa in a chapter of *A Preacher's Progress* which is entitled 'A Political Dissenter'. Kruppa states, 'From 1868 to 1884, Spurgeon was a prominent spokesman for political Dissent ... he played a significant part in helping to shape the politics of Nonconformity.'[37] Even stronger is A.R. Meredith who, in an unpublished PhD thesis, says, 'Politics and social issues were of central importance to Spurgeon.'[38] Both these statements exaggerate the extent of Spurgeon's political activity. It is true that he did not shy away from expressing political opinions advocating, for example, the disestablishment of the Church of England.[39] He also urged the importance of voting on all Christians who were qualified to do so. 'Every God fearing man should give his vote with as much devotion as he prays', Spurgeon declared in the *Sword and Trowel*.[40] He also enjoyed a measure of personal friendship with Gladstone, something that was celebrated by other Baptists.[41] It is also right to say that he was influential due to his immense standing.[42] Many biographies ignore Spurgeon's political activity completely and Kruppa and Meredith make an important point when they highlight this.

Nevertheless Spurgeon was not as active politically as many other nineteenth-century Dissenters, such as John Clifford.[43] He was not a significant figure shaping the politics of Nonconformity or, indeed, more narrowly, of Baptists. Rather, he shared the political views held by the majority of Dissenters and Baptists from the

---

[36] Nicholls, *Spurgeon*, p. 58.

[37] P.S. Kruppa, *Charles Haddon Spurgeon: A Preacher's Progress* (New York: Garland, 1982), p. 283.

[38] A.R. Meredith, 'The Social and Political Views of C.H. Spurgeon, 1834–1892' (unpublished PhD study, Michigan State University, 1973), p. 18.

[39] Spurgeon (ed.), *Sword and Trowel*, September 1874, p. 438.

[40] Spurgeon (ed.), *Sword and Trowel*, April 1880, p. 191.

[41] D.W. Bebbington, 'Gladstone and the Baptists', *Baptist Quarterly* Vol. 26, No. 5 (January 1976), pp. 233-34; and 'Gladstone and the Nonconformists', in D. Baker (ed.), *Church, Society and Politics: Papers Read at the Thirteenth Summer Meeting and Fourteenth Winter Meeting of the Ecclesiastical History Society* (Oxford: Basil Blackwell, 1975), p. 375. For some comments from Spurgeon on his relationship with Gladstone, see C.H. Spurgeon to an unnamed friend, 11 January 1882, in 'Original Correspondence of Charles Haddon Spurgeon, 1863–1886', No. 40, and C.H. Spurgeon to John Spurgeon, 20 July 1882, in 'Original Correspondence of Charles Haddon Spurgeon, 1851–1893', Spurgeon's College, Heritage Room (4G), No. 60.

[42] Meredith, 'Social and Political Views', pp. 66-67.

[43] See D. Thompson, 'John Clifford's Social Gospel', *Baptist Quarterly* Vol. 31, No. 5 (January 1986), pp. 199-217.

middle of the century onwards, which were, of course, staunchly Liberal.[44] He shied away from making party political comments from the pulpit and did not want the Tabernacle to be used for political meetings in support of Liberal candidates.[45] When compared to Spurgeon's other activities, the political dimension, although certainly present, does not loom large.

The evidence suggests that it is right to speak of a fourth and final period of activism, which extended from 1879 to Spurgeon's death in 1892. This period saw him increasingly incapacitated and unable to work. At the beginning of 1879 Spurgeon was struck by an especially severe bout of illness.[46] 1879 was the twenty-fifth year of Spurgeon's ministry in London, his pastoral 'silver wedding' as it was called. A number of meetings were planned for the beginning of the year which would include the presentation of a testimonial, but the 'jubilee celebrations' had to be postponed until May because of Spurgeon's continuing ill-health.[47]

Although he would still enjoy times when his health was better, as shown by the reports of the 1879 Orphanage fête, such times would become the exception rather than the rule, and of increasingly short duration. An obvious issue concerns the degree to which Spurgeon's punishing schedule up to and indeed beyond 1867 was a contributing cause of his various illnesses. Spurgeon himself thought it was a factor, as did those closest to him, and it is hard to believe this was not the case to some extent.[48] What is certain is that during this fourth period of ministry he was of necessity doing much less.

---

[44] For some of the background see J. Wolffe, *God and Greater Britain: Religion and Politics in Britain and Ireland 1843–1945* (London: Routledge, 1994), pp. 130-40, especially, pp. 131-32; J.H.Y. Briggs, *The English Baptists of the Nineteenth Century* (Didcot: Baptist Historical Society, 1994), pp. 369-405. D.W. Bebbington, 'The Baptist Conscience in the Nineteenth Century', *Baptist Quarterly* Vol. 34, No. 1 (January 1991), pp. 13-24, suggests that Baptist commitment to the Liberal cause became more overt from the mid-1850s onwards. From 1868 onwards this 'partisanship reached new heights'. However, Bebbington states that 'more militant' Baptists had been identifying as 'Liberals' well before 1850. See, especially, pp. 18-19.

[45] See C.H. Spurgeon to J.A. Spurgeon, 1 August 1885, in G.H. Pike, *James Archer Spurgeon D.D. LL.D. Preacher, Philanthropist, and Co-Pastor With C.H. Spurgeon at the Metropolitan Tabernacle* (London: Alexander and Shepheard, 1894), p. 159.

[46] See C.H. Spurgeon, 'This Year Also', *MTP*, Vol. 25, S. No. 1451, Luke 13.8, 'A Short Sermon for the New Year From the Sick Chamber of C.H. Spurgeon', p. 1; *Christian Signal*, 16 January 1879, in 'Spurgeon's Scrapbooks', Vol. 2, p. 1.

[47] Spurgeon, *Autobiography*, Vol. 4, pp. 15-16. The testimonial was presented on 20 May. Other significant meetings in connection with the silver jubilee were held on 18 and 19 May. See *Memorial Volume. Sermons And Addresses Delivered In The Metropolitan Tabernacle, Newington, In Connection With The Presentation Of A Testimonial To Pastor C.H. Spurgeon, To Commemorate The Completion Of The Twenty-Fifth Year Of His Pastorate ...* (London: Passmore and Alabaster, n.d. [1879]), pp. 3, 15, 27.

[48] C.H. Spurgeon, 'Be Not Discouraged', in *Sword and Trowel*, December 1879, p. 571; *Autobiography*, Vol. 4, pp. 63, 84-85.

On occasion, Spurgeon's chronic ill-health could lead him to rephrase his insistence that all Christians, if they were to be considered faithful, must be active. As early as 1876 Spurgeon was writing, in his preface to the bound volume of the *Sword and Trowel* for that year, 'Dear reader, are you serving the Lord with all your heart? If not, you are missing the only way of happiness. Even a religious life is not joyous unless the Lord be served either by active exertion or by *patient endurance.*' Spurgeon had alluded to his own 'infirmities' earlier in the preface.[49] The awareness that some believers might be unable to serve by 'active exertion', having instead to exhibit 'patient endurance', was linked with his own experience of suffering. Spurgeon sought to show such endurance himself. In a letter to his Tabernacle congregation, written on Christmas Eve 1891 from Mentone, Spurgeon spoke of his frustration at being unable to engage in 'activities' which had become part of his 'nature'. 'But', he added, 'as I cannot alter it, and as I am sure that infinite wisdom rules it, I bow before the divine will.'[50]

Still, the same emphasis on the importance of activism was present in a wide range of Spurgeon's later sermons.[51] One of these, entitled 'Everyday Religion', was preached in 1881. Spurgeon made the point that true faith would lead a believer to live an 'industrious life'. Biblical 'faith always worketh', Spurgeon insisted. Consequently, to speak of a lazy believer was a contradiction in terms. 'A believing man becomes an active man, or else it is because he cannot act, and, therefore, what would have been activity runs into the channel of patience, and he endures with resignation the will of the Most High.'[52] Again Spurgeon spoke of the 'patience' and 'endurance' of the one who could not 'act', but such an attitude was not the opposite of activity.[53] Rather, the faith which would, ideally, have worked itself out in a blaze of enthusiastic service was instead redirected into resigned (and yet, in a very real sense, active) trust in the perfect will of God. What was abundantly clear was that if a 'believer' manifested no 'zeal', 'perseverance' or 'endeavour to serve God' then

---

[49] C.H. Spurgeon, Preface, in Spurgeon (ed.), *Sword and Trowel*, 1876, p. iv. Italics added.

[50] C.H. Spurgeon to 'dear friends' (at the Metropolitan Tabernacle), 24 December 1891, in 'Original Correspondence of Charles Haddon Spurgeon, 1887–1892', Spurgeon's College, Heritage Room (4G), No. 157. Cf. C.H. Spurgeon to Eliza Spurgeon, 7 November 1881, 'Original Correspondence of Charles Haddon Spurgeon, 1851–1893', No. 53, 'We are all in divine keeping whether we live or die and so let it be.' See, also, C.H. Spurgeon to Eliza Spurgeon, 2 May 1883, 'Original Correspondence of Charles Haddon Spurgeon, 1851–1893', No. 67.

[51] In addition to those surveyed in this chapter, see, e.g., C.H. Spurgeon, 'Eyes Right', *MTP*, Vol. 34, S. No. 2058, Proverbs 4.25, delivered 14 July 1887, p. 690; 'The Servants And The Pounds', *MTP*, Vol. 33, S. No. 1960, Luke 19.12,13, delivered 24 April 1887, pp. 246-47.

[52] C.H. Spurgeon, 'Everyday Religion', *MTP*, Vol. 27, S. No. 1599, Galatians 2.20, delivered 22 May 1881, p. 282.

[53] Cf. C.H. Spurgeon, 'Something Done For Jesus', *MTP*, Vol. 36, S. No. 2126, Matthew 26.10, n.d., p. 55.

grave doubts ought to be expressed about the reality of their conversion.[54] Saving faith was active faith. If Spurgeon was not always active himself it was not because his emphasis on activity had diminished. Rather, to his deep regret, he was increasingly incapacitated and, even at his best, simply unable to work at his former pace.

This survey of the course of Spurgeon's activism has highlighted a number of points. He began his Christian life with a rush of activity and he found an increased sphere for this activity when he moved to London. Spurgeon's London activism had both evangelistic and social dimensions which were worked out through his preaching and pastoral ministry and what became the multi-faceted work of the Tabernacle. Spurgeon's health problems post-1867 curtailed his service and caused him to qualify his stress on activism slightly, supplementing it with an emphasis on the importance of 'patient endurance'. Nevertheless, a strong stress on activism remained, even post-1879 and the onset of yet more severe ill-health. In his final year of ministry Spurgeon preached a sermon entitled 'Wanted! – Volunteers' which was a sustained call to his hearers and readers to make it their 'life's work' to 'serve the Lord',[55] and in the last few months of his life he was working hard in order to finish his commentary on Matthew's Gospel.[56] Such a call and such activity were fundamentally congruent with the approach to activism Spurgeon had adopted in his pre-London period. Thus, whilst our survey has shown that the contours of Spurgeon's activism need to be drawn on the map of his ministry with care, this much was constant: activism was central to his spirituality.

Case Study: The Pastors' College

The nature of Spurgeon's activity can now be examined in more detail, beginning with the first case study, that of the Pastors' College. This was his first love. On one occasion he said of the College, 'This is my life's work, to which I believe God has called me.'[57] This quotation indicates the importance of the Pastors' College to Spurgeon's spirituality – it became a vital part of his *raison d'être*. The first student was Thomas W. Medhurst who had been converted under Spurgeon's ministry at New Park Street, not only as a result of Spurgeon's preaching, but also through an exchange of letters and a personal meeting. Writing to Spurgeon, Medhurst had expressed anxiety that he might not be one of the elect.[58] Spurgeon's response was characteristic: 'You have only to believe that Jesus is able and willing to save, and

---

[54] Spurgeon, 'Everyday Religion', pp. 282-83.

[55] C.H. Spurgeon, 'Wanted! – Volunteers', *MTP*, Vol. 37, S. No. 2227, 2 Chronicles 17.16, delivered 22 March 1891, pp. 542, 543.

[56] C.H. Spurgeon, *The Gospel of the Kingdom. A Popular Exposition Of The Gospel According To Matthew* (London: Passmore and Alabaster, 1905 [1893]), 'Introductory Note', n.p..

[57] Fullerton, *C.H. Spurgeon*, p. 227. Cf. Spurgeon, *Autobiography*, Vol. 3, p. 127.

[58] T.W. Medhurst to C.H. Spurgeon, 2 July 1854, in Spurgeon, *Autobiography*, Vol. 2, p. 142.

then trust yourself to Him.'⁵⁹ Following Medhurst's conversion and baptism he began to preach in the open air in the district surrounding New Park Street and two people joined the church as a result.⁶⁰ According to Medhurst, it was Spurgeon himself who suggested that he prepare for 'pastoral work'. In 1855 Medhurst was temporarily billeted with the Rev. C.H. Hosken, who lived in Bexleyheath, Kent. The student regularly travelled into London to be personally tutored by Spurgeon himself. Medhurst, who was twenty years of age, had just finished an apprenticeship as a rope maker and had little by way of formal education.⁶¹ He would become a type of the 'rough and ready' men that the College would train.

In 1857 Spurgeon enlisted George Rogers as tutor and Medhurst moved to Rogers' home in Camberwell, with a second student also accepted.⁶² The work now grew with Rogers becoming Spurgeon's 'beloved friend'.⁶³ Studies took place in Rogers' home until 1861, when the College was able to move to rooms in the newly built Metropolitan Tabernacle,⁶⁴ a relocation which enabled significant expansion of student numbers. In 1861 there were twenty students,⁶⁵ but by January 1865 there were eighty-three, with Rogers as principal leading a small team of tutors.⁶⁶ As president of the College Spurgeon remained actively involved in its life, especially through his Friday afternoon lectures⁶⁷ and, from 1865, an annual meeting of College alumni, the 'College Conference'.⁶⁸ Nevertheless, he did increasingly lean on others with regard to the day-to-day work of the institution.

One area in which Spurgeon remained crucial to the life of the College was that of raising support. By 1876 the cost of running the College had risen to approximately £6500 per annum.⁶⁹ Each month the *Sword and Trowel* carried lists of those who supported the College, together with the exact amount donated.⁷⁰ Spurgeon regularly

---

⁵⁹ C.H. Spurgeon to T.W. Medhurst, 14 July 1854, in Spurgeon, *Autobiography*, Vol. 2, p. 143.

⁶⁰ Spurgeon, *Autobiography*, Vol. 2, p. 145.

⁶¹ Spurgeon, *Autobiography*, Vol. 2, pp. 145-47; Vol. 3, p. 128.

⁶² Spurgeon, *Autobiography*, Vol. 2, p. 147.

⁶³ Spurgeon, *Autobiography*, Vol. 3, p. 128.

⁶⁴ Spurgeon (ed.), *Sword and Trowel*, October 1865, p. 462; April 1870, p. 146.

⁶⁵ Fullerton, *C.H. Spurgeon*, p. 230.

⁶⁶ The tutors, David Gracey and Archibald Ferguson, both joined the College in 1862. See Nicholls, *Lights to the World*, p. 11. Gracey became College principal in 1881.

⁶⁷ Spurgeon (ed.), *Sword and Trowel*, January 1865, p. 36. The lectures were published as C.H. Spurgeon, *Lectures To My Students* (3 Vols; London: Passmore and Alabaster, n.d.).

⁶⁸ Nicholls, *Spurgeon*, pp. 93-94.

⁶⁹ See Spurgeon, *The Metropolitan Tabernacle*, p. 103, where the College president estimated that the College needed £120 a week. Randall, *School of the Prophets*, p. 3, states that the figure in 1870 was £5,000.

⁷⁰ See, e.g., January 1865, p. 36; February 1865, p. 36. This practice was observed for all subsequent volumes of the *Sword and Trowel*. See, e.g., January 1874, p. 46; February 1874, pp. 95, 99-100. Randall, *School of the Prophets*, p. 3, notes that a weekly Tabernacle offering provided perhaps £2,000 of the £5,000 per annum needed. The amount given in each weekly offering was also faithfully recorded in each number of the *Sword and Trowel*. See, e.g.,

appealed for funds from his constituency,[71] as well as for 'fervent prayer'.[72] He was successful in recruiting and retaining a myriad of backers. Whilst Spurgeon remained central to the whole enterprise this success in raising support widened the circle of those he relied on still further. This created a degree of anxiety but, in general, for Spurgeon to know that so many others were standing with him in the work of the College was an 'inexpressible source of joy' to his own 'soul'. He was not interested in help grudgingly given. But when assistance came freely and willingly from those in sympathy with the basic aims and ethos of the College, Spurgeon believed that a real spiritual partnership had been forged and the gifts were 'love tokens' which 'knit' him to his people.[73] In 1874 the College moved to purpose-built premises in Temple Street, just to the rear of the Tabernacle.[74] By this stage the College was already an enterprise which was supported, in different ways, by a wide range of helpers. By 1874 the College was also having a significant, shaping effect on the religious scene in Britain.[75]

Part of that influence came through church planting, as already noted. The students worked under Spurgeon's direction and with his support. Figures assembled by Mike Nicholls suggest that a staggering fifty-three of the sixty-two new London Baptist churches established between 1865 and 1876 could be 'attributed to [Spurgeon's] work'.[76] Spurgeon's methods varied depending on the context, as Nicholls shows, but most often the establishment of a new work would begin with him sending a student to a district to preach regularly in the open air. Assuming sufficient interest had been shown amongst the local populace, a hall would then be hired. If the work developed further, a temporary building might be erected, followed by a permanent one. The funds to develop the work in each of its different stages would usually come thanks to Spurgeon, who would appeal for money for different causes through the pages of *Sword and Trowel*.[77] He also had his own lawyer who would help in drawing up the trust deeds for new churches.[78] Spurgeon's own passion for evangelism, something that was at the heart of his spirituality, found further expression through the church planting work of his students.

March 1872, p. 147. On the Tabernacle's support for the College, see also Fullerton, *C.H. Spurgeon*, p. 239.

[71] Spurgeon, *Autobiography*, Vol. 3, pp. 127-29.

[72] Spurgeon, *Autobiography*, Vol. 3, p. 129.

[73] Spurgeon (ed.), *Sword and Trowel*, March 1872, p. 145. Spurgeon was here talking specifically about a new year's gift to the College of £100 from the 'dear friends' at the Tabernacle.

[74] Spurgeon, *Autobiography*, Vol. 3, p. 125; Fullerton, *C.H. Spurgeon*, p. 232.

[75] See the figures quoted by Spurgeon himself in *The Metropolitan Tabernacle*, pp. 101-103

[76] Nicholls, *Spurgeon*, p. 98. For details see the Appendix, pp. 175-77.

[77] Often in the 'Memoranda' section of the magazine. See Spurgeon (ed.), *Sword and Trowel*, March 1872, p. 145; July 1872, pp. 336-37.

[78] Nicholls, *Spurgeon*, pp. 97-98.

As far as the type of training offered by the College was concerned, this also reflected Spurgeon's spirituality. The Bible was central to the College curriculum and the theology that was taught was described, by him, as 'Puritanic'.[79] Those trained needed to be well versed in the 'doctrines of grace'.[80] But, important as these things were, it was essential that the students' study of scripture and of theology led them into a deeper, living relationship with God. In Spurgeon's Friday lectures he urged them to be men of prayer, coming before God with a 'fervency of desire' and a 'simplicity of dependence'.[81] Continued communion with God was to be their aim.[82] Above all a minister was to know Jesus. Spurgeon urged students and ministers trained at the College to 'sit at [Christ's] feet' and consider his 'nature', 'work', 'sufferings' and 'glory'. In this way daily, continuing communion with Christ could be maintained and developed. This was his overarching priority. Nurturing and growing 'Fellowship with the Son of God' was crucial to a student's time at the College.[83]

The training was also practical and applied.[84] The College existed to equip preachers rather than to produce scholars, and it was vital that all the men were useful in the cause of Christ and his kingdom.[85] Spurgeon laid particular stress on the need for students who could reach and pastor ordinary people.[86] In an open letter written in 1862 for the purposes of soliciting increased funding for the College, he declared that he wanted to train

> men of the people, feeling, sympathizing, fraternizing with the masses of working-men; – men who can speak the common language, the plain blunt Saxon of the crowd; men ready to visit the sick and the poor, and able to make them understand the reality of the comforts of religion.[87]

Spurgeon's comments reflected his own commitment to champion the 'common man'.[88] To facilitate this identification with ordinary people amongst his students, they lived with different Tabernacle families for the course of their College studies. Few of these families could be regarded as wealthy, and Spurgeon believed this

---

[79] Spurgeon, *Autobiography*, Vol. 2, pp. 149-50.

[80] Spurgeon, *Lectures To My Students*, Vol. 1, p. viii; *Autobiography*, Vol. 2, p. 149.

[81] Spurgeon, *Lectures To My Students*, Vol. 1, Lecture 3, p. 40.

[82] Spurgeon, *Lectures To My Students*, Vol. 2, Lecture 1, p. 13.

[83] Spurgeon, *Lectures To My Students*, Vol. 2, Lecture 2, p. 34. This particular talk was given to existing and previous students. See p. 23.

[84] C.H. Spurgeon, 'President's Letter, 1867', in 'Maroon bound Scrapfolders, Vol. 1', Spurgeon's College, Heritage Room, p. 40; J.D. Douglas, *The Prince of Preachers: A Sketch; A Portraiture; And A Tribute* (London: Morgan and Scott, n.d. [1893]), p. 71.

[85] Spurgeon, *Lectures To My Students*, Vol. 1, p. viii; *Autobiography*, Vol. 2, p. 148; Vol. 3, p. 129.

[86] Cf. Nicholls, *Lights to the World*, p. 30.

[87] Spurgeon, *Autobiography*, Vol. 3, p. 129.

[88] For this stress, see D.W. Bebbington, 'Spurgeon and the Common Man', *Baptist Review of Theology* Vol. 5, No. 1 (Spring 1995), pp. 63-75.

policy of billeting students with ordinary people helped those in training remain connected with 'the struggles and conditions of everyday life'.[89] Spurgeon's championing of the 'common man' will be examined in more detail in chapter 9, but it should also be recognised here. His stress on producing men who could speak the gospel in the 'common language' and who would engage sympathetically with the poor was of a piece with his desire to turn out 'hard-working men' as opposed to 'fine gentlemen'.[90] In contrast to a 'gentleman' minister who might have aspirations to move amongst the cultured élite, giving sermons that were full of carefully turned phrases and which bore the impress of 'modern thought', Spurgeon's students were to be of a different stamp. As to work ethic, they were to be the most active men in the districts that they served;[91] as to practical usefulness, they were to be those could gather new churches and revive failing ones, preaching the gospel of Jesus to the common people with passion and practical effect.[92]

Overall, it was Spurgeon's aim to produce men who would share his own fundamental concerns, men who would grow in communion with Christ and who wanted to share Christ with other people. Spurgeon's students ended up working in a whole variety of different contexts, with a significant number serving overseas.[93] Not all former students continued to share the outlook or indeed the basic spirituality of their president.[94] Spurgeon's aim, however, was to fashion an army of ministers and missionaries who would share his Christ-centred, evangelistic piety.

---

[89] Spurgeon, *The Metropolitan Tabernacle*, p. 100.

[90] *Annual Paper Concerning the Lord's Work in Connection with the Pastors' College, 1885–86* (London: Passmore and Alabaster [1886]), p. 29; Randall, *School of the Prophets*, p. 20.

[91] *Annual Paper Concerning the Lord's Work in Connection with the Pastors' College, 1885–86*, p. 29; Randall, *School of the Prophets*, p. 20.

[92] Spurgeon, *The Metropolitan Tabernacle*, p. 101, in which Spurgeon quoted Lord Shaftesbury, who said that Spurgeon's students 'had a singular faculty for addressing the population, and going to the very heart of the people'.

[93] For example, William Higlett, Frederick Hibberd and C.H. Spurgeon's son, Thomas Spurgeon. All of these men served in the Antipodes. See K.R. Manley, '"The Magic Name": Charles Haddon Spurgeon and the evangelical ethos of Australian Baptists. Part 1', *Baptist Quarterly* Vol. 40 No. 3 (July 2003), pp. 173; 180. For details on Thomas Spurgeon in Australasia, see W.Y. Fullerton, *Thomas Spurgeon: A Biography* (London: Hodder and Stoughton, 1919), pp. 62-81 (Australia), 90-110 and 119-43 (New Zealand). For the commitment of the Pastors' College to world mission more generally, see I.M. Randall, '"The World is our Parish": Spurgeon's College and World Mission, 1856–1892', in I.M. Randall and A.R. Cross (eds), *Baptists and Mission: Papers from the Fourth International Conference on Baptist Studies* (Milton Keynes: Paternoster, 2007), pp. 64-77.

[94] See, e.g., J. Powles, 'Misguided or misunderstood?: The case of Charles Spurgeon Medhurst (1860–1927), Baptist missionary to China', forthcoming in *Baptist Quarterly*. A son of T.W. Medhurst, C.S. Medhurst left the Pastors' College in 1884 for missionary work in China. In the early twentieth century he became involved in the Theosophical Society and was ordained a priest in the Liberal Catholic Church. Cf. J.C. Carlile, *C.H. Spurgeon: An*

Case Study: The Stockwell Orphanage

The second case study which sheds light on Spurgeon's activism and the importance of this for his spirituality is that of the Stockwell Orphanage. If the College was Spurgeon's 'first love', the Orphanage was not far behind in his affections. Vital to the genesis of the Orphanage was a gift of £20,000 from Anne Hillyard, who, whilst being the widow of a clergyman, also had Baptist connections.[95] Hillyard's letters reveal her as a woman of deep evangelical piety,[96] who wanted to make her money available 'for the training and education of a few orphan boys'.[97] In the account in the *Autobiography*, a Tabernacle Monday night prayer meeting is also highlighted as being crucial to the founding of the Orphanage. The meeting, which probably took place at the end of August 1866, was attended by a student of the Pastors' College, Charles Welton.[98] According to Welton's account, Spurgeon stated, 'Dear friends, we are a huge church, and should be doing more for the Lord in this great city. I want us, to-night, to ask Him to send us *some new work*; and if we need money to carry it on, let us pray that *the means may also be sent*.'[99] A succession of students and deacons led the meeting in intercession, focusing on Spurgeon's words. Hillyard's initial letter to Spurgeon was written a 'few days' later. Welton's conviction was that the Orphanage was 'born of prayer', a view that Spurgeon certainly shared.[100] The Orphanage, then, is revealing both of Spurgeon's basic

---

Interpretative Biography (London: The Religious Tract Society and The Kingsgate Press, 1933), pp. 60-61.

[95] Anne Hillyard, née Field, was related to a number of Birmingham Baptists. She was, according to J.A. Spurgeon, baptised as a believer by his brother soon after her initial offer of money. She inherited one third of the estate of her uncle, hence her ability to give such a substantial sum. See F.W. Butt-Thompson, 'The Morgans of Birmingham', *Baptist Quarterly* Vol. 2, No. 6 (April 1925), p. 268; Shepherd, 'Spurgeon's Children', p. 89, n. 4 on p. 101; '"Report of Proceedings [sic]"' of the Laying of the Foundation Stone [For the Stockwell Orphanage] 9 September 1867', Held at Spurgeons (Spurgeon's Childcare), Rushden, p. 10. In an editorial slip, the *Sword and Trowel* gave the date of the stone laying as 9 August. See 'The Stockwell Orphanage', *Sword and Trowel*, October 1867, p. 466. Kruppa, *Spurgeon*, p. 170, records that Hillyard donated £10,000, not £20,000, but this is an error.

[96] See, e.g., A. Hillyard to C.H. Spurgeon, 17 September 1866, in Spurgeon, *Autobiography*, Vol. 3, p. 170.

[97] A. Hillyard to C.H. Spurgeon, 3 September 1866, in Spurgeon, *Autobiography*, Vol. 3, p. 169. Hillyard had read an article by Spurgeon, which touched on the theme of education, in the *Sword and Trowel*. See Spurgeon, *Autobiography*, Vol. 3, pp. 167-69; C.H. Spurgeon, 'The Holy War And The Present Hour', in *Sword and Trowel*, August 1866, pp. 339-45; Shepherd, 'Spurgeon's Children', n. 5 on p. 101.

[98] Identified only as 'C. Welton' in the *Autobiography*, Charles Welton was a student during the years 1865–67, before settling as pastor at Thetford, Norfolk. He died in 1929 and so was still alive at the time the *Autobiography* was published. I am grateful to Judy Powles for providing this information for me.

[99] Spurgeon, *Autobiography*, Vol. 3, p. 168.

[100] Spurgeon, *Autobiography*, Vol. 3, pp. 168, 173.

commitment to activism and also of the link he repeatedly made between prayerful dependence on God and fruitful Christian work.

In January 1867 a suitable site at Stockwell, close to the Elephant and Castle, was found and acquired although, to Spurgeon's discomfort, a loan of £3,000 was required to complete the purchase.[101] On the 18 March 1867 the trustees, the majority of whom were Tabernacle deacons, met formally for the first time.[102] Spurgeon had effectively committed himself to founding an Orphanage.

Fundraising for the new venture was uppermost in Spurgeon's mind as plans began to take shape. His short piece in the October 1866 *Sword and Trowel* was, in the main, an urgent appeal for money. As revealed in the 'Indenture' written out at the beginning of the Stockwell Orphanage Minute Book, most of Anne Hillyard's money was tied up in railway bonds which could not be easily accessed and, in any case, the aim was to use this money as capital, so providing the trust with an annual income.[103] Hence there were problems in purchasing the Stockwell site, a situation which explains the need for the loan.[104] The appeal of October 1866 was vigorously repeated in May 1867. Now that Spurgeon himself was willing to commit to this work, with the support of his trustees, he was unblushing in urging 'fellow labourers' to do the same.[105] Following this and other appeals, money began to flow, with the names of donors, together with the exact amount given, carefully recorded each month in the *Sword and Trowel* alongside the details of the College's supporters.[106] Regular updates on the progress of the work also appeared in order to 'strengthen the faith of believers in the power of prayer'.[107] All this was in addition to direct appeals to the readers of Spurgeon's printed sermons[108] and to the Tabernacle congregation, to whom a large number of 'collecting cards' were distributed.[109] The *Sword and Trowel* reported that, by the time of the stone laying ceremony on 9 September 1867,

---

[101] Spurgeon, *Autobiography*, Vol. 3, p. 172; *Sword and Trowel*, May 1867, p. 233.

[102] 'S.(tockwell) O.(rphanage) Minute Book No. 1. March 1867 – June 1876', held at 'Spurgeons' (Spurgeon's Childcare), Rushden, Minutes for 18 March 1867.

[103] 'Stockwell Orphanage Indenture, 18 March 1867', held at 'Spurgeons' (Spurgeon's Childcare), Rushden. The Indenture (i.e., The Trust Deed) covers the first twelve pages of the minute book. It recorded that Hillyard's investments actually totalled £19,100. The majority of this was tied up in railway bonds, for example, £4,000 with the Great Western Railway. The minutes for 18 May 1868 recorded that the initial figure had been revised and now exactly £20,000 had been received from Hillyard, £18,400 of which was in the form of 'railway and other debentures'.

[104] Spurgeon (ed.), *Sword and Trowel*, October 1866, p. 480.

[105] Spurgeon (ed.), *Sword and Trowel*, May 1867, pp. 233-34.

[106] See, e.g., Spurgeon (ed.), *Sword and Trowel*, July 1867, pp. 335-36; August 1867, p. 384.

[107] Spurgeon (ed.), *Sword and Trowel*, August 1867, pp. 378-79.

[108] See, e.g., C.H. Spurgeon, 'Believing To See', *MTP*, Vol. 13, S. No. 766, Psalm 27.13, n.d., p. 465. Although n.d., this was published in the summer of 1867 and the *Autobiography* confirms this message was preached sometime in 1867. See Spurgeon, *Autobiography*, Vol. 3, p. 173.

[109] '"Report of Proceedings"' of the Laying of the Foundation Stone …', p. 11.

about £5,500 in donations had been received and some of the immediate anxieties had been eased.[110]

The work moved forward. A matron had been appointed in June 1867 (a woman, Mrs Gilbert, who had been identified for the post by Spurgeon himself),[111] and by August the first six boys, who were to live temporarily in Mrs Gilbert's own house in Kennington Park, had been selected.[112] The main buildings – including an infirmary, 'play hall', dining hall, and a house for the headmaster – were, as already noted, completed in 1870.[113]

Peter Shepherd gives a good picture of the sort of boys who were admitted to the Orphanage and also of what life at Stockwell might have been like.[114] The evidence suggests the children were generally happy,[115] although there were some exceptions.[116] It is important to note that, as Shepherd states, 'Spurgeon's children' did not 'come from the very lowest strata of need'.[117] The applications procedure effectively screened out all children born out of wedlock;[118] usually the mother was still alive (repeatedly the phrase 'fatherless children' was used);[119] and, in response to a 'contemplated gift' from a group of Baptist churches, William Olney

---

[110] 'The Stockwell Orphanage', in Spurgeon (ed.), *Sword and Trowel*, October 1867, p. 467.

[111] 'Stockwell Orphanage Minute Book', 20 June 1867.

[112] 'Stockwell Orphanage Minute Book', 12 August 1867.

[113] The infirmary appears to be the last major building to have been completed. See 'Stockwell Orphanage Minute Book', 8 April 1870.

[114] Shepherd, 'Spurgeon's Children', pp. 89-102. Shepherd utilises some of the available primary material, and with profit. Less reliable, although it also includes information as to how the Orphanage work progressed in the first half of the twentieth century, is G.W. Hughes, 'Spurgeon's Homes', *Baptist Quarterly* Vol. 15, No. 7 (July 1954), pp. 297-310.

[115] See, e.g., the series of 'Letters from George Edwards to his Mother, 19 March 1885-29 November 1887', held at 'Spurgeons' (Spurgeon's Childcare), Rushden, some of which are cited by Shepherd, 'Spurgeon's Children', p. 100. The first letter, written on 19 March 1885, stated, 'I am very happy here.' Cf. 8 October 1886, 'I hope you are quite well and happy at home as I am myself at the Orphanage.' Overall, there is no suggestion in any of the letters that Edwards was unhappy. Of course, the nature of the evidence – letters home written under the supervision of the Orphanage staff needs to be borne in mind. George Henry Edwards was admitted to Stockwell on 1 October 1884 and left having been found work on 1 November 1891. I am grateful to Jean Bowerman at 'Spurgeons' (formerly known as Spurgeon's Childcare) for providing this information for me.

[116] Such as Thomas Pearce, whose name, according to Charlesworth, had become a 'synonym for mischief and insubordination' amongst the Orphanage staff. Pearce ran away from Stockwell because he 'wanted to live with his mother'. He was returned but continued to be 'insubordinate' and so was sent back home. See 'Stockwell Orphanage Masters Report, 1 Feb 1881-7 Jan 1887', held at 'Spurgeons' (Spurgeon's Childcare), Rushden, entries 961 and 964 (February-March 1881).

[117] Shepherd, 'Spurgeon's Children', p. 93.

[118] Shepherd, 'Spurgeon's Children', p. 93.

[119] 'Stockwell Orphanage Minute Book', 18 March 1867; 'Indenture', p. 2.

successfully proposed to his fellow trustees that they would 'at all times give the preference to the sons of deceased Baptist ministers provided that the necessities of the case, the health of the child and other matters are in accordance with our regulations'.[120] Some of those admitted were from decidedly middle-class families: according to information included in the *Sword and Trowel*, two of the boys who entered Stockwell in February 1869 were sons of a deceased surgeon and another boy was the son of a judge's clerk 'whose salary had been at least £600 a year'.[121] Consequently, and as Shepherd notes, Stockwell was a rather different operation from Barnardo's orphanage, where the policy was, famously, not to turn away any child in need.[122] Spurgeon was on good terms with Barnardo, as the latter's presence of the platform of the 1879 fête indicated,[123] but Spurgeon's vision for his Orphanage was a more 'respectable' one, arguably more in tune with the middle and lower-middle class Tabernacle membership and with the majority of his *Sword and Trowel* readers. Spurgeon's commitment to 'common people' thus needs to be qualified in the light of the Stockwell Orphanage. It was thrifty, hard-working, 'respectable' people that he especially sought to champion.

What were the different influences which came together to shape the work of the Orphanage? A number of interwoven strands can be discerned. Firstly, the Orphanage was a clear example of the 'evangelical activism' already outlined. The

---

[120] 'Stockwell Orphanage Minute Book', 18 May 1868. As Olney's comments indicate, some children were refused admittance to Stockwell on medical grounds. For an example of this, see 'Stockwell Orphanage Minute Book', 4 September 1874.

[121] 'Stockwell Orphanage', in Spurgeon (ed.), *Sword and Trowel*, March 1869, p. 133. But cases such as these were unusual and, of course, the decease of the father could leave a middle-class Victorian family facing severe financial hardship and uncertainty. The Orphanage *Annual Report* for 1885–86 lists the 'parentage' of the 1,099 children who had entered the Orphanage by that date. Of these, six had been children of surgeons or dentists, one the child of an architect and one the child of a 'gentleman'. But the vast majority were children of 'Mechanics' (261), 'Shopkeepers and Salesmen' (171), 'Manufacturers and Tradesmen' (161), 'Labourers, Porters, and Carmen' (159), and 'Warehousemen and Clerks' (117). See *Annual Report of the Stockwell Orphanage, 1885–6* (London: Passmore and Alabaster, 1886), as included in the bound volume of the *Sword and Trowel*, 1886, p. 461.

[122] Shepherd, 'Spurgeon's Children', p. 93. It ought to be said that Spurgeon avoided Barnardo's controversial policy of mass emigration for older children, as related with significant and surely justifiable anger in P. Bean and J. Melville, *Lost Children of the Empire: The Untold Story of Britain's Migrants* (London: Unwin Hyman, 1989).

[123] There is a letter in the folders of original correspondence in Spurgeon's College Heritage Room, written to 'My Dear Doctor', which is almost certainly from Spurgeon to Barnardo. Spurgeon appears to be turning down an invitation to speak on the grounds of ill health. Spurgeon was responding negatively to a whole host of such invitations at this point (1878) and felt that to accept Barnardo's request alone would cause great offence to others. But the whole tone of the letter is warm and supportive. A pencil note on the letter indicates that it was passed to Spurgeon's College by the 'Secretary of Dr Barnardos [sic]'. C.H. Spurgeon to 'My Dear Doctor', 13 April 1878, 'Original Correspondence of Charles Haddon Spurgeon, 1851–1893', No. 32.

desire to 'do more' for Christ was, of course, not just typically Spurgeonic, but also typically evangelical.[124] Spurgeon admired other evangelical activists, for example George Müller, whose orphanage work Spurgeon sought to take as a model for his own. Spurgeon had written an enthusiastic précis of Müller's annual orphanage report and included it in the *Sword and Trowel* for September 1866, a crucial month for Spurgeon as he wrestled with the possibility of founding his own Orphanage.[125] Also, children were admitted whatever the denominational allegiance of their relatives.[126] Furthermore, the basis of the Stockwell Orphanage was avowedly evangelical, with all trustees having to be members of 'Evangelical Churches dissenting from the Church of England and not holding Unitarian or Socinian views'.[127] For these and other reasons, Kathleen Heasman's description of Stockwell as a 'denominational home' needs to be qualified, although it is true that, in reality, all the active trustees were Baptists and that the Baptist credentials of the work could sometimes be asserted.[128] Heasman herself notes that the period between 1850 and 1900 saw evangelicals, perhaps especially Nonconformist evangelicals, leading the way in organised philanthropy. She estimates that as many as three-quarters of all charitable organisations in the second half of the nineteenth century in England were broadly evangelical in 'character and control'.[129] Spurgeon was a particularly prominent representative of this wider trend.

---

[124] See, e.g., D.K. Gillett, *Trust and Obey: Explorations in Evangelical Spirituality* (London: Darton, Longman and Todd, 1993), pp. 60-61; J. Wolffe, *The Expansion of Evangelicalism, The Age of Wilberforce, More, Chalmers and Finney* (Leicester: IVP, 2006), p. 19.

[125] 'Mr Muller's Report for 1865-6', in Spurgeon (ed.), *Sword and Trowel*, September 1866, pp. 400-406. As already noted, this was a summary of Müller's full report, although Spurgeon quoted from the original at some length.

[126] C. Spurgeon, *Story of Spurgeon's Orphan Homes, These Three-Score Years, 1867-1927* ([no details of place of publication or publisher], 1927) Charles Spurgeon noted that the largest number of admissions [had] always been from the Church of England' and described the Orphanage as 'unsectarian', 'catholic' and 'Christlike'. A copy is held at 'Spurgeons' (Spurgeon's Childcare), Rushden. Charles Spurgeon died in 1926 and so his appreciation of the Orphanage work was published posthumously.

[127] 'Stockwell Orphanage Minute Book', 18 March 1867; 'Indenture', p. 8.

[128] K. Heasman, *Evangelicals in Action: An Appraisal of Their Social Work* (London: Geoffrey Bles, 1962), p. 91. For a statement of a more Baptist flavour see, e.g., J.A. Spurgeon as quoted in the '"Report of Proceedings"' of the Laying of the Foundation Stone ...', p. 10. Anne Hillyard began as a trustee and was still listed as such in 1875 but did not attend trustees' meetings. See 'Stockwell Orphanage Minute Book', 28 May 1875. Charlesworth was, when first appointed as headmaster, an Independent.

[129] Heasman, *Evangelicals in Action*, pp. 13-14. Cf. D.W. Bebbington, 'The Growth of Voluntary Religion', in S. Gilley and B. Stanley (eds), *The Cambridge History of Christianity: World Christianities, c.1815–c.1914* (Cambridge: Cambridge University Press, 2006), pp. 60-61; I.M. Randall, *What a Friend We Have in Jesus: The Evangelical Tradition* (Darton, Longman and Todd: London, 2005), pp. 156-57.

Activism 209

The Orphanage was further marked as evangelical by the marrying of social concern with evangelistic passion. Although the primary focus was on social action, Spurgeon made sure that the boys (and later girls) had the opportunity to hear and respond to the gospel. Indeed, this had been part of Anne Hillyard's original vision, one that Spurgeon endorsed from the beginning and continued to promote as the Orphanage work grew.[130] During Spurgeon's lifetime, a steady stream of children were converted and subsequently baptized at the Tabernacle.[131] Some of the boys later entered the Pastors' College to train. John Maynard was one of the first boys to be accepted into the Orphanage, his application having been received by the trustees on 16 October 1867.[132] Maynard was converted whilst at Stockwell and baptized at the Tabernacle. He began training at the Pastors' College in 1882.[133] On 18 May 1885 Spurgeon enthusiastically commended Maynard to the Baptist Missionary Society (BMS).[134] He described Maynard as his 'son in the faith'. 'He loves the Lord and is wholehearted', Spurgeon continued, advising the BMS committee that they should have no doubts about accepting his student.[135] Maynard left Britain for cross-cultural missionary service in the Congo in later in 1885.[136] But within a month of arriving at Underhill Station on the Congo River, on 28 January 1886, Maynard had died of a fever.[137] His example of service and his reported dying words, which included, 'Tell the boys and girls of the Orphanage to seek Jesus ... tell the students to preach Christ, and Christ only ...', led to him being held up as a model of active,

---

[130] See, e.g., A. Hillyard to C.H. Spurgeon, 3 September 1866, in Spurgeon, *Autobiography*, Vol. 3, p. 169; Spurgeon frequently urged the children to trust in Christ. See, e.g., C.H. Spurgeon to 'Children at Stockwell Orphanage', 24 January 1874, in C. Spurgeon (ed.), *The Letters of C.H. Spurgeon* (London: Marshall Brothers, n.d. [1923]), p. 181. He also urged prayer for the conversion of the children. See, e.g., 'Stockwell Orphanage', in Spurgeon (ed.), *Sword and Trowel*, July 1885, p. 371.

[131] Spurgeon, *Autobiography*, Vol. 3, p. 178.

[132] 'Stockwell Orphanage Minute Book', 16 October 1867.

[133] *Annual Report of the Stockwell Orphanage, 1885–6*, as included in bound volume of Spurgeon (ed.), *Sword and Trowel*, 1886, p. 462.

[134] Letter from C.H. Spurgeon to A.H. Baynes, 18 May 1885. In the folder for H. Ross Phillips, application #81, 1885, Candidate Papers Box 71-98, 1884–1886, BMS Archives, The Angus Library and Archives, Regent's Park College, Oxford. I am grateful to Anthony R. Cross for drawing my attention to this and the following letter.

[135] C.H. Spurgeon to BMS Committee, dated 188[5], in support of the application of John Maynard. In the folder for John Maynard, application #76, 1885, Candidate Papers Box 71–98, 1884–1886, BMS Archives, The Angus Library and Archives, Regent's Park College, Oxford.

[136] *Annual Report of the Stockwell Orphanage, 1885–6*, as included in bound volume of Spurgeon (ed.), *Sword and Trowel*, 1886, p. 462.

[137] Spurgeon (ed.), *Sword and Trowel*, April 1886, p. 196; *Freeman*, 19 March 1886, in 'Loose-Leaf Scrap Folder, October 1885–March 1886', Spurgeon's College, Heritage Room (2G).

'ardent', evangelical piety at both Stockwell and at the Pastors' College.[138] Consequently, although primarily 'social', the evangelistic and social dimensions of Spurgeon's activism came together in the work of the Orphanage in what could be described as an example of integral mission. The overarching point should be clear: Spurgeon's christocentric evangelicalism fired and gave shape to his Orphanage work.

One aspect of evangelical piety which was embedded in the specific context of nineteenth-century evangelicalism was the faith principle. This was important with regard to financing the Orphanage. The faith principle, and Spurgeon's commitment to this, at least in theory, has already been set out in chapter 6. Müller did not overtly make the needs of his orphanage known. Although his approach to fundraising was more 'flexible' than is sometimes allowed,[139] he did not tend to appeal directly for money to fund his work. Spurgeon's application of the faith principle was certainly more fluid than Müller's. Rather than relying on the 'unsolicited willinghood [sic]' of Christians,[140] Spurgeon constantly appealed for funds, making many specific details known.[141] A central reason for this was the acute anxiety Spurgeon seemed to feel in relation to money, especially when there was a possibility he might not be able to satisfy creditors. Spurgeon described such a possibility, in a letter to W.Y. Fullerton, as being 'of all things my horror'.[142] This anxiety was rooted in aspects of Nonconformist culture,[143] but the tendency was certainly exacerbated by his temperament. It is ironic that, in the preface to the volume of sermons in which a paean to Müller's methods appeared, Spurgeon was vigorously commending the

---

[138] G. Edwards to mother, 17 February 1889, in 'Letters from George Edwards to his Mother, 19 March 1885–29 November 1887'. Students from the College had visited Stockwell and given a talk about Maynard.

[139] See 'Mr Muller's Report for 1865–6', in Spurgeon (ed.), *Sword and Trowel*, September 1866, p. 403. For further comments on Müller's fundraising, see N. Summerton, 'George Müller and the Financing of the Scriptural Knowledge Institution', in N.T.R. Dickson and T. Grass (eds), *The Growth of the Brethren Movement* (Carlisle: Paternoster, 2006), pp. 49-79; Randall, 'Ye men of Plymouth …'.

[140] 'Mr Muller's Report for 1865–6', in Spurgeon (ed.), *Sword and Trowel*, September 1866, p. 402.

[141] See, e.g., Spurgeon (ed.), *Sword and Trowel*, May 1872, p. 240; July 1872, pp. 335-36.

[142] C.H. Spurgeon to W.Y. Fullerton, 2 July 1885, in 'Various Spurgeon Letters', Spurgeon's College, Heritage Room (K1.9).

[143] Spurgeon's anxiety regarding money is noted by Kruppa, *Spurgeon*, p. 153. My research into Andrew Fuller brought home to me the extent to which 'failing to act honourably to creditors' was regarded with horror by many Dissenters. J.W. Morris, one of the Fuller's biographers, was declared bankrupt in 1808 due to the failure of his printing business and had to leave the pastorate. His reputation was ruined in the eyes of his friends, not least Fuller himself. Morris is just one of the examples of a Baptist disgraced by debt who could have been cited. On Morris see, P.J. Morden, *Offering Christ to the World: Andrew Fuller (1754–1815) and the Revival of Eighteenth Century Particular Baptist Life* (Carlisle: Paternoster, 2003), p. 2.

Orphanage to 'the generous consideration' of his readers.[144] Thus, despite his own rhetoric and the assertions made by the compilers of the *Autobiography* and some modern writers, for example Lewis Drummond, Spurgeon's commitment to the faith principle was far from total.[145]

Nevertheless, as evidenced by the purchase of the site for the Stockwell Orphanage, Spurgeon was willing to proceed 'in faith': he moved forward with his venture even though it was not certain he could fund it. Although it should be noted that Müller would have refused to take out a loan,[146] for Spurgeon as well as for Müller 'faith' preceded 'sight'. Müller's stress on praying for needs, apparent in his 1866 report and in his work generally,[147] was particularly emphasised by Spurgeon. Concern for his own Orphanage repeatedly drove the anxious Spurgeon to prayer and renewed trust in God.[148] It was a trust which, according to his later testimony, was not misplaced. A letter he sent out to subscribers and other donors in 1887 stated, 'DEAR FRIEND, – The Orphanage has a mouth which is for ever swallowing, and if it be not filled it will soon be crying out. This last calamity has never yet fallen upon me, for the Lord has supplied our needs from day to day most graciously.'[149] Thankfulness for God's 'day-to-day' provision echoes Müller's own confident, daily trust in God to send whatever was needed. Spurgeon believed that through his Orphanage he had tried and proved God's faithfulness. The needs of Stockwell and the accompanying potential for 'calamity' had driven Spurgeon to intercession; the answers which he believed had come had caused intense relief and, consequently, his trust in a gracious God had been increased. However inconsistently Spurgeon had applied it, he believed that the 'faith principle' had been vindicated by his own 'venture of faith', the Stockwell Orphanage.[150]

A further strand of influence can be discerned. Spurgeon's work for the Orphanage reflected the 'entrepreneurial' spirit of the age. This dimension of Spurgeon was highlighted in chapter 6, but it is relevant here as well. The Orphanage reveals Spurgeon – who had risen, as Robert Shindler's 'tombstone' biography put it, from 'the usher's desk to the Tabernacle pulpit' – as embodying some of the

---

[144] C.H. Spurgeon, Preface, *MTP*, Vol. 13, p. vii; 'Believing To See', p. 465.

[145] See Spurgeon, *Autobiography*, Vol. 3, p. 173. Lewis Drummond, *Spurgeon: The Prince of Preachers* (Grand Rapids: Kregel, 1992), pp. 420-22, suggests that Spurgeon followed Müller's principles fully.

[146] See 'Mr Muller's Report for 1865-6', in Spurgeon (ed.), *Sword and Trowel*, September 1866, p. 403.

[147] This aspect of the 1866 report was duly noted by Spurgeon. See 'Mr Muller's Report for 1865-6', in Spurgeon (ed.), *Sword and Trowel*, September 1866, p. 405.

[148] See, e.g., Spurgeon (ed.), *Sword and Trowel*, July 1867, p. 325-26; August 1867, p. 378; *Baptist*, 10 October 1879, in 'Spurgeon's Scrapbooks', Vol. 2, p. 126.

[149] C.H. Spurgeon to subscribers and donors of Stockwell Orphanage, 19 May 1887, in 'Original Correspondence of Charles Haddon Spurgeon, 1887–1892', Spurgeon's College, Heritage Room (4G), No. 82. Cf. C. Spurgeon (ed.) *The Letters of C.H. Spurgeon*, p. 214.

[150] A. Cunningham Burley, *Spurgeon and his Friendships* (London: Epworth, 1933), p. 104.

entrepreneurial, 'self-help' values which were highly esteemed in Victorian Britain.[151] He was deeply involved in founding and growing the Orphanage; he cast the vision for the 'business', established the principles on which it would run, raised funds and recruited staff.[152] As will be established, Spurgeon was certainly not acting alone as he did this, but, without question, his involvement was crucial. The industrial and business landscape and ethos of Victorian Britain helped shape Spurgeon's evangelical activism in particular ways. And, even in the wider context of what was being achieved elsewhere in Britain, Spurgeon was a particularly successful social entrepreneur. He was one of those Victorian evangelicals who, as David Bebbington puts it, 'turned philanthropy into a business'.[153] Once again, we see that an aspect of Spurgeon's spirituality was moulded by the spirit of the age. Overall, the work of the Orphanage reveals Spurgeon as a nineteenth-century evangelical activist, an entrepreneur who was committed to social concern alongside evangelism.

The Orphanage and Communion with Christ's People

It is important for this study to establish the extent to which Spurgeon relied on others and the Orphanage provides a particularly good example of this. The fact that Spurgeon worked closely with others has sometimes been missed, not least because some of his own statements suggest he preferred to work on his own. Kruppa cites Spurgeon who stated, in 1884, 'Whenever anything is done, either in the church or in the world, you may depend upon it, it is done by one man.'[154] Mark Hopkins suggests that Spurgeon had a 'preference for working on his own' and cites William Williams, who recorded Spurgeon as saying the following, '"Lead me not into temptation" means, to me, Bring me not into a committee.'[155] Other similar quotations could be adduced.[156] Spurgeon appears, on the basis of these extracts, to

---

[151] R. Shindler, *From the Usher's Desk to the Tabernacle Pulpit: The Life and Labours of Pastor C.H. Spurgeon* (London: Passmore and Alabaster, 1892). The proofs of this work were revised at Mentone 'under Mr Spurgeon's supervision' with a final chapter added after the subject's death. See p. v (title page).

[152] Interestingly, Spurgeon noted, in his appreciation of Müller's Bristol Homes, that 'no first class business firm in London conducts its affairs with greater precision and punctuality. Let it be noted again that faith in God, and careful, methodical economy and diligence should always go together.' 'Mr Muller's Report for 1865–6', in Spurgeon (ed.), *Sword and Trowel*, September 1866, p. 400.

[153] Bebbington, 'The Growth of Voluntary Religion', p. 61.

[154] *Pall Mall Gazette*, 19 June 1884, as cited by Kruppa, *Spurgeon*, p. 176.

[155] M. Hopkins, *Nonconformity's Romantic Generation: Evangelical and Liberal Theologies in Victorian England* (Carlisle: Paternoster, 2004), p. 160; W. Williams, *Personal Reminiscences of Charles Haddon Spurgeon* (London: Religious Tract Society, 1895), p. 172.

[156] C.H. Spurgeon, 'The Holy War Of The Present Hour', *Sword and Trowel*, August 1866, p. 341. Cf. Kruppa, *Spurgeon*, pp. 175-76.

be the epitome of individualism and what a former Orphanage boy called 'manly self-reliance'.[157]

In one sense, analysis of the way the Orphanage developed gives some support to these statements. Certainly, the work at Stockwell would not have existed without Spurgeon and he was indisputably the leader. I have read the extant 'Minute Book' of the Stockwell Orphanage (which runs to June 1876) and I have not found one instance of the trustees making a decision against Spurgeon's wishes: indeed, once his mind was known all debate was ended.[158] According to the minute book, when Spurgeon was not present and contentious matters arose, decisions were deferred so that the president's views could be sought. One example of this concerned a decision regarding whether to give the boys a particular vaccination.[159] The Orphanage was not an enterprise run by a committee of independent-minded equals. The impression given is that Spurgeon was utterly dominant.

And yet a closer reading of the minutes and of other available primary material shows that, in another sense, these statements about Spurgeon's individualistic *modus operandi*, both from himself and others, are misleading. My contention is that, rather than revealing Spurgeon as working independently, even autonomously, the Orphanage shows that he relied heavily on trusted friends. Spurgeon may have been 'manly' but he was not self-reliant. One of the most important trustees was William Higgs, a Tabernacle deacon, builder and close personal friend of Spurgeon who had accompanied his pastor on his initial visit to Anne Hillyard.[160] On an early visit to the Stockwell site, on 17 April 1867, Spurgeon formally proposed to the other trustees that a temporary shed should be erected so that meetings could be held. It was Higgs who (not unnaturally) was tasked with drawing up a detailed plan.[161] One month later, on 20 June 1867, Higgs was able to report that 'he had prepared a plan of the shed and submitted it to the board of works'. Higgs now had a proposal of his own to make, saying that his workmen had offered to fund and build one of the orphan houses themselves. Spurgeon and Higgs formed a 'subcommittee' to make arrangements to move this forward.[162] Higgs was one of those trustees who was crucial in developing the work of the Orphanage.

But Higgs was not the most important Orphanage trustee. The most significant member of the group, excepting the president and 'perpetual chairman' (and even

---

[157] R.S. Latimer, 'Grateful Memories', in *Within Our Gates*, Spring 1894, p. 6. *Within Our Gates* was the quarterly magazine of the Orphanage which was begun by the new Orphanage president, J.A. Spurgeon, in 1894. Copies of the early numbers are held at 'Spurgeons' (Spurgeon's Childcare), Rushden. Latimer's comment that C.H. Spurgeon was 'manly' was perceptive, his judgment that Spurgeon was 'self-reliant' less so.

[158] Cf. Spurgeon, *Autobiography*, Vol. 3, pp. 176-77.

[159] 'Stockwell Orphanage Minute Book', 26 November 1869.

[160] Higgs's firm had built the Tabernacle and he would later holiday with Spurgeon. See Fullerton, *C.H. Spurgeon*, pp. 137, 177. Spurgeon described Higgs as 'my dear brother'. See Spurgeon, *Autobiography*, Vol. 4, p. 249.

[161] 'Stockwell Orphanage Minute Book', 17 April 1867.

[162] 'Stockwell Orphanage Minute Book', 20 June 1867.

this judgement could be questioned), was James Archer Spurgeon. In 1867, J.A. Spurgeon was the only active trustee of the Orphanage who was not a member of the Metropolitan Tabernacle. The official invitation he received, in January 1868, to become co-pastor of the Tabernacle made reference to the help he had already given regarding the Orphanage, and with good reason.[163] J.A. Spurgeon was a gifted administrator who combined an eye for detail with an impressive breadth of understanding of the business world.[164] This was in marked contrast to his older brother who 'when required to give attention to matters of business detail' became 'worried and pulled down'.[165] At the trustees meeting on 20 June 1867 already referred to, complex discussions of technicalities relating to a number of Anne Hillyard's railway bonds were necessary. At this point, according to the minute book, C.H. Spurgeon left both the chair and the meeting. J.A Spurgeon took over and, after some debate with fellow trustees, undertook to follow up the issues relating to these bonds personally.[166] This was an example of the sort of close, detailed work which J.A. Spurgeon would soon be undertaking for the Orphanage on a regular basis. The trustees as a body were, from the beginning, anxious to protect C.H. Spurgeon as much as possible from any work he found a strain. There were clearly concerns that he was finding it difficult emotionally to visit boys who had applied, through their mothers or another relative, for admittance to the Orphanage.[167] Accordingly, it was very unusual, from at least the beginning of 1868, for him to have any role in the application process. All the 'application papers and procedures for admission' had earlier been drawn up by J.A. Spurgeon and another trustee.[168] Rather than acting alone, C.H. Spurgeon was, even as the Orphanage work began to take shape, already leaning heavily on trusted associates and friends.

This reliance on others to take the Orphanage forward becomes even more apparent in the early to mid-1870s. Certainly C.H. Spurgeon was still involved. This involvement still occasionally included dealing with matters of detail, particularly with regard to the Orphanage building, where he continued to act in partnership with Higgs.[169] C.H. Spurgeon also took the lead in the appointment of key staff,

---

[163] Pike, *J.A. Spurgeon*, p. 88.

[164] G.H. Pike, 'Men and Women on Work. The Rev. James Archer Spurgeon, D.D., LL.D.', in *Family Friend*, March 1896, p. 37; Pike, *J.A. Spurgeon*, p. 80.

[165] Pike, *J.A. Spurgeon*, p. 86.

[166] 'Stockwell Orphanage Minute Book', 20 June 1867.

[167] Cf. Spurgeon, *Autobiography*, Vol. 3, p. 177; 'Stockwell Orphanage', in Spurgeon (ed.), *Sword and Trowel*, March 1869, p. 133.

[168] 'Stockwell Orphanage Minute Book', 20 June 1867. Later it was made quite clear, for example by Charlesworth in the 1884–85 *Annual Report*, that 'Mr (C.H.) Spurgeon cannot personally see any applicants and should not be written to'. *Annual Report of the Stockwell Orphanage, 1884–5* (London: Passmore and Alabaster, 1885), as included in the bound volume of Spurgeon (ed.), *Sword and Trowel*, 1885, p. 464.

[169] 'Stockwell Orphanage Minute Book', 6 February 1868, 17 February 1868, 24 February 1868.

personally selecting the headmaster, Vernon J. Charlesworth.[170] But, as 1869 wore on, C.H. Spurgeon was increasingly not present at trustees' meetings and, from the beginning of 1873, was absent more often than not.[171] In 1869, of the fourteen trustees' meetings, C.H. Spurgeon attended eleven.[172] But, in 1873, when there were twenty-four such meetings, C.H. Spurgeon was present at only four of them. In 1875, when there were again twenty-four meetings, he was recorded as being in attendance only once, on 28 May 1875, when the group gathered to elect some additional trustees.[173] C.H. Spurgeon took the chair on this occasion, as he always did when he was present. But, in his absence, the meetings were chaired by his brother. When J.A. Spurgeon was himself away, which was unusual, other trustees, usually Higgs or William Olney, would step in.[174] In other words, it was J.A. Spurgeon who took the lead in organising the affairs of the Orphanage from 1869 onwards. Day-to-day, from at least 1876, Charlesworth, who increasingly enjoyed the confidence of the Spurgeons and the rest of the board, had power to act. The headmaster appears to have taken an important role, not only in matters such as discipline, schooling and other details; he was also working on admissions and on finding 'suitable positions' for the boys when the time approached for them to leave Stockwell.[175] There was still oversight from the trustees, most obviously from J.A. Spurgeon, who often signed Charlesworth's notes and was clearly present at a whole host of meetings.[176] Evidence suggests that C.H. Spurgeon's involvement in the actual management of the Orphanage, from as early as 1869, was at best minimal.[177] This was partly because, by now, C.H. Spurgeon's views on most matters pertaining to the running of the Orphanage were known: his stamp remained firmly on what was regarded as his institution. But it is no exaggeration to say that, in the day-to-day management of the Orphanage, C.H. Spurgeon was entirely dependent on others.

C.H. Spurgeon knew this and expressed his profound gratitude especially to J.A. Spurgeon. 'I am so deeply indebted to you for looking into detail at Stockwell', C.H.

---

[170] 'Stockwell Orphanage Minute Book', 12 March 1869. Charlesworth had been one of those who had led in prayer at the 1867 stone laying ceremony. See, '"Report of Proceedings"' of the Laying of the Foundation Stone …', p. 5.

[171] Cf. the comments in Spurgeon, *Autobiography*, Vol. 3, pp. 176-77.

[172] Although not at all from October to December of 1869.

[173] 'Stockwell Orphanage Minute Book', 1869–1875. See especially, 28 May 1875.

[174] For example, 25 June 1869, when Olney was chairman. 'Stockwell Orphanage Minute Book', 25 June 1869.

[175] 'Stockwell Orphanage Master's Report, 8 September 1876–28 January 1881', held at Spurgeons (Spurgeon's Childcare), Rushden, *passim*.

[176] See, e.g., the entries for 1876. 'Stockwell Orphanage Master's Report, 8 September 1876–28 January 1881'.

[177] C.H. Spurgeon did get involved in the disciplining of Thomas Pearce (see n. 114) as a relative of Pearce had complained directly to Spurgeon about the boy's treatment. See 'Stockwell Orphanage Master's Report, 1 Feb 1881–7 Jan 1887', entries 961, 964, (February–March 1881). Spurgeon assured Charlesworth by letter that he approved of the headmaster's actions. See entry 964b.

Spurgeon wrote to his brother in 1882.[178] G. Holden Pike, who knew both men well, described J.A. Spurgeon as the 'helper' C.H. Spurgeon 'trusted and valued above all others'.[179] Pike's brief biography of J.A. Spurgeon (astonishingly, the only one which appears to have been written) undoubtedly descends into hagiography, but the correspondence written by the elder to the younger brother, some of which is included in this volume, gives ample evidence to support Pike's statement.

In these letters C.H. Spurgeon was at his most personal and unguarded, appearing in 'undress', as Pike put it.[180] The correspondence reveals, once again, the degree to which C.H. Spurgeon relied on his brother. In November 1871 C.H. Spurgeon wrote from Paris,

> DEAR BROTHER, – I am not very demonstrative in gratitude, but I must indulge myself with the pleasure of saying how much I owe to you and how greatly you contribute to my peace of mind. Your loving aid is beyond all thanks, although it desires none. Believe me, dear brother, I value you as God's best gift to me in this work.[181]

Spurgeon enjoyed a close personal relationship with his brother which was clearly aided by their familial ties. But, perhaps just as significantly, J.A. Spurgeon was a partner to C.H. Spurgeon in his 'work' and this working partnership was the context in which mutual regard and friendship developed still further.[182] Crucially, C.H. Spurgeon regarded his 'dear brother' as 'God's gift' to him – this was a 'spiritual' friendship. Their relationship remained strong right to the end of the elder brother's life, surviving the vicissitudes of the Downgrade Controversy (contrary to the misleading suggestions of some writers).[183] Theirs was an enduring spiritual friendship worked out in the context of shared Christian activity.

---

[178] C.H. Spurgeon to J.A. Spurgeon, 2 December 1882, in Pike, *J.A. Spurgeon*, p. 153.

[179] Pike, *J.A. Spurgeon*, p. 9.

[180] Pike, *J.A. Spurgeon*, p. 138. The correspondence is included by Pike on pp. 138-69.

[181] C.H. Spurgeon to J.A. Spurgeon, November 1871, in C. Spurgeon (ed.), *The Letters of C.H. Spurgeon*, p. 58 / Pike, *J.A. Spurgeon*, pp. 139-40. There are a number of other similar passages in the letters recorded by Pike. See, e.g., C.H. Spurgeon to J.A. Spurgeon, 18 May 1871; C.H. Spurgeon to J.A. Spurgeon, 2 February 1878, in Pike, *J.A. Spurgeon*, pp. 143, 147, and see also p. 171. Cf. C.H. Spurgeon's very similar comments as recorded by Burley, *Spurgeon and His Friendships*, p. 39.

[182] For example, C.H. Spurgeon to J.A. Spurgeon, 25 April 1887, in C. Spurgeon (ed.), *The Letters of C.H. Spurgeon*, p. 63.

[183] Ernest Bacon, *Spurgeon: Heir of the Puritans* (London: George Allen and Unwin, 1967), pp. 139-40, states that J.A. Spurgeon's attitude in the Downgrade Controversy was 'undoubtedly a keen disappointment' to his brother. But this, together with Bacon's assertion that J.A. Spurgeon effectively acted as mediator between the Baptist Union (BU) and C.H. Spurgeon in the dispute, is simply not true. For a reliable treatment of the Downgrade Controversy see M. Hopkins, 'The Down Grade Controversy: New Evidence', *Baptist Quarterly* Vol. 35 No. 6 (April 1994), pp. 262-78, and *Nonconformity's Romantic Generation*, pp. 193-248. Hopkins shows, with reference to a wealth of primary evidence, the

Although his principle debt was to J.A. Spurgeon, C.H. Spurgeon was appreciative of all the Orphanage trustees, Charlesworth, the other staff and, more broadly still, all who supported the Orphanage by their prayers, presence at annual fêtes and other events and, of course, their gifts.[184] All of these people were partners with him and with all he believed he enjoyed 'fellowship'. Together they were engaged in what Spurgeon described as a 'labour of love'.[185] As he surveyed the crowd who had gathered at the fête in 1878 he was profoundly moved. Here were a 'host' of 'faithful men and women' who had sustained the Orphanage and continued to do so. The *South London Press* reported that Spurgeon felt called upon to

> testify his gratitude for that divine grace which had bestowed so much happiness upon him. What a wonderful power divine grace was to make them brothers and sisters in sympathy and affection! They might not have known each other had it not been for the Gospel [sic], and certainly there would have not been that intimate bond of union which existed between them. How many had arisen to a new state of spiritual joy – had arisen out of the old state of lethargy – simply through the possession of the Power! Their thanks were chiefly due to God for His gift ...[186]

In Spurgeon's view, God had been at work drawing the Orphanage supporters together, establishing an 'intimate ... union' as he and they engaged in a common task. Moreover, God's power had been known, not through the action of an individual, but through a collective work. Most striking in this extract is the

---

extent to which the two brothers consulted and acted together in the dispute (see *Nonconformity's Romantic Generation*, pp. 218; 220-26). Bacon's assertions appear to hinge primarily on J.A. Spurgeon seconding a motion at the BU Council meeting of 20 April 1888, which C.H. Spurgeon later said he would have opposed if he had been present. But C.H. Spurgeon had been fully aware of the motion and the fact that his brother would second it, and had urged his supporters to vote in favour, writing to one, 'I hope you will not oppose the declaration wh[ich] it is sought to pass. That w[oul]d be a disastrous course for the Evangelical brethren.' See C.H. Spurgeon to B. Pifford, 4 April 1888, 'Original Correspondence of Charles Haddon Spurgeon 1851–1893', No. 95. J.A. Spurgeon was effectively outmanoeuvred by late amendments and the speech of the proposer, as Hopkins shows (*Nonconformity's Romantic Generation*, pp. 223-26) and J.A. Spurgeon clearly had grave doubts about what he was doing, even as he spoke in favour of the motion. C.H. Spurgeon's own verdict was that they (i.e., both he and his brother) had been 'entrapped by diplomatists'. See C.H. Spurgeon to Wright, 27 April 1888, as cited in Kruppa, *Spurgeon*, pp. 442-43, and Hopkins, *Nonconformity's Romantic Generation*, p. 226. C.H. Spurgeon remained warmly supportive of James both during and after the Downgrade Controversy. See, e.g., C.H. Spurgeon to J.A. Spurgeon, 7 June 1887, 8 December 1890, 8 October 1891, in C. Spurgeon (ed.), *The Letters of C.H. Spurgeon*, pp. 64-66. J.A. Spurgeon remained within the BU both during and after the controversy, as did the majority of students trained at the Pastors' College. This may account, in part, for Bacon's negative assessment.

[184] Spurgeon, *Autobiography*, Vol. 3, p. 180.

[185] C.H. Spurgeon to 'Dear Friend' (a circular to Orphanage supporters), 5 January 1888, in 'Original Correspondence of Charles Haddon Spurgeon 1887–1892', No. 87.

[186] *South London Press*, 22 June 1878, in 'Spurgeon's Scrapbooks', Vol. 1, p. 56.

emphasis on joy: the same emphasis we have already seen was the hallmark of much of Spurgeon's activity. This 'happiness' was felt by Spurgeon and, he was sure, by others present who had joined with him. The joy of wholehearted Christian activity – a joy experienced both as activity was carried out and as its fruits were surveyed – was a pleasure that was all the greater for being shared. Consequently, although Spurgeon had spoken about the importance of the heroic 'one man' who achieved great things for God, and although it sometimes suited him to portray himself in these terms, this was far from the reality of the Orphanage work.

Spurgeon lacked certain gifts, for example the ability to give sustained attention to detail in business matters, and he had weaknesses, for example, his anxiety over money. Perhaps most importantly, he was not temperamentally a solitary man. He could enjoy quiet contemplation and time spent alone with God, but he had to return soon to be around people – those who were like-minded and who loved him and supported him. Spurgeon was, quite clearly in my view, temperamentally an 'extrovert' rather than an 'introvert': that is, he was invigorated by being with others rather than being alone.[187] His visits to the Orphanage could be the means to a real revival in spirits. At the June 1879 Orphanage fête Spurgeon spoke of the 'affection' the boys seemed to have for him. The *Christian World*, reporting Spurgeon's speech, said that, 'As soon as [Spurgeon] showed his nose he was the centre of a sea of boys ... Whenever he was in the dumps nothing did him so much good as a turn in the orphanage.'[188] Spurgeon emerges from the material we have looked at as a thoroughly relational 'extrovert'.

Consequent to all this, Mark Hopkins' claim that Spurgeon had a 'preference for working on his own' needs to be challenged. Hopkins may have had Spurgeon's dominance as a personality and the fact that he always led 'from the front' at least partly in view here. But, as it stands, the statement in *Nonconformity's Romantic Generation* goes beyond this, with reference also made to Spurgeon's supposed 'aloofness'.[189] Yet analysis of Spurgeon's activism, undertaken through the lens of the Orphanage, does not support these assertions; indeed it points in the opposite direction. Spurgeon was always the dominant personality with regard to the Orphanage, but at no time, either in its founding or as it grew, did he work 'on his own'. The description of Spurgeon as 'aloof' is, I would submit, particularly misleading. Hopkins' comments at this point represent a minor flaw in what is an extremely perceptive and suggestive study. Spurgeon actually had a preference for working with others. As he collaborated with other people he experienced both 'communion' and joy.

---

[187] I am using the terms 'extrovert' and 'introvert' as they are defined in the 'Myers Briggs Type Indicator'. On this, see I. Briggs Myers with P.B. Briggs, *Gifts Differing* (Palo Alto: Consulting Psychologists Press, 1980), pp. 6-7 and *passim*.

[188] *Christian World*, 27 June 1879; cf. *Baptist*, 27 June 1879, in 'Spurgeon's Scrapbooks', Vol. 2, pp. 77-78.

[189] Hopkins, *Nonconformity's Romantic Generation*, pp. 160-61.

Activity and Christ

If the two case studies both especially highlight the ways that Spurgeon's activism linked with his stress on other people, analysis of his preaching is particularly revealing of the way his activism was focused on Christ. All work was to be done for Christ, out of gratitude, 'veneration' and love to him,[190] just as the aim of all work was, ultimately, to glorify Christ in the power of the Spirit.[191] Jesus was also the example for Christians as they engaged in activity for him. Particularly instructive in this regard are passages in Spurgeon's sermons where Jesus is presented as the exemplary worker. One message, 'The Blind Man's Eyes Opened; Or, Practical Christianity', is worthy of an extended treatment. In this message, preached in 1883, Spurgeon gave Christ the title 'THE WORKER' and described him as 'the chief worker, the example to all workers'.[192] As Spurgeon expounded his text he noted that Jesus had compassion on the blind man of John 9.1-12. Crucially, this compassion was active – it led to Jesus actually healing the man. Believers were to imitate Christ, not through a ministry of supernatural healing, but by alleviating the suffering of others through the ministry of caring. Rather than speculating about the cause of such suffering as Jesus' disciples had done,[193] Christians were to 'postpone the inquiries' and give practical help. This, as far as Spurgeon was concerned, was following the example of Jesus.

> I say that the Master was no speculator; he was no spinner of theories; he was no mere doctrinalist; but he went to work and healed those that had need of healing. Come, what have we ever *done* to bless our fellow men? Many of us are followers of Christ, and, oh, how happy we ought to be that we are so! What have we ever *done* worthy of our high calling?

Here Spurgeon had social action primarily in mind but, later in this message, he also spoke of the need for evangelistic endeavour. In an extraordinary passage he comes close to describing Jesus as 'driven' in his pursuit of souls. '[Christ's] mind, his soul, his heart, were all of a force which produced perpetual activity ... There was a sort of instinct in Christ to save men, and that instinct craved gratification and could not be denied. "I must work," he said.'[194] Whether the need was social or evangelistic, Christ the 'worker' sought to meet those needs and believers were to

---

[190] Spurgeon, 'Something Done For Jesus', pp. 51-53. Cf. C.H. Spurgeon, 'Christ's Motive And Ours', *MTP*, Vol. 29, S. No. 2232, 2 Corinthians 8.9, Philippians 1.29, delivered 29 November 1891, pp. 609-11.

[191] C.H. Spurgeon, 'The Holy Spirit's Chief Office', MTP, Vol. 40, S. No. 2382, John 16.14,15, delivered 26 July 1888, p. 484.

[192] C.H. Spurgeon, 'The Blind Man's Eyes Opened; Or, Practical Christianity', *MTP*, Vol. 29, S. No. 1754, John 9.3,4, delivered 12 August 1883, p. 675. For a similar emphasis see, 'Everyday Religion', p. 283; 'With The King For His Work!', *MTP*, Vol. 24, S. No. 1400, 1 Chronicles 4.23, delivered 1 November 1877, p. 114.

[193] John 9.2.

[194] Spurgeon, 'The Blind Man's Eyes Opened; Or, Practical Christianity', pp. 674-77.

follow. The challenge to work hard in imitation of Christ regularly recurs in Spurgeon's preaching.[195] As far as 'activism' was concerned, Jesus, the 'great master worker'[196] who 'never had an idle hour',[197] was the believer's inspiration and model.

Christ not only provided believers with an example to imitate; the living Christ also impelled believers to action. As Spurgeon brought 'The Blind Man's Eyes Opened …' to a close he pressed home his appeal in the following terms:

> Oh, that I could lay my hand – or, better far, that my Master would lay his pierced hand on every true Christian here and press it upon him until he cried out, 'I cannot sit here. I must be at work as soon as this service is done. I cannot only hear, and give, and pray, but I must also work.'[198]

Christ was pictured as being actively present, laying his 'pierced hand' on Christians and 'pressing' them to give themselves to a life of active service. Earlier in the message, Spurgeon had assured his hearers that God was at work in them in such a way as to make this life of passionate service possible. Christians were described as the 'workshop of Christ': Christ came to save them, and in each believer 'the works of God shall be made manifest'.[199] In another message, 'Farm Labourers', Spurgeon employed a different image to similar effect. Instead of describing believers as Christ's 'workshop', the church was pictured as God's farm. God had tilled and cultivated the ground changing the nature of the soil and making it fruitful. 'Kept by the eternal Spirit of God', a believer could produce a harvest of, amongst other things, 'usefulness'.[200] Whether the metaphor was industrial or agricultural, the point was the same. God himself (in 'The Blind Man's Eyes Opened …' the focus was specifically on Christ) was portrayed as the supreme worker, working in believers that they in turn might labour effectively at whatever God had given them to do.

Given these emphases, it is unsurprising that Spurgeon regarded active Christian work as a form of communion with Christ. In 'The Blind Man's Eyes Opened …' he had spoken of Christ enjoying 'unbroken communion with the Father' as he went about his work.[201] But in the message, 'Communion With Christ And His People', Spurgeon made it clear that believers could be caught up into this dynamic – of

---

[195] C.H. Spurgeon, 'Wanted! – Volunteers', p. 548. For an example from Spurgeon's earlier ministry, see 'The Spur', *MTP*, Vol. 16, S. No. 943, John 9.4, delivered 31 July 1870, pp. 421-32.

[196] Spurgeon, 'The Spur', pp. 423, 428.

[197] Spurgeon, 'With The King For His Work!', p. 114.

[198] Spurgeon, 'The Blind Man's Eyes Opened; Or, Practical Christianity', p. 682.

[199] Spurgeon, 'The Blind Man's Eyes Opened; Or, Practical Christianity', p. 683.

[200] C.H. Spurgeon, 'Farm Labourers', *MTP*, Vol. 27, S. No. 1602, 1 Corinthians 3.6-9, delivered 5 June 1881, pp. 319-20. For similar emphases, see 'The Ploughman', *MTP*, Vol. 59, S. No. 3383, Isaiah 28.24, n.d., pp. 577-86. Here, as in 'Farm Labourers', Spurgeon was explicit in saying that it was the Holy Spirit who 'ploughed' in people's hearts that they in turn might give themselves to Christian service (here, specifically, evangelistic service). See, e.g., pp. 577, 580-81.

[201] Spurgeon, 'The Blind Man's Eyes Opened; Or, Practical Christianity', p. 674.

experiencing activity as communion – themselves. Spurgeon insisted that Christians had 'fellowship with Christ' as they plunged themselves into active Christian service. How could this be the case? Spurgeon offered some specific examples of how he saw the dynamic working. For instance, all those who struggled to teach the 'ignorant' were, in the midst of their struggles, in communion with Christ. This was so because Christ, in his earthly ministry, had himself taught those who had repeatedly failed to understand him. Similarly, those who sought to restore 'backsliders' were in communion with the good shepherd who had ventured into the wilderness to find the one lost sheep and, having found it, brought it home 'rejoicing'. Spurgeon gave further examples to the small group who had gathered at Mentone. A Christian who had prayed for another 'night and day with tears' had known communion with Christ 'who has borne all our names upon His broken heart, and carries the memorial of them upon His pierced hands'. In short, whenever Christians cooperated with Christ in his 'designs of love' they were in 'true and active communion' with their Lord.[202]

Spurgeon regarded activity in the cause of Christ, then, as a real form of communion with Christ, just as he regarded prayer, reading the scriptures and the Lord's Supper as forms of communion. Even the happiness that was felt when engaging in activity was linked with the overarching theme of communion with Christ. In his Mentone message, Spurgeon spoke of how Jesus' work was his 'joy'.[203] Christians who followed Christ in giving themselves to his work would find that 'kind actions' made them 'happy'. In 'such joy', Spurgeon declared, 'we find communion with the great heart of Jesus'.[204] Overall, then, Jesus was the great worker, and when believers also worked – in obedience to Christ, in imitation of Christ and in the power of Christ – then they would know communion with him. This had been Spurgeon's own experience and, he believed, the experience of many of his hearers.

Conclusion

Although different periods of activity can be traced when the whole of Spurgeon's Christian life is surveyed, activism was fundamental to his spirituality throughout his ministry. This activity was a crucial outworking of his relationship with Christ, springing from a deep dependence on him. The focus of the activity was Christ and his kingdom. Although evangelism was paramount, social action was important too. Through preaching, personal work and the work of the Tabernacle and its

---

[202] C.H. Spurgeon, 'Communion With Christ And His People', 1 Corinthians 10.16-17, 'An Address at a Communion Service at Mentone', in *Till He Come* (London: Passmore and Alabaster, 1896), pp. 316-17. For a similar emphasis, see C.H. Spurgeon, 'Fellowship With God's Greatness', in [Anon.] (ed.), *Sword and Trowel*, October 1893, pp. 549-53; 'With The King For His Work!', pp. 114-15.

[203] With Hebrews 12.2 probably in mind.

[204] Spurgeon, 'Communion With Christ And His People', pp. 316-18.

institutions, a range of different people were reached and helped. Overall, the desire was to 'spend and be spent' in the service of Christ.[205]

As Spurgeon engaged in activity he relied heavily on others. This point could have been made with reference to the Pastors' College,[206] but this chapter has demonstrated this through analysis of the way the Orphanage operated. Due to issues of failing health, but also, and more fundamentally, temperament and gifts, Spurgeon worked closely with others. These were people who shared his basic commitments, were loyal to him personally and whose abilities complemented his own. As he engaged in activity with fellow workers he experienced spiritual friendship – communion – with these helpers. In Spurgeon's thinking, this communion embraced not only his close associates such as his brother and the Tabernacle deacons who were also trustees of the Orphanage, it also included the members of his church and wider constituency who were active supporters of the work at Stockwell. Christian activity was also a means by which communion with 'Jesus the worker' was experienced. If Christians wanted to know Christ more deeply then they had to work for him, in the church and in the wider world. For Spurgeon, there could have been no greater incentive to active Christian service.

---

[205] C.H. Spurgeon, 'A Good Soldier Of Jesus Christ', *MTP*, Vol. 16, S. No. 938, 2 Timothy 2.2,3, delivered 26 June 1870, p. 370; 'With The King For His Work!', p. 114.

[206] See, e.g., Carlile, *C.H. Spurgeon*, pp. 182-83, whose comments are based on his own time as a student of the Pastors' College.

CHAPTER 9

Holiness: 'Oh to be Christly! We do desire to live on earth the life of Jesus ...'

Spurgeon's spirituality was an active spirituality. One of the ways this 'activism' was worked out was in his quest for personal holiness. This chapter examines that quest. After an opening section which highlights the importance of holiness to Spurgeon, the chapter effectively splits into two halves, with two key questions considered. These are, firstly, 'What was Spurgeon's conception of practical holiness?', and, secondly, 'How was this holiness to be achieved?' In answering these two basic questions this chapter seeks to locate Spurgeon's approach to 'sanctification' within the larger context of nineteenth-century teaching on the subject. David Bebbington identifies four main 'traditions of spirituality' that were current in Protestant churches in nineteenth-century England with regard to holiness. These were the 'High Church mentality in the Church of England'; the Wesleyan tradition, which tended to be confined to Methodism; the 'Calvinist' approach, which encompassed both the Established Church and Dissent; and Keswick holiness teaching, which arose in the late-Victorian period and, like the Calvinistic tradition, enjoyed cross-denominational support.[1] Spurgeon engaged with each of these movements. Analysis of his life and ministry will show that his views were largely congruent with Calvinistic teaching (something unsurprising in itself), but with some features that were more particular to him. Overall, 'communion with Christ and his people' is the theme which helps us make sense of Spurgeon's approach to holiness, as it does the other dimensions of his spirituality. As will be seen, Spurgeon's understanding and practice of holiness was resolutely focused on Christ, as well as being a 'holiness of the people'.

The Central Importance of Holiness

Spurgeon never tired of insisting that the pursuit of what he termed 'practical' holiness was essential for the Christian.[2] This was a note he struck at the beginning

---

[1] D.W. Bebbington, *Holiness in Nineteenth-Century England* (Carlisle: Paternoster, 2002), p. 6.

[2] C.H. Spurgeon, 'Our Position And Our Purpose', *New Park Street Pulpit (NPSP) / Metropolitan Tabernacle Pulpit (MTP)* (London: Passmore and Alabaster, 1855–1917), *MTP*, Vol. 57, S. No. 3245, 2 Corinthians 7.1, n.d., pp. 178-79; 'The Sitting Of The Refiner', *MTP*, Vol. 27, S. No. 1575, Malachi 3.3, n.d., pp. 2, 11.

of his ministry³ and maintained right through to the end.⁴ God's grace in Christ did not leave believers 'in sin' having merely saved them from its punishment. Rather, salvation was 'from sin' and divine grace 'disciplined' all true believers to live holy lives.⁵ Sanctified living was not an optional extra. It was essential for every Christian.

It is worth underscoring Spurgeon's own heartfelt passion for holiness, something which is perhaps best done with reference to his public prayers. In one which was prayed at the Tabernacle on 16 August 1863, Spurgeon declared,

> Oh that we could be what we want to be. We are well aware that even our model which we have painted in our own mind, is not a perfect one, for we have not fully understood the perfection of the Lord Jesus, so as to set him before us as our example ... Yet, even to that poor ideal of Christ we never have as yet attained. Oh that we could reach it! Oh that we could become like Christ!⁶

Spurgeon was here leading his whole congregation in prayer, seeking to give voice to their desires as well as his own. But his words were deeply personal, as shown by the evident fervour with which he addressed God. Earlier in the prayer Spurgeon had spoken of the 'earnestness of desire' with which he longed for holiness. The conception of holiness as Christlikeness, which is clearly central to the section of the prayer cited here will be explored in detail later in this chapter. Suffice to say at this point that Spurgeon's desire for progress in personal holiness was deep, and that it was expressed in typically 'heartfelt' language.

Spurgeon was resolute in opposing any who sought to downplay the importance of holy living for Christians. From the beginning of his ministry he had to contend with antinomianism, the assertion that believers are exempt from obeying the moral law. The High Calvinism which was associated in Baptist circles with John Gill

---

³ See, e.g., C.H. Spurgeon, 'Salvation From Sin', 'Notebook Containing Early Sermon Skeletons, Vol. 1', Spurgeon's College, Heritage Room (K1.5), S. No. 33, Matthew 1.21. Cf. *Autobiography: Compiled from his Diary, Letters, and Records by his Wife and his Private Secretary* (4 Vols; London: Passmore and Alabaster, 1897–99), Vol. 1, p. 229-30. According to the *Autobiography*, this was the first sermon Spurgeon preached at Waterbeach.

⁴ See, e.g., C.H. Spurgeon, 'Scriptural Salvation', *MTP*, Vol. 36, S. No. 2145, Romans 10.11, delivered 18 May 1890, p. 285.

⁵ C.H. Spurgeon, 'The Two Appearances And The Discipline Of Grace', *MTP*, Vol. 32, S. No. 1894, Titus 2.11-14, delivered 4 April 1886, pp. 194-95; 204. Cf. M. Hopkins, *Nonconformity's Romantic Generation: Evangelical and Liberal Theologies in Victorian England* (Carlisle: Paternoster, 2004), p. 149.

⁶ C.T. Cook (ed.), *Behold the Throne of Grace: C.H. Spurgeon's Prayers and Hymns* (Marshall, Morgan and Scott: London, [1934]), pp. 39-42. Cf. [Anon.] (ed.), *The Contemporary Pulpit Library: Sermons by the Rev. C.H. Spurgeon* (London: Swan Sonnenschein, 1892), Prayer 6, p. 127, 'O Lord, our God, we have an intense desire to be rid of sin. We long after holiness'.

exhibited tendencies to antinomianism, at least on a popular level.⁷ These tendencies were clearly present at Waterbeach during Spurgeon's time there. In comments recorded in his *Autobiography*, he stated that at Waterbeach he knew a man who had once 'stood on the table of a public-house, and held a glass of gin in his hand, declaring all the while that he was one of the chosen people of God'. Spurgeon noted with approval that the other patrons wasted no time in throwing the man out. The young Spurgeon preached against antinomianism at Waterbeach chapel, saying that 'one of the first evidences that anyone is a child of God is that he ... seeks to live a holy, Christlike life.'⁸ 'Effectual calling', he maintained in one particular pre-London message, was a calling 'to holiness'. Continuing in this vein he exhorted all of his hearers who considered themselves 'Calvinistic Christians' to 'be holy'.⁹

This early opposition to antinomianism was maintained throughout Spurgeon's London ministry. In 1862 he preached a sermon entitled 'Holiness Demanded' from Hebrews 12.14, and the phrase 'holiness, without which no man shall see the Lord'. In the course of this message he ridiculed 'certain Antinomians' who by 'hacking at the text' attempted to argue that the verse in question actually spoke of the 'imputed holiness of Christ'. Rather, the context indicated that the holiness referred to was to be 'followed' and it was, therefore, 'transparent' that this following had to be the 'act and duty' of the believer.¹⁰ The contention that holiness was a 'duty' was an echo of the eighteenth-century pamphlet wars conducted between evangelical Calvinistic Baptists, such as Andrew Fuller, and their High Calvinist opponents. Fuller insisted that active faith in Christ was a 'duty' and also asserted the importance of holy living.¹¹ Spurgeon had read 'Fuller upon Antinomianism' within a year of his conversion and was clearly influenced by the eighteenth-century debates on this subject.¹² Hebrews 12.14, Spurgeon insisted, spoke of 'practical, personal, active,

---

⁷ For antinomianism in Baptist life, see P.J. Morden, *Offering Christ to the World: Andrew Fuller (1754–1815) and the Revival of Eighteenth Century Particular Baptist Life* (Carlisle: Paternoster, 2003), pp. 29, 50. For the wider context, see A.P.F. Sell, *The Great Debate: Calvinism, Arminianism and Salvation* (Worthing: H.E. Walter, 1982), *passim*, but especially pp. 42-54, 79-80.

⁸ Spurgeon, *Autobiography*, Vol. 1, pp. 258-59.

⁹ C.H. Spurgeon, 'Notebooks With Sermon Outlines, Vols 2, 4-9', Spurgeon's College, Heritage Room, (U1), 'Nonconformity', S. No. 223, Romans 12.2.

¹⁰ C.H. Spurgeon, 'Holiness Demanded', *MTP*, Vol. 50, S. No. 2902, Hebrews 12.14, delivered 1862, pp. 457-58. Spurgeon made the identical point from the same text in 'The Winnowing Fan', in C.H. Spurgeon, *Twelve Sermons on Sanctification* (London: Passmore and Alabaster, n.d.), S. No. 940, Hebrews 12.14,15, delivered 10 July 1870, p. 265.

¹¹ For Fuller's 'Antinomianism Contrasted with the Religion of the Holy Scriptures', see A. Fuller, *The Complete Works of the Rev Andrew Fuller, With a Memoir of his Life by the Rev. Andrew Gunton Fuller* (ed. A.G. Fuller; rev. ed. J. Belcher; 3 Vols; Harrisonburg: Sprinkle Publications, 3ʳᵈ edn, 1988 [1845]), Vol. 3, pp. 737-62.

¹² Spurgeon, *Autobiography*, Vol. 1, diary entry for 17 April 1850, p. 131.

vital, holiness', which needed to be actively pursued.[13] Antinomianism, wherever and whenever it surfaced, was to be opposed.

Spurgeon also wanted to reject the 'moralism' which he believed militated against true Christian holiness. Such moralism was associated with Latitudinarian religion which had a tendency to reduce Christianity to an ethical code.[14] In a message included in his book *Farm Sermons*, Spurgeon spoke severely of those who had not experienced personal conversion to Christ and yet were described as 'excellent moral people'. He believed it was impossible for a 'single ear of holiness' to be produced if the 'gospel seed' had not taken root in someone's life.[15] In other words, true conversion was a necessary pre-requisite to true holiness. In 'Holiness Demanded', he spoke in similar vein, insisting that the very best 'morality' could only 'skim the surface'. By contrast, true holiness dealt with 'the thoughts and intents, the purposes, the aims, the objects of men ... holiness goes into the very caverns of the great deep; holiness requires that the heart shall be set on God, and that it shall beat with love to him.' In provocative language he declared that the moralist was no better than a 'well washed corpse'.[16] Holiness and morality (as Spurgeon was defining morality in these sermons) were thus entirely different. If antinomians were guilty of accentuating God's work in salvation in such a way that the Christian's 'duty' to live a sanctified life was rejected, then moralists were guilty of seeking to live 'good' lives without the regenerating and renewing Holy Spirit within them. Both these positions were to be resolutely opposed.

This insistence on the need for personal, practical holiness was thoroughly evangelical. Spurgeon's dual rejection of antinomianism on the one hand and moralism on the other was, as Bebbington notes, especially typical of 'Calvinistic Evangelicals', who had to contend with antinomianism in a way that their Arminian counterparts did not.[17] But the stress on practical, 'experimental' holiness was shared by the whole evangelical movement. Raymond Brown observes that, during the first three decades of the nineteenth century, there were few books of sermons published by evangelicals which did not 'devote some attention to the theme' of holiness.[18] Later in the century, Spurgeon's contemporary, J.C. Ryle, declared in his widely read *Holiness* that sanctification was just as important as justification and that, 'Sound Protestant and Evangelical doctrine is useless if it is not accompanied by a

---

[13] Spurgeon, 'Holiness Demanded', pp. 457-58.

[14] Bebbington, *Holiness in Nineteenth-Century England*, p. 43.

[15] See, e.g., C.H. Spurgeon, *Farm Sermons* (London: Passmore and Alabaster, 1882), pp. 83-84.

[16] Spurgeon, 'Holiness Demanded', p. 459. Cf. C.H. Spurgeon, 'Consecration to God Illustrated by Abraham's Circumcision', *MTP*, Vol. 14, S. No. 845, Genesis 17.1,2, delivered 13 December 1868, p. 685.

[17] D.W. Bebbington, 'Holiness in the Evangelical Tradition', in S.C. Barton (ed.), *Holiness Past and Present* (London: T.&T. Clark, 2003), pp. 302-303.

[18] R. Brown, 'Evangelical Ideas of Perfection: A Comparative Study of the Spirituality of Men and Movements in Nineteenth Century England' (DPhil dissertation, University of Cambridge, 1964), p. 139.

holy life.'[19] Many other examples of this insistence could have been cited from right across the evangelical spectrum.[20] Although they differed among themselves regarding the precise ways holiness was to be both conceived and, especially, attained, there was common agreement on the basic point: holiness was absolutely vital.[21] In continually calling attention to the need for holy living Spurgeon was emphasising a central tenet of evangelicalism.

Spurgeon's Conception of Holiness

Personal holiness, then, was crucial to Spurgeon, but what was his conception of a holy life? To begin with, he wanted to stress the importance of complete consecration to Christ as the vital, foundational dimension of true holiness. In a sermon entitled 'Holiness, The Law Of God's House', Spurgeon stated, 'As Christians we are not our own, but bought with a price, and if we live as if we were our own we defraud our Redeemer.' He then proceeded to ask a series of questions,

> Will a man rob God? Will he rob Jesus of the purchase of his blood? Can we consent that the world, the flesh, the devil should use the vessels which are dedicated to God? ... No, let us feel that we are the Lord's, and that his vows are upon us, binding us to lay ourselves out for him alone.

Put simply, Christians belonged to Christ. Their allegiance was to him and to him alone. This was a high standard to set, but such consecration was, Spurgeon insisted, an 'essential ingredient' of holiness.[22]

As has been established, Spurgeon believed that believers should consecrate themselves to God at the beginning of their Christian lives.[23] Initially he regarded the Puritan-style prayer he had written on 1 February 1850 as his moment of consecration (see chapter 2).[24] But later he came to view his baptism as a believer on 3 May 1850 as the time when he had committed all to Christ (see chapter 4).[25] But

---

[19] J.C. Ryle, *Holiness: Its Nature, Hindrances, Difficulties, and Roots* (London: J. Clarke, 1952 [1877]), p. vii.

[20] For the nineteenth century specifically, see Brown, 'Evangelical Ideas of Perfection', pp. 35-254. For the more general evangelical stress on holiness, see I.M. Randall, *What a Friend We Have in Jesus: The Evangelical Tradition* (London: Darton, Longman and Todd, 2005), pp. 111-128.

[21] Randall, *What a Friend We Have in Jesus*, p. 111.

[22] C.H. Spurgeon, 'Holiness, The Law Of God's House', *MTP*, Vol. 27, S. No. 1618, Ezekiel 43.12, delivered 11 September 1881, p. 514.

[23] This stress is also to the fore in C.H. Spurgeon, 'On Whose Side Are You?', *MTP*, Vol. 26, S. No. 1531, Exodus 32.26, delivered 4 April 1880, p. 211.

[24] Spurgeon, *Autobiography*, Vol. 1, p. 129.

[25] Spurgeon, *Autobiography*, Vol. 1, p. 151-55.

Spurgeon also stressed that such consecration needed to be, firstly, maintained[26] and, secondly, deepened.[27] In a sermon entitled 'Loyal To The Core', he declared that a Christian should be able to say, from the heart and at all times, the lines from Frances Ridley Havergal's hymn, 'Take My Life',

> Take myself and I will be
> Ever, *only*, ALL for thee.[28]

The importance of complete consecration to Christ was a theme to which Spurgeon would return on a regular basis.[29] For him, such 'holy consecration' was the 'very cream of religion' and fundamental to true holiness.[30]

With the foundation of complete consecration in place, the faithful Christian could press forward to live a holy life. The overriding theme of this would be conformity to Christ. A vast array of material could be adduced to support this basic contention, only some of which can be surveyed here.[31] Spurgeon wanted to emphasise that Christians, consecrated as they were to Christ, were Christ's 'servants'.[32] As such, they were under the 'holy discipline of his house' with an obligation to do as their master bid them.[33] Obedience to Christ was, as always,

---

[26] See, e.g., C.H. Spurgeon, 'Consecration Of Our Substance', in C.H. Spurgeon (ed.), *The Sword and The Trowel: A Record of Combat With Sin and Labour For The Lord* (*Sword and Trowel*) (London: Passmore and Alabaster, 1865–92), September 1876, p. 426.

[27] C.H. Spurgeon, 'The Corn Of Wheat Dying To Bring Forth More Fruit', in *Farm Sermons*, p. 82. Spurgeon expressed a desire to 'rise to a condition of consecration more worthy of [the] Lord'.

[28] C.H. Spurgeon, 'Loyal To The Core', *MTP*, Vol. No. 26, S. No. 1512, 2 Samuel 15.21, n.d. (but must be after 1874 when 'Take My Life' was written), p. 8. 'Take my Life' was no. 1181 in the supplement to *Our Own Hymnbook* (London: Passmore and Alabaster, 1900 [1866 without supplement]). The emphases in the quotation from 'Loyal To The Core' are Spurgeon's own. For Havergal, see P. Friesen, 'Frances Ridley Havergal', in T. Larsen (ed.), *Biographical Dictionary of Evangelicals* (Leicester: IVP, 2003), pp. 294-95.

[29] See, e.g., C.H. Spurgeon, 'Our Motto', *MTP*, Vol. 25, S. No. 1484-5, Ephesians 6.7, delivered 20 July 1879, pp. 397-408, especially pp. 398-99; [Anon.] (ed.), *The Pastor in Prayer*, Prayer 8, 21 April 1878, p. 49.

[30] C.H. Spurgeon, 'The Sluggard's Farm', in *Farm Sermons*, p. 19.

[31] For other examples of the emphasis on 'Christlikeness', see, e.g., C.H. Spurgeon, 'Christ Put On', *MTP*, Vol. 36, S. No. 2132, Romans 13.14, delivered 23 February 1890, pp. 121-32; *The Treasury Of David: Containing An Original Exposition Of The Book Of Psalms; A Collection Of Illustrative Extracts From The Whole Range Of Literature; A Series Of Homiletical Hints Upon Almost Every Verse; And Lists Of Writers Upon Each Psalm* (7 Vols; London and Edinburgh: Marshall Brothers, n.d. [London: Passmore and Alabaster, 1869–1885]), Vol. 1, p. 198.

[32] Spurgeon, 'Holiness, The Law Of God's House', p. 514.

[33] C.H. Spurgeon, 'Obeying Christ's Orders', in *The Miracles of Our Lord* (2 Vols; London: Passmore and Alabaster, 1895), Vol. 1, S. No. 2317, John 2.5, delivered 13 July

fundamental to Spurgeon and it was certainly vital to his conception of holiness. Christ's orders had to be obeyed. But as well as being obedient to Christ's will as revealed in the scriptures, Christians were also to reflect on the example and character of Jesus and apply what they discovered to different situations they faced.[34] A Christian was to act as Jesus acted. To help them apply this principle to everyday life, Spurgeon encouraged his hearers to ask themselves questions such as 'What would the Lord have me do?' and 'What would Jesus Christ have done if he were in my circumstances?' if they found themselves in 'perplexing' situations.[35] Holiness was conceived of as conformity to Christ, and this meant obeying Christ's commands and following his example.

Spurgeon was surprisingly confident that he and his hearers could know how Jesus would have responded in the various situations they faced day-by-day. Once gained, this knowledge would, in his view, be the 'solution' for the most complex of ethical dilemmas facing the Victorian Christian.[36] Spurgeon's understanding of how conformity to Christ might operate in practice was not subtle, therefore. The way this conformity was worked out in his own life was shaped by number of factors other than the pure word and example of Jesus. Cultural factors shaped his approach in significant degree. One example of this would be Spurgeon's attitude to theatre-going, as discussed in chapter 2. Nevertheless, it should be clear that the importance of Christlikeness as an ideal was central to Spurgeon's vision of holiness.

Closely related to Spurgeon's stress on holiness as conformity to Christ was his insistence on what he called separation from the world. The theme of separation was dealt with in some detail in 'Holiness, The Law Of God's House'. Spurgeon was quick to point out that separation did not mean 'avoiding men with monkish fanaticism'.[37] Although (and as we have seen) he could encourage busy ministers to go on occasional 'retreats', a sustained attempt to 'get away from the ordinary associations of men' was inimical to true holiness, rather than being 'the noblest form of holy service' as 'Papists' believed.[38] This was of a piece with the rejection of the otherworldliness he saw displayed both in Roman Catholicism and the Oxford Movement. Writing on the Tractarians, Norman Vance contends that they had a tendency to downplay 'everyday human society as the proper sphere of Christian

---

1889, p. 341. Cf. 'The Work Of Grace The Warrant For Obedience', in *The Miracles of Our Lord*, Vol. 1, S. No. 1479, John 5.11, delivered 15 June 1879, p. 345.

[34] C.H. Spurgeon, 'Method And Music, Or The Art Of Holy And Happy Living', in *Twelve Sermons on Holiness* (London: Passmore and Alabaster, n.d.), S. No. 913, Colossians 3.17, delivered 30 January 1870, p. 65.

[35] Spurgeon, 'Holiness, The Law Of God's House', p. 514; 'Method And Music, Or The Art Of Holy And Happy Living', p. 65. Cf. [Anon.] (ed.), *The Pastor in Prayer*, Prayer 2, 2 December 1877, p. 16.

[36] See, e.g., Spurgeon's argument in 'Method And Music, Or The Art of Holy And Happy Living', pp. 65-66.

[37] Spurgeon, 'Holiness, The Law Of God's House', p. 513.

[38] Spurgeon, 'The Friends Of Jesus', pp. 454-55.

activity'.³⁹ Such a tendency was anathema to Spurgeon, who attacked High Church spirituality on just this point. His comments were couched in familiar terms. The concept of separation he saw displayed in Roman Catholicism and in Anglican High Churchmanship was, he averred, simply not Christlike. 'Nobody', he maintained, 'mixed more with sinners than did our Lord.'⁴⁰ Once again, Spurgeon's approach was predicated on the example of Christ. As he reflected on that example he was sure that separation did not mean withdrawal from everyday life.

Christians were, however, to live 'separate' lives in the sense of being distinctive. In a message, 'A Clarion Call To Saints And Sinners', Spurgeon described a Christian who sought to argue, 'If you are in the world you must do as the world does.' Spurgeon's withering response to such an argument was to ridicule such 'unhallowed conformity'. The challenge the preacher then gave to Christians to live differently was, significantly, couched in the language of separation.⁴¹ Spurgeon regularly talked of separation in this way – living differently in the 'world' (which he was here defining negatively as the sinful world).⁴² For example, in 'Holiness, The Law Of God's House', he wanted his hearers to think about whether they were 'different' from those among whom they 'dwelt'.⁴³ Again, his approach was linked with the example of Christ. 'Every action, every word, every movement betokened that he was another man from the sinners whom he sought to bless. So must it be with us.'⁴⁴ *Difference* was therefore crucial to Spurgeon's concept of separation, which can be defined as living a distinctive Christian life amongst, rather than apart from, non-believers.

This was an approach to holiness, viewed as a 'godly life' lived '*in* the world' with no division between the sacred and the secular which, as Gordon Mursell states, had a long and distinguished Reformed pedigree.⁴⁵ Spurgeon believed he was standing in the line of such Reformed thinking and often contrasted his views with alternative, 'Catholic' approaches. This contrast was in evidence as he made it clear that every aspect of daily living was to be brought under the rule of Christ. The question which regularly recurs in his sermons, namely, 'What would Jesus have me

---

³⁹ N. Vance, *The Sinews of the Spirit: The Ideal of Christian Manliness in Victorian Literature and Religious Thought* (Cambridge: Cambridge University Press, 1985), pp. 6, 31.

⁴⁰ Spurgeon, 'Holiness, The Law Of God's House', p. 513.

⁴¹ C.H. Spurgeon, 'A Clarion Call To Saints And Sinners', *MTP*, Vol. 37, S. No. 2225, Micah 2.10, delivered, 2 April 1891, pp. 519-20.

⁴² Spurgeon, 'A Clarion Call To Saints And Sinners', p. 518.

⁴³ Spurgeon, 'Holiness, The Law Of God's House', p. 513. Cf. 'The Friends Of Jesus', pp. 454-55; C.H. Spurgeon, 'Come Ye Out From Among Them', 'Notebooks With Sermon Outlines, Vols 2, 4-9', Vol. 2, S. No. 119, 2. Corinthians 6.17-18.

⁴⁴ Spurgeon, 'Holiness, The Law Of God's House', p. 513.

⁴⁵ See, e.g., G. Mursell, 'Holiness in the English Tradition: From Prayer Book to Puritans', in Barton (ed.), *Holiness Past and Present*, pp. 279-82, especially p. 280.

do about this?' was to be applied to 'everything'.[46] In a message appropriately entitled, 'All The Day Long', Spurgeon declared,

> Beware of serving Christ on Sunday, and Mammon on Monday ... many women, after a fashion, put on the fear of God with their new bonnet. When the Sunday is over, and their best thoughts are put away, they have also put away their best behaviour. We must have a seven days religion, or else none at all ... Some people ... are holy only on holy days, and in holy places ... May we become so truly gracious that to us every day becomes a holy day; our garments, vestments; our meals, sacraments; our houses, temples; our families, churches; our lives, sacrifices; ourselves, kings and priests unto God![47]

Spurgeon thus contrasted his vision of holiness with Roman Catholic and Tractarian approaches. High Church spirituality accentuated the importance of 'holy' days, 'holy' places, vestments and the like, so, in his view, unhelpfully separating 'sacred' from 'secular'. Spurgeon took this High Church language and turned it on its head. Every day and every place was holy, every Englishman's home was, potentially, a 'temple', and everyday work clothes were vestments, entirely appropriate garb for holy living. In this respect, Spurgeon's vision for holiness was a distinctively Protestant one.

As well as being for the whole of life, Spurgeon wanted to emphasise that holiness was for all Christians. Catholic approaches not only divided the sacred from the secular, they were elitist. In 'The Friends Of Jesus' he contended that all 'godly women' were, in reality, 'sisters of mercy', just as all 'Christlike men were of the Society of Jesus'.[48] Spurgeon took particular care to apply the principles of separation and conformity to the lives of ordinary working men and women.

One sermon in which he particularly sought to do this was preached in 1861, and entitled 'A Peal Of Bells'. Spurgeon's text was Zechariah 14.20 which includes the phrase, 'Holiness unto the Lord'. In this message, Spurgeon spoke of how people would sometimes come to him, having been 'stirred' by a sermon, to offer themselves for pastoral ministry or cross-cultural missionary service ('Mr Spurgeon, could I go to China? ... Could I become a minister?'). Many such people, continued Spurgeon, were quite unsuitable for this sort of service given that they 'had very little gift of expression, very little natural genius, and no adaptation for such a work'. His response to such zealous but misguided volunteers was to advise them, in the epigrammatic style which he loved, not to take a 'spiritual office' but instead 'to

---

[46] Spurgeon, 'The Friends Of Jesus', p. 455. Spurgeon was clearly advocating the use of this approach long before Charles Sheldon's *In His Steps* popularised the question 'What would Jesus do?' in North America. This was not until the late 1890s. On Sheldon, see A.E. McGrath, *Christianity's Dangerous Idea: A History From The Sixteenth Century to the Twenty First* (New York: Harper Collins, 2007), pp. 366-67.

[47] C.H. Spurgeon, 'All The Day Long', *MTP*, Vol. 36, S. No. 2150, Proverbs 23.17,18, delivered 22 June 1890, pp. 339-40.

[48] Spurgeon, 'The Friends Of Jesus', p. 454.

spiritualise [their] common office'. In a passage worth quoting at length he assured his hearers,

> Why, the cobbler can consecrate his lapstone while many a minister has desecrated his pulpit. The ploughman can put his hand to the plough in as holy a manner as ever did a minister to the sacramental bread. In dealing with your ribbons and your groceries, in handling your bricks and your jackplanes, you can be as truly priests to God as were those who slew the bullocks and burned them with the holy fire in the days of yore ... We do not so much want great preachers as good upright traders, it is not so much deacons and elders we long for as ... men who are deacons for Christ in common life, and are really elders of the Church in their ordinary conversation. Sirs, Christ did not come into the world to take all fishermen from their nets though he did take some, nor to call all publicans from the receipt of custom though he did call one, he did not come to make every Martha into a Mary though he did bless a Martha and a Mary too. He would have you be housewives still, be sisters of mercy in your own habitations. He would have you be traders, buyers, and sellers, workers and toilers still, for the end of Christianity is not to make preachers, but to make holy men.[49]

Despite the rather unflattering comments with which Spurgeon introduced these remarks, this was an affirming spirituality for the masses who attended the Tabernacle and who read his printed sermons. Spurgeon was careful not to denigrate so-called full-time Christian workers as a class. Of course, God did call some to serve as missionaries and ministers, and their role was vital. But a faithful cobbler who sought to do his work for Christ could be just as 'sanctified' as a pastor, and certainly they knew more of Christ and more of holiness than a minister who 'desecrated his pulpit' through unfaithful preaching. The fact that the ordinary actions of 'common' working life could be holy was fundamental to Spurgeon. Put another way, with regard to holiness, the particular calling was secondary. It was the way that the calling was lived out that was crucial.[50] This was a vision of holiness that was accessible to all. Conformity to Christ was just as much for a cobbler as for a minister; holiness could be worked out anywhere, except, perhaps, in a monastery or convent.

The statement, 'holiness could be worked out anywhere', an accurate reflection of Spurgeon's exposition in 'A Peal Of Bells', does need to be qualified when Spurgeon's overall approach to holiness is considered. As will be clear from chapter 2, there were, in practice, certain places that a Christian should not go, such as the theatre. Granted these were questionable leisure pursuits and not 'trades' but, by extension, they also marked out certain occupations, most obviously that of an actor, as being incompatible with true holiness. Spurgeon was sure that it was impossible to imagine Jesus going to the theatre or acting in a play. That this would have been

---

[49] Spurgeon, 'A Peal Of Bells', p. 413; cf. 'First Things First', p. 558, where Spurgeon is addressing the London Banks' Prayer Union. Spurgeon was clearly using the word 'publican' in 'A Peal Of Bells' in the sense of 'tax collector'.

[50] Cf. C.H. Spurgeon, 'Everyday Religion', *MTP*, Vol. 27, S. Nos 1599-1600, Galatians 2.20, delivered 22 May 1881, pp. 286-87.

Christ's attitude towards the Victorian theatre was not argued, it was merely assumed and stated. It is easy to see how Spurgeon's understanding of what might or might not have been acceptable to Jesus was shaped by his Protestant heritage and by other cultural factors. But, once these necessary caveats have been drawn, it is still right to define Spurgeon's conception of holiness as both a holiness that was focused on the example of Christ and as a holiness 'of the people'. Consecration to Christ led to conformity to Christ which was to be worked out in the midst of everyday life, not by withdrawal from it. Separation was being Christlike in the 'world'.

Spurgeon and the 'Common Man'

Before considering how, for Spurgeon, such practical holiness was to be achieved, his commitment to a holiness of the 'common people' needs to be opened up further. Frequently Spurgeon would state his belief that the path to sanctification was, in fact, *especially fitted* for the 'common man'. In 'The Holy Road', preached in 1886, he painted a picture of the way of holiness as a 'plain way', and as such a way which was eminently 'suitable for [the] common and unlearned'. Whereas some commentators spoke of religion as if it were 'a very difficult thing' only to be understood by the 'cultured few', Spurgeon took the opposite view. To illustrate his basic point, 'The Holy Road' included a story which exalted the simple piety of an 'old farmer', which was from the 'heart' and expressed in 'plain speech', whilst at the same time denigrating the 'learned' definition of faith offered by an Archbishop.[51] Repeatedly, in sermons and books, Spurgeon talked up the piety of ordinary people, those who were 'every-day saints'. Farmers and ploughmen featured often in his stories of those making progress in the life of holiness.[52] As an extension of this theme, his 'John Ploughman' books contained simple homilies self-consciously written for the 'toiling masses' in a 'rustic style'. Spurgeon's stated aim in these popular books was to eschew 'refined taste and dainty words' and instead rely on 'strong proverbial expressions'.[53] If the 'Holy Road' was especially fitted for the common people then Spurgeon's preaching and writing were well suited to encourage them and to guide them along the way.

Spurgeon's approach can be further illuminated by contrast with his pulpit contemporary, Joseph Parker. As already noted in chapter 2, it was Parker with whom Spurgeon especially clashed over the issue of theatre-going. But this was not Spurgeon's only problem with his fellow Dissenter. Parker's style of writing and speaking also came in for sharp criticism. In a review of *Detached Links: Extracts from the Writings and Discourses of Dr Joseph Parker*, which appeared in the

---

[51] C.H. Spurgeon, 'The Holy Road', *MTP*, Vol. 32, S. No. 1912, Isaiah 35.8, delivered 1 August 1886, p. 415.

[52] See, e.g., C.H. Spurgeon, 'The Saint Of The Smithy', in *The Spare Half Hour* (London: Passmore and Alabaster, n.d.), p. 118.

[53] C.H. Spurgeon, *John Ploughman's Talk; Or, Plain Advice for Plain People* (London: Passmore and Alabaster, n.d.), Preface.

Sword and Trowel for May 1873, Spurgeon described the extracts in question as 'more pretentious than profound; more verbose than edifying'. A significant proportion of Spurgeon's criticism was reserved for the compiler of the work, a Rev. Joseph Lucas. But, said Spurgeon, '[T]he very best carver cannot cut good slices from questionable meat ... If a man's style is so very magnificent that he cannot be quoted, it is unfair to attempt the task.' Spurgeon's ideal for such extracts was set out in the same review. They should have something of 'terseness, pith, and force in them'. The Parker volume was singularly lacking in these qualities. It might be 'tastefully bound' (a comment that was probably double-edged), but it certainly did not meet with Spurgeon's approval.[54]

Undoubtedly Spurgeon saw in the 'flamboyant'[55] Parker a taste for high culture which he personally disliked. One of Parker's biographers, W. Adamson, tellingly describes his subject's preaching as being full of 'chaste epigrams' and 'of a high style of literature'. Adamson compared Parker's messages with Spurgeon's sermons, which were constructed on 'the old model' and were 'popular'.[56] The City Temple itself was 'luxuriously decorated', said G. Holden Pike, so that it was difficult to imagine Spurgeon ever feeling at home in it.[57] All this provides additional evidence that Spurgeon championed a spirituality of the common people. In 'The Holy Road' he ridiculed what he regarded as the sham spirituality of much of the élite. Spurgeon's targets were, by turns, 'Papist Priests', 'scholarly critics', 'learned scientists' and anyone or anything that smacked of 'culture'. 'The gospel of the common people is the only gospel', Spurgeon thundered, before adding, 'The most educated must find their wisdom in the cross, or die fools.'[58]

This was of a piece with Spurgeon's general championing of 'the common man', highlighted in an article by David Bebbington. Spurgeon disparaged 'refinement' and 'aesthetic sensibility'[59] and stated, 'I hate the fashions of society ... and if I conceived it best to put my foot through a law of etiquette, I should feel gratified in having to do it. No we are men ...'[60] Spurgeon habitually dealt in language such as the following:

> Better far to give the people masses of unprepared truth in the rough, like pieces of meat from a butcher's block, chopped off anyhow, bone and all, and even dropped down in the sawdust, than ostentatiously and delicately hand them out upon a china

---

[54] Spurgeon (ed.), *Sword and Trowel*, May 1873, p. 234.

[55] The description is David Bebbington's. See his *The Dominance of Evangelicalism: The Age of Spurgeon and Moody* (Leicester: IVP, 2005), p. 220.

[56] W. Adamson, *The Life of the Rev. Joseph Parker, D.D. Pastor, City Temple, London* (Glasgow: Inglis Ker / London: Cassell, 1902), pp. 171-72.

[57] G.H. Pike, *Dr Parker and His Friends* (London: Fisher Unwin, 1904), p. 274.

[58] Spurgeon, 'The Holy Road', p. 415.

[59] D.W. Bebbington, 'Spurgeon and the Common Man', *Baptist Review of Theology* Vol. 5, No. 1 (Spring 1995), p. 66.

[60] C.H. Spurgeon, *Lectures To My Students* (3 Vols; London: Passmore and Alabaster, 1875), Vol. 1, p. 17.

dish a delicious slice of nothing at all, decorated with the parsley of poetry, and flavoured with the sauce of affectation.[61]

The words are startling enough written down. With Spurgeon's talent for mimicry, passages such as this must have been dramatic indeed in their original, oral form. As Bebbington states, it was quite natural that Matthew Arnold, son of the great headmaster of Rugby School and broad churchman, should roundly condemn Spurgeon for his 'pulpit vulgarities', his 'lack of taste' and his 'commonness'.[62] Arnold was far from alone in regarding Spurgeon in this way. The Liberal politician the Earl of Rosebery, who heard Spurgeon in 1873, described him as the 'apostle of the grocers'. George Eliot's comments on the pastor of the Metropolitan Tabernacle were similar. Spurgeon, she said, held to a 'grocer's back-parlour view of Calvinistic Christianity'.[63] Spurgeon himself was completely undeterred by such criticism and was proud to defend the common people. As Bebbington notes, Spurgeon was 'one of the most articulate' voices in the whole of the Victorian period who argued the 'claims of the people against the elite'.[64] Spurgeon's appeal appears to have been especially strong for the 'solid' middle and lower-middle classes and in this respect Rosebery's and Eliot's comments are particularly insightful.[65] These were the people who flocked to the Tabernacle week-by-week.[66] Spurgeon's unabashed, populist championing of the common people included within it an approach to holiness and a vision of conformity to Christ which shopkeepers and tradesmen could feel was especially appropriate for them. Spurgeon's remarkable and sustained appeal to the Victorian middle and lower-middle classes is illuminated by careful consideration of his approach to holiness. To sum up, his conception of holiness was focused on Christ and was very much 'of the people'.

Motivation for Holiness

The question, 'How was holiness to be achieved?' can now be addressed. A believer's motivation for holy living can be considered first. Spurgeon was clear that motivation was important and that if certain interlocking factors were kept in view then they would be a great spur to the passionate, ongoing pursuit of holiness.

---

[61] Spurgeon, *Lectures To My Students*, Vol. 1, p. 77; cf. Bebbington, 'Spurgeon and the Common Man', pp. 66-67.

[62] Bebbington, 'Spurgeon and the Common Man', pp. 63-64. Bebbington is summarising Arnold's arguments.

[63] Both as cited by J. Munson, *The Nonconformists: In Search of a Lost Culture* (London: SPCK, 1991), p. 99.

[64] Bebbington, 'Spurgeon and the Common Man', p. 75.

[65] For the phrase 'solid' middle class, see H. McLeod, *Class and Religion in late Victorian Society* (London: Croom Helm, 1974), p. 147.

[66] Cf. the comments of S.C. Williams, *Religious Belief and Popular Culture in Southwark c.1880–1939* (Oxford: Oxford University Press, 1999), p. 47.

Gratitude to Christ for all he had done was one such important motivation to holiness. In a sermon preached in 1860, entitled 'Election And Holiness', Spurgeon declared that an awareness of all that God had done for the believer in Christ would surely evoke intense feelings of gratitude. These would, in turn, 'nerve a man to piety'. He quoted lines from Isaac Watts' hymn, 'When I Survey the Wondrous Cross', which was, of course, an evangelical standard:

> Love so amazing, so divine,
> Demands my life, my soul, my all.[67]

The focus for gratitude was especially on the atonement. The rich mercy of God set forth in the cross constrained and compelled believers to 'walk in the fear of God' and thus in 'compassion', 'holiness' and 'love'.[68] As Spurgeon put it elsewhere, 'Gratitude leads to holiness.'[69]

Another, related motivation for holiness was simple love for Christ. In a sermon entitled 'The Sitting Of The Refiner' Spurgeon spoke of this in typically mystical vein:

> When the Lord fills his servant full of his love, and makes him to be joyed and overjoyed with the sweet consciousness that he is the Beloved's, and that the Beloved is his, then a holy jealousy burns within the soul, and the heart cries, 'Is there anything that can grieve the Beloved? Let it be slain! ...' Oh that we knew Christ better, and lived more in the light of his countenance, for then we should be purged as with the spirit of burning.[70]

Gratitude is still important here but, whereas in 'Election And Holiness' the stress was on what Christ had done in the past (albeit with continuing effect), in 'The Sitting Of The Refiner' the focus was on Christ's present action, whereby he fills the Christian with his love. It was this present consciousness of Christ's love which called forth the believer's own responsive love and which then created in him or her a renewed passion for holiness. Both what Christ had done and also what he was doing in the life of the Christian were vital incentives to holy living.

The extract from 'The Sitting Of The Refiner' displays Spurgeon's hallmark stress on communion with Christ and, unsurprisingly, this was a further motivating factor for holiness. In fact Spurgeon was explicit in saying this was a primary reason

---

[67] No. 282 in Spurgeon (ed.), *Our Own Hymn Book*.

[68] Spurgeon, 'Election And Holiness', *NPSP*, Vol. 6, S. No. 303, Deuteronomy 10.14,15,16, delivered 11 March 1860, p.140. Spurgeon had a particular focus here on gratitude for a believer's election.

[69] Spurgeon, 'The Hope That Purifies', *MTP*, Vol. 57, S. No. 3235, 1 John 3.3, not dated, p. 53.

[70] Spurgeon, 'The Sitting Of The Refiner', p. 3. Cf. H.F. Colquitt, 'The Soteriology of Charles Haddon Spurgeon Revealed in his Sermons and Controversial Writings' (unpublished PhD dissertation, University of Edinburgh, 1951), p. 242.

for Christians to press on towards greater holiness. Put negatively, he held that communion could not be maintained if a believer was not growing in holiness. This was a prospect that was abhorrent to Spurgeon. He declared that 'works' of holiness 'have much to do with your close communion with God. "How can two walk together except they be agreed?" If ye walk contrary to [God] he will walk contrary to you.' The horrifying prospect of 'walking apart' from God was set before believers so they would be motivated to prioritise personal holiness. But Spurgeon also put his point in a positive way. When there was progress in holy living, then joyous, felt communion would not only be maintained but also strengthened.[71] This was because the relationship between communion with God and holiness was a dynamic one. Spurgeon stated that, 'In proportion as you get near to Jesus, you will hate sin, and you will love him, who bore your sin, and carried it all away, that you might be free from it for ever.'[72] The more communion with God (here conceived of, as it most often was, as communion with Christ) was enjoyed, the more a believer could grow in holiness, and the more growth in holiness there was the more communion could be enjoyed. Thus the dynamic inter-relationship between holy living and communion with Christ can be pictured as an upward spiral: increased levels of holiness led to increased levels of communion which in turn would enable further growth in holiness. For Spurgeon there could be no greater spur to sanctification than this dynamic relationship between practical holiness and communion with Christ.

Holiness and Eschatology

One further motivation to holy living can be considered, namely the expectation of the future, personal return of Christ. This merits a separate section because Spurgeon's views on the second coming of Christ have not, in my view, been analysed with particular clarity before. Consequently, I will give this particular motivation for holiness a more extended treatment. Such a treatment is also warranted by the fact that Spurgeon's millennial views highlight some interesting influences on him, as well as adding to the argument that his motivation for holiness was thoroughly christocentric.

At the beginning of Spurgeon's ministry his eschatology was postmillennial, as shown by a message entitled 'The Power Of The Holy Ghost', which was preached at New Park Street on 2 June 1855. Here he dramatically declared that he was looking expectantly for a new outpouring of the Spirit that would usher in the 'latter day glory' which was Christ's kingdom, urging his people to pray and 'continually labour' for this.[73] But Spurgeon came to adopt premillennial views. In a sermon

---

[71] Spurgeon, 'A Call To Holy Living', p. 16.

[72] C.H. Spurgeon, 'Who Loves Christ Most?', *MTP*, Vol. 50, S. No. 2873, Luke 7.41-43, delivered 3 February 1876, p. 117.

[73] C.H. Spurgeon, 'The Power Of The Holy Ghost', *NPSP*, Vol. 1, S. No. 30, Romans 15.13, delivered 17 June 1855, p. 235.

preached in 1865 he set out his new approach, stating, 'I conceive that the advent will be pre-millennial', before adding the explanatory gloss, '[Christ] will come first; and then will come the millennium as a result of his personal reign on earth.'[74] In a review which was carried in the August 1872 issue of the *Sword and Trowel*, Spurgeon explicitly repudiated postmillennialism, stating, 'We are quite unable to shut our eyes to the teaching of scripture, which we believe to be dead against the post-millennial theory of the advent.'[75] Hopkins, who notes this shift in Spurgeon's thinking, states that the change had taken place 'by 1861', citing a sermon entitled 'The First Resurrection' which was preached on 5 May 1861.[76] But a passage in a message preached on 2 August 1857 (although not published until 1899) is clearly premillennial. In this message, Spurgeon spoke of those who expected to see an era of gradual and ultimately great progress for the gospel before the return of Christ as not having understood 'the prophecies [of scripture]'. Rather, he insisted, 'Jesus will first come'.[77] So Spurgeon's change of view can be dated with more precision.[78] In the two years between the summer of 1855 and the summer of 1857 Spurgeon radically revised his eschatology.[79]

Once established, Spurgeon's commitment to premillennialism continued to the end of his ministry.[80] He did not explicitly endorse any of the different varieties of premillennialism.[81] J.D. Douglas, who knew Spurgeon well, summed up his approach. Douglas stated that Spurgeon held with 'firm conviction' the view that

---

[74] C.H. Spurgeon, 'Justification And Glory', *MTP*, Vol. 11, S. No. 627, Romans 8.30, delivered 30 April 1865, p. 249. Cf. 'Watching For Christ's Coming', p. 159: 'I think the millennium will commence after his coming, not before it.' Spurgeon's premillennial eschatology is also noted by Colquitt, 'The Soteriology of Charles Haddon Spurgeon', pp. 261-62.

[75] Spurgeon (ed.), *Sword and Trowel*, August 1872, p. 385. Spurgeon was reviewing J.R. Wilkins, *The Voice of Inspiration on the Seven Last Things of Prophecy* (London: Hamilton Adams, 1872), a work which was postmillennial.

[76] See C.H. Spurgeon, 'The First Resurrection', *MTP*, Vol. 7, S. No. 391, Revelation 20.4,5,6; 12, p. 346; Hopkins, *Nonconformity's Romantic Generation*, p. 150.

[77] C.H. Spurgeon, '"Jesus Only" – A Communion Meditation', *MTP*, Vol. 45, S. No. 2634, Mark 9.8, delivered 2 August 1857, pp. 373-74. See, especially, p. 374.

[78] Spurgeon, '"Jesus Only" – A Communion Meditation', pp. 373-74. In this message, Spurgeon spoke of those who expected to see an era of great progress for the gospel before the return of Christ as not having understood 'the prophecies [of scripture]'. Rather, 'Jesus will first come'. See, especially, p. 374.

[79] Some comments in the Preface of *MTP*, Vol. 1, indicate that Spurgeon's views were changing in late 1855. See, n.p. [final two pages of Preface].

[80] See, e.g., C.H. Spurgeon, 'The Two Appearances And The Discipline Of Divine Grace', *MTP*, Vol. 32, S. No. 1895, Titus 2.11-14, delivered 4 April 1886, pp. 195-96; 'An Ancient Question Modernised', S. No. 2286, Ezekiel 24.19, delivered 4 May 1890, in *Twelve Sermons on the Second Coming of Christ* (London: Passmore and Alabaster, n.d.), p. 594.

[81] For an exposition of thinking of the two main schools, the 'historicist' and the 'futurist', see Bebbington, *Evangelicalism in Modern Britain*, pp. 85-86.

Christ's personal return would antedate 'the bright millennial day'. But, Douglas continued,

> [Spurgeon] did not ... enter into the details of prophetic enquiry; or take sides either with the Futurists on the one hand or the Historical School of Interpretation on the other. He had no theory with respect to the Book of Revelation; and though [we were] bold enough to think that we had discovered the key that could turn the lock of the Apocalypse, we failed utterly to awaken his interest in the discovery.[82]

So, Spurgeon was firmly premillennial, but he would not commit himself to a particular species of premillennialism, despite being pressed by his friends. Douglas's comment, that Spurgeon eschewed 'the details of prophetic enquiry', is an important one. Spurgeon was scathing about the speculative and, as he saw it, divisive approach to prophecy advocated by some among the Plymouth Brethren. He was particularly opposed to those Brethren (often termed Exclusive) who followed J.N. Darby, seeing in them, as he put it in 1869, 'malignant power'.[83] Five years later, in similarly critical mode, he asked, 'Ye men of Plymouth, why do you stand there looking up into heaven?'[84] The premillennial thinking Spurgeon most admired is represented by men such as Andrew Bonar and Henry Grattan Guinness. These men were, said Spurgeon, 'valiant defenders of the faith' and 'animated by that one blessed hope, "the coming of the Son of man in his glory"'.[85] Bonar and Guinness were both 'historic premillennialists',[86] but this was not the reason that Spurgeon warmed to them. Rather, he was attracted to them because, he said, they avoided speculative 'controversy', concentrating instead on 'spiritual unction' and 'simple words'.[87] A man like Guinness was also committed to practical action. Spurgeon

---

[82] J.D. Douglas, *The Prince of Preachers: A Sketch; A Portraiture; And A Tribute* (London: Morgan and Scott, n.d. [1893]), p. 188.

[83] Spurgeon (ed.), *Sword and Trowel*, June 1869, pp. 265-66.

[84] Spurgeon (ed.), *Sword and Trowel*, May 1874, p. 230; cf. C.H. Spurgeon, *An All-Round Ministry* (London: Passmore and Alabaster, 1900), p. 63. For further examples of Spurgeon's rejection of prophetic speculation, see 'The Ascension And The Second Advent Practically Considered', in *Twelve Sermons on the Second Coming of Christ*, S. No. 1817, Acts 1.10,11, delivered 28 December 1884, pp. 19-20; *Sword and Trowel*, July 1871, p. 332.

[85] Spurgeon (ed.), *Sword and Trowel*, June 1889, p. 288. For further contact between Spurgeon and Guinness, see I.M. Randall, '"Ye men of Plymouth ...": C.H. Spurgeon and the Brethren', unpublished paper, November 2006.

[86] For Bonar, see C. Gribben, 'Andrew Bonar and the Scottish Presbyterian Millennium', in C. Gribben and T.C.F. Stunt (eds), *Prisoners of Hope? Aspects of Evangelical Millennialism in Britain and Ireland 1800–1880* (Carlisle: Paternoster, 2004), pp. 177-202; for Guinness, see Bebbington, *The Dominance of Evangelicalism*, p. 186.

[87] Spurgeon (ed.), *Sword and Trowel*, June 1889, p. 288. Spurgeon had no time for prophetic speculation. See, e.g., *Sword and Trowel*, July 1871, p. 332. By contrast, Spurgeon visited the London headquarters of Guinness's 'Regions Beyond Missionary Union' with some of his students. See I.M. Randall, '"The World is our Parish": Spurgeon's College and World Mission, 1856–1892', in I.M. Randall and A.R. Cross (eds), *Baptists and Mission:*

took students from the Pastors' College to visit Guinness's missionary training centre, the East London Institute (aka Harley College), which was based in Bow. This was an enterprise of which he thoroughly approved.[88] For Spurgeon, premillennialism had to 'animate' people for practical action in the cause of Christ, not lead to divisive and energy-sapping speculation about future events.

Nevertheless, the fact that Spurgeon was premillennial should be clear. The links between nineteenth-century premillennialism and Romanticism are widely accepted. Indeed Bebbington comments that such premillennialism was 'part of the Romantic inflow into Evangelicalism'.[89] The stress on the potentially imminent, personal return of Christ appealed to 'poetic imaginations' with a penchant for the 'awesome' and the 'supernatural'. This Romantic approach was in contrast to that advocated by the enlightened mind steeped in the ideas of cause and effect and (perhaps crucial here) 'gradualness'.[90] Those schooled in such Enlightenment thinking were much more likely to espouse the postmillennial position. Thus, Spurgeon's espousal of premillennialism represented a significant modification of much Puritan[91] and older evangelical[92] millennial thinking, a modification which was linked with Romanticism.

The evidence shows that this Romantic-tinged premillennialism was more important to Spurgeon than has previously been realised. Bebbington contends that Spurgeon 'rarely mentioned this topic'[93] and it is certainly true that premillennialism was not a major theme of Spurgeon's preaching when compared to the cross or the resurrection. Even so, he still dealt with it in a surprising number of messages,[94] as

---

Papers from the Fourth International Conference on Baptist Studies (Milton Keynes: Paternoster, 2007), p. 71.

[88] Randall, '"Ye men of Plymouth ..."'. Grattan Guinness worked closely with his wife, Fanny. The East London Institute was founded in 1872.

[89] Bebbington, *Evangelicalism in Modern Britain*, p. 84, cf. pp. 83, 80-86.

[90] Bebbington, *Evangelicalism in Modern Britain*, p. 84.

[91] For Puritan postmillennialism, see I. Murray, *The Puritan Hope: Revival and the Interpretation of Prophecy* (London: Banner of Truth, 1971). Murray's view that the Puritans were 'postmillennial' has been challenged by C. Gribben, 'The Eschatology of the Puritan Confessions', *Scottish Bulletin of Evangelical Theology* Vol. 20, No. 1 (2002), pp. 51-78, who shows the diversity of Puritan prophetic thinking. Nevertheless, many Puritans, e.g. John Owen, espoused the basic position which would later become known as postmillennial. See Gribben and T.C.F. Stunt in 'Introduction', Gribben and Stunt (eds), *Prisoners of Hope?* pp. 7-8.

[92] Gribben and Stunt, 'Introduction', p. 9; J.A. De Jong, *As the Waters Cover the Sea: Millennial Expectations in the Rise of Anglo-American Missions, 1640–1810* (Kampen: J.H. Kok, 1970). Andrew Fuller, on whom Spurgeon leaned in his rejection of antinomianism, was postmillennial from at least the mid-1790s, having been influenced in this direction by the writings of Jonathan Edwards. See Morden, *Offering Christ to the World*, pp. 122-23, 138.

[93] Bebbington, *The Dominance of Evangelicalism*, p. 182.

[94] In addition to those mentioned elsewhere in this chapter, see C.H. Spurgeon, 'An Awful Premonition', in *Twelve Sermons on the Second Coming of Christ*, S. No. 594, Matthew 26.28, n.d., p. 575; '"He Cometh With Clouds"', in *Twelve Sermons on the Second Coming*

well as being involved in drawing up a post-Downgrade confession of faith which closed with the sentence, 'Our hope is the Personal Pre-millennial Return of the Lord Jesus is glory.'[95] Iain Murray plays down Spurgeon's commitment to premillennial teaching, stating that his subject 'never accepted the most common feature of nineteenth-century pre-millennialism, namely, that in point of time the advent and millennium were at hand'.[96] Murray is right that Spurgeon did not dogmatically state that the parousia was definitely 'at hand', but he certainly believed that Christ could return to begin his personal, earthly reign at any moment. In 'All The Day Long' he warned his hearers, in the vivid language characteristic of many of the premillennial utterances of this period, that before 'the word can travel from my lip to your ear Jesus may be here'. Dramatically, he continued, 'While you are in business, or on your bed, or in the field, the flaming heavens may proclaim his advent.'[97] Presiding at a communion service Spurgeon declared that 'he knew of no reason' why Christ should not come 'tonight'; indeed, he would not be 'surprised' if this were to happen.[98] Undoubtedly Spurgeon believed that Christ's personal return was potentially imminent. Spurgeon's commitment to premillennialism was stronger and more important to him than has previously been supposed. On one occasion he even said, 'I believe that our relationship to the Second Advent of Christ may be used as a thermometer with which to tell the degree of our spiritual heat.' The person who had 'burning' desires to see Christ's return could be assured that they were in a healthy spiritual state, but a person who had no such desires was most likely 'lukewarm'.[99] An expectant, deeply felt, premillennial hope was an important indicator of a lively spirituality.

One of the ways premillennialism specifically shaped Spurgeon's spirituality was by helping to mould his approach to holiness. In a message preached in 1886, entitled 'The Two Appearances And The Discipline Of Divine Grace', Spurgeon spoke about the relationship between the second advent and holiness. He began by stating that he and his hearers lived between the 'two appearings' of Christ. The first of these 'appearings' was the incarnation, the second the parousia. These twin truths taken together were, according to Spurgeon, 'the very best argument for a holy life'. Characteristically, his reflections on Christ's 'first appearing' focused almost

---

of Christ, S. No. 1989, Revelation 1.7, n.d., pp. 595-96; 'The Form Of Godliness Without The Power', *MTP*, Vol. 35, S. No. 2088, 2 Timothy 3:5, delivered 2 June 1889, p. 301; 'A call to communion – 1', in T.P. Crosby (ed.), *C.H. Spurgeon's Sermons Beyond Volume 63: An authentic supplement to the Metropolitan Tabernacle Pulpit* (Leominster: Day One, 2009), Song of Songs 8.13-14, n.d., p. 384.

[95] See '"Mr Spurgeon's Confession of Faith"', in Spurgeon (ed.), *Sword and Trowel*, August 1891, pp. 446-48.

[96] Murray, *The Puritan Hope*, pp. 259-60.

[97] Spurgeon, 'All The Day Long', p. 344.

[98] Spurgeon, 'An Ancient Question Modernised', p. 594.

[99] C.H. Spurgeon, 'Come My Beloved!', in *The Most Holy Place: Sermons on the Song of Solomon* (London: Passmore and Alabaster, 1896), S. No. 2360, Song of Songs 8.14, delivered 4 March 1888, pp. 559-60.

exclusively on the cross: the reason God became incarnate was to redeem his people through the atonement.[100] But Spurgeon wanted to look to the future as well. If, he declared, there 'blazes' before you 'the supernatural splendour of the second advent, and behind you burns the everlasting light of the Redeemer's first appearing, what manner of people ought ye to be?'[101] Both the backward look and the forward look would encourage the faithful believer to live a holy life in the present. As far as the second of these two appearings was concerned, in another message, 'Watching For Christ's Coming', Spurgeon suggested a variation on his well-worn maxim, 'What would Jesus do?' In addition to this, another question could be asked, namely, 'What would Jesus think of me if he were to come?'[102] Spurgeon was sure that if Christians reflected on this latter question more regularly then such reflection would lead to greater progress in holiness.

In a message, 'Preparation For The Coming Of The Lord', Spurgeon further urged Christians to think about the potential imminence of the second advent. The date of Christ's coming was 'concealed', but Christians were still to 'watch' and be 'ready'. Such readiness took the form of active holy living. Spurgeon continued,

> Should a Christian man go into worldly assemblies and amusements? Would he not be ashamed should his Lord come and find him among the enemies of the cross? ... Oh, that we may abide in [Christ] and never be in such a state that his coming would be unwelcome to us! Beloved, so live from day to day in duty and in devotion, that your Lord's coming would be timely. Go about your daily business and abide in him, and then his coming will be a glorious delight to you.[103]

This was how the question 'What would Jesus think of me if he were to come?' worked in practice as a spur to holiness. Keeping the personal return of Christ in view was an encouragement to holy living in the present.

In summary, Spurgeon's premillennial eschatology rejected prophetic speculation and was strongly focused on Christ and on practical Christian living. Indeed, his premillennialism acted as a significant motivator to holiness. This eschatology was shaped in part by Romanticism, and the adoption of this approach was a departure from Puritan thinking which, although not uniform, tended to be postmillennial. Consequently, Spurgeon, influenced as he was by nineteenth-century millennial thinking, cannot be defined simply as a latter-day Puritan, however much we can say (and should say) that he was influenced by 'Puritanism'. The eschatology of many

---

[100] Spurgeon, 'The Two Appearances And The Discipline Of Divine Grace', e.g., pp. 191-92.

[101] Spurgeon, 'The Two Appearances And The Discipline Of Divine Grace', pp. 196-97.

[102] C.H. Spurgeon, 'Watching For Christ's Coming', in *Twelve Sermons on the Second Coming of Christ*, S. No. 2302, Luke 12.37,38, delivered 7 April 1889, p. 162. The question, 'What would Jesus do?' was written up in the Stockwell Orphanage school-room, something Spurgeon noted with approval. It was, he said, 'a splendid motto' for the whole of life.

[103] C.H. Spurgeon, 'Preparation For The Coming Of The Lord', in *Twelve Sermons on the Second Coming of Christ*, S. No. 2105, 1 John 2.28, delivered 22 September 1889, p. 516.

eighteenth-century evangelicals was also often postmillennial, but Spurgeon did not choose to follow them in this area. Spurgeon's approach to holiness was shaped, as was his approach to other dimensions of his spirituality, by a number of different forces, including those that were rooted in the nineteenth century.

It is not difficult, however, to find a common thread which links together the four motivations to holiness which have been surveyed in this and the previous section. That thread is Christ himself. The themes of gratitude, love and communion were all focused on Christ: gratitude was for the past work of Christ, love was a response to the present work of Christ, and communion with Christ was needed for ongoing progress in sanctification. Finally, the potentially imminent personal return of Christ was also a spur to holy living. As far as motivation to holiness was concerned, Spurgeon's approach was to focus resolutely on Christ.

God's Work in Progressive Sanctification

As we continue to explore how, for Spurgeon, practical holiness might be achieved, it is important to stress that he put great weight on the importance of God's work in believers' lives. Jesus Christ was not only the motive for believers to live a holy life, he also gave what Spurgeon called 'constraining power' so that this life was possible.[104] It is true that God the Holy Spirit was 'the immediate agent'[105] of a believer's sanctification, but Spurgeon thought of the Spirit and the Son, as H.F. Colquitt observes, as 'equal co-workers' in this process.[106] In preaching, Spurgeon used an illustration of someone having a bath. The Christian was the one who needed to be washed, the bath water was the 'blood of Christ' and the one who did the washing was the Holy Spirit. Spurgeon was unashamed and unrepentant about speaking of Christ's blood in such a way, indeed he gloried in such imagery despite (or perhaps in part because of) the fact that many nineteenth-century liberal commentators would have found it distasteful. For Spurgeon, washing with Christ's blood was quite simply the only way a believer could be sanctified. The Spirit applied the work of Christ on the cross effectually to the believer, and so both Spirit and Son could rightly be spoken of as sanctifiers.[107] 'The more the blood [of Christ] is applied', Spurgeon declared in another message, 'the more we shall become sanctified in spirit, soul and body by the power of the Holy Ghost.'[108]

These emphases were brought together in a sermon Spurgeon preached in 1883, from Colossians 1.27, which was a sustained reflection on Paul's phrase 'Christ in you'. Christ was 'in' Christians in the sense that he was possessing, reigning and filling them. Indeed, Spurgeon asserted that believers were transfigured until they

---

[104] Spurgeon, 'Christ Put On', p. 123.

[105] Spurgeon, 'The Sitting Of The Refiner', p. 4.

[106] Colquitt, 'The Soteriology of Charles Haddon Spurgeon', p. 243.

[107] C.H. Spurgeon, 'Threefold Sanctification', *MTP*, Vol. 8, S. No. 434-35, Jude 1; 1 Corinthians 1.2; 1 Peter 1.2, delivered 9 February 1862, pp. 92-93.

[108] C.H. Spurgeon, 'The Saviour's Precious Blood', *MTP*, Vol. 60, S. No. 3395, 1 Peter 1.19, n.d., p. 102.

became 'like Christ himself'. This 'transfiguration' culminated in the perfection of heaven, but was progressive and could be experienced 'by degrees' as Christ occupied the whole soul. 'Christ in you' was nothing less than 'the sweetness of true godliness'.[109] In the 'Sitting Of The Refiner' Spurgeon described this process in the mystical language he regularly employed. 'Jesus reigns in the work of sanctification', Spurgeon declared, before describing his 'refining' work as a 'fire process, mysterious, inward, penetrating, consuming, transforming'.[110] Spurgeon spoke of sanctification as the will of the Father, performed by the Son and 'applied', progressively, by the Spirit, and so his understanding was trinitarian. But the particular focus on Christ was unmistakable and the extent to which Spurgeon pursued this marked him out from a contemporary who otherwise broadly shared his approach to holiness.

J.C. Ryle published his *Holiness* in 1877, largely to counter Keswick teaching.[111] Spurgeon's own response to Keswick will be considered later in this chapter, but we can note now that Ryle and Spurgeon's concerns about the movement were essentially the same and that there was much common ground between the two men regarding holiness more generally. Yet one difference between the two staunchly Calvinistic evangelical leaders can be seen with regard to their respective use of the phrase 'Christ in us'. Ryle was extremely cautious about using such language, a caution which was certainly heightened by the use of it on Keswick and proto-Keswick platforms. He asked the question, 'Is it wise to use the language which is often used in the present day about the doctrine of "*Christ in us*"?' His conclusion was that this 'doctrine' was often elevated to a position which it did 'not occupy in Scripture'. Ryle certainly did believe that Christ was, in a very real sense, 'in' the believer. This was something, he said, that 'no careful reader of the New Testament' could deny. Certainly, Christ dwelt in a believer's heart by faith, but what Ryle wanted to stress was that this 'inward' work was carried on by the Spirit. Christ was '*specially*' [sic] at God's right hand. Sanctification, Ryle insisted, was 'the special work' of the Holy Spirit. He was clearly uncomfortable about those who spoke, in his view too loosely, of 'some mysterious indwelling of Christ in a believer'.[112]

By contrast, Spurgeon was much less guarded when speaking of the indwelling Christ. In his message, 'Christ In You', preached in 1883, there is a passage, covering almost three pages of the *Metropolitan Tabernacle Pulpit*, in which he dealt with what he termed 'the sweetness of this mystery which is Christ in you'. In the course of these pages the following statement occurs. Spurgeon declared that, 'Christ in heaven, Christ free to poor sinners is precious, but Christ here in the heart is most precious of all.' He continued by insisting that 'Christ in your heart' was the

---

[109] C.H. Spurgeon, 'Christ in You', *MTP*, Vol. 29, S. No. 1720, Colossians 1.27, delivered 13 May 1883, pp. 273-74.

[110] Spurgeon, 'The Sitting Of The Refiner', pp. 7, 9.

[111] That Ryle wrote *Holiness* to counter Keswick teaching is shown particularly clearly by pp. x-xi of his 'Introduction'.

[112] Ryle, *Holiness*, p. xiii.

'cream of the matter, the honey of the honeycomb'. It was entirely appropriate for a Christian to speak of possessing Christ, being filled by Christ, and experiencing Christ 'in all his power'. In this sustained reflection on Paul's phrase, 'Christ in you', Spurgeon was clear that, amongst other things, this was the way a believer grew in holiness. Only once over the three pages in question was the Holy Spirit mentioned, when Spurgeon stated that a believer was to take Christ into their 'inmost soul by the Holy Spirit'. But far more representative of his preaching here were words such as these, 'Get Christ in you, curing your sin, Christ in you filling your soul with love to virtue and holiness, bathing your heart in comfort, and firing it with heavenly aspirations.' Here it was *Christ* who 'filled the soul' and 'bathed the heart'.[113]

It is hard to believe that Ryle would have been comfortable with such language, the isolated statement regarding the Holy Spirit notwithstanding. The date of Spurgeon's preaching – 1883, that is, eight years after the inception of Keswick – is significant. Even against the background of Keswick teaching, Spurgeon's desire to speak of the indwelling Christ was overriding. Theologically, Spurgeon would have admitted that Christ indwelt a believer by the Spirit, but as he preached his desire to focus on Christ effectively took over. Probably the fact that Ryle had written specifically for publication, whilst Spurgeon's words were originally preached, had a bearing on these differences. But that there was a difference between the two men should be clear.

The point to underline before moving on is that holiness was, for Spurgeon, fundamentally a work of God. Without God's action growth in holiness could not be achieved. Consequently, it was incumbent on believers to pray in order that they might grow in holiness. To cite just one reference, in 'The Hope That Purifies' Spurgeon encouraged believers to pray that God would give them 'tender consciences' which were 'sensitive to the very approach of sin'.[114] Spurgeon's impassioned public prayers for holiness have already been noted. One of these, from 9 June 1878, helps make the point. Spurgeon prayed, 'O Lord Jesus, deepen in us our knowledge of Thee. Thou hast made the first lines of Thy likeness upon our character; go on with this work of sacred art till we shall be like Thee in all respects.' A few lines later he said, 'Plough deep in us, great Lord, and let the roots of thy grace strike into the roots of our being ... Holiness of life we crave after. Grant that our speech, our thoughts, our actions, may all be holiness.'[115] Bringing about

---

[113] Spurgeon, 'Christ in You', pp. 272-74. For the sake of balance, it should be noted that on another occasion Spurgeon could say that 'real sanctification is entirely from first to last the work of the Spirit of the blessed God'. See C.H. Spurgeon, 'Our Lord's Prayer For His People's Sanctification', *MTP*, Vol. 32, S. No. 1890, John 17.17, delivered 7 March 1886, p. 153. Cf. Colquitt, 'Soteriology of C.H. Spurgeon', p. 244, who cites this statement, although his page reference is incorrect.

[114] Spurgeon, 'The Hope That Purifies', p. 57.

[115] [Anon.] (ed.), *The Pastor in Prayer: Being a Selection of C.H. Spurgeon's Sunday Morning Prayers* (London: Elliot Stock, 1893), Prayer 11, 9 June 1878, p. 67. Regarding the second of these two quotations, it is not clear whether Spurgeon was addressing the Father or, as he certainly was in the first quotation, Christ.

practical holiness in a believer's life was God's work. Spurgeon conceived of that work in trinitarian terms, but there was a particular christological focus.

The Believer's Struggle for Holiness

Alongside this emphasis on holiness as God's work, there was a complementary stress on believers actively cooperating in the work of sanctification, and this not only through prayer. This point was fundamental to Spurgeon's answer to the question, 'How was this holiness to be achieved?' Believers were actively involved in the pursuit of holiness. Colquitt's discussion of Spurgeon's approach to holiness is unbalanced in that it fails to give sufficient weight to this dimension of his thought.[116] But it was crucial to him. Spurgeon asserted that, 'The Christian man, while he is acted upon by divine influence, and is cleansed by the Holy Spirit, is also an active agent of his own sanctification.'[117] Christian believers were 'responsible beings' and as such had to purge themselves and live holy lives. 'Depend upon it', Spurgeon declared, 'you and I do not grow holy by going to sleep. People are not made to grow in grace as the plants grow, of which it is said, "They grow and ye know not how."' Rather, the Christian should be 'actively seeking growth', 'earnestly' and 'resolutely' striving after holiness. These comments illuminate Spurgeon's basic approach. Rather than being passive, believers were to strive vigorously after holiness.[118] The image of 'growth' is also instructive. Although Spurgeon deployed this, in part, negatively (the plant does not 'know' how it grows, unlike the believer who is consciously involved), the basic idea of growth in holiness was nevertheless affirmed, implying a step-by-step process over an extended period of time. Holiness, then, was to be achieved, from the believer's point of view, through effort. Furthermore, this pursuit of ever greater levels of holiness would be a lifelong quest.[119]

How did Spurgeon marry these two emphases, of holiness being God's work but also something the believer should earnestly strive for? The message from which the quotations in the previous paragraph were taken was entitled 'Our Position And Purpose', unfortunately undated. Spurgeon's text was 2 Corinthians 7.1, which contains the phrase 'let us cleanse ourselves'. The sermon provides a fine summary of Spurgeon's overall approach and is worth an extended treatment. Spurgeon began by referring to the 'glorious privileges' Christians enjoyed. These included 'divine communion', but also 'divine covenanting' and 'divine indwelling'. As to covenanting, Spurgeon declared, in language redolent of the Puritans, that God had

---

[116] Colquitt, 'The Soteriology of C.H. Spurgeon', pp. 239-45.

[117] All quotations in this and the following two paragraphs are, unless otherwise stated, taken from C.H. Spurgeon, 'Our Position And Our Purpose', *MTP*, Vol. 57, S. No. 3245, 2 Corinthians 7.1, n.d., pp. 172-78.

[118] Cf. Spurgeon, 'The Work Of Grace The Warrant For Obedience', p. 346.

[119] For further exposition of what, for Spurgeon, were recurring themes see, e.g., C.H. Spurgeon, 'The Winnowing Fan', *Twelve Sermons on Sanctification*, S. No. 940, Hebrews 12.14,15, delivered 10 July 1870, pp. 265-68.

entered 'covenant relations' with his people, binding himself to them. In turn they now belonged to him 'by the purchase of his Son' and because of the 'effectual conquest' of his grace. As far as indwelling was concerned, Spurgeon was at pains to assure his vast Tabernacle congregation that this really was a privilege they themselves presently enjoyed. Speaking to those who had trusted Jesus, Spurgeon declared, with evangelical certainty, that God 'resided' within them. Christ indwelt all of his people by the Holy Spirit, working holiness in each of their lives.[120]

Crucially, though, the indwelling Spirit made a Christian 'active' in his or her own sanctification; indeed, such activity was described as a believer's personal 'duty'. God 'works it in; you work it out; you have to work out in the outward life what he works in the inner springs of your spiritual being.' This 'working out' would involve the Christian in strenuous effort, indeed Spurgeon proceeded to augment the language of 'striving' and 'activity' with that of conflict and battle. Negatively, Christians had to 'fight' against the 'old nature', driving out sin 'as the Canaanites were driven out of Canaan by the edge of the sword'. The fight would be ongoing, for Jericho's walls did not fall 'without being compassed about seven days'. Nevertheless, the believer's aim in the battle should be to 'conquer', allowing no 'idols' to remain. The battles the Israelites had fought to clear Canaan of idol worship became an allegory of the believer's fight against indwelling sin. Some Christians, Spurgeon believed, had come to tolerate a certain level of sin in their lives effectively giving themselves a 'sort of spiritual indulgence, such as used to be issued by Rome'. Unsurprisingly, this was unacceptable to Spurgeon. In the imagery of his sermon, the Christian's aim was to take full possession of the land.[121]

Positively, Christians were to pursue 'perfecting holiness'. In line with Spurgeon's teaching elsewhere, the Christian's 'model' for perfection in this sermon was none other than 'the perfect Saviour'. Changing his imagery, he urged his hearers to press forward towards this goal (i.e., the imitation of Christ), adding, 'and God speed you in the race!'[122] Spurgeon did not develop the positive side of holiness in this message. Probably he felt he was running out of time and appears to have been unwell.[123] But elsewhere he dealt with this theme at length. In 'Christ Put On', his text was Romans 8.14 with its injunction, 'Put ye on the Lord Jesus Christ.'[124] Christians, declared Spurgeon, were to 'keep putting on Christ', that is, they were to wear 'more and more' of the 'character' of Christ as 'the dress of [their] lives'. As he proceeded with his message, he turned to Colossians 3.12 to describe what he called the believer's 'wardrobe', so that they might all see 'the articles' in their 'outfit'. This imagery might appear a little foppish for Spurgeon, but as he developed it he did so in a way that was congruent with his aforementioned stress on the 'common

---

[120] Spurgeon, 'Our Position And Our Purpose', pp. 172-78.

[121] Spurgeon, 'Our Position And Our Purpose', pp. 172-78.

[122] Spurgeon, 'Our Position And Our Purpose', p. 178.

[123] Spurgeon, 'Our Position And Our Purpose', p. 178, 'I cannot speak to you as I would wish tonight ...'.

[124] All further quotations in this paragraph are from Spurgeon, 'Christ Put On', pp. 599-610. See especially pp. 605-607.

man'. Nothing was to be left in the window 'to be stared at', for in 'true religion' everything was 'designed for practical use'. When describing the qualities of 'humbleness of mind' and 'meekness' he declared that those 'choice garments' were not as 'esteemed' as they ought to be. Sadly, it was the cloth 'Proud-of-heart' that was very fashionable, whilst the 'trimmings of Mr Masterful' were much sought after. For Spurgeon, the 'footman' (clothed with the 'practical', though wonderful, garment of Christlike 'humility') was better dressed than the 'master' (who wore the 'fashionable' cloth of 'pride'). As Spurgeon warmed to his theme he stated,

> I have read of a great man, that he took two hours and a half to dress himself every morning. In this he showed rather littleness than greatness; but if any of you put on the Lord Jesus Christ you may take what time you will in making such a toilet. It will take you all your lives, my brothers and sisters, fully to put on the Lord Jesus Christ, and to keep him on.

Spurgeon's description of the spiritual wardrobe was less Beau Brummel and far more appropriate to his own cultural preferences and those of most of his hearers and readers. Although he was conscious he was speaking to a mixed audience the imagery was properly 'manly' and appropriate for those artisans and middle-class traders who had no desire, time or money for the leisured lifestyle of the mannered Victorian dandy. In the course of his lengthy description of the Christian's wardrobe, Spurgeon even managed to bring in his favourite battle theme when he slipped in a reference to Ephesians 6.11 and putting on the 'whole armour of God'.[125] Crucially for us, the need for effort on behalf of the believer (as shown by the constant repetition of the imperative 'put on', which the preacher employed to great rhetorical effect) and of holiness as a lifelong pursuit (as Spurgeon stated, 'it will take you all your lives'), were, once again, to the fore. Holiness was God's work, but this had to be practically appropriated by the believer through a lifetime's 'putting off' sin and 'putting on' Christ.

Spurgeon and Nineteenth-Century Teaching on Holiness

We have already examined Spurgeon's attitude to one of the 'traditions of spirituality' identified by Bebbington, namely the 'High Church mentality in the Church of England'[126] (which has been considered alongside Roman Catholicism). Spurgeon's positive comments about 'perfecting holiness', which came in his message 'Our Position And Our Purpose', raise the question of his attitude to another of the movements of holiness mentioned by Bebbington. This is the Wesleyan holiness tradition with its claims to 'sinless perfection'. John Wesley actually rejected the term 'sinless perfection' and his teaching on sanctification is notoriously difficult to pin down, partly because he modified his early views in

---

[125] Spurgeon, 'Christ Put On', pp. 605-606, and cf. p. 608.
[126] Bebbington, *Holiness in Nineteenth-Century England*, p. 6.

several significant respects.[127] Wesley tended to focus on 'perfect love', understood as 'the humble, gentle, patient love of God, and our neighbour'.[128] This state of 'entire sanctification' was obtained by faith, although the ultimate state of 'perfection' was often only reached after a protracted and 'agonised wrestling' *en route* to the goal.[129] There were important differences between Wesley's own views and Wesleyan holiness teaching as it came to develop as the nineteenth century wore on.[130] For example, there was a tendency amongst some nineteenth-century Methodist teachers to downplay Wesley's emphasis that gradual progress towards perfection was the norm and instead 'preach up' the possibility of receiving sanctification instantly.[131] Later in the century other groups, particularly William Booth's Salvation Army, also propounded species of Wesleyan holiness teaching.[132]

Spurgeon's response was to reject all forms of 'perfectionism', although he reserved his strongest criticisms for the nineteenth-century variants of Wesley's views. Regarding the founder of Methodism himself, Spurgeon stated, 'I do not agree with Mr Wesley's opinion about perfection. It is very difficult to see how he could have done more than he did, but I do not doubt that even *he* felt that he might have been more like his Lord.'[133] More generally, in the course of 'Our Position And Our Purpose' Spurgeon asked the question, 'Can a Christian be perfect in this life?', before answering, 'No'. Perfection would come, but only at the 'resurrection of the just'.[134] Christians should certainly aim at perfection,[135] but they should be fully aware that in this life they would not attain it.[136] This did not mean that believers might not conquer 'the grosser shapes of sin'. But the day when there would no

---

[127] See H.B. McGonigle, *Sufficient Saving Grace: John Wesley's Evangelical Arminianism* (Carlisle: Paternoster, 2001), pp. 241-64; H.D. Rack, *Reasonable Enthusiast: John Wesley and the Rise of Methodism* (London: Epworth, 1989), p. 396; A. Skevington Wood, *The Burning Heart: John Wesley, Evangelist* (Sheffield: Cliff College Publishing, 2001 [1967]), pp. 268-69.

[128] J. Wesley, 'Brief Thoughts on Christian Perfection', in *The Works of the Rev John Wesley*, Vol. 11 (London, 1872), p. 446, as cited by I.M. Randall, *Evangelical Experiences: A Study in the Spirituality of English Evangelicalism 1918–1939* (Carlisle: Paternoster, 1999), p. 76. Cf. J. Wesley, 'Christian Perfection', S. No. 35, Philippians 3.12, in J. Wesley, *Sermons on Several Occasions* (London: Epworth, 1944 [1746–60]), 457-80.

[129] Bebbington, *Holiness in Nineteenth-Century England*, pp. 62, 65.

[130] See Brown, 'Evangelical Ideas of Perfection', pp. 37-55, 393-400; Bebbington, *Holiness in Nineteenth-Century England*, pp. 65-72.

[131] Brown, 'Evangelical Ideas of Perfection', pp. 42-43; Bebbington, *Holiness in Nineteenth-Century England*, pp. 65-66.

[132] Brown, 'Evangelical Ideas of Perfection', pp. 393-95.

[133] C.H. Spurgeon, 'A Sharp Knife For The Vine Branches', *MTP*, Vol. 13, S. No. 774, John 15.2, delivered 6 October 1867, p. 561.

[134] Spurgeon, 'Our Position And Our Purpose', p. 176. Cf. Colquitt, 'The Soteriology of C.H. Spurgeon', p. 246.

[135] E.g., C.H. Spurgeon, 'The Work Of Grace The Warrant For Obedience', *MTP*, Vol. 25, S. Nos. 1479-80, John 5.11, delivered 15 June 1879, p. 346.

[136] Spurgeon, *Farm Sermons*, pp. 301-302, 305.

Canaanites 'left in the land' (i.e., sinless perfection) would not arrive before 'the perfect joy of heaven'.[137] Spurgeon's own experience, congruent with all of his teaching on the subject, was of 'a daily struggle with the evil within'.[138] He delighted to tell stories of people who came to him claiming sinless perfection, only for them to become, in conversation with him, so angry that their claims were thoroughly disproved.[139] Spurgeon had a high regard for Wesley's own level of holiness,[140] but he could also be extremely blunt about those he called 'pretenders to perfection' in his own day.[141] To him such claims were arrogant nonsense.

Spurgeon's response to Keswick 'higher life' teaching, the final nineteenth-century movement of holiness noted by Bebbington, can also be examined. Keswick shared certain characteristics with nineteenth-century Wesleyan holiness teaching, but it nevertheless qualifies as a distinct strand of spirituality within evangelicalism. The first convention at Keswick, in the English Lake District, did not take place until the summer of 1875,[142] but the 'tradition' itself 'originated in the years around 1870'.[143] Key figures in this emerging movement were two American Quakers, Hannah Whitall Smith and Robert Pearsall Smith. Keswick teaching, according to Ian Randall, 'denied traditional Wesleyan convictions that Christians could experience entire sanctification'. Rather it tended to teach that 'sin was not eradicated but "perpetually counteracted"' through 'entry into "the rest of faith"'. A Christian could move on, if not to sinless perfection, then certainly to a 'higher Christian life' through a crisis experience. Contrary to the Calvinist tradition, resting faith rather than active works was the path to holiness.[144] Keswick teaching on holiness came to occupy a prominent place in the late-nineteenth century English evangelical landscape.[145]

---

[137] C.H. Spurgeon, 'Sin Subdued', *MTP*, Vol. 27, S. No. 1577, Micah 7.19, n.d., p. 35; Spurgeon, *Farm Sermons*, p. 305.

[138] Spurgeon, *Autobiography*, Vol. 1, p. 263.

[139] See, e.g., Spurgeon, 'Our Position And Our Purpose', p. 176; *Autobiography*, Vol. 1, pp. 262-63.

[140] Cf. Spurgeon (ed.), *Sword and Trowel*, September 1876, pp. 430-32, and the positive, and unusually lengthy, review of *Holiness Unto the Lord* by 'Miss Bosanquet', the wife of the eighteenth-century Methodist John Fletcher of Madeley. Fletcher himself is described as 'that holy man'.

[141] Spurgeon, *Autobiography*, Vol. 1, p. 263.

[142] From 29 June to 1 July. C. Price and I.M. Randall, *Transforming Keswick* (Carlisle: Paternoster, 2000), pp. 29-31.

[143] Bebbington, *Holiness in Nineteenth-Century England*, p. 74. Arguably, the origins of the tradition can be traced further back to the publication of W.E. Boardman's *Higher Christian Life* in 1859. See Brown, 'Evangelical Ideas of Perfection', pp. 401-402.

[144] Randall, *Evangelical Experiences*, p. 14. Randall is citing from J.S. Holden (ed.), *The Keswick Jubilee Souvenir* (London, 1921), p. 10, but his description still holds good as a summary of the founding principles of Keswick spirituality. Cf. Price and Randall, *Transforming Keswick*, pp. 14-15, 39.

[145] Price and Randall, *Transforming Keswick*, p. 60; Brown, 'Evangelical Ideas of Perfection', p. 188.

Spurgeon rejected Keswick teaching on holiness. In a sermon entitled, simply, 'Onward!', he spoke of those who had come to the 'complacent condition' of thinking that they had 'overcome all their sins by believing they [had] done so'. 'Onward!' was preached in May 1873, a full two years before the first meeting at Keswick, but Bebbington, who himself cites this message, is surely right to see Spurgeon's comments as an attack on the growing ethos which would lead to the convention's founding.[146] Spurgeon continued,

> [A]s if believing your battles to be won was the same thing as winning them. This, which they call faith, I take the liberty to call a lazy, self-conceited presumption; and though they persuade themselves that their sins are dead, it is certain that their carnal security is vigorous enough, and highly probable that the rest of their sins are only keeping out of the way to let their pride have room to develop itself to ruinous proportions.[147]

The quotation is revealing as to the reasons behind Spurgeon's rejection of Keswick. For him, battles with regards to holiness were ongoing and had to be fought. Again the motifs of struggle and fight, so important to Spurgeon and his understanding of holy living, were to the fore. The contention that those who claimed to have 'overcome their sins' by faith were guilty of pride and presumption was also important. In the *Sword and Trowel* of May 1883 Spurgeon quoted, with grim satisfaction, an extract from an American paper in which the writer asserted that, in his experience, those who claimed to be 'living the higher life' were actually most likely to stir up trouble in churches. Spurgeon added the comment that as soon as people began 'to brag about their holiness' they became 'wholly useless'.[148] Spurgeon detected a definite tendency to unguarded language about perfection in the Keswick tradition.[149] If they were guilty of no other sin, they were certainly guilty of pride.

For Spurgeon, both Keswick and Wesleyan teachers seriously downplayed the deep and pervasive nature of sin in the life of the believer. Such an approach was both theologically wrong and corrosive of true holiness, likely to breed 'self-satisfaction' in some and 'disappointed hope' in others.[150] Standard Keswick teaching held that Romans 7, with its depiction of the struggle with the sinful nature, described the life of a 'weak' and 'unestablished' Christian.[151] But Spurgeon believed that the chapter set out the authentic experience of a faithful believer

---

[146] Bebbington, *Holiness in Nineteenth-Century England*, p. 88.

[147] C.H. Spurgeon, 'Onward!', in *Twelve Sermons on Sanctification*, S. No. 1114, Philippians 3.13,14, delivered 25 May 1873, p. 286.

[148] C.H. Spurgeon, 'Professors of the Higher Life', in Spurgeon (ed.), *Sword and Trowel*, May 1883, p. 212.

[149] E.g. Spurgeon (ed.), *Sword and Trowel*, September 1875, p. 445.

[150] Spurgeon (ed.), *Sword and Trowel*, September 1875, p. 445.

[151] Price and Randall, *Transforming Keswick*, p. 212. Price, who wrote this particular chapter, is summarising J.C. Ryle's criticism of typical Keswick teaching.

striving after holiness. Though they were regenerate and therefore possessed of a new nature, Christians were still 'encompassed' with the 'body of death' and the 'old nature' remained in them.[152] Consequently, no one who really knew their own 'hearts' ever pretended 'to be perfectly conformed to God's will'.[153] In February 1876 Spurgeon attacked Keswick in the following terms:

> Some glib professors talk of having got out of the 7th of Romans; I hope they will grow in grace until they get into the 7th of Romans! ... The nearer you get to perfection the more horrified you feel because of the sin that still remains in you; and the more horror you feel at your sin, the more intense will be your gratitude to the bleeding saviour who has put that sin away; and, in consequence, the more intense will be your love to him ... I charge you, Christian people, if you want your piety to be increased, never to blunt your sensibility of sin.[154]

Spurgeon believed that Keswick teaching actually militated against true growth in holiness. He would have been confirmed in this view by allegations about the private life of Robert Pearsall Smith which were made following an indiscretion at the holiness conference at Brighton in 1875.[155] Pearsall Smith was counselled to return to America and he never ministered on the platform of the Keswick convention proper. That something untoward had happened became common knowledge in evangelical circles, despite being little spoken of publicly.[156] Spurgeon would certainly have been aware of the rumours and the *Sword and Trowel* for January 1876 contains what was probably an allusion to them. In the context of some negative comments about advocates of the 'higher life', Spurgeon said, 'If all be true that we have heard, presumption has received an awful rebuke already.'[157] Spurgeon was in the midst of making what for him was the overriding point in relation to Keswick: the 'higher life' teaching was, in reality, corrosive of holy living.

---

[152] C.H. Spurgeon, 'Moab Is My Washpot', *MTP*, Vol. 17, S. No. 983, Psalm 60.8, n.d., p. 184, 'The old nature so remains in us, that, if we were to become deserted by God, we should even yet become as the ungodly are'. Cf. Spurgeon's 'Exposition' of Romans 7.7-25 in *MTP*, Vol. 59, pp. 478-80.

[153] Spurgeon, 'Holiness Demanded', p. 458.

[154] C.H. Spurgeon, 'Who Loves Christ Most?', *MTP*, Vol. 50, S. No. 2873, Luke 7.41-43, delivered 3 February 1876, p. 114.

[155] This was a vital conference in the genesis of what became the Keswick convention. According to Robert Pearsall Smith, all that happened was that he counselled a young woman alone in his hotel room, in the course of which he put his arm around her. The woman then spread rumours that she and Pearsall Smith enjoyed some sort of relationship. See Price and Randall, *Transforming Keswick*, pp. 29-30; Brown, 'Evangelical Ideas of Perfection', pp. 412-14. The official history of Keswick, written sixty years after its inception, covers over what happened. See W.B. Sloan, *These Sixty Years* (London: Pickering and Inglis, n.d., [1935]), p. 13.

[156] Price and Randall, *Transforming Keswick*, pp. 29-30.

[157] C.H. Spurgeon, 'Welcome to 1876', in Spurgeon (ed.), *Sword and Trowel*, January 1876, pp. 2-3.

As will already be apparent, therefore, of the four major nineteenth-century 'traditions of spirituality' highlighted by Bebbington, Spurgeon's approach largely quadrated with Calvinistic teaching. Evangelicals from earlier in the nineteenth century who adhered to a moderate Calvinism habitually spoke of the struggle for holiness. Words and phrases such as 'perpetual warfare', 'exertion' and 'utmost efforts' peppered their teaching.[158] Romans 7.14-25 was interpreted as describing the Christian's lifelong battle against 'the remains of indwelling sin'.[159] Many of the criticisms of Keswick voiced by the Calvinistic J.C. Ryle could, as has already been noted, have been Spurgeon's own.[160] In *Holiness* Ryle contended that what he termed 'true holiness' did not consist merely of 'believing and feeling' but of 'doing'. 'Active personal exertion' was required, indeed he spoke of a 'holy violence, a conflict, a warfare, a fight, a soldier's life, a wrestling'.[161] The similarities with Spurgeon's own views are obvious. A careful analysis of Spurgeon's approach to holiness, with its regular exhortations to battle and sustained struggle, allows us to locate him firmly within the Calvinistic tradition.

Spurgeon's Distinctive Approach

Nevertheless, as has already been argued, Spurgeon's approach was recognisably different from the bulk of sixteenth- and seventeenth-century Puritanism and eighteenth-century Calvinistic evangelicalism. The focus on the personal, premillennial return of Christ represents one important point of departure. Moreover, there was another nineteenth-century movement with which Spurgeon certainly had affinities. His advocacy of a manly holiness carried with it, as Andrew Bradstock demonstrates, 'distinct echoes' of the 'muscular Christianity' associated with other nineteenth-century figures such as Thomas Hughes and Charles Kingsley. In addition to the general lauding of 'manliness', points of contact included the exaltation of moral courage and religious certainty, as well as some of the military imagery that Spurgeon habitually deployed.[162] Also, for Hughes and Kingsley, the negative 'converse' of 'muscular Christianity' was 'effeminacy', something they saw

---

[158] Brown, 'Evangelical Ideas of Perfection', pp. 143-44.

[159] Brown, 'Evangelical Ideas of Perfection', pp. 141-42. Brown's discussion of these issues is carried on with particular reference to Charles Simeon, Andrew Fuller and William Jay of Bath.

[160] That Ryle wrote *Holiness* to counter Keswick teaching is shown particularly clearly by pp. x-xi of his 'Introduction'. Ryle did not name Keswick and hardly ever mentioned particular personalities, although 'Pearsall Smith' is mentioned in passing on p. xvii.

[161] Ryle, *Holiness*, pp. x, xvi.

[162] A. Bradstock, '"A Man of God is Manly Man": Spurgeon, Luther and "Holy Boldness"', in A. Bradstock, S. Gill, A. Horgan and S. Morgan (eds), *Masculinity and Spirituality in Victorian Culture* (Basingstoke: Macmillan, 2000), pp. 212-13. For the concept of 'muscular Christianity', see D.E. Hall (ed.), *Muscular Christianity: Embodying the Victorian Age* (Cambridge: Cambridge University Press, 1994); J. Tosh, *Manliness and Masculinities in Nineteenth-Century Britain* (Harlow: Longman, 2005).

exemplified in High Church spirituality.[163] Once again there was a parallel with Spurgeon. Consequently, it is not that surprising that Spurgeon expressed what he called a 'kindly regard' for Kingsley despite their very different theologies.[164] It was almost certainly what John Wolffe has called Kingsley's glorification of 'English Christian manhood' which attracted Spurgeon.[165]

In his own battle with 'effete' Tractarian religion Spurgeon, as Bradstock shows, recruited Martin Luther to his cause. This was not so much because of Luther's theology, of which Spurgeon could be critical, but because the German Reformer was 'all a man'.[166] Luther's religion was, Spurgeon stated, 'part and parcel of his common life'. The Reformer's domestic life was visualised thus:

> I like Luther with a wife and children. I like to see him with his family and a Christmas tree, making music with little Johnny Luther on his knee. I love to hear him sing a little hymn with the children, and tell his pretty boy about the horses in heaven with golden bridles and silver saddles. Faith had not taken away his manhood, but sanctified it to noblest uses ... What if we do not wear canonicals, and so on? The best canonicals in the world are thorough devotion to the Lord's work; and if a man lives aright, he makes every garment a vestment, every meal a sacrament, and every house a temple. All our hours are canonical, all our days holy days, every breath is incense, every pulse is music for the Most High.[167]

Spurgeon's imaginative reconstruction of Luther's home life owes much to a rather mawkish, typically Victorian sentimentality. Also, the last part of this extract is very similar to one cited earlier in this chapter from 'All The Day Long'. Luther is invoked to serve Spurgeon's ideal of a homely, 'manly' piety which is both distinctively Protestant and, at the same time, distinctively Victorian. Certainly Spurgeon's approach to holiness was being shaped by his Protestant heritage but,

---

[163] So Bradstock, 'Spurgeon, Luther and "Holy Boldness"', p. 216, citing D. Newsome, *Godliness and Good Learning: Four Studies on a Victorian Ideal* (London: John Murray, 1961), pp. 97, 207. It would be too simplistic, however, to assume that Tractarianism and 'muscular Christianity' were diametrically opposed. See Bradstock, 'Spurgeon, Luther and "Holy Boldness"', p. 223 n. 46. We might note that the cult of Christian manliness can also be thought of, in part, as an expression of the Romantic temper. See Hopkins, *Nonconformity's Romantic Generation*, p. 256.

[164] See the review of J.H. Rigg, *Modern Anglican Theology*, in *Sword and Trowel*, December 1880, p. 618: 'We are pleased to mark [the writer's] kindly regard for Kingsley, in which we could never help sharing ... he had very little of the heretic about him but the growl.' Spurgeon was free, however, from the 'racialist undertones' which ran through Kingsley's novels. On these undertones, see J. Wolffe, *God and Greater Britain: Religion and National Life in Britain and Ireland 1843–1945* (London: Routledge, 1994), p. 179.

[165] Wolffe, *God and Greater Britain*, p. 187.

[166] C.H. Spurgeon, 'The Luther Sermon At The Exeter Hall', *MTP*, Vol. 29, S. No. 1750, Galatians 5.6, delivered 11 November 1883 (at the Exeter Hall), p. 635; Bradstock, 'Spurgeon, Luther and "Holy Boldness"', p. 212.

[167] Spurgeon, 'The Luther Sermon At The Exeter Hall', p. 635.

just as certainly, that Protestant heritage was being reshaped, consciously or unconsciously, by contemporary concerns before being packaged and presented in a way which served Spurgeon's nineteenth-century agenda. Luther appears in Spurgeon's illustration as a doting Victorian father, Protestant of course but also rather 'English' and 'manly', depicted in sharp contrast to the alternative, Tractarian vision.

Spurgeon could use the Puritans in much the same way. In a sermon, 'The Doctrines Of Grace Do Not Lead To Sin', Spurgeon lauded Puritan godliness. As he warmed to his theme he asked,

> Did they invent a Book of Sports for Sabbath diversion? Did they haunt the ale house and places of revelry? Every historian will tell you, the greatest fault of these men in the eyes of their enemies was that they were too precise for the generation in which they lived, so that they called them Puritans, and condemned them as holding a gloomy theology. Sirs, if there was iniquity in the land in that day, it was to be found with the theological party which preached up salvation by works. The gentlemen with their womanish locks and essenced hair, whose speech savoured of profanity, were the advocates of salvation by works, and all bedabbled with lust they pleaded for human merit; but the men who believed in grace alone were of another style.[168]

The example of the Puritans was written up in a particular way, replete with dramatic flourishes, bold generalisations and sweeping statements (for example, 'Every historian will tell you ...'!). Furthermore, this rather Romantic picture of the sixteenth- and seventeenth-century 'godly' was carefully painted, so that features which helped Spurgeon fight the battles of his own day were to the fore. The Puritans were those who stressed doctrine and had an emphasis on grace that led to holy living. Their opponents in theory exalted 'works' but in reality were characterised by loose living and, tellingly, 'womanish locks and essenced hair'. The depiction of Puritan piety is thus properly 'manly' (the powdered wigs of Puritan preachers were conveniently forgotten) and drawn in contrast to an exaggerated picture of the broad churchmen of the Restoration. Spurgeon's targets this time were perhaps not so much the Tractarians as certain Latitudinarian Churchmen. These were 'gentlemen' from the 'upper echelons'[169] of society who were rich, lethargic and, of course, 'unmanly'. Spurgeon contended for a holiness that was Protestant as opposed to Tractarian or Catholic, muscular and manly as opposed to effeminate, and 'common' as opposed to elitist, privileged and 'cultured'. The German Luther and the English Puritans with their significantly different theologies were alike enlisted to the cause.

---

[168] C.H. Spurgeon, 'The Doctrines Of Grace Do Not Lead To Sin', *MTP*, Vol. 29, S. No. 1735, Romans 6.14-15, delivered 19 August 1883 (at the Exeter Hall), pp. 448-49. Cf. Spurgeon, 'Scriptural Salvation', p. 285, 'The lives of the Puritans who taught the gospel of faith in Christ were infinitely preferable to the lives of those Cavaliers who believed in human merit'.

[169] Bradstock, 'Spurgeon, Luther and "Holy Boldness"', p. 215.

Spurgeon, then, sounded the clarion call for a particular brand of Protestant piety. His vision of holiness drew deeply from the past but it was also thoroughly Victorian. Perhaps most of all it was popular and 'manly'. As Bebbington has noted, Spurgeon drew the same sharp distinction between 'men' and 'gentlemen' as the novelist Elizabeth Gaskell classically articulated in her book *North and South*. To be sure, for Spurgeon the ideal was more the rural fens of John Ploughman than the industrial north of Henry Thornton, but Spurgeon still appeared as a spokesman for 'a similar provincial protest against the mannered life of the capital'.[170] Bebbington comments that Spurgeon's 'immense popularity ... flowed not only from his pugnacious loyalty to the basics of the gospel. It was also a result of his doughty championship of the common man.'[171] This groundbreaking conclusion is surely reinforced by much of the material covered in this chapter. Indeed, this argument with regard to Spurgeon's popularity can be pushed further. Spurgeon advocated a holiness of and for the common people. Although challenging, the vision of the holy life which he propounded and sought to embody was also affirming and, crucially, attainable. The spirituality preached in the Tabernacle week by week was an everyday spirituality particularly well suited to those who had initially flocked to hear him, and continued to do so throughout his ministry. Spurgeon's popularity in the nineteenth century certainly owed something to his 'championing' of the 'common man'. But this popularity was also linked with his advocacy of a spirituality that was particularly appropriate for his constituency.

Conclusion

Spurgeon's approach to holiness was both essentially Calvinistic and also shaped by a number of different nineteenth-century movements. Most of all it was focused on Christ and his people. In a prayer prayed at the Tabernacle on 7 April 1878, Spurgeon declared,

> Oh to be Christly [sic]! We do desire to live on earth the life of Jesus – sent into the world by Him as He was sent into the world by the Father. We would closely copy all His acts, words, and spirit; for only so are we saved, when we are saved from the power of sin and transformed into the likeness of Christ. Let no drunkard here imagine that his life ought to be spent in selfish endeavour to save himself from the flames of hell; but may he rather reckon that the grand object is to be saved from the power of sin, and to be consecrated unto God, and to live unto the glory of the most High.[172]

The prayer captures most of the central features of Spurgeon's approach to holiness. If a person was truly 'saved' they would 'desire' to live a holy life and make

---

[170] Bebbington, 'Spurgeon and the Common Man', p. 68; Bradstock, 'Spurgeon, Luther and "Holy Boldness"', p. 215.

[171] Bebbington, 'Spurgeon and the Common Man', p. 75.

[172] C.H. Spurgeon, 'The Reason Why Many Cannot Find Rest' in [Anon.] (ed.), *The Pastor in Prayer*, 7 April 1878, p. 44.

progress in that endeavour. The pattern for such holy living was Christ himself. Not only his words but also his acts and his 'spirit' were to be copied by believers. Such an approach would of necessity lead a Christian to engage with the 'world' into which Christ sent them, just as he had been sent into the world by his Father. The mention of the drunkard reminds us that, for Spurgeon, the life of holiness was, potentially, for all. Even such a person could be saved, not only from the penalty but also the power of sin. Here was a holiness which was continually focused on Christ who was the believer's model, motive and goal. Here also was a holiness which could be pursued by the common people.

CHAPTER 10

Suffering:
'Certain of us have had large fellowship with the Lord Jesus in affliction'

William Williams was, as has already been noted, a close personal friend of C.H. Spurgeon. Williams became minister of Upton Chapel, Lambeth, in 1877, and from this point onwards he was part of Spurgeon's trusted inner circle, with the two men enjoying what Spurgeon described as 'frequent communion' based on their mutual love for Christ.[1] As pastor of Upton, Williams made it his habit to go and listen to Spurgeon giving his Friday afternoon lectures to his students.[2] Williams took detailed notes on these occasions, and insisted that the published *Lectures* did not do justice to the experience of hearing the talks in person.[3] A number of the quotations Williams recorded, culled from various lectures, relate to the subject of suffering. For example,

> One secret of Solomon's wanderings was that he was not afflicted. The covenant mark he lacked.
> The tears of affliction are often needed to keep the eye of faith bright.
> Be willing if necessary to live in a spirit of perpetual martyrdom for Christ.
> Learn to love the burdens Christ gives you to bear.
> In the night of sorrow sinners are like owls, believers like nightingales, and they sing in the darkness.

---

[1] See W. Williams, *Upton Chapel Sermons: A Centenary Memorial, With Preface by C.H. Spurgeon ...* (London: Passmore and Alabaster, 1885), Preface, p. xii. Williams entered the Pastors' College in 1872, leaving in 1874. His call to Upton followed a brief pastorate in Derbyshire. Spurgeon believed that God had wanted to bless him personally by sending Williams to Upton. See 'Rev. W. Williams. Upton Chapel, Barkham Terrace', in *Christian Globe*, 19 April 1883, in 'Spurgeon's Scrapbooks, Numbered Volumes', Spurgeon's College, Heritage Room (2G), Vol. 7, p. 151.

[2] W. Williams, *Personal Reminiscences of Charles Haddon Spurgeon* (rev. and ed. M. Williams; London: Religious Tract Society, n.d. [1933]), p. 9.

[3] Williams, *Personal Reminiscences* (rev. edn.), p. 62.

> There is honey in every cup of affliction which God puts into the hand of the Christian; but generally he has to wait until he reaches the bottom before he can taste it.[4]

These comments from Spurgeon go some way to indicating the crucial place suffering occupied in his understanding of the Christian life. Supported by numerous similar statements in his writing and published preaching, they also hint at the extent to which he suffered personally. This final main chapter examines the relationship between suffering and Spurgeon's spirituality. It includes material on the nature of his suffering to supplement that already given in chapter 8. Overall, however, the focus is on the ways his understanding and experience of suffering connected with the integrating theme of his spirituality, 'communion with Christ and his people'. Spurgeon believed that 'affliction' had indeed kept his faith bright, drawing him closer to his suffering saviour. His suffering also drew him closer to others and he was especially keen to pass on the lessons he had learned through affliction, not only to his students, but also more widely through his preaching and writing. Moreover, bodily suffering would ultimately lead to death, which was the gateway to a glorious future when, for the Christian, all suffering would be over. Accordingly, the chapter concludes with some reflections on Spurgeon's conception of life beyond the grave, a conception which reinforces and adds to the argument of this study.

Spurgeon and Suffering

With regard to Spurgeon's physical suffering, a basic timeline was established in chapter 8 under the heading 'The Course of Spurgeon's Activism'. Four periods of activity were traced, although, in respect of Spurgeon's suffering, the first two periods of activity, which ran from 1850 to 1853 and from 1854 to 1866, can be treated as one. From 1850 to 1866 Spurgeon enjoyed relatively good health; certainly he was free of the long-term, debilitating, physical problems which would dog him later. 1867 saw the beginning of a new period in which physical suffering bulked larger in his experience. The beginning of 1879 ushered in the final phase of ministry. From this year onward the attacks of gout were both prolonged and acute. Spurgeon's arms and feet were regularly swollen.[5] In addition, he became increasingly troubled by kidney problems, initially undiagnosed. From 1879 until his death in 1892 he found himself frequently incapacitated. Spurgeon's later London ministry was heavily marked by debilitating physical suffering.

In this final period of ministry, the question as to whether or not Spurgeon would be able to take the Tabernacle service on any given Sunday became a weekly drama which was regularly played out in the press. Much information was carried in both religious and secular papers concerning the state of the pulpit celebrity's health. On Monday 21 March 1881 the *Daily News* reported that a letter from Spurgeon had

---

[4] Williams, *Personal Reminiscences* (rev. edn.), pp. 73-74. The quotations are given, by Williams, as isolated 'thoughts' taken out of context. Williams also provided outlines of some of Spurgeon's unpublished Friday lectures, see pp. 57-62.

[5] Williams, *Personal Reminiscences* (rev. edn.), pp. 83, 85, 95.

been read to his congregation the previous day explaining his absence from the pulpit. Spurgeon had written that he was being 'driven out upon the sea of pain' by repeated blasts from 'the tempest of disease'. 'My pains have at times been overpowering, and I have needed Divine succour to come through them.'[6] Spurgeon was effectively 'shut in' at home, unable even to go downstairs. Sunday preaching had been an impossibility in the first weeks of March and he had frequently missed midweek services too. One of those who filled in for Spurgeon was Williams, who took several of the Tabernacle's Thursday evening meetings that month.[7] In the letter reported in the *Daily News*, Spurgeon had written that he was recovering: a 'little longer and it will all be over', he had said.[8] But this was too optimistic. On Sunday 27 March Spurgeon was back preaching, but the press described him by turns as 'pale', 'weak' and 'very feeble'.[9] During the morning service he had insisted that he was now 'quite free from pain'[10] but, according to the *Baptist*, the results of his latest 'attack' were 'unmistakable on his countenance' as he tackled the platform stairs with the aid of a stick. It came as little surprise that Spurgeon was unable to manage the evening service.[11] Reportage such as this from March 1881 would be commonplace during the ensuing decade.[12]

Spurgeon, then, was often incapacitated by physical pain, but we need to note that his experience of suffering encompassed more than this. The 'mental anguish' referred to in chapter 8 was also significant. Spurgeon suffered from this in each of the three phases of physical suffering I have identified, although it became more acute from the mid- to late-1850s. The Surrey Gardens Music Hall Tragedy of 1856 was probably a significant trigger for this suffering.[13] Following the disaster, Spurgeon spoke of his thoughts being like a 'case of knives' cutting his heart 'in pieces'. This was a time of unrelenting 'misery' and 'darkness'. Then, suddenly, the

---

[6] *Daily News*, 21 March 1881, in 'Spurgeon's Scrapbooks, Numbered Volumes', Vol. 4, p. 77.

[7] *Daily News*, 11 March 1881, 28 March 1881, in 'Spurgeon's Scrapbooks, Numbered Volumes', Vol. 4, pp. 76; 80.

[8] *Daily News*, 21 March 1881, in 'Spurgeon's Scrapbooks, Numbered Volumes', Vol. 4, p. 77.

[9] *Daily News*, 28 March 1881; *Christian World*, 31 March 1881, in 'Spurgeon's Scrapbooks, Numbered Volumes', Vol. 4, p. 80.

[10] *Christian World*, 31 March 1881, in 'Spurgeon's Scrapbooks, Numbered Volumes', Vol. 4, p. 80.

[11] *Christian World*, 31 March 1881; *Daily News*, 28 March 1881; *Baptist*, 1 April 1881, in 'Spurgeon's Scrapbooks, Numbered Volumes', Vol. 4, p. 80.

[12] See, e.g., reports in the *Freeman*, 5 September 1884, 23 January 1885; *Christian World*, 18 September 1884, 29 January 1885, in 'Spurgeon's Scrapbooks, Numbered Volumes', Vol. 12, pp. 6, 56. Cf. C.H. Spurgeon, *Autobiography: Compiled from his Diary, Letters, and Records by his Wife and his Private Secretary* (4 Vols; London: Passmore and Alabaster, 1897–99), Vol. 4, pp. 351-52; Williams, *Personal Reminiscences* (rev. edn.), pp. 83-85.

[13] So J.D. Douglas, *The Prince of Preachers: A Sketch; A Portraiture; And A Tribute* (London: Morgan and Scott, n.d. [1893]), p. 63.

'burning lava' of Spurgeon's brain was cooled.[14] Nevertheless, from this time on Spurgeon experienced mood swings which could be violent and sudden, with ecstasy giving way to weeping and despair. Williams once mentioned to Spurgeon that he was going to preach on Proverbs 3.33, not knowing that this had been his friend's text on the night of the tragedy. Spurgeon's reaction (Williams spoke of a 'deep sigh' and Spurgeon's 'countenance' changing even before he had finished quoting the verse) led to a resolution from Williams never to speak of this text or the Surrey Gardens disaster to Spurgeon again. The mention of Proverbs 3.33 had, Williams believed, given a revealing insight into the 'furnace of mental suffering' his friend had endured and continued to endure.[15]

Others recognised that Spurgeon suffered from depression,[16] and Spurgeon himself was quite open about his mental suffering. For example, he wrote to his congregation from Mentone on 1 March 1885 about experiencing 'fits of deep depression' which were, he believed, the result of 'brain weariness'.[17] He also wrote about 'depression' in letters to family and friends.[18] Doubtless these feelings of depression were closely bound up with the physical pain, which was clearly one of the reasons why depression deepened in the final two phases of his ministry. Nevertheless, such depression could sometimes strike when least expected, as in the conversation with Williams about the Surrey Gardens tragedy. I have showed the material in this chapter to a psychiatrist, Dr Anil Den, as well as talking more generally to him about Spurgeon's insomnia and mental suffering.[19] Depression can be reactive, when circumstances become too much for a person. Such depression is transient and when circumstances change the suffering lifts. The second form of depression is endogenous (that is, from the inside), with the root cause an imbalance of brain chemicals. Although this form of depression can be brought on by a

---

[14] Spurgeon, *Autobiography*, Vol. 2, pp. 195-96. Cf. W.Y. Fullerton, *C.H. Spurgeon: A Biography* (London: Williams and Norgate, 1920), pp. 93-94.

[15] Spurgeon, *Autobiography*, Vol. 2, p. 220.

[16] See, e.g., Douglas, *Prince of Preachers*, p. 99.

[17] C.H. Spurgeon, 'Letter From Mr Spurgeon', 1 March 1885, *MTP*, Vol. 31, p. 132. 'Brain weariness' was a phrase Spurgeon often used. See, e.g., C.H. Spurgeon to unnamed friend, 29 December 1877, 'Original Correspondence of Charles Haddon Spurgeon, 1863–1886', Spurgeon's College, Heritage Room, (4G). For another example of Spurgeon's openness on the subject of depression, see C.H. Spurgeon, 'Be not Discouraged', in C.H. Spurgeon (ed.), *The Sword and The Trowel: A Record of Combat With Sin and Labour For The Lord* (London: Passmore and Alabaster, 1865–92) (*Sword and Trowel*), December 1879, p. 571.

[18] See, e.g., C.H. Spurgeon to Eliza Spurgeon, 2 May 1883, 'Original Correspondence of Charles Haddon Spurgeon, 1851–1893', Spurgeon's College, Heritage Room (4G), No. 67, in which he spoke of being 'a good deal depressed'.

[19] As revealed in, e.g., C.H. Spurgeon to an unnamed friend, September 1873, 'Original Correspondence of Charles Haddon Spurgeon, 1863–1886, No. 10, in which he speaks about 'becoming demented with the sleeplessness of a brain over-wrought'. Spurgeon regularly struggled with insomnia. See, e.g., C.H. Spurgeon to John Spurgeon, 8 September 1883, in 'Original Correspondence of Charles Haddon Spurgeon, 1851–1893', No. 69.

traumatic event and exacerbated by other illnesses, it remains even when these other factors are removed. Surveying Spurgeon's symptoms, Dr Den's opinion is that Spurgeon was suffering from a form of endogenous depression and that, if he had presented with such symptoms today he would certainly have been treated with a mixture of medication and therapy.[20] Thinking of Spurgeon as clinically depressed sheds new light on his mental suffering.

In addition to the physical and mental suffering, Spurgeon often battled an accompanying sense of spiritual depression. In a message preached in May 1885, a few months after the letter from Mentone just cited had been written, Spurgeon spoke of specifically *spiritual* struggles, what he termed an 'agony of soul'. The sermon was on Psalm 77.9 and the question posed in the text, 'Hath God forgotten to be gracious?', Spurgeon said,

> Pain of body, when it is continuous and severe, is exceedingly trying to our feeble spirits; but agony of soul is worse still. Give me the rack sooner than despair. Do you know what it is to have a keen thought working like an auger into your brain? Has Satan seemed to pierce and gimlet your mind with a sharp, cutting thought that would not be put aside? ... When Asaph prayed for relief, and the relief did not come, the temptation came to him to ask, 'Am I always to suffer? Will the Lord never relieve me? It is written, "He healeth the broken in heart, and bindeth up their wounds"; has he ceased from that sacred surgery? "Hath God forgotten to be gracious?".[21]

The mention of Satan and also of Asaph's temptation to doubt God's word highlight the spiritual depression Spurgeon experienced. His comments on this verse were clearly autobiographical and he believed that Psalm 77 mapped out his own experience.[22] As with Spurgeon's mental suffering, this spiritual depression was surely linked with his physical 'afflictions', indeed, the three different strands of suffering I am identifying were closely woven together. Nevertheless, Spurgeon here

---

[20] Personal conversation with Dr Anil Den, 22 October 2009, at Spurgeon's College, London. I am also drawing from printed notes provided by Dr Den entitled 'Mood Disorders', which are dated 7 November 2004. It is possible Spurgeon was bi-polar (a condition sometimes termed manic depression), but there is not quite enough evidence to make this diagnosis with certainty.

[21] C.H. Spurgeon, 'A Question For The Questioner', *New Park Street Pulpit (NPSP) / Metropolitan Tabernacle Pulpit (MTP)* (London: Passmore and Alabaster, 1856–1917), *MTP*, Vol. 31, S. No. 1843, Psalm 77.9, delivered 31 May 1885, p. 303.

[22] Cf. C.H. Spurgeon's comments on Psalm 77.2 in *The Treasury of the Old Testament* (4 Vols; London: Marshall, Morgan and Scott, n.d.), Vol. 2, p. 726. Spurgeon's exposition of this Psalm in the *Treasury of David* stated that Psalm 77 was a 'transcript' of the 'inner conflicts' often experienced by mature Christians. See *The Treasury of David: Containing An Original Exposition Of The Book Of Psalms; A Collection Of Illustrative Extracts From The Whole Range Of Literature; A Series Of Homiletical Hints Upon Almost Every Verse; And Lists Of Writers Upon Each Psalm* (7 Vols; London and Edinburgh: Marshall Brothers, n.d. [London: Passmore and Alabaster, 1869–1885]), Vol. 3, p. 411.

sought to distinguish clearly between pain of 'body' and 'soul'.[23] The latter involved doubting God's character and his word. Williams even remembers Spurgeon 'very low and depressed' and doubting his own 'standing in Christ', although as the two men talked Spurgeon did rally.[24] Spurgeon spoke, in a message entitled 'Strength And Recovery', of how the soul could sometimes be 'grievously diseased', infected by doubt, fear and 'lukewarmness'. Spurgeon believed the 'heavenly surgeon' was always waiting to heal believers. Nevertheless the periods of spiritual depression could be very real.[25] Overall, it should be clear that Spurgeon experienced considerable suffering – physical, mental and spiritual.

A Theology of Suffering

How did Spurgeon account for the presence of suffering in God's world, specifically in the lives of believers such as him? Spurgeon emphasised the fall of the first man and woman and the way this had brought misery and pain into the world.[26] There was a stress, then, on human responsibility for suffering, although Spurgeon also regarded its presence in the world as being the result of the devil's activity.[27] What he really wanted to emphasise, however, was that all suffering fell within the scope of God's sovereignty.[28] He especially stressed this principle as it related to the suffering of believers. Thus, in a sermon entitled 'Gratitude For Deliverance From The Grave', preached in 1887, Spurgeon stated that although a Christian's 'afflictions' were most certainly the result of a 'cruel enemy', the devil's actions were overruled by God and 'made to work for his [God's] good'.[29] In this message Spurgeon also spoke of the devil as the 'second agent' in suffering and God as the 'Great First Cause'. Others bore the responsibility for suffering, but God was sovereign over it.

---

[23] Cf. Spurgeon, *Treasury of the Old Testament*, Vol. 2, p. 726.

[24] Williams, *Personal Reminiscences* (rev. edn.), p. 32. As noted in chapter 3, this recollection is undated.

[25] C.H. Spurgeon, 'Strength And Recovery', *MTP*, Vol. 30, S. No. 1805, Zechariah 10.12, delivered 18 September 1884, p. 571. That Spurgeon was talking here from personal experience is strongly hinted at on p. 572, 'For my own part I blush ... confusion of face covers me that I should have so many advantages and yet grow so slowly.'

[26] C.H. Spurgeon, 'Honey From A Lion', *MTP*, Vol. 27, S. No. 1591, Romans 5.15, delivered 3 April 1881, p. 186.

[27] C.H. Spurgeon, 'The Roaring Lion', *MTP*, Vol. 7, S. No. 419, 1 Peter 5.8,9, delivered 17 November 1861, pp. 833-35. Note that the pagination for this sermon, in the bound copies of the *MTP* that I have seen, is not in sequence with the other messages in the volume. The message is inserted in between pp. 568 and 577, but its pages are numbered 833-840.

[28] C.H. Spurgeon, 'For The Troubled', *MTP*, Vol. 19, S. No. 1090, Psalm 88.7, delivered 12 January 1873, pp. 16-17.

[29] C.H. Spurgeon, 'Gratitude For Deliverance From The Grave', *MTP*, Vol. 38, S. No. 2237, Psalm 118.17,18, n.d., pp. 1-2.

The cross of Christ was the supreme example of the outworking of this principle. Here, as in all suffering, God was not to be blamed: the cross was the fault of the devil, as well as being an 'atrocious crime' committed by 'ungodly men'.[30] Yet the cross was also 'pre-determined in the counsel of God' and this was the fundamental reason why Christ had died. The precise relationship between human and demonic responsibility for suffering and God's sovereignty over it was not a conundrum that needed to be explained but a mystery that needed to be believed. Moreover, once believers accepted the mystery of the sovereignty of a loving God over suffering they would find it deeply 'consoling'.[31] The cross showed that Christians did not ultimately have to pay for their own folly, neither were they in the hands of the devil. Rather, they were in the hands of God who was gracious, suffering in their place to win them salvation. Working within this framework, Spurgeon held that a believer's trials were strictly limited, both in duration, for suffering would ultimately give way to a heaven guaranteed by Christ's death, and scope. With regard to scope, as well as affirming that Christ had taken the punishment that was due to sinful people, so that those who believed would never have to endure such agonies,[32] Spurgeon also wanted to insist that God's mercy limited the suffering of believers in other ways. He believed that he himself had never 'yet experienced a trouble which might not have been worse'.[33] A note at the beginning of 'Gratitude For Deliverance From The Grave' recorded that this message had been preached in connection with the dedication of 'Jubilee House', an addition to the Tabernacle buildings which commemorated the fiftieth year of Spurgeon's life. This was a life which, the preacher reminded his hearers, had often been 'threatened by grievous sickness'. Spurgeon may have suffered much, but he still believed that he had been repeatedly 'delivered from the grave'.[34] He was sure, despite his familiarity with suffering, that God had ameliorated or withheld affliction on countless occasions in his own experience.

Suffering was, therefore, an area in which Spurgeon's essentially Calvinistic theological frame of reference intersected strongly with his spirituality. This was certainly the case with regard to Spurgeon's early thinking and preaching on the subject,[35] but it was a feature of his later ministry too. In 1890 he declared, 'How

---

[30] Spurgeon, 'Gratitude For Deliverance From The Grave', p. 3; cf. C.H. Spurgeon, 'On The Cross After Death', *MTP*, Vol. 33, S. No. 1956, John 19.31-37, delivered 3 April 1887, p. 202.

[31] Spurgeon, 'Gratitude For Deliverance From The Grave', p. 3.

[32] Spurgeon, 'Gratitude For Deliverance From The Grave', p. 8.

[33] Spurgeon, 'Gratitude For Deliverance From The Grave', pp. 3-6.

[34] Spurgeon, 'Gratitude For Deliverance From The Grave', p. 1. This dates the sermon as having been preached in either May or June 1884. For details on 'Jubilee House', see Spurgeon, *Autobiography*, Vol. 4, pp. 237-52.

[35] C.H. Spurgeon, 'God's People In The Furnace', *NPSP*, Vol. 1, S. No. 35, Isaiah 48.10, delivered 12 August 1855, p. 275.

often I have read *Elisha Coles on Divine Sovereignty* ... when I have been ill!'[36] Spurgeon's focus on God's sovereignty provided an underpinning for his approach to questions of suffering, an approach in which Spurgeon was able to maintain, firstly, that God was not to blame for 'afflictions', which were the result of the fall; secondly, that God was still in control, being the sovereign 'first cause' of suffering; and, thirdly, that God was still good, limiting the suffering of believers. The doctrine of final perseverance is also relevant here. If someone belonged to God's elect (and if they had trusted in Christ that was proof that they were part of the elect) then they would persevere to the end: no suffering could ever separate them from God.[37]

At the heart of Spurgeon's theology of suffering was the belief that the cross, as well as being the supreme example of God's sovereignty over suffering, revealed that God himself had suffered in the person of his Son. Spurgeon regularly reflected on Christ's passion in his preaching and his writing, reflections which were often emotionally charged.[38] A passage from *Evening By Evening* provides an example:

> 'He humbled Himself'? Was He not on earth always stripping off first one robe of honour and then another, till, naked, He was fastened to the cross, and there did He not empty out His inmost self, pouring out His life-blood, giving up for all of us, till they laid Him penniless in a borrowed grave? How low was our dear Redeemer brought! ... Stand at the foot of the cross, and count the purple drops by which you have been cleansed; see the thorn-crown; mark His scourged shoulders, still gushing with encrimsoned rills; see hands and feet given up to the rough iron, and His whole self to mockery and scorn; see the bitterness, and the pangs, and the throes of inward grief, showing themselves in His outward frame; hear the thrilling shriek, 'My God, my God, why hast Thou forsaken Me?' And if you do not lie prostrate on the ground before that cross, you have never seen it: if you are not humbled in the presence of Jesus, you do not know Him.[39]

---

[36] C.H. Spurgeon, 'Sad Fasts Changed To Glad Feasts', *MTP*, Vol. 38, S. No. 2248, Zechariah 8.19, delivered 7 September 1890, p. 141. Spurgeon republished Elisha Coles' *A Practical Discourse Of God's Sovereignty ...* (London: Passmore and Alabaster, 1866), adding a 'Brief Preface' of his own. Coles' work was originally published in 1673. See I.M. Green, *Print and Protestantism in Early Modern England* (Oxford: Oxford University Press, 2000), p. 312.

[37] Spurgeon, 'Gratitude For Deliverance From The Grave', p. 9.

[38] For further examples of such descriptions, see C.H. Spurgeon, 'Our Sympathizing High Priest', *MTP*, Vol. 32, S. No. 1927, Hebrews 5.7-10, delivered 31 October 1886, p. 591; *The Treasury of the Bible: The New Testament* (London: Marshall, Morgan and Scott, 1962), pp. 387-401. Spurgeon also spoke about Christ's sufferings more broadly. E.g., see C.H. Spurgeon, 'The Suffering Saviour's Sympathy', *MTP*, Vol. 33, S. No. 1974, Hebrews 2.18, n.d., pp. 410-11. Here the preacher dealt with how Christ suffered as he was tempted in his humanity. But Spurgeon's normal practice was to focus on Christ's passion when describing his sufferings.

[39] C.H. Spurgeon, *Evening By Evening: Or, Readings at Eventide for the Family or the Closet* (London: Passmore and Alabaster, 1868) (3 June), Philippians 2.8, p. 155.

Christ's suffering here was physical, as shown, for example, by the piercing of hands and feet; mental, as shown by the 'mockery' he endured; and spiritual, as shown by, amongst other things, the cry of dereliction. This, of course, corresponded with Spurgeon's own threefold experience of suffering. The difference between Christ and Spurgeon was in the degree of affliction, although one senses that the astonishingly vivid language and imagery Spurgeon employed was shaped not only by his fertile imagination but also by his various experiences of suffering, including his finely balanced mental state. His descriptions of Christ's passion certainly came from the heart. Williams recalled that Spurgeon would sometimes publicly weep 'even to sobs' because his 'sympathies' with Christ's suffering were 'so real and intense'.[40] The wisdom of some of these emotional reflections on the details of Christ's passion was, according to Williams, questioned by George Rogers, the Pastors' College principal during Williams' time as a student. The more cool and rational Rogers thought the inclusion of such passages in sermons and books a 'mistake'. He believed they did little good, as 'all souls were [not] as responsive to Christ and full of love to him as [Spurgeon's] own'. Williams, loyal to a fault as far as his commitment to Spurgeon was concerned, disagreed with Rogers.[41] Spurgeon himself believed that there was 'nothing more likely' to win people to Jesus than 'beholding him in his sorrows'.[42] As for people who were already Christians, if they were not moved by Christ's afflictions then he believed there was something badly wrong, as the extract from *Evening By Evening* just cited indicates. Elsewhere he quoted Bernard of Clairvaux, 'The more vile Christ hath made himself *for* us, the more dear he ought to be *to* us.'[43] A deeper appreciation of the horror of Christ's sufferings would surely increase a believer's love for their Lord.

Christ's suffering also provided believers with a 'pattern' for faithful discipleship. In a sermon based on the words said to Christ on the cross in Matthew 27.43, Spurgeon insisted that it would 'do his hearers good' to paint the picture of Christ being mistreated on the cross in their own minds, adding, 'I shall not complain if imagination heightens the colouring'. Seeing Christ thus would undoubtedly remind believers that Jesus' suffering was redemptive. But in this message Spurgeon also wanted to say that Christ's sufferings were a model for Christians who were called to

---

[40] Williams, *Personal Reminiscences* (rev. edn.), p. 103. Williams is specifically remembering Spurgeon at Communion services. For an occasion in a sermon where C.H. Spurgeon might well have wept when describing Christ's sufferings, see 'The Shameful Sufferer', *NPSP*, Vol. 5, S. No. 236, Hebrews 12.2, delivered 30 January 1859, p. 95. As Spurgeon spoke of Christ's suffering he said, 'I must pause, I cannot describe it. I can weep over it, and you can too.'

[41] Williams, *Personal Reminiscences* (rev. edn.), p. 98.

[42] C.H. Spurgeon, *My Sermon Notes ... From Matthew 4.3 To Acts* (London: Paternoster and Alabaster, 1886) No. 182 (John 19.14), p. 162.

[43] Spurgeon, *My Sermon Notes ... From Matthew 4.3 To Acts*, No. 145 (Matthew 27.29), p. 54

know the cross and its accompanying shame in their own lives.[44] Spurgeon regularly insisted that Christians were called to take up a cross.[45] A Christian's cross-bearing was not, of course, for salvation, as Christ's sacrifice was once for all time.[46] Nevertheless, a Christian still bore a cross in order that God's purposes might be accomplished in them and, through them, that God might be known in the world.[47] Spurgeon's statements on this subject were often accompanied by evidence that this was a theme close to his heart. In *The Gospel of the Kingdom* he closed his comments on Matthew 10.38 with a direct address to God: 'Lord, thou hast laid a cross upon me, do not permit me to shirk from it, or shrink from it.'[48] In the light of this, a further strand needs to be added to our understanding of Spurgeon's theology of suffering. Christians were called to cross-bearing in response to both the example and direct command of Christ. When a Christian suffered they were both following in the footsteps of Christ and suffering for Christ. This kind of suffering was, Spurgeon believed, a high calling indeed.

In continuing to set out Spurgeon's theology of suffering, we need to note that for him the cross affirmed that there was a purpose in suffering. One of the points Spurgeon made as he preached on Christ's afflictions was that Jesus learned 'obedience through the things ... he suffered'. Spurgeon made much of this thought as he preached on Hebrews 5.7-10 in 'Our Sympathizing High Priest'. Moreover, as Christ had learned obedience through suffering, so believers would do the same. Spurgeon made his basic point by way of an analogy: in the same way that swimming could only be learnt in the water, so obedience could only be learnt through suffering. Given the high premium he placed on obedience, the analogy was a remarkable one, even allowing for a degree of hyperbole. Obedience, which was crucial for Spurgeon's conception of the Christian life and so crucial for Spurgeon's spirituality, could be truly learned only through suffering.

In a powerful passage, Spurgeon expanded on how he saw this dynamic working in practice. If a Christian prayed for healing for a chronically sick spouse or child only to see their loved one die, how ought they to respond? Resentment or bitterness might be natural responses, but they would be entirely inappropriate for the Christian. Here was an opportunity, said Spurgeon, to 'learn obedience'. The Christian was being called to a deeper faith and a more thoroughgoing obedience,

---

[44] C.H. Spurgeon, 'Let Him Deliver Him Now', *MTP*, Vol. 34, S. No. 2029, Matthew 27.43, delivered 17 June 1888, pp. 337-38. For the same dual focus, with the sacrifice of Christ on the cross seen in terms of both substitution and example, see 'The Shame And The Spitting', *MTP*, Vol. 25, S. No. 1486, Isaiah 50.6, delivered 27 July 1879, pp. 426-31.

[45] In addition to the other references in this paragraph, see, e.g., C.H. Spurgeon, 'Jesus Declining The Legions', *MTP*, Vol. 33, S. No. 1955, Matthew 26.53,54, delivered 27 March 1887, p. 191.

[46] Cf. C.H. Spurgeon, 'The Only Atoning Priest', *MTP*, Vol. 18, S. No. 1034, Hebrews 10.11-14, delivered 4 February 1872, pp. 76-77.

[47] Spurgeon, 'Let Him Deliver Him Now', pp. 338, 348.

[48] C.H. Spurgeon, *The Gospel of the Kingdom. A Popular Exposition Of The Gospel According to Matthew* (London: Passmore and Alabaster, 1893) (Matthew 10.38), p. 75.

one that endured even when fervent hopes had been disappointed.[49] 'Who knows what it is to obey God to the full until he has had to lay aside his own will in the most painful and tender respects?'[50] Unquestioning faith and obedience formed Spurgeon's ideal. By stripping away a range of different motives for obedience, a believer would learn to obey whatever the circumstances. This may have been in Spurgeon's mind when he once thanked God in prayer for bringing him low because by this means the 'little buildings on the rock had been swept away, and he had come to the solid granite itself'.[51] *In extremis*, a believer was left with bare trust in God and his goodness. This had been the lot of Christ, who had not been spared 'the last ounce of crushing sorrow' on the cross. In such desperate circumstances Christ continued to trust and in this he was the supreme example to believers.[52] Overall, Spurgeon had a theology of suffering in which Christ, and especially the cross, was central. The cross displayed God's sovereignty over suffering and his love for the world. It also set forth an example for believers to follow and provided a dynamic by which Christians could grow in obedient faith. Viewed in the light of the cross, suffering was both bearable and beneficial.

The Benefits of Suffering

Spurgeon held that suffering could, potentially, result in many benefits for the Christian, the learning of obedience being just one of these. He believed that, whilst prosperity softened a Christian, adversity had the opposite effect, bracing the soul and strengthening it.[53] Once again, this was a principle which was deeply rooted in his own experience of suffering. On the last Sunday of 1888 Spurgeon was in Mentone and had a serious accident when his stick slipped at the top of a flight of marble stairs. In the ensuing fall Spurgeon rolled over at least twice and was badly bruised and shaken, losing two of his teeth.[54] One of the sermons he gave on returning to London was on Exodus 15.22-27 and entitled 'Marah Better Than

---

[49] On the specific issue of deepening faith, see 'Thursday Evening At The Tabernacle', *Baptist*, 6 August 1886, in 'Loose-Leaf Scrap Folders', March 1886–October 1886, Spurgeon's College, Heritage Room (2H), pp. 49-50. On the occasion reported, Spurgeon gave an extended reflection on how faith is strengthened in trials.

[50] Spurgeon, 'Our Sympathizing High Priest', p. 597. C.H. Spurgeon used the swimming analogy again in 'Two Good Things', *MTP*, Vol. 27, S. No. 1629, Psalms 119.71 and 73.23, delivered 17 June 1880, p. 640.

[51] *Christian Commonwealth*, 16 April 1885, in 'Spurgeon's Scrapbooks, Numbered Volumes', Vol. 12, p. 102.

[52] Spurgeon, 'Our Sympathizing High Priest', p. 597. Cf. 'The Shame And The Spitting', pp. 429-30.

[53] C.H. Spurgeon, *The Saint And His Saviour: The Progress of the Soul in the Knowledge of Jesus* (London: Hodder and Stoughton, 1889 [1857]), p. 419.

[54] G.H. Pike, *The Life and Work of Charles Haddon Spurgeon* (6 Vols; London: Cassell, 1894 [1892–93]), Vol. 6, pp. 308-309; C.H. Spurgeon to Newman Hall, 20 January 1889, in C. Spurgeon (ed.), *The Letters of C.H. Spurgeon* (London: Marshall, n.d. [1923]), p. 195.

Elim'. Spurgeon referred to his Mentone fall in the sermon's introduction, saying that, soon after his tumble, an unnamed friend had spoken to him. The friend had compared Spurgeon's experience with that of the Israelites who had encountered the bitter water at the springs of Marah (Exodus 15.23). Spurgeon agreed, but both he and his friend concurred that 'Marah' was actually better than the clean springs of 'Elim', as described in Exodus 15.27. This was because there was more lasting benefit to be gained from the former than from the latter. As Spurgeon reflected further on his text he made comparison between the two contrasting experiences of God's people. There had been a miracle at Marah, but no corresponding miracle at Elim. God had made a 'decree' for his people at Marah, saying that if they were faithful to him then they would not be inflicted with the plagues the Egyptians had experienced (Exodus 7–13), but there had been no such decree at Elim. The contrast in favour of Marah was further shown by the fact that Elim was given only one verse in Exodus, whilst Marah was given four. For Spurgeon the message was clear: 'bitter' experiences such as his serious fall could be times of God's special blessing, where he dealt with his people in a particularly thoroughgoing and lasting ways.[55]

Spurgeon's handling of Exodus 15.22-27 gives evidence that his own personal experience of suffering was shaping his reading of the biblical text. Earlier, in 1880, he had insisted that his own 'affliction' had been spiritually beneficial for him. He believed this, he said,

> [N]ot because we have been told so, but because of personal proof; and we assert it now, not as young beginners who are buckling on the harness, and who think themselves certain; but as those who have gone some distance in the pilgrimage of life, and know by actual test and matter of fact that it is even so.[56]

As Spurgeon said elsewhere, 'We have never reaped such a harvest from any seed as from that which fell from our hands while tears were falling from our eyes.'[57] He believed that suffering was good for believers, he believed this strongly, and, finally, he believed this on the basis of personal experience.

Spurgeon spent considerable time in his preaching setting out specific ways in which suffering benefited the Christian. He held that affliction was often God's way of getting the attention of sleepy Christians. Some believers were apt to stumble through their Christian lives in a spiritual lethargy. Such people needed 'awakening and arousing' and trials did this. For other believers who were making more progress, but were tending to pride, suffering acted as a salutary reminder of the old nature. A glass of water might look clear, but a little stirring disturbed the sediment and made the water cloudy. So it was with believers: the agitation caused by

---

[55] C.H. Spurgeon, 'Marah Better Than Elim', *MTP*, Vol. 39, S. No. 2301, Exodus 15.22-26, delivered 4 April 1889, pp. 145-46.

[56] Spurgeon, 'Two Good Things', p. 637.

[57] C.H. Spurgeon, 'The Pitifulness Of The Lord And The Comfort Of The Afflicted', *MTP*, Vol. 31, S. No. 1845, James 5.11, delivered 14 June 1885, p. 325. Cf. 'Certain Singular Subjects', *MTP*, Vol. 29, S. No. 1718, Joshua 24.4, n.d., p. 251.

suffering brought the sin and compromise, which had been present before although not visible, to light. Whether a believer was sleepwalking aimlessly through the Christian life or boasting of sinless perfection, suffering acted as a spiritual wake-up call.[58]

Having been suitably awakened, the faithful believer was then led to search his or her heart for possible sin. Spurgeon believed that suffering could be occasioned by specific sin, although he was clear that this was often not the case.[59] But whether a believer's sin had been a cause of their trials or not, certainly the trials should be accepted as 'chastisement' and used as an opportunity for confession, 'for the best of us have much to mourn in the presence of the Most High'.[60] Growth in humility and holiness was thus achieved.

Spurgeon's conception of holiness was, as has been shown, closely associated with Christlikeness. Suffering afforded an important opportunity for the development of Christlike character.[61] It gave, for example, opportunities to show courage, a virtue Spurgeon believed was exemplified by Christ.[62] The point about suffering and courage was brought out in the aforementioned sermon, 'Gratitude For Deliverance From The Grave'. In this Spurgeon declared,

> We cannot show our courage unless we have difficulties and troubles. A man cannot become a veteran soldier if he never goes to battle ... Rejoice, therefore, in your tribulations, because they give you opportunities for exhibiting a believing confidence, and thereby glorifying the name of the Most High.[63]

Trials gave an opportunity for a believer to display a properly 'manly' courage and, also, a believing confidence in God. These were two virtues that Spurgeon prized highly, as has been shown. Without adversity there would be no opportunity for them to be tested and to grow. Patience was another virtue which was both epitomised by Christ and developed through suffering. Christ had shown patience through suffering and in this he was the pattern for believers.[64] The connection between patience and suffering was a theme taken up by Spurgeon writing as John Ploughman. After asserting that 'the disciples of a patient saviour should be patient themselves', Spurgeon's *alter ego* insisted that affliction was a God-given

---

[58] Spurgeon, 'Two Good Things', pp. 640-42.

[59] Just as Spurgeon believed that accidents were not, usually, to be regarded as God's judgments. See Spurgeon, *Autobiography*, Vol. 4, p. 214.

[60] C.H. Spurgeon, 'For The Sick And Afflicted', *MTP*, Vol. 22, S. No. 1274, Job 34.31,32, n.d., pp. 40-42. Cf. 'For The Troubled', pp. 18-20.

[61] C.H. Spurgeon, 'God's People In The Furnace', *NPSP*, Vol. 1, S. No. 35, Isaiah 48.10, delivered 12 August 1855, p. 273; 'For The Troubled', p. 22.

[62] See, e.g., Spurgeon, *Gospel of the Kingdom*, Matthew 20.17-19, p. 170, and the description of the 'resolute and vigorous' Jesus heading for Jerusalem contrasted with the 'timid' and trembling' disciples.

[63] Spurgeon, 'Gratitude For Deliverance From The Grave', p. 2.

[64] C.H. Spurgeon, 'The Sheep Before The Shearers', *MTP*, Vol. 26, S. No. 1543, Isaiah 53.7, n.d., pp. 349-53.

opportunity to show and develop patience.[65] Elsewhere Spurgeon confessed he could not see how patience would be produced 'apart from affliction'. As a veteran warrior was the 'child of battles', so a patient Christian was the 'offspring of adversity'.[66] These comments on patience are similar to those Spurgeon made with regard to courage. Virtues such as these could only be shown in trials which required their particular use. Going through the fire of suffering was, therefore, an essential part of the process of Christian growth and sanctification.[67] Christ had shown courage and patience in the face of suffering; Christians were to do the same, thus growing to become more like Christ themselves.

The sort of toughening up that Spurgeon was sure suffering produced was, he believed, essential preparation for future service. Adversity prepared the soul for 'greater heights of service';[68] for 'future usefulness' it was essential that 'present sorrow' was born.[69] This last mentioned comment was from a sermon entitled 'Certain Singular Subjects' in which he also used the phrase 'sanctified trials'.[70] The idea of afflictions being sanctified to the believer was an important one for Spurgeon.[71] Two Christians could have similar experiences of suffering and yet respond in markedly different ways. There was a real danger that suffering would make a believer impatient, hardened and bitter. It could also, potentially, lead them to despair. Worst of all, a believer might blame God or slip into what Spurgeon described as a 'kind of atheism', saying that if God was real he would not allow such suffering.[72] For the 'fire' to purify and not consume it had to be sanctified to the believer. For this to happen God had to be at work in a believer's life as they experienced trials. In the sermon, 'The Sitting Of The Refiner', the 'refiner' is clearly thought of as being Christ, acting by the agency of the Holy Spirit.[73] Believers had to respond to this work by accepting suffering 'humbly'[74] and 'willingly'[75] just as Christ had accepted his suffering.[76] Following the example set by

---

[65] C.H. Spurgeon, *John Ploughman's Talk; Or, Plain Advice For Plain People* (London: Passmore and Alabaster, n.d.), 'On Patience', pp. 36-40.

[66] Spurgeon, 'Two Good Things', p. 640.

[67] C.H. Spurgeon, 'The Sitting Of The Refiner', *MTP*, Vol. 27, S. No. 1575, Malachi 3.3, n.d., p. 4; C.H. Spurgeon to W. Cuff, 7 March 1891, in C. Spurgeon (ed.), *The Letters of C.H. Spurgeon*, p. 152.

[68] C.H. Spurgeon to W.J. Mayers, 25 July 1874, in C. Spurgeon (ed.), *Letters of C.H. Spurgeon*, p. 170.

[69] Spurgeon, 'Certain Singular Subjects', p. 251.

[70] Spurgeon, 'Certain Singular Subjects', p. 251.

[71] Cf. Spurgeon, *The Saint And His Saviour*, p. 361.

[72] C.H. Spurgeon, 'Patient Job And The Baffled Enemy', *MTP*, Vol. 36, S. No. 2172, Job 1.22, delivered 28 August 1890, pp. 604-10; cf. 'The Sitting Of The Refiner', p. 4.

[73] Spurgeon, 'The Sitting Of The Refiner', pp. 1, 4.

[74] Spurgeon, 'For The Sick And Afflicted', pp. 38-41.

[75] C.T. Cook (ed.), *Behold The Throne Of Grace: C.H. Spurgeon's Prayers And Hymns* (London: Marshall, Morgan & Scott, n.d. [1934]), 'Praise At All Times' (3 November 1889), p. 81.

[76] Spurgeon, 'Jesus Declining The Legions', pp. 186-87.

the earthly life of Christ a Christian was to cooperate with all that the risen glorified Christ wanted to do in their lives through the refining work of suffering. If a Christian did cooperate in this process, then they would become purified through affliction. Where a believer was enabled to have the right attitude to suffering, they would become more like Christ and more useful for Christ as a result of their trials. Overall, for Spurgeon, suffering was not only immensely beneficial; approached in the right way it would lead to growth towards Christlike holiness.

Influences on Spurgeon's Approach

Spurgeon freely acknowledged that this vision of the Christian life – one that laid great stress on the importance of suffering – was not one that all would find attractive.[77] In a sermon reflecting on the life of the Old Testament character, Joseph, the pastor of the Metropolitan Tabernacle insisted that the road 'to all true honour' was difficult.[78] There was, he insisted, simply no way around this. But, far from seeing this as a drawback, Spurgeon made a virtue out of this, viewing the prospect of hard trials in a positive and 'heroic' light. This much can be seen from the following quotation from 'The Pitifulness Of The Lord And The Comfort Of The Afflicted':

> We count that man happy who has passed through trial and hardship with a brave endurance. Such life is of an interesting and manly kind; but life without struggle and difficulty is thin and tasteless. How can a noble life be constructed if there is no difficulty to overcome, no suffering to bear? What was there about Dives, and his fine linen, and sumptuous fare, to make life of? Who envies him? Studying the lives of eminent men, we come to this conclusion, that on the whole it is good for a man to bear the yoke; good for a man to breast the billows; good for a man to pass through fire and through water, and so to learn sublime lessons. When we see what poor, paltry things those are who are nursed in the lap of luxury and consequently never come to a real manhood, 'we count them happy that endure.' No wise man would seek to be exempted from the healthy discipline of trouble any more than an intelligent child would wish to be excused from school and to be allowed to play all day and every day in the meadows. No: we are not butterflies that flit from flower to flower; life is real, life is earnest, and the tonic of sorrow braces and strengthens us to make it so! As a matter of faith and even as a matter of reasonable judgment, 'we count them happy which endure'.[79]

Spurgeon's words are worth citing at length as they emphasise his basic contention: suffering was an opportunity for the development of Christlike character.

---

[77] Spurgeon, 'For The Troubled', p. 23: 'I know while I am preaching some of you have said, "Ah, these people of God have a hard time of it."'

[78] C.H. Spurgeon, 'Trial By The Word', *MTP*, Vol. 22, S. No. 1277, Psalm 105.19, delivered 6 February 1876, pp. 73-74.

[79] Spurgeon, 'The Pitifulness Of The Lord And The Comfort Of The Afflicted', pp. 327-28.

They are also suggestive of the wide range of cultural influences which helped shape Spurgeon's approach. In this respect it is interesting to note that immediately before the words cited, he directly appealed to the 'more sensible part of mankind'; that is, he was arguing for the place of trials in developing character in a way which he expected would resonate with many of his fellow Victorians, not necessarily only those who were committed Christians. The cultural influences which can be identified in this extract have all been noticed and subjected to extended treatments elsewhere in this study. What is remarkable about Spurgeon's comments from 'The Pitifulness Of The Lord ...' is the way in which the different influences can all be discerned in one quotation.

It is worth taking time to note the cultural movements which informed Spurgeon's thinking in 'The Pitifulness Of The Lord ...'. There is a suggestion of the 'Christian manliness' associated with Charles Kingsley in the use of the word 'manly' and the mention of 'real manhood'; an echo, too, of the exaltation of Samuel Smiles' 'self-made man' in the comment about the lives of 'eminent men'. The emphasis on the 'common man' over and against the cultured élite is also present, especially in the references to Dives' 'fine linen' and 'sumptuous fare', in the negative words about 'the lap of luxury' and, perhaps, in the comment about butterflies which 'flit from flower to flower'. Rather than envying the cultured ease of the dandified élite, the artisans and the solid middle-class could rejoice: the struggles they faced in business and in life in general did not make them inferior; rather, the reverse was true, for their supposed betters were, in reality, 'poor and paltry things', enfeebled by idle luxury. Enlightened common sense is also present in the extract, with the appeal to 'reasonable judgment' in the final sentence. There are Romantic references too. The phrase, 'life is real, life is earnest' is an echo of American poet Henry Wadsworth Longfellow's A *Psalm of Life* with its lines,

> Life is real! Life is earnest!
> And the grave is not its goal[80]

Longfellow was both Romantic and popular. His second wife, Frances Appleton, had died horrifically in a fire at the family home in 1861, with Henry unable to save her.[81] The tragic story was well known in Victorian society, and it is possible that in citing Longfellow's lines Spurgeon was consciously alluding to this context of suffering.

What is clear, however, is that the whole extract from 'The Pitifulness Of The Lord ...' has a Romantic tincture in the way that it consistently evokes a 'heroic' ideal. The faithful Christian pilgrim is one who passes through 'trial' and 'hardship' with 'brave endurance', battling through fire and water, learning invaluable,

---

[80] H.W. Longfellow, *A Psalm of Life: What the heart of the young man said to the Psalmist*, in, e.g., H.W. Longfellow, *Favourite Poems* (London: Routledge, 1878), p. 12. I am grateful to David Bebbington for pointing out this reference to me.

[81] C.C. Calhoun, *Longfellow: A Rediscovered Life* (Boston: Beacon, 2004), p. 215.

character building lessons along the way. Some of this imagery is redolent of Bunyan, but the spirit and tone is also shaped by a popular Romanticism which exalted the heroic. The Christian believer was like Sir Walter Scott's Ivanhoe, battling through against the odds. As Spurgeon wrote elsewhere, as knights were made 'by a stroke from the sovereign's sword', so Christians would 'become princes in Christ's realm' as Christ laid 'his cross on their shoulders'.[82] This was a heroic, Romantic vision of the Christian life.

There is something instructive in seeing so many of the different streams which helped feed Spurgeon's spirituality converge and intermingle. Mark Hopkins has written of the 'cross-currents' produced by the confluence of Enlightenment and Romantic emphases in Nonconformist life.[83] Hopkins gives some attention to Spurgeon in his analysis and I want to affirm that Spurgeon's life and ministry exhibit evidence of both Romantic and Enlightenment influences, with the two often coming together. This is true of his approach to suffering, which is our particular concern here, but it is also true of his spirituality more generally. Moreover, there are more cultural currents present than the Romantic and the enlightened (although it is true that the cult of manliness, for example, was in itself an expression of the Romantic temper). Spurgeon emerges from this analysis as a complex figure, one whose spirituality shows evidence of different influences. The fact that suffering gave the opportunity for a heroic Christian life can also be underlined. This was a further benefit which could accrue through suffering.

Suffering and Communion with Christ

Suffering could lead to many benefits but, unsurprisingly, Spurgeon prized suffering most for the way it could bring Christians into closer communion with their Lord, and it is specifically to this theme that this chapter now turns. In a sermon entitled 'Job Among The Ashes', Spurgeon asserted that a believer's suffering could lead to a clearer sight of God. Prosperity was a 'painted window' which shut out 'the clear light of God'. Only when the paint was removed did the window become 'transparent', enabling God to be seen with a new clarity. This had been Job's experience: he had lost everything and this 'paved the way' to him receiving a fuller revelation of God. The principle on display was that in 'the absence of other goods the good God is the better seen'. Again, Spurgeon stressed that the suffering had to be 'sanctified': affliction did not lead to a clearer view of God in every case. But where God was at work and where a believer responded faithfully to this, then spiritual perception would be heightened. Those who gained a spiritually 'enlightened eye' would learn to thank God for the process of suffering by which this sharpened spiritual vision had been attained. Spurgeon turned to the New Testament to provide another example to set alongside that of Job. 'Who would not go to

---

[82] Spurgeon, *Gospel of the Kingdom* (Matthew 27.32), p. 248.

[83] M. Hopkins, *Nonconformity's Romantic Generation: Evangelical and Liberal Theologies in Victorian England* (Carlisle: Paternoster, 2004), p. 256.

Patmos if he might see the visions of John?' The deprivations of exile were the context in which John had received his revelation of Jesus Christ. Therefore, it was the witness of both Testaments that suffering could lead to a new vision of God, one which made the trials eminently worthwhile.[84]

Moreover, this was also Spurgeon's own testimony. In 'The Pitifulness Of The Lord ...' he declared,

> [T]he Lord has a choice way of manifesting himself unto his servants in their times of weakness. I speak what I do know; for I have trodden ... the path upon which shines the inward personal revelation of God. He draws the curtain about the bed of his chosen sufferer and, at the same time he withdraws another curtain which before concealed his Glory![85]

Scripture and Spurgeon's personal experience agreed. God revealed himself to suffering believers, and did so in a particularly 'choice' way.

In 'Job Among The Ashes' Spurgeon had spoken of how a fuller revelation of God enabled a new closeness to him. The sermon is unusual for him in that it lacked a strong christological focus. Elsewhere, however, there was a clear stress on suffering as a means to increased closeness to Christ himself. Jesus could be seen more clearly in and as a result of an experience of suffering, and, crucially, he could be known more deeply through it too. In 'The Pitifulness Of The Lord ...' Spurgeon insisted that

> [T]hose of us who have done business upon great waters and have endured abundant pain count them happy that endure, even while they are enduring. The people of God find themselves more buoyant in the saltiest seas of sorrow than in other waters. The cross of Christ doth indeed raise us nearer to God when it is sanctified.[86]

Suffering was especially prized because, when it was considered as a cross given by Christ, it drew a believer closer to God. As Spurgeon continued his message he spoke specifically of closeness to Christ. 'Sorrows reveal to us the Man of Sorrows. Griefs waft us to the bosom of our God.' For Spurgeon, there could be no greater prize, for the 'most delicious of sensations outside of heaven is to faint away on the bosom of the Lord'.[87]

---

[84] C.H. Spurgeon, 'Job Among The Ashes', *MTP*, Vol. 34, S. No. 2009, Job 42.5,6, delivered 19 February 1888, pp. 100, 107. Elsewhere Spurgeon used slightly different imagery but the point was essentially the same: it was in the 'thick darkness' of suffering that the 'brightness' of the Lord's presence could be best seen. See Spurgeon, 'Trial By The Word', p. 77.

[85] Spurgeon, 'The Pitifulness Of The Lord And The Comfort Of The Afflicted', p. 329.

[86] Spurgeon, 'The Pitifulness Of The Lord And The Comfort Of The Afflicted', p. 328.

[87] Spurgeon, 'The Pitifulness Of The Lord And The Comfort Of The Afflicted', p. 329.

How did Spurgeon believe this dynamic worked? Part of the answer was that 'sorrow and adversity' drove the 'children of God to their knees',[88] thus fostering increased communion. Similarly, suffering would lead the faithful Christian to search the scriptures as he or she sought comfort and help.[89] A believer, then, was led to seek Christ more diligently in the midst of trials. This was only one half of the dynamic, however, for Spurgeon was sure that as a suffering believer drew near to God, then God would draw near to them, doing so especially in the person of his Son who was present to the believer by the Spirit. Jesus had shown compassion to suffering people in his earthly ministry, so he would have compassion on his suffering people in Spurgeon's day.[90] In 'Trial By The Word' Spurgeon offered the following analogy. A faithful mother, he declared, loved her young child at all times. Nevertheless, it was when the child was sick or injured that her full 'tenderness' was seen. 'If you would read all her heart, you should see her when [the child] scarcely breathes, when she fears that every moment will be its last. Then all the mother is revealed. How she fondles it, and what a store of sweet words she brings forth.'[91] Spurgeon's imagery was both intimate and daring, but he believed it was entirely justified, employed as it was to describe the closeness which could exist between God and a faithful, suffering believer. Again, as Spurgeon spoke of God drawing near, it was Christ whom he especially had in mind, for Christ's suffering gave him a special 'sympathy' with other sufferers.[92]

The sympathy Christ had with suffering believers was a theme Spurgeon returned to repeatedly.[93] In one of the sermons in which he spoke of this he quoted lines from a hymn by Henry Milman,

> When our heads are bowed with woe,
> When our bitter tears o'erflow,
> When we mourn the lost, the dear,
> Then the Son of Man is near.
>
> Thou our throbbing flesh hast worn,
> Thou our mortal griefs hast borne;
> Thou hast shed the human tear,
> Son of Man, to mourners dear.[94]

---

[88] Spurgeon, 'Certain Singular Subjects', p. 251; cf. 'The Pitifulness Of The Lord And The Comfort Of The Afflicted', p. 329.

[89] C.H. Spurgeon, 'My Comfort In Affliction', *MTP*, Vol. 31, S. No. 1872, Psalm 119.50, delivered 7 July 1881, pp. 644-45.

[90] Spurgeon, 'The Pitifulness Of The Lord And The Comfort Of The Afflicted', pp. 333-34.

[91] Spurgeon, 'Trial By The Word', pp. 77-78.

[92] Spurgeon, 'The Suffering Saviour's Sympathy', p. 417.

[93] In addition to the other sermons cited in this section, see C.H. Spurgeon, 'Consolation Proportionate To Spiritual Sufferings', *NPSP*, Vol. 1, S. No. 13, 2 Corinthians 1.5, 11 March 1855, p. 99.

Suffering

Jesus the man had suffered, for example mourning and weeping at the tomb of a friend. When his children mourned, or when they suffered some other 'mortal grief', the suffering God, the 'Son of Man' drew near.[95] He was with his people in the 'furnace', just as he had been with Shadrach, Meshach and Abednego in Daniel 3.[96] Suffering led to 'near and dear communion' between the believer and Christ.[97]

As this communion was enjoyed, Christ would not only comfort and strengthen the Christian, but the believer would gain yet deeper insight and knowledge of Christ. In 'Communion With Christ And His People', Spurgeon declared,

> Certain of us have had large fellowship with the Lord Jesus in affliction. 'Jesus wept': He lost a friend, and so have we. Jesus grieved over the hardness of men's hearts: we know that grief. Jesus was exceedingly sorry that the hopeful young man turned away, and went back to the world: we know that sorrow. Those who have sympathetic hearts, and live for others, readily enter into the experience of 'the Man of sorrows'. The wounds of calumny, the reproaches of the proud, the venom of the bigoted, the treachery of the false, and the weakness of the true, we have known in our measure; and therein have had communion with our Lord Jesus.[98]

Once again, the note of personal testimony is unmistakable. The thought that Christ comforts believers in 'affliction' is also surely present. But the dominant motif in this extract appears to be that a believer entered into the sufferings of Christ when he or she suffered. A believer's suffering led to them knowing an increased depth of sympathy with Christ. In Spurgeon's thinking and experience, communion with Christ was always a dynamic concept. As far as the communion which could be known through suffering was concerned, a clearer sight of Christ would lead to increased communion, which would in turn lead to an even fuller revelation. So the dynamic would continue. Suffering had a vitally important role in developing communion with Christ for Spurgeon.

---

[94] Spurgeon, 'The Suffering Saviour's Sympathy', p. 417. Surprisingly, 'When our heads are bowed with woe', which was written in 1827, is not in *Our Own Hymn Book*. Henry Hart Milman was dean of St Paul's Cathedral from 1849. It is possible that Milman's sympathy with aspects of liberal biblical criticism militated against the inclusion of his hymn, although, clearly, Spurgeon was quite happy to cite it when preaching. For Milman, see C. Smyth, *Dean Milman* (London: SPCK, 1949).

[95] Spurgeon, 'The Suffering Saviour's Sympathy', p. 417.

[96] C.H. Spurgeon, 'God's People In The Furnace', *NPSP*, Vol. 1, S. No. 35, Isaiah 48.10, delivered 12 August 1855, p. 275. Cf. 'Trial By The Word', p. 77. Christ was in the 'midst of the furnace with his persecuted ones'.

[97] Spurgeon, 'The Pitifulness Of The Lord And The Comfort Of The Afflicted', p. 329.

[98] C.H. Spurgeon, 'Communion with Christ and His People', in *Till He Come: Communion Meditations* (London: Passmore and Alabaster, 1896), 1 Corinthians 10.16-17, 'A Communion Address at Mentone', p. 317.

Suffering and Communion with Christ's People

How did suffering link with the second aspect of the theme, 'communion with Christ *and his people*'? First of all, Spurgeon's own experience of suffering meant that he had to rely increasingly on the help of others as his ministry progressed. This was set out at some length in chapter 8 and does not need to be rehearsed again here. As I have already argued, Spurgeon's desire to work closely with others was linked with underlying issues of character and temperament: even if Spurgeon had not suffered in the ways set out in the opening section of this chapter, he would still have sought communion with Christ's people as he engaged in different activities for Christ. But there is no doubt that suffering, especially the incapacitating physical suffering Spurgeon experienced, heightened the necessity of this 'communal' way of working.

Fundamentally, though, the theme of suffering connects with 'Christ's people' because of Spurgeon's insistence that believers' afflictions uniquely fitted them to be a source of comfort and strength for others. This did not happen automatically. Just as suffering had to be 'sanctified' in order for it to do the believer good, so God had to be at work in and through the believer if they were to help others. Nevertheless, when God was at work in this way, suffering believers would become a rich source of blessing to fellow pilgrims.[99] There were, Spurgeon believed, numerous instances of this dynamic at work in scripture. Regarding the Psalmist, David, Spurgeon said, 'What a mercy it is for us all that [he] was not an untried man! We have all been enriched by his painful experience ... May it not be a blessing to others that we also are tried? If so, ought we not to be right glad to contribute our quota to the benefit of the redeemed family?'[100] Spurgeon's point was that David's painful experiences, as shared in many of the Psalms attributed to him, had been of great benefit to those (like Spurgeon himself) who had read them and received help from them. Those who suffered in Spurgeon's day could be glad that they too had the opportunity to minister comfort and strength to others. The supreme example of the sufferer reaching out to help others in affliction, however, was not David but Christ himself. Spurgeon spoke of Jesus learning not only obedience but also 'sympathy' through sufferings.[101] Christ had repeatedly reached out in compassion to others,[102] even doing so when he was on the cross.[103] Suffering believers were to follow his example.[104]

---

[99] This theme has been expounded by a range of Christian spiritual writers. Its classic expression is probably found in H. Nouwen, *The Wounded Healer* (London: Darton, Longman and Todd, 1994 [1979]).

[100] C.H. Spurgeon, *My Sermon Notes: A Selection From Outlines Of Discourses Delivered At The Metropolitan Tabernacle ... From Genesis To Proverbs I to LXIV* (New York: Fleming H. Revell, n.d. [1884]), No. 54, Psalm 143.9, p. 327.

[101] Spurgeon, 'The Suffering Saviour's Sympathy', p. 409.

[102] Spurgeon, *Gospel of the Kingdom* (Matthew 14.14), p. 113.

[103] C.H. Spurgeon, 'Christ's Plea For Ignorant Sinners', *MTP*, Vol. 38, S. No. 2263, Luke 23.34, delivered 5 October 1890, pp. 313, 317.

[104] Spurgeon, 'The Suffering Saviour's Sympathy', p. 410.

Christians who were, or had been, 'afflicted' in their journey of faith were able to help other struggling Christians in a number of different ways. If they patiently endured through intense suffering their example might act as a spur and encouragement to others. Spurgeon believed that some were especially chosen to suffer and so 'to be monuments of the Lord's special dealings; a sort of lighthouse to other mariners'.[105] Spurgeon thought of the Protestant martyrs in this way. As seen in chapter 2, their stories had been first mediated to him in printed form by John Foxe's *Actes and Monuments*. The courage these martyrs had shown as they faced death for their beliefs was inspiring to him.[106] By showing fortitude and faithfulness in suffering, then, a Christian would give an example which others could follow.[107]

As far as Spurgeon himself was concerned, he was clearly regarded by fellow Christians as an example of someone who bore suffering patiently and heroically. This was how he was viewed by many of his students, in particular.[108] It was not enough, however, to suffer silently. The lessons of suffering had to be actively shared. Spurgeon sought to do this through his books and preaching.[109] He also got alongside people more personally. This latter point can be seen through letters he wrote to those who were afflicted. In *The Letters of Charles Haddon Spurgeon*, the editor, C.H. Spurgeon's son, Charles Spurgeon, included a section headed 'Words of Sympathy'.[110] For this section, the editor selected twelve letters, eleven of which were written to bereaved friends. In these, Spurgeon sought to express his own grief, comfort the family member or friend, and encourage them in their ongoing Christian pilgrimage.

The letters are revealing. In them Spurgeon expressed his own grief at various situations faced by his friends. He assured his son, Charles, that he would 'never forget the day' he heard of the death of one of Charles' children, his grandchild;[111] and he wrote to Thomas Olney saying that he 'felt stunned' by news of William Olney's death: 'I could not realise it; indeed, I cannot now', he said.[112] He also

---

[105] Spurgeon, *My Sermon Notes ... From Genesis to Proverbs*, No. 37, Job 3.23, p. 230.

[106] C.H. Spurgeon, 'Chastisement', *NPSP*, Vol. 1, S. No. 48, Hebrews 12.5, delivered 28 October 1855, pp. 366-67.

[107] Spurgeon, *Autobiography*, Vol. 1, p. 23.

[108] J.C. Carlile, *C.H. Spurgeon: An Interpretative Biography* (London: Kingsgate Press, 1933), pp. 130-31.

[109] For further examples from C.H. Spurgeon's writing, see, e.g., *John Ploughman's Talk*, 'On Patience', pp. 36-40; 'Men Who Are Down', pp. 88-93; *Evening By Evening*, 2 Timothy 2.12 (July 3), p. 186.

[110] C. Spurgeon (ed.), *The Letters of C.H. Spurgeon*, pp. 166-72. Cf. other letters to those who were suffering, e.g., C.H. Spurgeon to unnamed friend, 24 July 1873, No. 9a; C.H. Spurgeon to unnamed friend, 3 June 1882, No. 44, both in 'Original Correspondence of Charles Haddon Spurgeon, 1863–1886'.

[111] C.H. Spurgeon to Mr and Mrs C. Spurgeon, 11 September 1890, in C. Spurgeon (ed.), *The Letters of C.H. Spurgeon*, p. 166.

[112] C.H. Spurgeon to T.H. Olney, October 1875, in C. Spurgeon (ed.), *The Letters of C.H. Spurgeon*, p. 167.

offered comfort. This included practical help, sending a cheque to help defray funeral expenses, for example.[113] He repeatedly assured grieving friends of his prayers,[114] and sometimes recorded the nature of his petitions in the letter. 'I beseech the Lord to minister comfort both to you and your sorrowing wife', Spurgeon wrote to William Cuff, a former student, following a family bereavement.[115] He gave encouragement too. He was especially quick to say that he believed the Lord would comfort his friends in their grief,[116] and wanted people to know, in line with the theological framework outlined at the beginning of this chapter, that their suffering did not fall outside of God's sovereignty. Indeed, suffering could be a sign of God's special love. To Cuff he wrote,

> It must be a very severe stroke to you, and it is a sign that our Father loves you very much and thinks a great deal of you. I had a watch once which I allowed to lie at ease and never worried it with cleaning for I thought it worthless; but one which keeps time to a second gets wound up every night with a key which touches its inmost springs, and sometimes it gets taken to pieces – for it is worth it.[117]

Such a passage can sound like inappropriate moralising, but such a letter appears to have been well received by the recipient and, indeed, treasured. The fact that Cuff made this and other letters available to Charles Spurgeon with permission to publish is, in itself, evidence of this.[118] William Williams wrote positively of the help Spurgeon gave to suffering Christians, saying that his friend 'was as familiar with the glades of grief and the dark narrow gorges of depression as any man, or he could never with such consummate art have ministered comfort to the suffering …'.[119] Spurgeon had himself learnt the lessons he sought to share with others; suffering had become a crucial aspect of the way he related to God. People knew this: it was part of his psyche to share what he had learned and experienced with others. That which he had come to know 'experimentally' he believed he was called to share, from the pulpit and also more personally with individual friends. J.C. Carlile's comment on Spurgeon's battles with suffering is worth quoting: 'The greater part of his career was lived in fellowship with physical pain. How bravely he endured his cross, and

---

[113] C.H. Spurgeon to E.H. Bartlett, 14 December 1887, in C. Spurgeon (ed.), *The Letters of C.H. Spurgeon*, p. 169.

[114] E.g. C.H. Spurgeon to T.H. Olney, October 1875; to W.J. Mayers, 25 July 1874, in C. Spurgeon (ed.), *The Letters of C.H. Spurgeon*, pp. 167; 170.

[115] C.H. Spurgeon to W. Cuff, '30 November [no year]', in C. Spurgeon (ed.), *The Letters of C.H. Spurgeon*, p. 170.

[116] E.g. C.H. Spurgeon to T.H. Olney, October 1875; to J.W. Harrald [n.d.], in C. Spurgeon (ed.), *The Letters of C.H. Spurgeon*, pp. 167, 171-72. Cf. C.H. Spurgeon to W. Baldock, 6 October 1886, 'Various Spurgeon Letters', Spurgeon's College, Heritage Room, (K1.9).

[117] C.H. Spurgeon to W. Cuff, '30 November [no year]', in C. Spurgeon (ed.), *The Letters of C.H. Spurgeon*, p. 170.

[118] C. Spurgeon (ed.), *The Letters of C.H. Spurgeon*, 'Introduction', p. 9.

[119] Williams, *Personal Reminiscences* (rev. edn.), p. 24.

made suffering contribute to the comfort and the strengthening of others.'[120] The letters collected by his son show how the lessons of suffering were shared, one-to-one, with some of Christ's people.

Spurgeon also believed that the lessons of suffering could be shared in evangelism. On one occasion he pictured a believer, who had displayed Christian graces when under severe trial, being questioned by an unbeliever.

> 'I saw how happy you were, dear friend, when you were in trouble. I saw you sick the other day, and I noticed your patience. I knew you to be slandered, and I saw how calm you were. Can you tell me why you were so calm and self-contained?' It is a very happy thing if the Christian can turn round and answer such a question fully. I like to see him ready to give a reason for the hope that is in him with meekness and fear, saying – *'This* is my comfort in my affliction.' I want you, if you have enjoyed comfort from God, to get it packed up in such a form that you can pass it on to a friend. Get it explained to your own understanding, so that you can tell others what it is, so that they may taste the consolation wherewith God has comforted you.[121]

It was not just other Christians who could be helped by a believer's suffering. Rightly shared, a believer's faithfulness in difficulty could have an evangelistic impact on the non-believer. Spurgeon's approach to suffering thus connected both with those who were already Christ's people and those who had yet to experience 'God's consolation' for themselves.

The End of Suffering: Perfect Communion

Part of the previous section dealt with how Spurgeon sought to bring comfort to grieving friends. Unsurprisingly, this comfort included assuring them that their loved ones, assuming they were Christians, had entered heaven and were with their Lord for ever.[122] Spurgeon also believed that all infants were 'saved', even if they were born to non-Christian parents.[123] Consequently, he had no hesitation about giving this assurance to those of his friends who had lost a very young child.[124] This certainty regarding the future was also present in the only letter included in Charles Spurgeon's 'Words of Sympathy' section which was written to someone who was terminally ill. The recipient was Thomas Curme. Spurgeon had heard of Curme's illness and that there was no hope of his recovery. Spurgeon wrote to his friend of his deep sadness, offering what he called a 'loving, tender prayer' for Curme, 'Lord, comfort Thy dear servant …!' But the primary way Spurgeon sought to minister to

---

[120] Carlile, *C.H. Spurgeon*, p. 130.

[121] Spurgeon, 'My Comfort In Affliction', p. 643.

[122] E.g. C.H. Spurgeon to F.J. Feltham, n.d., in C. Spurgeon (ed.), *The Letters of C.H. Spurgeon*, p. 171.

[123] Spurgeon, *Autobiography*, Vol. 1, p. 175.

[124] E.g. C.H. Spurgeon to 'Mr Higgs', 18 March 1886, in C. Spurgeon (ed.), *The Letters of C.H. Spurgeon*, p. 171.

his friend was to encourage him with the sure and certain hope of heaven: 'You have nothing to do but go home; and what a home!'[125] The end of physical suffering, namely death, was also the gateway to heaven.[126] This chapter concludes with an analysis of Spurgeon's view of what the life to come would be like for believers, a vision which was focused on the overarching theme of his spirituality. 'Communion with Christ and his people' was to be enjoyed throughout the Christian pilgrimage, but it was only an anticipation of the perfect communion which was to come.

Spurgeon's millennial views have already been dealt with in chapter 9 and will not be rehearsed here. H.F. Colquitt gives further detail on Spurgeon's eschatology, and does so competently. When Christ returns in person, Christians who had died would experience a 'resurrection of the body, at which time the soul which has been separated from the body in the intermediate state, will unite with the body'.[127] Those still alive would be transformed, also receiving new bodies.[128] These new bodies would be patterned on Christ's own resurrected body.[129] As for the 'ungodly', there was for them another, second resurrection to a 'damnation'[130] which was eternal.[131] Spurgeon's conception of hell can be summed up quite simply. There was, he said, 'no communion with God in hell'.[132] For Spurgeon, there could hardly be a more chilling sentence. The thought of being 'away from Jesus' for eternity filled him with horror.[133]

If the greatest terror of hell was the absence of communion with God, then 'heaven' was the realisation of perfect communion with Christ. For Spurgeon, to think of heaven without Christ was inconceivable. A passage from a sermon entitled 'For Ever With The Lord' makes the point well. It was impossible, Spurgeon said, to imagine heaven without Christ. To try to do so was completely 'absurd', analogous to thinking of the 'sea without water' or the 'earth without its fields'. He continued, 'There cannot be heaven without Christ. He is the sum total of bliss; the fountain

---

[125] C.H. Spurgeon to T. Curme, 12 June 1884, in C. Spurgeon (ed.), *The Letters of C.H. Spurgeon*, p. 169.

[126] Cf. C.H. Spurgeon 'No condemnation', in T.P. Crosby (ed.), *C.H. Spurgeon's Sermons Beyond Volume 63: An authentic supplement to the Metropolitan Tabernacle Pulpit* (Leominster: Day One, 2009), Romans 8.1, n.d., p. 329.

[127] H.F. Colquitt, 'The Soteriology of Charles Haddon Spurgeon Revealed in his Sermons and Controversial Writings' (unpublished PhD dissertation, University of Edinburgh, 1951), pp. 261-62.

[128] C.H. Spurgeon, 'Though He Were Dead', *MTP*, Vol. 30, S. No. 1799, John 11.24-26, delivered 14 September 1884, p. 498.

[129] Colquitt, 'Soteriology of Charles Haddon Spurgeon', p. 263.

[130] C.H. Spurgeon, 'The Coming Resurrection', *MTP*, Vol. 15, S. No. 896, John 5.28,29, delivered 17 October 1869, p. 585.

[131] C.H. Spurgeon, 'The Lord No More Wroth [sic] With His People', *MTP*, Vol. 36, S. No. 2176, Isaiah 54.9, n.d., pp. 652-53.

[132] C.H. Spurgeon, 'The Bridgeless Gulf', *MTP*, Vol. 9, S. No. 518, Luke 16.26, delivered 5 July 1863, p. 381.

[133] C.H. Spurgeon, 'For Ever With The Lord', *MTP*, Vol. 19, S. No. 1136, Philippians 1.23, delivered 12 October 1873, p. 571.

from which heaven flows, the element of which heaven is composed. Christ is heaven and heaven is Christ. You shall change the words and make no difference in the sense.'[134]

The association of 'heaven' with 'Christ' could hardly be closer, indeed the two words were essentially interchangeable. The 'bliss' of heaven was the bliss of enjoying communion with Christ, a point which Spurgeon went on to elaborate. Though the communion which a believer enjoyed with Christ 'in the body' was wonderful, it was only an anticipation of the perfect communion which was to come. In this life, a believer could know Christ, be near Christ and have 'intimate intercourse' with Christ. But in the next life these things would be known with an intensity that would make present communion seem pale by comparison.[135] Spurgeon was here talking of the 'intermediate state'. He held that believers who had died found themselves immediately in the presence of Christ and were conscious while they waited for the resurrection of the body.[136] Thus, whether it was before or after the resurrection to eternal life, it was conscious enjoyment of Christ's presence that was the outstanding feature of life beyond the grave for the believer.[137] In a sermon, 'The Elders Before The Throne', he again set out his views on the 'intermediate state', declaring,

> We believe, then, that the condition of glorified spirits in heaven, is that of nearness to Christ, clear vision of his glory, constant access to his court, and familiar fellowship with his person. Nor do we think there is any difference before the throne between one saint and another. We believe that all the people of God, apostles, martyrs, ministers, or private and obscure Christians shall all have the same place *near the throne*, where they shall for ever gaze upon their exalted Lord, and for ever be satisfied in his love.[138]

Those who had died in Christ would be near Christ, would see Christ and would have 'familiar fellowship' with Christ. This was the essence of heaven and it would be forever satisfying. The egalitarian aspect of Spurgeon's vision of the future parallels his vision of equality around the Communion table.[139] There would be no

---

[134] Spurgeon, 'For Ever With The Lord', pp. 570-71.

[135] Spurgeon, 'For Ever With The Lord', pp. 571-72.

[136] That this was Spurgeon's view can also be seen from C. Spurgeon (ed.), *The Letters of C.H. Spurgeon*. See, e.g., C.H. Spurgeon to T. Curme, 12 June 1884, p. 169; C.H. Spurgeon to R.J. Feltham, n.d., p. 171.

[137] See verse 6 of C.H. Spurgeon's hymn 'Immanuel' which is no. 1107 in [Anon.] (ed.), *Supplement To Our Own Hymn Book* (London: Passmore and Alabaster, 1898).

[138] C.H. Spurgeon, 'The Elders Before The Throne', *MTP*, Vol. 8, S. No. 441, Revelation 4.10,11, delivered 23 March 1862, p. 172, italics original. Cf. Colquitt, 'Soteriology of Charles Haddon Spurgeon', p. 270.

[139] Spurgeon's exposition of the 'parable of the talents' in the *Gospel of the Kingdom* (Matthew 25.22,23), p. 226, had a similar emphasis. In Spurgeon's view, the servant who had doubled his two talents and the servant who had doubled his five were 'equally praised and blessed'.

hierarchy; all Christians would be equally close to Christ, equally his 'favourites' and his 'friends'.[140] This would be a heaven for the common people.

Colquitt includes a number of well chosen quotations emphasising heaven as communion with Christ although, as with much of his study, one wishes for more analysis of the material he is citing. Moreover, in Colquitt's survey of Spurgeon's eschatology, he does not bring out the importance of heaven as a place where communion with Christ's people is experienced. This latter dimension of Spurgeon's thinking can in fact be seen in the extract from 'The Elders Before The Throne' which was cited in the previous paragraph. All of God's people would, together, be near Christ. Elsewhere Spurgeon elaborated on this theme. Heaven, he said, would consist 'largely in the communion of saints'. Some Christians, he averred, were like icebergs, cold and living in majestic isolation. Such people needed to be drawn into the 'gulf stream of divine love' so they might 'melt away' into 'Christ and his people'. This was preparation for heaven, which would be the consummation of this experience of communion.[141] In *Evening By Evening* Spurgeon wrote, 'Jerusalem the golden is the place of *communion* with all the people of God. We shall sit with Abraham, Isaac, and Jacob, in eternal fellowship ... We shall not sing solos, but in chorus we shall praise our King.'[142] Spurgeon's vision of heaven was of a community of saints from every age who would together praise and serve Christ. As indicated by the quotation from *Evening By Evening*, this communion with others included the biblical saints, but it also included personal friends. A repeated refrain in Spurgeon's letters to the bereaved was that they would meet their loved ones again.[143] To the terminally ill Curme Spurgeon wrote, 'I shall soon come hobbling after you, and shall find you out. We are bound to gravitate to each other whether here or in glory. We love the same Lord, and the same blessed truth.'[144] Spurgeon's vision of heaven, then, was one where believers related not only to Christ but to one another on the basis of their common love for their Lord. Christ had brought them to himself and also to one another. It was not only communion with Christ that would be perfected beyond the grave, but also communion with Christ's people.

Conclusion

'The rod of God teacheth us more than all the voices of his ministers', said Spurgeon in his sermon, 'Trial By The Word'.[145] Such a comment can seem surprising coming

---

[140] Spurgeon, 'The Elders Before The Throne', p. 172.

[141] C.H. Spurgeon, 'The Bridegroom's Parting Word', *MTP*, Vol. 29, S. No. 1716, Song of Songs 8.13, delivered 15 April 1863, p. 222.

[142] Spurgeon, *Evening By Evening* (2 Timothy 4.18), July 12, p. 195, italics original.

[143] See, e.g., C.H. Spurgeon to E.H. Bartlett, 14 December 1887, and C.H. Spurgeon to an unnamed 'friend', 24 May 1884, in C. Spurgeon (ed.), *The Letters of C.H. Spurgeon*, pp. 168-69.

[144] C.H. Spurgeon to T. Curme, 12 June 1884, in C. Spurgeon (ed.), *The Letters of C.H. Spurgeon*, p. 169.

[145] Spurgeon, 'Trial By The Word', p. 76.

Suffering

from one who had such a high view of preaching,[146] but it shows the vital importance of suffering to Spurgeon's spirituality. His life and ministry were heavily marked by suffering that was not only physical but also mental and spiritual. Both his theology and personal experience of suffering led him to emphasise the benefits that accrued to the believer through 'sanctified afflictions'. These benefits were christocentric and crucicentric. Suffering enabled a believer to grow in virtues such as courage and patience, virtues that were displayed perfectly by Christ in his passion. Supremely, though, suffering was a route to greater communion with Christ. Once again, Spurgeon believed that scripture and his own experience agreed: trials were often the context of a deeper revelation of Christ to a believer, a revelation which led to deeper communion. Suffering was a crucible in which increased communion was fashioned. The pain of the 'refining' was nothing besides the joy of fresh communion which this purifying process led to.

Christians whose lives were marked by suffering could be a particular source of comfort and strength to fellow believers. Spurgeon was regarded by others as someone who had persevered through great suffering, and he himself recognised that he had suffered more than many Christians. He believed that this gave him a special sympathy with those who were afflicted in different ways. He further believed that the lessons of suffering – for example, that a gracious God comforts sufferers, drawing near to them in Jesus – were to be passed on to others. For Spurgeon, this not only meant preaching and teaching on the subject of suffering, but also personal, one-to-one help for those in need.

Because suffering was the gateway of heaven, it has been appropriate to consider Spurgeon's eschatology in this, the final main chapter of this study. If his conception of heaven had been different from what I have maintained is the overarching theme of his spirituality, it would have called into serious question the argument of this study. This is because Spurgeon regarded 'heaven' as the consummation of the Christian's earthly pilgrimage, the end to which all the Christian's experiences led. What has been seen, however, is that 'communion with Christ and his people' dominates Spurgeon's conception of the life to come. 'Heaven' (whether the 'intermediate state' or the 'new heavens and the new earth') was closely associated with Christ in Spurgeon's mind, so much so that he could speak of the words 'heaven' and 'Christ' as being effectively interchangeable. Moreover, the perfected believer's experience of heaven was one which was shared with countless other believers. Spurgeon's conception of heaven was communitarian and egalitarian. Believers were united with Christ and also, whilst remaining distinct, united to one another as those who were alike in Christ. Thus, in his understanding of heaven, the two dimensions of our theme, 'communion with Christ and his people', fused into one. In death as in life, this phrase provides the integrating theme of Spurgeon's spirituality.

---

[146] Just as the comment that there was 'no sermon like the Lord's Supper', cited in chapter 7, can seem surprising.

CHAPTER 11

Conclusion:
'Love Christ and live Christ; think of Christ and speak of Christ'[1]

This study has considered the spirituality of Charles Haddon Spurgeon, the foremost popular preacher of the Victorian age. Arthur T. Pierson, writing in the *Sword and Trowel* for August 1892, declared, 'No man can dispute that Mr Spurgeon was pre-eminently a spiritually-minded man.'[2] Yet many attempts to understand him have not given due weight to his spirituality. I have sought to show that, when Spurgeon is examined through the lens of spirituality, considerable new light can be shed on the life and ministry of this important Victorian figure.

Spurgeon's spirituality was significantly shaped by his upbringing, something that he himself was clear about. The influence of his grandfather and mother was particularly important. Nevertheless, he believed that it was at the moment of conversion, and not before, that his Christian life truly began. Spurgeon's spirituality was strongly 'conversionist', therefore, and an appreciation of this is vital if his spiritual life is to be understood. But his spirituality was also 'Baptist'. Although he was not a sectarian Baptist, he saw his baptism as a believer as the moment he consecrated himself publicly to God. In addition, it was at his baptism that he felt properly joined to the visible church and able to participate in the Lord's Supper with a good conscience. Through upbringing, conversion and baptism the trajectory of Spurgeon's Christian life was set.

Once established, Spurgeon's Christian spirituality was sustained in a variety of ways. The Bible was foundational, and he gave himself to meditation on the scriptures. But prayer was also crucial for nurturing his spirituality, and often he would talk of prayer and Bible reading as closely aligned disciplines which together

---

[1] C.H. Spurgeon, 'The Bridegroom's Parting Word', *New Park Street Pulpit (NPSP) / Metropolitan Tabernacle Pulpit (MTP)* (London: Passmore and Alabaster, 1855–1917), *MTP*, Vol. 34, S. No. 1716, Song of Songs 8.13, delivered 15 April 1883, p. 228.

[2] A.T. Pierson, 'The Complex Character Of Mr Spurgeon', in *The Sword and The Trowel: A Record of Combat With Sin and Labour For The Lord* (London: Passmore and Alabaster, 1865–92) (*Sword and Trowel*), August 1892, p. 464. Pierson, an American Presbyterian pastor, was substituting for Spurgeon as the primary preacher at the Metropolitan Tabernacle at the time of Spurgeon's death. Pierson stayed on as pastor, working with J.A. Spurgeon, until 1893.

sustained him.³ Furthermore, and perhaps surprisingly in the Nonconformist setting of his time, the Lord's Supper had a vital role to play. Spurgeon had a distinctly 'non-sacramental' approach to baptism, despite the importance he attached to the rite. By contrast, his approach to the Supper, shaped not just by his Calvinistic heritage but also by his own experience at the table, was sacramental. His spirituality was not only sustained through the Bible and prayer, but also through his regular celebration of the Lord's Supper.

Thus shaped and sustained, the Christian life had to be lived. Spurgeon gave himself to Christian activity. Preaching was always central to this activity, but writing and the different agencies of the Metropolitan Tabernacle were also important. This work invigorated him. 'Activism', therefore, was not just an outworking of his spirituality; in and of itself it had a role in sustaining his spiritual life. He also vigorously pursued what he called 'practical' holiness,⁴ which, he believed, was 'indispensable'.⁵ In the outworking of Spurgeon's spirituality, his suffering was also significant. This suffering was not only physical but also mental and spiritual. His physical suffering progressively reduced his capacity for work from 1867 onwards, although activity, as much as he was able to manage, always remained important to him. His physical suffering also exacerbated his tendency to depression. Although he could experience intense joy, he would often feel, as he put it in a letter to his father in 1875, 'weary' and 'very sad'.⁶ In affliction he sought to be faithful to God by displaying a patient endurance and by sharing the lessons he had learnt in suffering with others.

Overall, both the inner and outer dimensions of what I have defined as 'spirituality' were vitally important to Spurgeon. A relationship with Christ, established at conversion and nurtured by spiritual disciplines was crucial. This relationship had to be lived out in concrete ways, in the church and in the wider world.

Diverse Influences

I have argued that Spurgeon's spirituality was shaped by a diverse range of factors. These include Puritan piety. This was imbibed to a significant degree from his upbringing, although he continued to be shaped by Puritanism in London, for example through his extensive library. The mature Spurgeon was self-consciously

---

³ See, e.g., C.H. Spurgeon, 'The Pure Language', in 'Notebooks With Sermon Outlines, Vols 2, 4-9', Spurgeon's College, Heritage Room (U.1), Vol. 4, S. No. 221, Zeph. 3.9; 'Renewing Strength', *MTP*, Vol. 29, S. No. 1756, 1756, Isaiah 40.31, n.d., pp. 700, 707.

⁴ C.H. Spurgeon, 'Holiness Demanded', *MTP*, Vol. 50, S. No. 2902, Hebrews 12.14, delivered 1862, pp. 457-58.

⁵ C.H. Spurgeon, 'Holiness indispensable', in T.P. Crosby (ed.), *C.H. Spurgeon's Sermons Beyond Volume 63: An authentic supplement to the Metropolitan Tabernacle Pulpit* (Leominster: Day One, 2009), 2 Timothy 2.19, pp. 492-505.

⁶ C.H. Spurgeon to John Spurgeon, 16 October 1875, 'Original Correspondence of Charles Haddon Spurgeon, 1851-1893', Spurgeon's College, Heritage Room (4G), No. 22.

Puritan. His essentially Calvinistic theology and the ways he conceptualised and practised piety were all shaped in some degree by Puritanism. Attempts to smooth out some of the more rugged features of his Puritanism leave us with a less than complete picture of the man. This study has shown that Puritan spirituality was important for Spurgeon.

However, Spurgeon was fundamentally an evangelical. His spirituality displays all the distinguishing marks of evangelicalism identified by David Bebbington, namely conversionism, biblicism, crucicentrism, and activism.[7] Just one way in which Spurgeon's evangelicalism can be seen is through an analysis of his approach to assurance. His doctrine of assurance of salvation certainly drew from Puritan covenant theology and the doctrine of final perseverance, but it was the more confident view of assurance typical of Calvinistic evangelicals that he adopted. Spurgeon was reading the Puritans through an evangelical lens. Calvinistic evangelicalism shaped his spirituality in other ways. Of significance were the eighteenth-century Particular Baptists who insisted on the importance of invitational evangelistic preaching in a Calvinistic Baptist context, and George Whitefield who provided Spurgeon with a model for ministry. But other evangelicals were important too. These included the Arminian John Wesley, whose evangelistic zeal and level of personal holiness Spurgeon appreciated, as well as nineteenth-century figures such as George Müller and J. Hudson Taylor, both of whom were associated with the Brethren. Spurgeon's spirituality was an evangelical spirituality, and the influences on him were wider than Calvinistic evangelicalism alone.

Spurgeon's approach to the Christian life was certainly a Protestant one, as shown by his thoroughgoing rejection of Roman Catholic ecclesiology and High Church ritual. Nevertheless, his spirituality was still influenced by certain High Church and Roman Catholic figures. These included the medieval Catholic Bernard of Clairvaux, the seventeenth-century Roman Catholic mystic Madame Guyon and some of the writers from the nineteenth-century High Anglican Oxford Movement. Certainly there was a 'mystical' strain in Spurgeon. This derived in part from Puritanism but was also connected to the High Church and Roman Catholic writers that he drew from. His evangelicalism was broad enough to encompass High Church influences. His spirituality was thus fed by a number of different religious streams.

A range of different cultural influences on Spurgeon's spirituality can also be discerned. These include the Enlightenment. Spurgeon's spirituality was influenced by Enlightenment patterns of thinking. As has been noted, for him, belief in transubstantiation was not 'rational',[8] the doctrine of baptismal regeneration was inimical to common sense,[9] and assurance was a matter of 'mathematical

---

[7] D.W. Bebbington, *Evangelicalism in Modern Britain: A history from the 1730s to the 1980s* (London: Unwin Hyman, 1989), p. 3.

[8] C.H. Spurgeon, 'The Witness Of The Lord's Supper', *MTP*, Vol. 59, S. No. 3338, 1 Corinthians 11.26, n.d., p. 38, and as noted in chapter 7.

[9] C.H. Spurgeon, 'Who Should Be Baptized?', *MTP*, Vol. 13, S. No. 2737, Acts 8.37, delivered (at New Park Street) in the 'summer of 1859', pp. 351-52, and as noted in chapter 4.

precision'.[10] The gospel, Spurgeon insisted, was addressed to 'intelligent individuals'.[11] All of these comments smack of enlightened thinking.

Other cultural influences were present too. Chief among these was Romanticism. True, Spurgeon resisted some of the Romantic influenced movements on the British religious scene. He stood against the ecclesiology and many of the practices of the Oxford Movement. He also rejected the 'New Theology' represented by a man like J. Baldwin Brown and, from the 1870s onwards, he resisted Keswick holiness teaching. But Spurgeon did embrace other Romantic developments. These included biblical infallibility, premillennialism, the 'faith' principle, and a penchant for the 'heroic'. In many of Spurgeon's statements, for example those inveighing against the mechanical, 'unpoetic' age in which he lived, he showed himself to be imbued with the Romantic spirit. Therefore, although this study accepts the influence of the Enlightenment over Spurgeon, I have argued he should not be seen as an enlightened figure resisting the inflow of Romanticism into evangelical life.[12] Spurgeon's spirituality evinced a decidedly Romantic tincture, even whilst he remained indebted to the Enlightenment.

The mix of Enlightenment and Romantic influences can be further seen by considering Spurgeon's championing of the common people (he habitually referred to the 'common man') and his espousal of Christian 'manliness'. The first stress can be seen as Spurgeon reacting against Romanticism, certainly against Romanticism as a movement of high culture. Spurgeon rejected taste and refinement and a new theology which seemed out of the reach of ordinary people. Instead he appeared as a spokesman for hardworking, common sense artisans, shopkeepers and business people. But the second stress, Christian manliness, was embedded in Romanticism. Spurgeon's championing of the common man was often couched in terms which showed his indebtedness to the Romantic cult of manliness. Thus the two cultural moods came together.

Spurgeon's temperament also needs to be given due weight in any consideration of his spirituality. His extrovert nature meant that he often engaged with scripture in the company of others. This also led him to stress the corporate dimensions of prayer and the Lord's Supper. Spurgeon's tendency to depression certainly impacted his spirituality. He was extremely sensitive, as he himself admitted,[13] an emotional man for whom feelings were always very important. This temperament, together with his experiences of suffering, helped shape the mystical dimension of his spirituality. Overall, the different streams that fed his spiritual life – religious, cultural and temperamental – joined and intermingled, flowing together to make the whole.

---

[10] C.H. Spurgeon, 'The Blessings Of Full Assurance', *MTP*, Vol. 34, S. No. 2023, 1 John 5.13, delivered 13 May 1888, p. 268, and as noted in chapter 3.

[11] Spurgeon, 'Who Should Be Baptized?', pp. 351-52.

[12] As suggested by D.W. Bebbington, 'Gospel and Culture in Victorian Nonconformity', in J. Shaw and A. Kreider (eds), *Culture and the Nonconformist Tradition* (Cardiff: University of Wales Press, 1999), pp. 57-58.

[13] C.H. Spurgeon, *MTP*, 'Patient Job, And The Baffled Enemy', Vol. 36, S. No. 2172, Job 1.22, delivered 28 August 1890, pp. 604-605.

Spurgeon cannot, therefore, be understood merely as a latter-day Puritan, an Enlightenment figure, a typical Victorian or, indeed, a Romantic. There is truth (in varying degrees) in all of these depictions, but on their own none of them tells whole story. Analysis of the influences on Spurgeon's spirituality reveals him to be a complex, many-sided character.

A Unifying Theme

Despite the multi-faceted picture that is built up through examination of the various interconnected influences on Spurgeon's spirituality, when the whole is viewed a clear two-dimensional theme can be discerned, namely 'communion with Christ and his people'. The first dimension of this theme has been brought out in each main chapter of this study. Spurgeon's upbringing prepared him for conversion which was conceived of as a simple looking to Christ. Conversion marked the beginning of communion with Christ, with a living relationship between the believer and Christ established through faith in his person and work. Believers' baptism, which was undertaken in obedience to Christ's command, was understood and experienced as the moment of consecration to Christ. Such consecration was important not least because it was essential to the maintenance of communion.

Thus established, the focus on Christ and especially on communion with him was resolutely maintained. For Spurgeon, the Bible was not only interpreted christologically but was also closely associated with Christ. Engagement with the scriptures was foundational to continued communion with Christ. His prayer life also fostered such communion. Christ's person and work were central themes of Spurgeon's prayers. Moreover, praise, thanksgiving and petition were often addressed directly to Christ. Contemplation of Christ was regularly practised. His theology was christocentric with a strong emphasis on the atonement. Finally, Jesus was spiritually and yet really present at the Lord's Supper, where Spurgeon enjoyed the 'nearest communion with Christ' he said he ever experienced.[14] His spirituality was sustained by the fellowship with Christ he experienced through the Bible, prayer and the Lord's Supper.

Activity, holiness and Spurgeon's suffering also related closely to communion with Christ. Activity in the cause of Christ was both an outworking of Spurgeon's relationship with Jesus and a means to further communion. Growth in holiness, understood as Christlikeness, was crucial if fellowship with Christ was to be deepened. 'Sanctified suffering' drew Spurgeon closer to the suffering servant who had died on the cross for him. 'Communion with Christ' was thus crucial to the inner and outer aspects of his spirituality, crucial to theology, prayer and practical action. Moreover, the 'pilgrimage' which was Spurgeon's Christian life was a journey to a heaven in which face-to-face fellowship with his Lord would be enjoyed. The communion with Christ known on earth was only a foretaste of what was to come.

---

[14] C.H. Spurgeon, 'Christ And His Table-Companions', in *Till He Come: Communion Meditations And Addresses* (London: Passmore and Alabaster, 1896), Luke 22.14, p. 277.

The second dimension of the theme, '... and his people', can also be traced through the different aspects of Spurgeon's spirituality considered in this study. The experience of conversion, so important to Spurgeon personally, had also to be shared with other people. Evangelism was paramount for him, with his gospel preaching shaped by his own experience of salvation and by the ongoing relationship he believed he enjoyed with Christ. His baptism was not just his personal consecration to Christ, for it also represented his connection with the body of Christ, the church. Although it has not always been recognised, Spurgeon's ecclesiology was very important to him. Tabernacle elder Thomas Cox wrote that, 'Next to Xt [Christ]' Spurgeon 'loved the church'.[15]

This stress on the church can be seen through Spurgeon's approaches to the Bible, prayer and the Lord's Supper. With regard to the Bible, he engaged with the scriptures with the help of the church triumphant (for example, Puritan commentators) and the church militant (for example, the helpers who worked with him on the *Treasury of David*). This study of the scriptures was undertaken with a view to edifying the church through preaching and writing. With regard to prayer, the Tabernacle's various prayer meetings were central to Spurgeon's practice of prayer. Vital too was the knowledge that his church and many others were interceding for him. As far as the Lord's Supper was concerned, it was vital that this was celebrated with others. He was not only committed to celebrating the Supper with his own church, but with believers from other churches too.

Spurgeon's spirituality was one that was actively worked out amongst people. In addition to evangelism, he wanted to share the love of Christ through social action, with the Orphanage the primary way that this found expression in his ministry. His conception of a holy life was of one that was lived passionately for Christ 'in the world'. Holiness did not involve withdrawal from everyday life but rather living differently amongst ordinary people.

Spurgeon engaged in activity not just *among* but also *alongside* other people. As well as prayer support, financial backing was vital to him, and for this he looked to his church and to his wider constituency of supporters, those who read his printed sermons and took the *Sword and Trowel*. Spurgeon also depended on a band of close associates who worked with him in ventures like the Orphanage. These were people who were prepared for him to take the lead and remain centre stage – even when in reality he might only be lightly involved in the day-to-day affairs of the institution in question. They were also people he regarded as kindred spirits, sharing a certain 'orthodox' view of the Bible and theology (although they did not have to be Calvinists or Baptists) and, most importantly, an experiential piety and love for Christ. But although Spurgeon set the agenda and was dominant, these people were nonetheless real partners with him and were essential to his ministry. Their gifts and personalities complemented Spurgeon's own. Spurgeon felt a deep sense of spiritual communion with his close associates, especially with those he worked with day-to-day, for example James Archer Spurgeon, Joseph W. Harrald, Vernon J.

---

[15] T. Cox, 'Notes on C.H. Spurgeon', Spurgeon's College, Heritage Room (B1.17), p. 3.

Charlesworth and George Rogers. Spurgeon always sought to work closely with other people. He did not only work in this way out of necessity because of his physical infirmities. It was his personal preference to be with others and work with them. For him the corporate dimension of spirituality was vitally important. This can further be shown through analysis of his conception of heaven. This was not one in which individual believers would experience communion with Christ in isolation. Rather, Christians would join with all of God's people, down the ages, and enjoy fellowship with one another even as they enjoyed fellowship with Christ.

Integration of Influences

Examination of the ways Spurgeon engaged with different religious and cultural movements further highlights the importance of 'communion with Christ and his people' as the central theme of his spirituality. Taking the Puritans as an example of a religious movement, it has been shown that Spurgeon appropriated certain aspects of their theology and practice, namely those that seemed to aid fellowship with Christ and with Christ's people. Conversely, he abandoned other elements of Puritan piety which did not seem to relate to his central concern or perhaps even, in his view, militated against it. So, Spurgeon embraced seventeenth-century Puritan commentaries which displayed an essential doctrinal orthodoxy in respect of the person and work of Christ and which, crucially, were 'experimental', with a focus on enjoying felt communion with Christ. Spurgeon also appropriated aspects of Puritan covenant theology. The fact that God had entered into covenant with his people guaranteed believers' union with Christ and thus provided a secure basis from which communion could be enjoyed. But, in respect of Puritan covenant theology, an important qualification needs to be made. Where this covenant theology seemed to undercut what Spurgeon regarded as an essential truth – that true communion only began at conversion – it was rejected. He believed that the theology of infant baptism held by the majority of those he considered Puritans took the focus away from conversion, thus causing confusion and obscuring something he believed was essential to communion.

'Communion with Christ and his people' also helps us make sense of Spurgeon's engagement with Roman Catholicism and High Church Anglicanism, an engagement which otherwise can seem quixotic. Certain devotional writers (especially those who expressed love to Christ in mystical vein) were prized because of the way they facilitated communion with Christ. The bulk of Roman Catholic and High Church literature, practices and ecclesiology were vehemently rejected, however. This was partly for cultural reasons, but this was not the whole story. Rather, a doctrine such as transubstantiation was rejected because it obscured the true meaning of the Supper, which was Christ and his spiritual presence, a presence that had to be perceived by conscious faith. Ritual, such as that beloved by the later Oxford Movement, obscured Christ. 'Priestcraft' was rejected because it interposed a barrier between ordinary people and the great high priest, namely Christ. Patterns of piety which involved 'withdrawal from the world' were rejected because this was not a spirituality of the people. Where High Church spirituality obscured Christ, for him and for other, 'ordinary' people, it was to be rejected. But on the occasions where it aided such communion it could be embraced. Thus, and I would argue only thus, can Spurgeon's vehement denunciations of the Oxford Movement and his appreciation of, say, J.M. Neale's work on the Song of Songs be understood.

The same essential dynamic was at work in Spurgeon's engagement with cultural movements. Of the two main movements which shaped him, Romanticism will be taken first. This cultural mood impinged on nineteenth-century Christian thought and practice in a number of different ways, as has been shown. Romantic developments on the religious scene which Spurgeon rejected included Tractarianism and the new theology of Baldwin Brown. Both of these movements, in different ways, seemed to obscure Christ, Tractarianism for the reasons set out in the previous paragraph, the new theology because it created doubt about the Christ of the scriptures. By contrast, Spurgeon embraced the Romantic notion of biblical infallibility because of the certainty it provided about Christ. Moreover, Spurgeon's Romanticism was resolutely popular. He rejected the Romanticism of high culture and embraced a manly spirituality which was of the people but still influenced by the prevailing Romantic temper as this percolated down through Victorian society.

Spurgeon's engagement with the Enlightenment is similarly illuminated when viewed through the lens of 'communion with Christ and his people'. A sacramental view of baptism seemed to undercut the centrality of conversion as the true and only route to communion with Christ. Enlightened arguments were deployed in favour of Spurgeon's view: baptismal sacramentalism, he insisted, was inimical to 'common sense'. Conversely he rejected an enlightened postmillennialism and embraced a Romantic premillennialism, performing a *volte face* on this issue in the early years of his ministry. The advent hope, that Christ might appear in person at any moment proved irresistible to Spurgeon, so intensely did he long for increased communion with his Lord. And yet, an enlightened pragmatism did continue to mark his eschatology. Prophetic speculation and misty dreaming about the future were alike eschewed. His premillennialism drove him to serve, practically. The focus had to remain on Christ and on his people.

This is not to argue that Spurgeon was consistent in the choices he made, or that he was theologically justified in making them. A biblical and theological evaluation of his thinking and practice would need another book. But the theme of 'communion with Christ and his people' consistently offers help in understanding and explaining Spurgeon. Thus the analysis of Spurgeon's spirituality undertaken in this study, with its identification of the unifying theme of this spirituality, provides an interpretative key which helps us open up and understand his engagement with an array of different and interconnected religious and cultural movements. Choices, both conscious and unconscious, which can seem strange and arbitrary when set alongside one another, begin to make sense if communion with Christ and his people is seen as the integrating theme of his spirituality. A deeper understanding of the forces which shaped the contours of Spurgeon's spirituality is reached. This in turn leads to a deeper understanding of his life and ministry.

Conclusion

Chapter 6 of Spurgeon's book *The Saint And His Saviour: The Progress Of The Soul In The Knowledge Of Jesus* is entitled 'Complete In Christ'. In this chapter, Spurgeon wrote,

> It is from oneness with Christ ... that we receive all our mercies. Faith is the precious grace which discerns this eternal union, and cements it by another – a vital union; so that we become one, not merely in the eye of God but in our own happy experience – one in aim, one in heart, one in holiness, one in communion, and ultimately, one in glory.[16]

The quotation helps us summarise Spurgeon's christocentric conception of the spiritual journey. Faith appropriated a 'vital union' with Christ that was predicated on the eternal union Spurgeon believed existed between Christ and the believer. Christian believers were one with Christ in their own experience and so could enjoy real, felt communion with Christ. This was a oneness with Christ which would receive its consummation in the life to come.

This journey with Christ and to Christ was also a journey which was to be undertaken in the company of other people who were on the same essential pilgrimage. In a dramatic passage in Spurgeon's sermon, 'An Ear Bored With An Awl', he declared,

> Beloved, some of us could not leave Jesus, not only because of what he is, but because of some that are very dear to us who are in his service. How could I leave my mother's God? How could I leave my father's God, my grandfather's God, my great-grandfather's God? My brother, how could I leave your God, to be separated from you, whom I have loved so long, so well?[17]

The *Metropolitan Tabernacle Pulpit* records, in what is a rare footnote to the main text, that at this point the preacher turned to J.A. Spurgeon, who was sitting on the platform with him. A few moments later C.H. Spurgeon declared,

> Our best friends are those with whom we go up to the house of God in company. Why, most of the friends that some of us have on earth we won through our being one in Jesus Christ; and we mean to stand fast for the grand old cause, and the old gospel, for the sake not only of Christ but of his people.[18]

These quotations nicely illustrate Spurgeon's love for and commitment to other people, especially those who had loved him and worked with him. The quotations also illustrate why the theme 'communion with Christ and his people' is a closely

---

[16] C.H. Spurgeon, *The Saint And His Saviour: The Progress Of The Soul In The Knowledge Of Jesus* (London: Hodder and Stoughton, 1889 [1857]), p. 167.

[17] C.H. Spurgeon, 'An Ear Bored With An Awl', *MTP*, Vol. 20, S. No. 1174, Exodus 21.5,6, n.d., p. 296.

[18] Spurgeon, 'An Ear Bored With An Awl', pp. 296-97.

connected, two-dimensional theme and not two separate themes. Those who were united with Christ and enjoying communion with him were also united with and in fellowship with one another. Thomas Cox had spoken, as we have seen, of Spurgeon having two 'loves', Christ and his church. In Spurgeon's thinking and practice these two loves were closely integrated. 'Communion with Christ and his people' is the dominant and unifying theme of Spurgeon's spirituality.

Bibliography

Primary Sources – Manuscripts

Angus Library, Regent's Park College, Oxford

'C.H. Spurgeon. Letters to his Father and Mother, 1850–84' (D/SPU)
'C.H. Spurgeon letter to J.A. Spurgeon, 13 February 1855' (D/SPU 5)
'My Visit to Spurgeon's Tabernacle, Thursday 25 February 1886', by 'Saladin' (D/SPU 9)
'C.H. Spurgeon to A.H. Baynes, 18 May 1885', in the folder for H. Ross Phillips, application #81, 1885, Candidate Papers Box 71–98, 1884–1886, BMS Archives, The Angus Library and Archives, Regent's Park College, Oxford
'C.H. Spurgeon to BMS Committee, dated 188[5]', in support of the application of John Maynard, in the folder for John Maynard, application #76, 1885, Candidate Papers Box 71–98, 1884–1886, BMS Archives, The Angus Library and Archives, Regent's Park College, Oxford

Spurgeon's College, London

Cox, T., 'Notes on C.H. Spurgeon' (B1.17)
'Cuttings on C.H. Spurgeon' (H1.01 and 02)
'Downgrade Controversy: Various letters in answer to questionnaire of 1888' (B1.16)
Letter, 'J. Ruskin to C.H. Spurgeon, 25 November 1862' (D.1.8)
'Loose-Leaf Scrap Folders' for 'April–June 1884', 'October 1885–March 1886', 'March 1886–October 1886' (2H)
'Family Register' in 'Spurgeon Family Bible' (*The Holy Bible with the Commentaries of [Thomas] Scott and [Matthew] Henry ...* (Glasgow: W.R. M'Phun, 1852) (Display Case 2)
'Maroon Bound Scrapfolders', 4 Vols (set out on tables)
'Original Correspondence of Charles Haddon Spurgeon' 1851–1893 (Vol. 1); 1863–1868 (Vol. 2); 1887–1892 (Vol. 3) (4G)
Spurgeon, C.H., 'Antichrist And Her Brood; Or, Popery Unmasked' (A2.06)
—, 'Extracts made ... from his mother's diary' (Display Case 2)
—, 'Manuscripts. Treasury of David. Vol. VII' (Display Case 8)
—, 'Miniature Cabinet with many of C.H. Spurgeon's pulpit notes' (L2.1)
—, 'Notebook Containing Early Sermon Skeletons, Vol. 1' (K1.5)
—, 'Notebooks With Sermon Outlines, Vols 2, 4-9' (U.1)
—, 'Original manuscript of "The cheque book of the bank of faith"' (Display Case 8)
Spurgeon, T., 'A Loving Tribute To The Memory of Mr. Thomas Cox ...' (B1.17)
'Spurgeon's Scrapbooks, Numbered Volumes', Vol 1, 1856–January 1879; Vol. 2, January 1879–December 1879; Vol. 4, August 1880–July 1881; Vol. 5, June

1881–March 1882; Vol. 6, January 1882–October 1882; Vol. 7, October 1882–April 1883; Vol. 9, October 1883–June 1884; Vol. 12, October 1884–May 1885 (2G). Vols 3, 8, 10 and 11 appear to have been broken up and material placed in different 'Loose-Leaf Scrap Folders'

'Spurgeon's Scrapbooks, Two Unnumbered Volumes', 1880–1890; 1890 (2G)
'Various Spurgeon Letters' (K1.9)

'Spurgeons' (formerly known as 'Spurgeon's Childcare') Archives, Rushden

'Charles Haddon Spurgeon: Obituaries – Newspaper Cuttings', Bound Volume
'Letters from George Edwards to his Mother, 19 March 1885–29 November 1887'
'Stockwell Orphanage "Indenture", 18 March 1867' (At front of Minute Book)
'Stockwell Orphanage Master's Report, 8 September 1876–28 January 1881'
'Stockwell Orphanage Master's Report, 1 Feb 1881–7 Jan 1887'
'S.(tockwell) O.(rphanage) Minute Book No. 1. March 1867–June 1876'

Primary Sources – Periodicals/Newspapers

The Baptist
British Weekly
Christian Commonwealth
Christian Globe
Christian World
Daily Bulletin
Daily News
Essex Telegraph
Family Friend
The Freeman
General Baptist Magazine
Glasgow Examiner
Kentish Mercury
Morning Advertiser
North American Review
Pall Mall Gazette
South London Press
The Times
Within Our Gates

Primary Sources – Books and Booklets

[Anon.], *Charles Haddon Spurgeon: A Biographical Sketch And An Appreciation By One Who Knew Him Well* (London: Andrew Melrose, 1903)

[Anon.] (ed.), *The Contemporary Pulpit Library: Sermons by the Rev. C.H. Spurgeon* (London: Swan, Sonnenschein, 1892)

[Anon.] (ed.), *The Pastor in Prayer: Being a Selection of C.H. Spurgeon's Sunday Morning Prayers* (London: Elliot Stock, 1893)

[Anon.], *Practical Reflections on Every Verse of the New Testament* (2 Vols; London: Rivingtons, 1882)

[Anon.] (ed.), *Supplement To Our Own Hymn Book* (London: Passmore and Alabaster, 1898)

Adamson, W., *The Life of the Rev. Joseph Parker, D.D. Pastor, City Temple, London* (Glasgow: Inglis Ker / London: Cassell, 1902)

Annual Paper Concerning the Lord's Work in Connection with the Pastors' College, 1885–6 (London, Passmore and Alabaster, 1886)

Annual Report of the Stockwell Orphanage, 1885–6 (London: Passmore and Alabaster, 1886)

Beddow, B. and C.H. Spurgeon, *Memories of Stambourne* (London: Passmore and Alabaster, 1891)

Brooks, T., *Heaven on Earth* (London: Banner of Truth, 1961 [1654])

Bunyan, J., *Grace Abounding to the Chief of Sinners ...* (Harmondsworth: Penguin, 1987 [1666])

—, *The Pilgrim's Progress, From This World to That Which is to Come, Delivered Under the Similitude of a Dream* (London: The Book Society, 1876 [1678])

—, *The Water Of Life; Or, A Discourse Showing The Richness And Glory Of The Grace And Spirit Of The Gospel ... With Preface By C.H. Spurgeon* (London: Passmore and Alabaster, 1868 [original work, 1688])

Campbell, J., *Mr Spurgeon Defended: Being a Series of Articles from the British Banner ...* (London: Passmore and Alabaster, n.d. [1856])

Carlile, J.C., *C.H. Spurgeon: An Interpretative Biography* (London: Kingsgate Press, 1933)

Coles, E., *A Practical Discourse on God's Sovereignty, with Other Material Points Derived Thence: Viz:- of the Righteousness of God, of Election, of Redemption, of Effectual Calling, of Perseverance, with Brief Preface by C.H. Spurgeon* (London, Passmore & Alabaster, 1885 [1867] [original work, 1678])

Cook, C.T. (ed.), *Behold the Throne of Grace: C.H. Spurgeon's Prayers and Hymns* (Marshall, Morgan and Scott: London, n.d. [1934])

Cowper, W., *Olney Hymns: In Three Parts* (London: Thomas Nelson, 1856 [1779])

Crosby, T.P. (ed.), *C.H. Spurgeon's Sermons Beyond Volume 63: An authentic supplement to the Metropolitan Tabernacle Pulpit* (Leominster: Day One, 2009)

Cunningham Burley, A., *Spurgeon And His Friendships* (London: Epworth, 1933)

Darlow, T.H., *W. Robertson Nicoll: Life and Letters* (London: Hodder and Stoughton, 1925)

Douglas, J.D., *The Prince of Preachers: A Sketch; A Portraiture; And A Tribute* (London: Morgan and Scott, n.d. [1893])

Durham, J., *Clavis Cantici; or, an Exposition of the Song of Solomon ... With a Preface by the Rev Gavin Parker* (Aberdeen: George and Robert King, 1840 [original work, 1668 and 1723])

Ellis, J.J., *Charles Haddon Spurgeon* (London: James Nisbet, n.d.)

Fuller. A, 'Antinomianism Contrasted with the Religion of the Holy Scriptures', in *The Complete Works of the Rev Andrew Fuller, With a Memoir of his Life by the Rev. Andrew Gunton Fuller* (ed. A.G. Fuller; rev. ed. J. Belcher; 3 Vols; Harrisonburg: Sprinkle Publications, 3rd edn, 1988 [1845]), Vol. 3, pp. 737-62

Fullerton, W.Y., *C.H. Spurgeon: A Biography* (London: Williams and Norgate, 1920)

—, *Thomas Spurgeon: A Biography* (London: Hodder and Stoughton, 1919)

Henry, M., *Matthew Henry's Commentary on the New Testament, with a Preface by C.H. Spurgeon* (London: William MacKenzie, n.d.), Vol. 1

Higgs, W.M., *The Spurgeon Family: Being An Account Of The Descent And Family Of Charles Haddon Spurgeon* (London: Elliot Stock, 1906)

James, W.H.C., *A Souvenir of Spurgeon's Tabernacle* (London: Hart and Straker, n.d. [1898])

Longfellow, H.W., *Favourite Poems* (London: Routledge, 1878)

Lorimer, G.C., *C.H. Spurgeon, The Puritan Preacher In The Nineteenth Century* (Boston: James H. Earle, 1892)

Memorial Volume. Sermons And Addresses Delivered In The Metropolitan Tabernacle, Newington, In Connection With The Presentation Of A Testimonial To Pastor C.H. Spurgeon, To Commemorate The Completion Of The Twenty-Fifth Year Of His Pastorate ... (London: Passmore and Alabaster, n.d. [1879])

Magoon, E.L., *'The Modern Whitefield': Sermons of the Rev. C.H. Spurgeon, of London; With an Introduction and Sketch of his Life* (New York: Sheldon, Blakeman, 1857)

Murray, I.H. (ed.), *C.H. Spurgeon: The Full Harvest 1860–1892* (London: Banner of Truth, 1973)

Norcott, J., *Baptism Discovered Plainly and Faithfully According to the Word of God: A New Edition, Corrected and Somewhat Altered* [with a Preface by C.H. Spurgeon] (London: Passmore and Alabaster, 1878 [original work, 1672]).

Pike, G.H., *Charles Haddon Spurgeon: Preacher, Author, Philanthropist* (London: Hodder and Stoughton, 1886)

—, *Dr Parker and His Friends* (London: Fisher Unwin, 1904)

—, *James Archer Spurgeon D.D. LL.D. Preacher, Philanthropist, and Co-Pastor With C.H. Spurgeon at the Metropolitan Tabernacle* (London: Alexander and Shepheard, 1894)

—, *The Life and Work of Charles Haddon Spurgeon* (6 Vols; London: Cassell, 1894 [1892–93])

'Printed Letter from Susannah Spurgeon Addressed to Women Candidates for Baptism at the Tabernacle', Spurgeon's College, Heritage Room (Display Case 7)

Power, J.C., *The Rise and Progress of Sunday Schools: A Biography of Robert Raikes and William Fox* (New York: Sheldon, 1863)

Ray, C., *A Marvellous Ministry: The Story of Spurgeon's Sermons* (London: Passmore and Alabaster, 1905 [1903])

"'Report of Proceedings [sic]" of the Laying of the Foundation Stone [for the Stockwell Orphanage] 9 September 1867', held at Spurgeons (Spurgeon's Childcare), Rushden

Rippon J. (ed.), *Selection of Hymns, from the best authors, Intended to be an Appendix to Dr Watts's Psalms and Hymns* (London, 1787)

Ryle, J.C., *Holiness: Its Nature, Hindrances, Difficulties, and Roots* (London: J. Clarke, 1952 [1877])

—, *Practical Religion* (Cambridge: James Clark, 1959 [1878])

Shirreff, W., *Lectures on Baptism ... with a Preface by C.H. Spurgeon* (London: Passmore and Alabaster, 1884 [1878])

Sibbes, R., *Bowels Opened; Or: A Discovery of Neere and Deere Love, Union and Communion betwixt Christ and the Church*, in A.B. Grosart (ed.), *Complete Works of Richard Sibbes* (Edinburgh: James Nichol, 1862 [*Bowels Opened* originally published, 1639]), Vol. 2, pp. 2-195

Sheen, D., *Pastor C.H. Spurgeon: His Conversion, Career, And Coronation* (London: J.B. Knapp, 1892)

Shindler, R., *From The Pulpit to the Palm-Branch: A Memorial of C.H. Spurgeon* (London: Passmore and Alabaster, 1892)

—, *From the Usher's Desk to the Tabernacle Pulpit: The Life and Labours of Pastor C.H. Spurgeon* (London: Passmore and Alabaster, 1892)

Sloan, W.B., *These Sixty Years* (London: Pickering and Inglis, n.d. [1935])

Smiles S., *Self Help: With Illustrations of Character, Conduct, and Perseverance* (Oxford: Oxford University Press, 2002 [1859])

Spurgeon, C. (ed.), *The Letters of Charles Haddon Spurgeon* (London: Marshall Brothers, n.d. [1923?])

—, *Story of Spurgeon's Orphan Homes, These Three-Score Years, 1867–1927* ([no details of place of publication or publisher], 1927)

Spurgeon, C.H., *Autobiography: Compiled from his Diary, Letters, and Records by his Wife and his Private Secretary* (4 Vols; London: Passmore and Alabaster, 1897–99)

—, *C.H. Spurgeon's M.S. Magazine, Written by Himself, When a Boy, Under 12 Years of Age. Facsimile Reproduction* (London: J. Barton, n.d. [original magazine written, April 1846])

—, *The Cheque Book of the Bank of Faith: Being Promises Arranged for Daily Use With Brief Experimental Comments* (London: Passmore and Alabaster, 1895)

—, *Commenting and Commentaries* (London: Banner of Truth, 1969 [London: Passmore and Alabaster, 1876])

—, *Evening By Evening: Or, Readings at Eventide for the Family or the Closet* (London: Passmore and Alabaster, 1868)

—, *Farm Sermons* (London: Passmore and Alabaster, 1900)

—, *The Golden Alphabet Of The Praises Of Holy Scripture ... Being A Devotional Commentary Upon The One Hundred And Nineteenth Psalm* (London: Passmore and Alabaster, 1898 [1887])

—, *A Good Start: A Book for Young Men and Women* (London: Passmore and Alabaster, 1898)

—, *The Gospel of the Kingdom. A Popular Exposition of the Gospel According to Matthew* (London: Passmore and Alabaster, 1893)

—, *How Spurgeon Found Christ* (London: James E. Hawkins, n.d. [1879])

—, *John Ploughman's Almanack* [for 1897] (London: Passmore and Alabaster, 1897)

—, *John Ploughman's Pictures; Or, More of his Plain Talk for Plain People* (London: Passmore and Alabaster, 1880)

—, *John Ploughman's Talk; Or, Plain Advice for Plain People* (London: Passmore and Alabaster, n.d.)

—, *Lectures To My Students* (3 Vols; London: Passmore and Alabaster, n.d.)

—, *The Metropolitan Tabernacle: Its History And Work* (London: Passmore and Alabaster, 1876)

—, *Metropolitan Tabernacle Pulpit* (London: Passmore and Alabaster, 1861–1917)

—, *The Miracles of Our Lord* (2 Vols; London: Passmore and Alabaster, 1895)

—, *Morning By Morning: Or, Daily Readings for the Family or the Closet* (London: Passmore and Alabaster, 1865)

—, *The Most Holy Place: Sermons on the Song of Solomon* (London: Passmore and Alabaster, 1896)

—, *My Sermon Notes: A Selection From Outlines Of Discourses Delivered At The Metropolitan Tabernacle ... From Genesis To Proverbs I to LXIV* (New York: Fleming H. Revell, n.d. [London: Paternoster and Alabaster, 1884])

—, *My Sermon Notes ... From Matthew 4.3 To Acts* (London: Paternoster and Alabaster, 1886)

—, *New Park Street Pulpit* (London: Passmore and Alabaster, 1855–1861)

—, *Only a Prayer Meeting: Forty Addresses at the Metropolitan Tabernacle and Other Prayer Meetings* (London: Passmore and Alabaster, 1901)

— (ed.), *Our Own Hymn Book* (London: Passmore and Alabaster, 1866)

—, *The Saint And His Saviour: The Progress Of The Soul In The Knowledge Of Jesus* (London: Hodder and Stoughton, 1889 [1857])

— (ed.), *Smooth Stones Taken from Ancient Brooks ... Being a Collection of Sentences, Illustrations, and Quaint Sayings, from the Works of that Renowned Puritan, Thomas Brooks* (London: Dean and Son, 1864)

—, *The Spare Half Hour* (London: Passmore and Alabaster, n.d.)

—, *Speeches at Home and Abroad* (London: Passmore and Alabaster, 1878)

—, *The Soul-Winner; Or, How To Lead Sinners To The Saviour* (London: Passmore and Alabaster, 1895)

— (ed.), *The Sword and The Trowel: A Record of Combat With Sin and Labour For The Lord* (London: Passmore and Alabaster, 1865–92)

—, *Till He Come: Communion Meditations And Addresses* (London: Passmore and Alabaster, 1896)

—, *The Treasury of the Bible: The New Testament* (London: Marshall, Morgan and Scott, 1962)

—, *The Treasury Of David: Containing An Original Exposition Of The Book Of Psalms; A Collection Of Illustrative Extracts From The Whole Range Of Literature; A Series Of Homiletical Hints Upon Almost Every Verse; And Lists Of Writers Upon Each Psalm* (7 Vols; London and Edinburgh: Marshall Brothers, n.d. [London: Passmore and Alabaster, 1869–1885])

—, *Twelve Sermons on Holiness* (London: Passmore and Alabaster, n.d.)

—, *Twelve Sermons on Sanctification* (London: Passmore and Alabaster, n.d.)

—, *Twelve Sermons on the Second Coming of Christ* (London: Passmore and Alabaster, n.d.)

Stevenson, G.J., *A Sketch of the Life and Ministry of the Reverend C.H. Spurgeon* (New York: Sheldon and Blakeman, 1857)

Upton, J. (ed.), *A Collection of Hymns Designed As A Supplement To Dr Watts' Psalms And Hymns* (London: Button and Gale, 1814)

Watson, T., *A Body of Divinity, Contained in Sermons Upon the [Westminster] Assembly's Catechism ... With a Preface and an Appendix by Pastor C.H. Spurgeon* (London: Passmore and Alabaster, 1898 [1890?] [original work, 1692])

Watson, W.H., *The Sunday School Union, Its History And Work* (London: Sunday School Union, 1869)

Wesley, J., *Sermons on Several Occasions* (London: Epworth, 1944 [1746–60])

Whitefield, G., *George Whitefield's Journals* (London: Banner of Truth, 1959 [1741])

Williams, W., *Personal Reminiscences of Charles Haddon Spurgeon* (London: Religious Tract Society, 1895)

—, *Personal Reminiscences of Charles Haddon Spurgeon* (rev. and ed. M. Williams; London: Religious Tract Society, n.d. [1933])

—, *Upton Chapel Sermons: A Centenary Memorial* [with a Preface by C.H. Spurgeon] (London: Passmore and Alabaster, 1885)

Young, D.T. (ed.), *C.H. Spurgeon's Prayers* (London: Passmore and Alabaster, 1905)

Secondary Sources – Books and Booklets

Bacon, E.W., *Spurgeon: Heir of the Puritans* (London: George Allen and Unwin, 1967)

Bean, P. and J. Melville, *Lost Children of the Empire: The Untold Story of Britain's Migrants* (London: Unwin Hyman, 1989)

Bebbington, D.W., *The Dominance of Evangelicalism: The Age of Spurgeon and Moody* (Leicester: IVP, 2005)

—, *Evangelicalism in Modern Britain: A History from the 1730s to the 1980s* (London: Unwin Hyman, 1989)

—, *Holiness in Nineteenth-Century England* (Carlisle: Paternoster, 2002)

Benedict, P., *Christ's Churches Purely Reformed: A Social History of Calvinism* (New Haven / London: Yale University Press, 2002)

Birkel, M.L., *Silence and Witness: The Quaker Tradition* (London: Darton, Longman and Todd, 2004)

Bouyer, L., *A History of Christian Spirituality, Vol. 3; Orthodox Spirituality and Protestant and Anglican Spirituality* (Tunbridge Wells: Burns and Oates, 1968 [French edn., 1965])

Briggs Myers, I. with P.B. Briggs, *Gifts Differing* (Palo Alto: Consulting Psychologists Press, 1980)

Briggs, J.H.Y., *The English Baptists of the Nineteenth Century* (Didcot: Baptist Historical Society, 1994)

Broomhall, A.J., *Hudson Taylor and China's Open Century* (4 Vols; London: Hodder & Stoughton, 1982)

Calhoun, C.C., *Longfellow: A Rediscovered Life* (Boston: Beacon, 2004)

Chandler, M., *An Introduction to the Oxford Movement* (London: SPCK, 2003)

Coad, F.R., *A History of the Brethren Movement* (Exeter: Paternoster, 1976 [1968])

Coffey, J., *John Goodwin and the Puritan Revolution: Religion and Intellectual Change in Seventeenth-Century England* (Woodbridge: Boydell, 2008 [2006])

Collinson, P., *The Birthpangs of Protestant England* (Basingstoke: Macmillan, 1988)

—, *The Puritan Character: Polemics and Polarities in Early Seventeenth-Century English Culture* (Los Angeles: University of California, 1989)

Cross, A.R., *Baptism and the Baptists: Theology and Practice in Twentieth-Century Britain* (Carlisle: Paternoster, 2000)

Davies, H., *Worship and Theology in England: From Watts and Wesley to Martineau, 1690–1900* (Grand Rapids: Eerdmans, 1996 [1961–62])

—, *The Worship of the English Puritans* (London: Dacre, 1946)

De Jong, J.A., *As the Waters Cover the Sea: Millennial Expectations in the Rise of Anglo-American Missions, 1640–1810* (Kampen: J.H. Kok, 1970)

Ditchfield, G.M., *The Evangelical Revival* (London: UCL Press, 1998)

Dix, K., *Strict and Particular: English Strict and Particular Baptists in the Nineteenth Century* (Didcot: Baptist Historical Society, 2001)

Drummond, L., *Spurgeon, Prince of Preachers* (Grand Rapids: Kregel, 1992)

Fiedler, K., *The Story of Faith Missions* (Oxford: Regnum Books, 1994)

Fowler, S.K., *More Than a Symbol: The British Baptist Recovery of Baptismal Sacramentalism* (Carlisle: Paternoster, 2002)

Gillett, D.K., *Trust and Obey: Explorations in Evangelical Spirituality* (London: Darton, Longman and Todd, 1993)

Gordon, J.M., *Evangelical Spirituality: From the Wesleys to John Stott* (London: SPCK, 1991)

Green, I.M., *Print and Protestantism in Early Modern England* (Oxford: Oxford University Press, 2000)

Hall D.E. (ed.), *Muscular Christianity: Embodying the Victorian Age* (Cambridge: Cambridge University Press, 1994)

Harris, H.H., *Fundamentalism and Evangelicals* (Oxford: Clarendon, 1998)

Heasman, K., *Evangelicals in Action: An Appraisal of Their Social Work* (London: Geoffrey Bles, 1962)

Hilborn, D., J. Thacker and D. Tidball (eds), *The Atonement Debate: Papers from the London Symposium on the Theology of Atonement* (Grand Rapids: Zondervan, 2008)

Hilton, B., *The Age of Atonement: The Influence of Evangelicalism on Social and Economic Thought, 1785–1865* (Oxford: Clarendon Press, 1988)

Hindmarsh, D.B., *The Evangelical Conversion Narrative: Spiritual Autobiography in Early Modern England* (Oxford: Oxford University Press, 2005)

—, *John Newton and the English Evangelical Tradition* (Oxford: Clarendon Press, 1996)

Hopkins, M., *Nonconformity's Romantic Generation: Evangelical and Liberal Theologies in Victorian England* (Carlisle: Paternoster, 2004)

Johnson, D.A., *The Changing Shape of English Nonconformity 1825–1925* (Oxford: Oxford University Press, 1999)

Kruppa, P.S., *Charles Haddon Spurgeon: A Preacher's Progress* (New York: Garland, 1982)

Lambert, F., *Pedlar in Divinity* (Princeton: Princeton University Press, 1994)

Manley, K.R., *From Woolloomooloo to 'Eternity': A History of Australian Baptists: Growing an Australian Church (1831–1914)* (Milton Keynes: Paternoster, 2006)

—, *Redeeming Love Proclaim: John Rippon and the Baptists* (Carlisle: Paternoster, 2004)

McGonigle, H.B., *Sufficient Saving Grace: John Wesley's Evangelical Arminianism* (Carlisle: Paternoster, 2001)

McLeod, H., *Class and Religion in late Victorian Society* (London: Croom Helm, 1974)

McGrath, A.E., *Christianity's Dangerous Idea: A History From The Sixteenth Century to the Twenty-First* (New York: Harper Collins, 2007)

—, *Christian Spirituality* (Oxford: Blackwell, 1999)

Morden, P.J., *C.H. Spurgeon: The People's Preacher* (Farnham: CWR, 2009)

—, *Offering Christ to the World: Andrew Fuller (1754–1815) and the Revival of Eighteenth Century Particular Baptist Life* (Carlisle: Paternoster, 2003)

Munson, J., *The Nonconformists: In Search of a Lost Culture* (London: SPCK, 1991)

Murray, I.H., *The Forgotten Spurgeon* (London: Banner of Truth, 1966)

—, *Heroes* (Edinburgh: Banner of Truth, 2009)

—, *Spurgeon Versus Hyper Calvinism: The Battle for Gospel Preaching* (Edinburgh: Banner of Truth, 1995)

Mursell, G., *English Spirituality: From 1700 to the Present Day* (London: SPCK, 2001)

Neill, S. and N.T. Wright, *The Interpretation of the New Testament, 1861–1986* (Oxford; Oxford University Press, rev. edn, 1989)

Nicholls, M.K., *C.H. Spurgeon: The Pastor Evangelist* (Didcot: Baptist Historical Society, 1982)

—, *Lights To the World: A History of Spurgeon's College, 1856-1992* (Harpenden: Nuprint, 1994)
Nockles, P.B., *The Oxford Movement in Context: Anglican High Churchmanship 1760-1857* (Cambridge: Cambridge University Press, 1994)
Noll, M.A., *Between Faith and Criticism: Evangelicals, Scholarship and the Bible* (Leicester: IVP, 1991)
—, *A History of Christianity in the United States and Canada* (London: SPCK, 1992)
—, *The Rise of Evangelicalism: The Age of Edwards, Whitefield and the Wesleys* (Leicester: IVP, 2004)
Nuttall, G.F., *The Holy Spirit in Puritan Faith and Experience* (Oxford: Basil Blackwell, 1947)
Peterson, E.H., *Christ Plays in Ten Thousand Places: A Conversation in Spiritual Theology* (London: Hodder and Stoughton, 2005)
—, *Subversive Spirituality* (Vancouver: Regent College, 1997)
Pinnock, C.H., *Flame of Love: A Theology of the Holy Spirit* (Downers Grove: IVP, 1996)
Price, C. and I.M. Randall, *Transforming Keswick* (Carlisle: Paternoster, 2000)
Price, S.J., *Upton: The Story of One Hundred and Fifty Years, 1785-1935* (London: Carey Press, 1935)
Rack, H.D., *Reasonable Enthusiast: John Wesley and the Rise of Methodism* (London: Epworth, 1989)
Randall, I.M., *Evangelical Experiences: A Study in the Spirituality of English Evangelicalism 1918-1939* (Carlisle: Paternoster, 1999)
—, *A School of the Prophets: 150 Years of Spurgeon's College* (London: Spurgeon's College, 2005)
—, *What a Friend We Have in Jesus: The Evangelical Tradition* (London: Darton, Longman and Todd, 2005)
Reardon, B.M.G., *Religion in the Age of Romanticism: Studies in Early Nineteenth Century Thought* (Cambridge: Cambridge University Press, 1985)
Rogers, J.B. and D.K. McKim, *The Authority and Interpretation of the Bible: An Historical Approach* (San Francisco: Harper and Row, 1979)
Rosman, D.M., *Evangelicals and Culture* (London: Croom Helm, 1984)
Rowell, G., *The Vision Glorious: Themes and Personalities of the Catholic Revival in Anglicanism* (Oxford: Oxford University Press, 2001 [1983])
Sasek, L.A. (ed.), *Images of English Puritanism: A Collection of Contemporary Sources 1589-1646* (Louisiana: Louisiana State University Press, 1989)
Sell, A.P.F., *The Great Debate: Calvinism, Arminianism and Salvation* (Worthing: H. E. Walter, 1982)
Sheldrake, P., *Spirituality and History* (London: SPCK, 1991)
Skevington Wood, A., *The Burning Heart: John Wesley, Evangelist* (Calver: Cliff College Publishing, 1993 [1967])
Smyth, C., *Dean Milman* (London: SPCK, 1949)
Spurr, J., *English Puritanism, 1603-1689* (Basingstoke: Macmillan, 1998)

Spyvee, H., *Colchester Baptist Church: The First 300 years, 1689–1989* (Colchester: Colchester Baptist Church, 1989)

Stout, H.S., *The Divine Dramatist: George Whitefield and the Rise of Modern Evangelicalism* (Grand Rapids: Eerdmans, 1991)

Stunt, T.F.C., *From Awakening to Secession: Radical Evangelicals in Switzerland and Britain 1815–1835* (Edinburgh: T.&T. Clark, 2000)

Tidball, D.J., *Who Are The Evangelicals?* (London: Marshall Pickering, 1994)

Toon, P., *The Emergence of Hyper-Calvinism in English Nonconformity, 1689–1765* (London: Olive Tree, 1967)

Underwood, A.C., *A History of the English Baptists* (London: Carey Kingsgate, 1947)

Vance, N., *The Sinews of the Spirit: The Ideal of Christian Manliness in Victorian Literature and Religious Thought* (Cambridge: Cambridge University Press, 1985)

Von Ruhr, J., *The Covenant of Grace in Puritan Thought* (Atlanta: Scholars, 1986)

Walker, M.J., *Baptists at the Table: The Theology of the Lord's Supper amongst English Baptists in the Nineteenth Century* (Didcot: Baptist Historical Society, 1992)

Ward, B.K., *Redeeming the Enlightenment: Christianity and the Liberal Virtues* (Grand Rapids: Eerdmans, 2010)

Watts, M.R., *The Dissenters: Volume 2, The Expansion of Nonconformity* (Oxford: Clarenden Press, 1995)

Wigram, C.E.M., *The Bible and Mission in Faith Perspective: J. Hudson Taylor and the Early China Inland Mission* (Zoetermeer: Boekencentrum, 2007)

Williams, S.C., *Religious Belief and Popular Culture in Southwark c.1880–1939* (Oxford: Oxford University Press, 1999)

Wilson, L., *Constrained by Zeal: Female Spirituality among Nonconformists 1825–1875* (Carlisle: Paternoster, 2000)

Wolffe, J., *The Expansion of Evangelicalism, The Age of Wilberforce, More, Chalmers and Finney* (Leicester: IVP, 2006)

—, *God and Greater Britain: Religion and National Life in Britain and Ireland 1843–1945* (London: Routledge, 1994)

—, *The Protestant Crusade in Great Britain, 1829–1860* (Oxford: Clarendon Press, 1991)

Secondary Sources – Articles and Essays

Bebbington, D.W., 'The Baptist Conscience in the Nineteenth Century', *Baptist Quarterly* Vol. 34, No. 1 (January 1991), pp. 13-24

—, 'Baptists and Fundamentalism in Inter-War Britain', in K. Robbins (ed.), *Protestant Evangelicalism: Britain, Ireland, Germany and America, c.1750–c.1950* (Oxford: Blackwell, 1990), pp. 297-326

—, 'Gladstone and the Baptists', *Baptist Quarterly* Vol. 26, No. 5 (January 1976), pp. 224-38

—, 'Gladstone and the Nonconformists: A religious affinity in politics', in D. Baker (ed.), *Church, Society and Politics: Papers Read at the Thirteenth Summer Meeting and Fourteenth Winter Meeting of the Ecclesiastical History Society* (Oxford: Basil Blackwell, 1975), pp. 369-82

—, 'Gospel and Culture in Victorian Nonconformity', in J. Shaw and A. Kreider (eds), *Culture and the Nonconformist Tradition* (Cardiff: University of Wales Press, 1999), pp. 43-62

—, 'The Growth of Voluntary Religion', in S. Gilley and B. Stanley (eds), *World Christianities, c.1815–c.1914* (The Cambridge History of Christianity, Vol. 8; Cambridge: Cambridge University Press, 2006), pp. 53-69

—, 'Holiness in the Evangelical Tradition', in S.C. Barton (ed.), *Holiness Past and Present* (Edinburgh: T.&T. Clark, 2003), pp. 298-315

—, 'The Life of Baptist Noel: Its Setting and Significance', *Baptist Quarterly* Vol. 24, No. 8 (October 1972), pp. 389-411

—, 'Response', in M.A.G. Haykin and K.J. Stewart (eds), *The Emergence of Evangelicalism: Exploring Historical Continuities* (Leicester: IVP, 2008), pp. 417-32

—, 'Spurgeon and British Evangelical Theological Education', in D.G. Hart and R.A. Mohler, Jr (eds), *Theological Education in the Evangelical Tradition* (Grand Rapids: Baker, 1996), pp. 217-34

—, 'Spurgeon and the Common Man', *Baptist Review of Theology* Vol. 5, No. 1 (Spring 1995), pp. 63-75

—, 'Towards an Evangelical Identity', in S. Brady and H.H. Rowden (eds), *For Such A Time As This* (London: Scripture Union, 1996), pp. 37-48

Bradstock, A., '"A Man of God is Manly Man": Spurgeon, Luther and "Holy Boldness"', in A Bradstock, S. Gill, A. Horgan and S. Morgan (eds), *Masculinity and Spirituality in Victorian Culture* (Basingstoke: Macmillan, 2000), pp. 209-25

Briggs, J.H.Y., 'Baptists in the Eighteenth Century', in J.H.Y. Briggs (ed.), *Pulpit and People: Studies in Eighteenth-Century Baptist Life and Thought* (Milton Keynes: Paternoster, 2009), pp. 1-24

Butt-Thompson, F.W., 'The Morgans of Birmingham', *Baptist Quarterly* Vol. 2, No. 6 (April 1925), pp. 263-68

Coffey J. and P.C.H. Lim, 'Introduction', J. Coffey and P.C.H. Lim (eds), *The Cambridge Companion To Puritanism* (Cambridge: Cambridge University Press, 2008), pp. 1-15

Coffey J., 'Puritan Legacies', in J. Coffey and P.C.H. Lim (eds), *The Cambridge Companion To Puritanism* (Cambridge: Cambridge University Press, 2008), pp. 327-45

—, 'Puritanism, Evangelicalism and the Evangelical Protestant Tradition', in M.A.G. Haykin and K.J. Stewart (eds), *The Emergence of Evangelicalism: Exploring Historical Continuities* (Leicester: IVP, 2008), pp. 252-77

Cross, A.R., 'Baptismal Regeneration: Rehabilitating a Lost Dimension of New Testament Baptism', in A.R. Cross and P.E. Thompson (eds), *Baptist Sacramentalism 2* (Milton Keynes: Paternoster, 2008), pp. 149-74

Friesen, P., 'Frances Ridley Havergal', in T. Larson (ed.), *Biographical Dictionary of Evangelicals* (Leicester: IVP, 2003), pp. 294-95

George, T., 'Controversy and Communion: The Limits of Baptist Fellowship from Bunyan to Spurgeon', in D.W. Bebbington (ed.), *The Gospel in the World: International Baptist Studies* (Carlisle: Paternoster, 2002), pp. 38-58

Gilley, S. 'Introduction', in S. Gilley and B. Stanley (eds), *World Christianities, c.1815–c.1914* (The Cambridge History of Christianity, Vol. 8; Cambridge: Cambridge University Press, 2006), pp. 1-9

Grass T. and I.M. Randall, 'C.H. Spurgeon on the Sacraments', in A.R. Cross and P.E. Thompson (eds), *Baptist Sacramentalism* (Carlisle: Paternoster, 2003), pp. 55-75

Gribben, C., 'Andrew Bonar and the Scottish Presbyterian Millennium', in C. Gribben and T.C.F. Stunt (eds), *Prisoners of Hope? Aspects of Evangelical Millennialism in Britain and Ireland 1800–1880* (Carlisle: Paternoster, 2004), pp. 177-202

—, 'Defining the Puritans? The Baptism Debate in Cromwellian Ireland, 1654–56', *Church History* Vol. 73, No. 1 (2004), pp. 63-89

—, 'The Eschatology of the Puritan Confessions', *Scottish Bulletin of Evangelical Theology* Vol. 20, No. 1 (2002), pp. 51-78

— and T.C.F. Stunt, 'Introduction', C. Gribben and T.C.F. Stunt (eds), *Prisoners of Hope? Aspects of Evangelical Millennialism in Britain and Ireland 1800–1880* (Carlisle: Paternoster, 2004), pp. 1-17

Haykin, M.A.G., 'Benjamin Beddome (1717–1795): His Life and His Hymns', in J.H.Y. Briggs (ed.), *Pulpit and People: Studies in Eighteenth-Century Baptist Life and Thought* (Milton Keynes: Paternoster, 2009), pp. 93-111

—, '"His Soul Refreshing Presence": The Lord's Supper in Calvinistic Baptist Thought and Experience in the "Long" Eighteenth Century', in A.R. Cross and P.E. Thompson (eds), *Baptist Sacramentalism* (Carlisle: Paternoster, 2003), pp. 177-93

Hedley, D., 'Theology and the revolt against the Enlightenment', in S. Gilley and B. Stanley (eds), *World Christianities, c.1815–c.1914* (The Cambridge History of Christianity, Vol. 8; Cambridge: Cambridge University Press, 2006), pp. 30-52

Hindmarsh, D.B., 'The antecedents of evangelical conversion narrative: spiritual autobiography and the Christian tradition', in M.A.G. Haykin and K.J. Stewart (eds), *The Emergence of Evangelicalism: Exploring Historical Continuities* (Leicester: IVP, 2008), pp. 327-44

Hopkins, M.T.E., 'The Downgrade Controversy: New Evidence', *Baptist Quarterly* Vol. 35, No. 6 (April 1994), pp. 262-78

—, 'Spurgeon's Opponents in the Downgrade Controversy', *Baptist Quarterly* Vol. 32, No. 6 (April 1988), pp. 274-94

Hughes, G.W., 'Spurgeon's Homes', *Baptist Quarterly* Vol. 15, No. 7 (July 1954), pp. 297-310

James, C.D.T., 'Spurgeon and Simpson', *Baptist Quarterly* Vol. 20, No. 8 (October 1964), pp. 365-68

Kapic, K.M. and R.C. Gleason, 'Who Were the Puritans?', in K.M. Kapic and R.C. Gleason (eds), *The Devoted Life: An Invitation to the Puritan Classics* (Leicester: IVP, 2004), pp. 15- 37

Keeble, N.H., 'The Pilgrim's Progress: A Puritan Fiction', *Baptist Quarterly* Vol. 28, No. 7 (July 1980), pp. 321-36

Lane, B.C., 'Puritan Spirituality', in P. Sheldrake (ed.), *The New SCM Dictionary of Christian Spirituality* (London: SCM Press, 2005), pp. 518-20

Larsen, T., '"Living by Faith": A short history of Brethren practice', *Brethren Archivists and Historians Network Review* Vol. 1, No. 2 (Winter 1998), pp. 67-102

—, 'The Reception given to *Evangelicalism in Modern Britain*', in M.A.G. Haykin and K.J. Stewart (eds), *The Emergence of Evangelicalism: Exploring Historical Continuities* (Leicester: IVP, 2008), pp. 21-36

Manley, K.R., '"The Magic Name": Charles Haddon Spurgeon and the evangelical ethos of Australian Baptists. Part 1', *Baptist Quarterly* Vol. 40, No. 3 (July 2003), pp. 173-84

McGowan, A.T.B., 'Evangelicalism in Scotland From Knox to Cunningham', in M.A.G. Haykin and K.J. Stewart (eds), *The Emergence of Evangelicalism: Exploring Historical Continuities* (Leicester: IVP, 2008), pp. 63-83

Morden, P.J., 'Andrew Fuller and the *Gospel Worthy of All Acceptation*', in J.H.Y. Briggs (ed.), *Pulpit and People: Studies in Eighteenth-Century Baptist Life and Thought* (Milton Keynes: Paternoster, 2009), pp. 128-51

—, 'C.H. Spurgeon and Baptism Part 1: The Question of Baptismal Sacramentalism', *Baptist Quarterly* Vol. 43, No. 4 (October 2009), pp. 196-220

—, 'C.H. Spurgeon and Baptism Part 2: The Importance of Baptism', *Baptist Quarterly* Vol. 43, No. 7 (July 2010), pp. 388-409

Mursell, G., 'Holiness in the English Tradition: From Prayer Book to Puritans', in S.C. Barton (ed.), *Holiness Past and Present* (Edinburgh: T.&T. Clark, 2003), pp. 279-97

Nockles, P.B., 'The Oxford Movement', in J. Hill (ed.), *The History of Christianity* (Oxford: Lion, 2007), p. 366

Nuttall, G.F., 'Puritan and Quaker Mysticism', in G.F. Nuttall, *Studies in English Dissent* (Weston Rhyn: Quinta, 2002), pp. 81-108

Pearse, M., 'John Foxe', in T. Larson (ed.), *Biographical Dictionary of Evangelicals* (Leicester: IVP, 2003), pp. 236-37

Pooley, R., 'The Wilderness of the World – Bunyan's Pilgrim's Progress', *Baptist Quarterly* Vol. 27, No. 7 (July 1978), pp. 290-99

Randall, I.M., 'Charles Haddon Spurgeon, the Pastors' College and the Downgrade Controversy', in K. Cooper and J. Gregory (eds), *Discipline and Diversity: Papers Read at the 2005 Summer Meeting and the 2006 Winter Meeting of the Ecclesiastical History Society* (Woodbridge, Suffolk: Boydell, 2007), pp. 366-76

—, '"The World is our Parish": Spurgeon's College and World Mission, 1856–1892', in I.M. Randall and A.R. Cross (eds), *Baptists and Mission: Papers from the Fourth International Conference on Baptist Studies* (Milton Keynes: Paternoster, 2007), pp. 64-77

Rogerson, J., 'History and the Bible', in S. Gilley and B. Stanley (eds), *World Christianities, c.1815–c.1914* (The Cambridge History of Christianity, Vol. 8; Cambridge: Cambridge University Press, 2006), pp. 181-96

Rosenblatt, H., 'The Christian Enlightenment' in S.J. Brown and T. Tackett (eds), *Enlightenment, Reawakening and Revolution 1660–1815* (The Cambridge History of Christianity, Vol. 7; Cambridge: Cambridge University Press, 2006), pp. 283-31

Rowdon, H.H., 'The Concept of "Living by Faith"', in A. Billington, A.N.S. Lane and M. Turner (eds), *Mission and Meaning: Essays presented to Peter Cotterell* (Carlisle: Paternoster, 1995), pp. 339-56

Sanders, C., 'Disciplined Spirituality', in M.A. Noll and R.F. Thiemann (eds), *Where Shall My Wond'ring Soul Begin: The Landscape of Evangelical Piety and Thought* (Grand Rapids: Eerdmans, 2000), pp. 61-70

Schneiders, S.M., 'Christian Spirituality: Definition, Methods and Types', in P. Sheldrake (ed.), *The New SCM Dictionary of Christian Spirituality* (London: SCM Press, 2005), pp. 1-6

Shepherd, P., 'Spurgeon's Children', *Baptist Quarterly* Vol. 42, No. 2: Part 1 (April 2007), pp. 89-102

Stanley, B., 'C.H. Spurgeon and the Baptist Missionary Society 1863–1866', *Baptist Quarterly* Vol. 20, No. 3 (July 1982), pp. 319-28

Stewart, K.J., 'The evangelical doctrine of Scripture, 1650–1850: a re-examination of David Bebbington's theory', in M.A.G. Haykin and K.J. Stewart (eds), *The Emergence of Evangelicalism: Exploring Historical Continuities* (London: IVP, 2008), pp. 394-413

—, 'Did Evangelicalism Predate the Eighteenth Century? An Examination of David Bebbington's Thesis', *Evangelical Quarterly* Vol. 77, No. 2 (April 2005), pp. 135-53

Summerton, N., 'George Müller and the Financing of the Scriptural Knowledge Institution', in N.T.R. Dickson and T. Grass (eds), *The Growth of the Brethren Movement* (Carlisle: Paternoster, 2006), pp. 49-79

Thompson, D., 'John Clifford's Social Gospel', *Baptist Quarterly* Vol. 31, No. 5 (January 1986), pp. 199-217

Tosh, J., *Manliness and Masculinities in Nineteenth-Century Britain* (Harlow: Longman, 2005)

Williams, G.J., 'Enlightenment Epistemology and Eighteenth-Century Evangelical Doctrines of Assurance', in M.A.G. Haykin and K.J. Stewart (eds), *The Emergence of Evangelicalism: Exploring Historical Continuities* (Leicester: IVP, 2008), pp. 345-74

Theses

Brown, R., 'Evangelical Ideas of Perfection: A Comparative Study of the Spirituality of Men and Movements in Nineteenth Century England' (unpublished DPhil dissertation, University of Cambridge, 1964)

Colquitt, H.F., 'The Soteriology of Charles Haddon Spurgeon Revealed in his Sermons and Controversial Writings' (unpublished PhD dissertation, University of Edinburgh, 1951)

McCoy, T., 'The evangelistic ministry of C.H. Spurgeon: Implications for a contemporary model of pastoral evangelism' (unpublished PhD dissertation, Southern Baptist Theological Seminary, 1989)

Meredith, A.R., 'The Social and Political Views of C.H. Spurgeon, 1834–1892' (unpublished PhD dissertation, Michigan State University, 1973)

Schwanda, T., 'Soul Recreation: Spiritual Marriage And Ravishment In The Contemplative-Mystical Piety of Isaac Ambrose' (unpublished PhD dissertation, University of Durham, 2009)

Unpublished Papers

Den, A., 'Mood Disorders' [unpublished printed notes: 7 November 2004]

Hopkins, M.T.E., 'The Downgrade Controversy: reflections on a Baptist earthquake' [unpublished photocopy: G.R. Beasley-Murray Memorial Lecture presented at the Baptist Union Assembly, Brighton, 6 May 2007], Spurgeon's College, Heritage Room (J2.28)

Larsen, T., 'Charles Haddon Spurgeon's Reading of the Sermon on the Mount', in T. Larsen, J.P. Greenman and S.R. Spencer (eds), *Reading the Sermon on the Mount through the Centuries* [Grand Rapids: Brazos, forthcoming]

Powles, J., 'Misguided or misunderstood?: The case of Charles Spurgeon Medhurst (1860–1927), Baptist missionary to China' [forthcoming in *Baptist Quarterly*]

Randall, I.M., '"Ye men of Plymouth ...": C.H. Spurgeon and the Brethren' [unpublished paper: November 2006]

Internet Sources

Adam, P., 'A Church "Halfly Reformed" – The Puritan Dilemma', The 1998 St Antholin Lecture, p. 2, www.masg.net.au/Documents/08_Adam_ChurchHalfly Reformed.pdf, accessed 9 August 2009

Papers from the July 2005 Evangelical Alliance symposium on the atonement, http://www.eauk.org/theology/key_papers/Atonement, accessed 3 July 2009

Index

Adamson, W. 234
Agricultural Hall, Islington 67
Alabaster, James 128, 134
Alleine, Joseph 23, 48
Andrewes, Lancelot 133
Angell James, John 48, 55, 70
Antinomianism 224-26
Appleton, Frances 273
Arminianism 38-42, 70, 226, 288
Arnold, Matthew 235
Artillery Street Chapel, Colchester 48-49, 59
Augustine of Hippo 20, 110, 132
Avrillon, John Baptist Elias 151

Bacon, Ernest 7
Baptist Missionary Society 6, 156, 160, 209
Baptist Union 7, 115
Baptists 19, 62-65, 77, 80-83, 101, 103, 115, 165, 167, 179, 196, 201, 206, 208, 224-25, 286, 288, 291
Balaclava, Battle of 97-98
Baldwin Brown, J. 115, 289, 293
Baptist, The 260
Barlow, John 33
Barnardo, Thomas 207
Baxter, Richard 23, 48, 62
Bebbington, David W. 1, 6-7, 53-55, 61, 70, 74, 114, 147, 223, 226, 234-35, 240, 248, 251, 253, 256
Beddome, Benjamin 86
Bernard of Clairvaux 169, 266, 288
Bernardo, Thomas 190
Birkel, Michael 149
Birt, Isaiah 103
Bonar, Andrew 239

Boy's Own Paper 1
Bradstock, Andrew 6, 253
Brine, John 62
British Weekly 153
Brooks, Thomas 43-44, 46, 72, 95
Brown, Raymond 226
Bunyan, John 24-30, 110, 119, 123-24, 153-54
  Works
    Grace Abounding 26, 55
    Holy War 26, 30, 119
    Pilgrim's Progress 22, 25-30, 45, 109
Burroughes, Jeremiah 32

Calvin, John 20, 32, 110, 124, 132, 134, 180
Calvinism 20-21, 62, 75, 88, 126, 223, 225-26, 250, 253, 264, 287-88, 291
Cambridge 17, 45, 192
Cantlow, William 77
Cardigan, Lord 97
Carlile, John C. 5, 31, 153, 280-81
Carlyle, Thomas 1, 124
Cassin, Burman 190
Chalmers, Thomas 33
Charlesworth, Vernon J. 96, 215, 217, 291-92
Charnock, Stephen 132
China Inland Mission 159
Christian World 52, 191, 218
Church of England 16, 19, 21, 79-80, 88-92, 165, 208, 223
Clifford, John 104, 179, 196
Coles, Elisha 31, 265
Collinson, Patrick 18
Coffey, John 18-20, 43
Colchester 16, 24
Coleridge, Samuel Taylor 113

Colquitt, H.F. 5-6, 243, 282, 284
Colportage Society 66, 194
Congregationalists (see 'Independents')
Cook, Charles T. 11, 144
Cowper, William 150
Cox, Thomas 130, 140, 291, 294
Crisp, Tobias 62
Cromwell, Oliver 20
Cross, Anthony R. 87, 103
Cuff, William 280
Curme, Thomas 281, 284

Daily News 259-60
Darby, John Nelson 239
Davis, C.A. 133
Davies, Horton 7
Den, Anil 261-62
Dickson, David 33, 35
Disraeli, Benjamin 1
Ditchfield G.M. 53
Doddridge, Philip 48, 55, 70, 101, 113
Douglas, J.D. 4, 238
Downgrade Controversy 7, 12-13, 115-17, 151-52, 216, 241
Drummond, Lewis 5, 211
Durham, James 34, 42, 175-76

Eaglen, Robert 50-51
Eld Lane Baptist Church, Colchester 81
Eliot, George 235
Elizabeth I 20
Enlightenment, The 13, 74-75, 111, 117-19, 126, 150, 158, 163, 240, 274, 288-90, 293
Essays and Reviews 114
Essex Telegraph 191
Evangelicalism 19, 53-54, 61, 70-76, 92, 95, 111-14, 123-24, 126, 147-48, 153, 158-60, 163, 179, 204, 207-210, 212, 226-27, 240, 243, 250, 253, 286, 288

Exeter Hall, Strand 28

'Faith Principle', The 158-60
Fellows, John 86
Field, John 134
Fowler, Stanley K. 88
Foxe, John 24-26, 279
Fuller, Andrew 65, 132, 225
Fullerton, William Young 5, 117, 143, 156, 158, 210
Fox, George 149

Gaskell, Elizabeth 256
Geneva 32
George, Timothy 179
Gibson, E.T. 133
Gilbert, Mrs (first matron of Stockwell Orphanage) 206
Gill, John 44-45, 62, 65, 86, 123, 224
Gillett, David 43
Gladstone, William E. 1, 196
Gleason, R.C. 19
Gordon, James 42, 146, 153
Gospel Standard 45
Gracey, David 133
Grass, Tim 79, 167, 180
Grattan Guinness, Henry 239-40
Gurnall, William 132
Guyon, Madame (Jeanne) 150-54, 169, 288

Harrald, Joseph W. 5, 128, 291
Havergal, Frances Ridley 228
Havers, Henry 21, 24
Haynes, W.B. 134
Hedley, Douglas 113
Henry, Matthew 36, 132
Higgs, William 213-14
High Calvinism 44, 62-66, 224-25
High Church spirituality 25, 88-92, 133, 147-48, 150-52, 154, 160, 168-71, 178-79, 188, 229-31, 234, 248, 254-55, 288-89, 292-93

Index

Hillyard, Anne 204, 209, 213-14
Hilton, Boyd 7
Hindmarsh, Bruce D. 54
Holden Pike, G. 4, 22, 128, 216, 234
Hopkins, Mark 6, 12, 16, 27-28, 41-42, 62, 65-66, 102-103, 109, 111-12, 129, 151, 212, 218, 274
Hosken C.H. 200
Hughes, Thomas 253
Hussey, Joseph 62
Hutcheson, George 33

Independents (Congregationalists) 16, 19-21, 79, 84, 165
Irving, Edward 159-60
Isleham Ferry, Cambridgeshire 77, 84

James I 23

Kapic, K.M. 19
Keble, John 133
Kelvedon 16
Keswick Convention 245, 250
Keswick holiness teaching 223, 245, 250-53, 289
Keys, John L. 128, 133, 135
King, Mary 45, 81
Kingsley, Charles 253-54, 273
Kruppa, Patricia 1, 5, 12, 19, 38, 56, 108, 162, 196, 212

Langford, Robert 81-82
Larson, Timothy 53
Lim, Paul 18-20, 43
London Missionary Society 159-60
Longfellow, Henry Wadsworth 273
Lucan, Lord 97
Luther, Martin 110, 132, 254-55
McCoy, Timothy 51
McGrath, Alister E. 3
Maidstone 16, 79-80
Manley, Ken 2

Marchant, FG. 133
Martyn, Henry 113
Maynard, John 209
Medhurst, T.W. 199-200
Mentone 166, 172, 178, 195, 198, 221, 261-62, 268-69
Meredith, A.R. 196
Metropolitan Tabernacle, Newington Butts 28, 41, 60, 66, 85, 103, 127, 130, 140, 157, 162, 165-66, 171, 181, 193-94, 200-201, 244, 259, 287
Milman, Henry H. 276
Morden, Peter J. 6
Müller, George 159-60, 163, 208, 201-11, 288
Murray, Iain 7, 241

Neale, John Mason 133, 151, 293
New Park Street Chapel, London 27-28, 31, 44, 52, 63 -64, 66-67, 73, 103, 171, 194, 200, 237
Newmarket 17, 45, 88
Nicholls, Mike 12, 201
Nightingale Lane, Clapham Common 128
Nockles, Peter 89
Noel, Baptist Wriothesley 87-88
Noll, Mark A. 19
Norcott, John 78
North American Review 1

Olney, Thomas 279
Olney, William 206, 279
Owen, John 110, 124

Page, W.H.J. 133-34
Parker, Joseph 37-38, 233-34
Passmore, Joseph 128, 134-35
Pastors' College 5, 38, 45, 96, 123, 128, 131, 133, 140, 158, 167, 191, 194, 199-203, 209, 222
Paul (the apostle) 20
Pearsall Smith, Robert 250, 252

Perkins, William 32
Peterson, Eugene 174
Pierson, Arthur T. 286
Plymouth Brethren 158, 239
Presbyterians 19, 166, 172
Primitive Methodists 50-52, 56, 66, 79, 81
Puritans 7, 13, 17-46, 48, 54-55, 60, 73, 75-76, 95, 123, 132, 147-49, 153-54, 163, 175-76, 240, 242, 246, 253, 255, 287-88, 291-92
Pusey, Edward Bouverie 89, 151

Quakers 149, 154, 250

Raikes, Robert 165
Randall, Ian M. 6, 79, 149, 162, 167, 180
Reformation 20
Rippon, John 86-87, 194
Robertson Nichol, William 153
Rogers, George 96, 128, 135, 200, 266, 292
Rogers, John 35
Rogerson, John 114
Roman Catholicism 18, 90-92, 150-52, 154, 168-72, 178-79, 188, 229-31, 247, 255, 288, 292
Romanticism 13, 113-14, 117-18, 124, 126, 160-61, 163, 240, 242, 255, 273-74, 289-90, 293
Rosebery, Earl of 235
Rosman, Doreen 38, 113
Rutherford, Samuel 154
Ruskin, John 113, 124
Ryle, J.C. 148, 226, 244-45, 253

St Andrew's Street Baptist Church, Cambridge 27, 83
Sanders, Cheryl 147
Sasek, Lawrence 18
Scott, Sir Walter 113, 274
Sheen, Danzy 50, 52

Sheldrake, Philip 2-3
Shepherd, Peter 206
Shindler, Robert 211
Shireff, William 78
Sibbes, Richard 32, 34-35, 42, 95, 175
Simeon, Charles 113
Skepp, John 62
Smiles, Samuel 162, 273
South London Press 182, 217
Surrey Gardens Music Hall 28-29, 260-61
Spurgeon, Charles (son) 279-81
Spurgeon, Charles Haddon
  and alcohol 38-39, 167
  and Arminianism 38-42, 70, 226, 288
  and atonement 56-58, 173-75, 264, 278
  and evangelicalism 17, 48, 55, 61, 70-76, 92, 95, 111, 123, 126, 147-48, 158-60, 163, 182
  and John Bunyan 24-30, 45-46, 55, 62, 109, 119, 123-24, 153-54
  and High Calvinism 44, 62-66, 224-25
  and politics 196-97
  and premillennialism 237-43, 289, 293
  and Puritan commentaries 31-37, 46, 123, 132, 175-76, 291-92
  and Puritanism 17-46, 48, 55, 60, 73, 75-76, 95, 100-101, 111, 117-18, 126, 147-49, 153-54, 158, 163, 175-76, 179, 202, 227, 242, 253, 255, 287-88, 290-92
  and Theatregoing 37-38, 232-33
  as 'John Ploughman' 10, 233, 256, 270-71
  Baptism as a believer 27, 77, 79-84, 104-105, 227

Conversion experience 47-52,
68, 100
Death 76
*Works (including those
posthumously published)
referred to in main text*
Autobiography 5, 8, 21, 42, 48-
52, 61, 73-74, 79-81, 88, 101,
194, 204, 225
Behold the Throne of Grace
144
Commenting and Commentaries
31-37, 132, 151
Evening by Evening 9, 37, 265-
66, 284
Farm Sermons 226
Gospel of the Kingdom 10,
119, 199, 267
How Spurgeon Found Christ
48, 51-53
John Ploughman's Pictures 9-
10
John Ploughman's Talk 9-10
Lectures to my Students 123,
258
Metropolitan Tabernacle Pulpit
8-9, 51-52, 116, 294
Morning by Morning 9
Most Holy Place 34
New Park Street Pulpit 8-9, 40,
51-52, 78, 107, 116
Our Own Hymn Book 10, 85-
87, 150, 183
*Smooth Stones Taken from
Ancient Brooks* 44, 46
Till He Come 9, 14, 167, 173-
75, 185-87
*The Letters of Charles Haddon
Spurgeon* 279
The Pastor in Prayer 139
The Saint and his Saviour 9,
36-37, 294
The Sword and the Trowel 10,
17, 22, 28, 38, 41, 80, 128,
159, 181, 186, 195-96, 198,
200-201, 205, 207-208, 233-
34, 238, 251-52, 286, 291
Treasury of David 10, 107,
111-12, 115, 125-6, 131-35,
155, 291
Spurgeon, Eliza (mother) 23-24,
55
Spurgeon, Emily (sister) 11
Spurgeon, James (paternal
grandfather) 16, 21-23
Spurgeon, James Archer (brother)
181-82, 195, 214-17, 291, 294
Spurgeon, John (father) 16
Spurgeon, Sarah (paternal
grandmother) 16
Spurgeon, Susannah (née
Thompson, wife) 5, 28, 128-29
Stambourne 16, 21, 24
Stanley, Brian 6, 158-59
Stout, Harry S. 71
Stockwell Orphanage 96, 158-59,
190-91, 195, 197, 204-18, 222,
291
Surrey Gardens Music Hall 28-29,
72-73
Swindell, John 81

Taylor, James Hudson 159, 162,
288
Taylor, Thomas 32
Tennyson, Alfred, Lord 1, 97-98
Toplady, Augustus 69
Trapp, John 132

Upton, James 86-87

Vance, Norman 229

Walker, Michael J. 57, 89, 168-69,
179-80
Waterbeach 27, 65, 73, 82, 85,
181, 192, 225
Watson, Thomas 32, 78

Watts, Isaac 110, 236
Welton, Charles 204
Wesley, John 20, 45, 70, 95, 148-49, 248-49, 288
Wesleyan Methodists 54, 70, 75, 165, 223, 248-50
'Westwood', South Norwood 45, 128, 134
Whitall Smith, Hannah 250
Whitefield, George 19-20, 64, 70-71, 95, 110, 132, 148, 288
Williams, William 4, 29, 133-34, 212, 258, 261, 263, 266, 280
Wilson, Linda 3
Wolffe, John 7, 148, 254
Wordsworth, William 113

www.ingramcontent.com/pod-product-compliance
Lightning Source LLC
Chambersburg PA
CBHW080726300426
44114CB00019B/2501